THE

ISLAND OF MAURITIUS

THE AUTHOR AND HIS COLLECTION.

SUB-TROPICAL RAMBLES

IN

THE LAND OF THE APHANAPTERYX.

PERSONAL EXPERIENCES, ADVENTURES, AND WANDERINGS

IN AND AROUND

THE ISLAND OF MAURITIUS.

By NICOLAS PIKE.

NEW YORK:
HARPER & BROTHERS, PUBLISHERS,
FRANKLIN SQUARE.
1873.

This Volume

IS MOST RESPECTFULLY DEDICATED TO

M. L. L.

AS A MARK OF ESTEEM AND FRIENDSHIP AND FOR THE VALUABLE ASSISTANCE RENDERED ME WHILST WRITING ITS PAGES; ALSO FOR THE KIND CARE AND ATTENTION BESTOWED UPON ME WHEN STRICKEN DOWN WITH FEVER ALONE IN A STRANGE LAND, AND WHICH NEARLY PREVENTED THEM BEING WRITTEN AT ALL

PREFACE.

THE PRESENT VOLUME of Sub-tropical Rambles is made up from notes taken on my voyage from America to Mauritius; information gained in the latter wherever possible; and my own experience during the years I have resided in it.

The 'Gem of the Ocean' is, in reality, but little known to the world at large. Small as it is, only a dot in a vast ocean, it is, or at least might be made, one of the most fertile and productive of the English Colonies. Its mountain scenery is grand, and its singularly formed rugged peaks supply an endless fund for reflection. Nowhere is the 'stone-book of Nature' more widely opened, so that 'he who runneth may read.' Its waterfalls, its caverns, its wild forest lands, must ever be sources of pleasure to all who choose to seek for them. Its coasts afford the naturalist never-ending stores for collection and study, and all these go far to make up for the many things so totally deficient in Mauritius; in fact, they make life bearable, which would be without them a dull monotone.

On my receiving my appointment as Consul to this Island, I sought in vain for information respecting it. With the exception of Baron Grant's work, written more than a hundred years ago ; notes by an old French officer quite as ancient, and a few scattered magazine articles, I could find nothing.

I therefore determined to note everything I saw ; and gain information of all kinds relative to this interesting place, and the present volume is the result. To those gentlemen who have assisted me so courteously by the use of their books, or with personal information, I beg to return my most sincere thanks.

In a second volume, nearly completed, I purpose treating more fully on the Fauna and Flora of Mauritius. I am aware much has been written on both, but am equally aware (often to my disappointment) that such writings have been mostly confined to articles sent to various literary institutions, that lie entombed in their records, unavailable to the general reading public.

I have tried to give a fair but brief account of everything without prejudice ; and if the reader, when he (or she) lays down my book, should say, he has gained new ideas, and a fair knowledge of the Island and its capabilities, or even had some hours' amusement, I shall feel my 'jottings by the way' have not been all labour in vain.

I would say a word about the title of my book.

Everybody has heard all about the Dodo, once existent in Mauritius, but many are not aware of the very beautiful bird the *Aphanapteryx imperialis*, coexistent with it, a sketch of which is on the title-page, and whose exquisite red silky plumage might vie with the handsomest birds of the present era.[1]

NICOLAS PIKE.

U.S. CONSUL, PORT LOUIS, MAURITIUS.
Nov. 1872.

[1] A full description of this bird will be given in a future volume.

CONTENTS.

CHAPTER IV.

PAMPLEMOUSSES GARDENS.

CHAPTER V.

THE RACES.

CHAPTER VI.

THE EPIDEMIC OF MAURITIUS.

CHAPTER VII.

THE CYCLONE OF 1868.

CHAPTER VIII.

A TRIP TO THE ARSENAL.

CHAPTER IX.

THE GEOLOGY OF MAURITIUS.

CHAPTER X.

THE MOHARRUM OR YAMSEH.

CHAPTER XI.

A VISIT TO ROUND ISLAND.

CHAPTER XII.

MY SECOND VISIT TO ROUND ISLAND.

CHAPTER XIII.

A CHINESE FESTIVAL.

CHAPTER XIV.

AN EXCURSION UP THE POUCE MOUNTAIN.

CHAPTER XV.

REDUIT.

CHAPTER XVI.

THE MARRIAGE CEREMONY OF THE MADRAS MALABAR INDIANS.

CHAPTER XVII.

FLAT ISLAND.

CHAPTER XVIII.

LA CHASSE.

CHAPTER XIX.

A HINDOO FESTIVAL.

PAGE

CHAPTER XX.

ACROSS COUNTRY TO THE DYA-MAMOU AND OTHER FALLS.

CHAPTER XXI.

ON THE SEA, IN AND NEAR PORT LOUIS HARBOUR, WITH DESCRIPTIONS OF SOME OF THE WONDERS THEREIN.

CHAPTER XXII.

A TOUR ROUND THE ISLAND.

CHAPTER XXIII.

VISIT TO THE ISLE DE PASSE, AND CONTINUATION OF TOUR.

CHAPTER XXIV.

THE HISTORY OF MAURITIUS.

CHAPTER XXV.

BRIEF SUMMARY OF THE GEOGRAPHY OF MAURITIUS, ITS DEPENDENCIES, CIVIL AND MILITARY STATISTICS, VARIOUS INDUSTRIES, COMMERCE, ETC.

CHAPTER XXVI.

THE GOVERNMENT OF MAURITIUS AND ITS VARIOUS ESTABLISHMENTS, WITH THE DIFFERENT RELIGIONS IN THE COLONY.

CHAPTER XXVII.

THE ROYAL COLLEGE, PRIVATE AND GOVERNMENT SCHOOLS, AND THE MUSEUM.

CHAPTER XXVIII.

IMMIGRATION.

CHAPTER XXIX.

SUGAR AND THE SUGAR-CANE.

APPENDIX.

LIST OF ILLUSTRATIONS.

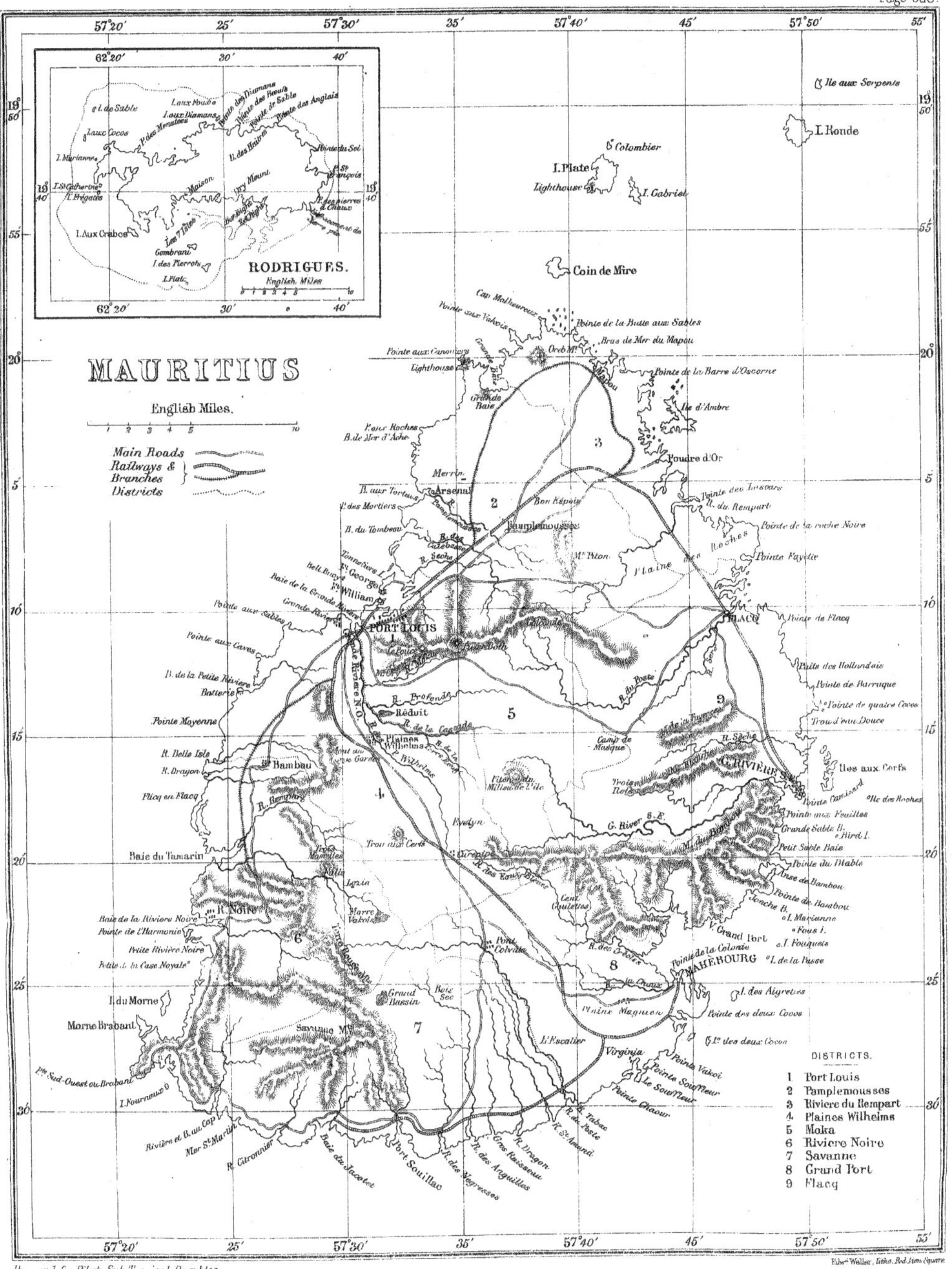

Prepared for Pike's Sub-Tropical Rambles.

Published by Sampson Low, Marston, Low, & Searle; Crown Buildings, 188 Fleet Str. London.

SUB-TROPICAL RAMBLES.

CHAPTER I.

Leaving Home—Ball at Piney Point—In the Gulf Stream—St. Thomas—Santa Cruz—Guadaloupe—Mr. Chaplain's Death—Barbadoes—Pernambuco—Oleuda—Rio—Description of the City—Public Gardens—Emperor's Garden—A Night in the Forest—Excursion up the Corcorada—Snakes—Descent—Public Squares—Departure from Rio.

On being appointed Consul for the Island of Mauritius, a passage, through the politeness of the Secretary of the Navy, was offered me in the United States steamer 'Monocacy,' of 1,030 tons, carrying ten guns, and commanded by Captain S. P. Carter, formerly Major-General Carter of the army.

This ship was built for river service, but not being completed before the termination of the war, she was detailed for foreign service.

As we put in at many places on my way to my distant appointment, I shall take a few notes at random from my journal, which may interest those whose tastes lead them to foreign travel, while their occupations prevent them visiting places so very foreign.

On August 18, 1866, we weighed anchor from the navy yard at Washington, and steamed down the Potomac, the day bright and calm as could be wished. We passed many fortifications on the Maryland side, now happily dismantled of their guns, and then slowly steamed by Alexandria. Before the war this was a thriving place of business. Now most of the stores are closed, and grass grows in the once busy streets. This city contained more rabid secessionists at the commencement of the Rebellion than any other. It was here the rebels planted on the Marshal House their bars and stars, which, to the annoyance of all true and loyal men, could be plainly seen at Washington.

In the evening we anchored off Piney Point, Virginia, and I went on shore with Captain Carter.

There was a ball at the hotel we visited, and we were politely invited to join in the dance, but declined the honour, and took our seats as spectators.

The band consisted of six darkies, playing a violin, cornet-à-piston, flute, banjo, bones, and triangle. An old grey-headed man called out the figures with most amusing gesticulations, and contortions of face and body, as he gave out at the top of his voice: 'Gemmen to de right, misses to de lef; go in dar boys, the war am over, we all broders once more!' and then, casting a look at me, 'Massa's from de North, good times am coming.'

The *ladies* were dressed in fashionable style, very *décolletées*, and the fun went on 'fast and furious.' Soon tired of this, we went into the bar-room, where two darkies were busily mixing brandy smashes and mint juleps for the waiting crowds. There were a good many boarders in the house, as the neighbourhood supplied excellent sport for the angler, and is noted for oysters. Most of the gentlemen were Southerners; but when they saw that we were United States Government officers, they treated us with great politeness, conversed freely on the late war, admitted that a great mistake had been made, and wished by-gones to be by-gones.

In the morning we left Piney Point, steamed through Chesapeake Bay, passed Fortress Monroe, and the Rip Raps, Norfolk, and Portsmouth, and entered Gosport navy yard. Here we coaled, took in eighty more men, the balance of our crew, and then went into the dry dock for some alterations.

The 'Monocacy' was a new, untried vessel; and from her conduct hitherto she had inspired the crew with great distrust of her sailing capacities and seaworthiness, but I confess I did not share their fears.

On the 28th we got in our shot and shell, and on the 29th were towed out to the Hampton Roads, and made fast to the Government buoys, whilst the deviation of the compass was ascertained.

I amused myself with capturing some of the pretty medusæ sailing round about the ship. Some of them I had never seen, particularly one of a chestnut colour, the body about three inches in diameter, with tentaculæ more than a yard long, and others of a pale blue, radiating all the hues of the solar spectrum. I caught up some sea-weeds too, prominent among which were the *Ceramium rubrum*, *Fucus nodosus* and *vesiculosus*, *Ulva linza*, *Entoromorpha intestinalis*, and several species of *Caltithamnium*, all common to our coast.

On August 30 the pilot took us out, and after passing Fort Henry we bade adieu to the United States, and were soon under way for the broad Atlantic.

It was with saddened feelings I looked my last on the shores of my native land, and thought, 'It may be for years, or it may be for ever,' I was saying adieu to home and friends.

Once out at sea, order began to reign in the ship; the men were mustered, and articles of war read, sails unfurled, and the monotony of ship life began.

By September 3 we were running down the Gulf Stream, with splendid weather. This remarkable stream has its fountain-head in the Gulf of Mexico, and its mouth in the Arctic Sea, and has a current more rapid than the Mississippi or Amazon.

The velocity of this current, however, varies greatly. According to Dana, 'Off Florida it is from three to five miles per hour, and in the Polar current has a rate of less than one mile. It is of great depth.'

Dr. Franklin was of opinion that the Gulf Stream was formed by the escaping waters, forced into the Carribean Sea by the trade winds, and that the pressure of these winds upon the waters of this ocean forced up a head sea.

It is stated that the chemical properties, or (if the expression be admissible) the galvanic properties, of the Gulf Stream waters, as they come from their fountains are different, or rather more intense than they are in sea-water generally. In 1843 the Secretary of the Navy took measures for procuring a series of experiments and observations with regard to the corrosive effects of sea-water upon the copper sheathing of ships. With patience, care, and labour, these researches were carried on for ten years, and the fact has been established that the copper on the bottom of ships cruising in the Carribean Sea and Gulf of Mexico suffers more than in any other part of the ocean. That is, the salts in these waters create the most powerful galvanic battery that is found in the ocean.

Professor Harvey states that the vegetation has a strong resemblance to that of the Mediterranean. 'Sea-weeds are borne on the Gulf Stream in such quantities, and thrown off the inner side of the current into the great area of still water in the centre of the Atlantic, that a part of it takes the name of the Sea of *Sargassa*, from the name of a common weed of the order *Fucaceæ*.'

On the evening of the 7th a heavy squall struck the vessel. Fortunately we were prepared for it, and had everything secured. It lasted all night; the rain fell in torrents, the thunder rolled deeply, and the vivid flashes of the lightning were blinding.

The gale reached its height at ten o'clock A.M. on the 8th, after which it gradually subsided, and land was sighted from the mast-head.

It proved to be St. Thomas, one of the islands of the West Indian group. Towards evening we were close in, but had great difficulty in getting a pilot, and it was ten o'clock at night before we were safely anchored.

The town of St. Thomas, which is the capital, is prettily situated at the base of a lofty ridge of mountains, which extends the whole length of the island, some of whose highest peaks rise to the altitude of 1,700 feet.

The island is about twelve miles long by three or four broad. It belongs to Denmark, is a free port, and has a larger commerce than any other West Indian island. It is the general rendezvous of our men-of-war, which have a special anchorage; there is also a government coal depôt there. It has a dry dock, but no iron-foundries, so that no metal work for shipping can be repaired.

On Sunday I attended the Episcopalian Church, where the minister gave a very impressive sermon from the second verse of the third chapter of St. James' Epistle. The principal thoroughfare of St. Thomas is King Street, containing English, French, and American stores for merchandise. I found everything at least thirty per cent. cheaper than in the United States.

VIEW OF ST. THOMAS.

The bay of St. Thomas is a fine one, open to the south, and can be entered at any time with the prevailing trade winds, and is perfectly safe except in hurricane months. Near the landing is a water-battery, and behind it an old Dutch fortification which commands the harbour, called Christian's Fort.

It is very ancient. Three or four hundred soldiers are stationed there, and it is a residence of the Governor. From a high hill at the back of the town, called French Hill, which I climbed, I had a fine view of the whole place.

The ex-President and General-in-chief of Mexico, Santa Anna, has taken up his quarters in a fine house on this hill.

On the spur of a mountain called Kiari is a remarkable stone tower named Blue Beard Castle, an antique-looking pile. It is 240 feet above the level of the sea, and, with the house adjoining, was purchased some years ago. It was in a sad state of dilapidation; but the owner, thinking it would make a good look-out or summer-house, put it in repair.

On excavating the earth, he found the tower had once been fortified, and eight or ten guns were dug out of the ruins. He had them cleaned, and mounted on earthworks round the tower.

It is supposed that it was built by the pirates and freebooters of the last century, as a stronghold in case of attack. It is well known that within the recollection of this generation they had places of refuge in the mountains.

Fruits and vegetables are exposed for sale under the trees in the square in King Street, and considering they are nearly all raised in Santa Cruz, at a distance of thirty-eight miles, all were very moderate in price.

I should say that, as fish abound on this coast, this was a capital place for a student of ichthyology.

I added to my collection some beautiful sea-weeds, from the tide-pools, to which the well-known lines of the poet beginning with 'full many a gem' apply admirably. Large piles of king-fish, from five to twenty pounds weight, are constantly for sale as well as the angel-fish (*Helicanthus ciliaris*), and quantities of snappers and grunts. There were the peculiarly-formed cow-fish (*Ostracion sex cornutus*), the peacock-fish (*Cheitodon vulgaris*), zebra-fish (*Eavaretas*), and the hog-fish—which in spite of its name is one of the most graceful of fish in the water, and capital for eating too—and, in short, a variety too numerous to mention.

We left St. Thomas, on December 14, for Santa Cruz, and let go our anchor in the harbour of Frederickstadt in the evening.

The singular clearness of the water here is very remarkable. We lay in a depth of thirty feet, yet we could distinctly see the corals and gorgonas at the bottom. Sharks abound; and a story was told us of an incident that occurred a few days before our arrival, of a Danish seaman, who was missing for two days; and a fisherman capturing one of these monsters, found portions of a human body in it, still undigested, and part of a shirt with the man's name on it. It was supposed he had fallen overboard, and been instantly devoured.

I called on the consul, Mr. Moore, and afterwards strolled about the place, which has a Spanish look, and reminded me of Vigo, in Spain.

Santa Cruz is called the garden of the West Indies. Most of the houses are of one storey, with prettily laid out grounds round them, and when viewed at a distance the island has the appearance of a highly-cultivated garden.

It contains about 12,000 inhabitants; exports sugar, molasses, rum and cotton, and supplies steamers with firewood. It is unfortunately subject to frequent droughts (possibly caused by the cutting down of the forests), and is said to be very unhealthy for strangers. I noticed in the churchyard that a large percentage of the deaths were caused by yellow fever, as incribed on the tombstones.

On the 17th we left Santa Cruz, and on the 18th were close to Basseterre, on the south-west of the island of Guadaloupe, and reached Point Petre that night.

The upper part of the town is clean and well paved, and appears to have very comfortable buildings. All the lower parts reek in squalor and filth, and I do not wonder at the cholera having made such frightful ravages there. In 1865 it carried off 25,000 victims. The heat was most oppressive at this time; and the volcano, the Souffrière, was emitting flames and thick volumes of smoke.

The fish-market is a curious establishment. The vendors are negro women, who sit behind a grating of large iron bars under a tin roof. Crowds of whites and negroes are elbowing each other, and making a Babel of noise to get at the bars. A particular fish is pointed out by the purchaser, when it is weighed and priced, but never passed through till paid for. Exorbitant prices were the rule. I chose a Grauper of about two pounds weight, and they asked me two dollars and a half for it.

The Governor and Commander-in-chief of the military forces visited us on board, themselves and suite in full uniform; the former was certainly one of the handsomest men I ever saw.

A terrible earthquake occurred here in 1843. After the disaster that spread ruin on all sides, fire, the constant ally of earthquakes, broke out and completed the work of destruction. A shocking incident was related to me. A young girl rushed out of her father's house to save herself, when some timbers from a ruined building fell on her, and held her firmly to the spot by the lower extremities. She called loudly for help; and on a soldier trying to rescue her, and finding his efforts vain, she begged of him to cut off her legs so as to save her from the fire, which was advancing with giant strides. He drew his sword to comply, but his heart failed him and he fled, and in a few minutes the poor girl was consumed; 4,000 bodies were dug out of the ruins. Famine followed, and the survivors were reduced to eat the canes in the fields for sustenance. I was informed that one part of the harbour of Point Petre, which before this event was capable of admitting ships of the heaviest burden, became completely choked up with rocks, forced up from the bottom of the sea.

I intended visiting the crater, which is about fifteen miles distant from the harbour, but the weather was too sultry to venture on so much exertion; so went on shore in the evening to take a quiet walk with Mr. Chaplain, the chief officer of the 'Monocacy;' but he was suddenly taken so ill that we were obliged to return.

On the 22nd we steamed out of Point Petre bay, and ran along the coast, which looked beautiful with its fields of waving canes; and we found the change of temperature most delightful as we got out into the broad ocean, after being nearly roasted at Guadaloupe.

It was decided to run down to Pernambuco, a distance of

2,500 miles; but the next day Mr. Chaplain was worse. The doctor asked me to visit him, and when we entered his room he was taken with a severe fit. He then became speechless, and though every care was bestowed that medical aid could give, he soon breathed his last. His body was taken on deck, and a place was prepared for it abaft the starboard wheel. It was placed on a platform shrouded with the American flag, and his sword laid by his side.

Our colours were hoisted half-mast, and the ship's course changed to Barbadoes, where we soon arrived, and anchored at Bridgetown, the capital.

The news of the death spread like wildfire over the ship; the men spoke of it in hurried whispers. They could hardly believe that he who had so lately issued his orders in a stentorian voice from the deck should now be lying on it, silent for ever; that the man who had so gallantly defended his country against rebellion should be now powerless, conquered by a mightier hand. Officers and men were deeply affected; not a smile was on the lips of any of that rough crew. Many had been Mr. Chaplain's comrades in arms during the late war, and had witnessed his daring acts of bravery, and I can truly say he was most sincerely regretted. As soon as we arrived at Bridgetown, preparations were made for the funeral. A plain coffin, covered with blue cloth, received the remains, dressed in full uniform. A boat from H.B.M. frigate 'Buzzard,' with officers and men, came alongside to pay respect to the dead. After a short funeral service the coffin was lowered into the ship's launch, attended by the deceased's coxswain and boat's crew. It was towed by the cutter, rowed with muffled oars, the ensign trailing in the water, and followed by all our boats and those of the 'Buzzard.' Not a word was spoken, the rattling of the muskets of the marines, as they landed, alone breaking the silence. The coffin was placed on a richly-plumed hearse, and the marines flanked it, trailing their muskets. Mr. Chaplain's sword and epaulettes, on a cushion, were borne after it by his coxswain.

The Governor in his carriage, the Commander of the 'Buzzard,' and all the officers of both ships, with the principal Americans and English of the place, followed. The cortége passed slowly through the town to St. Leonard's, where the impressive service of the Episcopal church was read, and a short address was given on the uncertainty of human life, especially to a soldier or sailor, and the necessity of ever being prepared to meet death. On arriving at the cemetery, the coffin was placed in a leaden one, and as it was lowered to its last resting-place, the marines fired a salute, which the frigate answered with minute-guns. When the minister read the solemn words, 'Dust to dust,' each one threw a spray of green leaves into the grave, as he bid adieu to the friend to be left behind buried in a strange land, far from his home and kindred.

Barbadoes is an important part of the British West Indian possessions. The island is twenty miles long and twelve broad, and contains about 136,000 inhabitants. Like most other sugar-planting countries, the greater part of the timber has been cut down to make way for the canes. There is little high land, but it gradually declines from the centre to the coast. The highest point is Mount Willoughby, and that is only 1,000 feet above sea level. There is little indication of volcanic action. In the southern parts of the island the land rises in terraces, one above the other. The plains are highly cultivated, but the northern side has a very broken surface, and is much less fertile.

Considerable quantities of petroleum, which is used instead of pitch, and serves for lamp oil, are found here. There is also a burning spring similar to the Retsamola, in the Apennines.

The climate of Barbadoes is in general healthy, is less humid in consequence of the light calcareous soil rapidly absorbing the rain, and enjoys a greater immunity from epidemic diseases than the other West Indian islands. Tornadoes and hurricanes which cause great damage to the shipping, are frequent during the months of August, September, and October. Bridgetown, the capital, is about two miles in extent. It contains good roads and some fine buildings, and in the principal square is a statue of Lord Nelson. On the 25th we weighed anchor, and again proceeded on our way to Pernambuco. Little occurred on our voyage, except a court martial on two men for getting drunk; a sham fight; a temporary alarm of fire, happily quickly allayed; and an excitement from an iron pin in the rudder getting loose; all of which, though but little to relate, caused breaks in our monotonous life at sea.

When still far from our port of destination it was found that we had only five days' coal, and there was a question of our putting back to Cearà; as we were not only dependent on coal for steaming, but for the condenser, which supplied the whole crew with water for drinking. We fell in with the Brazilian packet 'Percemuga,' just from Pernambuco, with a pilot on board, whom the captain asked if we would take. We sent a boat for him, and were glad of his services, particularly as he spoke English well.

As we approached Cape St. Roque, the waves were dashing furiously over an almost perpendicular rock, apparently of red clay formation. The shore in the distance looked like glittering heaps of white sand. We were close enough to see the houses, and fine groves of cocoa-nut trees.

Close to the cape I observed a church, which the pilot told me was that of 'Nossa Senhora dos Navigatos.' In most Portuguese seaports, chapels, or niches enclosing an image of the Virgin, are built on the shore, where those about to embark pray for a prosperous voyage, while the friends and relatives offer up prayers for their safe return.

Numbers of natives on janguardas were fishing on the coral reefs; some of these are large and carry a sail; others so small that only one man can sit on them. As the fellows paddle along some distance from the shore, it seemed as if half their bodies were submerged, and it was only as the frail crafts rose on the waves that it could be seen they were not floating on the water. These janguardas are formed of four or more logs of wood bound together, having a mast and large awkward-looking sail. They have no sides, so that every wave can break over them, yet the fishermen go a long distance from land on them.

All along the coast are fish pounds, similar to those I had seen in Algarve (Portugal). They are circular enclosures, which admit the fish at high water. As the tide recedes, the fish swim into the deeper water in the centre. The fishermen at low water go on their janguardas, and take their prey in a dip-net and carry them alive to the markets, in boxes made for the purpose, which they tow astern of their frail vessels.

Here we began to notice the splendour of the Southern constellations. Venus, from her great brilliancy in these latitudes, especially attracted our attention.

On October 8 we arrived off the port of Pernambuco; but the pilot we had taken out at sea was not allowed to bring the ship into harbour, as there was a government officer for that express purpose; so we had to remain outside, pitching and rolling about in a heavy swell. Early in the morning the pilot brought us in, and we dropped anchor under the reefs.

The port contains a sort of natural breakwater, running in a straight line, for nearly three-quarters of a mile, directly in front of the city. This appears to be of tertiary formation, and lies just above the surface of the water. The Portuguese have built a strong brick wall on this reef, to protect it from the violence of the waves.

A large hulk neatly painted is moored in the harbour, and serves as a school-ship for the Brazilian navy. The reefs of Pernambuco run parallel to the shore, at about 800 yards distance, for many miles.

A small octagonal tower called the Tour de Picas, erected on the shore, mounts several guns. On the opposite shore is an old fort called Castel de Bruno, built in 1640, and with the Tour de Picas protects the harbour, as the channel is very narrow here.

Vessels drawing more than 16 or 17 feet of water are obliged to anchor outside, but to those that can enter Pernambuco offers a safe and excellent harbour. At its entrance, on the eastern side of the reef, is a fine lighthouse, which exhibits three distinct lights from sunset to sunrise. There are two white and one red, and these make a complete revolution every ten minutes, and are visible from twelve to fifteen miles at sea.

To the south of Pernambuco lies Cocoa-nut Island, that has acquired a sort of notoriety from two hundred and fifty American seamen having for some time resided there. Maffit the pirate, after destroying and plundering several unarmed American vessels, finding their crews getting troublesome on his hands, compelled a French trader to take them into Pernambuco, and hand them over to our consul, Mr. Adamson, who took charge of them and placed them on this island until arrangements could be made to send them home.

This is one of the most important provinces in the Brazils, second only to Rio and Bahia, and with proper care would yield immensely; but from the careless way in which everything is done, and its agriculture in as backward a state, scarcely enough is raised for the consumption of the people.

It contains 1,180,000 inhabitants, 250,000 of whom are slaves employed on the sugar and coffee plantations. In the western part the country people grow a coarse kind of sugar (*Mandixa farinhio*) and vegetables. It is said to be celebrated for a fine-flavoured grape, highly prized by the Brazilians.

The city of Pernambuco is divided into three districts, called San Pedro de Gonsalvo or Recife, Boa Vista, and San Antonio.

The principal buildings are seventeen Catholic churches, one English Episcopal church, two monasteries, three asylums for girls, six hospitals, a theatre, custom-house, dockyard, arsenal, marine and military barracks, with a Lyceum, two Latin and seventy-five primary schools. There are three newspapers issued daily, two of them in Portuguese and one in English, giving the general news of the day, and these as far as I could judge were very ably conducted.

The appearance of Pernambuco from the sea is not attractive; and, as a great part of it is built on low flat land, little of the city is visible. The large white tower of the arsenal on the Prayos, with some of the highest buildings, are first seen; but from the waves dashing over the reef and sending up showers of spray, their foundations are hidden, and they seem to rise from the waters.

I called on Mr. Adamson, our consul, and had a very pleasant hour's chat with him.

Captain Carter and myself attended the opening of the Exhibition by Dom Jose Perreira, and were introduced to the President, who received us courteously.

The address was well conceived, giving a general review of the improvements made in the province during the past year, and comparing them with those of former years. He then referred to the progress made in the United States in arts and sciences, the wonderful strides in agriculture, and the large amount of cereals we produce. Also to the great inventive genius of America, mentioning the singular fact that, during the late rebellion, in the short space of three or four years, we had completely revolutionised modern warfare! Our monitors, our great guns, our merchant ships and frigates, and our iron hearts and hands to man them, all were descanted on. I listened for more than an hour, in an atmosphere of 90° Fahrenheit, and was glad to be shown to the exhibition-rooms, where all the products of the country were collected. The President offering his arm to Mrs. Adamson, our consul's wife, we went down to the rooms, the band playing Dom Pedro's march.

The first thing that attracted our attention was a large case of elegant vestments which were wrought in gold and silver thread, probably for the clergy of the district, and a flag of silk richly embroidered, bearing the arms of Brazil in its centre. There were perfect models of ships, brigs, steamers, &c., made by the apprentices of the marine arsenal, and very creditably done. In one compartment were all the woods of the province, some very beautiful; but I was informed that they had never been introduced as articles of commerce. I tasted some excellent wine from the fruit of the cashew, which the manufacturer told me would be made in such quantities the following year as to yield sufficient for shipment. There were also fine samples of native oils and vinegars. The cereals were prominent—abundant and of good quality. There were fifty-two kinds of beans, several quite new to me. There were also very fair native paintings. On the whole it was a creditable exhibition, and pleased us greatly, as many articles were quite equal to European manufacture. Our time and the heat did not allow us to examine everything very closely, and we were not sorry to get into the fresh air.

The beautiful town of Olenda is about two miles from Pernambuco, and is situated on the sides of a very high hill, the summit of which is crowned by a large convent. For many years Olenda was the capital of the province, but, owing to its distance from the harbour rendering it unfavourable for commerce, the town of Recife has taken the preference. The pretty Lauristinus, or a plant very closely resembling it, flourishes here, and forms a beautiful contrast with the dusky olive and the graceful palm and cocoa-nut trees. The view from the hill is magnificent, looking down into the valley below and over the city of Pernambuco, which can be seen above the fine groves of mangoes and other trees.

The captain and I visited the monastery, and were politely and hospitably received by the Bishop.

A sumptuous repast was spread for us, and we were shown over the building, which is kept in fine order. There are two large organs in the chapel, and the seats and stands in the gallery, where the monks of old used to chant their services, are beautifully carved.

In Dom Pedro's time, when the monasteries were suppressed, the clock-work attached to the chimes in the tower was destroyed, the bells were melted, and the machinery all broken up, and this a priest pointed out to me lying on the floor, and sighed sadly as he told of its departed glories. It is still an open question whether the breaking-up of these monastic institutions did not do more harm to the labouring classes than the suppression of a few abuses did good.

I must not forget the Foundling Hospital, which stands at a little distance from the monastery. Near the door in a recess is a swinging cradle, with a bell-rope attached. When a child is brought, it is laid in the cradle, and the bell is rung. Silently the cradle is turned, and the child taken out, when a number is placed on its neck, and a corresponding one put into the empty cradle, as it swings back into its place. This is to enable the child to be identified at any future period. No one is visible, no question is asked; nothing is ever known of the anguish of those who thus leave their children to strangers' care. How many aching hearts may have stood beside that cradle, as the little one has been laid within, to save it from shame, starvation, or perhaps death; for infanticide was prevalent before the foundation of this asylum.

We did not enter, but I could see the nurses with their little charges on the lawn in front of the place, which was very quiet, and in a very wholesome condition.

Near this is a large convent, where young ladies of the best families are sent to be educated; and a fair proportion of whom become so in love with convent life as to refuse to leave it, and take the veil.

The luxuriance of the vegetation in the whole province of Pernambuco is remarkable even for the tropics. I will not attempt to describe what has been so often done by abler pens than mine. It would be but a repetition of magnificent trees covered with wild lianes loaded with blossom, orchids which imitate insects and moths, birds of the brightest hues, and the oppressive fragrance of a tropical forest.

Some of the streets of Pernambuco are wide and spacious, containing handsome buildings; but even the narrow streets were kept very clean, though I should mention I did not see it in the rainy season.

The Palace à Campo stands near the theatre, and is a fine well-arranged building, with large gardens attached, filled with rare and beautiful exotic plants. The Palace Square seemed, from its position, a very desirable place of residence.

The principal business part of the city is built on an island, and there is communication with the mainland by five large, well-built bridges. One of them is a massive iron structure, built by an English engineer.

October 17 we left Pernambuco, with a fair wind, for Rio, where we arrived on the 23rd. As we entered the harbour we found the U.S.S. flagship 'Brooklyn,' and fired a salute to the admiral of thirteen guns, which was responded to, and her brass band favoured us with 'Hail Columbia' as we passed her.

Soon after anchoring, Captain Carter went on board the 'Brooklyn,' and word was then sent to the 'Monocacy' to fire a salute of eighty-six guns to the Brazilian, Spanish, Portuguese, British, and French vessels of war then in the harbour. It was promptly returned from all their iron mouths, as well as from the Brazilian forts, so that our advent made some stir in the place.

As you enter Rio harbour, the scenery is grand and imposing. The Sugarloaf and Corcovada Mountains, with their bold precipitous cliffs, frown down upon you; the Organ Mountains lie in the distance, and a long range of hills borders the coast. The harbour is well fortified and studded with picturesque islands.

When we went ashore we landed at the Palace Square, where is the residence of the Emperor of the Brazils. There was a regiment of soldiers parading in it before embarkation for Paraguay, and such a motley set I never saw before. The officers wore brilliant uniforms, and cocked hats bedizened with gold lace and flaunting plumes.

Brazil was then at war with Paraguay, with the view of a complete destruction of the sovereignty, independency, and integrity of that country. For this purpose it had formed a secret alliance with the governments of Buenos Ayres and

Uruguay. This alliance becoming known, excited great indignation throughout the remaining republics of South America.

Soldiers were everywhere recruiting in the streets, as large bounties were offered to such as would fill up the decimated ranks.

The Brazilians consider themselves superior to the Portuguese; but in my opinion they have sadly degenerated from the parent stock, as the contrast between the Cascadores of Portugal and the flower of the Brazilian army is very great. Then again, the manners and customs are entirely different, and the language greatly corrupted, as I did not hear pure Portuguese spoken in any part of the Brazils.

The city of Rio was clean, and the sanitary laws are excellent, and seem rigidly executed. Just beyond the Palace Square there is an American restaurant, where all the fancy drinks, from an 'Eye-opener' to a Champagne 'corpse-reviver,' can be procured from sunrise to sunrise.

The principal business street of the city is the Rua d'Ouvidor. There you can purchase the choicest and richest merchandise of the world. The native costume is now rarely seen in Rio, as both ladies and gentlemen have gone into the extreme of French fashion; and Parisian milliners, tailors, barbers, &c., occupy the principal shops of the Rua d'Ouvidor. The diamond merchants, too, have their stores here; and, judging from the fondness of all classes for jewellery, I should think there was a flourishing trade.

There are two theatres, and in one of them I saw the *Barbe Bleu* performed very creditably by a French troupe.

Several daily papers are published, but education does not seem to progress rapidly under the present government.

The Misericordia Hospital is one of the finest and best conducted in the world. It is under the management of a company, and the nurses are the *Sœurs de Charité.*

It contains 1,500 clean and comfortable-looking beds, while the floors of boxwood, brightly polished, give a cool aspect that must be refreshing to a sick man in a tropical climate.

There are many hotels, some of them well kept up, and with good tables, at reasonable prices. Taken altogether, Rio is as cheap a place as one could wish. The people are polite and hospitable to foreigners, and at the time we visited it the city was very healthy.

Most of the merchants doing business in the city have their dwellings in the suburbs. Rio boasts of two public gardens, one called the 'Botanical or Emperor's Garden,' about eight miles from it, and the other the 'Passeio Publico,' within the city. The latter is enclosed by a handsome iron railing on the W. and N.; on the S. by a high wall; and the east is built up to form an esplanade, looking over the sea. As you enter the gardens through a large gateway facing the street, the stranger's eye is struck with the fine bronze statues, on pedestals of the same material, on each side of the entrance. Passing down the main avenue, shaded by gigantic palms, to our surprise we came upon a number of American larch, spruce, and arbor-vitæ, all thriving well.

There is a winding stream through the grounds, with pretty little islands formed in it, and on its waters floated numbers of aquatic plants brought from the mighty Amazon.

Black and white swans, native wild ducks, gulls, boobies, cranes, the white egret, and the scarlet ibis, all are to be seen about the grass near the water, or under the trees planted there to give them shade from the fierce heat of the tropical sun. In the stream there were two manittas, or sea-cows. These huge monsters were quite tame, and either lay basking in the sun, or in the shallow parts of the water, just showing their noses above the surface. It is very rare to see them in confinement; but these appeared quite happy, and were on the best terms with their feathered comrades, and followed the black swans about everywhere.

As we crossed the stream over a little bridge, we saw a flight of steps opposite to us leading to the esplanade, and at the foot of them were two cast-iron alligators, partially hidden by artificial rock-work, covered with ferns and creeping plants. From the mouths of these monsters flow streams of clear water, which fall into a large basin, wherein I found some interesting plants; amongst others, some *Tetraspora*, *Ulvaceæ*, two species of *Confervæ*, &c. &c. At the top of the steps is a statue of Cupid, with a flask in his hand, out of which he incessantly pours deliciously cool water, that we found most grateful, as the day was hot, and we were tired with our long ramble. The view from the esplanade looking over the bay, is very fine. You see in the foreground the two forts that defend the harbour; the pretty little church to 'Nossa Senhora dos Navigatos,' on the island mountain, and the buildings occupied by the pupils of the Naval Academy; and in the distance the village of St. Domingo, and the beautiful mountains of Jurajuba. A good refreshment-room is in this garden, provided with seats and tables under the shade of some beautiful trees, and where we tasted the native ale, which we found excellent. On leaving I saw the celebrated Vanilla-bean plant twining round the trunks of large trees, to which it clings like ivy, by very strong tendrils that shoot from the joints, and almost bury themselves like roots in the bark of the supporting tree. The Passeio Publico is quite a fashionable promenade in the warm summer evenings.

We visited St. Domingo, taking the ferry-boat, and landing at the floating-bridge, which is similar in construction to that at Fulton Ferry, in Brooklyn, New York.

In the principal square sat numbers of coloured women, with all the fruits of the season spread out on the ground before them for sale. I observed for the first time the singular Jack-fruit, *Artocarpus integrifolia.* We purchased one, but did not find it at all to our taste, though highly esteemed by the Brazilians. The large seeds are the best part of it. I have since often eaten them cooked, and liked them. The fruit, when cut, we could not be tempted to eat, though assured it was very nice. Being blessed with an acute scent, we could not get over its disgusting smell of putrid meat; and, strange to say, the meat-fly hovers round it, just as if it were a piece of carrion.

The tree is very handsome, and at a little distance resembles the magnolia; but the leaf is darker, and its foliage is so dense as to be impervious to the sun. The monster fruit grows on a very short stem, and hangs from the trunk of the tree. I have seen it more than two feet long, and twelve to sixteen inches in diameter.

After examining all the different fruits, we strolled through the streets, and were greatly delighted at the taste displayed in the residences and the fine gardens attached to them. We saw oranges and tanjarines growing everywhere, and for the first time the mammæ apple (*Papaya edulis*). The tree grows from ten to fifteen feet high, and looks not unlike the foliage of the castor-oil nut-tree, except that the leaves are of a thinner texture, and grow in a large graceful tuft at the top of the trunk, and the fruit hangs just under the crown. Many of these exceed a pound in weight, and when ripe are of a bright yellow, filled with brownish seeds in a pulpy bed. The taste is not unpleasant when eaten, but leaves a peppery flavour.

The Prayos seems to be a favourite walk of the Brazilian ladies, here still dressed in the graceful Spanish costume, with veils on their heads. In every case they were accompanied by slaves, either black or yellow, it not being etiquette for a lady to appear unattended by one or more. The country people were very polite, and willingly answered questions, and gave me any information I required.

From the Prayos I went to Jurajuba, a small place near Santa Cruz, inhabited chiefly by fishermen, who supply the markets at Rio. There is little variety of fish in the harbour. The principal are graupers, black and blue fish, and rays; one of the latter I saw caught, was at least twenty feet across his fins. There are large quantities of a small fish they call a sardine, very like the mossbunkers, and most unlike the sardine of the Mediterranean. They are certainly the best flavoured fish brought to market. The prawns of Rio are in abundance, and are probably the finest in the world. There are great numbers of edible crabs, which are nearly all sold by Chinese, who hawk them about in large baskets slung on their shoulders.

After passing through Jurajuba, I shaped my course up the mountain, towards a small opening in the woods. Bright coloured butterflies fluttered across my path, and now and then a gorgeous-plumaged bird would start up before me, and, uttering a soft plaintive note, disappear in the dense foliage.

The place was covered with noble palms, mangoes, and flowering shrubs. I walked for some distance in a southerly direction, but at length found it impossible to penetrate deeper through the dense underbrush. The vines and creepers were so thickly intertwined, I was obliged to retrace my steps. I collected a good many rare botanical specimens, and got a few snakes and lizards, which abound here, the former are most of them poisonous.

As night was approaching, I hastened on in hopes of reaching St. Domingo; but, after walking two or three miles, I found I had lost my way. The sun was fast sinking in the west; and the unpleasant idea of having to spend a night alone in a Brazilian forest was beginning to force itself on me.

As I had a Colt's revolver and a large knife in my girdle, I began seriously to contemplate taking up my quarters in a tree, should I not succeed in finding an opening. I walked on for about half an hour unsuccessfully, and as it was then quite dark, had just decided on going to roost, when I heard the voice of a muleteer singing to his mules in the distance. I lost no time in shouting at the top of my voice, and to my great joy was answered, and he soon came to my rescue. He told me I was ten or twelve miles from St. Domingo; that he was a slave going to market to sell fruit for his master; and that if I would accompany him, he would guide me. He was astonished to find I could speak his language, and still more that I was foolish enough to penetrate the jungle solus. The stories he told me of the ounce (*Felis onca*) were enough to frighten anyone, but fortunately I knew them to be mostly imaginary. Both the ounce and boa constrictor are common in Brazil, but rarely seen in this neighbourhood.

The only dreaded thing I met with was the terrible snake, the *Jararaca* (*Bothrops Neuwiedia*), which is a near relation to the rattlesnake, and which abounds on the grassy slopes. It makes a whistling noise as you approach it, and elevates its body like a cobra. Scarcely a clump of bamboos is without one of these reptiles, the bite of which is certain death. It is generally most prudent to get out of their way; but the sight of a snake always arouses my organ of combativeness, and I kill it whenever I can get a chance to do so.

My companion was very chatty, and told me no end of marvels. Amongst others, he said that when he first heard my voice he tied his mules high up the mountain, their panniers laden with fruit and vegetables, as he was sure no one would molest them there. I was curious to know the reason of this perfect security; so he told me it was because 'They were so near heaven,' and added, as a corroboration, that a 'man who was killed up there by an ounce went straight up to heaven, as purgatory was many hundred feet below him!'

We took a narrow footpath on our descent into the valley, which was a short cut, luckily well known to the man, for it was so dark I was obliged to keep close to the mules.

Being anxious to get back, I urged him on, and we got to St. Domingo at three o'clock in the morning; when there I at once put off in a boat for the 'Monocacy,' where my friends were beginning to think I was lost.

In spite of my exploring difficulties, I had been so charmed with what I had seen, that I determined to pay another visit to the Brazilian forests.

I had been constantly asked if I had ascended the Corcovada; and as I wished very much to do so, I tried to get up a party from the ship to accompany me, but unsuccessfully; so made up my mind the following Monday to be up early, and off to the mountain.

Before that time, however, the Rev. Mr. Schneider, the American missionary there, offered to accompany me, and requested me to call for him very early. I did so, but the Fates were against me; his wife was so ill that he could not leave her. Nothing daunted, I still resolved to go on alone; particularly as he assured me it was perfectly safe to do so, and gave me directions for the ascent.

In an hour's time I was fairly on my way up, my vasculum strapped on my back, and a good stout hickory stick to help me on. The road was good enough for carriages to drive along as far as the great aqueduct, which is supplied from a reservoir up the mountain, and carries in a sufficient stream of water for the whole of Rio.

I passed many gentlemen's residences, most of them under preparation for the reception of their owners during the summer months; the fine gardens attached to each were being put in order. Along the aqueduct were a great variety of herbaceous plants, ferns, and mosses. The tree-fern (*Trichopteris excelsa*) is found at this level, and everyone of the gigantic forest trees was covered from root to branch with orchideæ, cacti, and twining plants. The road crossed deep ravines over bridges. In their dark recesses the sun never shines, and the fronds of the ferns were some of them fifteen feet long by three or four broad. The luxuriance of these cryptogams tempted me out of my path; and I was climbing over a wall near a bridge in order to descend, when I heard a voice shouting to me not to venture, as it was full of snakes and other slimy monsters. I found my informant was a coloured man, lying under the shade of some banana trees. He was going up the mountain with a basket of provisions for the labourers working on the road. He told me no one ever dared descend into these ravines on account of the venomous snakes. He said it was common to meet the boa constrictor, but it was only the jararaca he feared.

Whilst speaking, one glided along the road, and made the peculiar whistling noise that warns of its approach. My companion at once crossed himself and began reciting his prayers, while I killed the reptile and popped him into my bottle.

The road is good as far as the reservoir, which is a fine piece of work of dressed granite, built on the side of the mountain. The main aqueduct is covered in with masonry till it reaches the city, a distance of some miles. After refreshing myself, I took leave of the old man, striking into a narrow winding path, which in some places is only cut out of the side of the mountain, and is there very steep and dangerous.

By eleven o'clock I arrived at the upper water-works, about 1,800 feet above sea-level. So circuitous had been my route, I found I had travelled about fourteen miles by my pedometer.

At this height there are a few small huts built, one of them occupied by a Portuguese naturalist, who had charge of the works.

He furnished me with refreshments ; and while I was resting myself, a group of seven or eight darkies made their appearance, who had been engaged all the morning in removing a large stone which had fallen in and impeded the water-course. They were all slaves, but the most jovial set I had ever met with. Never did the fetters of slavery sit lighter on any of the descendants of Ham. After eating some lumps of brown bread and salt fish, and washing it down with Canna aguardienta, they began singing and dancing, strange to say to the tune of 'Ole Dan Tucker.' An old grey-headed fellow kept time, by tapping on the end of a barrel with two sticks. They had the double-shuffle, all-hands-round, plantation dance, and many others. Finally, one of them sung a plaintive air about Massa Linkum, and they all appeared well acquainted with the tragic fate of him whom they called the 'father of the black man,' and I saw his portrait everywhere.

I was much amused with these coloured 'children of a

larger growth,' and passed on, earning their good wishes by giving a few patacãos to each, and entreaties to the Virgin to protect me; but they all advised me to keep out of the jungle. Up I went, and the higher I got the more bewilderingly lovely became the scene. I caught a view of the ocean from the SW. side, but soon lost it in the difficulties of the ascent. I reached the summit by one o'clock, and was richly repaid for the toilsome journey. The government had erected a sort of look-out and telegraphic establishment, with seats for visitors to rest themselves, but it had been abandoned for some years.

The peak rises to about 2,600 feet, and on its eastern face nearly two-thirds of it is a perpendicular precipice. Just as I arrived at the top, the men-of-war in the harbour were firing a salute, and the effect was very singular as the sound struck the bold cliffs of the mountain. The panoramic view obtained at this point is magnificent.

Looking down on the bay, studded with its tree-covered islands, the outlines of the distant mountain ranges, the ocean dotted here and there with merchant-ships making for the port; the lofty peaks of Tijuco and Gavea, with their precipitous sides clothed with mighty forests; the plantations of coffee, oranges, and mandiocca in the valleys; altogether made a scene never to be effaced from my memory.

The trees at the foot of the mountain are very large, but the vegetable growth sensibly lessens towards the summit.

I know not how long I should have gazed on the view before me, had I not been unpleasantly roused from my reverie by finding I had seated myself in such close proximity to a small grey snake, coiled up, that I could have touched it with my hand. I killed it with a single blow of my stick, and believe the snake was a very poisonous one.

I began to descend, collecting ferns, insects, and reptiles, till my vasculum and bottles were all full.

When I had reached the shoulder, there was a very inviting opening into which, of course, I went.

I had not penetrated far, when my attention was arrested by some large bright coloured butterflies on the tpomœas. Whilst waiting for them to settle, I was arranging my scaup-net on my stick, when I heard a singular noise near me. On looking down I discovered I was only about fifteen feet from a large snake half coiled under an aloe, with crest erected and mouth open.

I confess I felt frightened, and did not at all approve of coming to South America to be ignominiously swallowed by a snake. Determined however to sell my life as dearly as possible, I raised my old hickory stick, meaning to try it on his vertebræ if he approached, at the same time steadily beating a retreat.

When at some distance, finding he did not move, I lifted a large stone and hurled it at him, at the same time giving a tremendous yell. I missed him, but the brute uncoiled and slunk away into the thicket, and as soon as he disappeared I took to my heels, and made off as fast as I could, tearing my clothes and scratching my face, in my hurry to get away from the monster's quarters.

In the meantime my friend at the reservoir, alarmed at my long absence up the mountain, came to look for me. I heard him holloaing long before I got out of the wood, but I soon reached the main road, and it was not long before I was seated on the grass enjoying some capital rice and curry with him. Towards four o'clock I left, my friend escorting me some distance, lest I should again lose my way.

He told me that a few weeks before a party of ladies and gentlemen made the ascent to the shoulder on horseback for a pic-nic. When returning, a young lady and her companion had preceded the party, and in a narrow place her horse grew restive and refused to stir; the whip was applied, when he threw her off over the precipice, the sides of which were studded with trees. Luckily her dress caught in some branches, and held her suspended over the awful abyss below. She was soon rescued, and the cause of the horse's swerving was discovered in a large boa constrictor lying across the road, its head and tail invisible. They attacked it, but at the first blow it disappeared in the ravine.

After accompanying me for a mile or two, my friend Pedro Gonsalves left me. He was a good specimen of the kind-hearted and hospitable people of the country to which he belongs.

I had not gone far when the rumble of distant thunder

warned me not to loiter. The whole sky became overcast, and heavy rain-drops came pattering down. Seeing a light at some distance below, I made all haste to reach it, but did not succeed before the rain fell in torrents, the thunder echoed from cliff to cliff, and the vivid flashes of lightning almost blinded me.

I entered a small shanty on the roadside, but could see no one. I announced my arrival in the usual way by clapping my hands; and then as I advanced I saw behind a large wooden chest an old couple with their child kneeling, offering up prayers to their patron saint, to protect them from the storm fiends. I did not disturb them, but remained near the doorway till the rain had passed. They then came forward, and asked me how I came to be in such a lonely place, as they could not understand how anyone could go there who was not obliged.

The man was guardian to part of the aqueduct. He told me he was a native of Viana, in Portugal, and showed the greatest delight when he found I knew the place well. While conversing with him, his old wife busied herself with preparations for supper, and invited me to partake of it. It consisted of brouer or coarse bread, made of unbolted rye and Indian meal, and fried bachalau or salt fish. I was very hungry, so ate heartily, and washed it down with a good draught of water, for wine they had none.

I left two cruzados novas with the old couple, and earned a shower of blessings, and entreaties to San Antonio to protect me in my descent. It soon grew quite dark; and it was with difficulty I reached Rio by midnight, wet and tired. I did not go on board, but stayed at the hotel, and next day paid a visit to the Botanical or Emperor's Gardens, about eight miles from the city.

It is a pleasant drive, past all the pretty gardens and cottages, to the comfortable inn close to the place. The most prominent feature there is some rows of the Oreodoxa Regia palm, most of them nearly forty feet in height. They were planted by Dom John VI., who founded the gardens. There is a fine avenue of Casuarinas, rows of cinnamon and clove-trees, and the tea-plant.

These have been introduced with the view of cultivating them as articles of commerce; and I think, if properly managed, they will be successful, as the climate seems to suit them. At San Paulo is a tea-plantation, which already sends tea of good quality to the Rio market. A little stream flows through the grounds, bordered with clumps of the graceful feathery bamboo, that gives such elegance to tropical scenery. The Jack and bread-fruit trees grow very large. I was astonished to find a total absence of the thousands of beautiful indigenous plants, which could be easily collected in the immediate vicinity. Even the rare and lovely orchideæ of the country would make charming groups, and be of the greatest interest to the foreigner.

I was greatly disappointed with the gardens, and thought how different they would have been in either Europe or America, with such a wealth of material close to hand, enough to make them of world-wide fame.

In a fine square, the Campo di Santa Anna, is the national museum; but it was scarcely worth a visit, all the specimens jumbled together without any arrangement or order. This square also contains a theatre and a number of Government buildings.

In the Campo di Dom Pedro is a fine statue of this emperor in bronze, and the square is ornamented with beautiful trees and flowering shrubs. The country produces sugar, cotton, delicious fruits, and coffee; the latter is the principal export.

Rio contains about 175,000 inhabitants, the greater portion of which are coloured. It can boast of one of the finest docks in the world; hewn out of the solid rock, and cost many millions of dollars. It is the work of an English engineer. There is an iron foundry, which I visited, and its works will vie with those of European nations. This is also under the management of Europeans and Americans.

On November 19 we were ready for sea; our engines had been overhauled and put in perfect order, and we steamed up the harbour and anchored off Coal Island. At noon three Spanish frigates fired a salute in commemoration of the Queen of Spain's coronation. Their masts were lined with the flags of all nations, and they fired fast and regularly a hundred guns. On the 22nd the 'Monocacy' turned her head towards the sea, and we slowly steamed away.

When close to the stern of the English flag-ship, the admiral gave us a good-bye salute. Just as we left a clipper ship was putting into the port in distress, having lost her top-masts and bulwarks.

As we passed St. Cruz a swell set in from the west. The ship rolled heavily, as we were deep in the water, having 300 tons of coal on board, including 40 tons on deck.

SUGAR-LOAF HILL.

CHAPTER II.

EASTWARD BOUND.

Bad Weather—Catching an Albatross—Accident to Captain—Brilliance of Southern Constellations—Serious Consequences of killing an Albatross—Whale Brit—Tristan d'Acunha—Its History—Chemical Barometer, and how to make it—Arrival in Simon's Bay—Description of Country—Cape Sheep—Hottentot Venus—The Pilot—Baboons—A Night in the Mountains—Ascent of Table Mountain—Principal Features of Cape Town—Harbour Sights—A Cape Waggon—Churches—Masonry—The Government—A Dutch Boer—Road from Cape Town to Simon's Bay—Adieu to the Cape—A Hurricane—Hints on Cyclones—Mauritius at Last.

Again on the wide ocean, onward bound ; but we soon found it was not to be smooth sailing, for we had been but one day at sea when the weather changed.

On the night of the 23rd it was so rough, everything was rolling and pitching about, and keeping up such a clattering that sleep was impossible. The guns frequently dipped in the water, and the waves broke over the hurricane deck.

Many of both officers and men were sea-sick, myself amongst the number. I lay tossing from side to side, and wondering how people could like the sea. I thought of the song 'Some love to roam o'er the dark sea's foam,' but decidedly give me the 'Life in the woods.' My only consolation was that the waves which surged over our vessel, and the wind that whistled round us, carried us rapidly on our way ; this pleased our captain, too, for he was very anxious to get far to the SE., beyond the river La Plate, to avoid the Pampero which prevails at this season. This wind is so called from its blowing off the Pampas, and is dreaded by navigators cruising in these latitudes.

Towards noon of the 24th, though little squalls of rain continued, the barometer indicated a change for the better ; and I amused myself fishing with line and hook, baited with pork, for a large albatross which hovered round the ship. The hook had a bit of wood for a float, and the bird would gracefully sail round it, and then plunge at the bait; but as I was quite a novice at this kind of bird-catching, I failed in my efforts. He did not, however, quit us, but, in company with some petrels, kept round about the ship till dark.

The 25th rose bright and clear, and all was bustle and activity on deck, as the crew were being exercised at the guns. After this the men had their day to themselves. It was curious to watch them all, seated over the deck with their biddy-boxes of needles, thread, buttons, &c. Some were making shirts,

TABLE MOUNTAIN.

pants, or cap-covers; others cutting out new, or mending old clothes, and very deftly too; for a man-of-war's man can turn his hand to everything. During the day there was a sale of the effects of two or three sailors who had deserted at Rio. Beds, bedding, wearing apparel, every article, was put up separately, and knocked down to the highest bidder; and a good deal of fun was made as any rather out-of-the-way thing, or ragged garment, was held up.

Divine service was held by Captain Carter regularly every sabbath. All came aft in their best clothes, and seated themselves quietly and reverently. The American flag was spread over a table, and when prayers were read, officers and men joined in a hymn. It is, I think, a peculiarly impressive service, out on the deep blue ocean. There were 175 souls shut away from all the world, assembling, and uniting their voices in praise of their Creator. In the evening I sat in the ward-room with the officers, and we sang all the good old psalm tunes. They brought back younger days when, at the old fire-side at home, all the dear ones, now dead or scattered, joined in the holy songs.

No little excitement was one day aroused by an accident that nearly proved fatal to our captain. He was standing near the rail, watching the men cleaning a boat; and as they were hauling it into its place, one of the davits struck him and sent him overboard. Fortunately, he caught at a block and rope, and with difficulty saved himself. It was a narrow escape, as we were steaming along six knots, and had he gone down to the water there would have been little chance of saving him. Officers and men looked pale when they heard of it, for the captain was much liked, and they congratulated him heartily. His loss would have been a great grief to us all, and an irreparable one to our ship. Albatrosses and petrels were always round us. The men tried hard to get me one of the former, but for a long while unsuccessfully. One of our sailors named Benaro, at last caught one, and after great resistance he drew him on board; but not before it had taxed his utmost skill and strength.

In about half an hour another was hooked, and we let them go about on the deck together. They were fine birds, but looked very droll waddling along. I had been instructed to procure a fine specimen of this bird for one of our large public institutions. I was anxious to kill one without injuring his plumage, and so gave him a dose of cyanide of potassium about as large as a pea; in less than a minute he lay over on his side, dead without a struggle. We concluded to give the other his liberty; but first fastened a strip of copper round his neck, on which was engraved the name of our ship, and our lat. and long., and then sent him over the side. He was so astonished at finding himself once more in the water that he did not attempt to fly off, but kept swimming after us.

In these latitudes the zodiacal stars, such as Orion and Arcturus, give the mariner the E. and W. bearings, and the Southern Cross the N. and S. when Polaris and the Great Bear can no longer be seen. I had heard so much of the Southern Cross, I was anxious to see it; but confess if it had not been pointed out to me, I should not have discovered it.

Perhaps it may be more brilliant when we are more to the south. But the other constellations are magnificent, and it was one of my greatest pleasures on board to sit gazing up at the wonderful beauty overhead. How many queries are suggested to a reflecting mind when we take an attentive view of the celestial vault that overtops our world, with the planets and stars one after the other emerging from the blue ethereal, and gradually illuminating the firmament, till it is spangled over with its shining orbs, moving in silent grandeur at such immense distances as to be past the range of human comprehension! Who, while contemplating them, can doubt the existence of the Supreme Being who has created them, and guides these millions of worlds in their courses?

Then came the unanswerable questions, What purpose do they serve in the vast plan of the universe? How do their laws, physical and moral, differ from ours? Are they inhabited by sentient beings, like ourselves, actuated by the same hopes and fears, the same passions, and subject to dissolution even as we are? Here my meditations were cut short by a call to go aft, and look at the myriads of medusæ and squids swimming round the ship. Being disturbed by the motion of the vessel, they threw off a phosphoric light, so brilliant that their forms could be discerned. The sides of the vessel were illuminated till every bolt and bar was visible.

It was most interesting to watch them, and we could see that they continued to give out this electric light till they were far astern.

About eleven o'clock a large meteor crossed the heavens, at about 75 degrees, and took a western flight, till it sank below the horizon. It appeared about the size of a man's head, and left a train of brilliant light behind it like a sky-rocket. I seemed to hear a rushing noise as it passed through the atmosphere. The light remained for half a minute before it faded away. Many smaller meteors appeared the same evening, taking the same course, shooting with the greatest velocity.

On the 28th we had a squall that carried away our topmasts, which increased to a gale by night. Instead of the calm placid appearance of the preceding evening, we had the sea running mountains high, and the wind howlng through the rigging.

However, I turned in, and contrived to sleep soundly in spite of wind and weather. Up to December 3 we had continual squalls, when I found, to my utter astonishment, that to *me* was attributed a good deal of the contrariety of the elements! The sailors averred that it was all owing to my having killed the albatross. When the storm was at its height on the Sunday, they entreated me not to kill any more of these birds, as they are considered to be the spirits of seamen lost in the ocean; and who, dying unassoiled, have to wander over the face of the deep for an infinity of years; and they hover round ships in the hope of seeing some of their old comrades.

I could not help laughing at the superstition, which was partially shared even by some of the officers; but finding them so earnest in their belief, I promised that no other bird should be molested by me while on board. I was sorry for the sake of science; for I saw some of the yellow-nosed albatrosses and large petrels afterwards, which I should like to have got for the Long Island Historical Society, New York, but was obliged to allow the lost spirits to sail on in security, protected by the brave sons of Neptune.

Luckily for me they did not serve me like Coleridge's 'Ancient Mariner,' and hang the dead bird round my neck,

> For I had done a hellish thing,
> And it would work me woe;
> For all averred I had killed the bird,
> That made the fair breeze blow.
> 'Ah wretch,' said they, 'the bird to slay,
> That made the breeze to blow.'

For several evenings I saw the most brilliant meteors; and the long continuation of them seemed so remarkable, I suggested they should be noticed in the log. But no—the officer on deck could not be made to see 'the use' of recording 'falling stars,' as he called them. It is a pity our Naval Academy does not do more towards cultivating the minds as well as developing the physical powers of the men. As it is, as good or better men might be taken out of our mercantile marine to man our ships of war.

On the 4th I observed large red patches of what appeared like weeds on the sea, and got one of the sailors to take up a bucket of water containing some of the substance. I found it was alive with crustaceous animals which whalemen call Brit, on which the right whale feeds. The presence of this food accounts for our having seen so many whales. We were then in Lat. 36. 20, Long. 16. 15.

On the 5th, was heard the cheering cry of Land ho! from the mast-head, and on the windward beam we soon saw the mountain of Tristan d'Acunha appearing above the white clouds that hung on the horizon. Though we had a fair view of the islands, we could not approach them, as the weather was uncertain, and it is considered a dangerous coast; so we gave them a good wide berth to leeward, and proceeded on our course. I

TRISTAN D'ACUNHA.

collected, however, some information about them, which I will relate. There are three islands in the group, but one only is inhabited. They were discovered by the Portuguese. The mountain in the central island is said to be 8,356 feet high, accessible to its summit, although it is snow-capped a greater part of the year. Trees grow half way up, but the rest is a rugged peak. Captain Patten of the ship 'Industry' was there, sealing, from August 1790 to April 1791. An open bay lies on the west, with a fine beach of black sand, where the ship's boats were hauled up. There are two falls of excellent water, affording a supply sufficient for a large fleet; and from one of these cascades the water casks could be filled by means of a hose, without removing them from the boats.

There is a good deal of timber, though not high. The principal trees resemble the yew in foliage, with a wood like the maple,[1] and burns well. Wild celery, dock, sorrel, and parsley are found. Gannets, penguins, albatrosses, Cape cocks and hens, and a bird something like a partridge, only it is black, and cannot fly, are abundant. Such numbers of sea lions are on this coast, that Captain Patten said he could have loaded a ship with the oil in three weeks.

Between the shore and the foot of the mountain is a fine rich soil, of a red colour and good depth, well adapted for the growth of vegetables.

In 1811 one Jonathan Lambert, an American, by a singular edict, declared himself sovereign proprietor of the island. He sowed the ground with various seeds, and planted coffee and canes, both of which did well. He, however, soon abandoned it; and, at a later period, the British Government took formal possession of it, by a detachment from the Cape of Good Hope.

An old serjeant of artillery called Glass, was made Governor, and a little colony was formed of twenty-two men and three women.

In 1823 a British vessel putting in there was astonished to find Englishmen, and an abundant supply of vegetables, pigs, goats, fruit, and water.

Glass told the sailors if there were only a few more of the fair sex, it would be a Paradise.

In 1829 Captain Ben Morrell, of the U.S.Ship 'Antartic,' said he found seven families living there very comfortably under the administration of Glass; and keeping bullocks, sheep, goats, poultry, eggs, butter and milk, all which they sell to ships on very reasonable terms.

The inhabitants have increased to eighty-five, and the island is considered the healthiest known; no epidemic has reached it, and children have none of the diseases elsewhere common to them.

This island lies 1,320 miles S. of St. Helena, in Lat. 37. 2. 48, Long. 12. 18. 29.

[1] Possibly the Yellow-wood of the Cape, though that tree grows large and high in the forest.

After passing Tristan d'Acunha, we began to see the pretty black and white Cape pigeons, that swim round the ship like a flock of ducks, and greedily pick up any scraps the sailors throw overboard.

Every night, from November 27 to December 6, meteors were seen, some very large, leaving their long tracks of light behind. I especially mention this to those who are studying meteorology, for I believe it is very uncommon for so many to be seen of such dimensions in so short a space of time.

When about 600 miles from the Cape, we again saw the whale brit and large quantities of sea-weed.

I made a barometer on board, which showed any disturbance in the atmosphere with such unerring certainty, and indicated it as soon as either the aneroid or quicksilver barometer, that I here give the way to make one of these chemical weather-glasses.

Take a glass tube, perfectly clean, about twelve inches in length and one and a half in diameter, and stop one end with a fine clean cork. Dissolve 2½ drachms of camphor in 11 liquid drachms of alcohol, and set it aside. Put 38 grains of nitrate of potash and 38 grains of muriate of ammonia into 9 drachms of water, and, when perfectly dissolved, mix the two solutions together. Shake them well till thoroughly incorporated with each other, and fill the tube with the mixture. Cork it up carefully, sealing both ends with wax, and then make a small hole in one end with a red hot needle. When the weather is clear and fine, the liquid in the tube is transparent and bright; but on the least change, the chemicals, which form a sediment in the bottom of the tube, become disturbed and rise in beautiful crystals. By watching it carefully a few days, when changes take place, one soon learns to graduate it.[1]

On the 15th, land was descried ahead, and soon after we could make out the celebrated Table Mountain, Devil's Rock, and the Lion's Head and Rump at the Cape of Good Hope. We ran down the coast with the current, so as to make Simon's Bay before dark. The shore is high and bold, and the waves dash madly against the rocks, throwing up the foam, so that it can be seen at a great distance.

[1] This kind of barometer is well known in London, and sold in scientific instrument and even toy shops.

Simon's Bay is about twelve miles by sea from Cape Point, near the NE. corner of False Bay. It lies at the foot of Simon's Berg, one of a high ridge of mountains. Vessels that find it dangerous to anchor in Table Bay put into Simon's Bay, which is considered perfectly safe at all seasons of the year. Ships visiting this bay can always obtain refreshments from the well-furnished stores of the town, and excellent water from the tanks. There is also a patent slip, capable of taking up vessels of 1,800 or 2,000 tons.

A large square rock, called Noah's Ark, lies at the entrance of the bay; opposite is a lighthouse, and just beyond a fortification, called the Block-house. This is mounted with a few guns 'en barbette,' and in the centre is a small circular loop-holed tower. Simon's Bay is noted for fish. Our men caught abundance of silver-fish, mackarel, Cape salmon, and snook. The latter is peculiar to the Cape coasts, and large quantities are salted and packed for the Mauritius market; the vessels bringing back supplies of sugar. The houses are well built; and from the Admiralty House, the residence of the Commodore commanding the Cape of Good Hope Station, a fine view is obtained of the shipping and harbour.

Bent on seeing all there was to be seen, I left the ship, with my vasculum and a long strong stick, such as the Boers use when on a journey. I landed at the pier, and set off on foot along a fine road by the shore, towards Belvidere. Before arriving at the inn there, I met a large drove of Cape sheep led by an old ram. They came prancing down the road, their great tails swinging and bobbing about in so droll a manner that I was puzzled to know what they were, never having seen such queer animals.

Instead of the ordinary caudal appendages, they have a mass of fat, sometimes over a foot square, terminated by a pointed tip, turned up. The upper side only of the tail has hair. The true Cape sheep has coarse long hair, which however becomes woolly on crossing the breed.

They are rarely seen now, the farmers finding it more profitable to keep good woolled sheep. As the breed improves, the tail gradually disappears. When killed, the tip is cut off and the tail split in two, salted, and dried in the wide chimneys, and makes a very good substitute for bacon; or it is melted, and supplies the place of butter in cookery. The tip is carefully rendered down, and strained, when it is clear as crystal, and can be applied to any purpose for which neat's-foot oil is used.

I laid in a stock of refreshments at the inn, which is kept by an Italian and his English wife. He is an old Crimean soldier, pensioned by the British Government, having been through the whole war.

He gave me all the information he could respecting the natural history of the place, and accompanied me some distance, giving me advice as to taking care of myself, &c.

I passed on along a pretty road still skirting the bay, and came to an open grassy spot, apparently the site of a former dwelling. There were long rows of aloes in full blossom, looking like a file of soldiers in the distance, with their bright scarlet and yellow flowers. Hovering over them were a number of long-tailed delicate birds. The bill is very long and curved, which they insert into the bells of the aloe, each one containing a large drop of delicious honey. They are never seen to alight, but circle round the plant uttering a rapid twittering note.

They are called sugar birds, and have the most brilliant plumage. The body is excessively small, but covered with feathers of the richest scarlet, purple, and green or yellow tints, often overlaid with a golden sheen that flashes in the sun till they look like winged jewels.

Aloes are common all over the country, and form an article of commerce. The long, large leaves, deeply serrated and bearing a sharp spine at the point, are cut on a bright clear day. A hole is dug near the plant and lined with maize leaves, in which the cut aloe leaves are placed. They bleed freely, and the viscous matter that flows from them very soon coagulates, when it is collected for sale. It is said to be equal to the finest socotrine aloes. From the network of the leaves I have seen very fair paper made, and the heart of the plant is as sweet as a nut, if care be taken in cutting off the leaves, which are bitter as gall.

Two huge ribs of a whale were placed at each side of the road, forming an archway. Many other large bones were scattered about, this having been once a whale fishery, but now abandoned. As I ascended a little elevation I could see a number of small houses, but only two or three were occupied.

As I approached, I saw a Hottentot woman washing clothes. If it be rude to stare at the fair sex, I certainly was guilty of rudeness to the last degree. I found all the descriptions I had ever heard of the Hottentot Venus beaten to fits by the reality. Cape sheep are nothing to it! She was dressed in a skin of some animal, made very soft, and tightly drawn round her person from the waist to the knee, so that of course a perfect outline of her figure was visible.

Her nude baby was lying under a tree near her, and when I questioned her about the place, she rose to show me the way to the principal house. She coolly shook her vestment straight, and snatched up the child, placing it on the seat nature had provided for it on its mother's haunches. As it was restless, to quiet it she lifted up her breast, which the child clutched over her shoulder, and thus took his breakfast as we went along. I never witnessed such a sight, and wished for my camera to take off the picture.[1]

She told me the principal person there was an old Scotchman, called Captain John Miller, who was the pilot of the port. This place is called Allen's Point.

I found the old man busy salting snook in a little outhouse. I at once told him who I was, and where from, when he quitted his work and entered into a conversation about America. I found him intelligent and he led the way to his house, where I partook of his hospitality. He showed me all over his place, and said that, with the exception of a coloured boy he was trying to bring up respectably, and teaching to read and write, there was no one else near but the Hottentot woman and her husband.

He had a nice patch of vegetables near the house; but he told me the baboons were so troublesome, they robbed him of nearly all his crops. He was determined to put a stop to their depredations, and he built a little thatched hut so as to overlook the garden, and placed a man there with a loaded gun. But they were too clever to be caught so easily. They watched the time when the man went to his dinner and down

[1] I afterwards succeeded in getting one that will give some idea of the *lady* in question.

they would come, doing endless mischief in his absence. These animals are very crafty, and when out marauding, one party is sent thieving while others are despatched to the different points commanding the situation, as scouts. The thieves devour all they can and fill their cheek pouches, and carry off as much as possible if all goes well. On the slightest appearance of danger, or the approach of any one, a peculiar cry is given as a warning signal, when away they scurry and it would be a fleet foot that could follow. They make for the nearest bush or kranz, where they grin down in triumphant security.

To go back to my old man, who knew their cunning ways: one day when the guardian left for dinner, down they came as usual, grown bold by continued successes; but whilst they were devouring the pumpkins the man cautiously crept back, and soon succeeded in mortally wounding a large fellow about four feet high. The scene that followed was so painful, that Capt. Miller declared he would never shoot another if they eat up all his vegetables. He describes it as exactly like a human being in the death agony.

The poor thing looked up in his face so pitifully, whilst its plaintive cries asked for help as plainly as could a human voice, that he felt as if he had committed a murder.

Near to his house was an eminence, where he kept a sharp look-out for vessels entering the bay. At the foot of this hill were two solitary graves; one bore the inscription on the headstone: Ruth Santi, October 25, 1865. The poor woman had arrived there in an emigrant vessel bound to Australia, which was obliged to put in for help, having so much sickness on board. Ruth was taken on shore, but too late, and fell a victim to the dire disease, dysentery, and was buried in this lonely place.

The old man warned me against the snakes, which were numerous, but told me that a long black serpent from six to eight feet long was considered harmless, and that they were never killed, as they preyed upon other snakes and were capital rat hunters.

We went through the bush to a high bluff about three miles distant, and here we came upon a whole family party of baboons at play. The young ones were sliding down a grassy slope, rolling over like great fur balls, chattering and gambolling like so many boys at play; which in the distance they so greatly resembled, that I could have sworn they were children. One of the old ones was leaning on a stick watching the others. I wished for one of their thick skins to send home, but could not find the heart to shoot a baboon.

The captain accompanied me some distance on my way back; but when he left me, instead of going to Simon's town, I determined to pass the night in the mountains, and branched off up one of them. I reached an elevation of about 2,000 feet, just in time to witness a beautiful sunset. A long bank of heavy black clouds in the west was illuminated, as the sun sank below the horizon, till it appeared as if lined with silver and radiating all the spectral colours from its edges, which changed every moment.

The top of the ridge is flat table land, as smooth and grassy as a well kept lawn. It was now nearly dark, and, descending a little, I found a nice nook under a shelving rock, which I beat well with my stick to be sure there were no snake tenants; then took off my big coat and rolled it up for a pillow, lighted my pipe, and was fixed for the night.

I awoke about one o'clock much confused, either dreaming or hearing human voices. I sprang up, revolver in hand, and sallied forth. About twenty feet from me I saw some very suspicious looking people silently crossing the path: I called to them but got no answer, so fired, when a loud screeching was set up, and away they all scampered into the bush. I then found I had appropriated the bedroom of some baboon family, out for a spree, and on their return they had discovered me; and I suppose it was their vocal objections to my presence that had awakened me.

It was a glorious moonlight night, so I pushed on for Simon's Bay, soliloquising as I went.

From boyhood upwards I had read every book on African travels, from Mungo Park to Livingstone, and had longed to tread the wilds of Africa. Well, here was my dream realised, and the place had a perfect enchantment for me. I reached the Royal Hotel about daybreak, and had a sound sleep while they prepared me a capital breakfast.

When I called upon our consul, Mr. Graham, he had gone to Cape Town; but a few days after he came on board, and gave

Captain Carter and myself an invitation to spend Christmas-day with him at Wynberg.

On the 25th we left the ship, and found our consul waiting with a carriage for us. The morning was clear and bracing, and we soon reached the sands of the beach, when lo, our noble steed protested against proceeding further. With difficulty he was coaxed on and we were obliged to walk along the heavy sand till we got to Ralk Bay, where the road is smooth and level and winds round the base of a mountain. Near this, on a lovely spot, stands the country house of our vice-consul Mr. Martin. We stopped there a short time, and he showed me some curious geological formations on the beach near his house.

After a delightful drive, we arrived at Wynberg and had a good day of it, and a regular English Christmas dinner, and returned well pleased to the inn. I was so taken with the road, which is macadamised with stone containing iron ore in excess, and that makes it literally an iron road, that I determined to go to Cape Town and up Table Mountain.

The next day I drove to an hotel in Cape Town, and persuaded my landlady to give me my breakfast over night so as to pack it in my vasculum; starting off long before daylight, I was some way up the mountain by sunrise, and had a good view of the environs of Cape Town. The ocean was calm, the atmosphere clear; and when about 1,200 feet up I had my breakfast, without the fear of the 'table cloth' being let down over my head.[1] By 12 o'clock I reached the Plateau, which is about two miles in length and about a mile broad. A constant verdure is maintained by the moisture of the atmosphere. I there collected many species of the Amaranthus for which the Cape is noted, especially the delicate pink and white ones,

[1] This peculiar phenomenon is called the 'Devil's Table Cloth,' and is a thin sheet of white vapour, often seen rushing over the edge of the precipice, while the entire sky is blue and serene. The rapidity of the descent resembles water pouring over the face of a rock. The air begins to be agitated in the valley, and in less than half-an-hour Cape Town is filled with dust, and the inhabitants are obliged to shut up doors and windows. The lower boundary of the cloud is regulated by the wind and temperature in Table Valley. The cloud never descends more than half way into the hot amphitheatre of Cape Town; but on the side of Camp's Bay it may be seen rolling down in immense volumes to the sea.

It has a most singular aspect; continually rushing to a certain point, and then vanishing. Fleecy clouds are seen, torn by the winds, whirling over the town, but the main body remains fixed to the mountain.

the large silvery white, and yellow tipped with purple. Large proteas with their pale pink petals half covered with a many-leafed calyx of white downy satin; ericas of various hues; the silver tree leaves (*Leucadendron argenteum*) and in every cleft elegant ferns.

There are a good many dangerous places up the mountain; and many persons have lost their lives when night has overtaken them, enveloped in the 'table cloth.'

When descending I heard a deep growl, and, looking across a chasm, I saw a head about as large as a dog's, which I took to be a jackal's. I aimed steadily at it with my revolver, which sent a bullet crashing through the skull, when he sprang up and fell into the ravine below out of my reach.

I saw a number of wild animals I did not know sitting on their haunches curiously watching me till I approached, when they would bound over the rocks or disappear in the clefts. I found afterwards they were the Dassy or Rock rabbit, I believe a true coney. They can be easily tamed when young, but are very mischievous, quite equal to a monkey in cunning and agility.

All was new and curious to me, and I returned delighted with my trip in time for a late dinner at an hotel in Cape Town; and on the following day had hastily to collect all my notes on the place, and be back in the evening, as the 'Monocacy' was ready for sea again.[1]

Cape Town is built on a gradual slope, bounded on the NW. by Table Bay, and almost enclosed on the other sides by a cordon of mountains.

The Lion's Head and Rump can be easily ascended, as their sides slope gradually and overlook a great extent of country. There is also an ascent termed the Kloof, which offers, from its scorched sides covered with the silver tree, some very lovely scenery, including the far distant Blue Berg mountains, with their snow-clad summits.

From the anchorage Cape Town has a pleasing aspect, the charm of which is in no way dispelled on landing and passing up the principal thoroughfare, Adderly Street, and entering a fine

[1] As my time was very limited, I have copied the following information from the Cape Almanac.

avenue of oaks that is a quarter of a mile long, and near which are some of the best buildings.

Among the latter may be enumerated, Government House, St. George's Grammar School, Public Library, Museum, &c.

There are many places worth visiting, such as the Patent Slip, and Ice works, breakwater, harbour and dock works, Green and Sea Points, Robbin Island, Infirmary, and others.

It is the seat of Government, the capital of the colony, and the centre of all public business. It is connected by telegraph with Port Elizabeth, Graham's Town, King William's Town, and all the principal places in the eastern districts. It exports wool, copper ore, hides, horns, ivory, and ostrich feathers, to England and foreign countries; corn, wine, and brandy, to the Eastern provinces, British Kaffraria, and Natal.

Fine steamers run regularly to and from England with the monthly mails, and thus keep up a regular correspondence with the Mother-country. Two lines of railway, of about thirty miles each, branch off from the town, and fine roads scaling the loftiest heights connect it with the remoter districts.

The Royal Observatory is about three miles from Cape Town, prettily situated, and possesses much interest. The present manager is Sir Thomas Maclear, who has made it one of the most valuable colonial institutions of the British Government. It is furnished with very superior instruments, and the clear atmosphere of the Cape fits it in a remarkable manner for astronomical observations. Sir Thomas has added greatly to astronomical and meteorological literature.

A time-ball drops from the flagstaff at one P.M. Cape mean time, and a corresponding one on the Lion's Rump falls at nearly the same instant, at a point where it commands the sweep of the whole bay.

There are three lights, one on Robbin Island—a white fixed light of the first order, dioptric; a white light of the third order, flashing at intervals of ten seconds, and can be seen thirteen miles at sea, placed on Green Point; and a third on Mouil'le Point with a red light, fourth order. On Cape Point is an iron lighthouse, thirty feet high, having a revolving white light of the first order, visible thirty-six miles seaward. A fine breakwater is in course of construction, on the plan of that in Portland Bay, England.

In 1860, the first truckfull of stones was tripped into the sea by Prince Alfred. There are 1,820 feet completed. An inner dock is also far advanced, 1,025 feet long, by 250 and 500 broad. The whole of it has been blasted out of hard blue rock, and the stone carried into the sea for the breakwater.[1]

The streets are laid out at exact right angles, and, like all towns in south Africa, are wide and well kept. On account of the large waggons with their spans of twelve to fourteen oxen, there is a bye-law compelling streets to be of a certain width, to allow of room for turning the unwieldy vehicles.

A Cape waggon is certainly unique in make and appearance, but admirably suited to the country roads, which frequently descend deep ravines (or kloofs, as they are here called), mount steep hills, with only a rough path cut through the bush, or ford the stony beds of rivers. There are no nails in them; all is of the toughest wood, iron-bound, and so constructed as to yield to the exigencies of the road. The Trek-oxen are generally fine animals, and a farmer takes the greatest pride in having his span of twelve well matched. Jet black, chestnut, dun with black faces, or bluish grey are the favourite colours. Every ox has a name, to which it answers at the driver's call; or when deaf to that, he has a terrible weapon in the whip he uses. It is of stout elastic bamboo, twenty to twenty-five feet long, with a lash of the same length tipped with a foot of leather prepared in a particular way. It is a boy's first plaything, and it is considered quite a feat to clap well—though, if the stroke is missed, the lash recoils on the unskilful wielder. The clap[2] is like the report of a pistol, and a good ox won't need to feel it for he knows by experience the driver can hit the offender with unerring aim. There are three daily markets, to which all the products of the country are brought.

Cape Town boasts of eight half English and Dutch newspapers, and four published entirely in Dutch. Most are ably conducted, but the rival editors carry on an unceasing war.

'The English Church is under the supervision of a bishop, with large staff of clergy. The Dutch Reformed Church has its synod there; the London, Wesleyan, South African, and French

[1] Since this was written, the Breakwater has been opened for use by Prince Alfred in a late visit.

[2] Clap is the word used instead of crack in the Cape.

Missionary Societies, Ebenezer, Lutheran, and Scotch Presbyterian churches, Roman Catholics, Jews, and Mohammedans, all are represented there, and disseminate their doctrines far and wide over the vast colony.'

Masonry is carried on to a great extent. There are over fifty lodges and chapters of Masons and Oddfellows. Near the Parliament House is the Good Hope Lodge of Knights Templars, said to be one of the finest in the world; built about thirty years ago; elegantly frescoed inside—the work of an Italian artist—and it has a fine garden attached to it. The King of Holland is the Grand Master. This institution has about 12,000*l*. out at interest, which is loaned to orphan children of masons, to educate them; each child giving his individual note for the money, which becomes a debt of honour, to be paid when circumstances permit.

Adjoining the Lodge is an elevated ground, used by the members for the game of golf. It is played with balls, struck through rings with shinney sticks, and the champion generally gets a prize.

The museum, besides foreign objects of interest, has a fine collection of the animals and insects of the colony. In the same building is the library, containing 35,000 volumes, besides 5,000 valuable books of reference. I saw an original copy of Shakespeare, presented by Miss Burdett Coutts, which cost 716*l*. I think it is a pity that she did not give them the money instead, towards educating some of the poor children of the town. A full length portrait of Prince Alfred adorns the library.

I was greatly amused at the signboards in the streets, which bore the drollest names, one especially with Mr. and Mrs. Death on it.

Sir P. E. Woodhouse is the present Governor, and Sir R. P. Douglas, Bart., Lieutenant-Governor and commander of the forces. 'The colony is ruled by an Executive Council of five members, the Chief Judge presiding; a Legislative Council of twenty-one members chosen for ten years, the Governor its President; and a House of Assembly of sixty-six members, representing the country districts, elected every five years, and led by a speaker—the same as in the English House of Commons.'

A fine portrait of Sir G. Darling—a former Governor—is hung in the Hall of Assembly.

The former feeling of ill-will between the Dutch and English has nearly died out in Cape Town, and is so greatly modified in the provinces it is rarely met with ; indeed, the young Dutchman's greatest pride is to speak English well, and be dressed English fashion.

The Dutch language in Cape Town, where spoken, is high Dutch, but in the remoter districts it is a vile mixture of low Dutch, Hottentot, and bad English. From what I saw, Queen Victoria has few more loyal subjects than the descendants of the former possessors of the Cape of Good Hope. They are noted for hospitality, and as to the cleanliness and order of the houses of the Dutch, I cannot speak too highly in praise of them.

It is rare to see near the capital one of the true race of Boers, which, for the benefit of my friends, allow me to say, does not mean a rude churl, as with us, but merely a country farmer. The Boer proper is almost extinct. Occasionally may be seen men of athletic make, over six feet, dressed in moleskin pants, and short round jackets, a felt high-crowned hat, and velt schoons or shoes of undressed leather; accompanied by wife and children of all ages, in short skimp skirts, little round capes or kerchiefs, and monstrous cappies (*anglicè* poke bonnets), quilted, with a deep curtain to them, and a bunch of faded artificial roses pinned on top. They are a nineteenth-century wonder, and take you back to the early days of New York, till you fancy it is Rip van Winkle *in propria personâ*, risen again after another 200 years' sleep.

He certainly could not look more astonished at the progress of the present day, than an up-country Boer does at the various articles for luxury or comfort displayed in an English shop, when he condescends to visit one.

A curious story was told me of one of these old men, who was blest with several stalwart sons, all expert enough in ploughing, sowing, or reaping, but who knew little else than these arts. Some trader visited the far away farm, and told marvellous tales of the outer world, and advised the father to let his sons travel. The idea worked in his brain, but took long to develop. One day, greatly to his eldest son's astonishment, he told him to go to a neighbour's farm for a month, and amuse himself and see all he could of the world! and away went Jan well pleased. On the trader's return the old man told him he had followed his counsels, and sent his son to see the world. This aroused the man's curiosity, so he asked him to what country he had packed him off so soon, and if it had not been a great grief to part from him. 'Ach mein Gott, yah, but I think it will be for the lad's benefit to see the world, so sent him to Mynheir van Zwartes', twenty miles off, and told him to stop a month and see all he could!'

I bid farewell to Cape Town about eight o'clock; and as I had sent on my carpet bag &c. by the mail cart, I set off on foot anxious to see some of the places on the road to Simon's Bay.

I passed the observatory, but had not time to stop there, and went on to Wynberg, where I saw the establishment of Plumstead, formerly belonging to a Mr. Batts, an Englishman. He had laid out 150 acres in splendid gardens, with fine avenues of oak and other trees; and the houses must once have been handsome, but are now in ruins. He died in 1833, and, as is a common custom in the Cape, lies buried on the property, under a handsome monument of Sicilian marble, on each side of which are inscriptions from the Song of Solomon in letters of gold, but it is rapidly going to decay, and is half hidden in weeds and shrubs.

I saw some fine fields of tobacco, which is very largely cultivated. Great quantities of Cavendish, cigars, and cut tobacco are exported. The mulberry tree grows to a great size, and latterly silk cultivation is going on. The samples produced are very fine, and it has been found that the wild mulberry (*Morus latifolia*) is equally as good for the food of the silk-worm, as the true mulberry, and of much more rapid and easy growth.

From the numerous vineyards, I could have fancied myself in the south of France. The lovely village of Constantia lies in this neighbourhood, famous for its delicious Constantia and Pontac wines, which, to be thoroughly appreciated, should be drunk on the spot. Wynberg is fourteen miles from Cape Town, and is the terminus of one branch of the railway. I passed through Clermont, Mowbray, and other pretty villages, all of which had an air of neatness and comfort quite refreshing to see. At Rondebosch is the country seat of the Governor, a well wooded and cultivated demesne.

I arrived in Ralk Bay, hot and tired, but got a comfortable little dinner at an English hotel. This is a famous watering-place for the gentry, who in the summer months avail themselves of the cool sea-breezes and bathing. It is a pretty little tree-embowered village, close to the bay, and can boast of some good houses and an English church. I saw there some of the pretty girls the Cape is famous for; and in dress they were no way behind the mother-country in elegance and fashion.

After a rest I pushed on for Simon's Bay, passing several fishing villages, and enjoyed immensely the sea-breeze that tempered the midsummer heat, as I kept along the shore. I reached Simon's Town just after dark, and at once took a boat and went on board, where I found all ready for departure, and next morning we slowly steamed out of the bay. I should have liked greatly to have extended my stay in the Cape to botanise in some of the districts. The descriptions I had of them making me long to prove them realities.

Though some parts are sterile enough, others are strewn with the loveliest flowers. The Ericas must be seen in their rocky beds to be appreciated, particularly the scarlet one with its bells an inch long. It is the native land of the Gladiola, and in some places they literally cover acres of ground. Its lilies, from the purest white, through all the shades of pink, to the deepest crimson; the large blue and white lotus blossoms floating over the rivers, orchideæ, gesnerias, geraniums, especially the large ivy-leafed species; jessamines of countless varieties, the ritje peren, equal to the finest tuberose, clematis, bignonias, and thousands of others of earth's loveliest children, bewilder one with their beauty and perfume.

I saw air plants from the distant George District, of the species called the elephant's foot, with its clusters of pale green leaves and pinkish blossoms, and one about the size of a cricket ball in a dry vase on a lady's mantlepiece. It had shot out delicate stems and leaves till it reached the ceiling, and she had trained it like an espalier fruit tree, and it was just showing bunches of pretty lilac flowers. But I could not describe half I saw and heard of. As I stood looking back at the town, I felt regret at leaving it, for I had received much kindness and hospitality, and I hoped one day to revisit its shores.

On the 28th the barometers fell; the weather changed and it became thick and cloudy towards sunset, with a heavy swell on the sea. After dark the wind rose, and by midnight it was blowing a gale, and the waves broke over the hurricane deck with such fury that it was with difficulty the vessel could make way against them. Towards morning the storm abated, and then we had a few days tolerably fair weather, till January 6, when the sky became gloomy, dark, and threatening; clouds passed swiftly to the north, the sea rose, and the ship rolled heavily; and there were all the symptoms of an approaching storm of no ordinary force. The night fully justified our fears. Heavy blasts of wind, straight descending torrents of rain, lightnings forked and sheet, the creaking of the ship's timbers, the few sails set torn to ribbons and flapping loose, the thundering noise of the tremendous waves as they neared us, each one threatening to engulf our vessel—made up a wild and fearful spectacle, but yet grand and sublime in its very wildness.

The men worked hard at repairing and bending the storm sails, and standing by the pumps knee-deep in the water that washed unceasingly over the decks.

Daylight showed us the extent of our damages. The paddle-boxes were injured; the round-houses smashed in and washed away; the rail forward stove in, and the one-inch iron plates were bent double. The ring-bolts to which the heavy guns were secured started from the deck, and the guns threatened with each roll to break adrift from their lashings. A temporary lull gave time for a few repairs; and we hoped for a change of weather, as the five hours' rain had beaten down the sea considerably.

Towards evening, however, the tempest recommenced. A red lurid light spread all over the sky; and, shortly after the setting of the sun, the ocean rose again furiously, and announced its fresh vigour by breaking over our starboard, washing and sweeping away all before it, tearing away the gratings of the hatches, breaking the after skylight, and rushing down into cabins and wardroom, floating everything and drenching everybody. The wheel-ropes were carried away, and the ship, paying off before the wind, became unmanageable. The guys of the smoke-stack broke, and it was feared we should have the whole mass of iron descending on us, when a general smash would have taken place. The ship coming to again, filled her decks with water, and leaning over to port, remained so long in that position that the stoutest heart quailed, and anxiously counted the seconds, till at last she gallantly rose again on the crest of a wave.

Luckily the sea had stove in the lower ports, so that the immense quantity of water found a ready egress from the deck, and the vessel, lightened of the weight, rolled less. New wheel-ropes were rove, and the storm having exhausted its fury, by daylight it was greatly abated, and the sun rose red and gloriously. It was a dismal scene old Sol shone down on, but the puffing and snorting of the powerful engine showed that her working gear was uninjured; and the good ship, so severely tried, sped onward gracefully, throwing the splashing glittering spray from her bows back into the conquered ocean.

Reflecting calmly on these past dangers, I cannot omit to render thanks, next to God, to the cool and steady bravery in the hour of peril of our gallant commander and to many of the officers and crew of the 'Monocacy,' for safe delivery out of one of those terrible cyclones that occur in the South Indian Ocean.

Deeply interested in the laws of storms, I succeeded, by careful observations of the barometers and thermometer, noticing the changes of wind and temperature, and the rising and setting of the storm-wave, in ascertaining pretty correctly the centre of the hurricane, and reduced the aforesaid changes of wind and weather to the rules laid down by Messrs. Piddington and Redfield in their admirable treatise on the laws of storms.

The officers of the vessel kindly supplied me with a copy of the log, which greatly aided me in tracing the cyclone home to its vortex.

Taking a scientific view of hurricanes and cyclones and the management of vessels therein, it is clear that there are three ways of managing a ship in, or at the appearance of, a cyclone.

First, in order to avoid the same, (in case there is plenty of sea room) the vessel should be hove to on the proper tack; secondly, if a ship is caught inside of a storm-disc, the only changes to be adopted are, running before the wind, or heaving the ship to; and the latter, when, on account of the high or cross seas, the safety of the ship is endangered, the only course left is to run before the wind in a tangent direction towards the inner storm-disc, and then gradually to edge off to the outer limits of the cyclone; and, lastly, by running on the outside of the wind's circle, and even profiting by it.

But the question is how to know the approach of a cyclone, and how to find the proper bearings of its centre. Considering then every cyclone as a great whirlwind, the direction of every wind is rotary, of which the outer part is a common close-reefed topsail breeze, such as no good seaman cares for, and by which no seaworthy ship is injured. The violence of the wind increases with great rapidity as the centre is approached, till close to, or in it, when it becomes of a destructive fury. Even if this centre should have a diameter of fifty or sixty miles, round which the storm is revolving, the first care must be to ascertain how this point or centre bears, in order to guide future manœuvres. Now as the 'Monocacy' on January 6 was, according to her log, in lat. 32. 15 S. and long. 47. 45 E., with the wind marked as ESE., the centre of every common wind would lay, according to proved and established rules of storms, to the E. by N. or ENE.

In the remarks in the log it is said, 'Clouds accumulating, cloudy and damp, moderate breeze from SE. by E., sent up fore topmast; from 4 to 6, squally and damp, heavy swell from SE. by E., light winds; 6 P.M., a drizzling rain.'

But with all these clouds and dampness, we find the state of the barometer as shown in the diagram, stating the position of the ship and centre bearings: the storm-disc, with its hourly changing tangent angles, is named a moderate gale, the outside circle of a hurricane, accompanied by a slightly disturbed surrounding atmosphere.

The greatest signs of an approaching cyclone are the oscillations in barometer and sympiesometer, more especially a high barometer with gloomy threatening weather. In the trades or monsoons this is always a sure sign of a coming tempest.

The question naturally arises, Can the barometer assist in forming an approximative estimate of the ship's distance from the centre? On first consideration, it is evident that there are very great differences in the fall and rise of the barometer and sympiesometer in various storms, though they may be all true cyclones. Consequently, the variations of these instruments may very often mislead, but the shortness of time in which these changes happen is enough to make even the most careless seaman understand the danger and close approximation of the destructive centre.

The accompanying diagram shows the height and hourly change of both instruments, and the distance from the centre is worked out according to Mr. Piddington's rules. Certainly these calculations can only be made approximatively, but coming so near the truth that we may consider the result to be the true centre.

In the Southern Indian Ocean the rate of travelling of a hurricane may be stated to be little more than nine or ten miles per hour, and especially in the meridian between Mauritius and Madagascar the rate rarely exceeds eight; so it is evident from the little progress the 'Monocacy' made against a head wind and sea, the course to the N. and E. brought her nearer to the focus.

The weather during the following days showed no material alteration. I found the oscillations of the mercurial barometer and the vibrations of the aneroid very strongly marked, which are common signs during a cyclone.

On January 7 the water changed to a dark brown colour, and the sea was running furiously.

On the 8th, the storm having passed, no material danger threatened, and the barometer kept unusually high, and the sky wore a brighter appearance than ordinary. The air was charged with a great amount of electricity, and incessant thunder and lightning were the consequences. Before I conclude this description, I will add a word or two as to one of the supposed origins of Cyclones. It appears to me that a simply flattened spiral stream of electric fluid generates above, and, expanding in a broad disc, may amply account for the commencement of a cyclone, by its descending to the surface of the earth; and that likewise its onward motion, in such a direction as the laws of force and gravity drive it, may account for its continuance, and the oppression and exhaustion of its force for its termination.

The unequal motion is naturally the consequence of one side of the disc being more flattened, and causing the cyclone to advance more rapidly. The descent or settling down of

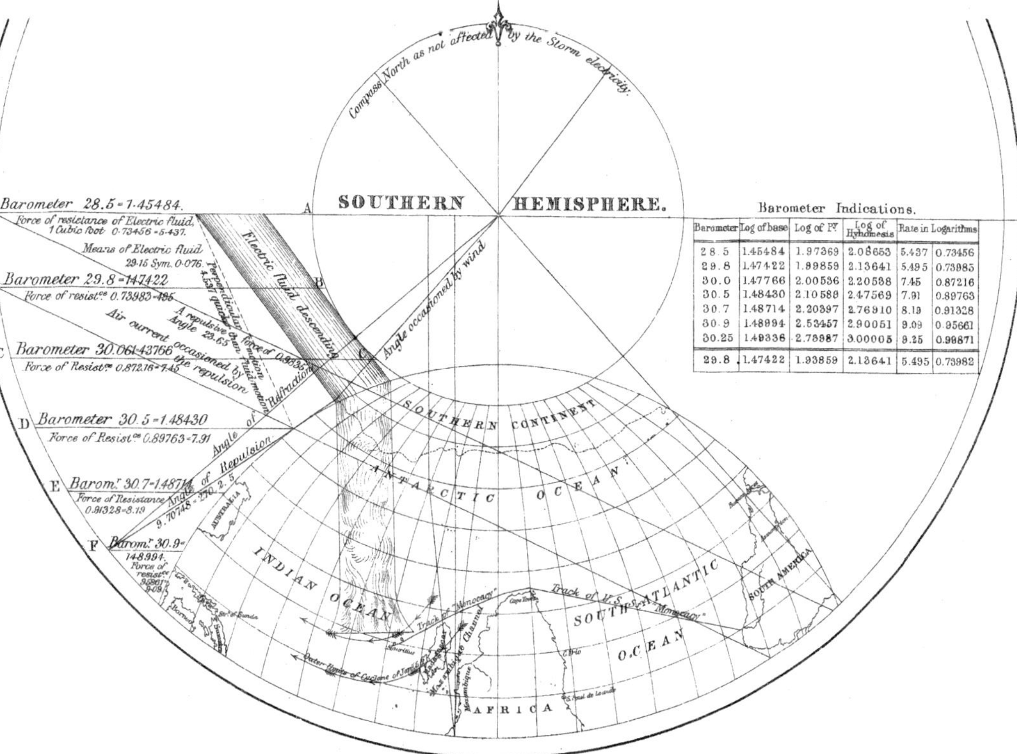

Barometer Indications.

Barometer	Log of base	Log of P.Y.	Log of Hyhomesis	Rate in Logarithms	
28.5	1.45484	1.97369	2.08653	5.437	0.73456
29.8	1.47422	1.89859	2.13641	5.495	0.73985
30.0	1.47766	2.00536	2.20538	7.45	0.87216
30.5	1.48430	2.10589	2.47569	7.91	0.89763
30.7	1.48714	2.20397	2.76910	8.19	0.91328
30.9	1.48994	2.53457	2.90051	9.09	0.95661
30.25	1.49336	2.73987	3.00005	9.25	0.99871
29.8	1.47422	1.93859	2.13641	5.495	0.73982

...ared for Pike's Sub-Tropical Rambles.

Published by Sampson Low, Marston, Low, & Searle; Crown Buildings, 188 Fleet Str.t London.

cyclones has in numerous cases been proved. The appearance of the vortices of violent tornadoes within the body of great storms is not unfrequent or new.

When about 400 miles from Mauritius, the sea was full of a floating mass of matter resembling brown *Ectocarpi*. It was very difficult to get up in a bucket. A few days later I saw much other matter floating about, of a gelatinous nature; the old sailors said it is frequently seen after tropical storms. It appears of the confervoid family.

By the night of the 11th, we neared the Round and Flat Islands, two apparently barren rocks, adjacent to the Mauritius; and little sleep was there on board, all being anxious to gain port again, after our long voyage.

Description of the Storm Chart.

The cords A A, B B, C C, D D, E E, F F, are the different currents of air, arranged according to their intensity; the logarithm annexed to the barometer-stand, is likewise the logarithm for the base of the triangle, A B C, which is formed by the descending electric fluid; the perpendicular erected on the surface of the globe, and the barometer-stand 29·8, or each following barometer-stand of decreasing intensity, necessarily increase the base, perpendicular and hypothenuse, but always keep in the same proportion to one another. The question how to find the angle B, the resisting force created by the pressure of the air, is solved by the following proposition: as base is to radius, so is the hypothenuse to sine of angle b, which increases proportionately with the base, and *vice versâ*. The atmosphere surrounding the earth creates a refraction of the electric fluid, similar to the refraction of the rays of light, and calculated on the same principle, but in this case always considering 29·15 as the mean of the intensity of the electric fluid; the rotation of the earth gives to the fluid a circular motion, and creates thereby, in opposite hemispheres, a reverse action, but forms at the same time a set of air currents, which are but the cotangents to the different storm-discs.

The only variations in the calculations that can arise, are those occasioned by local prevailing winds, and the air-currents that are thereby formed. But when, as in this case, the local prevailing winds are 'trade winds' or monsoons, the angle thereby occasioned can almost be guessed, within 10 or 12 degrees; and as the force of the wind acting upon the fluid is counteracted by its own spiral motion, the error in the calculation will be so slight that we may readily take the result for the true deviation of the fluid, and the veritable rate of the travelling of the cyclone. The electric fluid descending is represented in the same angle, as careful researches in the log of the U. S. steamer 'Monocacy' proved it to be on January 5, 6, and 7, 1867. The circles marked with arrows are the tracks of the cyclone extending from lat. 36 to 20 S., and covering an extent of from 40 to 45 degrees of longitude. The rate of the cyclone's travelling may be estimated at seven miles per hour, and the situation of the vortex in 57. 30 E. long., and lat. 27. 14 S.

MAP shewing the position of the United States Steam frigate 'MONOCACY' in the South Indian Ocean, during the CYCLONE of the 5th. 6th. 7th. & 8th. January, 1867.

By Nicholas Pike, United States Consul, Port Louis, Mauritius.

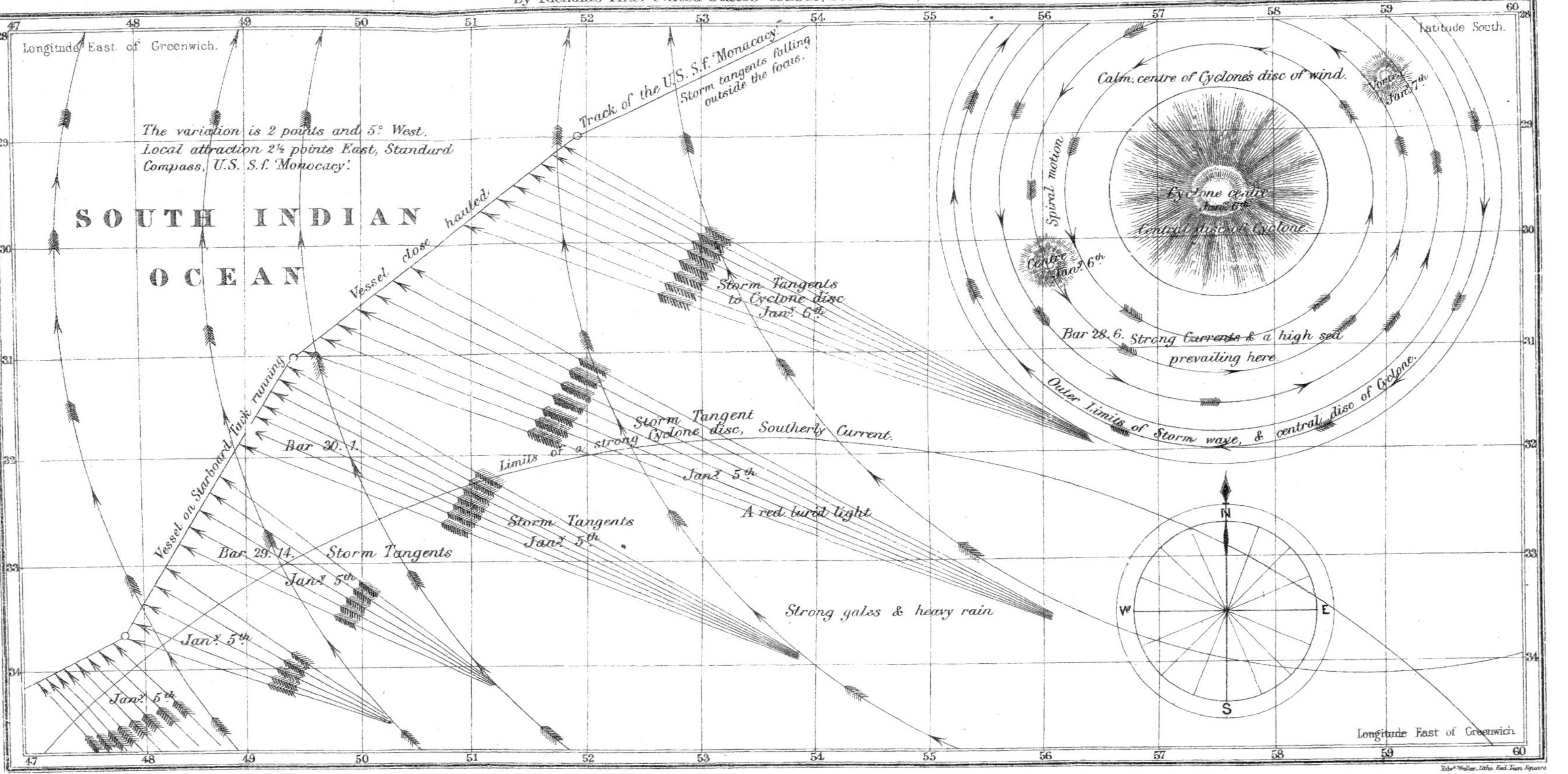

Prepared for Pike's Sub-Tropical Rambles.

Published by Sampson Low, Marston, Low, & Searle, Crown Buildings, 188 Fleet Strt. London.

Edwd. Weller, Litho. Red Lion Square.

CHAPTER III.

ARRIVAL IN MAURITIUS.

First Impressions of Port Louis from the Sea—Landing—A Night in an Hotel—The Harbour—Architecture of Houses—Chaussée—Principal streets—Place d'Armes—Government House—Government Street—Theatre—Champ de Mars—Labourdonnais Street—Mineral Spring—Water—New Town—Plaine Verte—Company's Gardens—Bazaar—Moka Street—Railway Depôt—Barracks—College—Churches—Mosque—Barbers—Masonic Lodges.

DAY dawned on January 12, 1867, bright and clear, and the sun rose brilliantly in a cloudless sky, as we hove in sight of Mauritius. On nearing the land, the fields of waving canes, topes of cocoas, and groves of Casuarinas, gave a pleasing impression of the place; but when approaching Port Louis harbour the beauty of the view is unsurpassed, and no easy task to describe.

The varied character of the ranges of basaltic hills reminded me of the far-famed Organ Mountains in South America.

The city of Port Louis lies in an extensive valley; and as we approached the Bell Buoy, the outermost anchorage for ships, a glorious scene presented itself. In the far distance was the world-known Peter Both Mountain; just behind the city rose the bold sweep of the mountain peak called the Pouce, to the height of 2,847 feet, wooded to its summit; to the east lay the gentle slopes of the Citadel Hill, bastion crowned; to the west, abrupt and rugged, the steep cliff called Long Mountain Bluff reared its signal-topped head (whence vessels are seen and signaled far out at sea)—all formed an entourage few cities can boast, and rendered it, when viewed from the sea, the most picturesque in the world.

We dropped anchor about noon inside the Bell Buoy, about a mile from Port Louis; and, as soon as we got pratique, numerous small plying boats appeared manned by Lascars, who clamoured for the honour of putting us ashore; but, as we had the vessel's boats at command, we declined their invitations.

At 1 o'clock the booming of the heavy guns of the frigate announced my departure from the good ship 'Monocacy,' which had carried me over so many thousand miles of ocean, and through many a storm.

I felt sorry to leave her and her gentlemanly commander, than whom a braver and more accomplished officer never trod the deck of a vessel.

As I landed at the granite quay, well adapted for the traffic of this busy mart of the East, with its ever flowing fountain of crystal water for the use of the shipping, I was forcibly struck with the conglomerate appearance of the people, and the jargon they spoke. Creoles and Coolies, Arabs, Cinghalese, Malagash, Chinese, and Malabars; all as eager as in other parts of the world to take the stranger in, and carry him off, body and baggage, to the nearest hotel.

I entrusted the latter to one of the most respectable-looking men; but, despite the offers of half-a-dozen cab and carriole drivers, I preferred walking with a gentleman well acquainted with the city, who met me on my arrival.

We wended our way to the Hôtel Univers, said to be the *best*, through a dirty narrow street; and, entering a low archway, we were ushered by a coloured waiter into a damp, ill-ventilated, low-ceilinged room, in which were a bar and three billiard tables; and gentlemen of colour were amusing themselves knocking over wooden pins placed on the tables with billiard balls.

Persons of various colours were smoking pipes and cigars, and drinking wine at little tables placed about the room. The landlord, a comely, well-spoken Frenchman, soon made his appearance, asked me to walk upstairs, and showed me into a room—one of a row facing a street through which ran one of the filthiest streams my eyes ever rested on. This room was about ten feet square, and contained an iron bedstead covered with mosquito netting, a table, and some chairs. Ventilation there was none except from the door, as not a window had evidently been open for some time. I made an agreement with the landlord for two dollars and a half per diem, and then went to

PORT LOUIS.

the Custom-house to see after the rest of my baggage. I returned about 6 o'clock, when I was shown into the dining-room, which had small tables placed on each side for the accommodation of the boarders, and a bill of fare was handed me.

Everything was brought from below in little dishes; for instance, I ordered a plate of roast chicken, and a leg was brought smothered in parsley, with one potato; a beef steak —and half-a-dozen such would not supply the appetite of a hungry man—and everything else was served me in infinitesimal doses, miserably cooked.

I strolled out in the evening into the 'Company's Gardens,' which are opposite to the hotel; why called gardens I knew not, as neither flower nor shrub grew there, only some fine banian and other trees shaded the place.

I returned to my dirty, uncomfortable hotel; and, after passing a miserable night, rose at daylight weary and sick. What with bugs, mosquitoes, and cockroaches, (to say nothing of centipedes six inches long!) the knocking about of billiard balls till late, and the loud laughter and gossiping of the coloured servants, sleep was impossible. The mosquito curtains were not properly beaten, and whole families lay in wait for their unsuspecting victim; the cockroaches ate my clothes, the ants got into my trunks, lizards crept over the walls, and rats, bold as lions, were all over the house!

What a delightful place to live in, I thought; if this is a specimen of the *first* hotel in Mauritius, Heaven bless those obliged to put up with the second and third class, which must contain vermin enough to destroy a regiment of soldiers.[1]

Port Louis is the only city of Mauritius, and is situated in the NW. of the island. It covers an area of about ten square miles, and is nearly enclosed by a ridge of mountains on one side, and bounded on the other by the sea. Its fine natural harbour is capable of affording anchorage to a large number of vessels of heavy burden, and they can ride safely even in ordinary hurricane weather with due precaution.

The entrance to the channel is through coral reefs, well marked out by buoys, and has an average depth of thirty-five

[1] It is but fair to state, things are managed better there now than when this was written.

to forty feet, and, within the harbour, of fourteen feet. It is well defended on the opposite sides by Forts George and William, and the citadel, which stands back of the city, also overlooks and commands it.

There are two lights as steering points for ships arriving at night, one at the light ship at the Bell Buoy, and another at Flat Island.

The streets of Port Louis are straight, and cross each other at right angles. They are mostly macadamised, but very roughly so, and kept tolerably clean, with the exception of the open sewers and drains, alike offensive to optic and olfactory nerves, and injurious to public health. The side walks are paved, and never obstructed by boxes, bales, or anything that can impede the progress of the pedestrian.

Several rivulets flow through the town, swollen to rushing torrents in rainy weather, bringing down masses of mud and debris; and in dry seasons almost stagnant, exhaling fœtid odours, and adding largely to the malarious condition of the city.

Most of the older houses are of one storey, built of wood; but the more recent buildings are of stone. To judge from their style, each individual must be his own architect, and follows the whim of the moment rather than any known rules: this does not at all contribute to the symmetry and beauty of the streets. I can safely say there is but one really handsome edifice in the colony, and that is on the Labourdonnais estate, in the vicinity of Rivière du Rempart.

The interior of the houses is very plain, and consists of drawing and dining rooms, and a few sleeping apartments, which all have the outer hurricane shutters, crossed with a strong Z shaped bar, that gives them a very monotonous appearance. Nearly all possess small dependencies called pavilions, which contain two or three bedrooms for guests.

The principal street for shops is the Chaussée, nearly the oldest part of the town, built chiefly of wood and old-fashioned-looking, a great contrast to the interior of the shops. There, all is of the latest Parisian fashion, and you may purchase any article for a lady's toilette, from a Lyons silk dress to plain English calico. Jewellers' shops shine resplendent, where objects of French *luxe* are to be found up to any price: gold and gems, especially diamonds, the favourite creole bijou, dazzle the eyes and set you wondering how so small a place can find purchasers for such luxurious articles.

A curious feature in this and other streets is the juxtaposition of one of these elegant magazines with a Chinese store, where are retailed, salt fish, charcoal, wines, porter, cocoa-nut oil, rice, wood, lard, and the thousand etceteras required in a household; all of which are sold in the smallest possible quantities for the convenience of customers. I am obliged to confess that all the Piver's essences in the one shop do not overpower the abominable odours of the other; Port Louis at times can rival Cologne in the latter item.

STATUE OF LABOURDONNAIS, PLACE D'ARMES.

Between the Chaussée and Royal Street lies the Place d'Armes, in front of the quays, shaded by banian, boisnoir (*Acacia Lebbeck*) and the flamboyant of Madagascar (*Poinciana regia*).

I gazed on the latter when I landed, in astonishment; they were covered with their magnificent scarlet, yellow, and white flowers, lying on the soft delicate green of the foliage and forming the loveliest bouquets I had ever seen on one tree.

On the left hand of the quay are the Custom-house, marine stores, and large covered sheds, for the landing of goods and sale of merchandise; and on the right are merchants' offices, provision stores, &c.

Just facing the landing is a finely-executed statue, in bronze, of M. de Labourdonnais, the best and ablest of the French Governors, to whom Mauritius is largely indebted. It is the first object that greets the eye as you step on shore, and it does not need much stretch of imagination to fancy he is welcoming the stranger to the shores for which he spent so many years of untiring devotion.

On either side of the Place, are the Guard's room and offices of the Commissariat Department, the Chamber of Commerce, broker's and auctioneer's rooms, and the Oriental Bank —a large two-storied building—the principal bank here.

Seats are placed under these beautiful trees; and there planters and merchants discuss all the affairs of the island, and the ladies say all the gossip and scandal too! A wide macadamised road runs through the Place, and on each side of it is a cab and carriole-stand. The fares for these vehicles have a fixed and pretty reasonable tariff, except on certain holidays when the drivers are allowed to fix their own prices.

At the upper end facing the sea is the ungainly, miserably-constructed Government House—the city residence of the Governor—where the legislative councils, levees, government balls, &c., are held. It was in course of erection when the English took the island, and they seem to have completed it on the old French plan.

The continuation of the Chaussée, Royal Street, extends nearly to the limits of the city on the north side. Most of the stores and shops here are of stone, and marvellous is the variety of goods to be found in what would be a plain ironmonger's elsewhere. Adjoining Government House, are the offices of the Colonial Secretary and other officials, in a low shabby building, fortunately better-looking inside than out, or the gentlemen might feel they were sent to prison for so many hours daily of their official life.

A narrow street runs alongside Government House, and in a row of dirty-looking tenements are the Audit and Surveyor-General's offices, Savings Bank, and, meanest of all, the Post Office; then, a little higher up, the Police Court, Internal Revenue departments, and lawyers' rooms. There is a new Post Office in course of erection near the Custom-house.[1] It is to be hoped that this new light and airy place will give a proportionate impetus to the activity of the clerks on mail day.

[1] Now completed.

This small street opens out into the spacious one of Government Street, in which stands a theatre, once, they tell me, elegantly decorated; but alas! all its pristine splendour has departed, and it is now in a woefully dilapidated condition. Nearly every year a troupe of French actors and opera singers come from Europe, and divide their time between Mauritius and Bourbon. I cannot say much in favour of those I have heard. A curious spectacle is presented when the house is full, with its mixture of white and colour, all *en grande toilette*. The only English acting is when the officers and men of the different regiments give an evening's entertainment in the theatre, and they generally draw good houses.

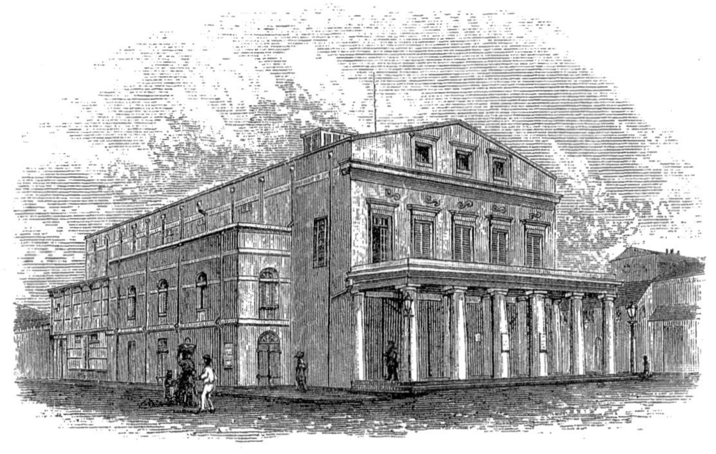

THEATRE, PORT LOUIS.

Opposite the theatre is Morillon's ice-house, where young Mauritius most does congregate between the acts, and consumes any amount of gâteaux, bonbons, ice-creams, &c., not forgetting either the stronger stimulants of sherry and soda and their congeners.

Above this are the large blocks of buildings, where the Courts are held, municipal business transacted, the head-quarters of the police, and the main entrance to the gaol.

There are some very pretty dwelling-houses higher up, with tastefully-decorated gardens in front.

Parallel with this are Church Street, of Flore Mauricien

fame (dear to all lovers of gâteaux, patés, &c.), Bourbon and Corderie Streets, all terminating in the Champ de Mars.

This is a fine grassy plain, unmistakably once a large crater, the walls of which on the north-west were broken out seaward. There is not a tree or shrub to be seen on it, strange to say; when, with a little trouble in planting trees round it, a splendid promenade might be made—so much needed in a place that suffers from heat eight months in the year, as Port Louis does. At the foot of the plain the Mauritius Cricket Club has erected a pretty pavilion, and laid out a square for that healthy and invigorating amusement; but, by the same perversity that seems to govern everything in this island, they seem to play most in summer, at a temperature when you feel disinclined even to walk, to let alone running insanely after cricket balls.

In the upper part stands a stone monument, twenty-five feet high, erected to the memory of M. de Malartic, one of the French Governors.

Round the Champ de Mars runs a race-course, kept in fine order by the Mauritius Turf Club. The race-stands are not permanent, but put up once a year just as they are required for the races.

Pretty country villas—the residences of the families of merchants, Government officers, and others—surround the plain. A road leads up the Pouce Mountain from the head of the Champ de Mars, and country houses are built a good way up. Two other fine streets are Rempart and St. George (which join at the top), and their continuation, Wellington Street, that runs up into the large plain of the Champ de Lort; but these are principally for dwelling-houses, most of which have gardens in front.

Nearly the only shops in these streets are the indefatigable John Chinaman's. In every angle of every street you will find him in his one, or at most two, rooms, which serve for house and shop; with the inevitable rows of sardines, olive oil, porter, and Warren's blacking.

Labourdonnais Street, that extends from mountain to mountain on either side of the city, crosses the above. At its extreme end, under the base of the Signal range, is the residence of Mr. E. Mayer, where the inhabitants formerly congregated in the morning to drink of a mineral spring, said to be equal to the famed Cheltenham waters in England.

It was discovered by Mr. Tiedman, and a careful analysis gives the following results:—

Carbonate of magnesia } „ „ lime }	5·50
Chloride of sodium	50·00
„ „ magnesium	6·00
„ „ lime	7·75
Sulphate of magnesia	32·00
„ „ lime	6·25
Oxyde of iron	6·75
„ „ silica	1·75

I tasted the spring, and should think it would be very efficacious in the diseases such waters are used for. It has not been open to the public for some years, but the gentlemanly proprietor supplies the water gratis to anyone applying for it. Like many other good things within everybody's reach, little advantage is taken of it; although large sums are spent yearly in importing quack medicines of similar properties from Europe, not half so useful as this would be.

The whole city is well supplied with water from three canals. One of them is brought round the base of the Signal Mountain, is led across the Champ de Lort, down a ravine, and up to the Champ de Mars, which it traverses, and then passes into the New Town behind the Citadel Hill.

Nearly the whole of this new part of the city, as far as the Valley Pitot, has sprung up within a few years, since the water was laid on. It was hoped that its healthy situation would soon render it quite a fashionable place—a sort of West End—and some very nice houses were built. One part rejoices in the name of the Boulevard Victoria, but it seems a failure as to its ever becoming fashionable.

The Plaine Verte runs at right angles with Royal Street, is about a mile and a half long, and is well laid out.

It was here in former days that executions took place, before hanging was substituted for beheading.

There is a little covered market-place, where meat, fruit, and vegetables are sold—a great convenience to those in this neighbourhood, who live a long way from the large market of Port Louis.

A fine promenade extends its whole length, well shaded with trees, and fountains at intervals; one, a nude female figure, with a cornucopia under her arm, from which gushes a limpid stream, is mounted on rough rockwork, about ten feet high, interlaced with ferns and creepers, and surrounded by an evergreen cassia hedge, but all sadly out of order.

In the heart of the town are the Company's Gardens, guarded at their entrance from the Chaussée by two stone lions. Once, they say, this was a delightful promenade for ladies, all planted with elegant flowering shrubs and creepers, with a fountain, from which meandered little rills in all directions, and every tree had a green turf bank at its foot, but, alas—turf, flowers, fountain, and ladies, are but things of the past! In a desert space, innocent of all verdure save the over-arching banian trees, stands a bronze monument of Mr. Adrien d'Epinay on a stone pedestal, and surrounded with an iron railing: a memorial of the dead in the place of the once life-giving fountain. Instead of fair dames, in their elegant Parisian toilettes, promenading, you see only groups of coloured nurses with their charges, scolding and gossiping, or chaffering with the vendors of cakes or cocoa-nut-water.

The gardens are traversed by a small street, dividing the old from the more modern part. The latter is laid out in winding shady walks, separated by high cassia hedges; and at the end is a fine bronze fountain, constantly playing into a large stone basin, round which are seats, where in an evening are groups of Creoles, smoking, chatting, and flirting, though the latter is principally confined to the alleys.

Opposite this fountain stands the Mauritius Club House, where the gentry, coloured and white, particularly those who reside in the country and come into the city daily for business, take tiffin, smoke their Havannah, sip their claret, or play a game at billiards.[1]

Near this is a large gloomy building, shaded by rows of the melancholy filas-trees, whence issues daily the 'Commercial Gazette,' the only English newspaper, printed by the only steam press in the island.

From the quays runs a narrow street, at the top of which are the Civil and Military Hospitals, and close to them the large depôt for Indian immigrants.

[1] This club has proved a failure, and the building is now used for merchants' offices.

The Bazaar, or Market House, is worthy of special notice. The whole is surrounded by tall iron railings, and a number of gateways give entrance from the different streets. A wide avenue traverses the whole of the bazaar; and on each side are large covered sheds, with a good raised pavement, on which the produce is exposed.

On the right hand from Queen Street are the fruit stalls, where some kinds of fruit are always to be found, according to season, except soon after a hurricane.

The principal are bananas, cocoas, costard apples, mangoes, litchis, pines, limes, citrons, alligator pears, sack, papaye, pistaches, and a host of other tropical fruits. With some few exceptions, I found them at first insipid or too sweet, in comparison with the fruits of more temperate zones. Oranges and grapes do not thrive here, though I have seen some miserable little bunches of the latter sold for a dollar a pound. Bananas are always in the market, and there is a great variety, from the little Gingeli, of two inches, to the red Plantain, over a foot long.

Oranges and apples are frequently for sale, but the former come from Seychelles, Cape, or Bourbon, and the latter from Australia, or brought in the ice ships from New York. On arrival, these fruits fetch from sixpence to a shilling each.

On the left hand side of the market are the vegetables, and I believe there is a better supply than in any market out of Europe. The principal are potatoes, native, Bourbon, and Australian; squashes, cabbages, red and white, brocoli, turnips, carrots, peas, beans, onions, patates, &c. &c.

There are numberless green vegetables sold, used by both Indian and Creole population. Many of them, called Bredes, are made into a sort of bouillon with a little salt meat, and form a standing dish from the highest to the lowest, eaten with rice, the invariable adjunct of the breakfast and dinner tables. The Brede Martin (*Solanum nigrum*) and a few others habit has rendered palatable; and they are, I believe, very wholesome, or as a Creole would tell you, 'bien rafraîchissants,' their definition of a dozen or two different bredes, tisanes, and messes of all sorts.

This is a busy, bustling scene; every one must go or send to market every day for fresh provisions, and the bargaining on all sides in the high-pitched voices of both Creoles and Indians make it a very Babel. Here sits a fine buxom Malabar woman, tempting you with her nice fresh greeneries, and thankful if you spend only a halfpenny.

There a sulky fellow who growls and snaps at everybody. In one corner a group of men and women chattering over some deficient sous, and whose attention you have a difficulty in attracting sufficiently to supply your wants, which at last they do, continuing their wrangle all the time.

In solitary state apart, sits another with a few shillings' worth of things before him or her, stolidly indifferent as to whether you buy or not.

Here you can purchase the strange stiff bouquets so much prized, from threepence up to five dollars.

Large cages of native birds, particularly the pretty scarlet cardinals with their brown mates, love birds; and greenish yellow canaries that sing so sweetly, are offered for sixpence a pair. Beautiful foreign birds are frequently for sale, brought by sailors from the Brazils, Australia, India, and the brightest of all from New Guinea, but they fetch high prices. Behind the fruit stalls is a place set apart for dried provisions, sold mostly by Arabs, who expose their wares on the pavement in small sacks, and strong Indian baskets.

Beans of almost every known species, rice, maize, spices, chilis, coffee, cigars, seeds, and drugs are in abundance—also dried herbs. There is scarcely a leaf or bark of indigenous or exotic plant or tree that is not used by Creole or Indian for some ailment. They have the most profound faith in herb teas or tisanes; and the latter know, unfortunately, too well the dire properties of the many vegetable poisons in the island, and use them freely too when prompted by revenge or other passions.

Beyond the Arabs is a long line of tables for bread, principally sold by Creoles, made into small French loaves, fetching a moderate price. Still further back is a row of stalls, kept entirely by young Malabars, of every conceivable thing in a small way. Most of them speak a little English, of which they are very proud.

Woe betide the unlucky stranger who goes into the line unprepared. A rush is made each one vociferating, 'What you want? Come to me, he no good,' and so on, offering you the most incongruous articles. Should you have been rash enough to ask for anything, you will be deluged with it. They have quick eyes to discern a stranger, and some of the young scamps quite patronise you. At least three or four times as much as is meant to be taken is asked, as they know they will be beaten down. I once saw a friend asked sixpence a dozen for buttons, and for fun he ran the gauntlet the whole length of the line, and by the time he got to the bottom, the fellow ran after him, and offered the same buttons for a shilling a gross!

Farquhar Street divides the upper from the lower bazaar. The latter is for meat, fish, &c. On the left hand of it are the meat stalls, where very fair beef, Creole and Madagascar, may be had from five-pence to ten-pence a pound. Mutton is sold by the joint, at extravagant prices, rarely fine; and goat's flesh is so often substituted for mutton, that a piece of the skin is generally left on to prove its identity. The veal is coarse and red, and pork is principally sold by Chinamen. Few English or French will eat the latter, as it is considered so unwholesome in a tropical climate; besides, the way of feeding pigs here makes one shudder.

Sometimes a fine pig is offered for sale from some newly arrived vessel, and then the pork is bought up readily. The Chinamen are the great consumers of pork, and at their numerous feasts roast five or six pigs, often, if not too large, whole.

Below the meat are, poultry, eggs, &c. Geese, turkeys, ducks, pigeons, guinea-fowl, manilla ducks and fowls, can be bought, but they are very dear, and miserably fed.

The opposite side is almost exclusively for fish, and like all the rest of the bazaar, is kept very clean.

A stream of water pours constantly over the sloping tables, so that the fish look always nice and fresh.

I suppose no place in the world can boast such a variety of fish, and many of them of such brilliant colours, that I can only compare them to the gorgeous plumaged birds of India or South America. The most esteemed are the mullets, Dame Berry, red and spotted vieilles, corne, cordonnier, rougets, pike, eels, and others. Fine crabs and crayfish (called here lobsters) are very abundant; small shellfish, indifferent oysters, and the cat fish, are sold in great quantities. Large sharks, rays, and other monsters are also cut up in slices, and sold to the Indians.[1]

Below the fish stalls is a space set apart for the sale of cattle and goats, but few of them are in fine condition.

In the centre of this market is erected a stand, on which is a large pair of scales, attended by a municipal officer, and any one being aggrieved by receiving short weight, can have the article re-weighed, and if found wanting, the seller is arrested, heavily fined, and loses his standing in the market.

The bazaar is well regulated, and under the supervision of inspectors who examine everything before it is allowed to be offered for sale, and any article not perfectly fresh is at once condemned and confiscated. A small tax is imposed for the rent of the stalls, as well as on all dead and live animals. By an ordinance of September 1, 1855, in consequence of cattle disease at the Cape, whence came large supplies to the colony, all persons having beasts for slaughter, are compelled to have them examined by a veterinary surgeon, at the municipality slaughter-house, some distance out of the city. They must, after passing the surgeon, who has the right to decide if fit or not, be killed immediately. Should any animal after death present symptoms of disease, the carcass is ordered off, and taken in a boat to the Bell Buoy, and flung overboard, when it is quickly devoured by the sharks which swarm outside the reefs. The greater part of the vegetables sold in the bazaar are grown by Indians, in the environs of Port Louis, Aux Pailles, Moka, &c., and are brought in small donkey carts long before daylight.

In one corner of the fish market is always a plentiful supply of coffee, cocoa tendre, or the soft white substance in the cocoa before the nut sets hard in its shell, and cocoa-nut milk, rice, and other cakes, with which the vendors regale themselves, and these often form the only food they take till their return home towards noon, of course including the inevitable pipe,

[1] Some years ago a calculation was made of the amount of fish supposed to be consumed daily in Mauritius. The following was the result:—

2,000 lbs. of fresh sea fish,
1,000 „ salt „ „
150 „ fresh water „
600 paquets shrimps and camerons,
300 „ oysters.

The above amount gave the annual sum of $220,000. A correct calculation made at the present day would most likely give a great increase on the above. This does not include imported salt fish.

too often filled with opium, gunga, or some other deleterious narcotic.

From the lower end of the bazaar runs Moka Street, and in it, facing Rempart Street, stands the old French Government House, a two-storied stone building, with a large dome in the centre, which lights the interior. It is now occupied by a firm of English merchants as a warehouse for the storage of goods. It is of considerable interest in connection with the history of the island, being the only city residence of the French Governors during their possession of the Isle of France. Moka Street is long and dusty, the great outlet to the city on the western side, with more traffic than perhaps any other, but principally filled with little provision shops, held by Chinamen or Lascars, canteens, &c. &c. Nearly every shop in it (unlike the rest of the city) is lit up at night, and I have often strolled up it after dark, greatly amused watching the strange manners of the various races. All Eastern nations are just as much addicted to story telling as in the old days of Haroun al-Raschid, and in nearly every little shop in the streets are groups eagerly listening to some one relating stories as marvellous as the Arabian Nights.

At gunfire, or eight o'clock, all the Lascars burn a kind of frankincense in their scales, and about the shops, muttering prayers over it, to keep away the devils, to bring them good sales the ensuing day, and render the house lucky.

Leading out of this street is the Central Railway dêpot, a fine stone building, well arranged and convenient. From this station all the trains leave for both Northern and Midland lines. The fare for the north line is three dollars and three quarters, and for the other four dollars and a quarter. The roads are admirably laid, its rolling stock is first class, and it is well conducted. Its numerous stations, plainly but substantially built, and well constructed bridges, reflect great credit on the firm of Messrs. Brassey and Company, the contractors for this railway. Telegraphs have been lately added, and few places in the world can boast a more convenient and comfortable arrangement of carriages, &c.—whether it will ever be a profitable concern remains to be seen.

Just beyond the dépot are the Line Barracks, built of stone, on one side two stories high, and the whole substantially enclosed with strong walls; having two large gates, one in Barrack and the other in Moka Street. The square contains twelve acres, and makes a fine parade and exercising ground for the troops. They are capacious enough for some thousands of soldiers; but since the epidemic, the military have nearly abandoned them, and now they are partially occupied by the police. There is a talk of pulling them down, and building new ones on the high land at Plaines Wilhems, which I should think is a much more sensible arrangement; for it seems to me to have been a great mistake to have a barracks in the centre of

CATHEDRAL, PORT LOUIS.

a densely populated city like Port Louis. Along the southern walls runs a ditch, which may originally have been intended as a moat, but now receives a good deal of sewage water, making it a most unpleasant locality.

In College Street, in a large enclosure, stands the Royal College, an irregular building, dating from 1791. One side of it is employed as a Museum, and here the meetings are held of the Royal Society of Arts and Sciences.

The principal edifices for religious worship in Port Louis are St. James's Cathedral, on a slight rise between Pondrière Street, Denis and Labourdonnais Streets; the Roman Catholic Cathedral, in Government Street; the Church of the Immaculée Conception in St. George Street; the Scotch Church, a little above the bazaar; the Independent Chapel, in Poudrière Street, and the Mohammedan Mosque, in Royal Street. There are a few other temporary places of worship, which are mentioned elsewhere, and a Lascar temple near Plaine Verte.

Taken altogether, Port Louis is a quaint, old-fashioned place, and I fear it is not destined, at all events for some time to come, to be much modernised and improved.

A painful picture is presented by the endless notices of 'To Let' on almost every other door in many of the streets. Fine old stores, once heaped with costly merchandise, and let at fabulous prices on lease, now fetch a few dollars a month for one or two rooms (all the rest shut up), let most probably to some coloured cobbler or cigar vendor, where he works, and resides with his generally numerous, and with rare exceptions, noisy and dirty family.

The depreciation of property in Port Louis has gone steadily on since the fever. The white population is gradually deserting it for the healthier districts. I do not think the day is far distant when it will be almost entirely in the hands of the coloured races, unless a total change is made in its sanitary condition, either by drainage or some other means of altering the present defective sewerage. The Indians also must be compelled to conform to European habits of cleanliness, and utterly give up their own antagonistic ideas on the subject, before this city can be a desirable residence, in spite of its being the capital of the 'Gem of the East.'

CHAPTER IV.

PAMPLEMOUSSES GARDENS.

M. Poivre—Description of Gardens—Centre Avenue—Obelisk—Lakes—Sago Walk—Avenue of Fine Trees—Effects of Hurricane—Nursery—Boabab—Grassy Slope—Mr. Horne's Cottage—Curious Trees near it—Dr. Meller's House—Fernery—Bernadin St.-Pierre—Loss of the St.-Geran—Captain's Death—And that of the Two Lovers—Tombs of Paul and Virginia.

At the distance of seven miles from Port Louis, in the district of Pamplemousses, are the celebrated Botanical Gardens, founded by M. Poivre in 1768. The island is greatly indebted to this gentleman for the introduction of the clove, nutmeg, and other spices, besides a large variety of useful and ornamental trees, procured with great difficulty and expense, from both hemispheres.

These gardens have been from time to time replenished from the various botanical gardens of Europe, Cape Town, Australia, and India, and now form the special attraction of the colony.

The numerous and shady avenues, and the comfortable little thatched pavilions scattered in all directions, impervious to the weather, render this a favourite resort of the citizens of Port Louis, on Sundays and holidays, especially during the intense heat of summer.

These gardens have been recently enclosed with a substantial iron railing imported from Europe. The entrance is through massive iron gates, and on the right there stands a pretty little lodge for the gatekeeper.

As far as the eye can reach, a long straight avenue extends, thickly lined on each side with the *Latania glaucophylla* palm (Mauritius), and towering above them to a great height are the slender stems of the areca-nut palm (*Areca catechu*), sometimes, but erroneously, called the Betel nut, with its small tuft of feathery leaves forming its crown. Below these leaves are clusters of bright yellow fruit, which the Indians and Malays chew, with the leaf of the Betel plant (*Piper Chavica*) and lime. This fruit possesses intoxicating properties, and powerfully stimulates the salivary glands and digestive organs, and diminishes the perspiration of the skin.

In the far distance, in the centre of the avenue, is an obelisk, erected to the memory of those who have introduced into Mauritius either useful plants or animals.

Round this monument are some fine specimens of a rare and beautiful palm, the *Latania aurea* (Duncan), from Rodriques. The natives of that island build their houses with the outer slabs of its trunk; make the rafters of its leaf-stalks, which sometimes attain the length of six to ten feet, with a diameter of two to four inches thick, and thatch them with its leaves.

From the obelisk we pass over a little bridge, spanning a clear stream, down a long winding path, so densely shaded by the Traveller's Tree (*Ravenala Madagascariensis*), Vacoas (*Pandanus utilis*), Raffias (*Sagus Ruffia*), and others, that it is impervious to the sun at noonday, and gives a better idea of tropical scenery than any part of the gardens. Here and there are clumps of the feathery Bamboo, which prettily conceal little pavilions with seats and tables, where you may breakfast or dine quite undisturbed by passers by.

The extension of this walk is bordered with the Stevenson palm (*Stevensonia grandifolia*), and passes the new rosary, where are thousands of rose trees grafted or budded with all the varieties of Europe, except the loveliest of all, the Moss rose, which has either not been introduced, or will not thrive.

There is a small lake, surrounded by a grassy bank, and full of blue and white lotus plants, that in the season cover its surface with their large blossoms. There are also some fine specimens of the lace, or lattice leaf plant (*Ouvirandra fenestralis*), with its curious skeleton leaves, dichotomous spiked inflorescence, and pretty white flowers which show their heads just above the water.

Further on is a large lake, containing several pretty islands, two of which are approached by bridges, and have seats under the trees for visitors. The centre islands are inaccessible, and are covered with the traveller's tree, palms, casuarinas, and a tangle of flowering shrubs and underwood. There are two fine white swans on its waters, presented by Lady Barkly, and a handsome black Australian swan, which some time ago unfortunately lost its mate. It follows the white ones about, but the poor fellow gets terribly snubbed by his snowy comrades. They are all quite tame, and eat from the hand. This lake is full of the celebrated gouramier, and golden dace, also of monster eels, one of which is so tame that whenever the swans come to be fed, he pops up his ugly head, and takes his share too.

Half encircling this lake is a winding alley of fine sago palms (*Cycas circinalis*), and rare shrubs and flowers are planted between it and the water's edge in clumps in the grass. The fruit of these palms is eaten in the Moluccas, and an inferior kind of flour is made by pounding its kernels in a mortar. It also yields a gum which, when coagulated in the air, is applied to malignant sores, and it excites suppuration in an incredibly short time.

Terminating the sago walk, rise about a dozen magnificent specimens of the *Oreodoxa regia* palm (Cuba), far exceeding in beauty those of the King's Gardens at Rio Janeiro.

The walk round the other half of this lake, is bordered with rows of the *Licuala horrida* palm, rightly named, for every stem and leaf is bristling with thousands of sharp spines.

In a corner between this lake and the garden wall is a small plantation of the China grass cloth plant (*Boehmeria nivea*), the fibre of which is said to be worth in the European and American markets, about 80*l.* to 100*l.* the ton. It is cultivated here as an experiment, for propagation and distribution to the planters.

Turning to the left on entering the gardens, are two walks shaded by magnificent trees, the most remarkable of which are the following :—the *Lecythis minor*, with its large fruit in the form of an urn, from which the top spontaneously separates like a lid. The *Bassia latifolia*, or Illipie tree, the fruit of which, when pressed, yields a large quantity of fatty oil, used in India for lamps, soap making, and food, and also employed medicinally in cutaneous disorders. The *Strychnos nux vomica*, or Strychnine tree, which produces the well-known poison-seeds ; its bark is also supposed to be very poisonous, though they say the pulp in which the deadly nuts are imbedded is eatable. The Camphor tree (*Camphora officiarum*), from which the Chinese obtain camphor by boiling pieces of its roots, wood and branches, until the camphor begins to adhere to the stirring rod. This is a noble umbrageous tree, from three to five feet in diameter. (The hard camphor of Sumatra and Borneo, is obtained from the *Dryobalanops Camphora*, quite a different tree). The *Hymenæa Courbaril* and *Hymenæa verrucosa* : the former is the West Indian Locust tree, with a close-grained, tough wood, in great request for tree-nails, used in the planking of vessels, and the latter is an East Indian tree; both yield the copal used for the well-known varnish. The *Chrysophyllum*, or Star Apple, producing a fruit much esteemed in its native country (India) as an article for dessert. The *Semecarpus Anacardium*, the 'marking nut tree' of commerce; from its seeds the varnish of Sylhet is obtained; it is extremely dangerous to some constitutions, as the skin when rubbed with it becomes inflamed, and covered with pimples that are difficult to heal, and the fumes are said to produce painful swellings and inflammation. The *Tectona grandis*, or Teak tree, that yields the well-known and valuable timber. The *Adenanthera pavonina* and the *Pterocarpus santalinus*, both giving red and scarlet dyes; the pretty smooth bright-red seeds of the former are made into necklaces, baskets, &c.; and the *Pterocarpus draco*, or Dragon's Blood tree, that furnishes the dragon's blood of commerce, which is sometimes, but improperly called gum dragon.

The ground under the shade of these interesting trees has been recently laid out in beds for the better cultivation of shade-loving plants, or rather plants that require shade in so hot a climate, such as begonias, fuchias, gloxinias, gesnerias, &c. &c. This pleasant spot is close to another alley of fine palms, arecas of different species, and at intervals are seats, from which a good view of the Peter Both Mountain is obtained. Many of these palms are 100 years old. Sad destruction was made among them by the hurricane of March 1868, and as it would take a great amount of time and labour to replace the old trees by young ones, and the soil would require entirely renovating, mahogany trees are being planted in their places. These handsome trees are grown from seeds sent by Dr. Hooker, Director of the Royal Gardens at Kew, and are, I believe, the first planted in Mauritius.

Near to this alley are two other newly introduced trees, the *Siphonia elastica*, or India-rubber tree. Nearly the whole of the India-rubber used in England is procured from the Siphonias of Brazil and Guiana.

In the centre of the gardens, a portion of ground is set apart for a nursery. This produces a large supply of young plants for distribution in the colony. In 1865 over 50,000 young

TROPICAL LAKE SCENE.

trees were distributed. New varieties of the sugar-cane are also propagated in this nursery, to enable the planters to replace the exhausted varieties now cultivated in the island.

To the right of the main entrance are rows of new exotics and beds of bright-coloured flowers and shrubs, all classified and named. Beyond these is one of the pleasantest parts of the gardens; a grassy slope extending downwards to another large lake, that has also a pretty island encircled with rock work, Raffias and Vacoas.

From the leaves of the Raffia, before they are fully unfolded, the Malagash make hats, mats, and a great variety of useful and ornamental articles. The scales of its pericarp, when polished, are sometimes used as an ornament for the outsides of workboxes, baskets, &c.

Its petioles or leaf stalks are employed for palisades and rafters in hut building, and when kept dry will last from twenty to thirty years. The vacoa is often called the Screw pine, from the peculiar spiral form the leaves assume in their convolutions round the trunk. Under the crown hangs the beautiful but uneatable amber-coloured fruit. The leaves are narrow and flat, and the natives plait them into mats, baskets, and sugar bags. The latter are universally used in the packing of sugar, and one would imagine ought to be a source of profit to the poor in the country; but, like so many other useful productions growing with little trouble over the island, its cultivation is so much neglected, that the greater part of the bags used are imported from Madagascar, and some other of the adjacent islands.

Out of this lake flows a stream, with a pretty fall of water that passes under an iron bridge into the ravine below.

A very attractive feature on the grassy slope is a gigantic baobab (*Adansonia digitata*), measuring thirty feet round at the collum. It has a singular fruit, about a foot and a half long, covered with a rough brown coat, and hanging from a very long thread-like stem from the branches. In Western Africa, its native country, it is said to live thousands of years, and grows so large that whole families can reside in its hollowed trunk.[1]

Scattered over the turf is a small collection of coniferous trees, natives of both hemispheres. Many of them have only been planted about three or four years, but they would scarcely be excelled in beauty in their own climates.

There are very fine specimens of araucarias, dammaras, pinus, two or three specimens of thujas, cupressus, juniperus, and callitris.

This collection is being added to yearly; and the graceful forms of these exotics mingled, with groups of bananas, travel-

[1] Adanson notices one which three centuries before had been observed by two English travellers, and on excavating the trunk of this tree, there was found an inscription they had written, covered with 300 ligneous layers; from this they were enabled to judge how much the gigantic plant had grown in 300 years, and comparing it with the diameter of the tree, it was estimated that the probable duration of its existence was upwards of 5,000 years.

ler's trees, and the more regular-shaped exogens, particularly the fine tamarinds (*Tamarindus indica*), have a picturesque and striking effect to a stranger's eye.

In the midst of all this wealth of tropical vegetation, here and there one starts with delight, as one finds some of our northern climate's pet flowers. Close to the monstrous Baobab is a bed where the English honeysuckle blooms in wild profusion, and most of us are tempted to break the strict rules against gathering flowers, in order to take away a spray that recalls so vividly 'auld lang syne.' Passing along the upper part of the grassy slope, over a stone bridge, covered with the large blue thunbergia, you see the cottage of the sub-director on the left, with the chief's offices.

In front of Mr. Horne's, is a fine Satin-wood tree (*Swietenia Chloroxylon*), which, in its native country, grows to the height of 100 feet; and a handsome plant of the Cow-itch (*Mucuna pruriens*). Not far from the cottage stand two splendid Bread-fruit trees, not only the oldest in the island, but supposed to be the parents of all the rest of this beautiful and useful tree in Mauritius. Near these, by the side of a canal, grows one of the *Carludovica palmata*, from the unexpanded leaves of which are made the famous Panama hats.

Then come rows of the elegant feathery cocoa-nut, and *Cocos plumosa*, and the majestic Talipot palm (*Corypha umbraculifera*). The Cinghalese make mats from the leaves of this palm, which serve to construct their temporary huts. These mats are so light that a man can easily carry enough for a tent capable of containing twenty people; and, with a few sticks from the nearest jungle, two or three men will run it up in about twenty minutes.

There is another walk shaded by the Gommuti palm (*Saguerus saccharifer*), from which sugar (called 'jaggery' in India) is made in the Moluccas, Ceylon, and the Philippine Islands. Its juice, when fermented, produces 'toddy,' that arrack is distilled from in Batavia. A fine tree has been known to yield ninety pints of toddy in a day. From its trunk, when exhausted of its sweet juice, a good deal of the sago of commerce is obtained, and one tree will give about 200 pounds of sago.

The hairy-looking fibre that envelopes its trunk at the base of its petioles is used by upholsterers as a substitute for horse-hair to stuff cushions, and is called gommuti or giou fibre, and serves also for caulking vessels, and making ropes.

There are some of the *Caryota urens* palms, which also yield sugar, toddy and sago. The palms giving the largest quantity of sago are the *Sagus lœvis* and *S. genuina*, the former of which often produces as much as 800 pounds from one trunk.

In a pretty enclosure on the right is the house of Dr. Meller, the Director of the Gardens,[1] with its verandah completely hidden behind masses of the lilac bourgainvillæa, the scarlet ipomæa, and monster passion flowers.

Under the supervision of this accomplished botanist, and the energetic management of Mr. Horne, the gardens have greatly improved, and new and useful plants are being constantly introduced into the colony.

Close to Dr. Meller's house is the Fernery, admirably situated on a rocky descent, with a pretty sparkling stream at its foot. It contains many hundreds of ferns and orchids, about 150 of which are natives of Mauritius. Here may be seen the celebrated Coco de mer, from Seychelles, with its great twin nuts. From the delicate fibres of the leaves, the elegant baskets, fans, hats, &c., are made. There are several squares planted with nutmeg, clove, and other spice trees, that all bear prolifically. The mangosteen of India grows here, but it must be either a very different or very inferior fruit, if one can judge of it by the descriptions given by travellers.

It would be a hopeless task to try and give a more detailed account of all the beautiful trees, shrubs, creepers, &c., of these gardens, as there is no printed guide to them, and except the late additions none are named, so that it is an *embarras de richesses* when one attempts a description of them.

In a work on Mauritius, it would never do to omit all mention of the tombs of Paul and Virginia at Pamplemousses.

Bernadin St.-Pierre's world-known and interesting romance has spread a sort of halo round Mauritius for well nigh a century; and to those who never visited the island, it will still have

[1] Since this was written the colony has had to deplore the loss of Dr. Meller, who died whilst on a visit to Australia to purchase fresh canes to replace the exhausted and diseased species in the Island. The gardens are now ably managed by Mr. J. Horne.

charms. But one has only to be there a few days before the positive absurdities in it strike one forcibly.

Writers of romances, when about to draw largely on their imaginations, should be very careful to conceal the actual whereabouts of their stories; for this very realistic age, when steam and electricity annihilate time and space, when the most distant corners of the earth are better known than Scotland or Ireland a century ago, is sure to take the romance of mystery out of them, and display their ridiculous side when reduced to fact.

The following narration will show on what St.-Pierre founded his tale.

In 1744, drought and locusts had occasioned a terrible scarcity in the Isle of France, and the 'St.-Geran' was sent from the mother-country, to assist the Governor, Mahé de Labourdonnais, richly laden with arms and provisions. This was doubly needed, on account of the failure of several large vessels, just returned from India, in procuring a supply of rice.

The 'St.-Geran' was in sight of Round Island at four P.M., and the captain, M. de la Marre, wished to profit by a fine moonlight night to enter Tombeau Bay, but it was afterwards decided to lie to till the next day. In consequence of ignorance of the dangerous coast, the ship touched on the reef, towards three in the morning, about a league from the coast, and the same distance from Isle d'Ambre. The sea there generally runs high, and drove the ship with violence on the breakers.

Every effort was made to lower the boats, but the crashing down of the masts stove in their bulwarks, and carried them away. The keel soon after breaking in the middle, engulphed the centre, and fixed the extremities of the ship on the reefs.

At M. de la Marre's request, the chaplain pronounced a general benediction and absolution, and the 'Ave Maria Stella' was sung.

Numbers of the crew flung themselves into the sea, on planks, yards, oars, or anything that offered a hold; but, carried away by the currents, beaten and tossed by the waves, nearly all found a watery grave.

A sailor named Caret made the greatest efforts to save M. de la Marre. He implored him to take off his clothes, but he persistently refused, saying, 'It did not become the dignity of his position to land without them.'

Caret at length succeeded in placing his captain on a plank, and the intrepid fellow swam a long time through the strong currents dragging the plank after him.

Encountering a raft laden with the crew, M. de la Marre thought he would be safer on it, and left the brave Caret for the raft. Plunging to avoid collision, the latter, as he slowly rose to the surface again, found to his horror that raft and men all had disappeared, engulphed in the boiling waters.

There were on board two lovers, a Mdlle. Mallet and M. de Péramon, who were to be united in marriage on arriving at the Isle of France.

The young man, as anxious and agitated as the girl was calm and resigned, when the others left, was making a sort of raft on which to save her who was dearer than his own life. On his knees he implored her to descend with him on to the frail but sole hope of safety; and to ensure a greater certainty, he begged her to take off the heavier part of her garments. This she steadily refused to do. When he found his most earnest solicitations vain, and consequently all hope of saving her lost, though she entreated him to leave her, he quietly took from a pocket-book a tress of her hair, kissed it, and placed it on his heart. With his arm round her to shield her as far as he could to the last, he calmly awaited the terrible catastrophe at her side; nor had they long to wait, for they were soon washed from the deck, and their bodies were picked up at Tombeau Bay.[1]

Eight of the crew and one passenger were all that were saved, and made known the details of the shipwreck. This disaster was the more frightful as it took place at a season of the year which is always calm in these regions, and it can only be attributed to the imprudence of the officers and their entire ignorance of the coast.

The two tombs shown as those of Paul and Virginia are two common-place brick and mortar structures, whitewashed, or at least they were so, years ago. They are situated in what

[1] It is said this bay derived its name, the Bay of Tombs, from the number of bodies washed on shore there from the St.-Geran.

was once a fine garden, a little rivulet flowing between them, and shaded by beautiful palms and feathery bamboos.

I had a special mission from a romantic young lady to send her some flowers from the tombs, as precious relics! Sad to relate, when I visited them there had been heavy rains—the whole place was a swamp, and I could not get within a hundred yards of them. However, I gathered a few rose leaves from another part of the garden, which, I do not doubt, answered equally as well.

Now, instead of the silence and seclusion once surrounding this show-place for all visitors, a railway station is within a few yards of it; the iron horses go thundering by, and the progress of steam has caused a consequent decline in romance in Mauritius as well as elsewhere.

THE RACES AT THE CHAMP DE MARS, PORT LOUIS.

CHAPTER V.

THE RACES.

The Beginning of Racing in Mauritius—Unprofitableness of Races—Horses very Inferior—Rules and Regulations up to Newmarket mark—No Information to be got—Preparations for Races—Race Monday—General Excitement—The Race—Jockeys—The Loges—Saturday—Scenes in Bazaar—Costumes—Nautch Girls—Toilettes—Painful Case of take in—Return Home.

The commencement of the racing era in Mauritius was in June, 1812, under the direction of Colonel Draper, a member of the English Jockey Club, and the fine field of the Champ de Mars was appropriated to the sport.

How matters were then carried on I know not, but I doubt if the racing was ever much to boast of. It is true that for years fresh blood from Europe, the Cape, and Australia has been imported, but like the human race, the equine degenerates rapidly here, and racing does not appear to have been a profitable speculation, for some of the most energetic importers have entirely ceased and given up their studs.

I have witnessed two of these exhibitions of horse-flesh, and considered the whole affair as got up by a few private speculators. All the horses I have seen entered were a poor lot, and so far from being fit for racing, I question if any gentleman in Europe or America who valued his turn-out would have ridden them either in the Central Park, New York, in Hyde Park, or the Bois de Boulogne.

It must be, however, understood that the failure is not from any want of forms and rules, for there is a Turf Club, which issues printed regulations on the strictest Newmarket principles, and they are supposed to be carried out to the letter.

I can give very little information as to what goes on in the Mauritius racing world, either in the present or past times.

I have applied over and over again to some of the principal members for such knowledge, who were lavish in promises; but the only result I have attained, after waiting many months, is a copy of the aforesaid regulations. So I must perforce draw a veil over the racing history of the island, and will only describe the field of strife.

Formerly the races were held in September, then in August, and latterly in July; a more sensible arrangement, as there is generally in the last named months a prospect of fine weather, without the mid-day heat of the former. For some weeks previous to the races great preparations go on. A long row of stalls or lodges, and the judges' stand, are erected near the winning post. The course is put in first rate order; confectioners lay in ample stocks of eatables and drinkables, not forgetting ice; milliners and dressmakers are at work night and day to—spare your blushes, ladies, I will not dare to intrude on such sacred ground. On that head I will confine myself to describing only the brilliant results when you dazzle our bewildered eyes on the long prepared-for day. Meetings of the Turf Club, bettings, watching the horses cantering round the field on early mornings and showing off their paces, and so on, till the eventful Monday, the first day of the races, arrives.

From daylight every street is crowded with loads of chairs, tables, benches, and stands. Private carriages are driven up and left horseless within the cordon near the loges. Tents rise on the surrounding eminences as by magic, flags fly, tomtoms beat, the whole city is in a ferment. One loge is set apart for the governor, another for the council, mayor, officers of the regiment, &c.

By 11 o'clock knots of anxious and horsey-looking men may be seen near the betting stand; horses may be heard neighing in the distance, the loges and carriages begin to fill, all is confusion worse confounded, everyone rushing madly about, not a calm face visible. Men, women, and children, horses and dogs, swell the crowd on the course; the wretched police, sweltering under the brilliant sun in their closely buttoned cloth coats, hoarse with their efforts to clear it.

Up goes the Royal standard, a carriage dashes along, and his Excellency and lady are ushered into their loge.

Vehicles of every description set down their gorgeous burdens, and the whole place is soon a flutter of ribbons, silks, and muslins. 'Way there,' and on come the prancing horses led by their jockeys and owners, with difficulty soothed into an equable frame of mind fit for their duties in the Babel of sounds around them.

Headlong goes the crowd at last. The course is clear even of the inevitable old woman who will go every way but the nearest off, and the howling dog pursued by the whole police force. The jockeys and saddles properly weighed and weighted, 'Are you ready?' responded to, and the magic 'Off!' uttered, and away they go. A great silence falls on the assembled multitude, till the horses begin to turn towards the winning post, when a gradual hum steals through the silence, and it ends in a roar of applause as the winner comes in, though I believe not more than a third of the multitudes present know when the horses do run. The jockeys return to be weighed, and all the forms usual on such occasions in the mother country are gone through. The jockeys (save the mark, for only one I have seen who knew anything about riding) are dressed in such fantastic colours, it is enough to make the quietest horse shy when he is mounted, in astonishment at such a flutter of silks and ribands.

The gentlemen who keep private carriages appear to take more pride in their horses than the racing community in theirs; and till a better system of stabling and training is adopted, the Mauritian Newmarket will be ever at a low ebb. It has one good side, it is profitable to trade, and is a general holiday and festival, and where there is such a lack of amusement, I do not wonder at its being kept up. I will turn, then, to the pleasantest part of the affair—the loges, where are the fashion and beauty of the island. The French ladies, and the English who follow French fashions, certainly dress with exquisite taste. From the fluttering lace above the chignon (or waterfall, as we call it in Yankee-land) down to the points of their Canots' boots, or the tips of their dainty Jouvin or Boudier's gloves, all is rich, well chosen, harmonious; only to a Northerner's eye, a *leetle* too rich for out-of-door costume.

There are generally three or four races, and by 4 or 5 o'clock all is over until Wednesday, when much the same programme is gone through, except that there is not such a large concourse of people as on the first and last days.

With the single exception of New Year's day, Saturday, the third day of the races, is the grand holiday for all classes and colours. Peons, cooks, household servants, claim a release from work, the two latter but too often regardless of Monsieur or Madame's entreaties to be home in time to get dinner ready. Lucky is the housekeeper who has this day taken the precaution to have that meal cooked beforehand.

From gunfire at dawn of day every inlet to the town swarms with carts and carrioles, literally crammed with Indian women and children; the men walking alongside, and all dressed in a superabundance of extra finery. They come in from the villages and estates.

The first point of attraction is the bazaar, and thither I also went for household purposes. I confess that bad beef and worse mutton (the fare in the market on that day) had less charms for me than watching the busy scene around. Outside the gates stood rows of little carts, drawn by sleek-coated donkeys, their headgear adorned with flowers. These were filled with very small Indian children, put there to keep them out of the crowd, while pater and materfamilias were having a gossip within the gates. Each cart was a picture. Such a number of grave, self-possessed atoms of humanity I never saw. Every one of them in a new costume, glittering with jewellery, their bright black eyes sparkling with anticipated delight, but unlike European children—nearly all silent.

Inside all was bustle and gaiety. Wherever Indian delicacies were sold, there mirth was rife—everybody laughing, joking, bargaining, eating, and gossiping in a Babel of dialects. All was hurry and fun, as the bazaar closes early on that day, and woe-betide the housekeeper that neglects to send to market early. Every bit of fruit is swept off, either by customers in haste to go to the Champ de Mars, or by the vendors, who hope to realise larger profits by selling it on the race ground.

Here and there a grave couple are seen smoking and telling their adventures since their last meeting, and if you want their wares you must wait till the speech is finished before they will answer you. Commend me to a group of Malabar women out for a spree, for gossiping. If it be true that out of the ten measures of speech given by the Gods, women got nine, it is quite certain that the Indian fair sex appropriated seven of them. Their tones are so sharp and high, that any stranger would suppose them quarrelling.

Between seven and eight o'clock, up Bourbon, Church, and Corderie Streets, that run direct from the bazaar to the Champ de Mars, goes a stream of coloured people of all nations.

The grave, stout Arab, generally in a carriage drawn by a good pair of horses, with his little boys, in beautifully gold-embroidered robes and caps (no Arab woman is ever visible in Mauritius); the Parsee in long white dress and singular tall cap, hollow at the top—and even he has a smile on his stern handsome face, and thousands of Indians of different races, most of them in native costume; but a few indulging in coats, particularly old cast-off soldiers' red coats, with a yellow or white waist cloth and bright head dress, the ends sticking out horn-fashion, looking quite happy and unconscious that a coat requires a nether garment. The stout, heavy Malagash, small creole Indian, pig-eyed Chinaman, French and English creoles, and American, English, and French, *pur sang*, all have representatives at this Mauritian carnival.

The centre of the Champ de Mars is devoted to other amusements than racing. Swings, merry-go-rounds, greased poles, even Aunt Sally has found her way there. Look down on this varied scene from one of the surrounding eminences, and you get a sight almost unique in the civilised world.

This vast plain is lined on two sides with pleasant looking houses, every window and garden overflowing with visitors, the hill at the upper end covered to its summit with tents and booths. The Citadel Hill, which overlooks it, is crowded with pedestrians, and the different streets that diverge from it at its foot swarm with carriages and people going and coming. Bacchus and Comus reign supreme. In every corner are Indians vending indescribable confectionary, eagerly devoured. Immense baskets of fruit and pistaches disappear, and oceans of lemonade and other not so innocuous drinks.

Between the races may be seen a dense crowd, and in its centre three Nautch girls performing their dances and singing songs unfit for ears polite, but luckily in the Hindoo tongue, to the great delight of the circling faces. They are accompanied by five musicians, with fiddle, cymbals, and drums fastened to the waist by cloth girdles. The girls were fantastically dressed in bright-coloured muslin skirts and very short bodices, showing the plump brown skin between the two, and the long scarf-like 'Capra' floating round them, striped and trimmed with gold lace. Their faces were painted, and anklets and wristlets encircled with rows of silver bells that tinkled with every movement. An old fakir went with the girls, dressed in ragged coat and patched trowsers, and a cap covered with strings of beads that hung to his waist, and his face hideously streaked with white paint. Between the dances he sang and told stories, which, judging from the warm reception they received from the audience, must have been of a very questionable character; and it is well known the accredited story-tellers, whose name is Legion, have a *répertoire* that beats Eugène Sue or Paul de Kock out and out.

After the most indescribable postures and gestures, one of the girls would throw herself on the neck of some bachelor bystander, who was obliged to give her money before he could make his escape from the jeers of the crowd. These wretched women are set apart from childhood for the Nautch, under the charge of the ugly old fakir, and are obliged to work very hard, and to give all their earnings to him.

On this day the real fun is not with the horse races, which few out of a certain set care about, but with the pony, sack, and donkey races. In the former generally one at least discharges its rider, and makes off to the hills, when the chevy that follows is the best part of the race. The soldiers most frequently contest the sack races; but the greatest fun is when the donkeys run, in which the pretty little animals, mostly ridden by boys, are as erratic in their movements as their brethren in other countries, and few arrive at the goal.

The stalls are filled with the *élite* of Mauritian society from the Governor downwards, dressed in the very acmé of Parisian fashion. Behind these stalls are refreshment rooms, where every delicacy is procurable, and a plentiful supply of iced drinks, most acceptable with the thermometer at 90° even at the beginning of August during the day, though it falls to 75° in the evenings.

Numbers of carriages draw up here beneath the stalls, and

offer a curious sight to English eyes. Almost every one contains a party of splendidly dressed women; and in among them you stroll, as being one of the most attractive features of the course, and more accessible than the fair dames in the stalls. Presently you see a delicate, mignon, white-gloved hand on the side of an irreproachable turn out; the tiniest soupçon of a lace bonnet and a resplendent silk dress, and with pardonable curiosity you approach nearer, trusting to meet a face to match the exquisite toilette, when lo! a pair of bright black eyes look round at you, set in a face of some shade of brown or black, with a thick down of violet powder on it, and you at once collapse.

Colour certainly carries the day on the race ground. The sports generally continue till quite dark on this day, but not so late as formerly. The Indians now take advantage of the trains, which are altered to a later hour on race days, so that the great influx from the country is obliged to leave the ground earlier than they otherwise would.

Those who do not go to the Champ de Mars, amuse themselves by watching the carriages drive home through the city, and doubtless commenting thereon; the tired owners glad to get home, the fair sex to dream of the boxes of gloves lost and won on the races—well for them if paterfamilias has not to muse on heavier losses.

CHAPTER VI.

THE EPIDEMIC OF MAURITIUS.

On Fevers generally—Malarious Fever in 1866—Distress in the Districts—Symptoms of the Fever—Complications—Effects of Quinine—Remedies—The Fever, Malarious—Causes of Fever—Spores—Ague Plants—Causes of Malaria at Port Louis—At Grand River—The Lowlands—Destruction of Trees—Sad Scenes—Funerals—The Western Cemetery—Fête des Morts—Cemetery of Bois Marchand.

Fair isle of the sea, who that views thee could dream
That thy beauty like apples of Sodom doth lie ;
That no life-giving draughts are supplied by thy stream,
And pestilence hangs 'neath thy bright fairest sky !

FEVERS, once almost unknown in Mauritius, are now fast becoming its bane; particularly since the great increase of the coloured population by immigration from India.

The Indian races have a well-known proclivity to febrile diseases. The hundreds constantly arriving from the worst hot-beds of malarious disorders, bring with them the germs of the different fevers prevalent in India, which favourable circumstances develop from time to time into activity. The true Bombay or bilious typhoid fever, so frequently fatal, especially when followed by its deadly ally dysentery, is supposed to have been introduced about thirty years since, and at intervals has broken out on different estates. Remittent fevers have been constant in the island, and typhoid, or enteric fever, has become almost endemic in Port Louis.

In 1863 a contagious fever amongst the Indian labourers carried off numbers of victims; but the best medical authorities state that no case of intermittent fever had occurred for twenty years till the year 1866.

With all these elements of fever ripe for development, aided by peculiar atmospheric influences, and aggravated by a combination of malarious causes (to be explained later), it is little wonder that the intermittent fever of 1866 changed in the early hot months of 1867 to the virulent epidemic form it then assumed.

Malarious fever was rife in Black River, Grande and Petite Rivière since 1866, and then spread to Port Louis, Pamplemousses, Flacq, and other low-lying districts, from certain circumstances peculiarly favourable to its progress, and took an intensity and deadliness unparalleled in Colonial history, its prevalence increasing as the means of resistance grew less and less, and the death rate attaining the high figure of 240 per diem in the city of Port Louis alone.

A great difference between the epidemic of 1863 and that of 1867 was the constant relapses: in that, it was death or cure; in this, the disorganisation engendered repeated attacks, assisted by the scarcity of good food and water from the long drought.

In every district dispensaries were established for supplying food and medicines to the poor sufferers. It was a difficult task to provide for the thousands whose religious prejudices prevented them from partaking of other than certain meats; and where whole families were stricken down, it often occurred that there was not one strong enough to go the distance to fetch the help held out. From shortness of hands, the Government was unable to send visitors from hut to hut, and hundreds died from sheer inanition.

Honour to those who were thoughtful enough at such a time of trouble to send in a quantity of deer shot in the woods, which gave many a dish of broth to the poor wretches who could take no other meat!

A total failure of quinine at a most critical moment proved a great source of anxiety to the medical men, as to that alone would many of the most obstinate cases yield. A marked contrast between the Bombay fever and this epidemic was, that whereas this would generally cede to the effect of quinine, the symptoms of the other would be aggravated by it.

The commencement of the fever was rarely without premonitory symptoms. Generally a day or two previously the patient suffered from languor, lassitude, and a feeling of general indisposition; but the relapses were frequently very sudden, without any apparent exciting cause.

The complications in most of the cases of the intermittent

fever were manifold, and depended on the disposition of the patient to any slumbering disease, and by far the greater number of deaths occurred from the subtle agency of some other malady combining with the fever.

In most of the cases of bilious remittent, the remission was well marked, and lasted several hours; but in the intermittent, when it had assumed the most virulent form, the remission was scarcely perceivable, and disappeared, but very slowly, after days of active medical treatment.

In the earlier months of the epidemic, whilst the treatment was yet uncertain, numbers were carried off by congestion of the brain. The cold or ague stage rarely appeared at the first attack, but was seldom absent more or less in all relapses. It was ushered in by languor and chill, and a sensation as of a stream of cold water running down the back; the skin was shrivelled and the papillæ prominent (vulg. goose skin); the teeth chattered, the nails became blue, and the whole frame was shaken. The countenance appeared anxious, features shrunken and pale, eyes dull and hollow, respiration hurried and oppressed; great irritability; frequent hysteria or delirium, and a general feeling as if death must ensue.

The duration of this stage was from half an hour to three or four hours; it was only to be subdued when severe by heaping on blankets, bottles of hot water, hot drinks, and other active treatment, when it was gradually succeeded by the hot state, or reaction. The surface of the body became dry and intensely hot, generally accompanied by sickness at the stomach, and inclination to vomit; a bounding pulse that rose far above the natural standard; the mouth parched with excessive thirst; great restlessness; fulness, or violent throbbing in the head, and frequently delirium at intervals. This stage rarely lasted less than three hours, and when at its worst, often extended to thirty-six hours, but the ordinary time was from three to six hours.

Then followed the sweating period. Slowly a little moisture spread over the breast and neck, gradually extending over the whole body; pulse and breathing became natural, headache and thirst abated, and the patient felt for the moment as if suddenly restored to health, so great was the relief; a mistake but too quickly rectified, as exhaustion utter and complete succeeded; profuse sweats, necessitating frequent changes of personal and bed linen; and to prevent collapse, broths or other nourishment, and even wine, were obliged to be given constantly in small quantities.

Numbers of Indians died in the exhaustion following the fever. Their nature and habits at all times disincline them from over exerting themselves; and the system was so prostrated, and the disgust to food was so great, that even a strong-minded white man could scarcely be roused sufficiently to force himself to take nourishment. It is not then surprising that the Indian, who rarely fears death, should prefer sinking out of life to taking the trouble to rise and eat.

I know this as a fact from my own domestics, that they could be with the greatest difficulty induced to take food or medicine, unless I administered it myself. They said, 'Life was not worth the trouble of exerting themselves to eat.'

The above were the ordinary symptoms, but besides these, on many occasions, asthenia characterised the case, either resulting favourably or otherwise in patients where the heart had lost its contracting power from extreme debility. Delirium, insomnia, and other cephalic symptoms, were frequent at first; gastric irritation with gastro-hepatic derangement and vomiting, latterly. Loss of appetite, nausea, and tenderness on pressure over the epigastrium and right hypocondrium, appeared more or less in every case of intermittent fever.

At the commencement of the epidemic fulness of the liver and spleen did not exist, but after repeated attacks of fever, derangement of both were almost sure to follow. Dropsy of the feet and legs was another painful consequence, particularly in those who had taken immoderate and incessant doses of quinine. The eyesight and hearing were also affected by the same cause.

The tongue was usually coated with a thick, yellowish-brown or creamy, and sometimes a black, fur. The creamy appearance often remained, notwithstanding treatment, for a considerable time after the disease abated; the fact of the edges of the organ being redder, and of a more healthy hue, alone indicating the ending of the fever.

For some time diarrhœa and dysentery were rarely complicated with the fever; but these pests of hot climates increased in like proportion with it, and during its decline, and even to the present time, it is very prevalent.

Frequently the whole intestinal tract from the mouth downwards was ulcerated, and then no remedies were of any avail. Water on the brain, inflammation of lungs or stomach, and Bright's chronic disease, were also adjuncts of the fever, modified according to different temperaments after the height of the epidemic had passed.

Cinchona and its preparations administered in excess will often establish some local disease. If in a perfect state of health, and taken in small doses, no obvious effects are produced, save perhaps some slight stomachic derangement, a little thirst and temporary excitement of appetite; but if the dose be increased, the alimentary canal becomes disordered, indicated by nausea, vomiting, thirst, and constipation, and a febrile state is set up, or manifested by the excitement of the vascular system; the tongue is dry, and the cerebral and spinal organs become deranged, as is shown by throbbing headaches and giddiness.

As a prophylactic, quinine is seldom used with success. Persons who have taken this drug in the hopes of escaping the fever have, almost invariably, been attacked sooner or later.

To my knowledge several instances of death occurred from the system being overdosed with quinine before the fever had appeared.

The best prophylactic measures are: clothing neither too heavy nor too light; avoiding night or damp air; occasional purgatives, a good regular diet, and a very moderate use of stimulants.

The most successful treatment was by purgative medicines, James' powder, and calomel; mustard poultices, or mustard foot-baths; and quinine on the subsidence of the fever in moderate doses. With a sluggish or dormant liver the use of calomel and emetics was imperative, as in these cases experience has long shown that quinine is not only wasted but injurious unless purgative medicines have been previously used.

From four to eight grains of quinine carefully injected into the subcutaneous areolar tissue has often produced beneficial results.

According to Dr. Murehead, one drachm of liquor arsenicatis may be used as an equivalent to twenty grains of quinine. Such a dose can scarcely be given without risk (albeit the doctors gave from thirty to fifty grains sometimes in their prescriptions), therefore he suggests that a relapse might be prevented by quinine, and moderate doses of arsenic be given to complete a cure.

In intermittent fevers, the febrile exacerbations are of much longer duration than in the remittent. The object then is to shorten the period of exacerbation and lengthen that of remission. This may be done by saline and effervescent draughts, cold drinks, iced water in small quantities, bits of ice in the mouth, lemonade, cream of tartar water, and cold applications to the head.

As soon as the body is covered with perspiration, the bed and body clothes should be entirely changed, taking care not to weary the sufferer, and clear chicken broth be given at intervals, not of long duration.

Intermittent fever is rarely thoroughly cured without a recurrence of the disease. Hundreds, supposed to have been cured, and in apparently good health for months, have had relapses without any perceptible cause.

Experience teaches us to regard with great caution what is called a perfect cure, as it is well known that persons who have suffered severely from this fever in tropical climates, on returning to Europe and elsewhere, have been attacked again with the identical fever peculiar to the districts where it was contracted, leaving no doubt that the germ of the disease was carried for a long time in the system.

A stranger fact is, that people who had passed unscathed through months of the fever in Mauritius, and then left for England or France, congratulating themselves on their escape, had sharp attacks of it some time after their arrival.

It is well known that the Madagascar fever remains in the system for years, is in fact almost ineradicable after having suffered from it severely in that island.

The cases are very rare where no relapses have taken place, and still rarer those who have escaped altogether, though such lucky fellows are to be found; but they are like 'angels' visits, very few, and very far between!'

In the case of persons just recovering from fever arriving at any place where it had not declared itself, the disease rarely spread from infection.

I may give an instance of this, at Crêve Cœur, where the Rev. Mr. Hobbs and his family reside. The estate lies very high, and he constantly received invalids into his house, most of whom are indebted to the kind attentions they received there for a return to health; yet neither he nor any of his family caught the fever.

Crêve Cœur, and a neighbouring estate, the 'Lucia,' are both elevated, and free from dense clusters of trees; and the free ventilation prevents the accumulation of water in stagnant pools and their emanations. Whilst the population in the surrounding estates was almost decimated, these places nearly escaped, from their favourable natural position.

The opinion of all the medical faculty in the island is, that the epidemic now waning is malarious, and of the intermittent form, generally at first distinct, but essentially malarious.

Everywhere one heard the questions, 'What have been the predisposing causes of the epidemic? and what are the existing causes of its long continuance?'

Whatever may be the difference in opinion as to the origin and modes of propagation, all agree that certain states of the air favour the disposition of the body to receive intermittent and remittent fevers, and rivet them into the constitution, which baffle all attempts at complete cure, and induce a tendency to relapse from apparently slight causes.

The concurrence of cold with a moist atmosphere; heavy rains after long dry weather; weakness of body, whether owing to poor and unwholesome diet, fatigue, severe evacuations, or previous diseases; anxiety of mind; inactivity, intemperance, or restlessness, all increase susceptibility; while hope, confidence, cheerfulness, whatever can excite mental energy, lessen it.

Differing as intermittent and remittent fevers do in many points, particularly in their rate of mortality, they yet agree in their origin as occasioned by effluvia emanating from putrid, stagnant waters, swampy low grounds, and animal matter. It is found in the tropics that malarious diseases are most common in the seasons succeeding heavy rains, when the temperature is high, and where the surrounding country abounds with jungles, and insect life is rife.

It is now well ascertained that gases, emanating from decomposed vegetable and animal matter, generate confervaceous as well as diatomaceous plants, such as *Tetraspora Nostoc* and all the genera *Agaria*.

These cryptogams are never found in *dry* warm situations, but where it is *damp* and warm, and they develope themselves especially where organic matter is in a state of putrefaction.

Some of these plants live on the surface of stagnant waters, but very many on the surface of low lands. Others are parasites on plants, which they destroy, as is shown in the diseases of the vine and potatoe.

In *Oidium Tuckeri* the spores are so small that Ehrenburg, the great microscopist, was scarcely able to detect the form of a thousand of them, grouped together, with the highest power of his microscope. Our knowledge of the elementary structure of organisms is exclusively based on microscopic discoveries, and modern physiology is the result. Organic chemistry has materially participated in the development, but the microscope excels the chemical re-agents in practical usefulness, both as to precision and facility, and has firmly established its superiority in hystiology and physiology.

Through the medium of these fundamental branches it has benefited medical science at large, and of late has lent material aid as well as diagnosis.

Sometimes it may delude and give rise to erroneous inferences, but the chances are in such a case it is the performer or an imperfect instrument that is in fault.

It more frequently reveals the true state of elementary structure, and its derivation from the normal state, and thus aids as well as corrects pathological knowledge.

In a long-continued series of observations, in cases of persons who have died of fever, when particular organs and their secretions were submitted to minute microscopic examination, it was almost invariably found that the membrane lining the stomach was covered with a multitude of very minute plants, closely resembling the *Alga*, *Cryptococcus Cerevisiæ*. These parasites often covered the whole intestinal tract; some were perceptible on the surface of the lungs, and some could be detected in the blood. In the latter, it sometimes happened that there were epithelial cells, apparently containing fatty and pigment molecules.

On living patients, in the advanced stage of the fever, they may be detected, by one well acquainted with the microscope, in the substance which is formed at the corners of the mouth and eyes.

Some of the parasites appear quite hollow, others contain nuclei and spores, and others show cell-articulations.

In the secretions of entirely healthy persons they cannot be detected.

Water taken up in well-cleaned basins out of some isolated pools at Grand River, or where its waters mingle with the sea, and subjected to the rays of the sun till stagnant, developed a green superficial film. Under the microscope this film showed plants so nearly related in shape and structure to those in and on the different organs of the human body, that there is no doubt of their being of the same genera, and it is equally certain that they were exciting causes of the epidemic.

Myriads of these plants were generated all over the island; and when matured, the spores became free, and were taken up by the wind and carried from place to place. These spores were thus inhaled, and if the stomach was not in a morbid condition, they would pass out without effecting or undergoing any change, or be destroyed by the gastric juices; if, on the contrary, it contained material highly susceptible of fermentation (which the universal rice and vegetable diet here tends to), the spores would germinate and grow, produce inflammation, and fever readily ensued.

Unlike phænogamous plants, which absorb carbonic acid gas, depositing the carbon in the plant, and throwing off the oxygen into the atmosphere, all the lower class of cryptogams absorb oxygen, and consequently give out carbon, thus vitiating the atmosphere we breathe.

It may not be out of place to mention here, that the physiological effects of the cinchona bark, and its alkaloids, on vegetables, animals and men, should be borne in mind, as the connection of these effects with the therapeutical influence of the bark in fever were until lately inexplicable.

Decandolle states that leaves of plants immersed in an infusion of pale bark were dried in twenty-four hours; and others, plunged into a solution of quinia water, presented evidences of contraction in from six to eight hours.

It is evident, therefore, why this remedy, when used in malarious fevers, acts so beneficially. By its contraction, or process of withering, it destroys the fast growth of the poisonous fungoids in the system, and, if there is no complication, eradicates the disease.

This fever is only contagious under certain circumstances. Knowing how it is germinated, it will be readily perceived that when a person is attacked with it, in damp unventilated places, it follows as a matter of course, that from the moment the spores in or on the patient become free, all the inmates of the same place, and especially when they are crowded together and filthy in their habits, will be subjected to the disease; and in so far only is it communicable.

Since writing the above, I met with an interesting article on 'The Causes of Ague,' and as it bore so forcibly on what I had written, I transcribe some of its paragraphs at length.

'The fertile source of desolation and disease consists of incalculable myriads of microscopic cells, suspended in the atmosphere over waste, marshy, and fen districts. They are minute oblong cells, single or aggregate, and having a distinct nucleus, with a clear interspace, apparently empty, between it and the cell wall. They are of the algoid type, strongly resembling the *Palmella*, and are consequently amongst the very lowest organisms known. Sometimes several of these cells or spores are contained in an outer cell or wall, or delicate investing membrane, to form a plant.

'Of these "ague plants" is formed the greyish film whereever damp, black earth is turned up and exposed to the sun. These spores or minute seeds (germinating cells) rise into the air, carrying pestilence with them.[1] There are several species of the "ague plant," which have been called Gemiasma, from the Greek for earth, and the word miasma. The white, and a yellowish green variety, occur usually in a non-calcareous soil, and produce agues of but slight intensity, and are the only ones known in England. There are also red, green, and lead-

[1] These spores may be found, I believe, in the expectoration of people seized with ague.

coloured "ague plants," and one singular species, the "*Gemiasma protuberosa*," which has larger spores, "and consists of groups of jelly-like protuberances."

'These latter kind habitually occur in rich calcareous soils, and produce fevers of a dangerous and congestive character.

'The cells with their spores produce visible incrustations of mould on the surface of recently exposed marsh earth. The danger from these growths is greatest in a hot dry season following a wet one. The wetter and hotter, the worse for man, and the better for malaria.

'The marsh demon is verily "The pestilence that walketh in darkness." It seems almost certain that the spores of the "ague plant" only rise with the evening dews. Microscopically tested, the day air is free from those organisms.

'In different parts of the world these cryptogamic spores rise in the night mists to definite heights.

'In the United States they seldom rise from above thirty-five to sixty-five feet above the low levels; in England, not more than from fifteen to thirty feet.

'These spores are found throughout these vapours, but do not extend beyond them, and are found in the greatest abundance in their upper strata.

'Intermittent or ague fever has actually been produced in men by causing them to inhale the spores of these algæ.

'It has long been known that malaria is movable by the wind. The spores of the "ague plants" having risen and become entangled in the mist, spores, mist, and all are blown along together, far perhaps from the place of germination.

'This fact admits of considerable practical application in tropical climates, where the wind usually blows for a long time from the same quarter. It is easy to see how a volume of vapour or fog, laden with its deadly burden of poison-cells, may roll up and hang suspended on the side of a hill, towards which a wind blows across an adjacent marsh.

'Instances have occurred where the poisonous vapour has been blown over a hill, and deposited on the other side, to the unmitigated disgust of the inhabitants, who imagined themselves secure from their pestilential neighbour.'

The above article applies peculiarly to Mauritius, as I shall endeavour to show by a slight description of the numerous hot-beds of the 'ague plants' with which the island abounds at the present day.

I will begin with the very focus of malaria, Port Louis, and mention a few of the numerous causes of infection in that city alone.

The foul streams flowing through it in all directions are, two-thirds of the year, almost stagnant; the other third they are swollen by the torrential rains, and bear along masses of vegetable and animal matter from the hills and Indian camps, which, as the waters subside, lie festering in the sun, poisoning the atmosphere.

The emanations from the open drains, the imperfect drainage of the houses, and the defective method of disinfecting the night-soil, load the air with mephitic vapours.

The gradually filling-up of the east end of the harbour, from the mud constantly pouring into it, and the tide not being strong enough to wash away the impurities that lodge in the muddy bottom, adds its quota to the malaria.

The low shores to the west of the city are only covered at high tides, and are strewn with decayed sea-weed and filth, washed in from the shipping.

Between Port Louis and Fort William lies a swamp, that receives into its rank vegetation the streams that flow from the cemeteries and another swampy land at the back of them. These cemeteries contain in themselves a very sufficient cause of malaria. The emanations from them are at times most deadly, owing to the circumstances that the dead are not interred deeply enough, and the loose earth and coral which cover them permit the escape of the gases evolved by their decomposition.

It has been frequently remarked that the health of the city has invariably suffered when the miasma from its western side has been blown over it.

Between Port Louis and Grand River are low lands, prolific in the germs of malaria. After heavy rain the Grand River swells, and receives into its floods filth of every kind, which is swept down, or deposited all over its course, or left in pools to decompose in the sun.

Near its entrance to the sea, where the waste water spreads out over the wide embouchure made by the torrents of ages, and the rapidity of the flood abates, it has not power to sweep away all the débris, and part always remains filling up its channel, and impeding its proper egress to the ocean. The whole of this district, and the neighbouring one of Petite Rivière, lies low.

Just before the fever broke out at Petite Rivière, there was a large camp of Indians located there, reeking with indescribable filth. The huts crowded to excess, men and beasts herded together; and with the ordinary dirty habits of the men, and the scarcity of water in that district during the severe drought at the end of 1866, the wonder is the fever left any of them alive.

Very few indeed were spared; and it was a melancholy sight, at the end of 1867, to pass by the camp. Here and there you met a poor squalid wretch, or a few weakly children; but nearly all the huts were destroyed that had contained whole families, now swept away, and the few that remained shut up—it looked like a city of the dead, after teeming with busy noisy life as it did some months previously.

The ill effects of allowing the Indians to wash their clothes and bathe in the running streams, thus polluting the waters in their whole course, was well shown during the epidemic, as Death with unceasing energy stalked amongst those who lived near such waters, and used them unfiltered.

'The marshes of Pamplemousses and West Savanne; the moist lowlands of Petite Savanne; the shallow tidal lagoons west of Black River; and all the low coast-line receiving the drainage from the central watershed, gave out their poisonous exhalations.'

During 1867 some parts of the island entirely escaped; most probably lying above the spore level, or fever line, which I see Dr. Reid, the chief medical officer, places at 600 feet above the level of the sea.

In his report on the fever, he mentions a curious fact about the spread of the fever into a section of Black River and Savanne, always known as the healthiest part of Mauritius. Between these districts and the infected ones lies a barrier of forests and woody elevations. He writes, 'During the first week of January 1868, occurred a hurricane, the main force of which was from the SE. and E., in that extremity of the island, sufficiently strong to spoil the forests of their leaves, and make gaps in this barrier of wooded highlands, and thus carried in the fever germs from the part of Black River, where fever was rife, to the hitherto healthy inhabitants.'

I could add greatly to these details; but those I have mentioned are sufficient to show that, with all these existing powerful agents to malaria lying dormant, and so many spore-beds waiting for peculiar atmospheric influences to set them free, the heavy rains, and then subsequent excessive drought followed by hurricanes, would act on them with fatal certainty, and thus strike the whole island with this terrible plague, converting, for the time being, the once 'Gem of the Ocean' into a very pest-house.

Dr. Reid also mentions in the same report a circumstance which would seem to corroborate the fact alluded to in p. 120, as to the effects of the cinchona, as stated by Decandolle.

He says, 'The waters of the few remaining woodland marshes of Mauritius, the Mare aux Vacoas, aux Joncs, and Bassin Blanc, are deeply tinged and impregnated with tannin and resinous matters, and the inhabitants around and near these marshes entirely escaped the fever.'

He suggests, and very properly, 'May not this exemption be due to the tannin, and other products of the débris of the surrounding forest, being present in those localities, and preventing the fever germs from flourishing therein? May not the removal from the humus and marshes of the lowlands of similar substances, which they received when the island was well wooded, have been one of the changes which prepared them for the reception and development of malarious germs?'

I do not doubt it; and it is most likely owing to the withering effects of the different barks in solution, that prevented the germination of the fever-spores in those marshes, and caused the consequent immunity of the neighbouring inhabitants from the disease.

It is well known that the indigenous forests contain many trees, the barks of which produce similar effects on fever to those of cinchona.

While on this subject, I may as well mention a great source of the changes in climate the Mauritius has undergone, viz. the one alluded to by Dr. Reid—the cutting down of the forests.

The mania for cane-planting, to the exclusion of nearly all other articles of export, has been carried to such an extent, that where once stood magnificent forests, with streams running through them, are now wide treeless and waterless plains, whenever the frequent droughts occur.

For a hot climate, I never saw one so denuded of tree life. Formerly, in different parts of the city, were trees, affording welcome shade to foot-passengers and carriage-horses. But a raid was made on the greater part of them by the municipality, on the plea that they injured the sewers and pavement, as if the open stench-giving gutters did not do fifty times more injury. Why, in the Cape, I noticed the finest trees planted at the edge of the gutters, which there pour along clean streams instead of dirty, and in most tropical climates trees grow in all the streets. Oh, Goths and Vandals! to destroy, ruthlessly, one of the Creator's best gifts for the health and comfort of his creatures!

Here and there one certainly sees clumps of shrubs and underwood about the country; but these become a harbour for all the filth and refuse of the place, and of course when rain falls they are muddy nuclei of infection.

There are endless *talkings* and suggestions as to what ought to be done to bring about a difference in the sanitary condition of the island, and it is to be hoped that *action* will follow.

If stringent measures are not soon taken, the prosperity of Mauritius must come to an end. Ships already avoid coming here for fear of infection, and all the millions of dollars spent to render it the 'half-way house to the East' for all nations, may as well have been flung into the ocean.

What the Creator made 'very good,' man has all but ruined.

> Where shall we turn, O Nature, if in *thee*
> Danger is masked in beauty—Death in smiles?
> Here year by year the secret peril spreads,
> Disguised in loveliness its baleful reign;
> And viewless blight on many a landscape shed,
> Gay with the riches of the South in vain.
> Youth, valour, beauty, oft have felt its power,
> The loved, yet chosen victims; o'er their lot
> Hath fond affection wept. Each blighted flower
> In turn was loved, and mourned, and is forgot.
>
> . . . .
>
> Yet those who perished left a tale of woe
> Meet for as deep a sigh as Pity can bestow.

Those who inhabited Port Louis during the terrible mortality in 1867 and 1868 will never forget the sad spectacles the city presented daily. Fever, fever, was the only word on every lip, the only thought in every heart. Mourning and desolation everywhere. Scarcely a person visible that did not wear the garb of woe. Song and laughter had ceased.

Port Louis was once remarkable for the number of pianos heard in every street in an evening, from the Erard's grand and semi-grand to the humblest cottage instrument.

At this time it was literally 'The daughters of music were brought low, and the voice of mourning was heard in the streets.'

Funeral trains were met at every corner. Relays of men were kept night and day digging the graves.

The owners of undertakers' shops that sold mourning, and apothecaries, must have made fortunes. The numerous druggists' shops were so crowded day and night, and so short of hands, it was with difficulty medicine could be procured. Offices were opened in all directions for the distribution of food, medicine, or advice to the destitute; but all the efforts made by the municipality and private charities could not keep pace with the strident progress of the wretchedness and distress.

There was no mistaking the appearance of one who had suffered: the pallid, drawn features, the skeleton, bloodless fingers, as if the bright life-stream had been dried out of them, and the slow dragging step, marked but too plainly the victims.

It was distressing to pass through the streets; in every corner was some poor creature, suddenly struck down, and crouching on the ground to die.

In the outskirts of the city and country roads the victims were so numerous, that the police and sanitary committees were insufficient to succour half the poor wretches, and many died by the roadsides before help could be brought to them.

Near Roche Bois I have seen them lying in groups, dying and dead. Not a house, within a radius of half a mile from the one I then occupied, had a living person in it, except at a shop belonging to three Chinamen, two of whom died later. In many cases, as soon as a Malabar got the fever, he would hasten to his house and shut himself in to die; for such was the fear of it, to be attacked was the tocsin of death to him.

I visited many families, and the scenes I witnessed will never be effaced from my memory. A poor Indian, whom I had cured for the time being, came and entreated for help to a comrade. It was night, and I was tired and had gone to bed; but the poor fellow begged so hard, that I dressed and went with him. After a long walk we came to a hut, and as I approached I heard groans and lamentations. When I entered, the scene baffled all description. A small cocoa-nut oil lamp dimly lighted the interior, adding horror to the scene.

It was inhabited by a man and his wife, with a number of children. The mother lay dead in the middle of the hut, the man hanging over her in an agony of grief. Her baby, still living, was clasped to her heart, and seeking to draw its life-sustenance from her cold breast. The other children were all stricken with the fever, and in its last stages, past human help. Of course all I could I did, but help had come too late to do little more than assist in their burial.

One dreaded to ask the news, as one was quite sure to hear of some friend ill, dying or dead, and often buried before you knew of it. Parents had to rise from their sick beds to nurse their children, and these again had to drag their weary limbs to follow a beloved parent to the tomb, though frequently too weak even to do that.

No change of weather seemed to arrest the plague. Intense heat or cold, heavy rains or dry, mild calm days, or sharp breezes, all were alike fatal. The brightest morn brought no more hope than the wildest night.

For months the death-rate in the city alone averaged nearly 200 per diem. In every street could be seen the mourning weeds outside the doors where death had struck his victim; and this was often the first intelligence you had of the loss of dear friends—no time for ceremony then. May I never witness again the sad sight of those incessant funerals, slowly wending along from morn till night.

Here was a group of Malabars bearing along some poor fellow, preceded by a priest muttering a prayer, and followed by a few women bearing a copper dish of rice and fruit, and a jug of water, to place on his grave.

There comes a slow and stately train with black-plumed hearse, and a long line of carriages behind it—one of the rich and respected of the land; anon, a little simple bier, bearing a baby's coffin covered with a simple white muslin pall and wreath, with perhaps only the father and nurse as mourners; then a white-covered hearse, its white plumes and the horses' sweeping trappings showing that some fair girl had been cut off in early womanhood.

Occasionally would pass a Chinese funeral, the bier supported by stout Malagash bearers, in their long black gowns and flowing weepers, looking as stolid as if of stone; a few carioles following with Chinamen in them, and a person always preceding it, scattering pieces of paper about three inches square, often gilt or silvered, all along the road, to scare away evil spirits, and prevent their following the corpse to its last resting-place.

To the west of the city lie the European, Arab, Chinese, and Lascar cemeteries. At the entrance of the first stands a long avenue of the melancholy filaos, fit trees for a burying-ground, with the wailing, mournful notes that pass through them with the slightest breath of wind.

This cemetery is divided into the new and old, and is surrounded by high stone walls. The latter is so crowded with graves and vaults, all placed indiscriminately, that one can scarcely walk without treading on them. Shrubs and creepers grow in rank confusion over them, and many names are quite obliterated by time. I never enter the old part of the cemetery without the following lines occurring to me:

> I pray thee lay me not to rest
>   Among these mouldering bones;
> Too heavily the earth is prest
>   By all these crowded stones.

The very air oppresses one. There is no look of quiet repose about the place, as is seen in a northern burial-ground. The absence of tall trees and shade, and the bright glare of a tropical sun, destroy the feeling of rest that such a place should give.

I was surprised once, when reading over the names, to come upon one of a countrywoman of my own,—a name well known in America, and for those to whom she is still a household name, I copy the inscription on her tombstone:—

SACRED TO THE MEMORY OF MRS. H. ATWOOD,
WIFE OF THE REVD. S. NEWELL,
MISSIONARY AT BOMBAY.
BORN AT HAVERHILL, MASS. U.S. AMERICA,
OCT. 10, 1793;
DIED AFTER A DISTRESSING VOYAGE
FROM INDIA TO THIS PLACE,
NOV. 30, 1812.
LONG DEVOTED TO CHRIST, HER HEART BURNED FOR THE HEATHEN.
FOR THEM SHE LEFT HER KINDRED AND HER NATIVE LAND,
AND WELCOMED DANGERS AND SUFFERINGS.
OF EXCELLENT UNDERSTANDING, RICH IN ACCOMPLISHMENTS
AND VIRTUOUS, THE DELIGHT OF HER FRIENDS,
A CROWN TO HER HUSBAND, AND AN ORNAMENT TO THE MISSIONARY CAUSE,
HER SHORT LIFE WAS BRIGHT, HER DEATH FULL OF GLORY.
HER NAME LIVES IN ALL CHRISTIAN LANDS, AND IS PLEADING
WITH IRRESISTIBLE ELOQUENCE FOR THE HEATHEN.
THIS HUMBLE MONUMENT TO HER MEMORY
IS ERECTED BY THE
AMERICAN BOARD OF COMMISSIONERS
FOR FOREIGN MISSIONS.

The new part of the cemetery is in much better order, the tombs being principally placed in rows; and it is not likely to be overcrowded now, as none are permitted to be buried there except those who have vaults, and they are not allowed to be opened till a year has elapsed from the time the last corpse was interred. A great deal of care is bestowed on the graves; handsome vases are fastened with iron clamps[1] to the tombstones, flowers and shrubs are planted, and on the anniversaries of deaths splendid bouquets are placed on every tomb the inmates of which have a relative left.

On the 2nd of November, the Fête des Morts, the whole Catholic community goes to the cemeteries to place flowers on the graves. I once went with a lady who was accompanied by a servant bearing on her head a large basket of bouquets.

These were each placed with a prayer on the tombs of every relative and intimate friend; and when the basket was exhausted, a few still being unremembered, she laid a small spray on the rest, not forgetting a word of sorrow to each.

I will confess I was not a little tired before it was over, and

[1] Shame to say, but for this precaution they would be stolen.

envied her patience. Formerly candles were lit at every grave; but a terrible accident happening, this was forbidden by the authorities. A young girl kneeling between a row of lights, her muslin dress caught fire, and before she could be rescued she was so severely burnt that death ensued.

In sad contrast to the Western Cemetery, where each tomb is loaded with tokens of affection, each vault jealously guarded by locked iron railings—by everything love can devise to show reverence for the departed—is the new cemetery at Bois Marchand, a short distance from Port Louis.

In consequence of the overcrowded state of the old cemeteries, and the danger of constantly opening the graves in a densely populated city during the epidemic, land was purchased for a new burial-ground; and there thousands of the victims of this fearful plague lie buried in long rows, each grave slightly separated from its neighbour.

It was with difficulty the dead could find sepulture, when the living had hardly strength enough to follow their nearest and dearest.

By the hurricane in March the raised mounds were almost entirely levelled, and now it would be impossible to say whose were the relics of humanity covered by the bright red earth and long grass. That widespread 'God's acre' will for ever remain a record in itself of the fell disease that for so long a period devasted the 'Gem of the Ocean.'

LINES ON THE CEMETERY AT BOIS MARCHAND.

THEY lie in thousands side by side,
On that wild desert plain;
The loved, the cherished, nameless there,
By raging fever slain.

In tombs of their ancestral dead
Their bones may never lie;
No marble records shield their graves
Beneath that torrid sky.

O'er that blent mass of human clay
No mourners bend in tears;
No wreaths, no votive offerings there,
Though the loss will be felt for years.

For there the gray-haired grandsire lies,
  With the darlings he loved so well;
And there the bride of a few short hours—
  Of *such* griefs what tongue may tell?

The mother with her first-born babe,
  The father in manhood's pride;
The fairest and best were swept away—
  Our friends so trusted and tried.

Long, long will the 'Gem of the Ocean' rue
  The fever-fiend's deadly rage;
For sadder sights than its shores have seen
  Rest not in History's page.

April, 1868.[1]

Outside, under the filaos of the Western Cemetery, are the houses of the guardians; and the stone-cutters sit there all day, plying their trade of perpetuating or preserving the memory of the dead.

Past the Indian burial-grounds is a very melancholy corner, where are interred suicides and criminals who have been hung. Rank grass grows over them, and no flower but the wild, deadly *Strammonium* flourishes near them; though I once saw a little bouquet placed on the grave of a murderer, telling the tale of some heart grieving even for the poor wretch whom human mercy could not spare.

TABLE OF MORTALITY DURING THE EPIDEMIC OF 1866, 1867, 1868.

Months	Total		
	1866	1867	1868
January	1282	1470	1802
February	1100	2851	2224
March	990	6671	2825
April	1064	10554	2036
May	1038	8109	2259
June	1035	3647	1940
July	1085	2383	1530
August	1002	1386	1164
September	949	1145	927
October	1042	842	808
November	924	873	740
December	1037	1169	756
Total	12548	41100	19011

[1] The Bois Marchand is now being greatly improved, and trees planted. 1870.

CHAPTER VII.

THE CYCLONE OF 186

The Direction of the Winds, &c., from Feb. 27 to March 5—Premonitory Symptoms—Changes from 5th to 11th—Direction of Cyclone—Its Track on the Ocean—Damages in Port Louis—Destruction of Churches, Warehouses, &c.—Effects in the Harbour—Irving Lodge—Scenes in the Streets—Grand River Bridge—Midland and Southern Districts—Reduit—Pamplemousses—Effects on the Sea-shore—Table of Losses, Deaths, &c.

THE cyclone which visited Mauritius the 10th, 11th, and 12th of March, and which left behind so many sad traces of its power, is considered, with the exception of that of 7th of March, 1848, to have been the most violent in its effects since the hurricane of 1806.[1]

On the 27th of February there were strong breezes from ESE. and SE. veering to SSE., SW., W., NW., N., NNE., and on the 5th of March E. ¼ NE.

From the 1st to the 5th of March there were continuous indications of a cyclone to the east of Mauritius. Cyclonic matter was abundant, and nearly constant. So excessive was the heat, and so oppressive the weather, one could almost say some unknown agency was at work against human existence. Fever increased, the rays of the sun were scorching, and the atmosphere was so overcharged with electricity that everyone felt uncomfortable.

On the 6th of March a cyclone still threatened, and the wind changed from E. ¼ NE. to NE. This weather, I apprehend, was owing to the existence of a cyclone polygène to the W. of Mauritius.

From the 6th to the 9th the wind changed from NE. to N. and NW., but after a storm wave without apparent discharge,

[1] For much of this information I am indebted to M. Bosquet's able paper on this cyclone, published in the daily papers.

it suddenly veered on the 9th to ESE., inclining SE., and accompanied by all the indications of a cyclone, and the barometer lowered to 758.69.

The atmosphere acquired fresh cyclonic matter, indicating the existence of the already-recognised polygène cyclone, which advanced to the E. of the island.

During the whole day of the 10th the weather was at hurricane point, the wind SE., inclining to SSE., and the barometer stood at 754.88.

On the 11th cyclone weather was very marked, after strong squalls all night, and the barometer lowered to 753.36. At half-past nine light oscillations were visible, the wind keeping to SSE., and clouds flying from the SE., one or two degrees south.

The centre of the cyclone presented itself in the latitude of Port Louis. From one to half-past the clouds passed rapidly from ESE.; and this observation confirms the idea of the polygenic nature of the cyclone recognised from the 5th to the 9th inst.

During the 11th, and up to noon of the 12th, the weather grew worse gradually. The squalls and gusts acquired additional strength, and the barometer slowly descended from 746.29 (its height at 10 P.M. of the 11th) to 734.60 at 9 A.M. of the 12th. The wind blew furiously all night, keeping about SSE., but towards six in the morning it veered in all directions. At the moment of the minimum (the mercurial column always oscillating) the squalls were terrific from the ESE., but they diminished by afternoon, though the elements still kept up their strife, and the wind suddenly varied without any apparent order from S. to SW., W. to SW., S., &c.

At one o'clock, during a momentary calm, the superior currents indicating the wind from ENE., I concluded that the second cyclone of this polygène cyclone was presented by the meridian of Port Louis.

The first was directed to the E. of Mauritius, passing by the latitude of Port Louis from 9 P.M. to 2 A.M.

The second closely followed the first, and presented itself about 10 P.M., and came very near the island, and turned first to the N. and then W. of it.

The superior current, the barometer, the continuous oscilla-

CYCLONE CHART OF THE 10TH 11TH & 12TH MARCH, 1868.
By Nicolas Pike, U.S. Consul, at Port Louis, Mauritius.

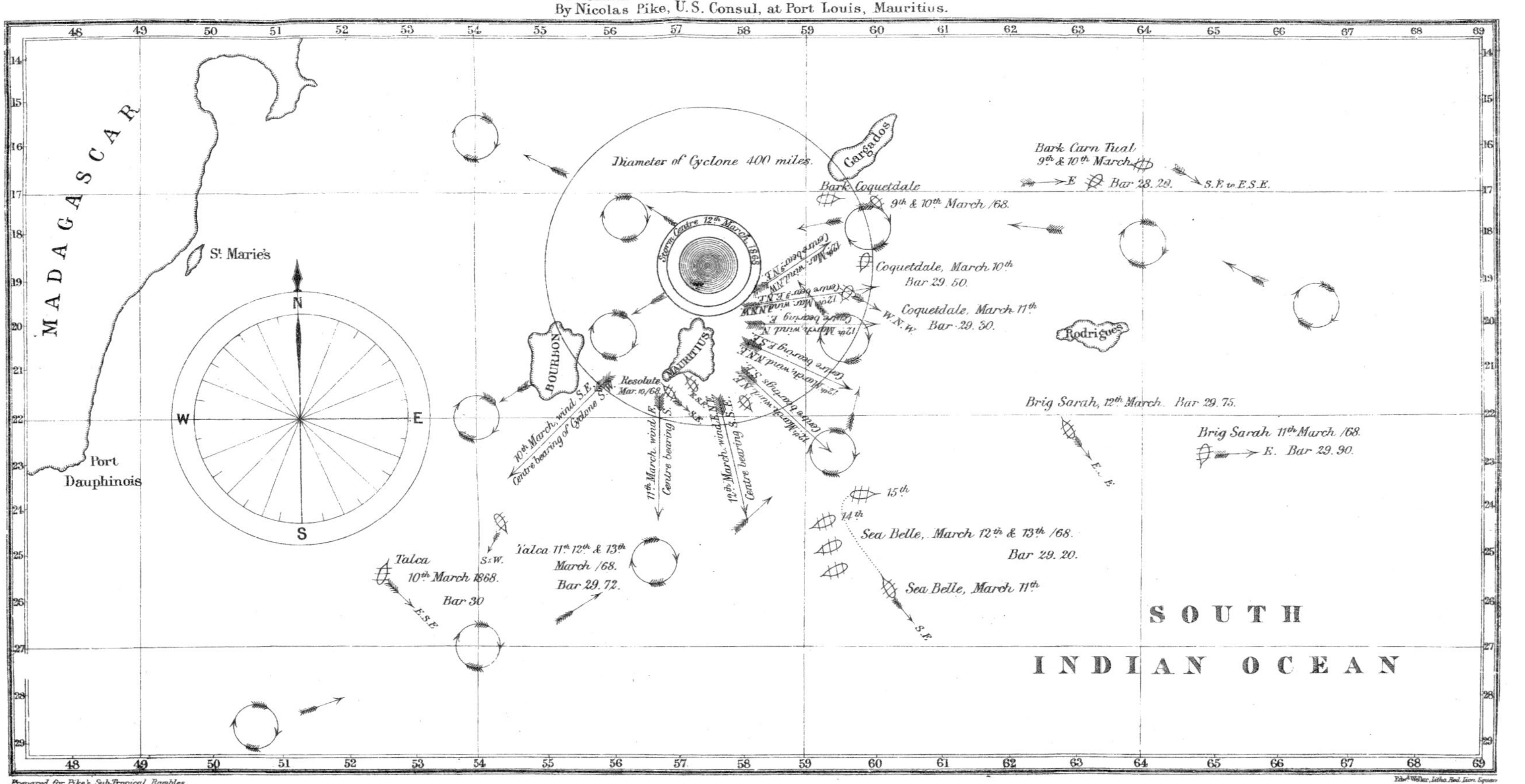

Prepared for Pike's Sub-Tropical Rambles.

Published by Sampson Low, Marston, Low, & Searle; Crown Buildings, 188 Fleet Str.t London.

tions of the mercury, and the weather, all confirm the opinion of the polygène cyclone; and from the end of February the irregular changes of the wind, the falling of the barometer, and the presence of cyclonic matter, as well as the ordinary indications which precede these terrible convulsions of the aerial ocean, prove the existence and development of it at a great distance.

The cyclone chart shows the direction of the track of the two cyclones which occurred in the Indian Ocean during the 10th, 11th, and 12th of March. The long arrows point to the centre bearings of the cyclone from Mauritius during the same period. The large circle denotes the diameter of the cyclone, which is worked out approximately to the law of storms.

Thus calculating that the cyclone commenced on Tuesday, the 10th, at 6 P.M., and exhausted its force (as far as Mauritius was concerned) on Friday the 13th at 6 A.M., allowing sixty hours for its duration, and considering the rate of travelling of a cyclone, in the South Indian Ocean, to be about seven miles per hour, it is safe to conclude that its diameter was about 420 miles.

It will be seen, by referring to this chart, that the centre of this cyclone passed directly over Bourbon; and, after its construction, news was received from that place confirming this fact, and stating that a great amount of damage was done there, though not equal to that in Mauritius.

The ships which are on the chart are those which were in the cyclone, and suffered severely before entering Port Louis Harbour.

An account of extracts taken from their logs will be found at the end of the chapter.

In the city of Port Louis the damage to property was very serious. Most of the ornamental trees in both private and public gardens were either blown down, uprooted, or so utterly denuded of leaves and their lesser branches that they seemed to have passed from the dense foliage of Midsummer to the depth of an European winter—a strange appearance for Mauritius, where there are so few deciduous trees.

Scarcely a dependency or Malabar hut in the various camps was left standing.

St. Mary's Church at Plaine Verte, built of iron, was severed from its foundation, and left an utter ruin; not any portion of its structure could be used again. The main part of the building was carried to some distance, while the chancel and vestries fell in on the floor of the church. The harmonium, reading-desk, pulpit, gas-fittings, &c., were all smashed to pieces. The parsonage and its dependencies stood roofless.

St. Paul's Church, near by, recently erected, and strongly built of stone, sustained nearly as much damage. The wall, exposed to the wind, fell in with a terrible crash, and, sad to relate, buried three men under its ruins. The roof fell, crushing in the gallery, and breaking up the organ till scarcely a pipe of it was visible.

The large iron warehouses in the docks were nearly all unroofed, and a large amount of merchandise (principally sugar) destroyed. On the morning of the 11th, the steady fall of the barometer caused the Port Officer to hoist his hurricane signals, and fire the gun, warning all masters of ships to be on board, and prepare their vessels for the coming storm. By this time, however, in consequence of the preceding day's threatening weather, all the ships had lowered their topmasts, yards, everything that the wind could lay hold of—with double anchors well down into the ground.

Towards noon the squalls varied very much, and struck the water with terrific descending force, but with little effect on the ships. Later, the wind hauled, and there seemed every probability that all the vessels (some eighty or ninety) would be driven to sea and lost, which nothing but a shift of wind, or the transit of the centre of the cyclone, could avert. By eleven o'clock, P.M., every ship in the harbour was adrift. The large 'Bethel,' formerly an English man-of-war, lying high out of the water, was the first to break from her moorings. The most inconceivable confusion and destruction ensued. The crashing of timbers and masts, and the roaring of the tempest, were terrific. The ships rolled on their beam-ends, and every blast seemed stronger than its predecessor, sometimes resembling explosions more than a progressive fluid, and tearing the surface of the water high up into curious spiral columns, revolving with incredible velocity.

When day dawned on the 12th the devastation was appalling; the ships had been driven across the harbour by the veering of the wind and were pounding into and ripping each other, causing masts and bulwarks to fall on all sides. The chain cables of some of the iron ships tore down the massive plates like paper, as the sea broke fearfully across the harbour, and along the reefs as far as the eye could reach, which was probably the storm-wave of the passing cyclone.

Many of the vessels, with their cargoes, were afterwards condemned, and the losses sustained amounted to many millions of dollars.

During the cyclone I was at Irving Lodge, a recently erected building, framed in America, and put together in the strongest manner, with a view to resist the terrible hurricanes so frequent here, and on which no expense had been spared by the American merchants, Messrs. Houdlette and Perkins.

On Wednesday evening, the gradual fall of the barometer, and heavy gusts of wind, with dark clouds passing swiftly from the SE., denoting certain signs that a cyclone was approaching the island, the servants were warned, and the hurricane shutters and doors were securely fastened, and every precaution taken for our personal safety; in spite of which, the roaring of the wind and heavy fall of rain made us all feel anxious.

Early on Thursday morning a violent gust of wind dashed in the shutters of a window, carrying away the inner blinds and sash, and tearing the window out of its frame.

Travelling across the room, it struck the door which opened into the dining-room, and broke it down, frame and all, destroying at the same time a fine chandelier which hung over the table, and smashing the table itself.

Up to this I had been peering through the hurricane shutters, watching the wind and clouds, and taking notes of them. The scene outside was frightful, houses being overthrown before my eyes; one was literally rolled over, containing three persons. Flying in all directions were parts of roofs, timbers, and branches of trees. The bath-house was actually blown away; large blocks of stone weighing two or three cwt., composing its foundation, were moved to the distance of fifteen or twenty feet by the force of the wind. Parts of the building struck the kitchen and started its roof; but it was so substantial that it fortunately resisted the violence of the storm.

About seven o'clock we deemed it proper to abandon the house, as the timbers creaked and shook so much that we were fearful it would fall on us. Taking advantage of the short lulls between the gusts, we retreated by the back door to the stable, about fifty yards distant, and we reached it with difficulty. This building was about seventy-five feet long, and fifteen high, used for a stable and servants' rooms. We barricaded ourselves in, fully expecting that, as the storm increased, the house and dependencies would all go. During the morning twenty families, whose dwellings had been all destroyed, sought refuge with us: and here we remained shut up, almost without food or drink, till Friday morning.

It was a never-to-be-forgotten night! The roaring and howling of the wind, and ever-increasing torrents of rain, were terrible. Our stable, though strongly built of stone, shook with every blast; and the poor women and children, cold and hungry, and their clothes all drenched and torn, were piteous to see.

On Friday morning, the violence of the storm having passed, though the wind still blew sharply, we ventured out to the house. The wind and rain having had free access to the interior, had drenched everything, destroying the new and costly furniture.

Had the storm lasted a short time longer the house must have gone; as it was, the whole of the south side had started.

Fifty buildings within a radius of half a mile were destroyed. As I passed along on Friday morning to return home, my heart sickened at the scenes that met my gaze on every side. Every street was obstructed with roofs, broken timbers, and trunks of trees; and every conceivable thing scattered about, made 'confusion worse confounded.' Groups of poor people, wet and weary, were huddled together in corners, in the greatest distress, homeless and miserable, with extended hands imploringly asking alms, they having lost everything but the few rags that scarcely covered their persons. My heart ached for the poor creatures, many of them showing in their pallid faces traces of recent fever, and but too many have been since relieved by death.

On arriving at my lodgings, I found them thoroughly drenched from the rivers of water that had leaked under the doors, and run plenteously down the walls, damaging books, clothes, and papers.

On the 16th I took a carriage and drove through the district of Pamplemousses, and the following day went southward; but wherever I passed, I saw but a repetition of scenes of destruction, and evidences of the violence of the cyclone.

The new and beautiful bridge over Grand River, built of iron, was partially destroyed. Two of the immense iron girders, about 200 feet in length, were blown off the columns into the river, and were in such a state as to be useless. There must have been a pressure of 100 lbs. to the square foot upon these girders to have raised them from their bed, as they weighed over 300 tons. The stone abutment on the west bank was also severely injured, probably by the weight of the girders striking it as they fell.

The station-house was unroofed and otherwise damaged. The depôt for the rolling stock of the Midland line was a large building of dressed stone, so substantial, one would have thought nothing but an earthquake would have started its walls; yet the wind blew in the SE. side, moving large stones from their foundation, carrying them some distance with incredible force, breaking and destroying a considerable quantity of rolling stock and machinery.

At Pailles scarcely a house was left entire. St. Peter's Church was partially unroofed; the large east window blown in; seats driven to the farther end of the church; all the glass smashed; the pulpit upset; and ruin and confusion on all sides.

The Black River, Grand Port, and other districts on the south, all suffered severely. To describe one, needs only a change of names to describe all the rest.

Fields of canes levelled to the ground, or torn up in masses; fine old trees broken or uprooted; roads impassable from the rain having washed deep gullies in them; sugar-houses, dwellings, dependencies, unroofed or otherwise injured; horses, mules and cattle, killed or wounded; the direst destruction everywhere.

On the Yemen estate, the vast sugar-houses were destroyed; walls and roofs crushing in on the machinery, and ruining about 60,000 lbs. of sugar.

The Indians fled from the camp, and about 300 of them sought refuge under the arch which formed the entrance to the furnaces, but were soon driven from their shelter, and had barely time to escape with their lives, as it gave way; one man, as it was, had both arms and legs broken. The much-admired avenue of fine tamarind trees leading to the establishment at Black River was half rooted up, and the rush of water from the mountains cut canals six feet deep in the road, which will take a long time to repair.

The inhabitants of the tamarind village were obliged to seek refuge in the artillery barracks, where they were miserably housed for want of room; but even thus they were better off than those who had no shelter to fly to, and were exposed for hours to the storm.

The state of all the villages was most deplorable, as numbers of horses, mules, and cattle were killed by the falling buildings, and from want of help were left long under the ruins. This, and other noxious matter round the temporary huts erected by the Indians, doubtless encouraged the terrible epidemic still raging at that time.

Government House, at Reduit, built in 1768, which had escaped hitherto, suffered so severely in the hurricane that at one time the lives of the inmates were in danger.

The elegant gardens attached to the house were a scene of devastation; and a large number of the beautiful trees that shaded the walks, and the variety of graceful shrubs and rare exotics, were twisted and broken, and in many places uprooted. These beautiful grounds, which were in such fine order, suddenly presented the appearance of winter, as scarcely a green leaf remained.

The crops in the districts of Pamplemousses, Rivière du Rempart and others in the N. of the island, received little damage, not many of the canes being uprooted; and a few bright days recovered those that were only bent by the wind.

The losses in all kinds of buildings was very great, as will be seen by the table at the end of this chapter.

Many of the small wooden houses, built on two or three courses of stone, were lifted up and carried bodily from their foundations, to the distance of some yards. One tolerably large house on the Pamplemousses road, with a good shingle roof, was literally turned bottom up, and stood on the ridge of the roof. The walls of many thatched dwellings fell flat inwards, and the roof, with not a bundle of thatch dislodged, covered the whole, as if placed there, looking, not inaptly, like the grave of the former residence; and in reality in several instances this was the tomb of some of the former inmates, unable to escape from the ruins.

It was sad enough to witness such a loss of property, but worse to note in every hut—every corner where only the remains of a roof slanted, and afforded a little shelter—some poor wretch shivering with ague or burning with fever; or sitting up, rolled in a ragged sheet barely enough to cover him.

The faces of all who were engaged, in a slovenly way, trying to patch up these miserable places, bore the unmistakable traces that they had also passed through the fiery ordeal of this terrible epidemic.

The effects of the hurricane were very visible on the sea-shore. The large kilns, erected for burning coral for lime, were much injured, and the piles of coral collected to supply them were washed back into the ocean from which they had been taken with so much labour.

A pretty little creek I had often examined for several curiosities, always full of algæas, and glowing with all the delicate tints only a sea-garden can show, was entirely filled up. A land-slip had taken place, from the torrents of water pouring down, and disintegrating masses of red earth on the shelving banks above; and as they fell they had covered even the boulders and rocks in the vicinity, and coloured the sea to some distance.

The destruction amongst cocoa-trees was very great. On one estate a fine tope of seventy-five young trees, just in full blossom, was utterly rooted out.

I cannot close this brief summary of the disasters caused by the cyclone without mentioning that everyone, from His Excellency the Governor to the lowest member of the community who had the means, did all in his power to alleviate the distress and misery caused by this terrible visitation.

RETURN TABLE OF DAMAGE DONE IN THE CYCLONE OF MARCH 11, 12, 1868.

DISTRICTS	Blown down, or carried away							Damaged						Killed or Died					
	Sugar-houses and Stores	Store-houses	Wooden Houses	Out-houses	Huts	Bridges	Boats	Sugar-houses	Store-houses	Wooden Houses	Out-houses	Bridges	Boats	Men	Women	Children	Oxen	Horses	Mules
Port Louis	2	57	411	477	1319	0	3	0	99	547	376	6	1	20	4	9	14	2	8
Pamplemousses . . .	1	52	258	190	3926	9	23	27	101	290	150	3	4	5	0	0	8	0	0
Rivière du Rempart . .	1	2	11	37	102	2	11	16	8	28	45	0	3	0	0	0	2	0	0
Flacq	2	22	87	66	3212	2	11	24	39	194	95	5	13	1	2	1	20	2	3
Moka	2	9	260	373	5236	0	0	13	12	243	143	2	0	8	2	1	19	5	47
Grand Port	7	0	57	58	2707	4	0	11	3	36	14	0	0	4	1	2	47	3	5
Savanne	4	13	41	26	1023	17	17	13	3	18	7	0	0	1	0	3	109	0	11
Black River	1	13	93	32	1263	22	20	13	37	97	9	1	1	11	2	1	79	1	9
Plaines Wilhems . . .	4	18	88	100	1400	0	0	27	41	160	51	1	0	9	2	0	23	0	8
Total	24	204	1306	1359	20188	65	85	144	343	1613	890	18	22	59	13	17	321	13	91

Notes of Cyclone at Bourbon.

'The sea was very rough on Monday, March 9, 1870, and this was the precursor of the tempest which burst over Réunion on the 12th and 13th. The centre of the cyclone passed over St. Pierre, describing its trajectory from NE. to SW. On Tuesday the wind blew with violence from the SE. till about 3 P.M.; then a calm intervened, which lasted till six in the evening, accompanied to the last moment by a suffocating heat. This was the passage of the centre, indicated perfectly by the excessive lowering of the barometer to 719 millemetres, the first time it had been known to descend so low since 1806. On the 12th the storm returned with fury from the NW., and it was only towards noon the next day that it began to calm.

'Great damage was done to buildings in the towns and villages, sugar-houses, gardens, &c.; a detail of which would only be a repetition of such scenes in Mauritius.'

Report of the Ship 'La Marie,' Capt. Horveno.

This vessel received the cyclone on Friday 13th, in 23° 16′ S. lat. and 57° 54′ E. long. to the S. of Réunion. Towards one o'clock in the morning the centre of the cyclone must have passed over this ship, the barometer marking 736 millemetres, and then rising. Thus it appears, from the time the hurricane passed us, and that at which it struck the 'Marie,' it must have travelled very slowly.

Capt. Horveno gives an account of a vessel in distress he fell in with and assisted. He says:—

'At 11.30 Saturday morning I perceived ahead of me a ship with only a mizen-mast left standing. It was the "Résolu," Capt. Durand, from Callao to Mauritius, loaded with guano, 103 days at sea.

'This vessel had passed through the centre of the cyclone on Thursday the 12th, at 1 P.M., that is 24 hours after I did. She had lost all her masts but the mizen, and in falling they had carried away all the boats.'

Report of the 'Nereida.

'The centre passed over this ship at 4 A.M. of the 17th, in lat. 31° 36′ S., and 53° E. long., nearly 200 leagues S. of Bourbon. At this time the storm had nearly expended all its force. The barometer fell only to 754 millemetres, and the wind blew from ESE., and then from WNW., but not strong enough to oblige the "Nereida" to change her course.'

CHAPTER VIII.

A TRIP TO THE ARSENAL.

Our Road—Arrival at Balaclava—Description of House and Grounds—Flour Mill—Distillery—Patent Fuel—School for Indian Children—Lime Kilns—Geology of the Coast.

WE left town by the Grand Baie and Cannonier Point road, which is rather picturesque, being lined on either side by wild camphor-trees. After passing Terre Rouge, much of the land is uncultivated, from the scarcity of water in the district, and most of the houses are in a more or less dilapidated condition; which, with the neglected gardens, give one the impression that the life and energy of the place have died out. Everything here is either quite new or rapidly decaying, and climate and animal life are so destructive to all the works of man, that were Port Louis itself left for a few years, it would be an uninhabitable heap of ruins, a jungle of grass and wild lianes.

Turning off the road at the Point aux Piments, we saw a catholic church terribly injured by the hurricane, but in which little groups of pious worshippers were constantly to be seen offering up prayers to the Virgin or Saints.

We soon arrived at Balaclava, the country residence of one of the merchants of Mauritius.

On entering the property you drive along a lane bordered with high hedges of the cassia, and pass in through a handsome iron gateway, made on the estate, and before the late storm covered with English honeysuckle. There is a carriage-road through the beautiful gardens up to the house, and you drive along avenues of rare exotic trees and shrubs, and on every side a wealth of roses and delicate flowers charms the senses.

There are the greater part of the indigenous trees of the island to be found here. The ponds are filled with Gourami and gold-fish; and at one end of the garden is a magnificent banian tree, which spreads its gigantic arms over the ovens of the old Arsenal battery, now scarcely visible through the mass of creepers over them.

The house, which stands on an eminence at the head of Turtle Bay, was built by the French. It originally formed part of an arsenal, constructed by Mahé de la Bourdonnais. There was also an iron-foundry and powder-mills, whence issued all the arms and defences of the colony, as well as a supply of ammunition for the ships the Frenchman fitted out for his Indian expedition.

A terrible accident, from the carelessness of a workman, caused an explosion of the powder-mills, almost entirely destroying the whole arsenal, as well as killing and wounding nearly 300 people. The present proprietor has added wings to the old building, converted a part of the ruins into a billiard-room, and surrounded the whole with a spacious verandah, till it has become, as by enchantment, a charming summer villa.

The whole property is now well supplied with water by means of a hydraulic ram from the Citron river; and where the pipes are brought into the garden in a sort of tower, its very unsightliness has been made to add another ornament to it, by being covered with climbing roses and sweet creepers, that flaunt out their wild masses of blossoms in the season, and perfume the air.

The French constructed a large dam of dressed stone, in 1743, which has been raised 2½ feet higher, and gives a lavish supply of water for mills and distillery. The surplus rushes over the dam in a wide sheet of twenty-five or thirty feet high, then goes dancing down the rocks, forming the loveliest, most capricious little cascades, till it joins the sea. A walk has been made round the dam, and a stone seat erected just where the water dashes down; willows are planted near it.

It was once graced by a little fairy form, the pride and darling of the place, fair as the flowers around her, but who faded away as quickly, touched by the poison breath of the dire epidemic then raging. It made me very sad, while I listened to the mournful tale, as I thought of my own little one, nearly the same age, so far away from me.

The view from the house seaward is of great beauty, the little land-locked bay always studded with fishing-boats; on one side a long sweep of turf to the water's edge, shaded with filaos, on the other a gentle rise covered to its summit with shrubs, its foot fringed with cocoa-trees, overhanging the bay; the wide ocean in the distance, and in the foreground the busy life of the mill and distillery; the superintendents' houses, and the fine trees everywhere, make a *tout ensemble* most picturesque. To be seen in its most charming phase, you should recline in one of the luxuriant oriental chairs in the verandah, on a bright moonlight night, when the bay lies before you, like an enchanted lake of rippling silver; and with the sound of the falling waters in your ears, you may dream away a summer's evening delightfully.

Descending a long flight of steps from the garden to the shore, which is masoned round for the three chasse-marées belonging to the place to lie alongside to take in their cargoes, on the right is a large mill for grinding the wheat brought principally from Australia, which is spread out for cleaning on the flat roof of the mill, laid level with bitumen, called here orgamasee.

There is a large water-wheel of thirty-eight feet, and one of twenty feet in diameter, that drive six stones, capable of grinding 300 bags of 150 lbs. each per day. The whole machinery, from the self-feeding buckets on a large wheel that carry in the wheat to the mill, to the separation of the different sorts of flour, is most complete. There was one very curious feature I noticed, where the shaft of a large cog-wheel had been broken. Its place was supplied by an old cannon, now sending forth streams of life sustenance, instead of belching forth flames and missiles for Man's destruction.

There is a tramway to the sea for bringing up the corn from the boats; one of the first, I believe, constructed in the island. The store-house can contain 10,000 bags of wheat, and is often full. Outside the mill is a fine grove of bananas, and the turf is dotted over with cocoas, palms, banians, &c., between it and the distillery on the left. Here we see the whole secret of rum making, for which no pains and expense have been spared to replace manual labour by machinery, as far as every modern appliance can do it.

The first thing we saw was the molasses as it was brought in from the sugar-houses, being poured from the casks into large troughs; black dirty-looking stuff, to be tested by the saccharometer; and if under 40° strong, it is rejected and thrown out. If up to proof, it is strained three times and run into large vats, of which there are eighteen, of sixty casks each, lined with lead, and where the molasses is mixed with water and yeast to cause it to ferment. After fermentation, it runs into the still, at the bottom of which is placed a hydrometer, which is covered with a glass case, under lock and key, in the hands of a government official, who is on the premises from 6 A.M. to 6 P.M.

A capital arrangement is made for filling the tonnels, which are twenty in number, of 1,100 galls. each. A copper vacuum-pan is connected with the pipes going down into the reservoir, and also similar pipes leading to the tonnels. Steam is let on, and then exhausted in the receiver, which causes the rum to pass up the pipes like a syphon. There is an indicator in the receiver, which denotes when the tonnel is full.

As soon as the rum is ready for market, it is drawn off into casks, measured by a government measure, and marked by the officer, when it is sent off by boats to Port Louis. As the rum leaves the still, it is about 30 per cent. over proof. When the vats are emptied, it is necessary to clean them; but thirty-six hours must elapse before the men dare enter them, on account of the great quantities of carbonic acid gas they contain; they are generally whitewashed before being filled again. Three boilers are employed, two of twenty-five and one of fifty horse-power, the steam for which is condensed and returned to them.

They burn three tons of coal per day, principally Australian. The dust from this coal is mixed with cowdung, one part of the former to two of the latter, and pressed by machinery into blocks of eight pounds each, then dried in the sun, when it becomes very hard, and forms excellent fuel; and a man can make a ton of blocks a day.

There is a cooperage on the place, where all the casks are manufactured, and the iron hoops wrought. The estate comprises about 1,800 acres, and ninety-five men are constantly employed in the mill and distillery.

The proprietor took the initiative in opening a school for the children of his Indian labourers. They are in school from 6 or 7 to 10 A.M.; and though now many are very regular, at first it was a chevy every morning to catch the little rascals, who objected to the discipline after their curiosity was satisfied, and the parents gave little help towards compelling them to attend. Most have made good progress, and in writing, sums, and reading, they would put to shame many a school of higher pretensions. The room is large and airy, with a thatched roof, and the walls are hung with maps, slates, &c. The pencils used are the large spines of the *Echinus manullatus*, plentiful in the Bay.

The old French fort of seven guns is turned into store-houses for lime, and close by are three large and three small kilns,

POND SCENE.

capable of burning 1,000 barrels of lime, in ten days, white as the driven snow. The coral for making the lime is brought in flat-bottomed boats from the reefs in the vicinity each making two or three trips a day.

There are fine quarries on the estate of grey stone, out of which the entire material used for building one of the churches of Port Louis was quarried gratis, by the liberality of the owner.

The shores of this bay are very interesting in a geological point of view. Traces are visible of vast streams of lava overlying each other, as well as numerous boulders, water-worn and incrusted with what was once molten matter; and in the interstices are many fragments of madrepores, which show that, at not a very remote period, they were submerged. But their present position, which is so many feet above the level of the sea, is wholly attributable to upheaval.

We returned home late in the evening, highly gratified with our day's entertainment, and each with a large bouquet courteously presented by our host.

CHAPTER IX.

THE GEOLOGY OF MAURITIUS.

Extinct Craters—Cessation of Volcanic Action—Upheaval—Deposits at Timor and other Islands—Force of Volcanic Agency—Mountain Peaks—Flacq—Craters —Dr. Ayres on Flat Island—Original Formation of Mauritius—Submersion— —Fossil Casts.

LIKE most other islands in the Indian Ocean, the Isle of France is of volcanic production. Endless are the peculiar characteristics of its mountain peaks, and the abrupt gigantic fissures which separate them, and of the beds of lava of different thickness and nature which are found everywhere.

Extinct craters of the different eras filled with earth are more or less abundant, and are seen in numberless situations in the island. The hills and mountain peaks, which impress their peculiar character on the physical aspect of the land, have been formed, at different times, by volcanic eruptions, on which the now extinguished fires have left ineffaceable traces of their existence.

The great fissures in the sides of the hills, which have given rise to the waters of the interior, and formed the beds of the rivers and ravines now seen, have undoubtedly resulted from disruption.

Although volcanic action has entirely ceased, there is no doubt that the volcano which formed the island was submarine, and that its formation was not sudden, but the work of successive ages; and the general appearance of its surface indicates these facts.

In many parts of the interior, particularly in the vicinity of the Chamarel Mountains, I have found corals in a perfect state, buried in a débris of cretaceous formation, but none of the species of which now exist in the warm tropical seas where they once lived.

Between Grand River and Port Louis beds exist more than fifteen feet in thickness; the Custom House is built on a formation of this kind; and, in fact, these corals are found in nearly every part of the island. I observed, near the River de Poste, in the interior, at an elevation of more than 1,000 feet, a stratum of plastic clay, twelve feet in depth, underlying a thick bed of gravel.

It is difficult at first sight to account for these facts, but it is evident that such deposits could have been formed only under water, and as they are now found hundreds of feet from the present level of the ocean, we must admit one of two things; either that the water was elevated above those points a sufficiently long time to form thick beds there, or that these beds were raised up from the bottom of the sea to the height where we now find them.

Nothing in the present time warrants a belief that the sea, which has not changed its level within the time of History, could have been so elevated long enough as to form considerable deposits; it must therefore be admitted that the only reasonable supposition is upheaval, an idea supported by positive events that have taken place in our own times.

In Flat Island blocks of volcanic rocks and masses of coral rise everywhere above the vegetation.

These coral blocks are found on the north side of the island, forty or fifty feet above the level of the sea.[1]

At Timor are deposits of madrepores thirty feet thick, also in New Holland, Van Diemen's Land, at the Marian and Sandwich Isles, &c., where they rest on argillaceous schist, sandstone, limestone, and volcanic products. In the Isle of France a similar bank, twelve feet thick, is placed between two currents of lava.

Similar deposits are found in many other places of the same species of madrepores, in the interior of land, at an elevation of from 900 to 1,000 feet. The existence of deposits in such situations evidently indicates that all these islands have been upheaved from the bosom of the waters at different periods, for banks of coral at various levels are often found.[2]

[1] See Dr. Ayres' 'Geology of Flat and Gabriel Islands,' in a letter to the Royal Society of Arts and Sciences, 1860.

[2] See Ruschenberger's 'Geology.'

The enormous incandescent mass forming the interior of the Globe, oscillating from side to side, beneath its thin crust, could emboss it in every direction, and nothing more than this would be required to raise continents out of the sea, and vary their surface into every conceivable form.

Amongst numbers of other modern instances, I may mention the upheaval, in the course of sixteen days, of White Island, Neo Kammeni, King George's Isle, and Aphröessa in the Gulf of Santorin.

We have in the present day astonishing proofs of the force of volcanic agency in Hawaii, one of the Sandwich Islands, itself an upheaval originally, and which has gained its vast mountain peaks by accretion. The well-known Mauna Loa rises to the majestic height of 13,750 feet above sea level. This most terrible of modern volcanoes has many craters, but the largest one is that of Kilauca, three and a half miles long, two and a half wide, and 1,044 feet deep. It is completely surrounded by a wall of hardened lava, and at the bottom is a lake of liquid fire, constantly surging up.

The whole interior of Mauritius was one vast crater, and the remains of the walls which encircled it, as it emerged from the ocean, now water-worn and degraded, forming gentle slopes, and filling the valleys with débris, are still evident to the eye of a geologist.

The mountain peaks were the first to rise out of the deep, and the enormous fissures made by rivers of liquid fire, forcing their way to the ocean, leaving behind large plains of lava, are visible in all parts of the island.

At Flacq the flow of the lava currents is distinctly seen, and these streams I have easily traced to the grand crater in the central districts.

Near Turtle Bay, there are many large boulders, twenty feet above the level of the sea, of ancient formation, and much water-worn, which present the appearance of having been for a length of time submerged. Numerous corals fill their cavities, built there by the animals that inhabit the cells. These boulders are covered with a thick encrustation of lava, and in some instances are embedded in it.

Between Mount Ory and the Corps de Garde Mountains a stream of lava, many miles in width, flowed to the sea. Then, again, between the Corps de Garde and Rempart Mountains, there is another break in the great wall, through which a current of molten matter discharged itself. Similar phenomena occur in various parts of the island.

After the great volcano became extinct, leaving high inward-curved walls, a number of lesser but very active volcanoes appeared on the sea-board side of the walls, in the opening occasioned by the subsidence of the great crater.[1] These lesser ones are termed adventitious craters: a remarkable instance of which may be seen in the large crater of Vesuvius, where an adventitious one opened in its centre in 1829. Port Louis lies in one such crater, and the Vallée des Prêtres in another; and I have counted at least ten distinct craters between that city and the Morne. Rempart Mountain forms the NE. and Tamarind Mountain the SW. limit of a crater some miles in

[1] The late eruptions at Mauna Loa were on such a magnificent scale, and prove how much may be effected in a few months by volcanic action, that I quote some passages from an interesting paper on these convulsions in a *New York Herald*.

In January 1859, three new craters were formed. Streams of lava were hurled upwards from 200 to 800 feet, and when they fell, they traversed a distance of five miles, and went sheer down a precipice in a torrent of fire, a mile wide; drove back the sea and usurped its place.

On January 27, 1868, Mauna Loa was observed to be very active. In twelve days there were 2,000 shocks of earthquakes, followed by immense tidal waves, that rose over the tops of the cocoa trees on the Rona coast, and swept away whole villages, with much destruction of life. The slope and part of a mountain were lifted bodily and thrown over a forest for a distance of 1,000 feet. Down the sides of the dread Mauna Loa swept a stream of lava, seven feet in width, and an eruption of moist clay the width of a mile that spread over 2¾ miles of ground in three minutes.

On April 2, immense bodies of earth were tossed about to great distances, as if they were feathers. Precipices of fearful height were levelled to the ground, and gigantic chasms and fissures have been formed from the rending and upheaving of the earth. The masses of lava that flowed from the crater, covering the roads with the fiery streams, rushed down to the sea and drove back the water violently. The ground thus gained formed a point a mile in length, and the lava continuing to pour over it, converted it into a part of the island. Huge rocks were hurled from the crater, with torrents of lava, to the height of 1,000 feet, and then rushed down to the sea with frightful velocity.

On March 27, a new crater two miles in circumference was formed, which also vomited rocks and streams of liquid fire. A current of lava flowed underground six miles from the sea, and the gases from the rents in the earth destroyed all vegetation.

The smoke that rose from the craters was a dense cloud, and floated off in a line of 1,000 miles across the sea. It was so thick at 500 miles from Hawaii, that Captain Stone of the brig 'Kamekameha V.' was unable to take an observation.

diameter, with a good-sized adventitious one in the centre, just at the back of Tamarind Bay.

The bold promontory of Brabant and the Island of Fourneaux are the only remaining portions of the wall seaward of a crater more than two miles in diameter. The mountain sides of the crater looking south are almost perpendicular. Four aux Cerfs, Grand Bassin, and others are all small adventitious craters.

At Baie de Cap there is a well-defined one, the walls rising to some hundreds of feet in height. There is a bluff at the head of this bay, about 300 feet perpendicular, formed of beautiful tabular basalt, which can only be viewed to advantage from a boat. Large columns are constantly being detached and falling into the bay from the degrading action of the waves at the foot of this bluff, which is one of the finest basaltic rocks in the island.

In the bay at Grand Port is a large crater, the walls of which are distinctly visible on a fine day from a boat. It appears about 300 yards in diameter, is of great depth, and the hue of the water changes to a dark shade, almost black, just over its centre.

Dr. Ayres, in his 'Geology of Flat and Gabriel Islands,' gives the following interesting notices :—'In Flat Island, nearly facing Round Island, we find the fossilised remains of an extensive forest, consisting of stumps of trees closely planted, about two feet high, hollow in the centre to the base, and some of them two feet in diameter.

'The greater part of them are endogens, presenting the appearance of the enlarged bases of palms, though many of the roots appear to possess an exogenous character.

'The outer crust is hard, lined on the inner and hollowed surface by a loose intertwined network of coarse fibres, such as are seen in the interior of cocoa and other palms, and screw pines. On some parts of the denuded surface of the volcanic rocks, roots are thickly interlaced, and the still finer fibres of the roots appear to form the chief part of the stratum, which is about fifteen feet deep. It is hard and structureless, resembling a muddy substance recently calcified.

'Here and there a perfect stump is visible, intermixed with masses of loose coral and shells of existing species. On the ground above the lava, covered with grass and herbage, trunks of trees are visible, broken and lying on the surface, one of them, four or five feet long, presenting the appearance of the trunk of a palm. No sea shells are found in this stratum occupied by the roots of trees, though abundant in the coral strata below.'

From the foregoing facts, the following ideas suggested themselves to me, as to the original formation of Mauritius. A terrific convulsion of a power almost inconceivably great must have upheaved it, and the adjacent islands, Rodriguez, Bourbon, and perhaps even Madagascar itself, in one vast tract of cones of various elevations, columnar masses, &c.

This is not at all impossible when we consider that an earthquake was sufficient to raise nearly 200 leagues of coast in Chili; and another, in India, upheaved a hill fifty miles long by sixteen broad, turning aside the course of the Indus; and a thousand other well-known incidents.

In process of time, the sloping sides of the great crater, and the currents of lava as they cooled, were covered with layers of earth, in which sprang up the gigantic palms and other trees, forming vast, voiceless forests; for we have no traces of animal life at this epoch, if we except the few land shells that have been found.

Fresh convulsions, causing these elevated cones to split and topple over, buried the forest in their débris, and submerged the whole once again in the depths of the ocean. But the volcanic action, terrific as it must have been to cause this submergence, was evidently unequal in force in different parts of this large tract of land.

On the side from Flacq to Flat Island, the superincumbent masses on the buried forests were so great as to isolate them in the earthy débris, and in the course of ages they became fossilised without any mixture of marine deposits from the surrounding ocean, as is proved by the stratum in which they are found being destitute of sea shells and corals.

Strange to say, the two species of land shells, the *Caracalla Lesteri* and *Helix rufa*, are precisely similar to the living species that are now found, the former infesting the cocoa trees on the sea-board of Mauritius. The volcanic action on the south side of the island was evidently different in character and intensity. The submergence of the forests there may or may not have taken place at the same time as those on the north. It is possible there were fewer elevations there in the primitive upheaval to be overthrown, and the subsidence may have been so gradual, as to allow of their becoming enveloped in the detritus from the shores, débris of sea shells and fragments of corals, which in time formed a compact mass round them. As the trees rotted they left the indelible impression of their forms in the plastic mass, which, as it fossilised, left a cast as perfect as if taken in plaster of Paris. This has deceived many into taking what is in reality only a cast of the original tree, for the fossil tree itself.

These casts abound in the islands near Mahébourg, particularly in the Isle des Aigrettes. I collected specimens, and submitted them to severe chemical tests with acids, and failed to discover anything like fibrous tissue.

I found only fragments of corals, broken shells, and minute foraminiferous shells, all of which I feel convinced are only deposits of débris that abound in the bay and coasts even at the present time.

A similar formation exists near Petite Savanne, which shows traces of submergence, and in this as in other cases rests on a bed of lava.

For what length of time the whole of this vast tract lay in the abysses of ocean none can tell,—when the upheaval took place which separated it into groups and isolated islands, or when it became habitable for animal life, none may know save He who 'taketh up the isles in his hand as a very little thing.'

CHAPTER X.

THE MOHARRUM OR YAMSEH.

Its Origin—Whence the name Yamseh—The Find in the Latanier River—The Disposal of their 'Bon Dieu'—Procession for Alms—Gouhns—How built—The Little Procession—Orgies at Plaine Verte—Colours worn by Indians—Grand Procession—The Lion—Breaking the Gouhns—Return Home—Ignorance of the Actors in the Yamseh.

One of the principal Mahommedan festivals in Mauritius is the Yamseh. It took its rise from the disputes among the followers of Mahommed, on the question of prophetical succession.

The Turks and Arabians recognised Abou Beker, Omar and Osman, as the rightful successors of the Prophet; the Persian and Indian Mahommedans denounce these three Caliphs as usurpers, and regard Ali, the Prophet's son-in-law and minister, as his religious and political heir.

The disputes only ended in a sanguinary contest, in which Hossein and Hossan, the sons of Ali, were slain with sixty of their relatives.

The name Yamseh, unknown in India, is but a local corruption of the cries of 'Ya Hossein! Oh Hossan!' used in the procession, which combines a religious ceremony with the funeral rites to the memory of the slain brothers and the rejoicings of the victorious party.

The night of every eleventh new moon is eagerly looked for by all classes of Mahommedans, who spend days in fasting, ablutions, and preparations for its appearance.

As soon as the slender crescent is visible, a procession is formed, headed by the priests, which proceeds to the River Latanier, at this time a shallow stream just outside of Port Louis.

A priest dives down to bring up their 'Bon Dieu,' buried the past year in some sort of place hollowed in the bed of the river.

THE MOHARRUM OR YAMSEH.

Two stones, or two lumps of some paste hardened so as to be impervious to the water, are brought up, and they have a dual signification, as they not only represent their God and Prophet, but also the two slain brothers.

The priests conduct their newly found treasure with great ceremony to the Temple at Plaine Verte, and for ten days and nights strict watch is kept over it.

During this time prayers are offered up incessantly, and all pay a small sum for every prayer the priests recite for them; certain food only is allowed to be eaten, and constant ablutions are exigent. Processions round the city are made, to levy contributions to defray the expenses of the Yamseh, and the making of the Gouhns.

The men and children dress up in all the fantastic finery that can be procured, and with their faces painted, making most barbarous music with their tom-toms, they put one in mind of the procession of sweeps on May-day, in former times, in England.

These Gouhns are a species of pagoda on wheels, made of bamboo bound very strongly together, and covered with gold and silver tinsel and many-coloured papers.

They consist of several stories, the one at the base largest, and gradually diminishing in size upwards, terminating in a dome. Pretty Chinese paper lanterns are hung from all the corners, and, when to be used at night, are lit up from within also. One very large Gouhn, handsomely adorned with gold and silver paper, flowers and tinsel, is constructed with great ceremony.[1]

The three stories are each built in a separate hut, and when completed the side walls are thrown down, to allow each part to be carefully lifted out, lest by any accident the threshold of the door should be touched, which would bode evil. They are then firmly bound one over the other, and taken to the Temple, where the two river-found God and Prophet representatives are placed in it, and a watch is placed over it night and day till the Yamseh is over.

On the evening of the ninth day, the 'Little Procession' (as

[1] The form of the Gouhns, however, varies greatly with the taste of the constructors, as will be seen in the illustration of one made on an estate.

it is called) takes place. The inferior Gouhns are carried on the heads of negroes hired for the purpose, not Mahommedans. Lighted lanterns, flags, brass crescents, and stars are carried aloft on sticks, and men, half nude and daubed with paint, fight with clubs and give and parry strokes with great dexterity. They parade through all the suburbs of the city, dancing and screaming till midnight, when they join the revelry at Plaine Verte.

There those who have not been in the procession enjoy what they call a 'little amusement,' by way of breaking the monotony of the long religious festival.

Large fires are lit, and in an enclosure of ropes hundreds congregate. The women and children sit round the fires, eating rice, cocoa cakes and sweetmeats, watching the men, and criticising in tolerably broad language their skill as they engage in single stick, leaping, dancing, and all kinds of rough games; laughing, gesticulating, and shouting in all the dialects of the East.

The impression left after witnessing the scene is, that one has spent a few hours on the confines of Pandemonium.

Watch the weird flickering lights of the fires, spreading an unearthly hue over everything; the groups of the half-nude savages (I say savages advisedly, as for the time being all trace of civilisation is lost); men, women, and children all more or less intoxicated, the latter mingling their shrill voices with the howling of the men—and at times there comes a stifling smell of incense, mingled with other odours indescribable; and it needs little imagination to believe it a living, acted scene from Dante's Inferno, or the wild orgies and unholy revels of the Brocken on Walpurgis Night.

The tenth is the grand day for which so many preparations have been made, and so many thousands of ells of crimson, pink, and yellow calicoes, muslins, and even silks have been sold for Indian vests and waist cloths. Black is never worn by the Indians in their native costumes. Green is a sacred colour, worn only by the higher classes, and by them for a badge of mourning alone.

The procession is formed at the Temple, and the principal Gouhns are brought out and carried steadily along, the priests monotonously chanting round them.

The smaller ones are carried by men who might be afflicted with St. Anthony's fire, for they unceasingly danced and whirled about like madmen.

One part of the procession is formed by mourners for the brothers, wearing a piece of the sacred green stuff round their loins, beating their breasts, howling, and uttering cries of 'Ya Hossein! Oh Hossan!' and contests with blunt swords and sticks go on in all directions, in memory of the ensanguined field.

The Lion that watched over the sacred remains of Ali's sons is represented by a brawny follower of the Prophet, whose skin is painted to imitate the tawny hide, and a goatskin thrown over his shoulders for a mane.

He utters the most hideous roars as he rushes about the crowd, restrained by a cord held by a priest.

Groups dressed in little more than horns and tails, monstrously streaked with paint, are supposed to be devils rejoicing at Hossein and Hossan's death, and they leap about, causing endless confusion.

The sham combats with swords and clubs go on till the procession reaches the river Latanier.

The inferior Gouhns that have been injured are flung into the river, after being torn to atoms by the children.

The large one is reverently lowered to the water's edge, and the god descends to his river bed, to sleep again for a year, and his pagoda is taken back to the Temple, to be decked up afresh on his awaking.

The whole procession is then broken up, and the rabble rout return to finish their day in feasting. On the morrow, all but a few *bons-à-rien* return to their work, though the events of these ten days serve for topics of conversation for months to come.

Formerly, real combats took place, and blood was often shed, till the police were obliged to interfere; and now it is a comparatively quiet affair, few of the higher classes of Mahommedans taking part in it.

The true Mahommedan element is fast dying out of this festival, and Indian superstition and idolatry usurping its place.

Not one in five hundred knows anything of the origin of all

this; when asked they tell you to go to the priests, as it is their business to know all about it.

They only know it as a recognised holiday, accompanied by unlimited strong drinks, feasting, and, dearer than even those to an Indian—noise!

On some of the estates the Yamseh is kept up with as much if not more preparation than in Port Louis, and the Gouhns are quite as fine, being subscribed for by all the Indians in the camp; and they get leave from their masters to go round to the various private houses in the vicinity to display them and get money. The combatants with single sticks, and performers who cleverly twirl a long slender pole round their heads, keeping it spinning for some minutes, dancers and howlers to the tom-toms, accompany the Gouhns; and they are generally well behaved, as a policeman is sure to put in an appearance where there is a group congregated. I once watched the painting of one of the *devils*: the fellow was seated in an old box, his arms straight down and head erect, while the *artist* knelt before him. He had just completed the body, with a heart over the chest, and white and coloured lines diverging from it in all directions, continued over the arms; and at the moment of my arrival he was standing, with folded arms, contemplating his work, quite regardless of the rain then beginning to fall. He then proceeded to the face, which was rendered as hideous as paint could make it, the fellow's eyes glittering out of heavy rings of white paint. I remained till half was done, but not a word could be got from either, it was far too serious a matter. That the work was *well* done I had positive proof, for I saw it exposed to a good sharp shower with but little effect on it.

CHAPTER XI.

A VISIT TO ROUND ISLAND

Departure from Port Louis—The Voyage—Arrival and Difficulty of Landing—Size and Formation of the Island—The Flora—Dinner—Preparations for sleeping—Fishing—Geological Description of the Island.

FROM the many accounts that had been given me of the remarkable geological formation of Round Island (which lies about twenty-five miles from Port Louis), and its peculiar Flora, differing in so many particulars from that of Mauritius and the neighbouring islands, I determined to avail myself of the first opportunity that offered and visit it.

On December 6, 1868, I made an arrangement with Mr. Vandermeesch, the proprietor of the island, and Lieutenant Robinson of the Royal Artillery, to proceed thither on the following day.

We secured a good boat of about ten tons, and a stock of provisions was placed on board sufficient for the subsistence of seven men for some time.

This precaution was especially necessary from the delightful uncertainty as to the result of our voyage. First, we might be overtaken by bad weather, when the island would be unapproachable, and there was just a possibility of our being driven out to sea; secondly, we might land and be unable to get off again for many days.

Precisely as the gun fired from the Fort, or 8 clock, P.M., the hawser which held our neat little craft to the end of the Mauritius Dock was cast off, and our sail hoisted.

The night was gloomy, and heavy clouds hung on the horizon indicative of rain, but now and then a few stars would peep out from the dark canopy, and cheer us on our way.

The wind failed, and the men had to use their oars through the labyrinth of vessels in the harbour of Port Louis.

All was still, save the plash of the sweeps, as we glided through the silent waters.

After considerable rowing, we reached the light-ship. Its rays flash brilliantly across the waves, and can be seen for many miles cheering the mariner on his way, or guiding him safely into port. Now we were fairly out in the deep waters of the Indian Ocean; and a light breeze springing up, the oars were laid by, and our pretty little boat, the 'Beautiful Jane,' sailed along like a duck. Our crew was selected from the most skilful fishermen of Grand Baie, and our skipper, an old Creole, knew every rock, reef, and current round the coast. The night being dark, a watch was set, lest we should run into any of the little fishing boats bound in a different direction.

The time passed away pleasantly, spinning yarns about sharks and other monsters, together with a highly coloured description of what I might expect to see on the morrow.

When daylight appeared we found ourselves some miles in a northerly direction from Gunner's Quoin. With us the sea was smooth, though there was a swell from the north.

Round Island then stood due east from us, at a distance of about ten miles.

We were favoured with a fine breeze, which increased as old Sol raised his head from the ocean. The morning was bright and clear, doubly welcome and refreshing to those who had been breathing only the heavy fever-laden atmosphere of Port Louis for some time; and especially to me, who had been suffering for some days from the epidemic. Though tolerably calm with us, we could see the white foam breaking over the Quoin as the waves beat against its bold cliffs.

> The gentleness of heaven is on the sea.
> Listen! the mighty being is awake,
> And doth with his eternal motion make
> A sound like thunder—everlastingly.

But the sunrise! Those who have never seen a sunrise at sea have reserved for them a glorious sight. This morning the orb of day rose in all his grandeur from out the wilderness of waters; so placid and tranquil was the scene that I was involuntarily struck by its contrast with the fearful heavy swell rolling in over the shoal water between the Quoin and Cannonier's Point, breaking on the rocks with a booming roar, threatening destruction to any craft that ventured near them, and warning us to bear away and keep a good distance from the land.

For the first time on this coast I saw a little stormy petrel, *Thalassidroma milanogaster*. One solitary bird was following in our wake, swiftly and gracefully sweeping over the waves. This interesting creature is aptly reverenced by seamen; for, diminutive as it is, it braves the fiercest storms, and 'skims o'er ocean's angriest flood.'

At noon we arrived at our destination on the SE. of Round Island, and made preparations to disembark.

I at once saw that what had been told me of the difficulty of landing was no exaggeration. Luckily our fishermen crew made their arrangements skilfully. The boat was allowed to drift within a few feet of the table rock, our landing-place, against which the waves were breaking.

At this stage we had to wait, and watch for an opportunity for one of our crew to jump ashore with a rope, so that the boat might be kept bow on and steady. When this was effected, the rope was securely fastened to iron rings placed there for that purpose years ago; and then our provisions, water, &c., were passed on shore.

When everything was safely landed, each one watched for the moment when the boat rose, and sprung on to the rock with a bound that made every nerve quiver; and it needed a sure foot and steady eye to alight firmly on the slippery stone.

If our little craft, which rose and fell some ten or twelve feet, had struck her bows on the precipitous ledge, she would have been hurled to Davy Jones's locker, and all in her in a few seconds. The depth of the water is about four fathoms here.

When all were safely on shore, the boat was taken out to some distance from land and anchored, with two of her crew left on board to take care of her.

Near the landing is a cave, made by an immense portion of detached rock having slidden off into the sea, leaving a cliff, which overhangs it, and forming a very good shelter from the fierce rays of the sun; and in rainy weather, the water rushes in torrents over it, but does not enter.

This cave rises from the sea, at an angle of forty-five degrees, for about a hundred feet, and is approached from the landing rock, on the right of it, by carefully stepping up the small projections on its sides. We descended about twelve feet, and then came to the floor of the cave, which we selected as the base of our operations. Into this we took all our worldly goods, and great care was needed to secure them from rolling into the sea. Lay down any solid article carelessly, and away it went, with a velocity that no efforts of ours could check, into the water, and was lost.

After giving our orders to the men to prepare a meal for us, we started off exploring, each in a different direction.

Round Island is about a mile long by three quarters broad, of extremely irregular formation, frequently intersected by deep fissures which increase in width towards the sea, when they form singular openings and caves. At a distance it appears like one great solid mountain.

The passage from the base upwards, through a gulch about 700 feet, is rough and difficult. The most curious geological phenomena are to be seen in this gulch, which has, in the course of ages, been worn away by the elements.

Distinctly visible are the different strata lying on each other, and well defining the different periods. The peculiar forms which these rocks take are very remarkable. Some parts resemble the ruins of old Gothic structures; others of a series of elegant pulpits, carved out of Red Sandstone; and many are like baptismal fonts, similar to those used at the present day, the whole forming a unique and singular formation. At this elevation is a tolerably open spot, easy of ascent.

The whole island is covered with endogens, palms, vacoas, &c., among which I particularly noticed the following: one palm, supposed to be the *Areca alba*, or 'Chou palmiste,' which grows in Mauritius;[1] a second, which is indigenous to Round Island, in fact, unknown in any other part of the world. This palm has long been called the *Jubœa spectabilis*, but this name is now proved to be an error.[2]

[1] With respect to this palm and others of the Round Island trees, I will quote some of the notes made by the Governor after their expedition, when he and Mr. Horne studied the botany of this place. He was inclined to consider the one in question, not the *Areca alba*, but a separate species; and says, 'It struck me at once, on seeing it in flower, that its red petals were quite different; and Mr. Horne, on subsequent comparison, has found other structural variations in the blossom, also in the large anthers.'

[2] The slightest comparison will show the discrepancies between this palm and

A third palm, the *Latania glaucophylla*, grows in great abundance, and is believed also to be indigenous. A few plants have been found on Flat Island, but they are conjectured to have sprung from seeds washed up by the tides.

The *Pandanus Vandermeeschii* is very numerous. This was discovered by the gentleman of that name (our companion), who sent specimens of it to the Botanical Gardens at Ghent, where they received the above name. This is quite different from the vacoa used for making sugar bags, the *Pandanus utilis*: this latter I did not see, though I am told that some few plants have been found.

Round the summit of the mountain I saw a species of aloe which I have not met with in Mauritius.[1] A report on Round Island was written twenty-five years ago by a Colonel Lloyd, an engineer, who went there for the purpose of examining it. He mentions a belt of forest trees, such as bois rond, ebony, benzoin, &c.; but they must have been nearly all cut down or destroyed, as we found few traces of them.[2]

A few patches of rough grasses enliven this rugged island, and on them feed numbers of rabbits and goats, but wild as the proverbial 'March hare.' The *Ipomœa maritima* grows at an elevation of 800 feet, the seeds, doubtless, having been brought hither by birds.

The only fern I found was a small species of the *Adiantum caudatum*, so common in Mauritius, which seems to flourish

the true *Jubœa spectabilis* of Chili, which is stated to be a lofty palm, whilst the Round Island tree never exceeds fifteen feet. The spathe surrounding the blossom of the former is monophyllous, that of the latter has eight or nine leaves, and the flowers differ in almost every particular. The fruit of the one is a little cocoa-nut with three perforations at the top, that of the other a small green berry: from the latter, as well as from other circumstances, indeed, I fully expect to hear that the Round Island palm turns out to be a species of Areca, an idea in which I have been confirmed by learning from Mr. Horne that the somewhat similar palm from Rodriguez, styled *Jubœa speciosa*, has been recently described in Holland as the *Areca Verschaffeltii*.

1 'It is proved to be quite different from the "Socotrine du pays" of Mauritius, and is probably new.'

2 'The belt of hard-wood timber mentioned by Colonel Lloyd is confined to the central ridge of the summit, a few trees only existing. The presence of that narrow belt of trees, with the analogies and discrepancies they present when compared with those of the adjacent main island, is certainly one of the most puzzling problems presented by this curious little islet.'

best among rocks in the hardest and driest soil.[1] The Round Island fern appears a variety from the Mauritian type.

I captured a number of lizards, spiders, scorpions, phasmas, and other insects, but will give an account of them later. One of my comrades killed a snake of the Colubra tribe, about two feet long, and two inches in circumference. The back was mottled with black and white spots, and the belly reddish with black markings. It was what a naturalist would call an ugly customer : it does not run from you, but elevates its head at your approach, and prepares to give battle. A large one was seen by one of the fishermen, who said it was six or seven feet long, and as large round as his arm. He was carrying a long pole on his shoulder, at each end of which were suspended several Pailles-en-queues, or tropic birds (*Phaëton rubricauda*). The snake reared his head to attack him, when he dropped the pole to pick up a stone to throw at it; but the birds made such a noise that the reptile slunk away into a heap of vacoa leaves near by, and he lost it.

Towards the NE. I came suddenly to the edge of a deep gorge before I was aware of it, formed by torrents of water pouring down it for ages. In some places it is 500 or 600 feet deep; and as I stood on its brink to look down into the abyss below, over the tops of the palms that fill its sides, I shuddered as I thought of the fall I should have had if I had gone over.

At the foot of the gorge, opening out to the sea, the rocks are shelving, and in little holes in them sat numbers of Pailles-en-queues on their solitary eggs. These beautiful birds did not attempt to move away from me, but merely uttered a shrill cry, and prepared for resistance if disturbed. They do not build any nest, but lay their one egg on the bare rock. It is of a reddish brown, speckled with dark spots, and is about the size of a duck's egg.

Young birds quite as large as their parents were easily captured by the men, who prized them for food, but I should fancy they must taste very fishy. The plumage of the young is quite different from that of the old ones, being mottled black and white. I did not see a single instance of a young bird on the wing; and I believe it is only in the second year that they get

[1] As my time was so limited, I was unable to do more than make a very cursory examination of the botany of the island; I will add extracts from the reports of the governor and Mr. Horne at the end of the chapter.

their full feathers. It was curious to see every ledge filled with young birds, from the downy fluffy ball, as large as a small chicken, to those of the size of the parent birds, each one sitting huddled up against the mother, and uttering notes of alarm in every sharp key their unmusical voices are capable of.

I saw a good many petrels (*Puffinus chlororhyncus*) sitting in the same locality. These birds also lay a single egg, quite white, as large as a hen's. There were no young about, and the eggs were all fresh that I took. I observed no other birds, and these seemed only to resort thither for the purpose of incubation at certain seasons of the year. I brought away eight or nine tropic birds, all taken sitting, and, strange to say, they were all males.

The Hon. Edward Newton, the Colonial Secretary, visited the island some years ago, and published a pamphlet on its ornithology, in which he states he observed the turtle dove (*Geopelia striata*) of Gray, petrels, and tropic birds; and he thought these were all ever found there.

I arrived at the top of the mountain, which is 1,000 feet above sea level by Elliot's barometer, and where stands a huge block of basalt, ten or fifteen feet high, which is the crowning point; up this I climbed, and a magnificent view lay around me. Looking down the almost perpendicular face of the NE. side of the island, thickly studded with small shrubs, and apparently inaccessible, thousands of the tropic birds were seen hovering about, uttering their sharp shrill cries, doubtless from the footsteps of man having intruded on what they had so long deemed their own domain. Westward lay Serpent's Island with its wintry appearance, white over with guano as with snow, which, though half a mile or more distant, seemed but a step from this elevated position. Flat Island and the Quoin appeared close by. The atmosphere was so clear that the coast-line of Mauritius, as far as Grand River, SE., was mapped out distinctly, and everywhere glistened the heavy billows of the brilliant blue ocean, and the white spray tossed up from every reef added beauty to the scene. Being hot, tired, and hungry, I descended, with the determination of studying the geology of the island on the morrow.

As soon as I reached our cave, I was delighted to find my friends with everything prepared to satisfy the inner man. I cannot refrain from saying a few words in praise of our Commissary-General, who deserved a *cordon d'honneur* for his excellent arrangements for our comfort. I then first ate the heart of the cabbage palm cut up into salad, and found it delicious, worthy of all the encomiums I had heard lavished on it; but it must be eaten when fresh to be tasted in perfection.

We did full justice to the viands, and then began our arrangements for the night. This is a very ticklish place for a somnambulist or a nervous person to sleep in. A roll—a turn over—and down you must go into the surging billows at the foot of the rock, with the pleasant anticipation of the immense sharks, and other monsters of the deep that swarm round the place, ready to take you in at a mouthful or two the moment you touch the water. Thus, as I said before, it is a ticklish place, and required great care in arranging our beds. Two small hammocks were ingeniously swung from the sides of the cave for two of us; but my other comrade, though a young soldier, is an old campaigner in this line, and preferred to sleep on the bare rock under the cliff, which he did. We passed a pleasant night, lulled to sleep by the monotonous roar of the waters round us.

We were up at daylight, but the morning broke gloomily, and dark clouds indicated rain; the barometer had fallen, and the sea ran high, making us uneasy, as we feared a coming storm. A smart shower of rain, however, accompanied by thunder and lightning, smoothed down the sea considerably, and, soon after, a magnificent rainbow spanned the dark arch of heaven.

As the weather was so uncertain, our skipper would not let us go exploring, as he said he might want us to embark at any moment; so I amused myself fishing at the entrance of our cave.

Fish in myriads were swimming about the detached rocks. I never saw a more beautiful sight. The splendid *Helicanthus Imperadore*, a marvellous variety of Cheitodons, many of the genus Serranus, Dame Berris, and others, all bright-coloured, were swimming about gracefully in the transparent waters.

I have seen the bright-plumaged birds and insects of South America in their native wilds, but the fish of the Indian Ocean can vie with the most gorgeous of them. They lose their beauty so rapidly when caught, that to be truly appreciated they must be seen in their native element. Now and then a shark would show his ugly head, when the rest disappeared as if by magic. The brute would look at me with his bright eye, and grin, showing his ghastly maw, as if in anticipation of the meal he hoped to get out of me should I slip over the ledge.

About 200 yards from ours was another cave, inaccessible to man. The waves would rush into it for some distance, when the confined air would force them back to the opening with a thundering roar, and throw the water up in volumes of spray for a hundred feet around. I thought, as I watched the foaming, seething mass, that the Souffleur at Grand Port in its angriest moments could not be compared to this. At 7 A.M. the clouds dispersed, the sun shone out brilliantly, and our skipper thought it safe, after breakfast, to make another excursion, of which permission I lost no time in availing myself.

This island is evidently formed by upheaval from the bottom of the ocean; it is in fact a crater of upheaval or elevation, which formation lies in strata or laminated beds of friable brownish volcanic sandstone and tufa. These beds are here found inclined all round the axis of the cone, rising more and more from the base to the summit. In one of the fissures to the NE. immense numbers of lines of stratification are distinctly seen, indicating the different periods at which they were formed.

More than six hundred feet from the surface, I observed pieces of detached basaltic rocks imbedded in the sandstone, which is entirely sedimentary deposit. For ages upon ages the formation of these beds was going on, and layer on layer was piled up, almost every one of which has a deposit of lava and scoria on its surface, and these are well seen wherever openings or fissures occur.

My opinion is that, at the time of upheaval, the whole mass was in a plastic conglomerate state. This conclusion I have arrived at from the peculiar undulating position in which the stratified layers are found, and that is visible almost everywhere.

Not a fossil or water-mark could I see in the different strata below the surface; but above it were fragments of a white rock, similar to variegated marble, in which lay fossil shells, mostly microscopic. These were evidently compact masses of limestone, probably having undergone a partial metamorphic process. The fossil shells are indefinite in outline, and appear mere patches of white crystalline carbonate of lime, which a few centuries longer of exposure would doubtless leave merely as white veinings or blotches.

The general geological features of Round Island stand as a key, to open out to us the immensity of the periods in which the volcanic action was going on here and at the Mauritius, and are a convincing proof that since these isolated rocks were upheaved an immeasurable interval of time must have elapsed.

Near and round the top and centre of the island are groups of volcanic rocks, many tons in weight, but there is no appearance of any flow of lava. These rocks may have been thrown from some neighbouring volcano, and deposited where they now lie, before the upheaval of the island. There is not the least sign of any depression, or indication of a crater, on the summit. Long after the upheaval of Round Island, volcanic action was still vigorous at Mauritius and in its vicinity. Submarine volcanoes were active, which rose above the sea and were again depressed. The Diamond Rock and others, appearing so near the surface that the waves break over them in the calmest weather, are evidently the tops of very high submerged mountains which were once, in all probability, united to the main-land. At the Table Rock, where we landed, is a flow of lava from the SW., which is filled with detached pieces of scoria, similar to that at the Mauritius, but differing from that in the strata of this island.

The current of lava flowed back against the bold and inaccessible sides of Round Island, cooling in waves, and remaining a silent witness to the wonderful agency at work at that time. Although this current was many feet in thickness, the little bluff or table rock is all that remains of it, as the volcano which furnished it, and the flow of which this is a part, disappeared below the sea.

Islands thus formed by upheaval are likely to disappear as suddenly. Most of them do so after a longer or shorter period, either by being abraded by the constant wash of the waves, or disintegrated by the elements, especially by the chemical action of light, or by their mass sinking into an abyss formed beneath them.

This last circumstance must have happened to one of the

Azores, elevated in 1719, and which disappeared in 1723, leaving in its place a depth of seventy fathoms; and to another island in the same region in 1638, where there is now a fathomless abyss.

The vapour, ashes, and scoria ejected from the volcanoes of Mauritius and its neighbourhood, which continued through all the successive periods of the deposits forming Round Island, as

A FERN.

shown by the sprinkling of them in each layer of the sandstone, must have been dense enough to darken the sun, and intercept the light of day. I do not believe it possible for man to have been a witness of the horrors accompanying the eruptions and convulsions of the early ages of this planet. We have here, I think, another proof of the Divine forethought for man, that the greater part of these terrific convulsions took place before the era of human life—convulsions on so fearful a scale that man could scarcely look on them and live; yet they prepared the earth for him to have his being on it.

We have, occasionally, eruptions and earthquakes awful enough when they do occur; but still even the worst of them, within historic record, are as nothing to what geology teaches must have taken place in the Pre-Adamite world. May they not have been sent as warnings of the instability of even the earth itself?—warnings from the Great Power, 'which removeth the mountains and they know it not, which shaketh the earth out of her place, and the pillars thereof tremble;' and that surely as 'the mountain cometh to nought, and the rock is removed out of its place; as the water wears the stones, and washes away the things that grow out of the dust of the earth,' so even may man's hope be destroyed if he lift not up his heart for help 'from Nature unto Nature's God'?

CHAPTER XII.

MY SECOND VISIT TO ROUND ISLAND.

Invitation—The Voyage—Arrival—Object of Visit—My Share of the Work—Dinner—Departure of the 'Victoria'—*Our* Preparations for the Night, and the *Storm's*—'In Thunder, Lightning, and in Rain'—Our Exodus from the Cave—Night and Morning—Preparations for Breakfast—Entomology under Difficulties—Sail ho!—Homeward bound—In Port Louis at last—Fauna of Round Island—Extracts from Sir H. Barkly's Report.

EARLY in November of 1869, I received an invitation from H. E. Sir H. Barkly to accompany him, with several other gentlemen, to Round Island. This expedition was entirely for scientific purposes, to make collections of the fauna and flora of that island.

The 'witching hour of night' of November 9 saw us all assembled on board the port steamer 'Victoria,' commanded on this special occasion by the superintendent of the mercantile marine. We slowly steamed out of the harbour, the silence of night broken at intervals by the words of command—'port,' 'starboard,' or 'steady,' as the case might be. A very pleasant party His Excellency had assembled on the little craft, where everything had been put in capital order, and his aide-de-camp was untiring in his efforts to make everyone as comfortable as possible.

Merrily, merrily flew our barque
Over the bounding sea.

And though Luna had long retired to rest, the sky was cloudless. Some of us remained aft, smoking, most of the night, indulging in pleasant anticipations of our sojourn on the island, and laying out plans for our work.

We arrived at our destination soon after daylight, dropped anchor, and prepared at once for landing. By this time our cloudless sky had given place to strong indications of rain, and heavy clouds hung over the mountain top. The sea was, however, perfectly smooth, most remarkably so for this quarter, and our landing on the old table rock was effected without difficulty. The present lessee of the island was there, waiting to receive us, and, in honour of the Governor's visit, had previously erected a curious and ingenious landing bridge, in order to avoid the trouble and danger we had formerly experienced. The contrivance answered admirably, and in a short time all were landed, with our scientific apparatus.

We proceeded at once to the cave of former pleasant memories, and, to our surprise, found still the same kindly forethought awaiting us that had designed the bridge. A table was erected, with a supply of excellent *café au lait*, &c., particularly refreshing after our voyage, and to which all did ample justice.

Soon after, we separated into groups, each person with some definite object in view. The Governor, with a small party of assistants, started off botanising; several other gentlemen, shouldering their guns, strode off to wage relentless warfare against the feathered tribes.

While all my friends were thus engaged in the pursuit of scientific knowledge under the most agreeable aspects, I was not idle. I had been entrusted with the zoological department generally, and was determined nothing should escape me. I was well prepared for action, with jars, bottles, and implements of taxidermy, so that specimens could be preserved on the spot. I commenced operations by climbing up the ledges of rocks, and, down on all fours, was soon busy robbing the Fouquets and Pailles-en-queues of their young and eggs, and poking them out of the holes of the rocks with a long stick; thus exciting the ire of the parent birds, which displayed itself in a peculiar sobbing, mournful cry, and by showing fight with beak and wings. Frequently, in routing them out, I met with a different customer, such as a snake, lizard, or spider, all of which were game to my net. The taxidermist at the college was my auxiliary, and the old fellow looked with astonishment as I pulled out the birds without getting bitten. Scattered over the island as we were, our party was enabled to do a great deal in a short space of time. Many curious plants were discovered by the botanists, and I understand one entirely new palm was found by His Excellency.

After exploring the deep gorges, and scrambling up the steep mountain's side, all re-assembled in the cave for rest and refreshment, some notably showing fatigue, arising from being unaccustomed to rough climbing. I had a great advantage there from long habit; for, though I had been on the move all day, I was still fresh, and highly delighted with the additional knowledge I had gained of the island.

Slight showers had fallen in the day; and towards three o'clock there were unmistakable signs of a coming storm, and our captain proposed our leaving at once, not even deeming it prudent to wait for dinner. The latter proposition was, however, negatived, *nem. con.*, and with anxious looks he was obliged to give in; but dinner over, which every one was inclined to make the most of, the excitement about the weather giving a double zest to our viands, our captain would hear of no longer delay, and preparations were quickly made for returning. He declared that if the boat did not soon leave, embarkation would become impossible. About two o'clock my own barometer showed sudden change, and the captain was equally aware of it, and, as an old practical seaman, was anxious not to be caught in such perilous quarters in a storm. I think the whole party may thank his judgment, in hurrying matters, for their all getting off safely.

Not satisfied with my own investigations in the one day, Mr. Vandermeesch and myself, with servants, resolved to remain that night on the island, and ascend to the top of the mountain by daylight next morning, to examine the north side, which I had not been able to do in my first visit.

As the 'Victoria' left, we gave our parting friends three cheers for a safe and speedy homeward passage, to which they heartily responded in good wishes for us; and it was with not a little regret I quitted such pleasant society.

When we had watched the steamer some distance, we all set to work with a will to make preparations for the night at the extremity of the cave described in my first visit.

Provisions and water enough for forty-eight hours had been left us by H. E., and the Surveyor-General's boat, with six men in it, was placed at our disposal, and lay at anchor about half a mile from the shore. Busy as we were, the elements were collecting their forces more energetically still; and at half-past six the sea suddenly began to roll in heavily, and very soon volumes of water ten or twelve feet deep poured over the table rock, where our party had embarked only two hours previously. The wash of the waves swept off our water casks, that were about fifty yards from it, and at an elevation of about twenty-five feet; and they were not long before they surged into the cave, nearly reaching the spot where we stood watching the scene in dismay, and cutting off our retreat.

The captain of the boat, as soon as he saw the sudden change in the weather, raised his anchor and scudded off before the wind, and we soon lost sight of him in the heavy rolling billows.

All efforts now were turned to securing everything as far as was practicable; but the night was well set in before we had finished, and the whole sky was overcast with heavy clouds. The reverberations of the deep rolling thunder made the mountain tremble, and the vivid flashes of lightning occasionally lit up the foaming, seething mass of waters below us, madly dashing against the rocks, the spray thoroughly drenching us.

Then came the rain in a deluge to add to our troubles; and it was not long before the torrents rushing down the mountain poured over the precipice forming the roof to our cave, in a cascade twenty feet wide, bringing with them stones of all sizes, that struck the bottom of the cave with great force, and then bounded off into the sea, now and then giving us a sharp blow. Here we remained, the sea gradually encroaching on our quarters, till we were obliged to crowd in the farthest corners, and hold on to prevent our being washed away. Matters were getting too exciting to be pleasant, and we felt some effort must be made to escape from our perilous position.

The day before, a long rope had been strongly attached to the rock above, and one end was hanging down over the precipice; but unluckily it had been placed on the lowest part, where the heaviest body of water was falling. Fortunately the rope was long, and my comrade emerged from his hiding-place, and, watching his chance, seized the rope, and, holding on like grim death, managed to draw it in, and worked it along away from the cascade, thus succeeding in hitching it over the projecting side of the rock, which showed a perpendicular face about thirty feet high. I never saw anything more bravely done, and at the risk of his life, for, a false step, and nothing could have saved him; as it was, he got a severe contusion on his head and side from a stone striking him.

Nothing daunted, the plucky little fellow, as the smallest and lightest man amongst us, was the first to ascend the rope; and I confess the time we were waiting for the welcome signal of his safe arrival was one of awful suspense, for it was a mere chance if the rope held out, or if he could fight against the wind and driving rain.

At last, to our great joy, above the roar of the elements we heard his welcome 'all right!' I next ascended, and, divested of all but an old blue shirt and trowsers, I grasped the rope and swung on to the projecting cliff, and commenced mounting, hand over hand. It was nervous work, swinging thus in mid air, between life and death, as a slip would have sent me into the yawning gulf below. I was soon high enough to rest my feet on the side of the rock, and could hear my friend urging me on in a voice that seemed to come from the clouds. I felt deeply thankful when I arrived at the top, in spite of my hands and feet being lacerated and bleeding, and my body bruised all over, to say nothing of the loss of the greater part of my unwhisperables. We then managed to get up the four men, fortunately without further accident than bruises and rags similar to our own. I must say the men all behaved well, and showed a resolute spirit to battle with the unpleasant position we were in; and luckily for us, for one coward might have imperilled the lives of all.

It was after midnight, as well as we could guess, when the last man reached the top; and our troubles were far from ended. The rain, thunder, and lightning were incessant, and our foothold was very precarious, and compelled us to hold on to the projections of the rocks. To thoroughly appreciate our position, it should be understood that the mountain here rises at an angle of about sixty degrees, and the sticks and stones rushing down with the torrents of water as they swept by us, added to our bruises, and assisted wofully in the desintegration of our garments.

The roar of the sea was deafening, and every high wave that struck the rock sent its spray over us, high up as we were; and we dared not advance, lest we should fall into one of the gorges that are frequent cn the mountain side, so there was nothing for it but to hold on.

> Pluck and patience must now prevail;
> 'Twas no use quaking and turning pale.

The ocean round us was so white with foam, that as the glare of the lightning revealed it to us it resembled a vast field of billowy snow. Though we were in such a perilous position ourselves, we forgot it momentarily to think of the little boat that lately left, and shuddered to conjecture its possible fate, as no boat built by human hands could have lived in so wild a storm.

There we clung till daylight gradually unfolded our piteous plight—six half-drowned, ragged, and bruised, miserable specimens of humanity, lying face down to the wet rocks, waiting for it to be light enough to grope our way above the reach of the salt spray. But moving was no easy matter, sore and stiff as we were. To add to our troubles, we began painfully to realise that we were without food and water.

The sea still beat against the rocks heavily, but the sky was clear and cloudless; and very welcome we found the cheering rays of the sun. The bridge, erected with so much care, was washed away, as well as the table in the cave where we had so heartily enjoyed our dinner the day before, and everything not swept out of the cave was thoroughly drenched. A fishing net we had used in the afternoon was still safe, and the men managed to drag the pools in the cavities of the rocks, into which numbers of fish had been thrown up in the storm, and captured some; but how to cook them was the question, which was settled by the men collecting dead palm and vacoa leaves, and spreading them out to dry for fire-wood. My friend and I hobbled about in search of Pailles-en-queue eggs and fresh water; the latter unattainable till we got to the summit of the mountain, where we found a pool of rain water, from which a herd of wild goats was drinking. We collected a quantity of eggs, but were at a loss how to carry them, till necessity, stern mother of invention, came to my aid, and, with the help of a leathern strap round my waist, I made a bag of my shirt.

To our great delight on our descent, we found the men had lit a fire with a common tin metal tinder-box, luckily kept shut and dry, and were broiling the fish. Our eggs made a capital *omelette à l'Isle Ronde*, and with a palmiste salad we fared sumptuously. The sun, in the course of the day, dried up everything outside, but our cave was still inaccessible, as the sea had not yet subsided; so we had to look out for sleeping quarters, which we found in a hole high up in the rock. Hard as our bed was, we slept soundly till next morning, in defiance of the cold breeze which played over our rag-covered limbs. By daylight all were up, anxiously gazing round the horizon for a sail, as we hoped our boat had gone to Mapou Bay, and would come for us when the storm was over—but no boat greeted our longing eyes. My hands and feet were so swollen that I could scarcely use them, and my poor friend's eye and face were in a sad state; but we still managed to crawl after more fresh eggs, while the men drew the net again. The sea was sufficiently down for us to enter our cave to collect the few things not washed away; and I was delighted to find that my jars of insects, &c., collected the first day, and which I had wedged in a crevice of the rock, were still intact. Near my sleeping berth that was to have been I found a good-sized snake, and, a little higher up, a large scorpion over four inches in length, both driven in by stress of weather. One of the men brought me a five-inch-long centipede in his bare hand, and was about to break off the mandibles, when I begged for the specimen entire. Afterwards I saw many that had been carried down the side of the mountain in the streams.

Time hung heavily with us, which it certainly would not have done but for our disabled state, so we selected a nice cool place, and lay down to rest our weary bones; exploring was out of the question. We had made up our minds we should have to remain for some days, so determined to make the best of it. We had found a place where a cliff projects over a gully, and where, in the absence of rain, we could make a comfortable sleeping-place—barring the snakes, lizards, and centipedes; and here we lay, snugly ensconced in our holes, with a full view of the ocean.

About two o'clock, a fishing-boat was seen to the north of us, and we tried to attract attention by hoisting a flag made of one of our ragged garments. They soon saw us, but were afraid to come close in; yet, after some pressing, they consented to take one of us who would spring off the rock into the boat, it being too rough to allow it to touch. I proposed that my friend should go and leave me with the men, but he said he preferred remaining to see what he could save; and besides, he wanted to come direct to Port Louis, and the men would only go to Mapou. There was no time to lose, so, wishing my brave comrade good-bye, and promising to send him relief as soon as possible, I watched my chance as the waves receded, and sprang to the deck of the boat, but came down with such a shock that I should have pitched head first but for the skipper's catching me in his brawny arms. The boat headed for Mapou, where I landed about six o'clock, barefooted, coatless, and ragged, and was obliged to take refuge in a Chinaman's shop from the wondering gaze of all the coloured ladies of the village! After buying a loaf and box of sardines, I was glad to hide myself in a carriole and start for the city, thankful that the moon had not yet risen.

On my arrival at Port Louis, I learnt that the Surveyor-General's boat had not returned. I at once sent off the carriole man with instructions to the fishermen to leave by daylight in the morning to fetch the rest of the party, and I had the pleasure of seeing my friend safely (if not soundly) back on Sunday.

On the night of our adventure, our boat was carried out to sea, and it was only with the greatest skill and care it had been kept afloat in the storm; and it was not till two days later that the captain was enabled to reach Mapou Bay, with all hands safe.

I should state that the 'Victoria' steamer had great difficulty in reaching the harbour safely, on account of the high wind, and heavy sea and intense darkness. The atmosphere was also so fully charged with electricity that the compasses were seriously affected by it.

When I came to examine the various specimens of natural history I had collected in my two visits to Round Island, I found them most interesting.

I had four distinct species of lizards,[1] one of which was over a foot in length, mottled gray on the back, white on the belly and feet, and excessively plump and clumsy, and which bears the

[1] As I then thought, from their varied size and colours

name of *Scincus Telfairii.* I met with it in almost every part of the island, and very tame; so much so that it was easily captured. It was difficult, however, to get a perfect specimen, on account of the animal throwing off its tail when handled—a peculiarity of this genus. It had a curious jerking motion, running a little way, and then stopping abruptly.

The second in size which I captured was about six inches in length; it is a pretty active little creature, generally found in the steep rocks on the sides of the mountain, but not so numerous as the first-mentioned. These lizards deposit from six to twelve white eggs, the size of an ounce musket-ball, in a row on the branches of the *Latania glaucophylla*, which I could not detach without breaking, so firmly were they glued to the bark. I believe this lizard is as yet undescribed.

The third species, the *Scincus Bojerii*, is very small, of a dark colour, with light stripes across the back. This is very active, and with difficulty captured: it was, however, numerous though shy. I looked in vain for the eggs of this lizard, as well as for those of the *Telfairii*, turning over stones and heaps of cacoa leaves without success. This lizard is the same as the one so common in Mauritius (*Platydactylus Cepedianus*).

The fourth lizard is about four inches in length, slender and active, darting about in every direction, but not easily caught. Its colour was dark olive, with longitudinal light stripes. This is the *Scincus Boutonii.*

These Scinci, with the exception of the *Bajerii* and Platydactylus, I have never seen in Mauritius, nor do I think they exist here.

I mentioned having found one species of snake in my first visit, but in my second exploration I obtained four other different snakes; one of them about four feet in length, and six inches in circumference. Another small serpent reared and flattened its head so much that I concluded it was poisonous. It was very pugnacious and bold. At that time, however, I had lost my glass, and could not examine its teeth; but later inspection induced me to believe it was also a Colubra, and harmless. Unlike any other snake that I know, it glides with extreme rapidity over the ground, with its head elevated.

Mauritius might well have been visited by the Irish saint; for not any snake has ever been known here, as native, which makes it so remarkable when they are so very abundant in a little island within twenty-five miles of it.

I was fortunate enough to find a great number of Gasteropoda of the genus Cyclostoma, which bear the name, I believe, of the Chœmiostoma; and it is not found anywhere else in the known world, except at Flat, and perhaps at Serpent Islands. It has a red mouth, and is twice the size of the *C. Lesteri*, found at Mauritius.

I took several species of spiders. The largest were, I think, of the genus Phryne, noted for the excessive tenuity of the anterior feet, flattened bodies, and palpi resembling feet terminating in claws, and bearing a resemblance to scorpions deprived of their tails. This genus is, I believe, principally known in America, Seychelles, and the East Indies, but I know nothing like it in Mauritius.

In the 'Dictionnaire des Sciences naturelles,' at p. 56, is figured a *Phryne reniforme*, resembling the Round Island spiders, except in the termination of the palpi. The latter end in two long forked spines, and three short simple ones, exclusive of the sharply-pointed claw; and the palpi are of a uniform thickness, and covered with short bristly spines: whereas the *Phryne reniforme* has the palpi small at the base, but increasing in bulk to the claw, and edged with a fringe of long spines. M. Vinson, who has written a large work on the 'Mascarene Arachnids,' does not even mention the genus.

One spider very much resembles the Mauritian *Olios leucosa* in form, colour, and manner of holding its egg-bag; another has the silver bands on the body, very similar to the *Epeira Mauritia* (Vinson); and one is, I think, very similar to the genus Thomisus (Duméril), but I do not recollect meeting with it in Mauritius.

On the broken leaves of the cacao I saw a number of small scorpions, two of which I caught. They seem entirely different from those in the main island, or from specimens I have seen from the rest of the Mascarene group or the East Indies.

On my first visit to Round Island I captured a scorpion of a bright green, just the colour of the leaves of the Jubæa palm it was disporting on. The creature was very active and defiant, and it was with difficulty I caught him. The length of tail is remarkable compared with all the others. I think it must be rare, as I diligently searched for it during my second visit, but without success. Though I failed to find another green one, I came upon a formidable and ugly-looking animal—a third species of scorpion. It appears to be common in the crevices of the rocks, and under the stones round the summit of the mountain. It is most pugnacious, and, when headed off from its retreat, shows fight by raising the palpi, and clapping them together, making a clicking noise like a crab.

This scorpion measured 8½ inches from the tip of the palpi to the tail. The palpi measure 3¾ inches in length, and are 1¾ in circumference. The body and legs are brown, and the palpi black. I tried hard to capture another that was running off very fast over the stones, with what I took to be a *Scincus Boutonii* in its claws.

I have examined some specimens of scorpions in the Museum, but I can find nothing exactly like the large Round Island one.

Centipedes abounded. The large one I got from one of the men had its full complement of legs, namely, twenty-one pairs, giving forty-two feet. It is, I believe, the *Scolopendre mordante* of Duméril (*Scolopendra morsitans* of Linnæus). It appears to me to differ from the Mauritian centipedes, but resembles some I have seen from Rodrigues and the East Indies.

During my visit in 1868 I caught a singular bee on the flowers of the *Ipomœa maritima.* Its general colour was a deep crimson, striated on the body with bright yellow. There are many specimens of bees in the Museum from different parts of the world, but I could find none resembling it in colour and markings.

I saw only one dragon-fly on the island—a common Libellula in Mauritius. It is very possible this may have been blown from the main island, as it is an insect of such strong and rapid flight.

I captured a Gryllus somewhat resembling the *Truxalles nasus* of Duméril, but it has the tail-like appendages of the locust, and much finer antennæ. The common male cricket (*Gryllotalpa vulgaris*) is numerous, and just like the Mauritian one, which is indigenous here.

The 'dry-stick' insect, or Phasma, is common at Round Island. The nearest approach I can find to two I caught is the *Phasma géant* of Duméril, though in this species the tubercles on the corselet are very prominent in five pairs, and there are two pairs on the thorax. In those from Round Island the tubercles are very numerous, and almost microscopically small, extending nearly over the whole back to the abdominal extremity, where the appendages are marked differently to the Mauritius one. Two other Phasmas I procured I at first took to be of different species, as they varied so greatly in colour—one was of a bright green, and one a brown; but on careful examination later, I concluded that they were the same. I presume the diversity of colour may be owing to the difference of age or sex, or probably from the peculiar food it might have partaken of when in the larva state, which is well known to affect other insects. I see that the Governor, in his report, mentions that this change of colour is not uncommon in this genus, as Cuvier, speaking of the *Phasma rossia*, from the south of France, says it is either of a yellow green or greyish brown.

I have compared my Round Island specimens of Phasmas with twenty-seven others in the Museum, but all differ essentially. I got a number of Coleoptera, one only resembling those at the Mauritius, which, though in form like the Round Island one, and the marks on the elytra are the same, the white spots on the abdomen are wanting; a small black beetle whose name I do not know; and one brown beetle, about 1½ inch in length, tubercled all over—but I can find neither figure nor description of it, nor do I think it is in Mauritius.

I have no doubt but for the untoward weather I should have added considerably to my specimens. What I did procure and have noted may be of assistance to future explorers in the lesser Mascarene Islands, about which, in the scientific world, a good deal of interest appears to be felt.

Extracts from Sir H. Barkly's Report on Round Island, delivered before the Members of the Royal Society of Arts and Sciences, Dec. 15. 1869 :—

'The number of plants collected by us at Round Island, exclusive of two sea-weeds, *Sargazzum vulgare* (?), and *Conospora fastigiata* (?), common, I believe, to the coast of Mauritius, was twenty-nine, comprising specimens of the following natural orders :—

ACROGENS.	Musci	1	
	Lycopodiaceæ	1	
	Filices	1	
		—	3
ENDOGENS.	Graminaceæ	5	
	Cyperaceæ	1	
	Pandanaceæ	2	
	Palmaceæ	3	
	Liliaceæ	1	
		—	12
EXOGENS.	Ebenaceæ	3	
	Asclepiadaceæ	2	
	Convolvulaceæ	1	
	Myrsinaceæ	1	
	Asteraceæ	2	
	Combretaceæ	1	
	Myrtaceæ	1	
	Cinchonaceæ	2	
	Homaliaceæ	1	
		—	14
			29

'The first point in the above list which attracts attention is the very large proportion borne by Endogens, or internally growing, to Exogens, or externally growing plants. Humboldt quotes approvingly the estimate of Robert Brown, that in the tropics Monocotyledons, which represent the former, are in the ratio of one to five to Dicotyledons—synonymous with the latter—whilst we see above that they are at Round Island as twelve to fourteen, or more than four times more numerous. Again, in a recently published Flora of the Sandwich Islands, out of the 554 flowering plants, 75 belong to the Monocotyledons, and 479 to Dicotyledons, showing the former to be less than a seventh of the whole! This feature becomes the more prominent when we find, on further examination, that whilst the Endogens differ so much that few, if any of them, can have been recently derived from Mauritius, several of the Exogens are identical with those of this island; some, too, in all probability, having been introduced into both from foreign countries.

'With a view to a closer appreciation of genera and species than I could otherwise have ventured on, Mr. Horne has been good enough to compare the whole of our specimens with those in the Colonial Herbarium, which was removed about a year ago from the Royal College to a building in the Botanic

Gardens at Pamplemousses. I annex Mr. Horne's observations upon each, with which mine will be found in most cases, in the following portions of this paper, to accord.

'To begin with the three orders of Cryptogams, each represented by a single individual, I can say little as to the moss even by way of comparison, the family being omitted altogether in the "Hortus Mauritianus," and no classification, so far as I am aware, of the Mascarene species having ever been made. I presume it to be a Sphagnum,[1] apparently differing but little from some which may be seen on trees in this island.

'The Lycopod belongs to the section Selaginella, and is probably new. I took it at the time for a dwarfed form of the common Mauritian *P. S. concinna*, but gave up the idea on looking over my specimens, with none of which it could be identified. It may, however, perhaps, be Bojer's *S. mnioides*, with which I am unacquainted, no specimen having been left by him.

'The fern is *Adiantum caudatum*, a wide-spread fern, found in Mauritius and most other islands of the Mascarene group. I may, however, remark in passing, that its habit at Round Island is so much changed, especially in the young stage, that I could scarcely at first recognise it.

'Turning next to the flowering plants, and commencing with the Monocotyledons, or those having one-lobed seeds, we have five grasses composing the scanty herbage of the islet. Strange to say, that which is most common, growing on tufts amongst the trees at the summit, appears identical with the Indian Citronelle, or Lemon-grass, *Andropogon* or *Cymbopogon Schœnanthus* of Bojer; who, however, distinctly states it not to be a native of Mauritius, nor can it even to this day be said to be naturalised here. Unluckily, the specimens brought away have been lost. The next grass, No. 5, of Mr. Horne, is not to be found in the Royal College Herbarium, and is supposed by him to be new.

'The third, numbered 7, is the Cynodon, mentioned by Colonel Pike; and we all, judging from its mode of growth, referred it to that genus; but it will be seen to differ totally from the Chien-Dent, or Petit Chien-Dent, so common here.

[1] I believe it is the *Hypnus acicularis*, Linn.

Of Mr. Horne's number 8 only a single imperfect specimen was obtained, which has been sent to Dr. Hooker, at Kew, unidentified with any in the Herbarium.

'The single Sedge, on the other hand, appears to be *Cyperus maritimus*, common to Mauritius.

'Proceeding next to plants of more perfect structure, having two-lobed seeds, we find that Round Island possesses three Ebonies resembling severally the Mauritian species *Diospyros pterocalyx*, *melanida*, and *chrysophyllus*. Their growth, however, like that of all the hard-wood trees, is stunted, and their branches gnarled and twisted. This is due probably to the wind, for there seems a sufficient depth of vegetable mould to enable them to grow more luxuriantly.

'Two trailing Asclepiads, with inconspicuous flowers, festoon the rocky surface of the islet in many places. One Mr. Horne identifies with the Sylophora (*Asclepias asthmatica*) of the Royal College Herbarium, which, however, is given by Bojer as a "Ceylon species cultivated in gardens principally by the Indians;" no doubt as a drug, since Dr. Roxburgh declares it to be one of the most valuable medicines in India. The second was originally regarded by Mr. Horne as a Periploca, possibly Mauritian, the "Spéca du Pays;" but he has since considered it to belong to another foreign section of the family, the Streptocaulon, on the authority of the late Dr. Meller, who thus classed a plant growing at Curepipe which it strongly resembles, though of a much stouter habit in every respect, as will be seen by comparison.

'Possibly, as the genus has downy seeds, both these Asclepiads have been conveyed to Round Island by the wind. Such may have been the case with the "Goatsfoot Convolvulus," *Ipomœa maritima*, common to most parts of the world.

'The Myrsinaceæ or Ardisiaceæ are represented at Round Island by a small tree, according to Mr. Horne, near the *Badula ovalifolia*, a Mauritian species, of which there is, however, no specimen in the Royal College Herbarium.

'Of the Asteraceæ, or composite-flowered plants, are found two, both evidently introduced. First, a species of Sonchus or European sow-thistle; not, however, the 'Laiteron,' so common here and all over the world, but a smaller and more prickly sort, which grows on Flat Island. Secondly, in large quantities, though mostly dead from the drought, an Ageratum, an American genus not mentioned in the "Hortus Mauritianus," but which has of late years run wild in the cane-fields and near old clearings in the forest, having probably spread from the Botanical Gardens, where Mr. Duncan gives, among the flowers cultivated, *A. conyzoides*, which I find from gardening-books has the light grey flowers of the one so common here.

'In the next order, Combretaceæ, there is a Terminalia; no doubt the one Colonel Lloyd meant when speaking of "Bois Benzoin," the name given to the species indigenous to Mauritius, from the wood being used for incense; but from which, as well as from all other Mascarene species found by us at Round Island, it widely differs, as will be seen by the specimens being more nearly allied, according to Mr. Horne, to the Indian Terminalias, though probably new and undescribed.

'The only three trees seen—although the trunk of the largest was not above four feet in height and eighteen inches in diameter—had great lateral expansion, their branches extending horizontally between five and twenty to thirty feet.

'Among plants allied to the Myrtle we found only a *Sossinia*, forming a small shrubby tree varying from six to ten feet in height, the leaves of which do not agree with those of any of the genera in the Royal College Herbarium, and which is probably therefore also new.

'Of the Chinchona family there were two: the first and commonest we at once pronounced to be the *Ternelia buxifolia* of this island, which it much resembles. The second, a Pyrostria, said by Mr. Horne to be nearer to *P. polymorphia* than to anything else in the Royal College Herbarium. The only other dicotyledonous plant observed by us was a small tree about twelve feet in height, somewhat resembling the Mauritian genus Blackwellia, belonging to the Homalineæ, but which Mr. Horne cannot trace to any known species.

'We saw no signs of the "Veloutiers" mentioned, I think, both by Colonel Lloyd and by Colonel Pike, though there seems a strong presumption in favour of their having existed, seeing that, according to Bojer, one of the commonest kinds here, *Scævola Plumierii*, is known as "Veloutier de l'Isle Platte."

'Having thus completed a description of the scanty Flora of Round Island, I must at once guard against a most incorrect idea as to the general character of its vegetation, which might be drawn from the bare enumeration of genera and species, by pointing out that if the number of individuals be taken into account, the Exogens are totally overwhelmed by the Endogenous plants.

'Taken as a whole, its Flora is no doubt essentially Mascarene, nay, even Mauritian, as far as genera are concerned; but the species, both in Endogens and Exogens, are frequently peculiar; and, as may be gathered from Mr. Horne's remarks, even when in all probability identical, varying more or less from the typical Mauritian standard.'

Since this chapter was completed, a letter has been received, by the Secretary of the Royal Society of Arts and Sciences, from Sir H. Barkly; and, as it has been already made public, I quote some passages from it relating especially to Round Island.

He says, 'The *Palmiste gargoulette*, Dr. Hooker has at last satisfied himself, is the *Hyophorbe amaricaulis* of Van Martius and others, the habitat of which has never been previously clearly ascertained.

'With respect to the Fauna, Dr. Günther refers all the snakes to one species (the difference in size and colour being due to age or sex), as it was furnished forty or fifty years ago from a head in the Paris Museum, but of which no other or perfect specimen was known, *Leptolon Dussumierii*. Dr. Günther will soon contribute a complete description of it to the Zoological Society, and it will be figured in the "Proceedings." The lizards are reduced to two, many of the specimens being different ages and sexes of *Scincus Telfairii*, which was first described from Madagascar under the name of *Leopopis Ballia*. The small lizards, both in spirits, and preserved by Colonel Pike, are the *Gongylus Bojerii*, previously sent home by Mr. Newton. Though the number of Round Island reptiles is thus more limited than I at first supposed, yet two curious features still remain. It has a genus of snakes of which no other species is known, and whose nearest congener, Dr. Günther considers, is only found in the Loyalty Islands in the South Seas; and its ordinary lizard is peculiar to its own shores and to distant Madagascar, and does not exist either in Mauritius or Bourbon, close by.

'Pray tell Colonel Pike I purpose writing to him, directly I get out to the Cape, about the insects, most of which are new.'

CHAPTER XIII.

A CHINESE FESTIVAL.

Preparations—Joss—Description of Temple—Ceremonies—Gambling—Opera—Pantomime.

At the Salines, not far from the artillery barracks, the Chinese have purchased about an acre of ground, and erected in the middle of it a good-sized building of stone, with numerous small dependencies round it. These are all dedicated to Joss, and once a year there is a general gathering of all the Celestials in the city. Lesser ones take place frequently, but these are principally for gambling.

For some weeks before this festival active preparations go on amongst the small-eyed but sharp-sighted Chinamen, on a grand scale, for a good time.

Pigs and poultry are in great requisition, and the night before all the cooks are in their glory ; and a queer sight it is to watch them, with their skinny, dirty, yellow forms, hovering over the seething pots. Pigs, when not too large, are frequently roasted whole, and ducks and fowls are in abundance ; so that the savour of the viands is very appetising, or would be, but for a subtle odour of opium diffused over the whole place. Rice is cooked in every conceivable form, and curious suspicious-looking vegetables are in piles ; fruits, and everything that can tempt a Chinese palate.

John Chinaman is generally the most economical of men, frugal to a proverb ; but on the occasion of this gala day he spares no expense. Every carriage and carriole to be had is engaged for transport to the festive scene. Very jaunty, too, the young Celestials look in the scrupulously clean and generally new costume for the day, one very noticeable feature of which is the whitest of stockings and brightest of varnished leather shoes.

The road to the Salines swarms with merry groups, all wending their way to the Joss-house, which has been thoroughly cleaned. Joss himself is regilt ; inside and out all is furbished up, and scores of little tables are placed outside, which are loaded with provisions. Gongs and cymbals make a deafening din, and jollity reigns supreme, for the demon of gambling has not yet made its appearance.

The room that Joss occupies is hung round with banners bearing all sorts of Chinese characters, and long scrolls of paper each with some wise saying written on it. Joss is a large wooden figure about ten feet high, sitting cross-legged on an elevated platform, surrounded by little silk or satin flags with curious devices on them. The whole place is decorated with bouquets, and on a table before the Joss are large vases filled with artificial flowers.

Candles highly ornamented are sold to the devout ; and at the time I was present they were being offered to him with dishes of meat and rice, till he was the centre of an illumination. Instead of these being offerings to a god, as I at first supposed, I found that Joss represents the devil !

The Chinese say God is always good and kind, and watchful for man's benefit, therefore does not need propitiation. It is the devil who is always seeking to do harm, to whom all these presents were made in order to please him, and make him their friend.

Early on the day of the feast a procession is formed, banners are borne aloft, gongs and cymbals clanged on all sides ; and each Chinaman, bearing a bowl of rice, passes with slow and steady step before Joss, invoking his friendship. After this is over the feasting takes place ; and then comes the serious business of the day, the real attraction to the greater part of those assembled—viz. the gambling and opium-smoking.

Opening out of the Joss-room is a small apartment with several bunks in it, and seats, always filled with stupefied wretches almost insensible from the quantities of opium inhaled from the long-stemmed pipes lying at their sides. The room is filled with dense smoke from the noxious drug.

The front, or principal room, is a very large one ; paintings decorate its walls, and a number of very handsome Chinese lanterns are suspended from the ceiling. Long rows of small tables are on each side—a crowd round every one of them. At the foot of every table sits a pale, hollow-eyed, cadaverous-looking individual, with a countenance so perfectly expressionless, he might be a statue, but for the few words that drop from his lips of stone, and proclaim his profession—gambler.

In front of him lies a quantity of copper cash, or round coins with holes in them, a tea-cup, and two small pieces of wood like Joss-sticks.

In the middle of the table is a board; on it are marked squares with Chinese characters, and at the sides of the board are slips of paper, with corresponding numbers upon them. The person who wishes to bet takes one of the numbered slips of paper, and places it on the same figure on the board. For instance, if he puts one dollar on number six, he can double it by covering it with a corresponding number. The board is filled with the slips of paper, and when all is ready the keeper of the bank removes from the pile of cash as many as he can cover with the tea-cup. They are shuffled about under the cup for a minute; it is then raised, and the cash carefully removed one by one with the thin sticks and counted. Should it come out an even number, all who have betted on even numbers win and the rest lose.

The room is generally filled to overflowing. I have seen from six to eight hundred gambling at one time in it. Silence profound reigns from one end of the place to the other, all intently watching the game.

I have carefully studied their countenances, but could not judge from them who won or lost. The same stolid look on every face, not a muscle moved. Sometimes after losing his ready cash, a Chinaman will stake his whole stock and trade—and lose. I remember an instance of this reckless gambling mania. A shop close to my house was owned by a very respectable Chinaman, a quiet fellow, who had his place well stocked with groceries, wines, &c., and owned one assistant, a boy of about twenty, as quiet and steady as his master.

For a few days his shop was shut, much to the inconvenience of his neighbours; and on enquiry, I found it was the annual festival, and both master and man had attended it. At length Mr. Lung-Fo re-opened, but, to every one's astonishment, he was busy sweeping out his shop, and weighing out charcoal and lard to the customers, while the youngster sat leisurely smoking and making up the day-books. It appeared they had been gambling from the time they left home. Lung-Fo had lost to his servant all his money, his whole stock and house; and then having nothing more, he wagered himself, and if he lost he was to be servant to the other—and he did lose. But there was no appearance of triumph on the boy's face; master and servant reversed their places with the most perfect sangfroid.

This is no uncommon case; but though numbers are constantly reduced to beggary, as soon as they are in that condition they set steadily to work again, and will earn before the next festival the wherewithal to induce Fortune to turn her wheel once more in their favour.

Adjoining the gambling-room is another, set apart for theatrical performances. One or more are sure to take place at this season, though generally it is only a continuation of one piece during several days.

I was fortunate enough to be present at a first-class opera, and all the Celestial talent in the country was in request. It was written by Mr. Ahong, a doctor and opium-dealer in the country; and the music was composed by Mr. Ching-tang, a dealer in snook and cocoa-nut oil in Port Louis.

The opera was of the dramatic order, the scene laid in Pekin, and the following were the *dramatis personæ*:—

Mr. Chow Chow, a student, son of a mandarin.

Pluchow, servant to the above.

Mr. Ahow, a rich mandarin, guardian of Miss Chin Sing.

Mr. Oulong, secretary to Ahow.

Miss Chin Sing, niece to Ahow.

Mr. Chow Chow, a young gentleman already deeply learned in all the lore of Confucius, occasionally pays a visit to Mr. Ahow, his father's friend, and there he meets the moon-faced Miss Chin Sing; and as philosophy has not closed either eyes or heart, he falls over head and ears in love at first sight (a thing not quite unknown among the barbarians of the West). He discovers from the elegant little feet, covered with the tiniest of jewelled slippers, that twinkle in and out from under her rich garments, that she is of rank, and that it is useless for him to aspire to her hand. She is jealously watched by Ahow; but when did an old guardian stop a young lover from finding means to impart his passion.

Pluchow, his faithful servant, manages to convey any number of letters to her, to all of which she replied in the elegant bouquets that silently express so much to the Chinese heart. She also contrives to let him know that her uncle has promised her hand to Oulong, in return for sundry services by which he has been able to enrich himself at the barbarian's expense. Poor Chow Chow is in such despair at this intelligence, that he threatens to commit suicide if his lady-love will not consent to elope with him.

She intimates she is willing. But just as all is arranged, the plot is discovered, Pluchow bastinadoed, and Miss Chin Sing locked up in the topmost room of the house. But love laughs at locksmiths ; and as her place of confinement overlooks a large garden, shaded with immense trees, Chow Chow contrives to converse with her from the top of a golden apple-tree, and flings her a silken cord, with which she manages to descend into his arms.

As soon as Ahow discovers his loss, he kills himself from shame at the disgrace ; Oulong follows suit, and the lovers are happy ever after.

The orchestra consisted of two gongs, two triangles, two Chinese fiddles, four cymbals, two guitars, and two kettle-drums. The opera commences with an overture, which resembled a grand crockery crash—which made me start, but greatly pleased the audience.

After two or three of these crockery-smashing crashes, a faint tinkling sound of a fiddle and triangle was heard, and scene first commenced.

Miss Chin Sing waddles across the stage, and prepares to arrange her toilet. Paints, powder, pomades, and twenty-four brushes are brought in by her maids, and her hair was soon arranged *à la théière*, and a dozen little gilt sticks, and a bunch of flowers, were stuck all over it. She looked quite gay and festive, and all the time the operation was going on she was singing a love-song in a delicate falsetto.

Scene No. 2.

Miss Chin Sing and Pluchow.

The latter unrolls a letter a yard in length from his master, which she covers with kisses.

The duet in this scene was most ridiculous—both voices in a weak falsetto, with singular gesticulations ; and whenever they stopped, a crash fit to make a nervous man's hair stand on end would ensue, a little fiddling, and a blow or two on the kettle-drums, as a sort of variation, evidently to the great delight of the Celestials present, who sat as still as so many children, with upturned eyes fixed on the scene.

Scene No. 3.

Mr. Ahow enters, in the full dress of a wealthy mandarin, his pigtail hanging to his feet, adorned with gold thread and lace. The old fellow struts across the stage, giving orders to his numerous servants, who bow humbly before him. Miss Chin Sing is sent for, and severely reprimanded, and sent weeping away. Chow Chow enters singing; but Ahow, puffing himself up into even greater dignity than before, a low earnest duet follows, and then both leave the stage, holding paper handkerchiefs to their faces to dry up their tears.

Scene No. 4.

Garden at night. Miss Chin Sing at an open window, Chow Chow perched on the top of a tree. He throws her a cord, and she throws herself into his arms, and he carries her off, it being impossible such tiny feet could walk. An interval of ten minutes was allowed; and all withdrew to take a whiff of opium or tobacco and a cup of tea, which was served in a side room, in the smallest of cups.

Scene No. 5.

Old Ahow and Oulong appear with the police and servants. The direst confusion ensues : everyone rushes about, and everybody sings something on his own hook, quite regardless of his neighbour's tune. Gongs clashed, drums beat, and the spectators clapped their hands in ecstasy. Ahow stalks about, supplies swords to all, and rushes off, vowing vengeance to the missing couple.

Scene No. 6.

Mr. and Mrs. Chow Chow are discovered in an arbour, drinking tea, and billing and cooing like two turtle-doves. A pretty little duet is sung, accompanied by a sort of mandoline [1] and a fiddle. The most plaintive of ditties in the faintest of voices, but all falsetto. While the happy couple are so blissfully engaged, Ahow and Oulong appear, and after a shower of reproaches, and just when they seem about to immolate the lovers, they change their minds. Ahow rushes on Oulong's sword and dies, and Oulong jumps out of a window and drowns himself. This does not at all distract the others; they merely walk off, looking very happy. The play is continued through the whole of their married life, but I did not go to see the other acts.

In the rear of the Joss-house a large stage was erected, intended for a pantomime performance at night. It was dimly lighted by pieces of cloth dipped in flat dishes of cocoa-nut oil, and set fire to—a very primitive sort of torch. There is a low covered house at the back of the stage, to conceal the actors. The stage is lined up each side by rows of Chinamen, and crowds stand round it.

A curious beast issues from the covered den, said to be the pet lion of Joss. I doubt if Cuvier ever even dreamt of such a specimen of the *Felis Leo.*

It dashes round the stage, its monster eyes glaring and mouth wide open, to the terror of the youngsters. It is about twelve feet long, by five or six feet high. It is covered with cloth to imitate skin; one man under the shoulders to work the head, and one under the tail; the undulations of the body being most eccentric. I pity the poor fellow who *personated* the tail, the peculiar jerk of which was inimitable, as he had to scamper after the mad leapings of the head. Head seats himself on a table, and eats grass; but by when tail has gathered up the long body and hopes for a rest, off rushes head to the

[1] These instruments are not at all like their European namesakes, but have some pretty soft notes when not accompanied by the gongs, &c.

farther end of the stage, poor tail tumbling off the table as he best can. Head sits down and eats fire, grins and bows; tail waggles all the time, keeping the spectators in a roar. The same thing is repeated over and over for hours, and still a sea of upturned faces surrounds the stage.

The Celestial Empire may boast of being the oldest under the sun, its wise men excelling in literature, its mechanics in skill; but, save in the art of making money, all the Celestials I have seen are yet in the lowest depths of ignorance and superstition, though as easily amused as children, and perhaps more harmless than the denizens of the West under a similar condition; at least, they are so here, where of course they are amenable to British law

CHAPTER XIV.

AN EXCURSION UP THE POUCE MOUNTAIN.

Early Morning—Begin our Ascent—Cardinal's Nest—Old Forts—Tunnel under the Pouce—The Shoulder—The Summit—Ferns—View—Entomology of the Mountain—Descent—Echo—Notes on different Ascents of the Peter Both Mountain.

On a fresh clear morning in June, I set off for a trip up to the top of the Pouce. I left my residence at daybreak with my Indian Bopchia, to carry my vasculum and the wherewithal to replenish the inner man. Passing through the still darkened though far from silent streets of Port Louis, where milkmen were shrieking 'du lait' at every corner, and produce-carts arriving from the country, I hurried on, hoping to be able to reach the shoulder of the mountain before the sun was high enough to render climbing unpleasantly hot work. I was soon joined by three friends—a Scotch engineer, a barrister-at-law, and a member of the press, all eager and ready for the ascent.

After traversing a filthy noisy Malabar camp above the Champ de Lort, our route lay through a large Mango grove, and down a ravine, where we crossed a limpid brook murmuring over the rocks, and began our ascent through a wilderness of the red and yellow-flowered Mimosas that filled the air with delicious fragrance, doubly grateful to our senses after the odours of the camp we had left. There had been copious showers in the night, which had thoroughly wetted the long rank grass, and our extremities were soon particularly 'moist and unpleasant.'

A small bird here flew across our path, and attracted my attention by its plantive cries. It was a female Cardinal, *Fouclia Madagascarensis*, which we disturbed from two pretty pale-blue eggs in a nest made of fine soft grass, neatly fastened to a branch by threads of cotton, which she had secured in her search for material for the home of her little ones; and the feathered ends were extended and crossed over the entrance, forming a shady archway to protect it from the rain.

We soon entered the old military road constructed by the French, but now so overgrown with long grass and shrubs as to be very troublesome to the pedestrian excursionist. By Elliot's barometer we were now 800 feet above the level of the sea. The view from this point is unobstructed by trees, and the whole city lay like a map before us. Passing through a dense growth of underwood and over loose rocks, we soon gained a height of 1,200 feet. Here on our right rose the bold side of the mountain, almost perpendicularly for 1,100 feet, the little scattered spots of verdure on it sparkling in the morning sun. Ferns now began to appear: the *Nephrolepis acuta* waved its graceful fronds on every side of us; the *Polypodium phymatodes* was abundant amongst the rocks, and the breeze was perfumed with the wild jessamine, which ranks over all the tall shrubs.

About 150 feet from the base of this mountain cliff, an excavation was made in its side of about 20 feet deep by 50 wide, with the view of making a tunnel for conveying water from the Moka river into Port Louis. A survey was made, in 1852, by the Surveyor-general and civil engineer, and it was expected that the undertaking would conduce greatly to the general welfare of the city and its neighbourhood.

It would also have served as a means of transit through the country, and have given the farmers an opportunity of conveying their produce to market, it being not only intended for a water way, but for foot and carriage passengers, to shorten the distance between Moka and the city.

The strata through which the tunnel was to pass is basaltic rock, easily worked. It was supposed a large quantity of valuable stone would have been extracted, suitable for public works, and when sold would have contributed towards defraying the expenses of the undertaking.

It was calculated the tunnel would be 816 yards long, and that 49,264 cubic feet of stone would be quarried out of it, and easily sent down by tramway to the Champ de Lort, for sale for building purposes. It was recommended that this should be done by the worst class of condemned prisoners out of Port Louis jail, as a proper mode of punishment for such criminals. The estimated expense of the whole was about 60,000 dollars. Like many another scheme in Mauritius it came to nought, and the hole in the rock is all that remains to tell the tale.

On reaching the shoulder we came to a large open space, formerly cultivated, but devoid of trees and shrubs except here and there a few clumps of aloes. A purling brook, clear as crystal, from which we refreshed ourselves, runs down the side of a footpath, leading round the west of the shoulder. Its banks are thickly set with the pretty *Odontosoria tenuifolia* and several species of Nephrodiums, whilst the most luxuriant mosses abound, and the ground is strewn with dead Pupa shells.

Amongst the mosses I gathered here and higher up are specimens of the *Polytrichum commune*, many of the stalks from seven to eight inches long; but I only found a single flower, as I was nearly two months too early for its flowering season. The *Hypnum brevirostrum* and *aciculare* were most abundant, and constantly with them is a very pretty species of Jungermannia. The curious *Macronitum subtortum*, that looks as if it was threaded on long strings, with its bright orange-pointed fairy caps for flowers, grows sparsely here, but I have seen it in large tufts at Curepipe. The *Metzgeria furcata* and three species of Dicranum were also amongst my treasures.

Our route was soon impeded by a deep gorge of recent formation. We were told it was formed in 1865 by a large waterspout bursting over this spot, carrying away immense quantities of earth and stones, and sweeping everything before it. Long will it be ere the recollection dies away of that terrible night, when the torrents descended from the mountain, swelling every stream into a roaring river in Port Louis and its vicinity; and, without a moment's warning, inundating all the lower parts of the city and causing terrible destruction of life and property.

We crossed the gorge with difficulty, as a strong stream gushed out of the cliff, at least twenty feet above the surface of the earth, from some subterranean source. Farther up, facing the north, and commanding the road lately ascended as well as the valleys below, was the site of an old French fort; and still higher up the cliff is another. We passed round the brow of the shoulder, and here a magnificent view burst on our sight, as we stood on the brink of a precipice 2,000 feet high, overlooking the highly cultivated districts of Flacq, Moka, and Plaines Wilhelms, as well as the different mountain ranges traversing the island.

It is very evident that the whole of this plateau was once a lake of liquid fire, and I do not doubt that the interior of it was the crater of one of the extinct volcanoes that form Mauritius.

We now took a footpath through a wood of stunted trees, on our way to the summit. At this altitude we found a different vegetation altogether; in fact, the zones are tolerably well marked up the mountain. Grasses and ferns here changed their character, and a great variety of Orchideæ were found. I gathered here many species of lichens and mosses,[1] some quite new to me. I procured some fine pinnæ of the fronds of the Cyatheas, both *excelsa* and *canaliculata:* unfortunately it is impossible to secure an entire frond, both on account of fragility and size. Aspleniums, *longissimanum*, *affine*, and *lineatum*, were in the greatest abundance; *Aspidium capense*, *Cœnopteris vivipara*, and others: in all seventeen species I added to my Herbarium.[2]

As we approached the summit it had the appearance of being covered with a white flowering shrub, but on nearing it we found it to be the Velouta (*Tournefortia argentea*), the white velvety leaves of which glittered in the sun. Here, for the first time, I found a modest little red Erica (*Andromeda lilicifolia*), with one exception the only known species of heath in the island.

The path to the summit is narrow and steep, a mere scramble up rocks; and when there we found only a little plateau about ten feet square. The whole island lay around us; and it was a glorious sight to look down on it from that giddy pinnacle, so calm and lovely in the far distance, and not a sound saving our own voices to break the silence.

[1] On the trees of this thicket, or forest, as Mauritians would call it, I collected the following funguses and lichens:—*Schizophyllum commune*; five species of Cladonia; two Stictinas, *tomentosa* and *retigera*; two Rorellas; *Ucasolia herbacea* (Huds.); four Stictas, *damæcarnis*, *macrophylla* and *dichotoma*, the fourth not named; *Usnea barbata*; *Physcia leucomela*; and a species of Biatira.

[2] For the names of the mosses and lichens I am indebted to the kindness of J. Tyerman Esq., Curator of the Botanical Gardens, Liverpool, to whom I sent specimens of the varied Botany of Mauritius.

All heaven and earth were still, but not in sleep,
But breathless, as we grow when feeling most;
And silent as we stand in thought too deep for words.

The city lay at our feet in a northerly direction; the plains of Pamplemousses, and Rivière du Rempart, to the NE., were green with waving canes; and the large plantations, many of them over 1,800 acres, looked only as so many cultivated gardens. The Moka and Black River districts to the W. presented a similar scene.

In close proximity to the summit of the Pouce is Peter Both Mountain, which only exceeds it in height by about twenty-five feet. The various spurs of the Calebasse chain could be distinctly recognised, as well as all the principal peaks. The Latanier and other rivers in their serpentine course meandering slowly to the sea appeared as silver lines intersecting the country. The tracks of the railways were just visible, and as a train passed, no sound reached us; but as the iron horses rushed puffing along, they seemed like children's toys rather than monster engines.

My aneroid barometer indicated 2,725 feet above sea level.

I gathered a good many land shells, many of them alive, and captured several curious insects. One, a Mantis, about half as large as the ordinary ones, of a dark brown colour, striated on the body with beautiful scarlet diagonal lines; the eyes of an intense prussian blue, abdomen greyish white, and wings pale-yellow, with numberless spots studded on the tips. I caught an Argynnis for the first time, its dull orange wings thickly strewn with black, and disturbed several moths in the long grass. These little creatures are as cunning as possible; the instant the net goes over them they slip down the grass stems, and run along with such celerity that it is a difficult matter to catch them.

We were heartily glad of a good rest, and we loyally drank the healths of Her Majesty the Queen, and the President of the United States. One of our party made a most flowery speech in praise of these eminent personages and their respective countries, but I fear that, under the circumstances, it was not highly appreciated by his small audience.

The air was cool and bracing, with a considerable difference in the temperature at the summit from the base of the mountain. It seems to be my fate to encounter storms on mountain sides. Before we were half rested, a large black cloud, and the deep roll of thunder which echoed from peak to peak, warned us of an approaching storm, and we reluctantly began our descent.

This was one of my first mountain experiences in Mauritius, and I was vexed to have to quit such a grand view so quickly. It was a new view of the city to me with all its surroundings: the harbour and its forest of masts, the wreaths of foam marking the coral reefs; the forts; and the broad expanse of the Indian Ocean, all glittering in the brilliant tropical sunshine—for there was no storm down below. We began our descent about eleven o'clock, and it required more care than we had any idea of. We hurried down to the shelter of the stunted trees, but not before we had all got well drenched did we reach it. Soon, however, it passed away, and a rainbow was the result of the sun breaking from the passing clouds. As the glorious arch spanned the heavens, it awakened in my soul thoughts of confidence, and trust and love, as I gazed on its brilliant hues—symbols of a brighter reality of Hope and Heaven.

Every step disclosed some new object of admiration—a moss, a lichen, a fern, an orchid; even a monkey or two appeared in the distance, but disappeared with an angry chatter at our disturbance, and gave us no chance of a nearer inspection. Very few birds were observed, and I concluded it was too cold for them. We heard the shrill whistle of the Boatswain, or Paille-en-queue birds (*Phæton candidus*), as they gracefully sailed over head. They build their nests in the hollows of the cliff, on the south side of the mountain. The place they had selected for their nests was inaccessible to all but a samphire or eider-down hunter, though our presence so alarmed them that they did not cease their cries till we reached the open space of the shoulder. Here we selected a grassy spot within a few feet of the precipice forming the south of the mountain.

From this place we could look directly down into a number of large sugar houses on the plains below, which had been unroofed in the March hurricane, and to us they looked like houses in miniature. The rain had ceased, all the clouds dispersed, and the atmosphere was delightfully cool and clear, and we heartily enjoyed our breakfast. Fortunately my friends had also a supply of provisions; for of my boy, that I had sent on ahead of us, we had never even caught a glimpse.

This part of the mountain, especially round the spur, is an interesting one, and affords a fine field for investigation to botanists.

At one o'clock the sun shone out in all its splendour, casting his fiery rays upon us; so we hastened our descent, and about 1,000 feet lower we halted for a rest.

Near this spot is a fine Mapou tree, on the trunk of which is cut in large letters the word 'Echo.' On hallooing we found the echo to be complete, caused by the sound reverberating from the high cliff before us.

A little lower down we found Bopchia stretched out in the grass, fast asleep. He had lost us on the ascent, and being tired of looking for us, leisurely resigned himself to a comfortable nap, awaiting our return, in oblivion of the fact that he had the greater part of our wine with him in my vasculum, and that I had to stuff my pockets with ferns, shells, mosses, &c. We arrived in the city about half-past two, all of us very sufficiently wearied, but so well pleased with our trip as to be willing to renew it on a future day.

To see the Pouce under the aspect above described, it must be in fine weather after some weeks' succession of heavy rains. I have ascended it several times since, but with very varied luck. The last time it was dreary in the extreme, from a long drought: scarcely a fern was to be seen, except on the rise above the shoulder, and there I missed many of my former friends. My object then was to hunt for land shells, so, instead of descending by the ordinary path, I struck into the ravine, and keeping down near the water-course, I was tolerably successful. With a good deal of trouble I found many specimens of the Pupas, *elongata*, *Mauritiana*, and *sulcata*, and one of the small but rare *clavulata*, two varieties of Hydrorœna, the *variegata* and *rubra*: the *Parmacella Mauritiana*, and dozens of the common Bulinus, Achatinas, and different species of Helix.

A great many were alive, and nearly all the Pupas. The *P. Mauritiana* is bright red when living, but changes to green when dead.

I also procured some fine specimens of the *Atrophyum Boryanum* fern, that I had hitherto found principally at

Curepipe. The *Polytrichum commune* was in full seed for the first time I have been able to get it in that condition, with the single exception previously mentioned. The mosses, in such beauty near the shoulder on my first visit, were now all dried up, the water-course was a bare furrow, and only a little rough coarse grass in the place of the lovely ferns on its banks.

The Peter Both Mountain.

It would appear that the grand feat to accomplish in Mauritius is to ascend this mountain. I have, nevertheless, hitherto preferred viewing the island from other peaks, almost equally difficult to climb—in the case of the Morne quite so.

Casual visitors seem especially attracted, and fired with the ambition of leaving their names on the all but inaccessible pinnacle. The first who led the way was a French mechanic named Claude Penthé, who conceived the then unheard-of idea of scaling the formidable rocky walls, and, with only a single negro, succeeded in placing the French flag on the summit, on September 8, 1790. Very possibly his description of the difficulties in the way deterred his countrymen from following his daring example; however that may be, I believe no other attempt is recorded till September 1832. On this date a party of British naval and military officers, with a large staff of men and accessories, essayed the ascent; but it was only on the second day that they were successful, and then, for the first time, the red cross of St. George flaunted triumphantly from the head.

In the years 1848 and '58, navy and army again united, and, with some gentlemen of the Island, went up. In the expedition of 1858 they were three days before they reached the top. In 1864, when some of the officers of the 24th Regiment and others arrived at the head, they left, for future climbers, a strong tin box, containing a visitors' book, and a piece of lead with the names of former explorers scratched on it. I do not think the book requires to be a verv bulky one. The hoary peak is not likely to be intruded upon very frequently. Some of the 86th Regiment went up in 1869, and I believe there have been two or three unrecorded ascents, but I do not know of any others save those I have mentioned. It is more than possible that this mountain will one day be quite inaccessible, from the gigantic basaltic rocks constantly toppling down, worn away by the elements. That day is doubtless distant, and before it arrives we shall hear of many an ascent, for the 'Irrepressible Saxon' delights in overcoming unheard-of difficulties in the way of a mountain climb.

A BUTTERFLY.

CHAPTER XV.

REDUIT.

Its Vicissitudes—Reason of its first Establishment—Alleged Establishment Its Interior and Exterior—Its Change under M. de Brillane—Anecdote of Bartolomeo—Difference of its Treatment under Sir R. Farquhar and his Successors—Mauritius threatened with Monsters—Destruction of the Cause of the Threat—Sir W. Gomm's Rule—Reduit in the Hands of Sir Henry Barkly and his Lady—Description of Scenery—Geological Features—Ghosts—Mynas—Ferns and Fernery—Ravages by Cyclone of 1868.

FEW PLACES in Mauritius have undergone the vicissitudes which Reduit, the present country residence of the representative of royalty, has experienced.

In the early ages of the French dynasty in the Isle of France, the *maison de plaisance* of the governors was at Montplaisir.

In 1749 M. David, who then held the reins of government, a gentleman reared in all the gallantry of the Court of Louis XV., sought a retirement where he might create a second Parc-aux-Cerfs de Paris, and found a romantic spot near Moka, just suited to his purpose.

To prevent objections to the large outlay required for the expenses of the building, he alleged as a reason for it, that he wished to provide a secure retreat for the ladies of the colony in case of an attack on the island by the British ; an event considered very probable at that time. It is to be supposed the excuse was accepted, as Reduit was completed, and Montplaisir deserted.

Though containing every appliance luxury could furnish to suit the gay revelry within its walls, it was not devoid of defences, should circumstances require it as a strong-hold. Outwardly it was a veritable *château* of the feudal age, defended by moat and drawbridge, thus carrying out the *soi-disant* reason for its construction.

After M. David's departure, Reduit was for a time neglected, with the exception of a permission given by M. Bouvet, in 1755, to M. Poivre to plant there some nutmeg trees, which he had procured with great difficulty from Manilla. It was also used for a time as a college. In 1756, M. Magon, finding its quiet and retirement refreshing after the oppressive cares of his troubled administration, spared neither pains nor expense to enrich its gardens with a great variety of useful and valuable trees and curious plants.

It suffered again an interregnum of desertion after M. Magon left till 1776, when Le Chevalier Guerin de Brillane entirely changed its fate and aspect

Moat and portcullis, all that gave a feudal character to the building, were swept away.

Again its star shone brilliantly, and its alleys were the resort of the beauty and gallantry of the day.

In 1789 Reduit had its share of the disasters caused by the terrible hurricane that then burst over the Isle of France, and it was shorn of much of its beauty.

A curious anecdote was related about this time of the celebrated traveller, Bartolomeo, who visited the island. He writes, 'Private persons purchase small plots of ground from the King, live as planters, and construct for themselves habitations, all of which are called Reduits.'

In 1810, Mr., afterwards Sir R. Farquhar, the first British Governor, took great pleasure in embellishing Reduit; but it experienced fresh vicissitudes at the hands of the Major-Generals Hall and Darling.

In February 1813 Reduit was the scene of the wildest terror and commotion. The peace of Mauritius was threatened! Vague rumours had spread of serpent monsters rearing their crested heads, but no one could give any reliable information. The 'Gem of the Ocean,' hitherto as free from deadly reptiles as if St. Patrick himself

Had banished them for ever,

now to be infested with such vermin! Impossible! They must be hunted out, or Mauritius would be uninhabitable! The bravest turned out, armed to the teeth, and with beating hearts set forth to seek the dread unknown. When found, the enemy proved a formidable one, nothing less than a Boa Constrictor, comfortably ensconced in the vegetation at the foot of the Cascade. However, he was slain and brought in triumph to Port Louis by MM. Fleurot and Cazelins. It was 14 feet 8 inches in length, and 14 inches in circumference. It appears the reptile had been brought from India in a vessel that was wrecked some years previously at Grand River Mouth, and supposed to have been destroyed, but which must have swum ashore, and made its way to the spot where it was killed.

Reduit was not simply abandoned, but numbers of its finest trees were allowed to be cut down or mutilated; and not till 1823 did it again find a protector, when Sir Lowry Cole restored it to the favour it has ever since possessed. He hired the most experienced gardeners for it, renewed its fountains, and planted the rarest trees and flowers.

From this time all savans, and men of any note who have visited Mauritius, have spoken of the cordial reception they have always met with at Reduit.

In 1846, it was not only in a prosperous state, from the great care bestowed on it by Sir William Gomm, but it at length enjoyed, what it had so greatly needed, the graceful presence and gentle influence of a noble Chatelaine, the Lady Elizabeth Gomm. It has continued the summer retreat of succeeding governors from the intense heat of the city, as it possesses a climate of from six to ten degrees difference in temperature.

In the hands of its present occupants, Sir Henry and Lady Barkly, it keeps up its reputation, both for the care bestowed on its grounds and the hospitable welcome that worth and talent receive when visiting Reduit.

It is situated in the district of Moka, at an elevation of 950 feet above sea level, and at the juncture of the rivers Profonde and La Cascade, whose waters unite and fall into Grand River, which carries them on to the sea.

It stands on a tongue of land, between two ravines, formed by the above-named rivers.

It commands a wide extent of country: to the right lies a range of mountains, most of them covered with verdure to their summits, stretching from Mount Ory to the celebrated Peter Both; and on the left rises the magnificent line of the Corps de Garde Mountains.

The eye wanders with pleasure over the intervening scenery.

The forest land; the numerous well-shaded habitations and sugar mills; the tender green of the cane fields; near the house, the stately avenues of Filaos and Mangoes; and the spacious lawn dotted here and there with fine palms—all form a landscape of rare beauty. Neither must the wide expanse of the blue Indian Ocean be forgotten in a description of the view from the Reduit. From the verandah can be distinctly seen the great currents of lava from the original crater, which, breaking down its walls for miles, flowed on to the sea.

The whole neighbourhood is exceedingly interesting to a geologist.

Traces of terrible volcanic action exist everywhere, extinct for ages, but which may one day burst forth again, and perhaps again submerge the whole or part of the island. On the sides of the ravines tufa is in abundance, also large water-worn stones, covered with a soft coating of sedimentary deposit, and small pieces of pumice stone are sometimes found.

Having several times been the recipient of the kindly hospitalities of Sir Henry Barkly and his fair consort, I can speak feelingly of the natural beauties of Reduit, as I enjoyed them so heartily.

During one of my visits I was informed that in a certain room in the NE. end of the building a student committed suicide, also that a lady's maid was found dead in her bed in the time of the occupation of Reduit by Sir W. Stevenson. I was told that this room was haunted by their spirits and others, black, grey, and white, according to the servants' belief, who all studiously avoided it. I, however, chose this apartment, and did all I could to invite some one of the ghosts to give me an audience, but unsuccessfully; so I presume when they made their visits I was in the arms of Morpheus. Or, it may be that the presence of a real live Yankee (a *genuine* one) was so great a rarity, they had not the courage to face such a curiosity. Possibly my total unbelief in spirits and their rappings made me an impracticable subject. At any rate my sleep was sweet and refreshing, so their gambols must for once have been carried on in other rooms where timidity reigned supreme.

On the slopes of the ravines are pretty walks where I have strolled delightedly, inhaling the fresh breezes of the early morning, the only really enjoyable part of the day in the summer at Mauritius. Then all nature looks glad, and every tree and shrub shines freshly out after the cool night. Every bird is busy and carolling at the top of its voice, as if it knew the scorching heat of the sun would soon reduce it to silence.

Of all merry birds commend me to the Myna (*Accidotheres tristis*) or Martin. I can only compare these jolly little creatures to rooks in a rookery.

Like them they are gregarious, and they equal them in noise. It is almost deafening to stand under a tree where they have taken up their quarters. The first thing in the morning they begin, and it is most amusing to watch the scolding, chattering, fighting, and flirting that go on before the bird business of the day begins, and each goes off on some quest of its own.

Sometimes a little blue monkey would be visible, but so shy it was impossible to get a closer acquaintance with it.

All along the margins of the ravines is a luxuriant growth of shrubs and lianes, but the latter making such a tangle that they were in some places almost impassable.

In many parts the clear waters of the river ran over and through the rocks with considerable force and noise; in others glided on in silence, without a ripple on their surface; and again, down they plunged with a sullen roar to a great depth.

Close to the water the ground is encumbered with rocks, all covered with mosses and uprooted trunks of trees, on which grow lichens and rare fungi.

Many ferns grow here peculiar to the island, some amongst the disintegrated rocks and some in the soft vegetable mould; the fronds, delicate and perfect as the most elegant plumes of feathers, waving gracefully in the light breezes playing through the ravines.

A short distance from Reduit are THE FALLS *par excellence*, which, in the rainy season, send a heavy body of water into the deep basin below, that is fringed with still finer ferns, from the spray always dashing over them. In some places on the sides of the ravines the Malabars have cleared the land, and made fine vegetable gardens, the produce of which is sold in Port Louis.

The lover of the pastoral, the admirer of rocks and ravines, the sentimental seeker of shady glades, purling streams, or brawling brooks, the venturesome scalers of mountain heights, and the explorer of subterranean caverns, may all find their various tastes gratified in this neighbourhood.

Attached to Reduit is a beautiful fernery, containing not only the greater part of the ferns indigenous to Mauritius, but many introduced from foreign countries. The native orchids are there also, as well as many fine specimens from Madagascar. It is kept with the greatest care, and is especially under the auspices of Lady Barkly, who takes particular interest in it. At most of the flower shows may be seen a collection of ferns, orchids, and lycopodia in her name, for which she has carried off several prizes.

There is also an aviary, containing all the native and accli-

TROPICAL SCENE.

matised birds of Mauritius, and many lovely foreign ones, principally from India and Australia.

Since my first visit, Reduit has suffered terribly by the cyclone of March 1868.

The right wing of the house was nearly destroyed, and this caused great alarm to the inhabitants.

It was of wood, like most old houses here, but it is now being substantially rebuilt of stone.

The gardens too were sadly damaged, and many fine trees of nearly a century's growth were uprooted.

Fortunately nature soon spreads a new covering of leaves over the ravages made by the elements ; but the real injury to fruit-trees is serious, as it destroys all blossom for the season, and in place of the mango and other trees being laden with their luscious burden, we have only masses of leaves.

Taken altogether, Reduit is one of the pleasantest retreats in the colony, and does infinite credit to the taste of M. David, who selected so delightful a spot for a summer residence.

CHAPTER XVI.

THE MARRIAGE CEREMONY OF THE MADRAS MALABAR INDIANS.

Permission to visit a Wedding-feast—Preliminary Ceremonies—Initiation of Bridegroom—Initiation of Bride—Intermediate Ablutions and Change of Dress—Description of the Bride's second Appearance—The actual Marriage—Presents to the Groom, and his Share of the Proceedings—Only Food allowed the Wedded Pair—Sprees on the Third Day—Consummation.

I HAD never seen a Malabar wedding, nor could I get any information from my friends about one ; so I instructed my servant, who is a Madrassee himself, to give me notice when one would take place among his own friends, and get me permission to witness it.

One day I was informed there was to be a grand gathering in Moka Street, as a wedding was in contemplation. Better still, the happy man was an intimate friend of Bopchia (mentioned in my trip up the Pouce), and I had full permission to see the whole ceremony if I chose.

Great preparations were made, and an infinity of presents collected for the occasion. A house was hired for the three days during which the wedding festivities are kept up. On a day, sunshiny enough to satisfy any bride, at eleven o'clock, a large party set out in procession, bearing aloft the presents on their heads.

These consisted of wreaths of flowers, bananas, pine-apples, cocoa-nuts, areca-nuts, betel, different coloured powders, incense, pumpkins, &c., all of which were arranged with flowers, and placed on trays covered with white cloths.

When some distance from the house the company halted, the presents were uncovered, and one of the party entered to inform the bride's mother of their presence. A band of music was sent to escort them, consisting of a tom-tom, two clarionets, and two pairs of cymbals, and then the procession moved on to the entrance. This was a doorway leading to a large yard, with the never-failing cocoa-nut and banana leaves to adorn it.

On passing in, at the rear of the house was seen a large place enclosed with canvas, where a concourse of Indians, dressed in their best, was assembled.

On approaching this tent the music ceased and an Indian appeared, demanding a piece of money, which was instantly given; and I found it was the value of the bride, or the stipulated present to the father of the woman, which takes the form of purchase, and converts the whole affair into a bargain or sale. This state of things I learn stands prominently out in certain phases of Indian society, under which social system large sums are frequently given by the father of a daughter of a lower caste to induce a man of higher class to consent to his son's marriage.

In a few minutes two young dancing-girls came out, handsomely dressed in white Dacca muslin chemises, with long graceful robes of Indian figured silk, and their heads arranged with gold ornaments. I could not help admiring their small delicate forms and tiny hands and feet, as they stood holding up a dish of a liquid like blood, made of saffron and lime, and singing a plaintive melody.

When they had finished, the band struck up some lively tune, and then the whole party entered the tent.

In front of a sofa sat a Brahmin priest, cross-legged, a number of cocoa-nut oil lamps burning round him, and between them a large round stone used for preparing curry, representing a goddess, and dishes filled with rice and fruits. When he had arranged all to his liking, the music played quickly, and the bridegroom made his appearance, attended by his nearest friend. He was a young man about twenty-two years of age, slightly built, with long flowing black hair. He had on a bright yellow dress edged with gold lace, and wore on his head a most curiously-constructed white turban. He seated himself cross-legged on the sofa, and a few women then came in. The mother of the bride had a van[1] in her hands, containing oil and other articles for bathing purposes, small manioc cakes, and a bunch

[1] A van is a sort of flat basket for cleaning rice.

of dried grass. Taking a position directly before the bridegroom, she anointed him with the oil by touching his knees and shoulders, then on the top of his head, repeating a prayer for his future prosperity and happiness, and was followed by the other women, who had previously stood behind him: they repeated the same ceremonies.

The bridegroom, who had been sitting all this time patiently, retired, and the bride put in her first appearance, looking very downcast and sad, led in by her attendants.

She was about eighteen, good-looking and plump, and was placed cross-legged also on the sofa, and all the same rites were gone through with her.

The Brahmin priest then blessed her, and a tray was brought forward containing the marriage-string, the wedding garments, wreaths, &c.; and a brass pot full of boiled rice was also brought in, and pieces of banana leaves were spread out. A woman filled each leaf with rice, adding milk, cream, ghee and sugar; the priest, lighting a few coals in a censer, and sprinkling incense (benjamine powder) over them, waved the censer backwards and forwards over the rice, as also a piece of burning camphor as an offering to the gods and goddesses, said to be present in the tent, to witness the marriage, and invoked their blessings on the pair. The bride was then led away to an adjoining room, to prepare her for the rest of the ceremony.

Meantime her lord and master soon to be was busy washing his body in the yard, and then all returned to the tent; after which the bridegroom broke a cocoa-nut and burnt a piece of camphor, to invoke the Sun's blessing on the pair; the music playing vigorously whilst waiting the re-appearance of the bride. Her dress is always changed at this stage of the ceremony, for fear of any spot of dirt on it, which would be unlucky.

Presently in she came with her attendants, dressed in a beautiful robe of crimson and gold-figured silk. On her head she wore a plait of rose and other flower-buds, extending from her forehead to her shoulders; across it was laid an ornament about six inches long and two wide, with gold and silver rosettes dangling from it; at the end of each was a little dove holding a bunch of flowers in its beak, and those fell round her face so as almost entirely to hide it from view, and I presume to spare her blushes.

I pitied the poor thing under such a load in a hot day, particularly when they told me it had to be worn for three nights and three days, during which time it is supposed not to wither if she is a good girl; should it do so she must pay a fine to Bramah, but I believe it is not often enforced. Her arms were bare, and smeared with a paste of sandal-wood ashes, also for luck. When she was properly seated, the groom took his place beside her on the sofa. The priest then lighted a small fire and poured oil over it, which he dipped from a basin with a maize leaf. (This is *his* invocation for the babies.) He then sprinkled rice over the shoulders of bride and groom, and held towards them a copper dish filled with rice, bananas, and cocoa-nuts. They both had their hands filled with the mixture, then they put some in each other's hands, and after this the dish was carried round, and everyone, down to the smallest child, placed both hands in it. This is to show that there are plenty of witnesses to the compact, and that if they break their oaths there are numbers to prove the perjury.

The bridegroom then placed a yellow silk cord round the bride's neck, which is her wedding-ring and proof of her marriage. At this a general clapping of hands took place, the band played some quick tune, and everyone looked pleased.

The priest again came forward and tied the ends of their robes together to prevent the demons from touching them; and two of the brothers, one for each side, sat down before him while he repeated the names of the newly-married couple, Thomas[1] and Pomona. They (the brothers) then vowed to give notice to all the world that they were satisfied with the match, and had witnessed the marriage. They rose, and the groom filled their hands with rice, washed their feet in water, with lime infused into it, and threw rice over them, and the bride did the same.

The happy pair were then marked on the forehead and conducted by two girls, neatly dressed in white, three times round the place, one carrying a lighted taper, the other a dish of fruit, to receive the congratulations of their friends. When the third round was completed, the bride placed her foot on the

[1] Thomas was a Catholic, and had a service in the church; but as his wife was a Malabar, he was obliged to go through all her ceremonies as well as his own.

curry-stone above alluded to, representing a goddess, and the brother handed the bridegroom four silver rings, which he placed on the second toes of each foot. This was an oath taken before the goddess that all was fair dealing between the families, and to impress on them not to deceive each other.

An unmarried woman may wear as many armlets and earrings as her caprice, the length of her purse, or liberality of her lovers will permit; but the toe-rings are the privilege of the wedded state only.

Once more the newly-married pair were seated in state on the sofa, and one of the girls held up the dish of saffron, to keep away all evil eyes, and sang a song which seemed to give great satisfaction to all present, and then the friends each threw a small quantity of rice over the patient couple.

Now came the crowning point in the ceremony, as far as the groom is concerned. Presents of money are given by every one of the assembled relatives and friends, and a considerable pile was soon accumulated—luckily for him, for the wedding cost him about a hundred and fifty dollars, besides as much rice as could be consumed in three days.

A dance was performed by the girls of the family only, and then the feasting began.

The groom is compelled to give food for three days to all his guests and relatives, such as rice, vegetables, milk and fruit. No meat is allowed to be eaten, and wine is utterly forbidden, under a heavy penalty to the groom. If a man chooses to go and drink outside he can, but no intoxicating liquor is allowed to enter the sacred precincts. Thus, though the noise and fun are fast and furious, drunkenness is unknown.

But to return to the happy (?) pair. *They* are only permitted to take bananas, milk, or vegetables, *once* a day, towards evening, for the three days. They are kept in state, and guarded by the relations.

On the third day, in the afternoon, a regular spree takes place. They all go to a river, where the bride's wreath is thrown in, which answers the same purpose as the slipper thrown with us, viz. for good luck. All return, and the now free man and wife take an active share in the fun. They are allowed to sprinkle every one near them with the saffron mixture, which they do in right good earnest, and which is taken as a hint to be off, and then he carries her away to his own house to commence the honeymoon.

How would our fair belles of Europe or America like to undergo such an ordeal? I guess that many a damsel would hesitate before saying 'yes' to a three days' ceremony such as just described.

CHAPTER XVII.

FLAT ISLAND.

Our Skipper—View inland—Turtle Bay—Old French Fort—Grand Baie—Whales—Cannonier's Point—Land near Grand Baie—Fishing—Gunners' Quoin—The Pass—Our Welcome—Quarantine Station—Water Supply—Wells—Plants and Trees—Our Quarters—Landing-bridge—Columba Rock—On the Reefs—Corals—Polyps—Zoophytes—Algæ—Palisade Bay—Lighthouse—Cemetery—The Mountain—Geological Features—Caves—Gabriel Island—The Quoin—Detached Rocks on Mountain—Volcanoes supposed to have been in this Vicinity—Return.

THE Surveyor-General's department has a fine yacht used for Government purposes; and as one of its officers was about to proceed to Flat Island on business, I gladly availed myself of an invitation to visit it. In April 1869 we sailed out of the Fanfaron, with a fair breeze and a flowing sail.

The old and careful skipper of the boat was sick with fever, and his place was filled by a young creole, who was probably more daring, and hoisted all sail, which, though it sped us on our way, made it somewhat uncomfortable on deck, as we were constantly taking in water. This, with the gloomy morning and occasional showers, frequently drove us below, where we found very jolly quarters.

We sailed along the outer edge of the reef till we reached Tombeau Bay, when we steered to the north. There we had a fine view inland of the Black River range as far as the north-eastern spur of Montagne Longue; and I think this view, which takes in at a glance all its singular peaks, is one of the grandest in Mauritius. Behind us the Pointe aux Canes, in the distance, looked like a long narrow promontory extending far into the sea.

The country NE. of Tombeau Bay is flat, and presents nothing near the coast but a few fishermen's huts with a lime-kiln or two, and some scattered corca and filoa trees. We next passed the pretty little arm of the sea called Turtle Bay, on account, it is said, of the great numbers of that Chelonia of aldermanic repute formerly caught here, as they visited these shores to deposit their eggs. There are, I suppose, still some in the neighbourhood, as once a week an hotel-keeper in Port Louis advertises 'Real genuine turtle-soup ready this day at noon;' but I should doubt its approval at the Mansion House or Fifth Avenue Hotel!

The residence, with the flour-mills and distillery, spoken of in another chapter, stand at the head of this bay; and someone displayed great taste by adorning its shores, one side with filoas, and the other with cocoa-nut trees.

The land is covered with rank coarse grass, and at the Point aux Piments the shore is steep and rocky, the waves breaking directly upon it. The ruins of an old French fortification stand on this Point. Only a portion of the walls of the officers' quarters and the north-west end of the building remain.

Then comes Grand Baie. Whales are occasionally caught very near this part of the island. On the 20th of this month Captain Sherman, of the American bark 'Young Phœnix,' when about to come to anchor off the Bell Buoy, heard the welcome cry from the mast-head of 'There she blows!' Immediately all was bustle on board; the boats were lowered, and in a very few minutes they were rowing away from the ship, which was put about, and the pilot, who was already on board, took to his boat and returned to Port Louis. Away went the bark after her boats, which were pulling vigorously, each straining to get in the first harpoon; and it was not long before they killed five of these monsters of the deep. They were soon cut up and boiled, and the ship netted 10,000 dollars.

Running out some distance into the sea is Cannonier's Point, a ledge of rock over which the waves foam and surge turbulently. On the Point stands a lighthouse with a fixed catoptric light—a most needful beacon to warn mariners against the reefs to the NE. and SW. of the Point, also to indicate the dangerous shoal in its vicinity. There is a quarantine establishment for vessels arriving with small-pox or any other contagious disease. It is also a military post, so that a number of houses have been built, very conveniently situated for the garrison, as well as the isolated buildings for immigrants.

Grand Baie is inhabited principally by fishermen, famed for their skill in the management of their boats and pirogues. Most of the land in the vicinity is cultivated with canes. It is a marvel how anything can grow, judging from its appearance, for it is covered with boulders of every size, up to masses many tons in weight. Huge cairn-like piles of rocks lie in all directions, and are intersected by what appear to be low walls, but which are in reality the aforesaid boulders rolled together, and the only earth for planting lies between them. This, however, is rich loamy soil, and suited to most tropical productions.

Before the railroad was opened, great quantities of sugar were shipped hence to Port Louis from the Pamplemousses district. A great part of the fish sold in the city market daily is brought from Grand Baie, Point aux Piments, and Tombeau Bay.

We now steered for the Gunners' Quoin, or Coin de Mire, and were soon opposite this curious rock. The sea was very rough here, but our craft danced bravely over the waves, though at times standing at an angle of ten degrees. I shall speak of the singular formation of this cliff later on. A small cave has been hollowed out of it on the NW. side by a fisherman,[1] who sometimes remains there all night pursuing his occupation. At one point, when passing through the channel between the Quoin and Flat Island, a side view of the rock gives an excellent profile of the Iron Duke. There he is with his *chapeau* on, and his very prominent nose standing out in such good relief as to produce an unmistakable likeness. I should prefer giving it the name of Wellington Rock, in honour of one of the greatest men of his time.

The current in this channel, which sets in a westerly direction, greatly retarded our progress, and a heavy cross sea made us pitch and toss about most uncomfortably; and as we rounded the Pass between Gabriel and Flat Islands, the sea rolled and broke over us, drenching our decks. Our skipper, however, skilfully carried us in alongside the stone jetty lately built by the Government. I confess I was not sorry to find myself again on *terra firma*. We were received by Captain Green, who has the charge of the island, and Mr. Edwards, the lighthouse-

[1] The probability is, that the man has enlarged one of the many natural cavities to be found on this coast.

keeper, who gave us a cordial welcome to their limited territory.

We were told that at times the Pass is so dangerous, that often days elapse when boats dare not enter, and they are obliged to lay at anchor outside—a very miserable position, I should think, on account of the heavy swell caused by the sea rolling in over the shoal coral-beds. Not long since a boat upset and broke to pieces, and the occupants, two ladies and a gentleman, were drowned. There is a signal station here, to give notice if it is practicable for boats to enter.

Flat Island is also a quarantine station, and the Government has erected numerous substantial buildings, made roads, planted trees, sunk wells, and beautified the place so as to make it pleasantly habitable. Works containing a condensing apparatus stand near the jetty, in which 12,000 gallons of pure water can be condensed in twenty-four hours. A donkey-engine is used for this purpose; and after the water is condensed, it passes through an iron filter three feet deep by eighteen inches in diameter, and is then conveyed into iron tanks, each containing 400 gallons. The whole establishment is in excellent order, and must have cost the Government a considerable sum of money.

Wells have been dug for cattle, some of them from eight to ten feet deep, which are cut through the loose volcanic rocks and a lower strata of conglomerate, composed of fine particles of various marine substances in process of solidification, similar to that I observed near the jetty, and resting on a bed of coral. We were informed that the waters of these wells were unwholesome for man, as they possess deleterious ingredients that frequently act as a purgative. I concluded they contain a large quantity of lime, from passing through the decomposed coral and shells, which abound everywhere under the surface.

We proceeded over a good road laid out on an elevated dune, which reaches from east to west on the north-west shore. Everywhere we saw patches of a pretty little shrub, whose bright green leaves relieved the eye from the glare of the sun. The *Psiadia glutinosa*, or Flat Island Balm, which takes its name from the place, and is used by the Creoles very successfully for cuts and other wounds; the Citronella (*Andropogon Schœnanthus*), and sundry coarse grasses, were abundant. We also found plants of the *Ipomœa maritima*, *Eugenia cordifolia*, *Wœnigia maritima*, and *Purina maritima*. I gathered only two ferns, the *Adiantum caudatum* and *Phymatodes vulgaris*.

The *Latania glaucophylla* flourishes here, the seeds of which are constantly brought by the currents from Round Island, and grow very rapidly. These, with filaos and cocoa-palms, were planted in the valley, and added much to the miniature landscape.

We were shown to what had been the doctor's quarters; and, after depositing our vasculums and traps, and making ourselves presentable, we went to Captain Green's house, where we found a capital breakfast prepared for us, most welcome to hungry voyagers.

Flat Island is nearly a mile wide, and the valley extends almost across it. The Quarantine-houses are on the south-west, and near them, on the beach of a small inlet, the rocks have been removed, and an elevated bridge built, which runs out for about 100 feet, in order to facilitate the landing in rough weather. The bridge is ascended by a ladder about twenty feet high, so that generally a safe debarcation can be effected.

Near this point is the curious Columba or Pigeon Rock, whose top is white with guano. The sides appear almost perpendicular, but could, nevertheless, be easily ascended if a safe landing could be secured. When we saw it, the waves were madly breaking against it, throwing up columns of spray, and the current swirling rapidly round its base. This is an isolated basaltic cliff, about half a mile from the shore, and rises to the height of 110 feet; the top appearing nearly level. On the shore opposite the Columba a ridge of detached basaltic rocks extends, piled up irregularly, but all resting on coral.

Being the full of the moon, the tides were unusually low, with a strong trade wind blowing, so that some parts of the reefs were nearly uncovered, and by jumping from rock to rock I managed to reach them. Polyps in myriads were around me, and in some places I could see the various madrepores and meandrinas at work, carrying on their never-ending-still-beginning process of building. The animals of the latter begin to work in a circle, and gradually, by the slowest stages, they build up the walls within and without, finishing the whole with a dome-like covering. How slow the operation is may be imagined, when Professor Agassiz writes, that 'an inch in fourteen years, or a foot a century,' is the average rate at which corals are formed.

The little star-shaped creatures of the madrepores radiated the loveliest colours from their tentaculæ, as they moved in and out of their habitations, and with a strong lens every movement could be seen.

Thousands of a fleshy polyp covered the rocks, making the scrambling over them slippery work. They were in patches, and each community was about an inch in diameter. Their colour was a reddish purple, with a pink mouth and tentaculæ, and they were an interesting sight. Though these animals live in communities, and are imbedded in a jelly-like matrix, each appears to have a perfectly independent existence. Cut them in a dozen pieces, and they will still go on multiplying, as you only destroy the bodies you actually separate.

I noticed a number of zoophytes which I believe to be Flustras; their beautiful leaf-like forms could easily be taken for the Pavonia coated with lime. Echinoides, star-fish, and crabs were in myriads. I collected many specimens of Algæ from the rocks and pools, including the following genera: Eucheuma, Gigartina, Caulerpa, Ceramium, Pavonia, Ulva, Sargassum, and Digenia. I found here, for the first time, the curious *Eucheuma horridum* of Agard. This plant is of a deep livid purple when alive, but turns to a greyish purple, variegated with orange, when dried. It resembles in external structure one of the thorny cacti, but the thick fleshy stems are scarcely recognisable when dry. The shells I found were small and insignificant of their species. I quitted the reef at last, very reluctantly, but the returning tide warned me of the danger of delay, and I sought the shore in all haste.

At this side of the island is Palisade Bay, and from it to the jetty are found strata of basaltic sandstone. Near the jetty I observed large slabs, which appear to have been detached from their original beds. This sandstone is formed by the aggregation of fragments of broken shells, corals and disintegrated volcanic rocks, and other matter thrown up from the sea, and agglutinated by the carbonate of lime in it.

Further out on the coral beds a similar formation is still going on, and very rapidly too. In Dr. Ayres' account of Flat Island, he mentions that the engineer informed him 'that the holes excavated for the piers of the jetty were immediately filled with sand, which in a very short time was converted into solid sandstone.'[1]

On the east of the island is its one mountain, and on it stands the lighthouse, built on a small plateau, at the height of 370 feet above sea level. It shows a revolving catoptric light of the first order. On this plateau is a grave cut in the sandstone, in which lies buried Mrs. Sarah Creed, the wife of a former keeper of the lighthouse. She died of cholera in 1854, and the present

LIGHTHOUSE ROCK, FLAT ISLAND.

keeper still tends the lonely spot, and has adorned it by planting flowers round the grave. The cemetery lies to the east of the island, and but too many have found a resting-place there. A short time since the skeleton of a man was found when making the road; it was in a sitting posture, and was supposed to have been a victim to some assassin, possibly in the old days

[1] This volcanic sand, or 'Pesserine,' is composed of comminuted basaltic rock, decomposed corals, and minute foraminiferous shells, and is more or less over the whole island; that near the mountain containing most of the volcanic material, the rest with a larger proportion of sea and crab-shells, Echinoides, &c.

when piracy was rife in these seas. They carefully gathered his bones, and laid them in a nameless grave in the cemetery.

On ascending the mountain the same phenomena present themselves as at Round Island. Between the different strata volcanic stones and pebbles lie in great regularity, indicating the various periods of activity of the neighbouring volcanoes.

On the summit Mr. Edwards, at my request, cut out of the solid formation several species of coral, which had been imbedded in it when in a plastic state below the sea, and all were well preserved. Most of these corals can be found in a living state in the neighbourhood of the island on the reef. One specimen of Astræa was as perfect as if just taken from the beach. Madrepora, Porites, Meandrina, and Millepora were

THE GUNNERS' QUOIN.

very numerous, not only on the top, but on the deep fissures which occur on the south of the mountain, and even in the solid sides of the cliffs. Large masses of disintegrated coral and shells are also frequently met with in process of change to a hard compact limestone.

The west and south sides of this mountain are steep; the latter a little sloping, the former almost perpendicular. The dip of the strata is from east to west and north, at an angle of about 30°. The colour of the rocks varies as greatly as their formation; the harder and unstratified being brownish black or grey blue, and others, showing more decided stratification, are of a reddish ferruginous hue. The latter is so friable that it was with difficulty I could bring away good specimens, as it crumbled easily in my hands.

On the eastern slope are groups of huge detached rocks, heaped at random in a semicircle, which are true basalt, deposited there by the volcanic agency of which I shall speak presently. Many of them have been rolled into the valley below, and others into the sea. Degraded rocks and *débris* have been washed down in immense quantities from the sides of the mountain, filling the valley to such an extent that the sea has been gradually driven back, and the dry land formed. Even at the present day many parts of this valley are little above the level of the sea, and in some places ponds which are seldom dry are met with of brackish water.

At the base of the mountain are several small caves caused by the action of the waves on the basaltic rocks, and towards the west is a three-chambered cavern formed by the sea forcing its way through the interstices of the rocks and wearing them away, as is constantly seen in upheavals of this description.

A great part of the island is covered with volcanic sand, but to the east lie dunes nearly thirty feet in height, which form a barrier to the sea. These dunes are as undulating as the ordinary sand-dunes of Europe. They are of recent formation in comparison with the age of the Lighthouse mountain, and in all probability, when the drifts first assumed sufficient tenacity to accumulate, the sea must have rolled between them and the mountain, over the coral beds on which they rest, and which are distinctly seen cropping out at low water mark.

Across the narrow-boat channel from the jetty, at about half a mile distant, lies Gabriel Island; to the north the chain of basaltic rocks, and the reefs are nearly uncovered at low tides. I am of opinion that Gabriel Island was once a part of the headland of Flat Island. At an early period it was covered with palms, vacoas and other endogenous trees, traces of which are now seen on the eastern side, represented by casts similar to those I observed at the Kesaux Aigrettes and Passe, near Mahebourg. Such casts are nowhere to be found at Flat Island, though I looked carefully for them, and enquired for them. These remains prove beyond a doubt that Gabriel Island was submerged and again upheaved.

South-west of Flat Island, about four miles distant, stands the towering rock of the Gunner's Quoin, rising perpendicularly from the ocean to the height of 550 feet. Its formation resembles that of the Lighthouse Mountain, a crumbling volcanic sandstone. The strata lie in a south-easterly direction, at an angle of about thirty degrees, and are better defined than those on the mountain, as they are distinctly visible from the sea level to the summit. Part of the island of the Quoin at the eastern base is covered with volcanic stones and lava that once flowed over it from some volcano in its neighbourhood.

I noticed the remains of a similar flow at the Table Rock at Round Island, and another at Amber Island, off the shore of the Rivière du Rempart district in Mauritius. They all indicate without doubt that a large and very active volcano existed between these islands. Another rose between the Quoin and Flat Island: the soundings of the channel by Mr. Corby, the Government surveyor, prove the presence of deep holes where this has subsided. The semicircular group of detached volcanic rocks mentioned on the eastern summit of the Lighthouse Mountain entirely differ from the formation on which they lie (being pure basalt), and appear to have been deposited at a very recent date. They are little changed by the elements and show no indications of being water-worn. I think it is most probable they were ejected from the crater of the last-mentioned volcano.

There is every reason to believe that the steep sides of the Pigeon Rock are parts of the wall of another volcáno, the rest of which has disappeared beneath the surging billows, perhaps in some future age to rise again, its peaks abraded and water-worn.

I have already stated that corals and marine shells are embedded in the different strata shown on the sides and top of the Lighthouse Mountain, many of them in good preservation, thus proving that they were deposited under water in horizontal beds. This mountain and the Quoin were doubtless once as round and perfect as Round and Serpent Islands, but the former were most likely divided at the time of their upheaval; parts breaking away in violent storms and subsiding into the sea, their sides and general appearance warranting the belief.

Upheavals which have a cone at their base often occur, but are not uplifted with sufficient force to break through the bed.

This is evidently the case at Round and Serpent Islands, or perhaps there was force enough to cause them to open in the centre, but not to separate as in the Quoin and Flat Island. If this had been the case traces would, in all probability, have been visible, even if such openings had been filled by the effects of erosion. Such upheavals are among the results of lateral eruption around great volcanoes near the sea.

I was but too soon obliged to quit my researches in this interesting island and obey a summons from our skipper, who was homeward bound. I was very sorry my time was so short, for I could have spent many days here very profitably and pleasantly; but my friend was obliged to return to Port Louis, so I had no alternative but to return also.

OLD SLAVE CREOLES.

CHAPTER XVIII.

LA CHASSE.

The Hunting Season in Mauritius—Game preserved—An Invite—On the way to the Meet—Our Posts—The Quartiers militaires—How I obeyed Orders—Our Game—Ferns—Our Comrades' Luck—*Our* Count—A Wild Boar—Return from the *Chasse*—Distribution of Game—Description of Cochon Marron.

Hark! hark! who calleth the maiden morn
From her sleep in the woods and stubble corn (*i.e. canes*)?
The horn! The horn!
The merry sweet ring of hunter's horn.
And a hunting we will go, my boys,
And a hunting we will go.

Deer-hunting in Mauritius is quite an institution, and is popular with both Europeans and Mauritians; indeed, with the latter it amounts to a *grande passion.* When a *chasse* is proposed, no need then to complain of the ordinary indifference or laziness; on the contrary, every one is roused to no end of activity. The hunting season begins on the 15th of May, and terminates at the end of August.

In some of the districts of the island there are yet dense forests and jungle that have escaped the ruthless hand of man, and where Nature still revels in all her glory. The various hunting-grounds are strictly preserved and guarded with jealous care by their owners; and woe betide the unlucky wight trespassing on them, or indulging a taste for venison, without having a *porte d'armes* in his pocket. Every particular ground has its hangar or hunting-box, which is the rendezvous for the *chasseurs.*

Invitations are sent out some days previous to the hunt; the hour and place of the meet are specified—of course before the sun is up, and at the nearest point to the ground which is to be hunted over.

I received an invite to one of these gatherings, and, after acceptance, one's first care is to provide a license to shoot for the season, for which ten dollars are demanded. Having looked well at rifle and ammunition, I started for the Moka district, to dine and pass the night with a Scotch friend and a young army officer. The former is an old sportsman, and as fine a fellow as one could wish for a comrade; and with him I was to proceed to the meet on the morrow, and make my *début* as a *chasseur* in Mauritius.

Up by daylight, a hasty cup of coffee, and away we sped as fast as two fleet horses could go over the seven miles intervening between us and the hangar of the gentleman who gave the *chasse.* All along the road were carriages full of gentlemen armed with guns and *couteaux de chasse*, carts containing the dogs, servants with baskets of refreshments on their heads; all was bustle and gaiety, in anticipation of a good time, and my host had to exchange salutations with almost everyone we met.

When about half-way to our destination one of the horses cast a shoe, and we had to turn aside to Bonne Veine to have it put on again. Here we were hospitably received, and though our spirits were already excellent, a decanter of fine brandy was brought out, with cool sparkling soda-water, which raised them a little higher. Our friendly host also furnished us with an extra gun and ammunition. The shoeing did not take long, and, thanking him for his attention and kindness in our need, on we went. I must say I have found that hospitality and friendliness are universal amongst both English and French planters.

The morning broke gloomily with showers of rain, notwithstanding which a large party was assembled when we arrived at the Quartiers militaires. Here we left our carriage and went to the hangar, which was at some distance, on foot, by a narrow pathway through the wood. Soon all were assembled, and after a few words with Dr. N., the proprietor of the grounds, the business of the day began.

About thirty of us were told off in squads and placed under the charge of a *piqueur* (a coloured man supposed to be well up to his work), to be posted. Along we went through the woods, sometimes over the dry bed of a river; now and then across a swamp filled with tall grass and weeds; anon sinking to one's knees; wading across streams, and again forcing our way through trees, ferns, or canes.

In some places the latter were so thick that it was with difficulty we could get through. Vegetation is here in the wildest luxuriance; it was perfectly enchanting. I was delighted beyond measure. The magnificent ferns and orchids hanging from every tree, with here and there a bright-coloured flower contrasting with the dark foliage, drove all thoughts of *la chasse* out of my head; I lagged behind—I could not help it, there was so much to admire. In vain my companions kept calling to me that I was pretty certain to get shot if I stopped behind them; I was so bewildered with the beauty of the place, that it was most reluctantly, at last, I pushed on with my comrades.

One after another was posted till our party dwindled to three --my host of the morning, his young friend, and myself.

At last W. was placed on an elevated spot of about two acres in extent, near an open swamp, on one side about five or six hundred feet across, with a small opening on the other, bordered by a dense jungle. Our conductor had received instructions from his master to allow me to remain with W.; so I was left with strict injunctions to keep perfectly still, and not, on any account, to quit my post.

I found it was an impossibility to obey such an order, and am sorry to say I broke the rules very soon after I was posted. Supposing there had been no attraction, I don't think I could have stood there the whole day, on the wet ground, and with a heavy shower now and then by way of variation. I soon set about exploring, and the result was two or three of that pretty land-shell, the *Helix pagoda*, all of them alive; also the *Pupa sulcata*, the largest and best specimens I ever obtained; *Carocolla semicirculata*, *Pupa lyoneciana*, *Helix aspersa*, and two or three of the genus Helix unknown to me.

In a stream I hastily examined, I took some *Neretina longispina*, and a few water-plants, two of the genus Tetraspora, one Entromorpha, two of Rivularia, and one of Ulvacea; and had I had time enough, I should have gathered (to me at least) many rich treasures.

I had strolled so far from W. and my own post that I suddenly came upon my other friend the Lieutenant, fast asleep on the grass, his rifle at his side, and his pipe on the ground just as it had dropped from his mouth. My first idea was to hide his rifle, and then fire mine over his head; but on second thoughts I did not like to play such a trick on a comrade, but preferred awakening him by the drawing of a cork, a sound familiar and welcome to his ear.

A drink and a pipe, and then he began to tell me his experience in tiger-hunting in India, all of which I respectfully listened to. I had been a hunter all my life on our western prairies, great seaboard, and immense rivers, and recommended my friend to go to America, if he wanted to have his passion for sport gratified to the utmost. The buffalo, and grisly bear, the North American panther, and Moose deer, are all more difficult and dangerous brutes to hunt than the Bengal tiger.

It ill betides the unlucky fellow who misses his shot with these animals, and woe to the huntsman who fails to keep very wide awake: to fall asleep would be certain death. Stag-hunting in Mauritius is one thing, but moose and carribo-hunting on the frontiers of North America is quite another.

After a comfortable smoke and chat with my sociable companion, I started back to find my friend whom I had so long deserted. 'Halloo,' said he, 'where have you been?' 'Stag-hunting,' was my reply. 'What luck?' 'I only saw one stag, but did not like to molest him!' We sat down to have something to eat; but whilst doing so, he sprang up, and told me to follow him, as a stag must be near, the dogs were all in full chase.

I ran to the edge of a marsh with a small clump of trees intervening between me and the woods. A noble stag bounded out of the copse into the open, the dogs in full cry after him. They were about 600 yards off, but coming in an oblique direction towards me. 'Shall I fire?' I asked. 'Do you see him?' 'I do.' All the time the stag was bounding before me. I raised my rifle, and fired. The ball took effect, and with one convulsive leap in the air, he fell dead on the spot. We both ran up. 'A good shot, and a long one; you have killed a fine stag,' said W., who cut a notch in his ear for identification.

The ball had entered the fore shoulder, and killed him in-

DEER IN THE JUNGLE.

stantly, and a guardian soon made his appearance, to mark the spot were our game lay.

We returned to finish our breakfast, and before we were well through, my friend, who is familiar with the Mauritian chase, was up again, and told me to keep quite still, as game was near. A faint yelping was heard in the distance, which soon grew very distinct on our right. Along came two or three beautiful does with theirs fawns, but we let them pass, as it is against the rules to kill them. Directly after came a fine stag, the dogs only a little distance behind. His career was soon cut short: W. raised his rifle, and sent a bullet so well home that he only ran a few yards and then dropped. We went up, but found he was not dead; and he tried to use his horns, but W. quickly dispatched him with his knife. Two noble stags falling under our guns, we felt very well satisfied with our day's work, but still eager for sport. Like the mariner I once made a voyage with, who took a drink of whiskey whenever he sighted a lighthouse, we considered we ought to have a bumper of wine whenever we killed a stag, which we did.

Our stags were not, however, so numerous as the lighthouses were to the old salt.

No more game appearing, I laid down my rifle, and wandered away again in search of ferns. This is one of the richest districts for Cryptogams in Mauritius. I soon had my hands full, and having no means of preserving them, I was obliged to make a packet and sling it round my neck. To give a description of them would be to mention half the ferns of the island; they must be seen in their native wilds to be fully appreciated. The long ribbon-like fronds of the *Ophioglossum pendulum*, the large deeply-indented ones of the *Lonchitis pubescens*, as soft as if rich pile velvet; Aspleniums, Nephrodiums, Trichomanes, Gleichenias, the graceful *Ochropteris pallens* with its most delicate foliage; Davallias, Polypodiums—I could extend the list *ad infinitum*, and every fern a treasure, many peculiar to Mauritius. Elegant Lycopodiums shot forth their fronds from old trees, their tassels often four or five inches in length, tossing saucily about with every wind, even the lightest zephyr. Orchids hung from many a branch; Hibernias, Cryptopuses, and a host of others. Lianes entangled my feet at every step, their forms and names utterly unknown to me; and occasionally a tree fern would rear its magnificent head, a crowning beauty to the whole.

I only regretted I was not at the *chasse aux plantes* instead of *aux cerfs*. The prickly raspberry was troublesomely abundant, and it scratches rather hard when its clumps are invaded; but flavourless as it is, I found the slight acid grateful. Numbers of guava trees grow wild, and were laden with fruit, and very good too. At times I had to scramble over some fallen giant of the forest, but its withered form was so covered with parasitical foliage it was, if possible, more beautiful than when alive; its stately head was reared far above the surrounding shrubs that now shaded it from the ardour of the sun. The bark was so closely covered with mosses as to be almost invisible, and it, in its turn, formed a shelter for the roots of the delicate little *Trichomanes Barklyæ*, discovered by Sir Henry Barkly, and named after him. Dense masses of the sombre Jamrosa gave shade impervious to the sun's rays, and I noticed some fine *Diospyros Ebenum*, or black ebony, amongst other large trees.

In a little pond near our post, I saw some wild ducks, probably the *Anas Melleri* (*Sclater*), introduced from Madagascar. They were evidently breeding there, and though I should have liked a specimen, I refrained from molesting them. If not hunted for a few years, they will be numerous enough to afford the sportsman a pleasant day's shooting.

On our left the *chasseurs* were keeping up a perfect fusillade. Bang! bang! every minute.

W. observed, 'There must be many deer in these woods, and terrible slaughter going on; look well to your rifle—it will be our turn soon.' Sure enough, in a few minutes another stag made his appearance, but when he got near us, he swerved off from his track, to an opposite direction. My friend, however, ran and headed him at a great distance, and sent a bullet through him, but he bounded on about a hundred yards before he fell. 'Hurrah for our party! three stags; but three are unlucky, we must have four; we must look out sharp for another, said I.

In the meantime our companion had joined us with bitter lamentations. He had shot by mistake a doe, which unfortunately had fallen on another property, and the guardian had secured it. We three were posted on the outermost limits of Dr. N.'s grounds, and we were told not to fire in a certain direction. Our friend had forgotten this, and finding it poor fun to be sitting all day in the rain, without doing something, he had fired at the first living thing he saw.

We afterwards discovered that our comrades on the right were in much the same predicament, and had been amusing themselves with shooting at old stumps; and one hunter had fired eleven shots at a target, he told me. This was the fusillade we had heard earlier in the morning.

BUTTERFLY.

We had now been on foot over six hours, so we concluded it best to make our way back to the hangar, for the rain had set in heavily, with no hope of a clear sky for that day. As we passed along the woods, we stopped at the different posts to listen to the yarns of each one's prowess. One gentleman swore he had shot six stags, but unfortunately they all sloped; another had shot two, both of which a neighbour had fired his gun over and claimed.

One old French gentleman positively asserted he had shot *eight*, but could only show us *one*, the rest having disappeared in the long grass; his one was, however, a noble animal.

At every post we examined the different firearms, and discussed the merits and demerits of the Queen's arms, muzzle-loaders, English and American revolving rifles, breech-loaders, &c., all of which were represented in our party.

One old fellow looked quite annoyed when we told him we had killed three, and meant to get another. Every hunter we met had killed from two to eight, so we began to multiply our *bonâ fide* three to ten—six Stags, and four Does shot by accident.

One of the party, however, before we reached the hangar, showed us a species of game no one had counted on being in this quarter—a fine wild boar. We were afraid to add pig to our list of *ten* deer, but by our arrival at the hangar most everyone had seen some, if not shot at them, and one only just missed a sow, with a litter of no end of young ones. We laughed, as we passed along, to see an old fellow, wrapped up in a coat and big woollen comforter, hugging a tree for shelter, and peering anxiously to right and left for a deer, regardless of the rain falling in torrents. He told us the dogs had run down a fawn, and that he was sure he had shot the doe, but that she mysteriously disappeared in an impervious thicket. We left him still on the look-out.

We crossed a plain covered with wild guavas, which very likely is the attraction for the wild-pigs; the one which was shot was very fat, doubtless from feeding on this fruit.

We halted about a mile from the hangar, to give the *piqueur* time to bring up the game, much of which was far off in the woods. By about half-past four the men began to bring in the deer, slung on poles, and by them it was all collected; twelve goodly stags, and nine does and fawns (the latter accidentally shot), lay in evidence that there had been good shots and true.

One of *our* stags was missing, it having fallen a few feet over another man's ground, and he refused to give it up. A curious scene is presented at the disembowelling, which took place when all were assembled.

The yelling of the dogs for their share of the spoil; the swearing and chattering of the Creole and Malabar men; the restive mules in the carts brought to carry home the game; the hunters claiming this or that stag; everyone talking and gesticulating at once, would have made a capital picture as 'The

Return from the Chase,' and I wished for my photographic apparatus to catch so piquant a scene.

As soon as the carts were loaded we took up our line of march for the hangar. Here the deer were cut up. It is customary to give the head and horns to the person who claims to have shot the stag, and the carcase is divided into quarters, the proprietor presenting a piece to each guest. When all was finished we made our way back to our carriage, and, wet and weary, were not sorry to exchange the mud and rain of the forest for a warm comfortable room and good dinner.

The wild boar I mentioned as having been shot by one of our party belongs to the race called *cochons marrons*, supposed to be descendants of domestic pigs escaped to the woods at a very early period.

Not having come in contact with this animal myself except on this occasion, I will quote an account of him, written by an old colonist:—

'They occasionally attain great size, some males weighing so much as four hundred pounds, and have tusks nine inches long, measured outside the curve. They feed on worms, grubs, the seeds of the ebony and guava, and whatever else they find in their marauding excursions. They often do a great deal of mischief in the plantations of Savanne, Black River, and Grand Port.

'Their fondness for guavas has caused the spread of these trees, which are not indigenous. The wood is of unrivalled excellence for shafts and poles of carriages.

'Great caution is required in hunting these *cochons marrons*. They possess keen scent, and, when hunted, retreat to the fastnesses of woods and marshes, and it is very difficult to dislodge them. If started, they lead dogs and men many a weary mile, and often make them pay dearly for their sport when they catch them.'

Since writing the above I have attended many chases, and most on a different plan. Those given by Messrs. Currie,[1] Autelme, and others, are on a very different plan. There is generally a meeting at the hangar, where refreshments are provided for the *chasseurs* before proceeding to the woods, and on

[1] I have received three invitations from these gentlemen, but some unforeseen contrariety always prevented my acceptance of them.

their return they sit down to a handsome dinner, where the incidents of the day's sport are related over the best wines to be procured in the colony. Sometimes the *chasse* lasts several days, and beds are provided at the hangars for guests.

At Flacq a party of gentlemen formed themselves into a sort of hunting club, and I have received many invitations. There the members draw for their stands on the ground before proceeding to the *chasse*, and they draw for their venison when the game is cut up.

During the season there is a *chasse* about once a fortnight, and I have seen as many as thirty-six deer killed in a day. After the day's sport was over, it being too far to return to Port Louis, I joined some friends, and shall not easily forget the hospitality I have received, nor the pleasant evenings spent, at Richemare.

CHAPTER XIX.

A HINDOO FESTIVAL.

Deities principally worshipped at this Fête—Temple at Roche Bois—Dress of both Sexes—The Old Man and his Jugglery—Burning and Flogging—Priests and Dancing Girls—Indian Musical Ideas—Walking through Fire—Sham Human Sacrifice—January Fête—Crowds in Attendance—Gouhns—The Priest's Blessing—Refreshments—Jewellers plying their Trade—Idols—Torture as a Means to fulfil a Vow, or secure future Benefits—Rolling round the Temple—Breaking Cocoa-nuts—The Tank—Ordeal by Diving—Sinnatambou—Precepts of the Shastras in Reference to these degrading Rites.

In the Tamil month of Audi, corresponding in English with the month of August or September, the Madras and Calcutta Indians hold a religious festival in honour of Doorga. Before describing it, I will give a slight account of this goddess, and of the two gods Kartikeya and Ganesa, all of whom play a prominent part in these revels. Doorga, also called Kallee or Throwpathy, is the chief among the female deities, and indeed the most potent and warlike member of the Hindoo pantheon. The Greeks worshipped Minerva, an armed and martial goddess, but she was a meek and pacific maiden compared with the spouse of the Indian Destroyer.

The wars waged by the latter, and the giants who fell beneath the might of Doorga's arm, form prominent themes in the wild records of eastern mythology. Her original name was Parvati, but hearing that a giant called Doorga had enslaved the gods, she resolved to destroy him. He is said to have led into the field a hundred millions of chariots and one hundred and twenty millions of elephants. In order to meet this overwhelming force, she caused nine millions of warriors, and a corresponding supply of weapons, to issue out of her own substance. The contest, however, was ultimately decided by her personal struggle with the giant, whose destruction she then succeeded in effecting; and in honour of this achievement, the gods conferred upon their deliverer the name of the huge enemy she had overcome.

Doorga has equalled Vishnu in the variety of shapes she has multiplied herself into, and of names by which she has been distinguished. The most remarkable being with whom she has shared her identity is Cali or Kalee, who, under her own name, is a principal object of Hindoo veneration. Every fierce characteristic in her original is in Kalee heightened and carried to the extreme. She is black, with four arms, wearing two dead bodies as earrings, a necklace of skulls, and the hands of several slaughtered giants round her waist as a girdle. Her eyebrows and breast appear streaming with the blood of monsters whom she has slain and devoured.

Horrible as this picture is, India has no divinity more popular, nor one on whose shrine more lavish gifts are bestowed. Not content, as the male deities usually are supposed to be, with offerings of rice, fruit, milk, and vegetables, she must see her altars flow with the blood of goats and other animals. The ancient books contain directions for the performance even of human sacrifices to this cruel goddess.

The bands of robbers that infest Bengal hold Kalee in peculiar honour, looking specially to her for protection and aid, and invoking her blessing on their unhallowed exploits by dark incantations.

Kartikeya is the god of war. He rides on a peacock, has six heads, and brandishes numerous weapons in his twelve hands. He presents a striking specimen of the fantastic forms in which Hindoo superstition invests its deities.

Ganesa is a fat personage, with the head of an elephant. But so important is this monstrosity, and so revered, that nothing must be begun without an invocation to him, whether it be an act of religious worship, opening a book, setting out on a journey, or even sitting down to write a letter.

To go back to our festival. Being curious to see all I could of this singular people, I attended one of these fêtes held in an open square at Roche Bois, where there is a temple erected to the goddess Doorga.

The whole of the rites form an inferior kind of Hindoo pantheistic worship. By their Indian laws the worshippers ought to live entirely on rice, milk, fruit, and vegetables; but (like the Catholics) they can purchase a dispensation to eat fowl and mutton; the Calcutta natives eat pork, but rarely the Madrassees.

Large sums of money are collected yearly. Almost every prayer has its price, and nearly every attendance in the temple must be accompanied by some offering. These people are in the grossest ignorance; few of them can read or write, and never was any nation more priest-ridden. One reason for this is that, though they believe Brama and the other gods and goddesses would not quit their magnificent temples in India to reside in these hut substitutes, yet they have implicit faith that they are aware of all their actions through the priests; so the more conscientious a man is, the more he is in fear of them.

Their religious rules are read to them, and they are very reluctant to speak about their religion, in dread that the priests may find it out.

Like all idolaters, they are extremely superstitious, and have a firm belief in witchcraft, evil eye, charms and spells, which is not to be shaken.

When very ill they generally make solemn vows to offer a sacrifice to Doorga when well. The breaking of such a vow is almost unknown, as they have not only the fear of the priest before their eyes, but they devoutly believe a broken vow will be followed by some dire punishment, such as blindness, leprosy, &c.[1]

[1] I once witnessed the fulfilling of a vow. A friend was very ill with fever, and an old attached servant was in great grief, and vowed, that if his master should recover, he would offer up a fine cock he had bought for the purpose and duly fattened. Before he was able to carry out his intentions, himself and all his family were stricken well-nigh to death. He then made an additional vow, to sacrifice a goat. As soon as all were well again, he bought a fine animal, and began his preparations; and these show pretty clearly whence their origin.

The goat, like the Paschal lamb, must be a he-goat without blemish, and fed for some days on the best food its owner could afford. As many guests were asked as could eat it up, because, should a morsel be left on the premises, some dire calamity would befall him or his. It was killed on soft ground, where the blood could sink into the earth and leave no trace. It was then cut up; a large piece was sent to his master, who had been very kind to him when ill, and the rest was roasted. Each guest had as much as he could eat, then his family, and lastly himself; what remained was given to the friends to take home. The cock was sacrificed later in the day, and eaten. Nothing would induce him to use the bird when ill, and required soup himself. He said 'No, he had vowed it when he thought his master dying, and as God had heard his prayers, and saved him, the bird was sacred, and he had rather die than touch it.'

The gods Kartikeya and Ganesa are also worshipped, but with fear and trembling: they hesitate even to pronounce their sacred names.

The temple at Roche Bois is about a hundred feet square, with a large dome in the centre, and ornamented with minarets painted in different colours. Workmen were still engaged on the unfinished interior when I saw it.

Thousands of Indians were assembled on the grounds with their yellow, pink, or scarlet robes wrapped in graceful folds around them. The men had massive gold or silver ear, toe, and finger rings, anklets, &c. The women wore the same, with the addition of large necklaces, often of heavy coins; bracelets half up their arms; many of them with a blaze of jewellery in their jet black hair, twisted into the curious one-sided knots that seem *de rigueur* in an Indian belle's toilet, and soaked in gingeli or other oils.

Some were seated crossed-legged in groups, others were amusing themselves singing, riding on wooden horses, swinging, dancing, or with the music of a small drum called the tom-tom, which is beaten at one end with a stick and at the other with the fingers.

A large circle was formed in one part of the square, in the centre of which was an old man entirely nude.

The old fellow's skin looked more like an alligator's than a human integument. He was fully six feet high, of large frame —all skin and bone, a most pitiable-looking object.

He built a fire between some large stones, and placed over it a brass kettle, in which were pieces of bark that soon ignited and emitted a pleasant odour like frankincense. Whilst the bark was burning, he took a roll of cloth, about a foot and a half long, and six inches broad, which he saturated in oil, and lighted at one end by the flame of a lamp. When it was in a blaze he placed it under his arm, and began dancing round the ring, chanting some prayers in some Hindoo tongue. Though his body was fearfully blistered, he continued for half an hour, till the torch was extinguished.

He then approached the kettle, and stirring its contents, he took out a handful of the ashes of the burnt bark, placed them in the palm of his left hand, and walked round the circle, holding out a plate in the right.

Men, women, and children pressed forward, and all placed a copper coin in the plate, when each received a small quantity of ashes, which they rubbed on their foreheads; then holding up the right hand to heaven, they repeated a prayer of thanksgiving that they had been blest by so holy a man, raised the left hand to the chin, and remained silent for about a minute.

The old man then took up a coil of rope braided in the form of a serpent, and addressed a few words to the crowd.

A well-dressed Indian soon came forward, and the old fellow muttered something, and then both set up a shout.

Taking one turn round the circle, he uncoiled his rope, and began lashing the man over the head and face, bringing blood at every blow. The victim (or happy man, as everyone else called him) never winced, but stood motionless till the flagellation was over. He was then marked with ashes and scarlet paint, and retired, one of the heroes of the day. Others followed, till the old man's strength was exhausted.

In the western part of the grounds were three houses, each about 100 feet long by 25, made of bamboo, and covered with palm-leaves. I entered one, and found it filled with a crowd of people, all in the height of Indian fashion. The nose-rings of some of the women were as large as saucers, which did not at all inconvenience them, as they eat through them. On one side sat three Indians, their heads shaved, and hideously painted.

The centre one was beating a tom-tom, the one on the right playing on a sort of clarionet, from which he produced three notes, while the man's instrument on the left could only give forth one melancholy squeak, and the three combined were not unlike a bagpipe.[1]

Opposite them sat, cross-legged, several Indians. They were dressed in European costume, of fine black cloth and white cravats, with a curious white muslin cap with wings. Some were Bramin priests, and wardens of the temple.

[1] St. Cecilia certainly never deigned to visit India, and bless its inhabitants by instilling a little music into their souls. All that I have ever heard consists of monotonous chants of two or three notes, varied only by a rise or fall of the voice, accompanied by beating time with the fingers on anything to hand, even a stick on a piece of wood, when no drum was to be had; and this they will keep up for hours at night, to the great annoyance of their neighbours who have musical ears.

Three young women entered, bowed to the priests, and passed to the back of the house, divided from the rest by a curtain. In a few minutes they re-appeared, with a small white mark in the centre of the forehead, and the parting of the hair painted scarlet. After salaaming all round, they began dancing and singing, the music going on vigorously all the time. They kept it up till tired out, and then disappeared behind the screen again.[1]

I intended visiting the other houses, but my attention was attracted by a crowd at the entrance.

It was caused by a young man about twenty years old, lying quite nude on the ground. On enquiry I found that he had been very sick and had made a vow that if he survived he would roll round the temple; and he was now about to fulfil it.

As he rolled along his wife went before him to clear away any chips or stones that might hurt him. He appeared in the last stage of consumption, and when he had performed the half of his task he fainted.

Buckets of water were dashed over him, and he was restored to consciousness, the crowd urging and encouraging him. He finished the circle of the temple, and then fainted again.

Four men removed him to the shade of a tamarind tree, where the women combed the dirt out of his long hair and washed his body. He was still speechless when I left, and I felt certain he could not long survive his task.

In the centre house six or eight drums and clarionets were making such a horrid din, the men hooting and howling at the top of their voices, that I feared to enter such a pandemonium lest I should be summarily ejected, or, still worse, kept in, when I should assuredly have been deaf in two minutes. Whilst I was looking about me, a rush was made to the centre of the grounds, where a large crowd soon assembled. Piles of wood were burning, which in about an hour became a bed of live embers. Two nude men, having long-handled rakes, were

[1] These women are set apart for dancing at these religious fêtes from childhood. They do not reside here, but come from India in time for the festival. They are a sort of nuns, and are compelled to lead a life of celibacy, apart from everyone, and eat only fruit, milk, and vegetables. They are kept at the public expense, and three different ones are sent every year, free passage being given them. Should any break their vows of celibacy, they are expelled the temple with the greatest ignominy, and their houses are razed to the ground.

employed in getting out the unburnt pieces of wood, and distributing the embers over a square of about twenty-five feet. An excavation was made on one side about a foot deep and six square, in close proximity to the bed of embers, and filled with water. During this raking, several people were employed dashing water over the men to prevent their being scorched by the heat, which was almost intolerable even where I stood.

Everything being pronounced ready by the priest who superintended the whole, music was heard in the distance, and a procession moved along the grassy plain, preceded by men bearing on their shoulders a small platform, on which was an image dressed in Indian costume, loaded with jewellery. They came on in silence, and halted near the burning mass. Presently another similar procession advanced from the opposite side, and faced the first. At a given signal, an old man, with only a cloth round his loins, bearing a child in his arms, stepped into the square, and walked unflinchingly across the glowing bed of embers. Three young men followed, and then a dozen rushed in and ran across, stopping for a moment to cool their feet in the trench filled with water. The contortions, screeching, and yelling of these latter were terrible, and I turned away sick at heart from the sight.[1] This part of the rites is called *thinnery*, or running upon fire.

It seemed to me literally the old worship of Moloch revived,

[1] Strange to say, the Indians persist they do not get burnt. For at least a month previously they undergo severe fasts, taking little except rice and milk; do not even touch grease or animal food; pray incessantly, get the priest's blessing, and then walk fearlessly over the burning embers. They say it is only those who have eaten forbidden food (especially salt fish), got drunk, or committed some unrepented sin, who get burnt.

They have each to pay four or five dollars for the privilege of passing over the fire. My domestic was quite grieved he could not be one of the performers; having my dinner to cook every day, of course he was unfitted to be one. It must, however, be remarked that the men who take part in such monstrous atrocities are but low-caste men.

An educated Hindoo gentleman, now on a business visit to this colony, wrote on this very subject in an article in the *Commercial Gazette* as follows:—

'Can it be said that it is no reproach upon the intelligence of the Indian public? Mr. Editor, to speak the truth, this kind of worship and service to the Hindoo deities is not enjoined in our own Vedas; but these blinded votaries, from a mistaken idea of invoking by dark incantations the protection and aid of the cruel goddess to bless their exploits of robbery, &c., subject themselves to the performance of inhuman deeds.'

and anything more heathenish and devilish I cannot imagine. I then entered the house I had previously passed by, as it appeared to be a great centre of attraction. On one side of it stood a curiously-painted wooden horse, and in the centre was a large block of wood, near which lay a copper dish and a formidable carving-knife. Soon after I entered the usual row of tom-toms began, with a queer sort of singing, and after every sixteen words there was a loud shout from all assembled. After a few minutes four men entered, bearing in something covered with a white cloth, which they laid on the floor.

Presently one end of it was raised, when, lo and behold! a man's head lay on the block. Two men danced and chanted a sort of funeral lament round the body, the instruments wailing out horrible discords; one of them brandished the knife, and at one blow severed the head from the body, which rolled on the floor, the blood flowing into the basin.

This was a sacrifice to Doorga. Probably in former times it was a real victim offered up—a sort of judicial sacrifice, as far as I could make out; now they make a very clever imitation of a human being, and go through the customary ceremonies.

In 1868, on account of the fever raging amongst the Indians, they were obliged to postpone their January fête. It was held in September, and as it was to be on a larger scale than ordinary I determined to be present at it.

This festival had been prepared for above a month previously. The priests had gone round everywhere, and each Indian that promised to attend was marked on the forehead with ashes, and paid a small coin. Thus not only were large sums collected, but a full attendance was insured, as none dared to break their promise to a priest. Every night, for a week before the 14th, small gouhns had been carried about, and sundry amusements going on, but on that day began the serious work. Crowds gathered from all parts of the island. Every railway train was full to overflowing, and very many more would have been too if the railway people had only had the bright idea of running an extra train or two on the 14th and 15th, and thus taking advantage of the great influx of passengers.

It was a sight to see when the overloaded carriages discharged their living freight, dressed in all the finery procurable for love, money, or credit, in the bright hues dear to Indian tastes, and decked with gold, silver, and precious stones in lavish abundance.

Hundreds could not be accommodated by rail, and those were lucky who could get carriole or carriage, for which they would pay any price, to get to Terre Rouge.

The priests have collected enough money to purchase about four acres of ground just off the main road leading to the arsenal. There they have erected several chapels and other buildings, suitable for their particular worship—if such a mass of superstition and idolatry can be called worship.

The principal part of the first day's proceeding was the fire-walking, previously described, but as I did not care for a repetition of such a scene, I went the second day.

It was with difficulty I could procure a conveyance to Terre Rouge, and no easy matter when there to make my way through the dense crowds; though I must say, however thickly congregated Indians may be, they will always make way for a white man, and generally with politeness.

My attention was first attracted by a number of very large gouhns, fantastically painted and gilded, mounted on huge wooden wheels, with ropes attached to the axles, so that they might be moved forward by the devotees.

On entering the grounds is a chapel, containing the image of some god made of iron, about three feet high, smeared with cocoa-nut oil and dirt, and mounted on a small altar.

At its side sat a villainous-looking priest, holding out a small tin box to all comers for coin, myself included. Two little dishes lay before him, filled respectively with powdered saffron and wood ashes. Everyone who gave a piece of money received a little of each powder, with which they marked their faces. (*Bien entendu*, *I* declined the favour.)

On both sides the path leading to the chapel were booths filled with cakes and sweets, dear to an Indian's, but very suspicious to an Englishman's palate.

Lemonade,cocoa-water, and cigar vendors did a good business; and in another booth, containing an immense variety of ornaments, the three salesmen appeared to be doing a thriving trade.

I saw as many as twenty bracelets placed on a young woman's arms, and a dozen small rings on a child's, still at the breast.

The men seemed to be quick, sharp fellows; they would take the measure of the arm or toe, cut the bracelet or ring of metal, fit it in a few minutes and solder it on, not to be removed till it sinks into the flesh as the arm enlarges.

At the entrance of this booth sat a group of men striking at each other with stout sticks, about three feet long. They managed to do this so as to let the blows fall in time to a sort of monotonous chant they were droning out.

I passed on to the main chapel, a building about fifty feet long, three sides of which were open. A small iron god stood at the entrance on a sort of altar decorated with flowers, and attended by a priest, who had also his collecting-box. Ten feet behind the first was a large and very ugly idol, partially covered with a piece of cotton cloth, an old broken iron lamp at its side, and guarded by a priest. There was a third that appeared to be the god actually worshipped—a doll-like image dressed in the Malabar costume, with a silk jacket and langouti, and jewels hung wherever it was possible to hang them. A large crowd of half-nude men and women were near it; dim oil lamps lighted it, and two hideously daubed Indians waited on it.

To enter these sacred precincts I was obliged to take off my shoes, and by thus respecting their prejudices I was assured a free access everywhere, and all were anxious to show me anything I wanted to see.

Just as I entered, a noisy flourish of tom-toms announced the arrival of a procession headed by a priest, and immediately behind him came the candidates for the honour of being tortured. They had on only the waistcloth, and each held at arm's length wires as large as a goose quill, four feet long, one end sharply pointed. On they came, and halted in front of the image in centre of the building.

There the wires were received by the priests and blessed, and they were then given to an attendant. A small stiletto was passed to another, with directions how to use it.

The first who approached was a well-built muscular man, and the stiletto was thrust through his flesh under both arms, about four inches below the armpits, then immediately withdrawn, and the wires inserted in the puncture. From one to three were placed under each arm, and, to drown the moans of the victims of an idolatry fit only for the darkest ages of the world, a crowd of spectators set up a howl.

At the same time there were others with skewers thrust through their cheeks, tongues, and lips, and one poor wretch had a sharp wire as thick as a large pin inserted in the forehead, and passed through the face downwards till it came out at the chin.

After all had been operated on they left the chapel, accompanied by the priests and men flourishing sticks round them. They appeared to suffer a good deal as they kept turning the wires in the wounds, in spite of the gangh and other intoxicating drugs given to deaden pain. Kettle-drums were then added to the other instruments, and with their din and the people's shouting and yelling, it was perfectly diabolical.

The poor tortured creatures began dancing and singing a sort of triumphant song, and advanced towards the open space at the entrance to the grounds, the men with sticks occasionally making feints to strike them over the head. Two men carried a copper dish containing some yellow wash, which they frequently applied to the wounds. This lasted over an hour, when all returned to the chapel, the wires were withdrawn, and after the wounds were dressed they bathed in water blessed by the priests, and their performance ended.

It is marvellous what fanaticism will enable its slaves to endure. These men paid two dollars for each wire thrust through them, besides other fees to the gods and priests.

I learnt afterwards that all these men had made vows the preceding year. Two who were married, and had no children, vowed a sacrifice if they were blest with one before the next festival, and the others were vows made during the fever time.[1]

[1] These frightful practices are endured annually to satisfy the cravings of the goddess Yellamah *alias* Throwpathy, who is represented to have tiger's teeth, cat's eyes, a dog's tongue, and a hideous countenance.

It is sensibly asked by one of themselves, 'Cannot this waste of time be prevented? Can this abuse of human energy not be checked? Cannot the Hindu mind be educated so as to run in a better channel? Cannot this festival be turned from dissipation of the lowest grade into a fountain of pleasure and instruction?' He says also, 'The cruel practices alluded to are not worthy of man, and especially of the Mauritian Christian Government, which seems to countenance them, although such monstrous festivals have been nearly put down even in the superstitious land of India.'

Occasionally there is the hook suspension, but it costs twenty-five dollars, besides exacting rigid fasts and penances.

My own domestic, though still a young man, said he had undergone it three times in India, and that if he had the money he would willingly do it again; only, he added, 'They did not know how do it properly here.'

In front of one of these images were numerous small dishes filled with rice, bananas, cocoa-nut and yellow-powder, all of which had been long before consecrated, and, most important of all, the inevitable money-box.

The candidate for the favour of the god presents himself kneeling, and holding out his joined hands. These the priest fill with rice, on which he lays a banana and piece of cocoa-nut, and marks him on the face with the powder. A piece of money is then tied with a string on the wrist, not to be taken off till the festival is over, when both string and money must be religiously kept, as they form a charm against all influences, human or diabolical.

The rice is held for a few minutes, and if the man's conscience does not accuse him of any sin since he was marked for the fête, it remains good; but if any unlucky peccadillo, such as tasting salt fish, or other forbidden dainty, returns to his memory, woe betide him: the rice withers in his hand, the mark is taken from his forehead, and dire will be his punishment.

If all is well, the rice is returned, with, of course, the customary obolus to the god (*i.e.* priest). This ends the ceremony, and the recipient of divine favour walks away with a light heart under the influence of the priestly absolution, though I do not know for how long a time it will hold good.

Just behind the chapel is a tank about twenty feet square, and the same in depth, containing four or five feet of water.

A flight of stone steps led down to it, and wreaths of flowers floated on the surface, and men and women were bathing in the filthy liquid, greasy from the emanations of their bodies, covered with different oils.

Having taken their bath, they prepared an offering to present to the iron god. Groups of men and women were seated on the steps, engaged in mixing flour in small copper pans with the *consecrated* water, and, beating up bananas with it, formed a sort of cream. Each person, selecting two attendants, took his or her offering, and, wet and shivering, went to the door of the temple, and placed a shilling in the box; then, prostrate before the priest, received a small green spray from the idol's neck. Afterwards they all laid down, and clenching their hands, began rolling round the chapel in the dirt. The kettle-drums beat loudly, and they rolled till quite exhausted, the women sometimes fainting. The latter frequently sweep the ground with extended arms, rise and make one step, then down again, till the whole circuit of the chapel is completed. As many as fifty people were rolling at one time, all smothered in dust, as may well be imagined.

After this performance a priest took his stand behind the chapel, near a large pile of cocoa-nuts. One by one the spectators go up to him for a nut, which he cracks; and if the shell happen to break crookedly, it is rejected as a sign that the man or woman has sinned during the festival, and the culprit is expelled; if, on the contrary, it break evenly, the applicant gets half, and deposits threepence in the other moiety as the priest's perquisite. When all are served, the broken bits are flung amongst the crowd, when a regular scramble takes place for the prizes. It is a most ridiculous scene, as they lie struggling over each other, as eager and excited as a band of children among whom a handful of nuts has been thrown. Outside the temple were three gouhns, about fifteen feet high, mounted on wheels, and containing seats. In the evening a god was placed in each, and a priest got in, and was dragged about, principally by children.

The day's proceedings terminate a sort of Lenten fast, and at sundown hearty dinners were being eaten in all directions. About ten o'clock at night the steps to the tank are lit up by cocoa-nut oil lamps, and a gouhn is placed in a little boat on the water, with the representative of Bramah in it.

A sort of paste is prepared, and any one who likes can throw a bit in. If he is a good man, Bramah permits the priest who dives for it to find it; but if a sinner, it is hidden for ever from human eyes, and the man is to be shunned. This water ordeal often lasts till past midnight.

The whole of this festival, and all connected with the Hindoo religion, is regulated by an old man called Sinnatambou.[1] All these scenes I witnessed within a mile or two of Port Louis; and the thought struck me that, instead of sending away *all* the missionaries from Mauritius to Madagascar, it would be better if they concentrated their forces against the hydra-headed idolatry and superstition rife over the island.[2]

[1] This man is a Hindoo of weaver caste, and is said to encourage these festivals, not from any regard to the deity or religion (in which he is no adept), but from desire for filthy lucre. He pockets the annual income; and as most of the managers of the temple are in some way or other under obligations to him, they dare not compel him to render an account to the public.

As usual amongst Indians, even this small community is not devoid of partisanship. At one time the most influential man was Mylapoor Moonisamy, who is now the head of the opposition party to Sinnatambou, and president of a small temple on the Nicolay road, dedicated to Siva.

[2] Since writing this chapter, I have been informed that these degrading rites and cruelties are not only disallowed by the high-caste Hindus, but that they are positively contrary to the precepts of the Shastras, in which it is stated that 'all those ignorant persons who regard as God an image of earth, metal, stone, or wood, subject themselves to bodily misery, and can never obtain final deliverance.' In the Bhagwat Gita it is also written, that 'He who worships matter becomes himself matter (*i.e.* a blockhead).' So far from approving such squandering of large sums of money yearly (sufficient, as a Hindu told me, to put every Indian child to a national school), there is a strong feeling against it, and a wish that so much zeal could be utilised to better purposes.

It is supposed that a thousand dollars were expended in fees alone this year (1870) for undergoing different tortures. Seventy-one victims passed through the fire, each of whom had to pay $2 50c. for the privilege, besides priests' fees.

CHAPTER XX.

ACROSS COUNTRY TO THE DYA-MAMOU AND OTHER FALLS.

Advice to Stay-at-homes—Invitation—Leaving the City—Into the Woods to Frésanges—Ravenalas—Dhoodie—Night and Morning—Rain no Effect on our Spirits—Contrast of Colour in Woods—Our Guide and Woodsmen—Ferns—Banks of the Rivière du Poste—Grand River, S.E.—The Dya-Mamou—The Caves—Cascade of Roche Platte—Back into the Woods—A Path for us, Death to the Shrubs and Creepers—Carias—Wasps' Nests—Swallows' Cave—A Skull—Story of Slave Woman—The Return—Incredulity of Friends.

WHO is there living in the Island of Mauritius that is fond of beautiful scenery, and yet has never visited the picturesque and romantic falls of Dya-Mamou, in the district of Grand River, SE.? If there is such an unfortunate individual, let me advise him to pack up his knapsack and be off 'over the hills and far away' the first holiday he can get.

These falls (like other lovely things I could name) are not to be lightly attained, but require infinite patience and perseverance before the prize is gained. Dense pathless forests must be traversed, and the tourist will find a difficulty in making his way without a guide.

In the month of June an invitation was given me to join a party of gentlemen all eager for, and equal to, a tramp across country to visit some part of the Mauritian forests to which they and myself were strangers, and also to see the famed Dya-Mamou and other falls in the neighbourhood; caverns, and many other curios that came in our way.

Arrangements were made to leave Port Louis by the 1.45 train, and go to a private station between Curepipe and Cluny, and permission had been granted our party to occupy a hangar about four miles distant from it.

All assembled at the station as agreed on, in spite of wind and weather (for it had rained all day), and a still falling barometer. We arrived at 4 A.M. at the small station, servants, baggage, all right, for we had taken the precaution of having food enough for two days, and a change of clothes.

We set off in high spirits, and soon met a servant of the owner of the forest, a guardian I presume, who led us into a narrow path which carried us directly into the woods. This man lived in a little thatched cottage, standing in an open space of about three acres, and close round about it were deer with their fawns feeding.

They did not seem at all alarmed at our presence; the stags merely tossed up their antlered heads and snuffed the breeze as we passed by and left the graceful animals to enjoy the sweet tender grass and scented herbs which were here in abundance.

The rain poured, and we had several streams to cross before we came to the hangar of Frésanges.

We only stopped here a few minutes, and then pushed on to Dhoodie, another hangar, where we intended to pass the night. Our servants had gone on with the baggage, and it took us three-quarters of an hour's hard walking through a most intricate forest before we reached the hangar. Just before entering the forest we crossed a plain covered with the Ravenala or Traveller's-trees as far as we could see. They stood in groups of eight or ten, many trunks springing from the same roots. I counted twenty-four full-grown trunks of about twenty-five feet in height, all appearing to shoot from the same root-stock.

This singular tree grows to great perfection here, seeming to rejoice in the swampy land. It struck me as one of the most curious vegetable sights I had ever seen. On a little elevation on the south side of the plain was a row of them, as even as if planted by hand, nearly all of the same height; and they stood like a file of giants, their dull green spiked leafage swaying with every breeze, and producing a peculiar creaking rustling sound.

Although we were wet through by the rain, we could not refrain from halting to gaze on this wild bit of tropical scenery. Just beyond this grove was another entirely of dark jamrose, in full flower, filling the heavy air with soft fragrance. I continually lagged behind, admiring everything, and was at last obliged to push on briskly to join my companions, whose patience I must have tried pretty severely on this journey.

A change of clothes, and a supper to which all brought good appetites, made us forget the discomforts of the rain, and we passed a pleasant hour in chatting over our recent walk and laying our plans for the morrow. Our sleeping-room was about 40 feet in length, on one side of which a platform is built three feet high, that we covered with soft dried grass, over which we spread our blankets, and lay down 'to sleep, perchance to dream.' I've no doubt my younger comrades may have dreamt of 'the sweet wee wife and tiny bairns' at home, but I know that a few minutes after my head lay on my pillow (made of a rolled-up overcoat) I slept far too soundly for dreams.

At daylight we were up and away to the river near by for a bath, and then back for cigar and coffee.

I sauntered about, inspecting the premises whilst inhaling the fragrant weed. There were six or seven houses at the hangar, all of native timber and thatched with vacoa leaves; one is the *salle-à-manger*, capable of containing tables for a large party of hunters; our sleeping-room, where at least forty persons could be accommodated; a kitchen and spare rooms for servants. These buildings are situated on a little bend of the Rivière du Bois, and are surrounded by trees, which grow to the water's edge.

Still the rain fell, and it looked gloomy and threatening, and a consultation was held as to what course to pursue. We had come to see the Falls, and nothing short of an earthquake or deluge should stop us, was the first resolution passed, *nem. con.* Our servants looked downcast and shrugged their shoulders, and talked of impossibilities; so we soon settled that question by deciding on sending them back to the hangar at Frésanges with our baggage, and gave them instructions to wait our return there.

By seven o'clock we started with our guide, fording the Rivière du Bois, just at the back of the hangar, and passed along a narrow footpath, overgrown with wild raspberries and ferns, into the depth of the forest. All along we saw tracks of the wild boar and deer, which abound in this vicinity, that lead into parts of the woods most difficult of access to the hunter. We disturbed numbers of the Myna-birds, and their shrill chattering whistle as they flew over our heads enlivened the silent forest. A few of the Coq de Bois were seen, and appeared very tame.

The continued rain had no effect on our spirits, and one of our party cheered us the whole route with bursts of song, now a ballad, now a snatch from an opera; and the more the difficulties of our path, the more the woods resounded with his voice. I, as usual, was always in the rear, clutching a moss here or lichen there, and, again, a root of a fern: the former were easily detached from trees and stones on account of the wet. We frequently encountered trunks of large trees prostrate in our path, covered with green mosses, and the eye would be instantly attracted by little groups of the *Eridia auricula Judæ*, or Judas' ears, which when wet are of the brightest scarlet. The contrast of colour is charming in these woods; the varied greens of the ferns, the yellow Sphagnums, the neutral tints of the lichens, the brown or moss-covered trunks, are inexpressibly beautiful to me. I often think what a great affliction it must be to those who have what is called 'colour blindness,' though to them who have never had the pleasure of a keen perception of colours it may not be so great a deprivation as to those who have.

Seeing me always in the rear, 'our friend lingers' I heard one say to the other, but I was neither tired nor deficient in a tramp. No! but every sense was absorbed in the surroundings. I was feasting on the scene and feeling, as I ever do when out in the wild, that this is truly a joy-giving world in which we live. Miserable mortals that we are, grubbing everlastingly after the 'almighty dollar,' and neglecting almost everything great and good, passing on and off this busy stage without enjoying, scarcely conscious of the beauty created expressly 'to give delight to man,' and to elevate and prepare him for a still brighter sphere.

My companions were all men of education and refinement, and appreciated everything as much as I did; but they were far wiser, for being wet and uncomfortable, they were hurrying along to our first halting-place, which we reached after passing through another grove of Ravenalas. The guardian of the place seemed to have expected us, for he came out to meet us, and offered his services.

This place much resembles the last, with the exception of the vacoa-thatched huts being smaller. The frame of a large hangar lay on the ground, and would soon be ready to replace the old one. A good many Malabars lived here, and there was a large pond, or basin, as they call it, filled with Gourami, so that fine fresh fish can be had at short notice. The trees and underbrush had been cleared away, and a very pretty view was had westward. Our refreshment got through, we agreed to proceed directly to the Falls, now about four miles distant.

They reckon distance by time, so they said it was about an hour's walk hence. The guardian, who was a very polite French Creole, set off with us, taking along with him several of his men. One strong stout Malabar preceded us with a sharp cleaver, to cut away the impediments from our path.

No sooner were we back in the forest than I was soon behind again. That fine fern the Langue de bœuf (*Aspidium nidus*) was growing on the top of an old giant, the largest tree I have seen here, with the exception of the Boabab. The tree was dead, and had been broken off about fifteen feet from the collum; it was covered completely with creepers, ferns and mosses, and crowned with this elegant fern. The fronds were many of them ten inches wide and five feet long, so green and luxuriant, and so incorporated in the old trunk, as to appear to be the leaves of the tree itself. A little farther on we came to a profusion of the *Callipteris prolifera*, one of the finest of its family. This species rapidly propagates by throwing off shoots at the joints of the pinnæ on the midrib, and when the small leaves appear on the shoots, they drop off and grow.

We soon reached the Rivière du Poste, which was somewhat swollen, but we forded it without much difficulty. As we crossed over to the right bank, we all exclaimed on beholding the beauty it presented. The bank shelved, and tier on tier of the lovely *Ochropteris pallens* rose one above the other, and over them the jamroses spread their branches till they nearly touched the water.

Intertwined in all directions was a species of purple convolvulus in full flower. It was a perfect picture: the dark leaves of the climber, and purple blossoms, the very pale greens of the ferns, the primrose tint of the jamrosa-flowers in their dark setting—the pen fails to depict it: 'we should need colours and words that are unknown to man.' Our guide was constantly calling attention to different plants medicinally used by the Creoles. He showed me one that he said would produce death in a short space of time after the juice had been taken into the system. I did not know its name, but found it a species of Euphorbia.

He said if a branch was bruised, and thrown into a pond, it would destroy the fish. He especially pointed out one that would cure a person that was addicted to the use of ardent spirits (pity it is not generally known), with many other wonderful things, to all of which we listened with becoming attention.

We soon began to hear the noise of falling water, and our guide told us to be careful, as we were on the banks of the Grand River, SE., just below the falls, and that the ravine was very steep. The woods hereabouts were more dense than ever, and it was with difficulty we could make our way. Our sapper and miner, who preceded us, slashed away right and left; and, advancing in single file, in about half an hour we reached the bottom, without any casualty except a few bruises and tumbles.

Then what a view opened out to us! The Dya-Mamou Falls, in all their magnificence, were before us. What a lovely romantic spot! I was fascinated, spell-bound! We crossed the river by jumping from rock to rock, till we reached an elevated position among huge boulders and rocks that lay in the wildest confusion, some in heaps just as they were tumbled headlong from the heights above. Our post was somewhat perilous, for the rocks were slippery, and facing us was a steep basaltic cliff looking down into a deep basin much disturbed from the volume of water passing through it, and a few yards off was the roaring cataract. On account of the previous day's rains (or perhaps in honour of our visit) there was a much larger body of water than usual: it foamed and hissed over the perpendicular basaltic wall of rock, and then thundered into the abyss below with terrific sublimity. These falls are about one hundred feet high, and I should say the sheet of water was fully fifty feet wide. The sides of the ravine just below the falls are bold, covered with immense detached masses of rocks, very difficult to clamber over. There is a pretty little cascade a few yards off in the river, but its beauty is lost in the magnificence of the Dya-Mamou Falls, which in my opinion are the finest in the island.

The sounding cataract
Haunted me like a passion: the tall rock,
The mountain, and the deep and gloomy wood,
Their colours and their forms, were then to me

An appetite; a feeling and a love
That had no need of a remoter charm,
By thought supplied, nor any interest
Unborrowed from the eye.

We feasted our eyes on the scene for some time; and our next move was to the caves on the left bank of the river, near the front of the falls. We had to make our way over the boulders at the edge of the river, and a false step would have plunged us into an involuntary bath; not that it could have made much difference in the condition of any of the party, for we had been 'dem'd moist unpleasant bodies' the whole day.

We reached this curious place, and there our guide told us the old story of a slave having made it his home for (some say) ten years. His retreat had been sought in vain, till smoke was discovered issuing from the cave, which led to his capture.

This cave is about twelve feet wide and twenty high, and appears to have been formed by a huge detached rock sliding out from the original formation to a distance of about twenty feet, and another much larger lossened above, which slid over the opening, forming a complete roof to the cave. Numerous ferns and creepers grew in the interstices of the rocks; and I made up my mind, if opportunity occurred, to pass a few days in this neighbourhood, making this cave the base of my operations.

Of course we heard the usual account of the monster eels in the basin, and which I believe is told of every river and pond in the island. I am aware there are large eels, having been at the death of one weighing forty-five pounds; but this is rare, and then they never attack man. After inspecting the cave, we ascended the ravine by a path hewn out of the bushes for us, and in a few minutes were again on the brink of the falls. It was a grand scene: the foaming, roaring waters below encircling a pretty little island studded with trees and shrubs; the deep black water in the back ground; rocks piled fantastically one on the other; large clumps of luxuriant ferns growing from the interstices; the sides of the ravine covered with trees, and a lofty mountain rearing its stately head in the distance. The long tortuous course of the river could be distinctly traced. Near the falls it is about two hundred yards wide, and very shallow; the bed filled with rocks and stones, over which the water rushed, forming rapids like miniature Niagaras.

Just above the falls, on a little flat formed of vegetable *débris*, I found the Erica growing, but not in flower; and groups of the finest bamboos I ever saw were there.

After enjoying the scene to the utmost, we visited another pretty little cascade called Roche Platte, about twenty feet in height, with an unbroken sheet of water passing over a perfectly flat table-rock into a basin below. We did not remain long here, but passed into the forest, which grew to the river's bank, our sapper still preceding us and spreading death and destruction around. With his sharp cleaver, which was about four feet long, he laid low hundreds of pretty shrubs and young trees; and many a delicate creeper was cut down and lay withering in his path that had so lately revelled in luxuriant grace.

I noticed many dead and dried trunks of large trees, with huge nests of the Caria, or white ant, surrounding them. These nests look like a great mass of cinders, and when broken are found honeycombed all through.

This species of white ant is very destructive in a forest, especially to vacoas, but I believe they generally attack trees in a sickly condition. The first signs of decay are the appearance of a fungus, which is caused by gases emanating from decomposed vegetable matter in the tree. Then the Caria is sure to follow, and the doom of the tree is sealed. They say portions of these nests are gathered by the Creoles, and prepared in some way as a decoction good for sore throats.

The servant to whom I had entrusted my fern treasures suddenly threw them all down, and disappeared in the thicket. I began to gather them up myself, somewhat vexed, when presently he emerged bearing a large wasps' nest full of young. He had not deserted me, but having espied the nest he had gone after it; and though the wasps had stung him, he carried off his prize. I was curious to know its use, for he took such particular care of it on the way back. The guide told me the Creoles esteemed them greatly, and broiled them over a quick fire, and then with a sharp-pointed stick picked out the young wasps and ate them! 'Delicious! sir, delicious!' he said; 'I shall try to get the next for myself, as I am very fond of them.' Well, white-ant tea and young broiled wasps may be good for those who like them—*chacun a son goût*—but I would rather be excused.

Three-quarters of an hour's hard tramp over streams of water and boggy ground brought us to within a hundred feet of another waterfall, the 'Cascade des Hirondelles.' It is very picturesque, but has not so large a body of water as the Dya-Mamou.

On the left bank of the river is a considerable-sized cave called the 'Swallows' Cave,' from those birds being supposed to build there in vast numbers; but I could not find one nest. It is about fifty feet deep and eighteen or twenty feet high. It has been formed by the freshets of the river having washed out the layers of tufa between the beds of lava. The names of numerous visitors were cut in the rocks. After seeing all that there was to be seen, we clambered up to take another look at the cascade. In the little pools I got, for the first time in Mauritius, that singular water-plant the *Hydrodicyton utriculatum*, whose delicate structure resembles a net, every mesh being precisely alike; also some specimens of Chara and two or three of the *Potamogeton utriculatum*, or *natans*.

After feasting our eyes on the scene a short time, we commenced the ascent of the ravine, which is steep there, and we heard the cries and chattering of monkeys. They frequently congregate in hundreds, and if disturbed will sometimes attack the intruder. We found the ground often covered with badanier nuts they had thrown down. Our guide told us this forest was formerly infested by maroon slaves, who committed great depredations on the surrounding plantations, driving off cattle, robbing the poultry-yards, and even white women had been taken into captivity by them. He pointed out a lonely spot where his grandfather was once hunting, when he saw a desperate maroon up in a tree, and as he passed near the slave threw down a little wooden image on to the rock at his feet. No notice being taken of this the man concluded that, though armed, the intruder was not after him, so came down. Many a tale of misery and woe could, doubtless, be told of this forest, where the caves and numerous hiding-places gave shelter to the runaway slaves, who, according to most writers, were horribly treated by some of the planters.

I managed to get some fine specimens of the following ferns

on our way back to the hangar: the *Odontosoria tenuifolia*, *Gleichenia dichotoma*, *Humata pœdata*, *Lonchitis pubescens*, Aspleniums, Trichomanes, and a host of others.

The soil about this region is of a reddish colour, and everything grows luxuriantly, from the constant showers. I noticed a curious geological formation cropping out in some parts of the forest, which was of bright red, a little harder than pipe-clay, and, contrasting with the bright-leaved shrubs, had a singular appearance. As I was searching after ferns I came upon part of a human skull. It was much decomposed, and had probably been for years exposed to the elements.

From the interstices grew a little white liane—life in death; and, after examining it, I laid it carefully back. I looked about, but could not find the other parts. It was a negro's skull, as their formation is unmistakable. 'Poor fellow,' I thought; 'you might have been a slave driven by your cruel master to this stronghold, there to die of starvation, and perhaps on this very spot welcomed death as an end to your miseries.' I turned away saddened, yet thankful that the foulest blot on humanity, the slave trade, is fast disappearing,[1] and will very soon be amongst the things that were.

The return path to the hangar was more open than the one we traversed in the morning; and we could see the Terre Rouge Mountains looming up before us covered with vegetation, with the exception of the western spur, which appeared quite barren, and from our position its shape resembled a Texan ranger's saddle.

I must not forget a story told by our guide of this same spur. He said that, many years ago, a slave woman had fled from her master to the woods for refuge near this locality. Being discovered and pursued, she fled to one of the barren cliffs on the side of the mountain, flung herself over the precipice, and was dashed to pieces.

My sympathies were not so vividly roused as might have been expected, knowing the wonderful propensity of this class for repeating marvellous tales; and I put it down amongst the monster eel and other stories of a similar kind.

For a few minutes the sun broke through the thick clouds, but evidently did not think it worth while to contend against the rain and gloom, so quickly disappeared.

[1] Of course it no longer exists in the Mauritius or in any British possession.

I regretted having only so short a time to pass in this locality, so varied and abundant was vegetable life, and changing its character constantly.

Here and there, on the edges of the openings, was a clump of towering tree-ferns. No matter how often one sees them, every fresh group attracts the attention, and calls forth exclamations of delight; and these, possibly from being sheltered from the winds, had more perfect fronds than ordinary.

After crossing an open space covered with high grass, we re-entered the forest by a narrow path cut by the *chasseurs* to enable them to penetrate to the interior of these wilds. Ravenalas were everywhere abundant, but their grand crests of leaves were often slit into ribbons. The flowers are very insignificant, whitish, and spring from horizontal sheaths, and have a dry banana-shaped fruit. The foot-stalks of the leaves, when cut near the base, yield a plentiful supply of liquid, not only to refresh the traveller in a dry and thirsty land, but to preserve the tree itself in hot dry weather.

We soon reached the Rivière du Bois hangar, and there quitted our creole friend, after thanking him heartily for the assistance he had rendered us. We pushed on rapidly, the rain giving us little respite, and found the streams considerably swollen by all the rain since morning.

However, our tramp was a jolly one, made so by the excellent conversational powers of my comrades. Sparkling chat, a song, a hearty laugh over a stumble—so time and the road slipped away. We took some refreshment at the Dhoodie hangar, and off again to Frésanges, where our servants awaited us. We made such good use of our time that we got up to Mr. Currie's station before the arrival of the train, and were glad enough to exchange our soaked, mud-bespattered garments for a dry suit.

I dropped my companions one by one at their different stations, but not before we had sworn a compact to renew our tramp on the first opportunity. I arrived in town in time to keep an engagement to dinner, where my friends, when I told them of my two days' excursion, put it half down to Yankee invention.

CHAPTER XXI.

ON THE SEA, IN AND NEAR PORT LOUIS HARBOUR, WITH DESCRIPTIONS OF SOME OF THE WONDERS THEREIN.

Start from Home—Embarking at the Trou Fanfaron—Docks, &c.—Landing Bullocks—Scarcity of Shipping—Timber-ship unloading—Abundance of Fish—Clearness of Water—Finding Caulerpa and Halisphila—Description of Hydrometridæ—Errantia—Coasts of Mauritius—Reefs and Fringing Corals—Their Polyps—Boat touching the Reefs—Sharks and other Monsters—Echinas—Fishing up Corals—Their Inhabitants—Fungi Agariciformis—Preparing Corals for sale—The Beauty of the Depths—Origin of Barkly Island—Its Shells and Algæ—Aquariums—Crabs under the Rocks—Surface Corals of Species I have not hitherto found—Champagne Bottles; the various Fumes equally mischievous to Man and Reptiles—Actimas—Pugnacious Eels—Breakfast—Tea *versus* Beer or Brandy—Dragging the Tide-pools—Flying Laffs—Gymnobranchiata—Soldier and Hermit Crabs—Leaving the Island—Examining the Contents of Fishermen's Bags—Ourites—Lobsters—Butterflies out at Sea—Holothuroidea—Overboard to dig up Pinnæ—Dolabella Rumphi Shells—Tropic Birds—The Mud Laffs—Terrible Wounds inflicted by them—Sunset Visions—Return to the Trou Fanfaron.

A DULL cloudy morning and a sprinkle of cold rain. These being often signs foretelling a fine day, or, as the Creoles say, only a 'petite pluie de bon matin, n'a rien ça,' I was in no way discouraged by the prospect. I had made up my mind to a day's thorough enjoyment, and with a friend of like persuasion I set off soon after daylight for an excursion on the sea. Two men, well used to aid me in such expeditions, bore our nets, rakes, bottles, fishing-tackle, long boots, and such-like gear, and a well-filled basket of provisions. Numbers of plying boats are always on hand from daylight to dark, manned principally by Arabs and Lascars, who all rushed forward at our appearance, pressing their claims to attention in a villainous lingo, half Creole, half English.

Many of the old men own several boats, and make a great deal of money plying to and from the shipping. So profitable is it, that after a few years' work some go back to their native countries (principally the ports on the Red Sea) with a comfortable independence. They engage young fellows about eighteen or twenty years old, and pay them a mere trifle a month, they themselves always collecting the fares; and many of these lads make good steady boatmen, though some—I may say most of them—are the sauciest rascals going.

We embarked in the large basin called the Trou Fanfaron, formerly only the outlet of a petty stream, but, enlarged and embanked, it then served for vessels to lie in for repairs not requiring a dry-dock. Within the last fifteen years great changes have taken place here. There have been built, at vast expense and labour, three dry-docks and two patent slips, and there are several spacious marine yards and boating companies besides. In the former vessels of large size can be repaired, and one of them can take in two ships at the same time. Unfortunately the whole have been little remunerative, on account of the fever. Its frightful ravages have spread such terror among sea-captains, that they are even yet reluctant to bring their ships here and expose their crews to its influence.

During the hurricane-season (supposed to last from November to April) the bullockers that trade to Madagascar for the beef supply of Mauritius are laid up in the Fanfaron, as the risk to vessels and their living freight would be too great at that period. At the moment of our embarkation a huge ship, lately arrived, was discharging her cargo of bullocks, and our men rest on their oars for us to witness the operation.

A broad belt is fastened round the body behind the monstrous hump (so noticeable a feature in Madagascar cattle), and then the animal is hoisted out of the hold by machinery, and quietly dropped over the side into the sea. The poor wretches look pitiable enough as they dangle helplessly in mid-air, all their limbs in a state of collapse, and they must feel wonderfully astonished as they find themselves plunging below the waves. Nevertheless, I should think the douche and subsequent swim to shore must be very refreshing to their weary limbs so long cramped in the vessel's hold, as well as a great purifier from the foul odours of their temporary stables. Across the Fanfaron extends the long railway-bridge on strong stone abutments, which excited the Creoles' fears to such a pitch when first opened, that two-thirds of them declared they never could or

S

would cross it, and that *that* alone would be sufficient to insure a failure on the north line. However, on completion, they soon learnt to subdue their feelings and even to cross the Grand River-bridge coolly, where an accident would precipitate the train hundreds of feet below, into the wide and deep river.

We slowly round the point to our left, where vast beds of coral crop out above the surface, and on which the Custom-house and other buildings connected with the marine stand. To the right runs out a long stone jetty, on which is in course of erection a church for the sailors.[1] The old man-of-war (when no longer fit to thunder forth defiance and death) that had been converted into a 'Bethel,' whence was given out the message of love, 'Peace on earth and good-will to men,' had come to utter grief during the last cyclone; so subscriptions were set on foot, and resulted in funds enough for this church.

We keep outside the shipping, which is ranged in tiers in the inner harbour. Formerly it was not without great care we could steer clear of the ropes of the thronging craft of all nations; but now, alas, they lie, like 'angels' visits, few and *very* far between.' The few there are show busy life, cleaning, painting, loading or unloading cargo, principally done by Malabars, all screaming at the top of their voices or chanting the monotonous notes in a high key, without which they couldn't move even a bag of sugar or rice.

Lines of mud-boats passed us, towed by a small steam-tug, taking their freight of filth from the harbour to be deposited far out beyond the Bell Buoy. We hug the shore towards Fort George on the right, and pass the coaling-station for steamers, which is close to the berth appointed for these vessels. Men and things in general wear a coally aspect; and I could not help smiling to see, in front of one of the overseers' huts, a clump of sugar-canes growing green and bright in the midst of the black dust. Close by is at this time an active scene. A large American ship has arrived from the East, laden with a freight of valuable timber, principally the far-famed teak wood from Moulmein. The spirits of the storm have been busy with her, and made wild work of her spars and rigging, and battering her hulk till she is obliged to unload her cargo. The giant logs,

[1] Since completed.

once the mighty monarchs of some Indian forest, are being rafted from her, and lie in hundreds, floating about and waiting to be piled on shore by the coolies.

Another sprinkle of rain, and out comes the sun, dispersing the mists on land and sea. The clouds roll away, leaving only a nightcap on the head of the Pouce, which, with the adjacent hills, half sunshine half shade, looms grandly in the background of the city. Clearly defined are the Peter Both with its royal head, and the Little Peter Both, which is a miniature likeness of its namesake. Sharply outlined against the sky stand the fire-worn cliffs of the Signal Mountain, and faintly visible in the distance are Mount Ory and the Corps de Garde, not yet cleared of mist. The sea is still as an inland lake, scarcely a ripple on its surface ; even the outer reefs are only marked by a slight crest of foam till they approach the Point aux Caves, where the waves are always breaking angrily.

Numbers of pirogues and fishing-boats are coming in rapidly for the early morning market, laden with the finny spoils of the preceding night. The whole harbour swarms with fish, and the strokes of our oars constantly startle shoals of mullets that spring out of the water, their silver sides glistening in the sun.

We now begin to see the corals on the bottom distinctly, but our present quest takes us near Fort George, away from these crystal waters, to a spot where I know a bank, not of odour-breathing thyme, but composed of the densest mud mixed with coal-dust this dirty harbour can produce. And now our work commences. Out come the buckets and dishes for washing ; and my friend waits, spectacles on nose, with magnifying-glasses, sea-weed hook, &c., all in readiness to clutch whatever my rake brings up.

I know of old that in this mud lies a bed of the precious *Haliotphila Madagascariensis* (Steidel). Up comes a mass—not of the coveted treasure—but of fine *Caulerpa denticulata.* It is quickly freed from its muddy coat, and the thick broad fronds show as bright a green as if grown in the clearest spring. Next, I bring up a quantity of *H. ovalis* (R. Brown), much of it in bud; but many times I have to try over a large space before the object of our search is gained. In vain for months have I hunted for this rare plant (which revels in the ooze), to find it in flower ; but to-day we are rewarded, and after getting some bucketsful of it, on close examination after cleaning, we found a few specimens in bud. Very carefully the best are laid in our book, and others placed in a bottle of sea-water for home inspection. A good omen this for our day's success.

As the sun by this time has warmed the water somewhat, we see numbers of what appear like little white dots on long legs, bobbing about and skimming over the surface of the water at the swiftest pace. These curious insects (for such they prove to be) are not easily caught, as on the approach of the net they disappear under the waves by magic; and when I had been lucky enough to secure some, they were so agile, and sprang up the net with such marvellous celerity, that I rarely captured more than two or three out of every dozen in the net. They belong, I believe, to the family of the Hydrometridæ, but of two species unknown to me. One is grey, striated on the abdomen with black lines, and a black patch on the back. The thighs are covered with shaggy down, and the two pairs of hind legs are very long, the front pair near the head very short. The antennæ are jointed like a spider's, and the palpi are visible above the head. Both are diamond-shaped, have prominent eyes, and are whitish on the under side. From this white showing so constantly, they would seem to possess the faculty of swimming on the back like the Notonectidæ, or water-boatmen.

The second species is yellowish brown, with two transverse black lines on each side of the back, and from them descend to the abdominal extremity a double row of lunular spots, also black, traversed by white lines. Two black dots lie behind the eyes, and below them, extending down each shoulder, is an elongated patch of the same. The legs are nearly black, with yellowish white base, and the palpi are so small that they are not visible without the aid of a powerful glass. I first saw this insect at fifteen or twenty miles from the shore to leeward of the island. At the beginning of summer they appear to come inside the reefs to breed, and in February and March may be seen in hundreds near the shore.

One of the men hauls up a floating mass, which proves to be a large Medusa; but being injured, we are about to return it to its native element, when some soldiers on the beach beg it, and carry it off as a great prize. One of them, however, laid hold of it with his hands, but let it drop like a hot coal, and doubtless it felt like one to him, as nearly all irritate the skin greatly when touched. We got a small one, that I brought home to sketch, of a pale buff, grey and white. It somewhat resembles the *Cassiopea Andromeda* (Tilesius), but the disc is perfectly spherical, the divisions grey with milk-white centres, and in the middle a circle with scolloped edges white within, a few pale buff markings showing on it. The edges of the disc are straight, with a cord-like border. The arms are eight in number, leaf-shaped, pale buff with darker edges, and rows of white suckers up them. It is very graceful in its undulating movements, and it remained alive for two days. The second day I could touch it harmlessly, and on the third dissolution began. The leaf-like appendages melted away gradually, but it was five days before the disc perceptibly diminished. We landed close to the fort, to give chase to some of the numerous scarlet-clawed crabs there; but they are so wary it is no easy matter to capture them as they rush to their holes. While the men were busy with them, I examined part of the moat, and fished up some pieces of coral covered with curious green-striated zoophytes. Here and there amongst them were a few fronds of the beautiful plant the *Acetabularia crenulata* (Lam.). I believe this is the first time this plant has been found in Mauritius. The fronds were barely an inch in height, and the exquisite daisy-like cups about half an inch in diameter.

We now turn our boat's head, and steer to the left for Barkly Island. Before we enter the deep mid-channel of the harbour, we hook up one of the Errantia[1] that lie thickly strewn over the coral bottom. Many are over five feet long, and look round and plump in the water, but when brought in on a stick hang limp and most repulsive-looking. They are fond of basking in the sun in shallow water, but hide themselves in the crevices of the coral rocks when disturbed. If they find escape impossible, they will contract into a heap, but float out again directly they are placed in water. Their Creole name is 'S'embrasse,' and truly they hug everything they touch. They are covered with hooked spines (acciculi), which are so small that to the naked eye they resemble only dots or tubercles all over the skin. The animal can evidently retract or protrude them at will, as at times different parts of the body are quite smooth,

[1] Or some genus near it.

but never all at once. This species is of a sandy and greenish gray colour, with dark lines, and a fine head of fleshy, olive-coloured tentacles, beautifully feathered at each edge, twelve in number, that cover a large pink mouth furnished with horny jaws. The body is in tubular segments, that appear capable of elongation at pleasure. I had one in a large bowl with some Holothuriæ, and on the first day they lay a hopelessly entangled mass, only their heads visible. On the second day the hooks seemed to begin to lose their power, and by the end of the third day they were scarcely perceptible. After death I could handle it, though when alive it caused violent irritation of the skin.

While we are crossing the deep water, and enjoying the tranquil beauty of the morning, I will say a few words on the coast of Mauritius and the coral-reefs.

Small as is the actual extent of the coast line of this island, it must ever be one of superlative interest to the naturalist, from the wonderful, ever-changing-never-ending field of research these vast encircling coral-reefs afford. The shores of Mauritius are, as a rule, the most disappointing and uninteresting I ever hunted over; the only exceptions being after heavy weather, when they are strewn with sea-weed. For weeks together I have explored them in my early morning rambles, and not found shell nor plant worth taking.

Yet it appears that all the world imagines both are to be had in abundance for the trouble of picking up, from the constant applications I have from friends in Europe and America —a woeful mistake, for it is a *great rarity* to find a good or perfect shell on the shore. The *débris* of the deposits of ages of shells and corals lie piled up on most parts of the coast, only making it the more provoking, as they show the incalculable wealth of conchological treasures in these seas, and the hopelessness of procuring them. Olives of the greatest beauty swarm on the reefs, yet in three years I have not found a dozen on the shore.

To acquire the treasures of the deep here, you must don a suitable dress, old and thick, not forgetting long and strong boots, and wade along at low water over the inner reefs; and there, if a true lover of nature, in a very short time you will forget the shore's sterility in the varied and wondrous forms of animal life you will meet at every step.

What marvels might be revealed to one with abundant leisure for the task, and the requisite amount of scientific knowledge, to examine the reefs carefully, noting down every discovery—a work of profit and pleasure to him who shall undertake it, and one that will open many a new page in marine zoology. It requires, however, infinite skill and patience, for the sea does not render up its secrets without considerable of both.

These waters appear to possess most favourable circumstances for the growth of the coral polyps. Being in the sub-torrid zone, they have the mean temperature (about 68°) which is supposed to be best suited to coral life. The whole island is surrounded by reefs, with breaks at the mouths of the rivers, with the exception of a small porton of the southern coast, which is precipitous, and where fresh-water streams are constantly pouring down volumes of mud into the ocean, both of which are antagonistic to the development of these polyps, especially the latter, as they require clear water to work in. The innumerable rivers of lava that in former times flowed far into the sea from the terribly active volcanoes in Mauritius, and the submerged cones of the great tract of land once in this vicinity, afforded foundations on which these vast sea-walls have been constructed.

The reefs extend from one to five miles from shore, and at low water it is shoal enough for the fishermen to ply their craft in all but boisterous weather.

A great part of the inner reefs lie a few feet from the surface, and some are partially exposed at very low tides. This does not appear to have an injurious effect on the polyps; indeed, I find it is an ascertained fact that some species of coral will endure temporary exposure to the sun.[1]

When we reflect on the wondrous power these minute animalculæ have of separating the calcareous matter from the ocean to build their cells, it is truly 'marvellous in our eyes.' Numerous as the coral polyps are, yet each one has not only its own peculiar form and manner of constructing its habitation, but its well-defined position in the reefs, as to the depth it requires to fulfil the position of its growth. From 40 to 60 feet is given as the general depth for reef-builders, though some writers go as far as 100.

[1] See Dana on coral formations.

Below this again are others that do not contribute to the height of the reef, but 'grow under its shelter and do not begin to work till it has a certain height, and then they fill the bottom towards the shore.'[1] The principal of the latter are the Dendrophyllæ (the 'shrubbery' of these sea-forests, as Professor Agassiz calls them). This writer, who has made corals an

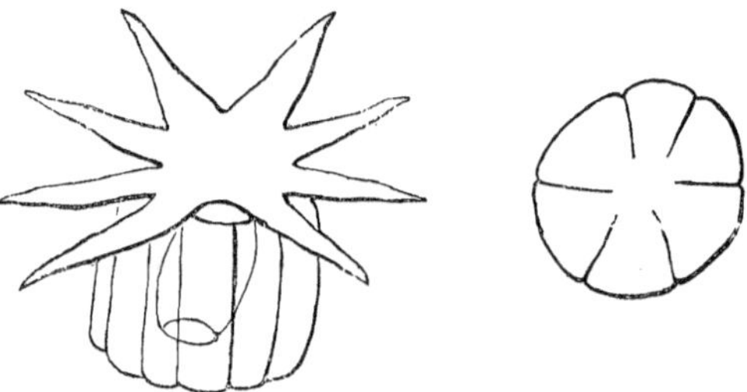

especial study during a long life, gives a most interesting description of the coral polyp, from which I quote some of the main facts.

He says: 'Corals are a part of the body of the animal,[2] as bones

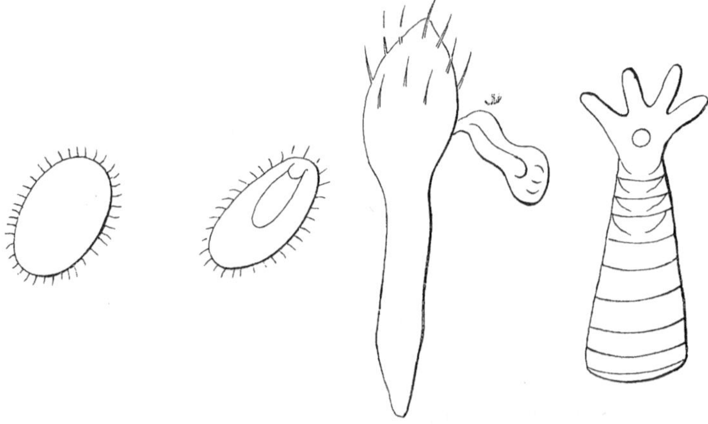

POLYP EGGS. DIFFERENT DEVELOPMENTS OF THE POLYPS.

are of our frame; they are the solid portion of it when alive. They are built upon a plan of radiation, and consist of a

[1] See Agassiz on coral life.

[2] So constantly but erroneously called 'an insect.'

number of equal parts, diverging from a vertical axis, and arranged in a perfectly symmetrical way. They have a central mouth, and a number of feelers surrounding the upper part of the body, which receive the food. This mouth opens into a sac, which is the digestive cavity, having a hole through which the digested food is carried into the main cavity of the body. This latter is divided by radiating partitions into a number of chambers communicating with one another at the centre, but not united there.

'Such an animal when soft is a sea-anemone, but let the walls be loaded with limestone and become stiff, then we have a coral.'

The Professor states another still more curious fact, and one still less generally known than the above, and which solves one of the most perplexing questions in the study of these animals —viz. Whence come the new corals that build up the various portions of the reef? He says: 'On examining these animals, we find along the partitions which divide the internal cavity bunches of eggs, and the young which are hatched from these eggs are free, and swim in the water. They are little pear-shaped bodies surrounded with innumerable fringes which keep them revolving in the water. They move about until they find a proper resting-place, where they fix themselves and grow.'

Whenever there is a reef which has grown up to the level, say of six fathoms, where the second set of corals come in, there will be found these little floating animals, which subsequently attach themselves to the reef at their proper level, and grow. Then another set will come in, in the same way, find their proper resting-place, and so build up the reef.

The outer and inner reefs present a widely different appearance. In the former a certain order is observed. Here are the gigantic Astreas, with their complicated inner structure and deep surface pits, the corrugated sides of which are lined with polyps so delicate and flower-like. These animals are short and cylindrical, with rounded mouths in the centre of the disc, and an indefinite number of tentacles, often spreading out to an inch in diameter, and yet not one interfering with its neighbour. There are several species here. I have found dead fragments with pits nearly an inch wide, and greatly resembling the drawings of *Lithostrotum Canadense* (Castelnau), in the St. Louis limestone of the sub-carboniferous period; and again I see others with pits varying from two to five lines.

The inner reefs are strewn with gigantic heads of Astreas wrenched from the reef-wall by some hurricane, often from fifteen to twenty feet in diameter, and weighing some tons. Many of these great blocks are far above the present sea level in the Black River valley—one of the numerous proofs of the rising of the island.

Next come the magnificent Meandrinas, of varied form and size, but generally heading like the Astreas. I frequently bring up large detached corals of this group covered with a polyp of the brightest green, which retain its colour for a long time by keeping it in the dark. All I get alive have the peculiar surface meanderings much smaller than those in the monster dead blocks I constantly find on the shore.

After the Meandrinas come Porites, Millepores, and other similar groups. This order must not be taken literally, as, though occasionally they may be found in pretty regular succession, and these are the principal of the reef-builders, yet they more frequently grow together promiscuously at different depths; some species of Astreas requiring deep water and others lying on the surface, and so on for all the others.

The above-mentioned are those principally used for lime, and it is curious to watch a large boat unloading, and see the monster blocks tossed on shore to be broken up. Many a precious weed have I found on examining them, which, but for this accident, I might never have seen in a lifetime. Many of the Porites are so solid and hard, it takes heavy blows to split them. The lime-burners frequently go to the outer reefs, and bring back a load of the loveliest of all the corals,[1] the Madrepores, the upper group, and the Fungi, which are not reef-builders.

They have a particular kind of hook for the purpose, and detach large branches of living corals, which they prepare for sale. This is not easy work, for enormous sharks swarm the vicinity, and it is a wonder more accidents do not occur. The corals are chosen that form handsome clusters or branches,

[1] I use this word as everyone here does, without any reference to its scientific signification, corals actually forming no part of the group Madreporidæ.

and they are buried in the sand for a certain number of days, when they begin to whiten. They are very particular as to the time, for if left too long they blacken and are spoilt. When dug up they are exposed to the full blaze of the sun, and every day sprinkled with sea-water, till they resemble masses of frosted snow. They are generally sold amongst the shipping, as the sailors give good prices for them to take home, the people there caring little for such things. The Creoles have a notion that a piece of coral in a house induces headache.

The destructive power of the periodical cyclones on the reefs is enormous; huge masses of coral are dislodged, and carried in towards the shore, where they still go on growing, though less vigorously than heretofore, and form an irregular surface, when sheltered from the force of the waves, but never a compact reef like that exposed to the ever-surging billows.

The reefs in Grand Port Bay, on the coast near Black River, and round the Morne, are the most extensive. In the first-mentioned they are making in rapidly, and in no very long period of time this bay will be impassable for any but the smallest fishing-boats. Not from the quick growth of the corals, which is of the slowest possible, as, according to the greatest authorities, hundreds of thousands of years have been required to bring the reefs to their present size. It is from the masses of loose coral, shell drift, coral *débris*, and sand brought in by every tide, and heaped up by every south-easter or hurricane.

A contemplation of the sea, even in persons who look on it only as a 'waste of waters,' generally induces a feeling of seriousness, if not of sadness. It has a powerful attraction for many who rarely give more than a passing thought to the countless hordes of living beings within it. What endless reflections, then, must it evoke for those who believe with Humboldt that the 'sea contains within its bosom an exuberance of life of which no other portion of the globe could give us any idea!' How truly does another naturalist remark, that 'science has so much to explore in it to carry the knowledge already acquired to the degree of perfection of which it is susceptible!'

How full are those vast prairies of the deep, those ocean forests, of organised beings, all enjoying life under conditions so utterly opposed to those of terrestrial origin; yet all luxuriating in those hyaline depths, whose profound beauty is nevertheless fraught with horror and death to man!

A French writer, I think Lamarck, says, 'we find in the sea unity and diversity which constitute its beauty; grandeur and simplicity which give it sublimity; power and immensity that command our wonder.'

A few more centuries, a nothing in the world's age, but in which the greatest of earth's dynasties may have crumbled to dust, when myriads no tongue could count of these frail architects, these tiny Acalephs and Actinoid Polyps, have perished, their bodies will form monuments that will outlast the mightiest fabrics ever raised by human hands.

They will exist, preparing new lands for new generations of men. The winds and waves, ceaselessly spreading ruin and devastation for *this* age, are hourly helping to accumulate and consolidate on the coral beds earth and vegetation for the lands one day to be inhabited by sentient beings whose intellects may far exceed ours, and to whom perchance the secrets of Nature hidden from our eyes may be laid bare.

A crunching sound—a shock—and I am suddenly brought back from speculations on the illimitable future to the actual fact that my inattentive steering has brought us into contact with the reefs on the opposite side of the deep channel. An unpleasant feeling comes with the shock, for in case of upset even the best swimmer has not a great chance of escape, for the deep water swarms with sharks. These scavengers of the deep are ever on the alert, as all the dead animals either in Port Louis or the shipping are brought out here and flung into the sea, when they are at once devoured.

The Tiger Shark is one of the most voracious of its tribe, a true man-eater, quite as ferocious as the *Zygœna malleus* (Shaw), or Hammer-headed Shark, also a native of these seas, but which is rarely caught. Young sharks are brought almost daily to the market, where they are sold, cut up in slices, to the Indians, who take a pleasure in eating them, out of revenge for the numbers of human victims made a meal of by the creatures yearly.

It is very rare for a shark to be seen inside the reefs in shallow water, but they infest the deep channels or breaks in the reefs at the entrance of every bay on the coast. The Bay of Tombeau, of 'Paul and Virginia' fame, has acquired a terrible notoriety for accidents—pirogues or boats frequently upsetting, and one or more of the occupants finding a grave in the hideous jaws of some monstrous shark.

I assisted at the capture of one of these brutes on board an American whale-ship. A bait was put on a large hook, with a strong chain attached to a three-inch rope as a line. When he felt the hook he ran out some fifteen fathoms from the ship and came near breaking the line. A boat was lowered, and one of the men sent a harpoon into him, when he made straight at the boat; but a whaleman's nerves are not easily flurried, and a steady blow with a whale-spade severed the vertebræ just behind the shoulder, otherwise he would probably have upset the boat. When brought on board and measured, it was fifteen feet long, and the jaws twenty-eight inches in diameter. On opening it, twenty-two young sharks were taken out of the creature, most of them two feet long. The liver filled a small barrel, and yielded a considerable quantity of oil. I have it from good authority that sharks twenty-five feet long have been caught off the harbour.

Dog-fish, skate, rays, and other voracious fish, are constantly captured, and all find ready sale among the black races.

As we slowly glide over the shoal-water we can see the corals bristling with Echini; and it is a lovely sight, as we gaze down between the great blocks, to see, at the bottom of pools from fifteen to twenty feet deep, numbers of Actiniæ in full blow and many-hued fish disporting among them. One lovely Actinia I see for the first time, the tentacles striated pink and white and yellow, and they appear very long, though that may be from the effect of the water. I try hard to detach one, but without success. Another animal, equally beautiful, I succeed in getting, but it resulted in the tube of an Annelide about two inches long, of a rough dirty brown. I suppose I injured it in forcing it from the rock, where it clung so tenaciously, as it never opened again.

I preserved the case, which, though rough outside, was smooth as satin within.

The Echini, both *mammillatus* and *esculentus*, are abundant; also one species I do not know, that has long fine-pointed spines nearly four inches in length, beautifully striated, claret-colour and white, crossing each other in all directions. They are very difficult to preserve, they are so brittle, and are most troublesome to the fisherman, as the spines are serrated, and when they break in the flesh are not easily extracted.

Another very common Echinus has a brown shell with white spines barely an inch long.[1] I have frequently taken them home, and laid them on the ground for the liquids to exude, when the small black ant would attack them, climb up the shell and detach the spines with the greatest activity, and each walk off with a load that must be equivalent to what a large beam would be to a man. When one could not manage his burden, several would help him down the shell, and then run back to their own work. It was most amusing to watch them detaching a firmly set spine, pushing under it with their heads, and rarely leaving it till they had succeeded.

There is a beautiful purple Echinus, plentiful at certain seasons, covered with hexagonal plates, exquisitely inlaid and edged with a border of elongated ones; and another of the same colour, with spines instead of plates. I have taken at different times nine other species of Echini, variously coloured, the names utterly unknown to me.

One of the men hauls up a great branch of the *Madrepore cervicornis*, and a busy scene takes place instantly. Out leap in all directions small glittering fish, the young of the *Holocentrum hastatum*, and others I do not know, green and white. The coral tips are all injured, so we proceed to break it up, and from every crevice creep crabs of all sizes and colours. Some, however, cling so tenaciously they will part with their claws rather than loose their hold. Disgusting-looking, flesh-coloured Annelidæ, covered with white hairs, that punish the intruding hand severely; Squillæ, those queer creatures that so much resemble the praying mantis; and shrimps, pink, olive, and bright green, make their appearance.

Buried in the crevices is the black *Ophiocornus erinaceus* (M. and T.); and how he manages to tuck in his five stiff armour-plated legs into such small holes is always a mystery to me, for when in the hand it is so rigid and inflexible, and the limbs or some of the joints break off with a touch.

Our next haul is too handsome to be treated so ruthlessly as the last, and with the greatest care (one of the men going

[1] The *esculentus*, I believe. I have frequently eaten it, and found it as good as an oyster.

overboard to lend a helping hand) we fish up a splendid branch of the same coral alive, the tips of pale lilac; and hanging in tufts all over it is a pretty little Elachista, which we first carefully detach. Clinging to it are a number of small, rough, brown crabs, so nearly the colour of the base of the coral that we do not at once notice them. They stick most pertinaciously, and are with difficulty got off, but their legs do not appear so brittle as those of many other species, so we got a good many perfect ones. The claws and eyes are enamelled of the same colour as the corals on which they are always found, but when dead they change to pure white. On many of the pieces of dead coral we saw large clusters of the *Digenœa simplex*, which looks so velvety when alive, but quite spoils in the drying.

Lying about on the bottom are hundreds of mushroom corals (*Fungus agariciformis*). They are very small on the inner reefs, and mostly flat, but when alive are curious and interesting. They have no apparent hold on the rocks they lie on, there are no tentacles visible, and, according to Rhymer Jones, 'they have no separate organs for the performance of the vital functions. The thin membraneous film apparently absorbs the materials for its support from the water, and deposits within its substance the calcareous particles which it secretes, moulding them to form its peculiar skeleton.'

I have taken them alive and kept them so for two days in a bowl of sea-water. Their 'gelatinous investment' scarcely contracts from merely lifting the mushroom out of the sea, but if touched with a finger it shrinks visibly. All the laminæ are filled with this gelatinous substance, of a brilliant mottled scarlet, green, and white, and when undisturbed it will overflow and cover them, and has a singular appearance as it oscillates in the water. At intervals on its surface are the soft sucker-like vesicles of a bright lilac colour, which swell out when at rest, but shrink into the mass if touched. These vesicles were once supposed to be rudimentary tentaculæ, but are now believed to be filled with air to support the animal in an upright position, as when overturned they appear to die; I have never found a live one reversed. Some of these Fungi of the sea are tinted lilac and green only.[1]

[1] I have taken two other species at different times of different colours.

Very fine hollow ones are taken from the outer reefs and bleached for sale. I have seen one over a foot across, which was mounted with a silver handle for a card basket, and it made an exceedingly pretty and unique ornament for a lady's table.

We drag up a netful of detached corals, and they are alive with small star-fish, scarlet, brown, greenish; the latter mottled, and always with two or three short arms and two very long ones, or some of them broken, but the wound healed, and the end rounded again, and not appearing at all to interfere with the creature's locomotive powers. From some bits of corals, worn till they resemble small flat stones, hang long wreaths of Sargassum, the disc-like root sticking so fast that it requires a knife to dislodge it. Every leaf is covered with a pale pink parasite, the *Jania antennina* (Kutz), and at first sight it is difficult to distinguish the plant.

One variety of Madrepore is of the palest rose, on the tips of the polyp cells, the upper ones of which are much larger than the lower, and all are elongated and narrow; whereas the lilac-coloured ones are rounder and the upper cells cup-shaped.

Twice only have I found a curious and, I believe, rare coral, a species of Galaxea. It is so fragile that it is quite impossible to get it up with rake or hook; so that, protected from cat-fish, lafs, or other troublesome customers by my long boots, I jump overboard and bring up the little beauty in my hands. Instead of branching, it is a series of slender but solid irregular-shaped tubes, about two inches long, that grow in tufts of ten or twelve dozen. These tubes are grouped together by being imbedded in a soft white honeycombed matrix for about a third of their length, as fine as, and greatly resembling, threads of lace. This small coral is indescribably lovely in the water when alive. The top of each tube is laminated, and is of pure white; the interstices of the laminæ are filled with a brilliant glaucous green and mottled white gelatine, very like the animal of the Fungi: the lower part is brown. The tubes are only laminated about two lines in depth, and the plates are shaped like a broad spear-point set on edgeways, every one being finely serrated. There are twelve large laminæ with a small one between each, the inner edges all meeting round a hollow centre. When living, a small tentacle, of the shape of a pin's head set on a point, appears above each plate, and they do not appear as sensitive as most of the Polyps, for they scarcely retract on touch. In one specimen I found two of the tubes united, and a number of little ones sprouting round the top like a hen-and-chickens daisy.

These tufts at once arrest the eye among the dingy masses of coral they rest on, and for the moment they forcibly reminded me of a bunch of snowdrops springing from the dark earth—a singular idea to cross one under a tropical sun; but there is no accounting for the vagaries of thought, which seems to delight in drawing comparisons between things of the most opposite nature.

The water is here so transparent that we can see to a depth of from fifteen to twenty feet in the hollows between the larger coral rocks; and we never tire of gazing into those deep pools, with their cool quiet beauty, so unlike the upper waters. We are nearing Barkly Island, and between it and the shore at Fort William the water is so shallow that the boat can only just pass at low tides. Beds of Ulvæ now show, and we run into a little inlet; and while our boatmen moor their boat with a primitive anchor made of a lump of coral, it will not be out of place to give some description of the origin of this singular islet.

The beginning of the year 1868 will be for ever famous in the annals of cyclones in the Indian Ocean. From January to March they were raging in one part or other of it. Twice they visited Mauritius, both times inflicting serious losses on shipping and sugar plantations. The first cyclone lasted from the 14th to the 16th of January, which, passing close to the island, created a tremendous sea, the waters breaking furiously over the N. and W. coasts. At the entrance of Port Louis Harbour, the waves were truly frightful, throwing up piles of coral *débris*, at the right hand (going in), and forming an islet three-quarters of a mile in length, in some places from four to six feet high. This was nearly united to the mainland, there being only a foot or two of water covering the banks opposite Fort William, and I have no doubt another hurricane will unite them altogether.

On the morning of the 16th I went with an American crew in a whale-boat, and after some difficulty, and several attempts, as the waves were still high, and the surf heavy from the reefs, we landed safely on the new islet. The appearance of the broken blocks of coral, shells, and marine *débris* was remarkable. The first thought that struck me was to give it a name, and that of the popular Governor suggested itself. I immediately, in due form, gave it the name of Barkly Island, in honour of that patron of the arts and sciences in Mauritius, and the rolling surf, as it dashed a volume of spray over it (and us too), gloriously completed the baptism. This name has been acknowledged, and will last as long as the islet itself.

The curious formation of Barkly Island has opened up to conchologists many beautiful and hitherto rare species of shells, and some quite unknown. A peculiar characteristic of very many of the shells when first discovered was their brilliant colour, particularly those of shades of yellow. As many as 350 species have been found here, the Cones, Cypræa, Mitras, Pleurotimas, and Tritons being very valuable. The place has been ransacked, literally dug over to some depth, till it is difficult to find any but the commonest shells, except at low tide.

This morning we are in luck, for it is lower than I have seen it for a long time, so that we can go far on the reefs. Out everyone turns, laden with bags, bottles, and sticks, to make loot of everything that falls in our way, except our two boatmen, who looking upon us as slightly *non compos* for giving ourselves so much trouble for nothing, bless Allah and his Prophet that they are more rational, and lie down at full stretch on the coral in the sun for a morning's nap.

It is a misnomer to call this an *island*, for there is not an inch of land on it, nothing but a pile of coral, and shell *débris* raised in the centre, and sloping to the reefs on either side. On the east the surf is always rolling in, but on the west side it is still water, the waves only rising with a gentle splash in ordinary weather, thus giving time for large beds of *Ulva Luiza* and *Entromorpha intestinalis* to grow and flourish, which afford shelter to innumerable marine animals.

My friend and I first explored the east, while the men dug in the centre for shells. The last night's tide has left a belt of sea-weeds which we pounce on at once, as we frequently find many plants here that, grown in deep waters, are rarely washed up on the coast—great wreaths of splendid *Turbinaria ornata* (Turner), two-thirds of the cup-shaped leaves filled with tufts of *Sphacelaria tribuloides* (Kuntz). Half-buried in the coral sand with them are heaps of Sargassum, principally the Myriocystum and Polycystum of Aghardt, with here and there a bit of the pretty little *gracile*; masses of Hypnæas, especially the very exquisite *divaricata* (Grev.), and its numerous varieties.

We find three species of Liagora, one the fine *pulverulenta* (Ag.), so deep-coloured when fresh, but which becomes a dingy grey very rapidly. Clinging to every plant, most difficult to dislodge, is the *Hypnœa valenta* (Turner), the pest of Port Louis Harbour. On detached corals are plants of the *Amansia glomerata* (Ag.), small, but resembling tufts of purplish red roses when just out of the water, but they shrivel and darken directly on exposure to the air. Decomposed, in large quantities, lies the beautiful *Hypnœa horrida* (Ag.); but it is impossible to procure a perfect specimen of it, unless you catch it when floating to the shore.

Occasionally we come on the pretty rose-spotted *Cypræa cruenta*; but more numerous are the young of the Tigris, the Mauritiana, and the Isabellas, with their orange tips and many hues. I have found the *C. Cernica* at rare intervals here, so highly valued by collectors at the present time. As we wade over the reefs we meet with various kinds of Tritons—on every ridge the dull grey shells of the *grandimaculatum* (Reeve) edged with its silky brown fringe, which is soon lost when dead on the shores. The striped varieties of the *T. ruticulum* (L.) are very handsome when taken alive, especially the scarlet and yellow varieties. The Tritons can be kept alive a long time in salt water, and open out readily, showing the curious animal, white, covered with various-sized brown spots. Also the small Surf Harp, which would make an attractive object in an aquarium, with its elegant pink mantle studded with yellow stars and spots. This attractive mollusc may be always found at low tides on the reef, and seems to be a favourite morsel with some fish. Whilst wading in the clear water, I saw a small Ourite dart after something invisible to me, and back again to his hole. I waited patiently for him with my hook-tipped stick, and presently captured him. In his stomach were three pretty little Surf Harps which the brute had only just swallowed.

How very few amongst the hundreds in the world who have

collections of shells know anything of the wondrous animals which once inhabited them; yet what a delightful study it is, possessing attractions which the mere students of their empty houses can never realise. I am glad to see that aquariums are becoming one of the fashionable necessities of the day. I say fashionable, because, when a thing is once stamped with that term, it is pretty sure to be carried out to its fullest extent, and numbers who scarcely ever took the trouble to think that a shell had an inmate before, will soon begin to take pleasure in watching the curious marine animals they are fortunate enough to procure. It may be the means of developing in many a mind the germs of a love for the study of Nature, which will be one good score to the credit of my Lady Fashion. It will be a great benefit for the present generation, for if the mothers are or can be brought to be deeply imbued with a true appreciation of the works of the Great Creator, their children will be sure to imbibe it. In my humble opinion, even at the risk of censure from the whole Sorosis Club, I hold that a woman would be far better employed in telling her girls of the beauties of a Bulla with its azure tipped-mantle, or of the gorgeous scarlet robe of *Conus fuscatus*, than in dinning the doctrines of woman's rights into their youthful ears, and training them to believe they are bound to wage perpetual war against our sex.

We come to a tolerably flat part of the islet, only bare at very low water, and here a new kind of hunt begins, and one generally very profitable. We turn over the loose lumps of coral, but unless there are few live crustacea or molluscs sticking to them outside our labour is in vain. Lift a large one gently with this outward and visible sign, and there is as much, if not a little more, below it than we know what to do with all at once.

Literally a mass of entangled living animals lies there waiting for the returning tide. First spring out the quick *Salarius Dussumerei*, difficult to catch as they bound about, and so slippery that you can scarcely keep them when caught: they are, however, harmless. Not so the eels occasionally there, which we let go, as we have already specimens of them. Crabs from a quarter of an inch to three inches long crawl off with alacrity, and some of them give a sharp nip if not carefully handled. Smooth and hairy annelides, star-fish, shrimps, and small but rare Echini, are all jumbled together. Stranger still, you may collect a handful of shells, rare Pleurotomas, Drillias, Mitras, and all alive! O lucky chance! with what delight we clutch and bag our prizes; how woefully disappointed we are on their examination may be guessed when I say that, though every shell has life in it, not above one in a hundred has its legitimate occupant—the legal owners have been long ago devoured by the little voracious Hermit Crabs, who appear to make their lair in these hollows, and thence make raids on the reefs, carrying in their victims and leaving the shells in a heap for the habitations of their young. They are born robbers, for we find the most minute shells with little crabs in them, that cannot long have been hatched, yet they cling as tenaciously to their stolen dwellings as the older ones.

One of the commonest of these Hermit Crabs is black with brilliant blue legs, one large white claw, and scarlet eyes. Another marauder has blue eyes and a black claw, which he raises defiantly when you intrude on him. The *Pagurus Bernhardus*, of various colours, often quite white, dies very soon when out of water—a slight injury kills it; whereas many of the large Soldier and Hermit Crabs are uncommonly lively for a day or two, much to my annoyance often, when I have been woke up at midnight, after a hard day on the reefs, by their falling off the table and clattering over the bare floors.

With my hammer I broke some of the large blocks of coral to hunt for Pholas, the curious and little-known Leptoconchus, and others only found in coral. I was very successful as to the Pholas: these singular molluscs have the peculiar faculty of boring into solid blocks, and preparing a house for themselves, and not a house only, but a grave also, for, when once located, they live and die there. The Leptoconchus is very rare; and one species found since the formation of Barkly Island is, I believe, new. I have never found a live one. On corals, bits of wood and shells, we find Serpulas innumerable, many of them dead, but occasionally we chance on a living one, which is a charming object, when the elegant feathery tentacles are spread out, rådiating the loveliest colours, but at the least approach of a hand they dart like a flash of light into their stony chambers. I believe some of the smaller species of Serpula may be yet unnamed.

In one block of coral I found a curious little yellow Chironectes, about one inch in length; and running over the rocks I caught a small black one, of which I can find no description; the pectorals and ventrals are used as feet, and the little creature scuds along at a great rate. I never succeeded in getting another, though I have often hunted for one.

Whilst busy amongst the corals, my friend made a bargain with a man fishing on the reefs for a very large and most villanous-looking red Chironectes—I think the *C. hirsutus* (C. and V.). It was so puffed out that I was curious to see the reason; so I cut it open, and found in the stomach a fish nearly as long as itself—a young Rouget (Surmullet). How the fish captured it, and, still more wonderful, how he swallowed it, I am at a loss to conceive. It was there in the stomach—proof positive he had swallowed it, yet the jaws did not appear to me capable of such great expansion. This Chironectes also uses the fins as feet, and, being armed with sharp claws, it moves very rapidly over the rocks.

We find numbers of the pretty *Hydatina physis* alive, its lovely blue and buff mantle forming an elegant trimming to the grey striated shells. One of the men brings us his findings amongst the dead corals, and we are glad to see many of the oddly formed Chinaman's Hats, or *Tectum sinense*: why 'Chinaman's,' I don't know, as I never saw one wear a hat of this shape. There are many of them quite perfect, and so are the pretty and rare *Neritopsis radula* and the equally rare *Murex Cummingi*, which I have never found alive here, but have received fresh specimens of it from Madagascar.

We find a few of the comical-horned *Aplysia depilans*, which we take especial care of, in order to get their delicate shells when dead, which lie in a fold of the back.

A few common shells, and a few tufts of Rhodymenia of various species, are all we find round the farther end of the islet.

Numbers of empty bottles drift here from the shipping, and are caught in the rocks. No sooner do they become fixed than they are taken possession of; and it is curious to see the various creatures that live amicably together in them, and on them. From some I got a small star-fish quite new to me; in the bottom of one was fixed a shell wherein was housed a fat White Crab: he was not, however, the sole tenant of his adopted tenement, for on each end of the shell was a large Actinia; and a small one, of a delicate yellow tint with white antennæ, hung over the front, where the crab protruded his eyes to look at his captor. One of the large ones had a lilac, brown, and white striated mantle clinging to the shell; above, it was of a plaided brown surmounted by lilac and fawn tentacles, beyond which at times the mouth extended. The other had the basal lines green, pink, and white, the same plaided appearance above, but the tentacles colourless, with a deep pink mouth. I brought home this curious family, and kept it in a shallow dish for some days: the crab did not trouble at all about his neighbours, nor did their weight affect him. The small Actinia soon disgorged its filamented interior and died. The large ones exuded small rose-coloured filaments from the pores in the mantle, and a small quantity from the mouth: the latter were, however, re-swallowed, and they opened their antennæ freely. Towards the end of the second day the mantles began to loosen, but on changing the sea-water they again adhered, and it was only on the fourth day that they collapsed, and slipped off dead: I do not doubt they would be very hardy in an aquarium. I once took one with seven Actiniæ on the same shell, the mantles of two partially over the opening; yet the crab's crawling in and out did not appear to interfere with them. I should like to know who was the first tenant.

Nearly every bottle had an eel in it, and most troublesome fellows they are to dislodge. I got out one, a foot and a half long and two inches thick, but how he managed to squirm in I know not, unless he went in thin, and fattened on the remains of the champagne. I had to break the neck of the bottle to get at him, and when I had wounded him he raised his head and showed fight, puffing defiance at me. A little terrier I had with me, seeing its threatening attitude, rushed to the rescue; but poor Quilp had to retreat ignominiously, howling pitifully, as his new enemy bit him in the cheek,[1] and I had to give him a second sharp stroke to keep him from wriggling into the sea.

There is a great variety of eels in this harbour: I have eighteen already in my sketch-book, and that is only a small portion of

[1] Leaving, where the sharp teeth had caught him, a long scar for life.

those I have seen. Amongst the rare ones I may mention the *Murœna tentaculata*, which takes its name from the feathery tentacles on the upper lip. The body is jet black, the dorsal fin of bright yellow, with a basal line of blue, and the anal fin is entirely of the latter colour. I had one sent to me alive in a basket of sea-water by the captain of a whale-ship, who caught it in the outer harbour. It was one of the most elegant creatures I ever saw, and every evolution grace itself; when I touched its mouth with a stick, it did not snap at it, as most of the eels do here, but seemed rather to try and avoid it.

One species is, I believe, new, a bright-green eel, spotted all over with yellow, a pale green dorsal fin, and bright crimson eyes, which gives it a most ferocious look. The only specimen I ever had was about a foot long. The Anguille à rubans, as the Creoles call them, are numerous and very varied. The bands or ribbons of black or brown are all at equal distances, but the large spots are very different. I have three drawings, one with two, one with eight, and another with fifteen large oblong black spots. Some have no spots, and these are the females, so the fishermen say.

The *Pœcilopteris variegata* is very common, and has also several varieties. When alive the markings are all irregular, running into each other, but when dead they take the regular form seen in drawings of this eel. The same thing I have noticed with others; a very common one, the Ciseaux (Creole), I had drawn from a dead specimen, and when I first saw a live one I proceeded at once to sketch it, taking it for a different one. Something interrupting me, I was unable to finish it till after it was dead, when I found it the same as the other, the confusion of brown lines and blotches having subsided into regular figures. Nearly all the eels I have here met with resemble snakes in their manner of elevating the head, and the fierce way they turn on man when disturbed. One cunning fellow, I think the *Anguille morèle*, often gives the unwary fisher a sharp bite. It grows about two feet long, and is of a sandy colour, with the tail tipped pink. The fin is scarcely perceptible round the tail, which is stiff and pointed, and with it he digs a hole in the muddy bottom, deep enough for him to stand on end in. Here he waits for his prey, with his head only visible, his keen eyes allowing nothing to escape him, and being so colourless under water he often catches the fishermen's legs or hands as they grope about after cat-fish. One day, when out at some distance from the reefs, I had the rare good fortune of watching an eel exude its spawn. I noticed the creature swimming uneasily about, and it excited my curiosity. Although my presence evidently annoyed her, it would appear this was the spot she had chosen to deposit her eggs. After gracefully and slowly circling round, she remained for a few moments perfectly motionless, and then the operation commenced, resulting in a beautiful spiral scarlet string of spawn, nearly ten inches in length, and over an inch in width. After all was completed, and the eel had carefully examined it, with a sudden dart it disappeared, and I was unable to capture it. I carefully collected the eggs, and preserved them in glycerine, but am sorry to say they soon faded to a faint yellow. The string resembles to the naked eye a delicate scarlet fabric of lace.

We emptied all the bottles we could find of their living contents, carefully replacing even the broken ones, as traps for future use. All this work, though exciting, was considerably fatiguing, and we were by this time hungry as wolves, so we called a halt, and proceeded to breakfast. An old sail spread over the rough coral served us for table and seats, and we made quick work of the contents of our dishes.

Here I would give a hint to fellow-hunters of the sea, on the proper thing to take on such an excursion. I pronounce it to be tea, that blessed drink that quenches thirst without causing inebriation. I have tried all kinds of liquids, and find that I work better, never get overheated, or headache from the sun, when I keep to tea, so always lay in a store of bottles of it. Brandy I take in case of accidents, but a still better remedy from the ill resulting from contact with the many noxious creatures we meet, pricks from spines, or stings, is a mixture of tincture of *Urtica urens* or of tincture of ledum (one part tinc. to five of water), and either will allay the consequent irritation like a charm, and will prevent inflammation. It is a decided and serious mistake to use beer, porter, wine, or ardent spirits when exposed to a blazing sun, as on such an expedition one necessarily is.

Breakfast and cigars over, we return to our work, and begin to drag the side pools on the west side of the islet. As we dip our nets we disturb shoals of brilliant little fish, but so active that I have never been able to catch one, though I have tried on each visit to this spot. They are silvery-white with a blue line from snout to tail—if full-grown or only the young of some fish I know not; but other prizes soon make up for their loss.

The men with their baskets caught two small lafs of the genus Pterois. They require most delicate handling to preserve them alive to carry them home for sketching. In the water they resemble winged creatures. The skin is a dead white, with vivid pink or scarlet and brown lines. The first dorsal fin is

SUBMARINE VIEW.

free with the exception of a small strip of bright-coloured membrane at the base; the pectorals are free half-way along the rays, and extend over the caudal of scarlet white and green; the latter with the second dorsal and anal fins are yellow, with rows of black spots, and the ventrals are jet black with scarlet tips and large white spots twice the depth of the body. Above the eyes are long striated filaments, which give its name (*Pterois antennata*), and from the mouth and preoperculæ float green and scarlet leaflets. When alive and every part is fully expanded, it is equally beautiful and curious, as it has a quick quivering movement, never quite at rest. No conception of it can be formed from a dried specimen. The upper lip when living overlaps the under, but immediately after death it shrinks back and alters the character of the face. Some have a deep maroon stripe passing through the eyes and down the cheeks. This Pterois is called the Flying Laff by the Creoles, but the true *P. volitans* differs somewhat from this. The fishermen say these fish grow large, but I have never seen one more than seven inches long. I have had some fine specimens of the Laf des brisants (*Pterois muricata*), which they say acquires its rich scarlets and greens by feeding on the Polyps of the outer reefs.

Scorpænas abound here, or Lafs de corail, of every vivid hue mingled together, marvels of colour; but we only found a dead one washed on shore. In this genus the dorsals and pectorals are nearly full, with the exception of the inferior rays of the latter, which are singularly rounded and flattened, as if they served also as feet, as the Creoles say they do, and they certainly have the appearance of it. The very name of Laff inspires dread, on account of the dangerous wounds inflicted by the spines of the genus Synauceia, but I doubt those of the Pterois and Scorpæna being of the same nature. I have several times pricked myself with the *muricata* and *volitans* when preparing them, but without any harmful result. Perhaps, when alive, they may be poisonous.

We found some of the finest specimens of animals of the order Gymnobranchiata I ever beheld. One was as large as a good-sized dinner-plate; it was white, with large chocolate blotches, and a pink mantle: unluckily it died too soon. Two others I succeeded in bringing home to sketch. I never saw any living animals with such gorgeous colours—the most vivid carmine and pure white, mixed with golden yellow in the bodies and mantles, and the gills of pale lemon colour and lilac. No painting could give an idea of the harmony of the shades as they blended into each other, or the undulating grace of the movements of the mantles. I have sat for an hour at a time watching them, lost in admiration, and frequently turning them over to see the expert way they would contract the elegant gill-branches, and re-open them as soon as they had righted themselves, but I could never decide which was the lovelier. Whilst I was busy with my net, my friend was raking up old shells and corals; and amongst the former were some large broken Doliums, all containing crustaceans of the Anomura group. None were very fine specimens, but later I was lucky enough to procure a fine male and female of two species. These large Hermit Crabs are not to be easily dislodged from their borrowed habitations; every whorl of the shell to the last must be broken—and most miserable the crab looks when out. He crawls helplessly about, but will make eagerly for any shell offered, if he can only get his tail in it, to hide which seems his great anxiety.

There is one species—I believe, the *Pagurus punctulatus*—which grows to a great size: the fishermen tell me they have taken it on the outer reefs over a foot long, with monstrous chelæ.

We add considerably to our stock of shrimps from the tide-pools. The beautiful *Stenopus hispidus* (Lat.), once so rare, has been often found lately close to this islet, and is a most attractive object, of pure white, with scarlet, blue, and lilac patches on the joints. We only saw a dead one on this day, but I have a fine collection of them, procured at different times. The beauty *par excellence* is a shrimp I have only seen twice, and found once, some time ago, and which I believe is still unnamed. The Hippolyte of Sowerby is the nearest thing I know to it; but it has a pair of foliaceous appendages in front, in three divisions, that float out gracefully when alive, but contract into little more than a mere coloured line when dead; and these mark it quite a different species, if not a new genus. It is exquisitely striated, edged with large patches of scarlet and brown, blue on a pure white ground, making it very brilliant when in the water.

All this time the men were getting up corals round the islet, and bringing them to us for inspection. To attempt any description of their varied forms and beauty when taken from the water would be quite useless, as I could give no adequate notion of them to those who have never seen live corals. Many were new to me, some possibly still undescribed by savans. We might almost say with the poet, as we examine the curious zoophytes we find amongst our treasures,

> Involved in sea-wrack, here you find a race,
> Which science doubting, knows not where to place;
> On shell or stone is dropped the embryo seed,
> And quickly vegetates the vital breed.

The tide rising rapidly, and the sun being in full blaze, we are glad to take to the shelter of our boat's awning, and we slowly leave the islet and steer towards Grand River mouth. One of the men has picked up a fine specimen of the Flying Gurnard (*Dactylopterus volitans*), not quite dead, so that we see the rich blue and scarlet shadings in the wing-like fins, which fade out soon after death.

Fishermen may be seen on some parts of the reefs any time in the twenty-four hours; fish being sold twice a day in the Port Louis market, and the best and freshest are to be got in the afternoon. Several men are just in our route, so we hail them, and ask for an inspection of their catches. I must say it is very rarely we get a rude or surly reply. One has a quantity of Ourites (Creole) or Poulpes only. They swarm all over the reefs, and incalculable numbers are taken, the small ones for bait, and the larger are sold for food, both fresh and salted. The implement for their capture is of the simplest, merely a long elastic stick with an iron harpoon-like head, and this they thrust into all the holes. When caught they dexterously turn the ugly brute inside out, and thread it on a string slung round the neck.

Another man has a large basket in which are two lobsters (homards), as they are erroneously called here (*Palinurus sp.*). There are six or seven species, some fine eating, and all brilliantly coloured. They have a mortal antipathy to the Ourite, and advantage of this is taken to lure them from their holes. A long tentacle of the latter is suspended at the entrance, when there is a likelihood of finding a homard; and no sooner does he catch sight of the dreaded weapon covered with suckers, than away he rushes in terror, and is soon caught by a noose of split bamboo firmly fixed over his tail, though not without a struggle, and the fellow can inflict a sharp wound with his powerful caudal spines. Care is taken not to place him near his enemy, or the flesh will be spoilt before he gets to market, the creature being literally sick from fright.

We pass a man who has collected curios for me a long time, and he shows us a fine basket of mullets caught by line, the *Mulet voleur* (Creole)—a delicate table fish when freshly caught, unlike the larger mullets (*Mulet sec*), which, as their Creole name denotes, are dry, and have a strong flavour from the coarse food they live on.

We are far from shore, yet above us, slowly winging its flight out seaward, is a large butterfly, the *Euploœ Euplone.* I have often seen the pretty *Danais chrysippus,* and even the stately *Phortante,* out nearly as far as the Bell Buoy, though what they seek over the restless waves is always a puzzle to me.

Hundreds of Holothuriæ lie on the bottom, particularly the common *Biche de mer.* It is of a dark brown, and I believe of the same species as the one so plentiful in the Chinese seas, and eaten by the Celestials. I am not aware of its being an article of food here. It is quite harmless, and will live a long while in a vessel of salt water. Very different is another species, the Gratelle, which may not be handled with impunity, for it causes most violent irritation of the skin when touched, and brings out an eruption and swelling; fortunately it only lasts a few hours, and if bathed at once with the 'Ledum' lotion, the pain soon ceases.

This Holothuria, about the size and shape of a small cucumber, is a mottled brown colour, and has to all appearance four fins when taken; but soon after capture it throws them all off, and they swim about quite independently of the trunk. I have at different times found at least twenty varieties of Holothuria in Port Louis harbour, many of the most vivid hues. I once kept a large one for inspection that was covered above with thick red blunt bristles, and underneath with black ones, having a flat white enamelled top. These bristles lengthened near the mouth, which was surrounded by a circle of twenty very dark maroon tentacles, with ciliated edges and delicate pink lining. All over it were minute white shells stuck fast in the bristles. Sand and small corals lay in the water, and I saw it pick them up by closing the tentacles round them, and drawing them into the bony-looking aperture. The intestinal canal terminates in an opening twice as wide as the mouth, and is so transparent that it can be traced, and its contents easily seen. In the same glass were two others of different species; but they both died in the night, disgorging their whole insides, and lying across the large one. They were so entangled that the live one could not move, and this caused such excessive irritation, that though I carefully removed them early in the morning, the thin membrane burst, and the whole of the viscera protruded. The delicate pink arborescent branchiæ were all forced out, and a bundle of snow-white and rose filaments several feet in length lay entangled *en masse* in this animal ruin. The sand and coral *débris* forms only a portion of their food, or perhaps may be taken only to assist digestion, for some of them are very voracious, and I have frequently found crabs and shrimps in their mouths.

We leave the flat reefs and pass over deep water, with occasional masses of rock, and then cross the deep channel opposite Grand River mouth. There we can see the famous Round Towers, part of the defences that once appeared so formidable, but which would be of little avail against appliances and contrivances of modern warfare. Soon a bottom of sand and mud is visible, and our curiosity is excited by black streaks in all directions over it. I plunge in my rake, and they prove to be the mouths of large Pinnæ, but the shells are so fragile that the teeth of the rake go through them; so, to procure some perfect specimens, I jump overboard and dig them up. The Pinnæ are another enemy to the poor fishermen (whose pedal coverings are often little more than old soles bound on with rags), as they stand straight up in the mud with only the mouth visible, and the edges of the shells make a gash like a knife.

I wade on to the shore, and here come upon one of our luckiest finds to-day. The late breezes had brought up a number of the curious *Dolabella Rumphi.* As its shell lies in the back, almost covered with flesh, it is impossible to get it till the animal is dead. We procure over a dozen fine ones, but having been dead some time, all the deep lilac liquid, which surrounds the shell in a membraneous sac when alive, had disappeared. From one Dolabella I took on Barkly Island, some time since, I got nearly half an ounce of the viscous liquid, which retained its colour even when dry. The very large ones would, I have no doubt, yield twice as much, and I should think could be used as a dye, for it stained everything it touched.

We stroll along the shore towards Petite Rivière; but a few common Venus and Nautica shells, some Hypneas and Ectocarpi, being all we can find, we return to our boat.

High overhead, so high that they appear like white specks against the deep blue sky, at intervals are seen the Boatswain or Tropic birds (*Phæton candidus*), slowly wending their way from the sea, where they have been feeding all day, to their inland mountain homes.

Occasionally one will swoop down with the rapidity of lightning on some too-daring fish which has imprudently displayed its silver sides, and with a plunge dexterously catching it in its powerful bill, it soars up again till almost out of sight, to bear it to his mate, who, sitting patiently on her one egg on some bristling crag, waits for her lord to bring her evening meal. It is, however, rarely they return so late as this, so I suppose the gentleman has been taking advantage of his liberty, and gone a-roving; or, having been unsuccessful in his fishing, dare not return to Materfamilias with empty beak. If a sharp voice is a sign of a vixenish temper, Mrs. Phæton can scold to some purpose when angry, her ordinary notes being a piercing screech.

It is quite time we are homeward bound, as we are far from

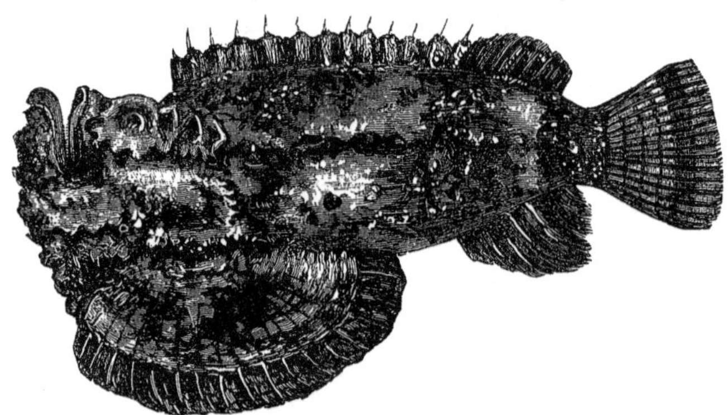

MUD LAFF.

the city, and a swell is rising that will put our men on their mettle to make the harbour before nightfall.

We pass a little pirogue tossing about on the waves with two men in it, one pulling and the other sorting his fish. As we pull by him, to our questions as to what he has caught, after showing us some packets assorted ready for sale, he held up one of the most dreaded fish of the coast, the Mud Laff (*Synanceia brachia*), abundant all round the island, and considered good food by the lower classes.

This most hideous and disgusting-looking fish averages from 16 to 18 inches in length. The spongy, wrinkled, leprous-like skin is ordinarily blotched with white-grey and brown, on an olive ground, but is generally so covered with mud and weeds that it is only after a great deal of trouble that it can be cleaned so as to show its true colours, as it seems to exude a glutinous matter which, attracting anything it comes in contact with, forms a thick coat over the whole body. The dorsal resembles an irregular row of tubercles, each with a spine rather than a fin, and the short wide puffed-out pectorals give it a dull appearance when swimming, as if it had a ruff round its neck. Being the colour of the mud, it is difficult to distinguish it at a short distance, and its very small bright eyes at the top of the head enable it to lie in wait unseen by its victims; the ventrals lie flat in the ooze, and the uncouth head is drawn back so that the great vertical mouth stands wide open to catch any unwary fish that pass his way. The prey is sucked in and swallowed and done for, but it is a sorry day when human hand or foot inadvertently touches it. I have hitherto managed to escape them in my wadings in search of marine curiosities, but I always keep a very sharp look-out, and wear the thickest of long boots.

Grand River, SE., is said to be especially infested with laffs, and during a visit there the fishermen cautioned me about going into the water, as I should be sure to be 'piqued.' However, I wished to make some experiments with this fish, so went expressly with the hope of capturing some. The truth of their abundance was soon verified, and an old expert that I had taken the caution to secure as assistant quickly procured me several specimens. We placed them alive in a vessel prepared for the purpose.

One large brute I laid on a dish, and tickled him under the pectorals, when the dorsal, which usually lies in a lumpy mass on the back when undisturbed, was quickly raised, and in a few seconds, when I touched the dorsal, the fish, with a spasmodic effort, ejected a greenish slimy substance through the hollow spines, and this I concluded to be the poison injected into wounds, making them so difficult to cure. To prove the dangerous nature of this poison, I punctured the ball of the forepaw of a kitten with one of the front spines (said to be the worst). The animal was immediately affected, and died of convulsions in an hour.

I saw a poor fellow near Tamarind Bay who had trodden on a laff, which wounded the ball of the great toe on the right foot.

It was much swollen when I looked at it. I at once opened the wound with a scalpel, and applied a strong solution of liquor ammoniæ to it. His comrades made a poultice of the leaves of the *Ehretia petioles*, and applied it; and in about an hour's time he began to feel a little relief. I gave him also a good glass of brandy to keep up his courage, for he was near fainting from the agony he endured, and his state of alarm lest lockjaw should ensue was pitiful to see. I afterwards learnt that he felt the effects of the wound for a very long time. I have seen

THE OCEAN.

several such cases since, and one especially terrible in the hospital, where the puncture was on the sole of the foot, and no aid had been given till some hours after. The foot and leg swelled tremendously; and after some days the wound sloughed, leaving a large hole. It was over two months before the man was able to be discharged.

There is a similar fish called the 'Laff des brisants,' of the general colour of the mud laff, but with blotches of bright scarlet on the body and pectorals, and the skin is tubercled all over, particularly on the operculars and cheeks; and even when dried, the tubercles are still visible. Laffs appear to be natives of all the warm waters of the Indian and Pacific Oceans, and everywhere are equally dreaded.

We approach some fishing-boats lying quietly in our route, and are greeted with shouts and invectives, and find we are all but entangled in their long seines, just laid out for the night's fishing. Plying boats are hurrying home from the vessels just arrived in the outer harbour, that have obtained *traffic-pratique*, but too late to be towed in. The sun is fast sinking below the horizon, and as he bids us farewell he sheds a parting glory over land and sea. Airy visions of snow-capped hills and sunny vales such as were never trod by mortal man, floating slowly over the sky, charm our tired senses—landscapes that fancy loves to sketch in the ever-changing sunset-tipped clouds—visions as fleeting as most of earth's brightest dreams.

At last the flaming orb vanishes, our cloud-land scenes melt into each other, snow and sunshine and storm curiously blent; sombre greys steal over the brilliant tints, and a feeling of chilliness creeps on us. We urge on our boatmen, and they have enough to do to pull up to the Fanfaron by dark, as twilight is of the most limited duration here.

CHAPTER XXII.

A TOUR ROUND THE ISLAND.

My Comrades and Preparations—Grand River—Kœnig's Tower—Race-jockeys—Denmark Hill—Point aux Caves—Caverns—Probable Origin of the Petite Rivière Caverns—Strange Sights—A Night on the Rocks—Fishing à la Patatrand—Plaines of St. Pierre—Grand Prospect from our Dining-room—Fight with a Tazarre—Rempart River—The Trois Mamelles—Catching Prawns—Tamarind River and Bay—Catching Olives—Raspberries—Rats and Tenrecs as Sharers in our Bedroom—Up the Bed of the River—Our Night's Lodging—Point Flinders—Account of Captain Flinders—The Tamarind Falls—Genêve Estate—Black River—The Morne—Flying Foxes—Baie du Cap—A Python Creeper—The Chamarel Falls—The Bel Ombre Estate—Jacotet Bay—Its Historic Interest—Effect of the Winds on the neighbouring District—River des Galets—Actinias—A Marine Garden—Night-fishing—Falls of the River des Galets—Bay of Souillac—The Savane—The Bois Sec—Tree Ferns—Grand Bassin—Savane Falls—River du Poste—The Coast near the Souffleur—Pont Naturel—Bras de Mer de Chaland—Point d'Esny—Grand Port—Isle Passe—Mahébourg—The Cemetery.

Having made up my mind to take a tour round Mauritius, I selected the month of July as most suitable, the heat being then not so oppressive, and the chances of rain less.

I invited an English officer, and a member of the medical profession, to accompany me. For our outfit, a round double-canvas tent, portable cooking apparatus (that had travelled many thousand miles with me before), a small photo-camera, and my tin vasculum, for the time-being filled with shirts and socks, were all that we required. As the above items were heavy and cumbersome, I employed two men with carrioles to carry our baggage, and meet us at certain points, which I had previously marked out as halting-places.

My object was to examine the coast, collect marine plants, with the view of naming and classifying the Algæ of the island, and to make short excursions into the interior, so as to obtain an accurate knowledge of the mountains and natural curiosities from personal observation, as well as to photograph them.

On a cool bracing morning I left Port Louis at daylight

and rode as far as Grand River, where my friends joined me. Over this river, which has its rise in the high lands of Plaines Wilhems, is a neat substantial suspension-bridge, and the view both seaward and inland is very pretty. Some distance up the river are seen the grand proportions of the railway-bridge, with the varied peaks of Mount Ory, and the Corps de Garde as a background, and the water ripples in tiny cascades over the rocky bed till lost in the sea.

This ravine, during the months the river is low, is filled with reeds and wild plants. One of the water-courses of the town runs along its left bank, which is very steep. Springs of water filter through it, and the constant moisture keeps it clothed with a most luxuriant growth of ferns, especially the lovely little *Adiantum Capillus-veneris*, which is very abundant. A curious pea grows among the rank herbage, with a large brown velvety seed-pod; but beware of touching it, for it is one of the cow-itch tribe, and the slightest contact fills the hands with innumerable minute hairs, which sting like a nettle, and quickly inflame the parts touched. The pools in the river-bed abound with the *Neretina longispina* and *coronata*, and the *Nerita zigzag*. The former it is very difficult to procure perfect, as they are devoured so ravenously by the rats which swarm in this locality.

The banks and dry stones look as if a snow shower had descended on them, for here are washed nearly the whole of the clothes of Port Louis; and watching the dhobies or washermen at work, vigorously beating every article on the stones, I no longer marvelled at my shirts and pants always coming home buttonless and ragged: no fabric ever invented could stand it.

Most of the cottages near the suspension-bridge have shrubs and trees round them. The flamboyant and elegant Poincillade (*Poinciana pulcherrima*), with the lilac Bougainvillæa, give patches of colour that relieve the heavy foliage of the Badaniers and Jamrosas. But the whole village looks desolate, so many houses are to let; and the few that are inhabited, mostly in disorder, give the place a ruinous look, considerably aided by the thick coating of stone-dust from the high road which runs through it. This, with the exception of the railway bridge, is the main outlet from Port Louis to Plaines Wilhems.

I noticed about here a very pretty sort of acacia, the *Moringa pterygosperma*, or Brede Morungue, as the Creoles call it. The leaves and white flowers are eaten as a vegetable, and the very long rounded seed-pods are considered a great delicacy when curried.

The view seaward extends many miles, and is enlivened by pirogues and boats manned by fishermen returning from their night's work for the early market in Port Louis. The former are exactly like the American Indian dug-outs, hollowed out of one solid tree, generally the Colophane (*Colophania Mauritania*). They require skilful handling, and considerable steadiness when once seated in them, as they easily upset; yet the fishermen skim along with them with a single paddle, dancing about from side to side, and rarely capsize them.

On the north bank of the river is a martello tower, commanding the whole bay at its mouth; and near this bridge is a large dam, from which an aqueduct carries a stream of water that supplies the west of the city.

Just beyond Grand River are the Lunatic Asylum, Police Station, and Vagrant Depôt.

Here we started afoot, turning down the road by the latter building, through a deep cut in the hill, passing close to the house of the Honourable Mr. Kœnig. This gentleman resides on the summit of a hill commanding a fine view of the ocean; and near his house he erected a large high round tower, which is still unfinished, and the joists which supported the staging for the workmen still extend from the openings for the windows.

I was informed that the Government would not allow the tower to be completed, as it was intended to occupy the various stories as sleeping-rooms, and it was feared that the lights at night would be seen far away at sea, and be mistaken for those at the entrance of Port Louis harbour, and cause vessels to strike the reef, which makes far out from the shore at this part of the coast.

The road winds round a small lodge in front of Mr. Kœnig's house, down through a grove of tamarind-trees out into the Plain of Petite Rivière. Here the Government had formerly a military station, and some six or eight of the buildings are still standing.

After we had gone about half a mile we came upon some jockeys on racehorses, who had preceded us on the road. They told us this was the finest ground for training in the island. They were exercising their horses for the races in August. After listening some time to the merits of their steeds, one of the jockeys informed us we should bet on 'Shadow,' as she was sure to win. 'Look at them 'ere legs,' said he; 'and there's a heye! Why, sir, she'll jump twenty feet at a spring; she'll go round that 'ere course like a swaller!'

We left them to their sport, and went on to make the most of the cool morning, over about three miles of ground, nearly to Denmark Hill, the residence of the Dutch Consul. A small lagoon interrupts the road, and on going round it we passed some lime-kilns on the shore. Nearly all the lime in the island is made of coral, which when burnt is of dazzling whiteness, but is very liable, when used for mortar, to render buildings damp, and discolour plastering and paper in wet weather. This inconvenience is caused by its containing too much muriate of chalk and magnesia, which, uniting with the marine salts, instantly attract damp, thus rendering houses unhealthy, and accelerating the destruction of the wood which enters so largely into the construction of all edifices here. Coral, when taken from the old beds, is better than the fresh when burnt for lime, on account of its being deprived of much of its saline property.

The road up to the Consul's is shaded with fine trees, and a large garden is attached to the house.

On the premises is a well, cut down through the solid rock to the depth of 130 feet, which supplies the place with water. Here we were most hospitably entertained, and did ample justice to our breakfast after our long walk.

When we left we kept along the shore wherever possible, and soon came upon the ruins of an old French fortification, an earthwork; and just in the rear were the remains of a number of houses, which I suppose were formerly occupied by the French soldiers, and round them rifle-pits, rudely constructed of loose stones set in mortar. I presume the object of this fort was to prevent the landing of men-of-war's boats, as it commanded an opening in the reefs, where boats could pass in nearly all weathers, as the sea rarely breaks across it.

We found many curious plants in the tide-pools, a number of which I secured for my collection.

The shore soon proved too tedious to proceed along it, being covered with huge boulders and detached rocks, and we were glad to go up on the table-land.

There we had a fresh enemy, for the long coarse grass is full of the most pertinacious of burs, that worked their way through our clothes, annoying us exceedingly.[1]

We started hares, partridges, and quails, but they objected to be shot. Hundreds of Nyna birds were whistling on the trees, but whether it was a morning song or a right royal row it would be difficult to say; the noise was deafening till we came near the Point aux Caves.

This bold headland terminates in huge masses of rock of every conceivable shape, the sea breaking directly upon them. The water is so deep that the Polyp that forms the coral has not been able to build its cells there.

The tide-pools in this vicinity are full of beautiful and rare fish, which I tried hard to capture with hook and spear. They were exceedingly active, but when not disturbed they remained floating perfectly motionless. The one we at last succeeded in catching was about five inches long, with large pectoral fins, similar to those of a flying-fish, only the rays were very far apart, of a bright blue; the web between was variegated, and the dorsal fin large in proportion. It looked more like a bird than a fish in the water, and had something the appearance of a laff (*Pterois volitans*).

Whilst gathering shells I was attacked by an eel, called the Anguille Morèle. He was about three feet long, and when I struck at him he came directly towards me, biting at my boots. I beat him off and speared him, having provided myself with a weapon in case of an attack from the Tazarre (*Sphyræna sp.*). This singular eel is banded black and white, edged with salmon colour, and has one round black spot on the white bands. It is a fierce voracious creature, bolder than a snake, and in his rage he runs his head out of the water like one. The bite of this eel is venomous, I am told, but I have not heard of any accidents from it.

[1] The *Anthisteria ciliata*, and *Andropogon lanceolatus.*

When we reached the Point aux Caves, we found our two men, Jumna and Baboo, with the carrioles, complaining bitterly of the hard time they had had to get there. The road, I know, was almost impassable for vehicles. Jumna said it was 'a thief's road, and needed gold to pass over it.'

We pitched our tent on the bluff, and not twenty yards from us

> The breaking waves dashed high
> On the stern and rock-bound shore.

When all was arranged, we sent our men to the nearest village to buy some rice and fowls for our dinner.

While they were gone I prepared a line and hook, baited it with a mussel, and threw it in the surf, and very soon caught enough fish for a meal, of a species of Vielle (*Serranus*). We soon prepared them, and very nice they were, and we had made quite a meal before the men returned. It was late ere they made their appearance, telling long tales of the misery they had had in their fowl search.

Towards nine we all turned in, well tired, and were soon asleep; but our slumbers were destined to be broken, for we had enemies on all sides. Rats swarmed, and the next morning we found the rock alive with them. A good plunge in the sea refreshed us after our disturbed night, and we enjoyed our coffee on the rocks, watching the fishing-boats drifting past.

As the name of this place imports, there is a large cavern, which can be entered on foot at low water; but it being then high tide, we were obliged to take a small boat. We found a number of the edible swallows'-nests and their eggs (the *Collocallia Francica*). I was soon satisfied this was only an entrance to the caverns running up to Petite Rivière. I had visited them once before and knew their locality, so proposed to my friends to proceed thither after breakfast. We put some lunch in our vasculums, and set off through a wild uncultivated tract, with here and there a few scraggy Bois noir-trees. We reached a Chinaman's shop, and provided ourselves with candles, and went on to the entrance of the cave, which is close to the railway station. The position is marked by clumps of aloes which grow directly over it.

Large loose rocks and stones lie all round the entrance to this cavern, which is of very remarkable formation. Creepers and ferns cover the interstices of the rocks, particularly the delicate plant the Amourette (*Quamoclit pinnatum*), with its bright scarlet stars.

Pretty little lizards (*Platydactylus cepedianus*) flit about in all directions, and soon after we entered the first cave we saw innumerable eggs of this lively animal in groups of threes; but it was difficult to detach them from the rocks on account of their fragility.

Cave No. 1 is about thirty feet wide and twenty feet high, and visitors' names were carved all over it. Rude walking-sticks were lying on the ground, left by former explorers, of which we availed ourselves. We each lit a candle and proceeded to examine this cave.

The bottom is of fine earth, but hard, smooth, and dry as a macadamised road, and there is no perceptible dampness on the sides. It is of an elliptical form, and has at first sight the appearance of being the work of man. Numerous cracks and fissures are visible. Small incrustations in the form of icicles cover the vault, and fall and crumble at the touch. They are composed of degraded rock and oxyde of iron, and formed by the water percolating through the porous formation overhead.

On each side of this cavern, more perceptibly at the entrance, there is a series of mouldings about two feet from the bottom, which extends its entire length. The roundings and polish of surface of these beadings were probably formed by the water being charged with carbonic acid gas, which is frequently disengaged through fissures in the earth, particularly after earthquakes or great volcanic eruptions.

We explored cave after cave till we came to an aperture so narrow that we had to pass on our hands and knees, and there we stopped; but I had seen enough to convince me that, though now blocked up, they once extended to the one that has its outlet at the Point aux Caves.

There is a perceptible slope downwards nearly the whole length of the caverns. We did not find any inconvenience from the heat mentioned by former explorers, though we remained in one of the inner chambers nearly two hours.

For the dimensions of the different divisions I will give an extract from Baron Grant's work, which on this point I find more accurate than some others I have seen:—'The second vault turns NE. quarter E., is 17 feet high and 21 feet broad,

110 long, ground dry, with a kind of causeway 2½ feet high. The third vault turns ENE. at one end, is only 4 feet high, but rises to 12 feet; it is 24 feet broad by 250 long; ground moist and damp, and contains small petrifactions. The fourth, 18 feet high, 27 broad, and 350 long; parapets on the sides. The fifth is 8 feet high, 18 broad, and 230 long; runs NW. The sixth, 10 feet high, 20 broad, and 90 long. The seventh runs W., 10 feet high, 16 broad, and 220 long. The eighth runs WSW., 16 feet high, 18 broad, and 90 long. The ninth runs SW., 7 feet high, 30 broad, and 170 long. The tenth, 12 feet high, 18 broad, and 96 long, runs NW.: part of this vault has to be crawled through. The eleventh, 2 feet high, 10 broad, 36 long: ground moist and vault in ruins.'

We found the curious plant that Baron Grant mentions 'as a singular plant full of milky juice, root thick as a finger, and ten feet long, without branches.'

There is no appearance of leaf or bud on it, the extremities are entire, and it is not uncommonly found in such places.[1]

As we returned to the mouth of the cavern, my impression was that this entrance had been formed by the falling in of part of the vaulted roof, as the large detached rocks proved In all probability an opening could be found to a much larger cavern directly opposite, this one lying in a SE. direction, and would be found to ramify with others extending over the whole island. I examined about 1,000 feet beyond the caves by removing the soil and tapping the rock with an iron crow-bar, and could follow what I conceive to be the continuation of them by the hollow sound produced. It appears to me there is reason to believe that this was, ages ago, the course of a subterranean river. We know for a fact that during earthquakes rivers as well as lakes disappear under ground, sometimes continuously, the water flowing through internal cracks, similar to those produced on the surface, which form canals for its passage.

This phenomenon is sometimes coincident with the appear-

[1] These plants are quite common in the interior of caverns in Virginia, and one of a different species I found, some years ago, whilst on an exploring expedition through the great Croton Aqueduct, New York.

ance of some abundant spring in a more or less distant place; but it often happens also that the water nowhere re-appears, and we must conclude it runs directly to the sea. This is not at all improbable in this case, when we remember the convulsions the whole island has undergone. Some river may have been swallowed up by the earth, after a superficial course of more or less extent, which forced its way through a subterranean canal, till some fresh upheaval turned aside its course, leaving the now empty caverns.

We have proofs of one subterranean river which makes its appearance on the south-west coast, where a considerable body of fresh water is forced up through the salt water that washes the shore at Savane. There is also one on the property of M. Ducasse, where there are two remarkable caves, not far from these mentioned above. I have not seen them, but will give a slight description of them, as I have heard it. One of them is still traversed by a subterraneous stream.

The other has two large dry chambers, one nearly fifty feet square, where it was said the festive board was often spread by its former hospitable proprietor. Such scenes have long passed away, and it now contains the tomb of the once generous Amphitryon. This tomb is of massive masonry, similar to an altar, on which, on the anniversary of his death, the friends and relatives place flowers and lighted candles, and pray for the repose of his soul. After passing this large cave, it is not possible to penetrate for more than thirty or forty feet. I do not doubt that all these caverns were formerly part of a continuous chain, extending at least through this whole district.

The railway crosses one part of these caverns, and as we left them we stopped at the station of Petite Rivière for a rest. Master and men expressed their surprise that we should have ventured so far into the 'womb of the earth,' as they termed it. Nothing would have induced them to face its dangers. Strange noises were heard there at night, and they were sure it was the abode of evil spirits. One of the Malabars at the depôt had beheld dread things only a week before. A tall pale woman, dressed in white, was seen, with two villanous-looking men following her with axes in their hands, and calling out 'La mort, la mort, la mort aux blancs!' Oftentimes music was heard, to which they listened for hours; and this was supposed to be the echo of the military band at Bourbon, as it was well known the cavern passed all the way under the sea to that island! I did not hear, however, of any one who had explored so far. All sorts of stories were told us, to which of course we listened with becoming gravity.

We diverged from the path we had traversed in the morning, but found the soil in this neighbourhood very poor and rocky, covered with small stunted trees, low bush, and tangled creepers, difficult to walk through. There are many sugar plantations about this district; but from the constant droughts and scarcity of water, a man must have great courage to undertake anything so arduous as sugar culture must be under the circumstances.

As we approached Point aux Caves, we started several hares. One was wounded by the lieutenant and secured by the doctor. We also saw a few quails and partridges, some of which we bagged, but they were troublesome shooting.

Next morning, long before the sun gave the least indication of his coming to light us poor mortals on our way, the lieutenant was stirring in true military style, and of course there was no longer sleep for us; so, after packing everything in its proper place, the men were sent on with orders to meet us halfway between Flicq-en-Flacq and Tamarind Bay. A strong cup of Mauritius coffee—which, by the way, let me say, is delicious (a present to us for our journey)—was soon ready; and it is very strange to me that more planters do not cultivate it extensively, for in the greater part of the island it grows well and bears prolifically. Enough could easily be grown for home consumption, if not for exportation. We lit our pipes, and strolled along the sands till we came to a favourable spot for a plunge, and afterwards set to work to look for curiosities. Alæ were abundant, and I found some fine specimens of the *Ceramium rubrum* and *Pavonia padina*. We hailed a pirogue to take us to the reefs, to collect shells and corals. As we glided over the clear waters, the rich beds of many-coloured madrepores, echinoides, &c., formed a sight worth a good deal of trouble to obtain. It looked like a parterre adorned with the richest flowers; but unfortunately there are so many laffs and sharp poisonous-spined fish lurking in every patch of sea-weed that the greatest caution is necessary before grasping the lovely treasures of ocean.

Here is another old French battery, some of the guns still lying about half-buried in the sand. The further I travel in the Island, the more I am astonished at the ease with which it was conquered by the British—forts at every coin of vantage, men enough to man them, the prestige of the impregnability of the place in their favour, and hatred to the English supposed to inflame every breast, all make the nearly bloodless victory the more marvellous.

The shores are everywhere lined with the *Ipomœa maritima* and a pretty large-flowered vetch, which with their bright green leaves and delicate flowers refresh the eye from the scorching glare of the sun on the beach. The elastic tendrils of the first-named plant are woven into a sort of net by the fishermen. This is, however, forbidden by law; yet, wherever it can be done clandestinely, it is practised. It is called fishing *à la Patatrand*, short for *Patate à Durand*, the creole name for the plant. This liane is stout and tough, and they knot the long branches together, which when cleverly done makes a net that sweeps in fish of all sizes, even to the smallest fry.

From Petite Rivière the shore is rocky and difficult to pass over, and as it approaches the River Belle Isle it is bold and steep. We forded this river, and at its mouth we found some curious plants, two species of the Bostrychia, and a few fine cones and other shells. We soon got into the plains of St. Pierre. This large tract of country is almost free from rocks, and possesses a very fair soil that could easily be cultivated, and streams run through it which would serve for irrigation. It appears to me cotton, maize, indigo, fruits, and vegetables would grow well there, and yet how much of it lies desert, when hundreds are all but starving. Nearly the whole plain is covered with long grass with sharp-spiked seeds, and different species of burs, which were so troublesome that we were obliged to return to the shore route. The wild jessamine (*Jasminum Mauritianum*) ranks over every shrub, giving out a soft perfume.

Soon after crossing the Rivière des Galets we found our men with the baggage. They were busy bathing the ponies as we got up to them ; and one, a spirited little piebald, got away, and off he set, prancing and bounding with delight over the plain, which formed a fine natural race-course.

He gave them a good deal of trouble before he allowed himself to be caught. Certainly no ponies in the world can beat these little fellows. Small and slight, active as a deer, scantily fed, and hardly worked, they will go through an amount of toil in this hot climate which would soon kill a strong English horse. Few are bred here; they are imported from Timor, Penang, and other Indian islands. The Arab ports on the Red Sea, the Cape, and Australia send also a great number of ponies and horses to the Mauritius yearly. Many Breton and Norman horses are used too, but few English, as they do not thrive well.

We pitched our tent near the sea, close to the Wolmar estate. Baboo and Jumna had brought fowls, rice, and all indispensables for curries and chutneys, and very soon such a dish of both was set before us as an Indian alone could concoct. We had had a hard day's walking, and enjoyed our dinner as only hungry travellers do. Very few dining-rooms can boast of such a view as we had before us. The Corps de Garde and Bamboo Mountain lay in the distance, and the Rempart Mountain, Trois Mamelles, and the long range terminating in the bleak cliffs of the Morne, were all visible. The oblique rays of the setting sun partially lighted up their steep sides; the heavy shadows were gathering slowly along the valleys, and here and there a clump of tall cocoa-nut trees or bamboos would stand out clear and distinct against the brilliant sky; and upon everything near lay the rich indefinable colour that frequently overspreads the earth at sunset.

It was a contest with us between eyes and mouth, and I fear that the savoury dishes of Messrs. Jumna and Baboo gave the victory to the latter for some time; but, the inner man once satisfied, we lay and gazed in silent admiration on the landscape nature had drawn for our benefit for the time being.

The reefs lie about a mile from the shore at this point, and at low water are quite bare. We lost no opportunity of adding to our collection from the tide-pools, but we had to be very cautious, as both the Anguille Patna and Morèle abound there. On all my excursions to the reefs I carried with me a good-sized harpoon, mounted on a pole eight feet long, a precaution of which

I found the advantage at this place. On the following day I was wading off to the reef in elegant costume—pants tucked up into a high pair of thick boots, an old flannel shirt and slouched hat, a bag over my shoulders for shells, in good fighting trim—when I was attacked by a tazarre, a fish something like a fresh-water pike.

The brute was a good-sized one, and came right at me like a bulldog. I had seen him a minute before, and so was ready for him, and planted my harpoon directly in his side; but he got away and made a second charge.

This time he was struck in the head, and I held him fast, though it taxed my strength. I did not well know what to do with him, as he wriggled on my weapon, so hailed a pirogue with two men in it. They said I had done well to capture it, as it was not easy to spear such a large one.

We agreed to make tracks for the Rempart River, and attempt the ascent of the Trois Mamelles. On our route we had to pass through a Malabar camp; and such a howling and yelling of cur dogs I never heard, and we all wished the Port Louis dog-killing laws were in force here before we got through.

From the bridge that spanned the Rempart River one of the prettiest views in the island is obtained. Looking up the stream, numerous cascades are seen as it winds through the ravine; on its banks are the graceful bamboos waving in the breeze that swept down the river, and the singular rugged peaks of the Trois Mamelles stood out clearly defined against the bright blue sky. This spot took my fancy so much that I obtained one of my best photographs here. We breakfasted on the banks of the river, in a spot covered with ferns, and close to a bed of deliciously fresh young water-cresses.

We crossed the valley, which is encumbered with rocks, till we reached the foot of the mountain, where we found a man cutting wood. He offered to guide us up, but declared it was impossible to reach the summit. We accepted his services, and found it pretty sharp climbing, even dangerous in some places. We ascended a narrow path, through thick underwood and loose stones and rocks, till we were a thousand feet above the level of the sea. Here we halted, and had a clear view over the plains of St. Pierre, with the Black River Mountains in the distance, and the sharp peaks of the Chamarel, which, with the

LES TROIS MAMELLES.

exception of the Piton de la Petite Rivière Noire, are the highest in the island, being 2,902 feet in height.

The highest peak of the Trois Mamelles is 340 feet, and the three are almost bare of vegetation to their summits, with the exception of the Orchilla plant, which covered them, and which if carefully gathered might be made a profitable article of commerce from the valuable dye it yields, and a few ferns. In the clefts of the rocks grow the Pterispedata and Radiata, a Nephrodium, and two Aspidiaceæ.

Towards the base ranked the Cascavelle (*Crotalaria retusa*), the *Dichondra repens*, and the *Tabernæmontana parviflora*.

From the rugged barrenness of this triple-headed mountain a geologist has little difficulty in tracing the volcanic action once at work on it. These rocks, which are basaltic, rise almost perpendicularly, and have the appearance of being cut straight down from the summit to the shoulder, the highest point we could attain. Seen from a distance they look like the ruins of some giant's stronghold. As I lay resting, I pictured to myself the time when the plain at the base of the inner side of this mountain was a lake of liquid fire surging up against the solid barrier, and in process of time thinning the mighty wall, aided from without by the action of the elements. As the seething mass cooled down and contraction ensued, probably the first fissures were made in the then thin crust. Fresh eruptions sent a boiling torrent of lava through the openings, forcing its way to the sea. Every succeeding hurricane hurled down masses of disintegrated rocks, and piled them in the fantastic heaps where they now lie. The powerful forces of light, air, and water have been silently at work through countless centuries, gradually wearing away the rough edges of the fissures, and degrading fresh material that appears waiting the slightest touch to fall on the audacious intruder in these solitudes.

The Rempart River takes its rise in one of the mountains of which range the Trois Mamelles form a part. The fountain-head falls into a small basin, forming a cascade, and then flows on through the underwood till it reaches what was formerly a forest, but now the trees are sparse and stunted. After our descent from the Trois Mamelles, we amused ourselves catching prawns (*Palæmon carcinus*), which abound in this river. They are here called 'Camerons;' that, I suspect, is the old Portuguese name for them. A noose is made of strong thread or split bamboo, and suspended over their hiding-places, and a bait (a bit of thread is the best thing) is put just in front of the snare. As soon as the prawn takes the bait the noose is drawn tightly over his body and he is secured. The large ones show fight, and strike so sharply with their tails as to draw blood if not carefully handled. The lieutenant, who had never seen them in their watery element before, enjoyed the sport, and was the first to take a fine large one. He held it up exultingly to the doctor and myself, saying, 'Look there, boys; come here and take a lesson how to catch prawns; it takes this individual to do it artistically,' &c. &c. We stood his chaffing quietly, waiting to see him take the prawn off the noose, when all at once the animal nipped him so severely that he let it drop into the water again, with an expletive more forcible than polite. It was our turn to laugh now, and we didn't spare our friend. This fresh-water prawn is indigenous to the island, and there is another species caught in the sea, but not so fine. It is also a native of the Seychelles.

Whilst busily engaged with our prawns, of which we snared enough for our supper, heavy clouds gathered round the summits of the mountains, and hid them from our view, and we had but just time to reach our tent when the rain came pattering down. After our day's climbing, fresh prawns and water-cress were not to be despised whilst waiting for Jumna's supper; and we didn't forget to toast the lieutenant's expertness in catching prawns. Thanks to our double tent, we could afford to laugh at the rain; and next morning we broke up our camp, and moved along the coast towards Tamarind Bay. The shore here is flat, and the reefs in some places run two miles out from it. We sent on our people to the left bank of the Tamarind River, near the bridge.

This is a fine bay, in some places very deep. We hired a pirogue at the lime-kilns, and embarked from a small jetty which ran out into the sea. The waves were breaking over the reef, and it wanted considerable skill to guide so ticklish a craft through them. Our object was to fish for Olives, which are so plentiful, and of great beauty and variety on the Mauritius reefs. We baited about five hundred feet of lines, and after a great deal of patience got a splendid haul. It is singular that though this animal is so abundant, it is rarely that the dead shells are found on the shore.

At the jetty I observed a curious black lizard, very active, about five inches in length, that seemed to feed on something in the water. It was very shy, and would hide below the rocks as I approached it. It appeared partly amphibious, and would dart into the waves, seize its prey, and return to its hole. I tried in vain to capture one. I was at first inclined to believe it was a triton, but the form of the tail did not warrant the conclusion, as it was very thick, and terminated in a point, and not formed for swimming. Round the whole of Tamarind Bay grow patches of the bright yellow-flowered creeper, the *Cassytha filiformis,* with an abundance of low shrubs and plants, but none needing special mention. On the right of the bay, just at the foot of the Tamarind Mountain, stands a small village principally occupied by fishermen. A brisk trade in fish is at present carried on, as the men can now take their produce by rail to the inland villages twice a day.

We passed the bay, and kept up the river, which was partially dry, and in many places encumbered with groups of boulders, and everywhere showed a rocky bed. The banks were covered with ferns, a species of Nenuphar and bright Amourette, while thousands of plants of the wild raspberry (*Rubus cœsius*), then in flower, filled the interstices between the rocks. Most deceptive of fruits! The leaf is totally different from the European species, and the plant only grows about two or three feet high, but the berry exactly resembles it, with only one exception. Hot and tired, you pluck a bunch, anticipating the delicious flavour of those of our northern climes, when you find, to your great disappointment, that it is almost tasteless.

We arrived at the bridge by the afternoon, which is placed in as romantic a spot as the one at Rempart River.

After dinner we found, to our annoyance, that we were not the only occupants of our tent. We killed two small scorpions without much trouble, but the rats were not so easily disposed of. First they ate up my arsenical soap; and though it gratified me to know it would be their last meal, having made it doubly strong on account of the insect plagues here, still I did not feel that indemnified me for its loss. Whilst we slept they devoured a great part of a fine boiled ham, and spoilt the rest.

I was awakened by some one calling out, 'Do the rats trouble you?' I answered 'No;' when the lieutenant said, 'I have started two, and shall strike a light;' and a pretty scene we had of it when we were illuminated. Our tent had been pitched on what I suppose must have been the burrow of a family of Tenrecs (*Centetes escaudatus*). The doctor killed one with the blow of a large knife; and the servants being called, we captured several, which grunted and squeaked like so many little pigs, and are said to be very good eating. They breed most prolifically, as each litter has from sixteen to twenty-five young ones; so I presume we had disturbed a mother and her babies.

Even the lieutenant's indomitable early rising was put a stop to for once, after our sleepless night. Baboo and Jumna had the best of it, as they had joined the two carrioles, supporting the shafts with their seats, and thus formed a capital bed under the covered tops. The old Creole who had guided us up the Trois Mamelles came in the night, and not daring to disturb us, stretched himself under the carrioles, and had a sound nap too.

As soon as we could rouse ourselves, and had had the unfailing pipe and coffee, we packed up eatables for twelve hours at least, making up our minds to a hard day's work. We started up the bed of the river, jumping from rock to rock till we came to where the water was barely ankle deep. But the lieutenant found it too rough for him, and turned back. When he was gone, the doctor and myself examined the pools in the river, and found some small perch, camerons, &c.; also three kinds of shells, the same as those in the bed of Grand River, the usual Conferva, two species of Chara, Thydrodicton, Utricularia, &c. The banks are here steep and high, and looked like impassable barriers; but our guide persisted in going on, as he said he knew the place well. We ascended the bank, grasping at old roots and stumps, anything to help us up, till we arrived safely at the table-land above.

We were now about two miles from the Tamarind Falls, too late to return, so we looked out for a shelter for the night, and as the sun was rapidly sinking we had to make the most of our time. The old Creole soon found us an unoccupied shanty, rough enough to be sure, but better than the open air. We cleaned it out, and covering the interior with boughs and bushes, soon made it comfortable, and then dispatched Jumna and the guide for bread and wine to a small village near. The doctor and myself meanwhile devoured the remnants of our tiffin, which were very slight, our appetite in the day having been prodigious. However, a pipe solaced us till the man returned with indifferent bread and worse wine, and some dried fish called 'Bombay Ducks' (*Saurus*), which they grilled; and hunger enabled us to make a hearty meal, and get a sound sleep on our cut bushes.

Out in the early morning, inhaling the sharp breeze, and eager to pay our visit to the far-famed Tamarind Falls. The ravine is almost impassable, as the bank rises abruptly from the river, which is here very deep; but we found a path just above the left bank, going through the estate of 'Mendrain.' From our position the Corps de Garde, Trois Mamelles, Mount Orey, and others, extending as far as the Peter Both, appeared as one vast continuous chain, and the intervening country was green with canes in every stage of growth. After working our way up to a good distance, we came to a spot called Point Flinders, where the bushes have been cut away to give a good view of the Falls.

This estate was formerly owned by a Mr. De Chazal, and here he entertained the celebrated navigator Captain Flinders, who had been taken prisoner by the French, and kept on *parole*. A small kiosque was erected for him on this romantic spot, for here he spent much of his time, and it has ever since retained his name Then it was covered with forest; now the forest is *non est*, and canes are; and what was once a rendezvous for artists and tourists is fast losing its celebrity.

The adventures of Captain Flinders were of so extraordinary a nature that I give a brief outline of them:—

Captain Matthew Flinders was appointed, in 1801, by the British Government, as commander of the 'Investigator,' to visit New Holland, or the Great South Land—to clear up all doubts as to the unity of this great region, open up new ports for seamen, and for the advancement of natural knowledge in various branches—besides laying down charts of the neighbouring seas, for the benefit of geography and navigation. In 1803 the 'Investigator' was so badly injured among the reefs near Torres Straits that she was condemned. He then tried to finish his survey with the 'Porpoise,' 'Cato,' and 'Bridgewater.' The two former were, however, wrecked at a place named 'Wreck Reef,' in lat. 23° 22′, long. 155° 34′, in August of the same year. 'The Bridgewater,' afraid of sharing the same fate, steered away; and, instead of remaining to see if there were any survivors of the catastrophe, her captain sailed to India, spreading the report everywhere that both vessels were entirely lost, with all on board. Strange to say, this ship in her next voyage was wrecked or sunk, and never heard of after—a fitting retribution, if cowardice or ill-feeling had prevented her captain from assisting his wrecked comrades.

Taking a small crew in one of the six-oared cutters, and leaving the rest in charge of Lieutenants Fowler and Flinders, Captain Flinders set out to make his way to Port Jackson for help. The men left behind were set to work to build two decked boats, in case that no tidings of the captain and his crew should arrive. They had to voyage in an open boat 250 leagues, along a strange coast inhabited by ferocious savages, a greater part of the way; but they succeeded in reaching Sydney in eleven days. The 'Rolla' was at once fitted out by the Governor, and sent to the relief of the men at Wreck Reef, who had been fortunate enough to save a good deal of property from the two vessels.

The schooner 'Cumberland,' a small Gravesend passage-boat of only twenty-nine tons, was given to Captain Flinders, who was anxious to make his way quickly to England to get further help to finish his work, as well as to contradict the reports of his death. The small size of the vessel made it necessary to stop at every convenient port; so Captain Flinders proposed Cœpang Bay in Timor, Mauritius, Cape of Good Hope, St. Helena, and some of the western isles. Governor King did not wish him to go to Mauritius, as he did not care to encourage communication between French colonies and Port Jackson. The master, however, was left to his own judgment, and two letters were given him for the Governor of Mauritius, in case of need. When near the island, he found his boat requiring repairs and stores, so much so that he was afraid of risking a longer voyage; and, ignorant of the fact that war had broken out between Great Britain and France, he steered direct for Mauritius, and made the land at Baie du Cap.

He did not speak French, but had a passport formerly given

him in that language, but unfortunately made out for the 'Investigator.' However, he presented it with the letters for the Governor, and told his tale of the daring feat he had accomplished. As soon as these papers were forwarded to Governor-General De Caen, and he saw a passport not made out for the 'Cumberland,' he refused to believe his story, called him an impostor, and seized the boat, putting Flinders in temporary confinement, and taking away from him all his papers, charts, log and journal, pretending that many passages in the latter proved him to be a spy. Many British vessels at this time were seized by the French in the Indian Ocean, and the prisoners taken were kept in a place somewhere at the Jardin Despeaux, Plaine Verte, and Captain Flinders was confined with them.

He wrote letter upon letter of remonstrance to De Caen, but received only abuse in reply. His sword, and even his spy-glass, were taken from him. Finding that it was hopeless to expect release, he begged to have his charts and books returned, that he might complete his work so far, while it was still fresh in his memory. The charts, after much delay, were sent to him, but the books denied.

To atone as far as possible for De Caen's severity, he was treated with the greatest kindness and sympathy by many French gentlemen; and whenever any officer had to bring any harsh message, it was done with perfect courtesy, and apologetically, as everyone pitied his hard case. After two years spent in Port Louis, as his health suffered much, he was allowed a residence at Vacoa, called the Refuge—on *parole.*

It appears that in 1804 a decree had been passed in Paris 'to approve the conduct of General De Caen, *but from a pure sentiment of generosity to grant Captain Flinders liberty and the restoration of the "Cumberland."*' This decision laid over till 1806 for the approval of the Emperor, but it was not till 1807 that it arrived in Mauritius, though it is said De Caen knew of it on its first passing.

Captain Flinders was at last allowed to return to Port Louis. His books, sword, and spy-glass were returned; but no entreaties could procure his despatches, log-book, and the third volume of his journal, though many gentlemen tried to intercede with De Caen for them. The 'Cumberland' was not given up to him, and every possible hindrance was thrown in the way of his leaving. It is supposed he was still detained on account of the war between England and France; and after the most vexatious harassings, it was not till March 1810 that the welcome news was brought to him that he was to sail in the cartel 'Harriet,' on condition that he would engage not to serve against France during the war. The 'Harriet,' however, was not forthcoming, and leave was granted him to proceed to the Cape in the sloop of war 'Otter,' in June. He had thus endured a captivity of six years, five months, and twenty-seven days—a lasting disgrace to the memory of De Caen, and which caused the greatest dissatisfaction amongst the people generally. He never succeeded in recovering either the log or the third volume of his journal. A most interesting account was written by Captain Flinders of his work and troubles at New Holland, his captivity in Mauritius, and his homeward voyage, and it is from these volumes that I have gleaned the above account of this celebrated man.

The Tamarind Falls are seven in number, and form a series of cascades of great beauty, and as they descend over the rocks at different heights, the various sounds blend with a strange harmony to our ears. One part of the Falls is formed by a break in the Tamarind River, and the others by streams that flow into it, and the united height of the whole seven is over 300 feet.

> Fretted with sands and rocks, and swept by the winds from the mountain,
> Numberless torrents with ceaseless sound descend to the ocean,
> Like the great chords of a harp in loud and solemn vibration.

The Falls were to our left, and before us rose a wall of rock. Its steep sides were partly bare of vegetation, with scattered tufts of verdure sown by the winds or birds; but its summit was covered with a dense belt of old trees, the many blasted heads and withered trunks bearing witness to their struggles with the elements. In the deep ravine below us lay the river, which, after receiving the turbulent waters of the cascade, flows silently on to the ocean. To the right stood out a gigantic beetling crag, flinging its broad black shadow right across the ravine, and forming a singular gorge with the opposite mountains. Through the opening is obtained a lovely picture, looking brighter and sunnier for the dark frowning hills we saw it through—a glimpse of the brilliant green waters of the ocean, as they touch a strip of dazzling coral sand, and then

THE TAMARIND MOUNTAINS.

gradually change to the deepest blue in the distance; the river joining the sea; a bridge; a few vacoas—things so slight in themselves, yet when combined as they are there, all made up a scene that held us entranced. On whichever side we looked was some beauty, each perfect in its kind, each different, which, with the elastic purity of the atmosphere, so acted on our senses, that I know not how long we should have remained if the demon of hunger, which the loveliest of scenery cannot exorcise, had not made his appearance; and with a sigh we rose, for we had a long way to go back to our quarters.

We made our way as well as we could over the rocks in the river, but were terribly fatigued on our arrival, and found the lieutenant somewhat alarmed at our long absence. Our description of the ramble made him regret he had not shared it, though he laughed at our enthusiasm about its beauty. Our next halting-place was to be the Black River; and thither we sent Jumna and Baboo, ourselves taking a less direct route.

We crossed a spur of the Tamarind Mountain, and had a fine view of the Black River valley, the craggy precipitous sides of the mountain, and the estate of Genêve; while the peaks of the Chamarel loomed in the distance, brilliantly lit up by the sun, which is the first land made by mariners coming from Madagascar.

We ascended to the Genêve sugar plantation, and examined the ruins of the fine mills, caused by the hurricane of 1868. This estate is nearly nine square miles in extent, and is about twenty-one miles distant from Port Louis. It has belonged to the same family for over half a century. It is the one mentioned by Bernadin St.-Pierre, and, if I recollect rightly, it was from this place Paul and Virginia walked one fine morning before breakfast to their home on the Latanier River, close to the city. I don't wonder at Paul having to carry her, unless the roads through the forests were different from their present state.

Deer and monkeys abound here, and are said to be very troublesome, though the greatest plagues are the wild hogs, which do much mischief to the plantations. The military post of Black River is on this estate. In former times this was considered one of the most important posts in the island, and its approach was strongly guarded. On the east was the battery of Lapreneuse, of six guns; about 600 yards farther back is another of these guns; a battery of two more flanked the cantonment, and on the opposite side of the anchorage was the La Harmoine battery, mounting twelve guns. Of all these formidable defences the only remains are a few rusty cannon and a heap of ruins. The country hereabouts is highly cultivated with fine cane crops, and the road passes along an avenue of large tamarind-trees, many of which were uprooted, and most of them severely injured, by the cyclone.

THE MORNE.

The road here winds round a small bay, and passes a plain covered with long grass, which, though troublesome, was a better path than the shore, which was very steep and rocky. The bold promontory of the Morne now rose before us in all its grandeur. The inner side, nearly perpendicular, is the only remaining wall seaward of a great crater, of which the Isle of Fourneaux, not far from the shore, once formed a part.

We had heard very much of the difficulty of ascending this solitary giant, but the trial looked so well worthy that we resolved to attempt it. Formerly, when densely wooded, it was considered one of the securest strongholds in the island, and was greatly resorted to by Maroons, who gave infinite trouble to the *gendarmes* before they could be dislodged. We got an old Creole, who lived near, to accompany us, and by his advice provided ourselves with ropes and hatchets to aid us in the ascent. We found the toil of climbing fully equal to anything we had heard of it. A greater part of the day was spent in our task. Sometimes our path lay through dense thickets and climbers intertwined in every conceivable form, and we were at times compelled to lay about us vigorously with our hatchets before we could pass.

Here grow the pretty little liane, the *Clitoria Ternatea*, the Cascavelle, and a species of Clematis; but the latter is not so fragrant as the European. The wild tobacco (*Solanum auriculatum*) flourished in the open spots, two species of Hibiscus, the *Horonga Thoninia*, and the common Mallow (*Malva crispa*), which is used here as elsewhere as an emollient. Sometimes, after an opening was made, we came suddenly on a perfectly perpendicular rock of fifteen or twenty feet, without foothold sufficient for a cat to scale. The only resource was attaching our good three-inch ropes to stones and flinging them up till they caught in the branches or roots above, and so hauling ourselves up. I believe the ascent of the Morne is quite equal in danger and fatigue to that of the Peter Both.

Weary and exhausted, we reached the little plateau at the top, and were glad of the spring there, of which we had heard but feared might be a myth.

As soon as we were sufficiently rested to appreciate our position, we felt that the spectacle from this giddy pinnacle was worth all the labour of mounting to it.

The broad blue ocean bounded our view on one side, glittering in the brilliant rays of the descending sun. The singular triangular-shaped island of the Morne was visible, and the Cap de Brabant, the SW. point of Mauritius. The encircling chain of coral reefs could be distinctly traced by the line of foam as far as the eye could reach, indicating the breakers that form so dangerous a fringe to the greater part of this coast. The white sails of passing merchantmen could be seen, India-bound or making for the Island, and numberless fishing craft. The view inland was, if possible, still more imposing. We could see the picturesque gorges of the Black River Mountains—all below in the deepest shadow, in strange contrast to the highly illuminated verdure crowning every summit. Nearly the whole range is basaltic, the Morne also. As I looked down from its steep sides, the only remains of what was once the vast wall against which the sea broke in vain till the action of fire within assisted the work of the waves, I could not help imagining the grand and awful sight it must have been when the boiling lava and the roaring waves met, when crag after crag went down, and contrasting it with its present peaceful aspect.

The little plateau is sheltered on one side by an overhanging cliff, and is nearly covered with trees and bushes: these we cut and piled up, and, with our good baskets of provisions, made ourselves tolerably comfortable for the night. It was bad enough to climb, but worse to descend; and we narrowly escaped coming to grief very often, there is so little surface soil; the roots, having slight hold, frequently gave way with our ropes round them, and occasionally expedited our descent far from agreeably. However, we escaped with a few bruises.

On this mountain also the Orchella plant grows, and a small tree of the Locust family, the dry pods of which are sweet, and we ate of them freely. Vast numbers of the Samlongue (*Syzygium Jambolanum*) grow here and on the Black River chain, and their dark foliage gives a sombre character to the scene. In the moist forest-earth grows the celebrated Fahame (*Angræcum fragrans*). According to Creole authorities, it contains within its slender fronds virtues to cure no end of diseases. Consumption itself must even yield to Fahame! The aromatic principle has been extracted from this fern by a chemist here, and the faculty all appear to agree that it is a very useful therapeutic agent.

Many fine indigenous trees grow in this locality of whose names and uses I am ignorant. I recognised only the *Mimusops Erythroxylon* and the *Callophyllum spectabile*. As we went down the valley of the Morne we came upon what had once been a sugar plantation; but sugar-mill and houses were all going to decay, and the desolate grass-grown place told its own tale of ruin. This valley was once a very large crater, two or three miles in width, but the revolutions of ages have nearly filled it up with detached rocks and *débris* from the deep sides of the Morne and Black River Mountains. There is every reason to believe that after the subsidence of the great crater in the interior, and the large adventitious ones, many smaller ones opened, which were very active. We see this just beyond the valley of the Morne, where there is a small crater of comparatively recent date.

The road we passed over was built by the Government, and is called the Military Road. For some distance it is ornamented with a hedge of Campêche on both sides. I wonder this shrub is not more used for this purpose, it grows so rapidly, and when cut looks well. We came out of this road into a grove of lofty Filaos; and we could not help noticing the profound stillness of the place, save for the melancholy soughing of the wind through the trees, and an occasional mournful cry of a ring-dove. As we pushed on we came suddenly upon an old man hoeing a small patch of maize; we saw no habitation, and from the curt replies we got to our questions as to our whereabouts, he seemed to think us intruders.

We struck out along the shore, which for some distance is rocky, but at length gained the open beach, and soon found a pretty spot to pitch our tent on a little promontory.

The spur of the mountains terminates here abruptly, the sides of which were covered with trees and shrubs—a wild-looking place. Under the craggy cliff two or three Creole fishermen live with their families in miserable thatched shanties. It was nearly dark before our tent was ready, and a steady rain came down that made us anxious about our men and horses. We offered to pay the Creoles to let them have an empty hut for the night, but they refused, as they said they did not want anything to do with 'les Anglais.' However, on Sumna and Baboo explaining that the horses belonged to them, they were immediately taken in and all comfortably provided for. Rats and Tenrecs disturbed our slumbers, and in addition we had the peculiar bat, called the 'Flying Fox' (*Pteropus edulis*). It makes a barking noise similar to the yelp of a lap-dog. Near our quarters were a grove of aloes, of which this animal is very fond, on account of the honey its flowers contain, I suppose;

it also eats the tender Badanier nut greedily, and when the Litchis are in season, they are so destructive that they will often strip a plantation in a night.

We killed one for a specimen, which measured three feet four inches from tip to tip of the wings.

Sleep being impossible, we all went out for a stroll on the beach. The wind was fresh from the SE. and the sea was breaking furiously over the reefs; and as the foaming waters caught the glittering rays of the moon, they were lit up with a magic brilliancy—

> Making the restless plain
> As the vast shining floor of some dread fane,
> All paved with glass and fire.

Soon after daylight we crossed a strip of beach, and emerged on a large grassy plain, on which grew numbers of the Veloutiers. Both kinds of the Veloutier flourish there, the *Scævola Königii* and the *Tournefortia argentea*; and the liane *Canavalia obtusifolia* ranks over all the shrubs. A sort of wild Betel, the *Ehretia petiolaris*, is also abundant. This plant grows on nearly the whole seaboard, and the fishermen make use of it as a remedy for the dangerous wounds made by the Laff. The leaves are macerated and made into poultices; but if really a cure for the poison of the spines of this fish I cannot assert, though I have seen it assuage the pain considerably. The *Indigofera compressa* is also wild in this neighbourhood, and does not alone possess its valuable dye, but is supposed to be a most efficacious medicine for asthmatical patients.

This plain lay between a spur of the Black River range and the sea, and extended as far as the Baie du Cap, which runs up a good way into the land. As we neared the bay, we saw the wreck of a small schooner which had been forced over the reefs by the breakers. In spite of the violence of the waves where it lay, men were busy at work, stripping it of its gear and all available booty. The bay forming an impassable barrier to our carrioles, we got a pirogue to take them round the Cape to the other side of the mountain, which forms the last spur of the range, and stands close to the coast. The craft was, however, too small, and we were obliged to send our men round the bay and over the mountain to procure us a ship's yawl, which they told us was kept there. This held us all, and the carrioles too.

THE CHAMAREL FALLS.

Rounding the Cape the wind blew very strong, and the current swept us back with such velocity that we came very near a capsize amongst the sharks and breakers, which made the bravest of us a little nervous. We were obliged to put back; and, crossing a sand-bar, ran right up to the head of the bay, and landed close to Mr. Strobe's house.

This is a lonely quiet spot, and the dwelling is in the midst of a well-cultivated garden, with abundance of fruit-trees. We went up to see the giant creeper, which grows on his place, and of which I had heard so much as one of the curiosities of the Island. Mr. Strobe not only gave us a guide to it, but allowed us to take as much fruit as we wanted from his garden. We crossed the river over a little temporary bridge, though, for all the water in it then, we could have jumped over it. The banks, however, were thickly covered with luxuriant vegetation, and some distance up are several pretty little cascades tumbling over the rocks into a small basin. Very near them at the foot of a hill is the gigantic Liane; the only one now here, though formerly there was one at the Savane, but it is long since dead. It was imported from the Moluccas many years ago. This python of a creeper is about two feet in diameter at the collum, and some of the roots extend for 100 feet round. It runs up the steep side of the hill, and covers over an acre of ground. Its trunks and stems are fasciated and whorled. It bears a cluster of white pea-like flowers, and produces a seed pod, about two feet in length and over two inches broad, containing a large brown bean. It flowers in April and May, and its botanic name is the *Entada Pursœtha.* It certainly is very curious, and it seems a wonder no one has thought of cultivating it elsewhere.

After leaving Mr. Strobe's we went up the river, and procuring a guide, pushed on for the Chamarel Falls, which are at no great distance. They are situated on the boundary of Black River and Savane, and are amongst the mountains of a branch line of the Savane chain. This cascade is formed by the Rivière du Cap rushing over a rocky ledge, sheer down a descent of three hundred and twenty feet. During heavy rains, when the river is swollen, the torrent, unbroken in its fall, thunders into the chasm below, and presents a scene that baffles description. In the dry season the foaming cataract gives place to a silvery stream; and, as the eye follows it, one has a more appreciative idea of the terrific depth of the abyss than when enveloped in clouds of spray.

> It mounts in spray to the skies, and thence again
> Returns in an unceasing shower, which round
> With its unemptied cloud of gentle rain
> Is an eternal April to the ground,
> Making it all one emerald. How profound
> The gulf, and how the giant element
> From rock to rock leaps, with delirious bound,
> Crushing the cliffs!

We returned slowly from the Falls, feasting our eyes on the surrounding scenery. It is beautiful now, but how much more so it must have been when the river flowed through a large grove of clove trees that once flourished there and perfumed the air with their fragrance!

The whole country around was interesting also in a geological point of view. We constantly came upon Madrepores and other marine productions, some quite perfect, but varying greatly from those now found in the neighbouring seas, and proving the submergence of the whole tract. In many places we found the beds containing these deposits with a superposed stratum of lava on them; thus showing their upheaval, and the subsequent overflow of the volcanoes then formed. These masses of coral extend from the base of the Tamarind Mountain in three distinct beds over three feet high. The lowest is divested of all traces of organisation, and so indurated that on being struck it gives out a metallic sound.

The others still retain their organic structure, with blocks of basalt imbedded in their substance. From the Isthmus that connects the Morne with the main-land the ledge of coral is continued to the Baie du Cap, and is termed Point de Corail.

The path back to the bay lay through the forest, a straggling, difficult road. Our men had gone round the mountain with the baggage, so we took a pirogue and pulled gently along the shore, to get a good view of the fine basaltic rock that juts out into the inner bay. It is of columnar basalt, and the long prisms are constantly becoming detached from the main body of the rock and falling into the waters below. We crossed the sand-bar which separates the inner from the outer bay, and sailed directly for a small opening at the side of the mountain.

BAIE DU CAP.

The waters of the Baie du Cap are so clear that we could distinguish the Madrepores at the bottom, different species of Algæ, many of them growing on the corals, and the many-hued fish disporting amongst them. Through this opening at the foot of the mountain, which extends into the sea forming the Cape, lay our road to reach our quarters for the night. It is an awkward place to mount and descend to the other side. In one part there is a narrow ledge giving barely a foothold, and a false step would send you sheer down the precipice till you struck the water 100 feet below—the pure atmosphere, the magical lines of colour in the spray tossed from the reefs as they combed along to the shore, forming a series of glittering arches, from which the 'Culprit Fay' might have filled his crimson cup with the falling drops, though I fear me the Ouphe would have had worse dangers than even 'quarl and scallop' to contend with on the reefs of the Baie du Cap.

The sun sank below the horizon as we approached the spot where our tent was pitched, near a group of cocoa-nut trees, on the soft sward peculiar to this part of the Island. I found a number of Algæ, particularly two very curious species of Caulerpa. The trunks of the cocoa-nut trees were covered with Cyclostomas, and many of them were riddled from their attacks, as they work their way to the very heart. The main road skirts the sea here, and we kept along it till we came to the 'Bel Ombre' estate. We crossed the Citronnier River over a neat little bridge, and came out on the plains of the 'Bel Ombre,' bordered on one side by rows of Filaos. The sugar-house and dwellings lay directly in our course, so we had a good opportunity of witnessing the process of sugar-making, which had then just begun. A crowd of women and children, all as merry as crickets, were engaged in spreading out the *bagasse* to dry on the grass. They saluted us as we passed, and looked astonished at seeing us walking there; but not half so much as we did, to see so many boys and girls in a perfectly nude state, and the mammas in scarcely a better condition, having on only the barest apology for a covering. It was so disgusting a sight that we hurried away from them. This estate occupies nearly 5,000 acres, and has had endless expense laid out on it to render it one of the finest in the Island. We returned to the beach road, which is delightful, the soft sward and shade of the Filaos being very pleasant after the rough roads we had traversed so long.

We came to the fine estate of Beauchamp, and it struck me as one of the most desirable residences in Mauritius. On a charming spot on the SW. bank, being the extreme point seaward of Jacotet Bay, we determined to fix our home for some days. The bay possesses historic interest, from its having been the scene of one of the most daring exploits of the war in 1810, when Captain Willoughby, R.N., with his boat's crew, effected the first landing of the English in the Island, took possession of a French fort there, and captured the officer in charge of it; then crossing the Rivière des Galets, he took the battery on the Souillac side, carried off its guns, towed out a schooner lying there, and got back to his frigate with the loss of only one man. On the bluff is the house belonging to the estate, overlooking the bay, and commanding a fine prospect inland. It was here that some of the former governors of the Island used to pass the summer months; and I am not at all astonished at it, for it is one of the loveliest spots in Mauritius. It was near this place that a planter was carried off prisoner by the boats of the 'Nereid.' He was afterwards exchanged for twelve or fifteen seamen. Another story runs that he was ransomed for his weight in vegetables! Being a very stout man, it may be fancied the amount of cabbages and onions the boats carried off!

The bay is circular, with an irregular-shaped islet in its centre. Numerous streams abounding with fish pour into it. The hills rise in the background one over the other, most of them well wooded; and in the middle distance clumps of palms and cocoa-nut trees varied the landscape, their long leaves swaying to every passing breeze. There is an abundance of trees round the bay; and the wild canaries, the only native *songsters*, in the Filaos made the air resound with their pretty warblings, as they feasted on the little cones they are so fond of. Some of their nests were shown to us.

Thousands of Myna birds roused us the first thing in the morning with their noisy households; and we had glimpses of the Cardinals, though the male had not as yet put on his bright scarlet mantle, which he changes for a sombre brown one as summer dies away.

The pretty little Pingoes, or Nutmeg Birds (so called from

the breast being of the peculiar shade of a fresh nutmeg when cut in two), were twittering on every bush.

From the configuration of the Black River Mountains the neighbourhood of the Baie du Cap suffers severely in hurricane weather. The mountains of Laporte, Le Fouge, and Canot, which extend along the bay and river, are of great height, in a direction nearly NE. and SW., and increase the violence of the winds which blow SE. and SW., presenting an obstacle to their passage, which causes whirlwinds that spread devastation around. When the winds take their ordinary hurricane circle, often from the north, these hills arrest the squalls momentarily, to precipitate them with greater force on the neighbouring plantations to the south.

In this district, which was formerly successfully cultivated, canes and cotton also thrive; but from the tenacious character of the soil it requires a large amount of labour to work it well. From the Black River to the Cape the earth is blackish; but in the gorges near the bay the change of soil and temperature is as great as if in different latitudes. In the latter is found only a light reddish-yellow earth, free from stones, and the frequent and abundant rains render it extremely fertile.

On the evening of our arrival we heard a great shouting of men and women's voices, and our attention was called to a party of Creoles in pirogues, in the small inner bay, near the bridge which spans the Rivière des Galets.

Torches were burning in the bows of the pirogues, and the men were beating the sides with sticks and shouting with all their might. The mullets and other fish, attracted by the lights and frightened at the noise, leapt from the water into the boats. We were greatly amused at this novel mode of fishing, and we remained watching till a large quantity of fish was taken.

The island in this bay is of curious formation, similar to that of the Isle des Aigrettes, a composite of coral *débris* and shells overlying beds of lava. It can be reached at low water on foot by approaching it from the east. It is covered with bushes, and on the outer side is bounded by very deep water. The rocks are covered with the *Ceramium rubrum*, and a curious Echinus.

The lovely Actinias are in all their glory. They well deserve the name of 'Sea Anemones'; especially a very common one on this coast, with tentacles of the richest imperial blue and the heart yellowish. The lines to the Blue Anemone would suit equally these beautiful sea-flowers :—

> Flowers of starry clearness bright,
> Quivering urns of coloured light,
> Have ye caught your cup's rich dye
> From the intenseness of the sky,
>
> . . . .
>
> From a long, long fervent gaze
> Up that blue and silent deep,
> Where like things of sculptured sleep
> Alabaster clouds repose
> With the sunshine on their snows ?

Masses of Astræas and Meandrinas form a contrast to the branching Madrepores and the trellised fan-shaped Gorgonas. All glow with lustrous tints, with softened shades, a painter must despair of imitating. All are blended and harmonised by the medium of the bright transparent waters of the ocean; but bring them into our atmosphere, and even as we clutch them they lose their beauty, withered by the gross touch of the human hand. How like yet how unlike a terrestrial garden! *This* is composed of luxuriant vegetation—trees, shrubs, flowers, all the wealth of vegetable life; in *that* nearly the whole landscape (if I may be allowed the word in such anomalous case) is composed of animal life, not flowers teeming with it outwardly as on earth, but the very flowers themselves existent, sentient beings. To carry on the simile, Parasites are not wanting. Flustras and Escharas cling everywhere to the coral branches, answering to the Orchideæ of the forest, and the Serpulæ mine along the securest dwellings of the Mollusca, even as the Carias do the noblest trees. Eels swim in and out of the green Ulvas, in their sinuous paths resembling glittering snakes. Damberries, with blood-stained fins and golden-scaled armour, float gracefully about, and ever and anon the Quarl, that fearful monster the 'Pieuvre' immortalised by Victor Hugo for all time, warily sends forth its long feeders from out some hidden, time-worn cave. Woe betide the incautious fish that plays within the sweep of its terrible arms—one touch from those dread suckers, and further struggle is in vain!

Crabs swarm everywhere, of many varieties, some quite new to me. One in particular, which we named the Jumping Crab, from its leaping two or three feet from rock to rock when pursued. It would take a baited hook readily, so that we easily caught some. As we sat fishing on the bluff, a good-sized Tazarre waited on us, remaining perfectly motionless within a few feet of the surface; and no sooner did we draw a fine fish from the deep water, than he would instantly snatch at it. We baited a large hook with a live fish, and threw it to him, but he was not to be done so easily, and refused it. I then watched my opportunity, and just as he was darting at a fine Damberry, I sent him a leaden pill from my revolver, and he soon disappeared, leaving us to fish in peace.

Some Creole fishermen offered to provide us rare sport from a fishing excursion to the reefs, if we would stand the expenses, which were only a few dollars, and to which we gladly assented; and active preparations in torches, &c. went on for the evening's diversion. Two good-sized pirogues were manned by four stout negro Creoles; and jolly fellows they were, regular sea dogs! A box of provisions, our pipes and tobacco, some good old rum, and Hennessy's best, with extra clay pipes for our men, completed our outfit. Spirits were an absolute necessity, as we expected to be wet through for hours. We pulled our pirogues about a mile out from the shore, to the outer reef, and anchored them, leaving one man as a guard. We all then jumped into the water, which was nearly up to our waists, armed with long spears, and we followed our guides cautiously, just keeping clear of the breakers. Suddenly there was a halt, and silence was enjoined. Our torches were lit, and in a hole close to us we observed numbers of fish that soon approached the light. 'Now is your time!—throw in your lances!' said our sable friends; and away they went like lightning, cleaving the water, scattering the Medusæ and jelly fish in all directions, that left behind a train of phosphoric light as they darted through the waves. A cord was attached to the lances; and as I drew mine in, I found I had speared a large fish of the genus Pseudoscarus, called here a Cateau, very handsome, but not very choice eating. We bagged several fine fish, none weighing less than from two to two and a half pounds. On we went, the Creoles evidently knowing every hole and break in the reefs. We disturbed myriads of little animals which appeared to have taken up their abode in the empty cells in the great coral beds. This sea garden was lighted up with millions of tiny sparks—the glow-worms of the deep, lighting the finny tribes of nocturnes to their prey, and presenting a pyrotechnic display on a small scale to us, but to them possibly equal to our brightest calcium light.

We were glad to hear that our old enemy the Tazarre never attacks at night. One of the Creoles hooked a large Ourite, or catfish (their Creole name), *Octopus vulgaris*. No sooner was it on the hook, than it darted its long tentacles up the pole, and wound one of its slimy feelers, with its double row of cup-like suckers, round his arm. The knife was instantly applied, and the limb severed from the body of the fish; but even then it was with difficulty that it could be detached, the suckers possess such remarkable tenacity. After removal, a sense of numbness remained for a good while in the arm. The brute was, however, dislodged from his hole, and proved to be a large one, measuring ten feet from tip to tip of the tentacles. I had often seen this animal on the reefs, but had always given it a wide berth, knowing it to be dangerous; and coming to close quarters with the disgusting-looking animal did not at all make me anxious for its proximity. A number of smaller ones were caught, and the fishermen despatched them by turning their bodies inside out, thus leaving an empty sack.

We fished until half-past two in the morning, having been between four and five hours in the water. We returned safely to our pirogues, which were laden with our night's spoils; but on the way to them I fell into a deep hole, and thus took an involuntary early morning bath, which did not, however, make me much wetter than I had previously been. A good draught of Hennessy, as we got into the boat, put us all to rights; and we got home well pleased with our excursion, but fully determined our next should be on a moonlight night. We fished up some large yellow cones on the reefs, the *C. betulinus*; and, amongst the sea-weeds I brought away, I found a curious specimen of Gigartina, some fine pieces of *Codium tomentosum*, and a rare one of Delesseria. The latter genus, though common in most parts of the world, had hitherto escaped my search, so I was greatly pleased to find a specimen at last.

A fine cool morning invigorated us, so that, in spite of our night's outing, we resolved to make the most of our time; and, after a hasty breakfast, we set off with a guide to visit the Falls

THE BAY OF SOUILLAC.

of the Rivière des Galets, which has its outlet near Jacotet Bay.

Our path was anything but a pleasant one, alternately forcing our way through liane-twined trees that impeded our progress every five yards, or out in the open through high grass, bearing a barbed seed (*Anthistiria barbata*), which worked its way into our flesh, and which we could not detach from our clothes without much trouble—a far worse species than that on the plains of St. Pierre. Much of the ground was also encumbered with large boulders; and with all these impediments, we found we had a guide who knew no more of the road than we did, so it may be supposed we did not make much headway.

Before reaching the Falls, our way lay along the side of a hill on which a path had been made. To make this road great masses of calcareous rock have been cut through, showing the successive layers, which vary greatly in thickness, but each one distinctly marked by lines of ferruginous earth. The river forms a very beautiful cascade, not like that of Chamarel, in one continuous sheet of water down into the depths below, but it is broken by huge craggy rocks covered with ferns and mosses, thus giving a more varied aspect to the scene. The height of the whole is little less than three hundred feet. Instead of the rude passage formed by a fallen trunk of a tree (as described by one traveller), a good pile bridge now spans the Rivière des Galets.

We left Jacotet Bay with regret, and pushed on to the Port of Souillac. Our road still lay along the shore, and we had a continuation of the turfy land, very pleasant walking. The Rivière de la Savane flows into the Bay of Souillac, and has a good bridge over it; the left bank is precipitous, and in the rainy season it must bring down a great volume of water to the sea. The village is picturesquely situated; it has a fine Roman Catholic church, of Gothic architecture, some good buildings, most of them with gardens attached; and here the District Courts are held. A good deal of business is done in this little place. It is the most southerly point of the island, and lies in one of the very finest cane districts. A number of coasters were lying there, waiting for freights, having discharged their cargoes at the quays constructed for that purpose. It was formerly the most convenient port for the planters to ship their sugar for the Port Louis market, before railroads were an established fact, and will continue so to this district till a branch line is made to the Savane. This port, which formerly could receive boats drawing eight feet of water even at low tide, is gradually closing so that craft only drawing five feet can now enter. The barrier is formed by large rocks and trees which are carried down the slopes by the descent of mountain torrents during the rainy season, and the daily degradation of the cliffs near the jetty and quays. The temperature of the Savane near the sea is generally warmer than in the upper parts. The south winds singularly affect both men and plants in this quarter. They are insupportable to people of asthmatic or consumptive tendency, and when they blow with violence for several days, trees and plants suffer severely from their withering influence.

About fifteen miles from Souillac is the famous Grand Bassin; and as we had none of us seen it, we set off to it, having previously got permission to use a large hangar in its vicinity. Part of our way lay through cane fields, and part through the woods. The Bois Sec, as this part of the country is called, answers very completely to its name. It is dreary in the extreme. Thousands of dried-up skeletons of trees blanched to a ghastly whiteness meet the eye on every side; and but for the tangle of lianes and plants at their feet showing life, it might be a forest of primæval days over which some blighting plague had passed,

> As falls the plague on man—

and left it as a memento to future ages of the dire ruin. The lianes *Premna scandens* and *Seea arborea* twine round the rugged stems and hide their barrenness. Formerly here grew the *Syzygium glomeratum*, spreading its lordly branches far and wide; but now it is rarely seen, being replaced by the *Syzygium scandens*, which is a mere climbing shrub. Two species of Lycopodium grow here. Acrosticheæ, Adiantums and Aspleniums are plentiful, and the elegant *Cyathea excelsa*. The trunks of the latter are covered with concave plates, whose sections are in waves, closely arranged in a circle next the bark. The stems are marked with long scars, broken into ragged projections, showing where the leaf has fallen, and thus produced these scars. It is not uncommon to see various Polypodia, Vittarias, and

GRAND BASSIN.

other ferns growing out of the scars, giving the tall bare trunks a singular appearance; or a delicate jasmine or other creeper will twine round the rugged stem, covering it with tender verdure; whilst over all spreads the exquisite crown of fronds, that makes it the King of Ferns in Mauritius.

Where we traversed the woods it was a most tedious kind of scrambling over fallen trunks and giant coils of roots, through thickets of climbers, and not unfrequently into deep holes. We passed the night at the hangar, and found the temperature so much lower that we felt the change sharply, our coverings being but scant. We paid our visit to the Grand Bassin early in the morning, along a private road cut through the bush. A troop of deer was quietly feeding on the rough grass, but our presence did not greatly scare it. This interesting lake lies at the height of 2,250 feet above sea-level, has an area of about 25 acres, and fills the crater of an extinct volcano. It is nearly surrounded with dense woods, which cover the slopes of the hills, part of the Savane chain. This great reservoir receives the waters of many streams in the rainy season: but the body of water varies little in depth the whole year, being fed from underground springs that percolate through the porous lava at the foot of the mountains. The accounts of its great depth are incorrect. I could not get soundings over sixty feet, though I tried in many places, as I swam over it, there being no boat there at that time. The water is delightfully clear and cold, and I think is the finest in the Island. We were told not to plunge in on account of the monster eels; but though we fished for them a good while, not one put in an appearance. There were plenty of Dame Ceres, or golden fish, and two fine black swans were sailing majestically about the lake.

Towards the centre of the Grand Bassin is a little island, on which grow a few Vacoas and shrubs, and the *Nymphœa stellata* adorns its edges. We turned away considerably disappointed, excepting for its geological interest. I think it has been greatly overrated. The accompanying view is taken from the SE. of the lake, taking in the whole Bassin at an angle of 90°, the Pitou Mountain in the distance.

The next day after our return to Souillac, we paid a visit to the Cascade of Savane in the neighbourhood. A wall of black basalt interrupts the course of the river of the same name, composed of the most regular geometrical prisms, by the action of the water separated and broken, and forming a thousand angular projections.

As the river surmounts the rocky barrier, and breaks into innumerable streams, flung back from point to point, and sending up showers of spray, sparkling in the sun with rainbow rays, it equals in beauty any in the Island, and even in the dry season is most romantic. As it descends into the Bassin below, the waters meander peacefully along, bordered with the large-leaved Nymphæas, and overhung with the elegant wild Bananas, Raffias, and Bamboos, and the scene changes to one of the most perfect repose.

> Beneath it sweeps
> The current's calmness: oft from out it leaps
> The finny darter, with the glittering scales,
> That dwells and revels in thy glassy deeps;
> While chance some water lily sails
> Down where the shallower wave still tells its bubbling tales.

After leaving Souillac, our route was still along the coast, boulders encumbering it as usual. We crossed several inconsiderable rivers, and halted near the Rivière du Poste, the boundary of the districts of Savane and Grand Port. A rock causeway traverses this river, which they told us was so dangerous during heavy rains, from the sudden swelling of the waters, that many lives had been lost there.

The ascent on the Grand Port side is so rugged and steep that it is called L'Escalier, and between it and the Rivière Tabac stands a fair-sized village. Beyond this lies a tract of country, in former times a dense forest, containing such fine timber trees that it obtained the name of Gros Bois. From the destruction of these trees even so early as the time of occupation by the Dutch, doubtless many species once abundant are now rare if not wholly extinct. The reckless way the trees were cut down by the crews of every vessel that touched here must have made great changes in the forests. During the present century the same system (or rather the want of any system) has prevented the growth to the full size of the best timber. In the Gros Bois are still fine specimens of the *Calophyllum spurium*, but they are rare. The small-leaved Tatamaka, the *Eleodendron orientale*, the *Jambosa venosa*, Colophania, and two species

CASCADE OF THE RIVER SAVANE.

THE SOUFFLEUR.

of ebony, yet abound, and a host of others which I could only admire and guess at their names.

We next camped at a pretty spot, shaded with Filaos and Bamboos, about thirty feet above the level of the sea, and within a mile of the Souffleur, a natural curiosity. The coast here is a line of abrupt rocks, rising up from the deep water, and the waves break against them with a wild and angry roar, as the surf rolls in unchecked by reefs; but it proved so soothing and musical to our ears that we all dropped off to sleep immediately after dinner, having had a fatiguing walk. In the morning the sea was still more boisterous, and dashed the spray right over our tent, so that we were obliged to pitch it higher up. From the action of the waves numerous caverns and fissures are worn in these rocks, even the mightiest boulders not being able to resist their violence, as they work their revenge on them for the time when, as molten rivers of fire, they broke down the giant crater walls, and forced back the waves of the ocean itself to a great distance, laying the foundation of the great coral reefs that are spreading far and wide.

The name Souffleur, or Rock Spout, has been given to an enormous block of black basalt, connected by a broken ledge of rocks with the mainland. It rises nearly forty feet above the sea, exposed to the full force of the waves, and is perforated to its summit by a cavity that communicates with the ocean. When there is a heavy swell the waves rush in and fill up the vacuum with terrific fury. Wave on wave presses on, and there being no other outlet, the water is forced upwards, and forms a magnificent *jet d'eau*, ascending to a height of fifty or sixty feet. The noise can be heard for two miles; and when the Souffleur growls and roars, it is a sure indication of rough weather.

The rocks are now greatly undermined, and the Spout is so enlarged that it is daily losing its former grandeur; but the day we saw it, they told us that it was performing its best. The wind had been blowing strongly from the SE. for several days, and the sea ran high, so we had a good view of it. When in action it emits a singular rumbling sound, and the rocks tremble and vibrate so much that it caused a most unpleasant quivering all over the body as we watched it from the adjacent rocks. So great are its powers of suction that a stone placed within ten feet of the adit was quickly drawn in. It is only when in a state of tranquillity that it can be approached without danger. The wet rocks are covered with slimy weeds (Cladophora, Valonioides, and *Fucus minimus*), which make the foothold very precarious.

At a little distance along the coast is another curious monument of the work of the ocean, the 'Pont Naturel,' as it is called. It resembles a real bridge, with a pile and two arches, through which the sea swirls and rushes with the greatest impetuosity. The formidable chasm is daily widening, the foaming billows breaking against the rocks, and the arches are being gradually undermined, so that some future cyclone will cause their total disappearance. I found some very fine Chitons on this bridge (*Chiton magnificus*). The slopes to the sea are covered with couch grass, the *Cynodon tenellus*, which appears to flourish most in the salt atmosphere. Troops of hares crop this saline herbage with great avidity, so we had no lack of game.

The whole of this part of the coast is strewn with rocks of basalt, many of which present the appearance of sudden refrigeration when in a state of such ebullition as to cause bubbles large enough to contain several gallons; and many of these vesicles may be found cohering, the *parietes* of which are scarcely thicker than paper, and the whole weighing but a few pounds.[1]

Our progress in returning from the Souffleur was very slow, as our route alternated between a scramble over rocks and a flounder through mud, much of the land hereabouts being marshy. The whole shore along this coast is also full of holes, burrowed by a species of land-crab, called Tourlouroux by the Creoles: they may be seen scampering in all directions, but always under protest, to judge from their defiant attitudes.

After the wild sea-landscape we had been so long gratified with, we came to one of quite an opposite character. A narrow arm of the sea runs up some distance into the land, and is called the 'Bras de Mer de Chaland.' It is a picture of perfect repose, its waters so clear that the rocks and fish at a depth of twenty feet are visible, and from their colour it has obtained the name of Blue Bay. A charming view is had of this place

[1] See Bolton's *Almanac.*

LE PONT NATUREL.

when going to Mahébourg by rail. It is nearly bordered with tall Filaos, and at a distance it looks like a lovely blue inland lake shut in by shading trees.

We took a pirogue here, and went off to the Isle des Cocos, shell-hunting. The whole of the southern coast is rich in conchological treasures. The finest Harps in the Indian Ocean are found in the deep waters round this part of the island. We had some difficulty in returning, for the tide set dead against us. After quitting this tranquil spot, we had once more a fine soft verdure under our feet as far as Point d'Esny. Here we pitched our tent, a little beyond the Military Camp, whence we had a capital view of the town of Mahébourg, which lies on a slope towards the sea. The white tower of the Catholic church shone out conspicuously against the dark foliage of the embowering trees, and the Creole Mountains made a fine background to the landscape. Before us, seaward, lay the sweep of Grand Port Bay; the intricate lines of reefs well marked by wreaths of foam, and the channels equally distinct by the still bright water. Point d'Esny is formed by a small bay making in from the larger one of Grand Port. From our quarters a causeway has been built that isolates this inlet, and converts it into a fish-pond. The soldiers of Her Majesty's 32nd and 86th Regiments were exercising on this fine plain, and practising with the Schneider rifles which they had lately received. Their range was about 800 yards, and many of them made capital shots. Grand Port is the largest harbour on the coast; but owing to its sand-bar and the difficult navigation between the reefs, which are spreading in all directions, it can never be of any importance for vessels larger than the coasting chasse-marées, though it was chosen by the Dutch and afterwards by the French as the principal port.

The Isle de Passe lies at the entrance of the harbour, and will be for ever famous in the naval annals of both England and France. On it there stood a circular fort and a barracks as a defence; but in 1810 it was stormed by Captain Pym, of the 'Sirius' frigate, and taken. It was kept by the British through all the thrilling events which occurred in the deadly conflict which took place in Grand Port Bay on the 25th and 26th August, in the same year, when the French gained their bloodiest but last naval victory over the English in the Indian seas. After the capitulation of the Isle de France, the barracks were occupied for some years by a garrison, but they have long been abandoned.

The adjacent island of Fouquets, which is about three miles from the nearest point of the mainland, has a lighthouse. The foundation line is thirty feet above the sea, and the light is at a height of 108 feet. There is a white dioptric light of the first order, facing seaward, and which can be seen sixteen miles off. This island is hollowed out by the waves in many places, forming caverns that undermine it for a good distance. I think the foundations of the lighthouse are unsound, for the walls are much cracked, and the whole building is off the perpendicular, so that I should not be surprised to hear that it had caved in during some gale. There is a large tank, which is capable of containing a supply of fresh water for the use of the keeper and his family, brought over in barrels from the mainland every day, when the boats take provisions, oil, &c., and stored there, as the place is often inaccessible for days together at high tides, and in stormy weather. A most extensive view is obtained from the top of the lighthouse. The whole sweep of the Bay, with its curiously outlined islands, Des Aigrettes, Vacoa, Marianne, De la Passe, Aux Cerfs, &c., and a long line of coast both to the north and south, are visible. The fine ranges of the Creoles, Camisard, and Terra Rouge Mountains are partially seen inland far behind the town.

The ruins of the Old Grand Port, dating from the time of the Dutch governors, were still standing in 1753, when they were entirely demolished, and their materials served to construct new quarters for the French Commandant and garrison. A new town was built in 1805, by General De Caen, who named it Mahébourg after Mahé de Labourdonnais.

The remains are still shown at Point de la Colonie; but to my eye the existing town is, or will soon be in many parts, almost as ruinous. In three-fourths of the place the streets are overgrown with grass, and the houses are in the most dilapidated condition, in fact so much so it is only a wonder how people can be got to inhabit them. What were once evidently well-cultivated gardens are now neglected, overgrown with weeds, and trodden down. Damp and decay have set a stamp on nearly the whole place. There are one or two pretty good streets, where the few shops are; and there is a small covered shed for a market-place, which seems well supplied with vegetables, poultry, &c. Since the opening of the railway a few new buildings have been run up, and it has a little improved; but even being the terminus of the Midland line has failed to give much impetus to the progress of the place. Socially speaking, Mahébourg is even more dead-alive than Port Louis itself. The station is, I believe, built on land reclaimed from the sea, which was previously a saline marsh, and the trains pass over a raised causeway of stone.

The place is considered generally very healthy, the death-rate even during cholera and the late epidemic being far less than in many other places. Mahébourg resembles most parts of this colony, very pretty in the distance, but, like Port Louis especially,

> 'Tis distance lends enchantment to the view.

The many umbrageous trees, especially the Badanier, the Nowruk, Sang Dragon, Samalonga, Flamboyant, and others, give it a most picturesque aspect; but enter it, and squalor and filth abound. It possesses a pretty little Episcopal church, the Catholic one before mentioned, and a neat little convent; but very little can be said as to the beauty of the private houses that are not dilapidated. Near the sea stand the barracks, good substantial buildings, in a fine square.

On a hill overlooking the town are the cemeteries. To arrive at them you have to mount a steep hill of red clayey soil, that must be terribly heavy for funerals to pass over in wet weather. The Protestant and Catholic grounds are all in one enclosure; the latter lie just at the entrance, and are nicely kept. Pretty shrubs and trees are planted about the tombs; and from this place you get a lovely view seaward, and you can mark the course of the Rivers Creoles and La Chaux, which intersect the town, by the steep banks of verdure to the water's edge, and the lines of waving bamboos.

Advance a little farther, and what a change meets the eye as you find yourself in the English Protestant burying-ground! Neither shrub nor tree shades the neglected graves, many of which are merely ill-made mounds of sandy earth. All looks desert—nothing to relieve the fierce glare of the sun; even the ground is in uneven hillocks, no order, as if every grave was dug at random; and you go stumbling over ruined vaults and old stumps, which show there were *once* fine old trees, why cut down no one could guess, and you turn back, disgusted, to the fresh greenery of the Catholic side.

We did not visit the Isle de Passe at this time, but on a subsequent trip I had an opportunity of so doing. How it occurred, and what I saw, as well as the continuation of our tour, I reserve for another chapter.

POINT AU DIABLE.

CHAPTER XXIII.

VISIT TO THE ISLE DE PASSE, AND CONTINUATION OF TOUR.

Preparation for Visit—River Creoles—Crater in Mahébourg Bay—Isle de Passe—The Return—Aground—En route again—Point au Diable—Mountain Ranges—Camisard—Its Geology—Ferns—Grand River SE.—The Falls—The Beauchamp Estate—Statue to the Virgin—Trou d'Eau douce—Point Hollandais—Annelides—Holothuriæ, &c.—Flacq—General Description—St. Antoine—Amber Island—Caverns—Islets in Mapou Bay—Polyp—Sunset—Arrival of English Fleet in Mapou Bay—Holicanthus semicirculatus—Battle with a Cave Eel—Situation of Pamplemousses—The Gardens and Churches—On the road to Port Louis—Cemetery of Bois Marchand—Peter Both—St. Croix—Olden Boundaries of Port Louis and Defences—The City and its Cries.

I HAD been spending a few days in Mahébourg, where I was most hospitably entertained by the officers of the 86th Regiment, when a pic-nic was proposed to the Isle de Passe. Most of them kept boats, and all were soon put in readiness for our excursion. Long before dawn on the day fixed, the Creole servants were conveying mysterious-looking boxes and hampers, to be stowed away in the boats, filled with everything requisite for a good time. At sunrise the officers made their appearance in the mess-room, dressed in suitable boating costume, but with more regard to ease than elegance. After snatching a hasty meal, we embarked on the River Creoles, in four pretty sloop-rigged boats. This river abounds with choice fish, gourami, carp, eels, mullets, and fine camerons. A light breeze carried us down the river, and across the sand-bar at its mouth out into the Bay; but we were obliged to stand off towards the Lion Mountain, and soon the wind hauled, and we had to take to our oars. I was not sorry for this, as we had a cool overcast morning, our company was all that could be wished, and we glided quietly along. As we rowed slowly over the coral beds, on which we could see most distinctly the many-hued molluscs and fish disporting themselves, I was able to hook up many interesting specimens of Algæ.

The curious Holothuriæ abound in these waters; but while I was watching them, the submarine scene suddenly changed to the blackness of darkness. Instead of the bright sparkling waters was a blackish-blue fluid showing deep water. We were, in fact, just over the often-described crater; but this being my first visit to it, I felt a curious sensation on coming to this deep hole, not unlike what one feels on inadvertently finding oneself at the edge of a deserted, uncovered mine. It is nearly circular, from three to four hundred yards in diameter, and said to be fathomless. The water at the sides, which are the walls of a submerged mountain, is a lighter colour, and we could see down for a few feet; the tops must be barely covered at low tides. We felt relieved as we could see again the bottom through the clear waves. This cavity is infested with monster sharks, that always make me shudder when in their vicinity.

We saw a very fine turtle (*Testudo imbricata*), and could easily have captured it. They formerly abounded on this coast, but are now rarely seen. After three hours' rowing we came to the Isle de Passe; the others not arriving so soon, as they had gone round by the Isle des Aigrettes. The place we landed at is rocky, and has been washed away by the sea to such an extent that there was danger of the boats being stove in, if the sea proved rough, by getting sucked in under the projecting rocks. We all proceeded to a small house that I took to have been the Commandant and soldiers' quarters. Two very large iron mortars, a broken gun-carriage, and an iron sixty-eight pounder, to which we made our boat fast, were all the warlike implements we saw on the island. In close proximity to this house was the magazine, with a strong high wall built around it. The arrangement for heating shot was very curious, and the whole work spoke of ancient times. Room was made seaward in the rock for guns *en barbette*, but I am of opinion that as a fort of defence it would be worth nothing now-a-days. Truly, it commanded the Pass, but a shell dropped in among the garrison would not only destroy the buildings, dismount the guns, but kill every soul on the island, as there was not the slightest chance of escape. Casemates could have been built, but in a military point of view it is not worth defending.

The soldiers who were quartered there had amused themselves by cutting their names, and the number of the regiment they were attached to, on the walls. There was scarcely a stone inside or out of the magazine but had one or more names on it. In the middle of the island were many graves; and I noticed the names of some of the brave 86th, who fought in the desperate engagements previously mentioned. There lay the remains of the poor fellows taking their final earthly rest in the desolate island, never more to start at the sound of the reveille, or the thundering din of battle:

> And though no stone may tell
> Their name, their rank, their glory,
> They rest in hearts that loved them well,
> And they grace Britannia's story.

Some kind-hearted fellow of the present regiment had placed a new head and foot-stone at one of the graves, and rudely carved on it: 'The 86th Regiment.'

MAHÉBOURG BARRACKS.

This island is also of upheaval, and of far more recent formation than Mauritius. It is composed of a friable greyish sandstone in easily traced strata, that appear to have been thrown over by a sudden convulsion. The dip of the strata is at an angle of thirty degrees, and inclined east and west. This and others of the group were most likely upheaved by the once very active volcano in Grand Port Bay. At one period they were much more elevated than at present, and covered with palms and cocoa-nuts. At the Isle de Fouquet are still found casts of them, the same as I stated to be found at the Isle des Aigrettes. They must all have been submerged and undergone a second upheaval, and lie about five miles from Mahébourg. It is not improbable that some centuries hence they may be joined to the mainland, as in many places the water is so shallow that even the light pirogues ground on the reefs.

After having examined everything worth seeing on the island, we returned to the house, where a bountiful repast was spread, and the popping of corks and rattling of dishes gave proof that the advanced guard had opened action, and in a few minutes the whole column was actively engaged doing its duty, as English and Yankees well know how. All were in the best of spirits, and it would be hard to find a jollier lot of fellows than the officers of the 86th. After thoroughly discussing all the good things under which our temporary table groaned, we found a goblet of iced champagne most welcome, as the thermometer had risen ten degrees since morning.

Some of us then set off shell-hunting, as all the islands of this bay are famous for curious specimens. Amongst others I found some of the largest Chiton shells I had ever seen, of the same species as those at the Souffleur. Our bright sky was however fast becoming obscured, and the wind rising; such warnings were not to be neglected, so we soon had all ready, and our boats set off together. The one I was in with the Major was a slow sailer, and in consequence the others soon shot ahead of us, and we found no efforts would keep us up. Of course we had to stand a good deal of chaff—asking 'If we wanted towing,' or 'If they should take messages ashore,' &c. &c. But if our course was tortoise-like, it was for the time sure. The wind freshened, and a steady rain set in, and very soon our boasting comrades, the hares, were hard and fast on the reefs, and all of them out in the water up to their waists, getting their boats off. We sailed merrily past them, and flung them some wine as a farewell gift, and got nearly to Creole River, when our short-lived triumph was over, and we were aground too. It was getting quite dark, but there was no help for it. The Major and I had to turn out into the sea with the men to push off our boat, the rain by this time pouring in torrents. However, we got in all safely after hard pulling, glad to find supper ready at the barracks.

And now to return to our trip after this long digression.

From Mahébourg we sent our carrioles round to Point au Diable, but we preferred sailing, although there was considerable sea on. The distance was about nine miles. This is a spur of the Bamboo Mountains, and received its name from early navigators, as it was said the compass here varied so much without apparent cause, which was probably owing to the large quantity of iron ore that the whole range contains. There is an old French fortification of stone, still in fair preservation.

We pitched our tents near this Point, in order to examine the coral reefs. We found large quantities of Sargassum, Cystophyllum, and for the first time *Turbinaria ornata*: there is but little variety of Algæ all round the coast, though Zoophytes are pretty numerous. The Sargassum is fine here, with its beautiful waving branches, covered with the nodes of air vessels resembling bunches of small yellow fruit; and amongst it I observed shoals of fish about an inch long, of a bright blue, which I took to be young Urasse, which swarm round the whole of Mauritius, and amongst them are the most brilliant-coloured of tropical fish. They come into shoal water at certain seasons, in order that the young may not be devoured by the large fish in deep water. I tried hard to catch some of these small fry; but as soon as I threw my net they would disappear amongst the weeds, as by magic, then when all was quiet they would recommence their gambols as actively as before.

I saw many Anguilles Morèles, but I took good care not to disturb them, so they let me alone. How the fishermen escape these eels I know not, probably from understanding their habits they avoid them. The reef at this part extends out some distance, with shallow water between it and the shore; but off the Point, near the fort, it is very deep.

To the north of Mahébourg is a magnificent range of mountains, extending from the centre of the island, where they have the name of Terre Rouge, to Grand River SE., changing their nomenclature to Creoles, Camisard, Bamboo, and Grand Port respectively. The Creole Mountains form a long spur off the main range, and make the background of Mahébourg itself. Numerous branches diverge to the sea; and amongst those of Grand Port rises the Camisard, supposed to have received its name from the Camisa, or shroud of clouds which it often wears; or, probably, from its having been the refuge of bands of Maroons, who there defied capture, as the Camisards of old who fled tc the Cevennes. The latter flying for liberty of conscience, and the former for personal liberty, not improbably gave the consequent idea of calling it the Camisard Mountain.

This singular mountain is double-headed, and is a curious feature in this range, standing out distinctly from the rest. I had been twice on the south side, but had never had the opportunity to explore its ravines. I now determined to visit it again to examine the curious formation of the north side. To do this we were obliged to make a *détour* round the base, crossing the western spur, and then force our way up the jungle to the highest points, which are quite bare. We planted the Stripes and Stars on one head and the Cross of St. George on the other. A regular road runs over the mountain, and through the gorge passable for man and horse; but we preferred to make a path for ourselves. When we had attained the summit, we were compelled to stand and admire the glorious prospect. Waving canes were planted nearly to the summit of some of the neighbouring hills. The mountain ranges to the north showed their varied peaks brilliantly illuminated by the same flood of sunshine that glinted the canvas tents of the soldiers at Point d'Esny, and fringed with gold the white-robed breakers, tossing madly over the dangerous reef barrier. The pretty little islands in Grand Port Bay sleeping calmly in the glare, and the chasse-marées, reduced by distance to tiny specks, dotted the ocean far beyond the reach of the surf.

> The solid frame of earth
> And ocean's liquid mass in gladness lay
> Beneath him, far and wide the clouds were touched,
> And in their silent faces could be read
> Unutterable love. Sound needed none,
> Nor any sense of joy.

Vegetation is luxuriant on this mountain; but my expectations had been so raised from the accounts I had heard of it, that I was somewhat disappointed. I had already climbed so many of the Mauritius mountains and seen so much of its Flora, that I saw little new or more interesting than in many other places. I found the following ferns, but, with the exception of the *Aspidium ebenum*, they were not finer than elsewhere—the universal Odontosoria, Aspidium, *capense* and *ebenum*, *Cœnopteris vivipara*, Nephrodiums, *Asplenium lineatum*, and a few other insignificant ones. Instead of numerous species fringing the road-side, waiting for the botanist to gather them, we had to hunt diligently for them. Good ferns are like fairies,

They that would find them, must search for them well!

I had hoped to find many of the rarer Orchideæ there, but we saw none, save those quite common on every mountain peak in the island. I picked up a good many land-shells; some particularly fine ones of the *Helix inversicolor* and *H. Staphylen* alive.

The north face of the Camisard is almost perpendicular, rising about 800 feet, and presents a magnificent specimen of columnar basaltic rock. It displays a congeries of hexagonal and pentagonal prisms, from two to six feet long, very regular, on the main part of the mountain, of a blueish grey tinge. From their size they must have once formed part of an immense mass of molten matter, the fissures, constantly occurring, having been caused by contraction in its cooling.

One section has the appearance of having been toppled over when in a partially cooled state, and the columns lie in irregular confused heaps inclined to the west, and resting on the columns of the main part. Ages ago when the melted rocks formed these prisms, the whole face of this giant cliff must have presented a picture equal to that on the coast of Illawana, New South Wales. The elements have played their usual part and made wonderful changes since that far-off time. Slowly but surely are they degrading column after column, forming a loose dry earth that is washed down continually to the plains; the ruin of the upper world of rocks spreading fertility and plenty on the lower regions where man resides. One by one those exquisitely formed prisms, once as perfect as if shaped by the most cunning tool ever used by man, are loosened, fall from the perpendicular and all shape is lost, bent into a mass of *débris*, scarcely recognisable. The transverse sections of these prisms are very distinctly shown where they have fallen and been broken off sharp.

About half-way down the mountain lies a huge block of blue basalt, which was detached from above and came crashing down like an avalanche, till it was arrested in its course at this spot, which is on the edge of a deep ravine. The footpath winds close to this rock, and as a portion of it projects, it forms a capital shelter from rain. Some time since an Indian and his wife sought refuge under it, and while quietly sleeping they were both cruelly murdered by Maroons, then infesting this neighbourhood, and their bodies were flung into the ravine below. The huge boulder is smeared all over with scarlet paint, and ashes and charred wood lie all round it. In front of it is a pile of small stones and broken boughs. Our men told us these were deposited by comrades out of respect for the dead, who whenever they passed the spot offered a prayer for them, adding to the pile at the same time. This is similar to the custom of the Catholics in Spain and many other countries, who always erect a cross on the spot where murder has been committed, every passer-by placing an additional stone at its foot, till I have seen huge piles thus formed heaped together on the site of some terrible tragedy.

We finished our descent by a narrow path, that led us to our rendezvous at Point au Diable. Here we left our men and carrioles to make their way as best they could along the rough road to Grand River SE., whilst we kept close to the shore, collecting marine plants, or making little *détours* inland, as some interesting spot tempted us.

We halted for a short time at Grand River SE., where is the terminus of the Northern line of railway, at a distance of thirty miles from Port Louis, and where the Government have built a substantial stone depôt. The village is very small, and principally inhabited by fishermen, and a small garrison of soldiers. The bay is large, and the reefs lie a long distance from the shore. There is a channel through them, where the chasse-marées enter, and water enough for them to come quite up to the village. We crossed the bay with all our traps, and pitched our tent on a grassy plain on Point Camisard, and near the military post. There were about fifty men of the 86th here, with their officers, who gave us a courteous reception. They have delightful quarters, and had made the most of them by planting the grounds with pretty-flowering shrubs, and round the house was a garden filled with flowers. The seeds had been imported from England, and I was pleased to see so many old favourites collected together.

About a mile from the post are the Falls of Grand River SE., formed by a huge wall of rock arresting the course of the river, which pours down it in a broad sheet in stormy weather. It is easily reached, except after heavy rains, and presents a curious phenomenon, often seen in the rivers here. In a ledge of rock, ordinarily dry, is a natural basin, scooped out of the solid basalt, about three or four feet in diameter, and as many deep. The pool that receives the waters of the cascade abounds with fish. We embarked in a large boat from the jetty, and rowed along to get a good view of the coast. The banks are high and bold, and almost covered with vegetation. Canes meet the eye everywhere. Near this is another 'Beauchamp' estate, one of the first sugar plantations in the time of Mahé de la Bourbonnais.

Fine ferns grew in all the interstices of the rocks; and on the side of a steep cliff, in a natural niche, about thirty feet from the water, some *dévote* had placed a white marble figure of the Virgin. The sailors that rowed our boat, as we neared it, laid on their oars, and reverently crossed themselves, repeating a prayer. This statue was placed in this spot in commemoration of one who was drowned, by a friend who made a vow to the Virgin, that if the body was recovered her image should be placed here, and he had well fulfilled his vow.

After passing the place, we came to a part of the river so rocky that it formed a barrier to our farther progress; luckily our sailors were familiar with the place, and steered us clear of the danger. We landed near the Falls, and strolled along the banks of the river, which takes its rise in the north of the Piton du Milieu. At a distance of seven miles are the Dya Mamou Falls, said to be of great beauty; but circumstances prevented our visiting them till a later date. The sea was too rough for an excursion to the four Isles aux Cerfs, which I had wished to visit, as I had heard so much of the quantities of pumice-stone found there.

After leaving the village of Grand River SE., we crossed the Rivière Sèche, which is fed by numerous mountain streams; and in a little bay that makes in here, we found quite a number of interesting plants, but the reefs lay too far off shore for a visit, so we pushed on to the Trou d'Eau douce. This is also a fishing village, and derives its name from a quantity of fresh water that bubbles up on the shore through the salt water of the tide.

Near this place are several Mares of brackish water, full of fish. The Mare aux Lubines rises and falls with the tide, but the Mare aux Fougères has good drinkable water. In the neighbourhood are large sugar estates ; and in this district are made many hundreds of sugar bags yearly from the Vacoas, which grow in great abundance. In former times there were establishments for the manufacture of indigo ; but this culture, like so many other useful ones, has been abandoned. One species of Indigo plant is indigenous to the island.

We encamped off Point Hollandais, near the old Dutch road. At a place called Palma, in this neighbourhood, is a natural well or opening in the rocks, about forty feet deep and eighteen in diameter at the top, which has been walled to prevent animals from falling in. This has also a communication with the sea, as the salt water flows into it at the rise of the tide. The Plaine des Hollandais is rendered fertile by an annual degradation of the mountains, which *débris* is washed down, giving a blackish earth peculiarly favourable to the growth of canes. While examining the reefs, I found some curious annelides, of a blackish brown colour, about half an inch in width and nearly eleven feet in length. I saw them in the tide pools, and when disturbed they would rapidly disappear in the crevices of the coral beds. Many of them were in process of multiplying their species by spontaneous division. I noticed that the animal buried as much of the body as he wished to separate ; but this division did not take place always in the centre of the body, as some writers assert, frequently not a fifth being thrown off. The anterior portion to be separated appeared to be in a dormant state, which gave me a good opportunity to examine the separation with a magnifying glass. This portion was very transparent, and all its parts, even the eyes and antennæ, appeared to be as perfect as in the original animal, but it was only connected with it by a small thread-like ligament.

I saw numbers of Holothuriæ, most of them a dirty brown, mottled with yellowish white. There are several species of this family here, some of them I had observed at Grand Port, of a beautiful orange colour, about six inches in length.

The Actiniæ were radiantly beautiful. One species was nearly eight inches in diameter and six in height, of a purplish colour, shaded yellow. The tentacles, when fully expanded, were tipped with scarlet, forming the most brilliant combination of colours possible.

We pushed on to Flacq, as we all had friends there. This is a military post, and some of the 86th, under the command of Colonel Lowe, were at this station then, and they gave us a hearty welcome and every comfort the place afforded, very grateful to tired wanderers. The whole district is one great cane field. There are some fine estates in it, and said to yield a very superior quality of sugar. The country is mostly an undulating plain, with scarcely a tree to relieve the eye, except

CAMPING.

round the houses ; and yet this was one of the best wooded parts of the island: but all have gone down before the almighty sugar-cane.

Large tracts of Flacq are so encumbered with loose stones and rocks as to have gained the name of 'Pavé.' The soil is greatly diversified, not only on the same estate, but not unfrequently in the same fields. In the lower portions the climate is in summer excessively hot, and droughts often occur; but in the more elevated parts rains are frequent, and the contrast is so great that there is often a difficulty in drying the sugar on account of the damp. Rice was in former days grown here to a large extent. As there is so much waste land, it might be cultivated to great profit. I find the Creole rice, as it is called, of superior quality. Its grain is very large, and pearly white. It is the sort named 'dry rice,' from its requiring little artificial irrigation, and is peculiarly adapted for the hilly uneven ground of this island.

I was informed that very many of the estates were mortgaged (the case unhappily too general at the present time), and are rented on money leases of a peculiar kind. The lessee cultivates the ground in canes; manures, cleans, and cuts them for the mill; the lessor, who is generally the owner of the mill as well as the land, mills the canes, manufactures the sugar, and advances what money the cultivator requires during the time the canes are on the ground. When the *coupe* is over, one half goes to the lessor, and the other to the lessee. My impression is, that these conditions are more favourable to the mill-holder than to the cane-planter.

With such a variety of soils as this district affords, it seems to me that the small landowners might grow many things more profitable than canes—leave the sugar to the large mill-owners, and grow other articles, particularly those for food for man and beast, and thus supply the large proprietors, instead of their being obliged to import almost everything. Vegetables grow very freely here; and as to the Patates, or sweet potatoes, I never saw finer. Great talk is made of the Flacq oysters, but for my part I cannot see in what their goodness consists. I think them small and flavourless, not worth the trouble of opening. In 1817, I find there was a splendid harvest at Trois Flots, in this district, of Nutmegs and Cloves: now there are few traces of the trees left.

During the occupation of Mauritius by the Dutch, a settlement was formed here, and it received its name from the flat surface of a great portion of the district.

According to Herbert, an early writer on this island, England had a prior claim to its possession. He says, the English had landed in this district before the Portuguese, who, when they took up their quarters there, found crosses put up in many parts of the island, thus proving that some Christians had been there previously, and the credit of it was given to the English; though I doubt the fact, for surely if England could have claimed possession she would not have waited until 1810 to enforce her claims.

Monkeys are numerous near the Rivière Sèche, and the Mare aux Fougères. In the rocky parts, rats and birds torment the cultivator, and weeds are very troublesome to the planter. Through the SE. of this district run two parallel ridges of hills, the principal of which are the Montagne Blanche and Montagne de la Fayence; the latter attaining the height of 1,338 feet. About a mile and a half from the military post is a railway station. I was very much astonished to find soldiers quartered in such a low swampy place. Not long before we were there orders came from the Surgeon-General that the soldiers should vacate their barracks, and occupy tents, which were accordingly pitched near the sea, and there they were encamped on marshy land, water running all round them, and in consequence sickness very soon prevailed amongst the men.

We left Flacq well pleased with our visit, and went on to Poudre d'Or, a squalid, deserted-looking place. It was formerly a station for troops, but had been abandoned. It owes its name, not to the colour of its sands, but to a peculiar kind of sugar said to be made from the canes of this district. They told us it was famous for elegant corals and shells in the hurricane season; but we found nothing to interest us at the village, so went on to some distance along the shore, and set up our tent, and here we added greatly to our botanical specimens. I found a fine species of Gigartina, I think the *Gigartina mamillosa*. The water is very shallow, and as the sea was calm, we ventured off a considerable distance. Eels, Holothuriæ, and crabs swarm over the reefs, and we had a try to catch a turtle we saw feeding on the Sargassum, but he soon disappeared in deep water.

In this vicinity lies Amber Island, celebrated as the locality where the St. Geran was wrecked; but, before our visit to it, we went to the estate of St. Antoine, where we were cordially received by its hospitable owner, M. Edmond de Chazal. This gentleman has a lease of Amber Island, and we felt a delicacy in going to it till we had obtained permission. No sooner was our wish known than not only was it acceded to, but a pic-nic was promptly organised to render our visit agreeable.

This estate is in fine cultivation, and the establishment has always been kept up in a style worthy of the true gentleman of the old French school, to which M. de Chazal belongs. His reputation for kindness and hospitality has spread far and wide —from the Governors of Mauritius downward all have shared his large-hearted hospitality. I must add one other mite of praise, like the 'Old English Gentleman,'—

> Although he feasted all the great,
> He ne'er forgot the small.

The family mansion is a good substantial one, with that great addition to comfort in this climate, a wide verandah, running its whole length supported on heavy columns, presenting a fine appearance as you approach it. A pretty fountain plays in front amongst the shrubs, and at the back is a large garden, surrounded with a hedge of the Roussaille (*Eugenia Michellii*), or Brazilian cherry, which, when in flower, resembles a cherry-tree, with its cloud of fragile white blossoms, though its bright scarlet ribbed fruit will not carry on the comparison.

Clumps of mangoes also gave shade about the place, and I only regretted it was not the season for their delicious fruit.

At some distance stands a two-storied house, also with a verandah. This is the Pavilion, for visitors, quite large enough for a Mauritian hotel, and I am told it is often filled with guests.

The sugar-mills were a good way from the dwelling, and they are fitted with all modern appliances.

There are several other houses about the plantations; and the servants' quarters are mostly stone, well ventilated, and the ground about them kept neat and clean, and showed the care bestowed on them by their master. Each family seemed to have its broods of hens and chickens, and some had goats. Good roads traverse the estate, and one of the young gentlemen informed me they were made under his father's supervision.

I should mention that our host has a fine family of twelve sons and daughters, several of whom are married, and following in their father's steps. When all are assembled, children, sons and daughters-in-law, grandchildren, and servants, my friend looks like a patriarch of old at the head of his household, which resemblance is heightened by a flowing white beard and a bald head; and his amiable wife will even yet bear comparison with her daughters.

On the morning after our arrival, preparations went on

vigorously for our excursion to Amber Island, which is about three miles off. Champagne baskets and sundry suspicious-looking packages were put into the carriages, and our guns carefully looked after by a servant, whose especial duty it was to see them all in order.

The morning was cool, and all were in high spirits. M. de Chazal's sons and the schoolmaster of the estate accompanied us, and off we started to see all that could be seen. After a pleasant drive through the plantation, we were dropped on the shore near a little jetty, built for the accommodation of visitors to the island.

A fine yawl was in readiness, and two men pulled us across the bay. The distance is about a mile, and we landed on an open sandy beach. A vast bed of coral extends from the shore to the island, and it will soon fill the whole bay. We disturbed numerous curlews and plovers, that wheeled over our heads, uttering shrill cries, but they kept out of the range of our guns.

Amber Island is composed of volcanic rock and lava, and was formed by an immense flow in this direction from the interior of Mauritius, as well as a flow from a large volcano now submerged, lying in a NE. direction: this is plainly seen on the E. side, where it has cooled in waves. We passed through very high grass to an elevated spot where there are three small houses, one for the guardian, and two for visitors. In one of these we partook of a capital breakfast prepared by our kind host, and after our meal set out to amuse ourselves. The whole place swarms with rabbits, and some of the party started off shooting, and some, with myself, went to examine a curious hole in the centre of the island. I had previously made up my mind to enter it, so had provided myself with a good stout rope, and one of our party and two of the servants accompanied me on the descent.

This opening is circular, about one hundred feet in diameter, and about twenty-five deep, containing water.

On the south side there is a dry place, and on this we intended to land. The side of this hole is rough and perpendicular, not a spot on which to rest a foot, and looks as if cut by hand. We fixed a rope to some bushes, and down we went hand over hand to the bottom.

A species of fern, the *Acrostichum aureum*, was growing ust where we landed, and on its fronds I captured a singular spider (*Tetragnatha pretensa*), then quite new to me. We disturbed a number of rats and crabs; and in the deepest water were mullets, many of them I should think over two pounds' weight.

The water was brackish, and rose and fell with the tides though at least half a mile from the sea. This opening has probably been formed by the falling in of the walls of a cavern, which doubtless traverses the whole of Amber Island. The masses of rock heaped up have choked any communication with either side, although not sufficient to arrest the flow of water. At some distance are several caverns opening into the sea, but I had not time to visit any of them. Near the landing-place Mr. de Chazal showed me a fissure in the rocks, a few inches wide, extending some hundreds of yards, and which he said was the top of a cavern containing water. We could hear its splash as we flung stones down the opening. We then took a pirogue, and poled along the bay to have a look at some other small islands, one of which we landed on. At low water the rocks are covered with Cypræa, particularly the Mauritiana and Tigris. In all directions were patches of a fleshy Polyp of a lovely peach colour. They were about six inches in length, and I, at first, thought they were plants of the genus Callithamnion, which they closely resembled. I attempted to pluck a handful, and soon found out my mistake, as they slipped through my fingers, and could only be separated from the rocks with a knife. Here again I saw the same lovely Sea Anemones as at Point Hollandais. I wished I had had time to sketch one, and at first I thought of taking one away with me; but as I watched the creature luxuriating in the gently laving water, every wave bringing it fresh life and vigour, as it had evidently been uncovered before the turn of the tide, I left it to its little life of enjoyment. I do not think this animal has been described, nor many of the Polyps of Mauritius. Their generic names are well known, but many of the species are quite new. The student of Natural History would find an interesting field of research in this branch of science. Catfish are numerous here; I frequently saw them with their long arms outstretched for their prey, but I took good care not to meddle with them. Caulerpas abound: one of a quite different species I found, the fronds of which are very small, and half-buried in the sand.

All these islands are volcanic, doubtless formed at the same time as Amber Island. The waters rush out of this bay, forming eddies and miniature whirlpools, so that it was with difficulty we could prevent the tide carrying our pirogue to the outer reef, where the waves dash with great violence. I used a small paddle, and our two men their poles, but it was some time before we could make any headway. It took a good hour's work to reach Amber Island, and the sun was setting before we re-embarked to return to St. Antoine. Dark heavy clouds were gathering in the west, their borders dazzlingly illuminated with the gorgeous rays of the rapidly descending sun. As the day-god sank into the waves, a crimson and gold lustre streamed across the ocean, lighting up the foam-crested billows near the reef, till one could fancy they were the white horses of Neptune, with waving manes and heads erect, saluting the departing majesty.

Sunsets in the tropics have been ever a fertile field for description, and I believe ever will be. They are sights that never pall, never weary, for there is such constant change and variety, no one ever saw the same *sky-scape* on different evenings. Words can give no adequate idea of the scene, and the noblest artist, when gazing on the picture bathed in such ineffable light, must lay down palette and brush, and acknowledge that it is beyond his art, that no earthly pencil can give more than the faintest rescript of aught so glorious.

We were forty minutes crossing the bay, but I had been so absorbed in the scene that it seemed hardly a moment before we reached the shore. We passed up a grove of Filaos and other trees to M. de Chazal's house, and a singular effect was produced by the faint rays of light as the sun sank below the horizon. A shadow was cast on the dark green foliage, and where the light struck the leaves, the shadow reflected a deep purple colour on them.

After sharing our host's large hospitality for the night, and taking leave of his family, we started off by daybreak in the direction of Mapou Bay: another spot most interesting in the history of the island.

To quote the words of an English officer:—

'On the 29th of November, 1810, the English fleet, consisting of seventy sail (chiefly men-of-war and Indiamen), anchored in the narrow passage formed by the island called Coin de Mer and the land. To cover the landing two brigs of war drawing little water anchored near the reef within one hundred yards of the beach. The boats containing the reserve, consisting of grenadiers and light infantry, collected outside the reef, and proceeded to the shore with parade precision. Before the evening closed, 10,000 men with three days' provisions, and their complement of guns, stores and ammunition, had disembarked without resistance. The column moved by the right along the beach of Mapou Bay for about a mile, and then inclining to the left fell into a close wood.

NEW MAPOU BAY.

This wood, like so many others, has gone down before the hatchet, much to the discomfort of pedestrians, for this is one of the dry hot districts, with the greatest scarcity of both wood and water. On the shore we added pretty largely to our collection of Algæ, amongst others we procured specimens of Ectocarpa, Schizonema, Zonaria, Asperococcus, and others new to me. On a little projection of rock running out into the bay, I amused myself watching the gambols of the small fish as they disported in the tide pools. In one little basin, containing about six feet of water clear as crystal, there were several small Chætodons, and amongst them two or three of the richly coloured *Holicanthus semicirculatus*. The body of this fish is of glossy black, with perpendicular lines from the top of the head to the pectoral fins, alternately of the purest white and brightest imperial blue. From the pectoral the lines begin to curve till they form perfect semicircles across the rest of the body to the tail, the alternate blue line changing to purple. The second dorsal is covered with a network of bright blue and yellow wavy lines on a ground of deep maroon. The caudal fin is half black, banded blue and white, terminating in a fringe of deep yellow. The anal fin is black, with curiously twisted blue lines. The effect of such a combination of colour when in the limpid water may be imagined. When not frightened, it will swim gracefully round and round in circles, glancing its bright golden eye at the intruder; but make the slightest movement, and, like a flash of light, it disappears to its hiding-place, and remains till the fancied danger is past. I was watching one of these lovely little creatures, almost breathless lest I should disturb it, when suddenly it vanished; and I was curious to see the cause of its panic, as I was quite innocent of it. After waiting a few seconds, I caught a glimpse of the head of an eel, not larger than a man's thumb, protruding through an opening in the coral bed four inches wide. Finding that the animal did not come out, and that he was evidently lying in wait for his prey, I determined to take him, if possible; so baited a good-sized hook, and suspended it over his hole. Hook and bait were seized, and I saw that I had an ugly customer to deal with, a large savage fellow. I prepared a cod hook with steel chain, and baited and attached it to a good-sized cod line. He seized greedily, and with a jerk I drew out his head. I called loudly to Jumna, who was a weak sickly little man, to hold on tightly to the line, while I jumped into the water to spear him. He didn't half like the job; however, he held on like grim Death. I carefully approached the hole when the brute came at me boldly. I was a little too quick for him, and planted my grains into his neck, about six inches from his head. We then began hauling him out, but it took all our strength to handle him, for he resisted furiously. We pulled away nine feet, and still saw no end to his body—ten feet! eleven feet! 'Why,' said I, 'we have caught a young sea serpent.' Twelve feet! and his tail began to wriggle out. I then quickly retreated to the rock, and we made for the shore, dragging our game; and even on land we had much ado to hold him, till I despatched him by severing the vertebræ with my hatchet.

This monster eel measured twelve feet three inches in length, and round the largest part of the head fourteen and a half inches. The head of this species terminates in a blunt point, the two small bright eyes not more than an inch from the end. The large mouth is filled with long sharp teeth, even the roof is covered with these formidable weapons. This eel is very dangerous, but not so common as reported. There are several species of this genus, but none so large as this. The fishermen call it the 'Cave Eel': its specific name I do not know. I was not a little proud of my game, so kept him, and on my return had him stuffed, and he now hangs on my office ceiling.

From Mapou Bay we turned inland over narrow paths leading through the various sugar plantations. The whole of this quarter suffers more or less from scarcity of water; and in some parts the borer and vegetable plague, the Herbe Caille, do infinite mischief. The country, as far as Pamplemousses, is only a succession of cane-fields, alternating with fallow land, or plantations of Manioc, or the Ambrevade (*Cajanus flavus*), which are grown as rotation crops—the former largely used as food for cattle, and the latter affording a small variegated pea (a favourite Creole dish), leaves for fodder, and the brushwood for burning, besides enriching the ground.

The district of Pamplemousses is a vast plain, bounded on one side by Mount Longue, L'Embrasure, Peter Both, La Nouvelle Découverte, and the heights of Villebague, and Piton, and stretching away to the sea on the other. There are two large marshes, the Peter Both and Nicolière, with some lesser ones near the village, caused by infiltration from the rivers and canals. These have been the source of the malaria, which has produced deplorable effects on its population, showing a death rate during the fever next to that of Port Louis.

The railway station at Pamplemousses is a few yards distant from the *soi-disant* tombs of Paul and Virginia, and a short stroll takes you into the heart of the village. Its appearance is pleasing, from the number of gardens and fine trees about it:

but here, as in every place in the island, two-thirds of the houses are in a ruinous condition. Standing in its midst are the Botanical Gardens, which form so conspicuous a feature from the abundance of fine flowering trees even on their borders, the branches hanging over into the public roads.

In the centre, on a slight rise, stands an old-fashioned-looking Catholic church, its white tower, which possesses a fine clock, forming a landmark for many a mile away. The grounds round it are nicely laid out, and surrounded with a capital

PROTESTANT CHURCH.

thorny fence, which overtops the wall, the *Helicteres hirsuta*, I think, a species of heliotrope, cut till it forms an impervious mass. The pink and yellow blossoms look very gay; but beware plucking them for their beauty, for not only do they bristle with sharp thorns, but they do *not* breathe odours of Araby.[1] A large cemetery is near the church, adorned with shrubs and flowers, and containing some fine tombs, unhappily but too much augmented of late years. A small Protestant church and parsonage stand on an eminence at one side of the village. Its tower is still incomplete, and it has little architectural beauty to boast. The only other noticeable building is a convent, with

[1] The Creoles give it the name of 'Vieille Fille.'

the best kept garden in the place. After resting in one of the summer houses of the only hotel, and refreshing ourselves after a long tramp to see all there was to see, we at last turned our faces homeward, and set off on the high road to Port Louis.

Since the establishment of the railway, which diverged from the former route, this road has little traffic, and very hot and dusty we found it. For a good way canes lined the sides of our path, but the waste lands were more numerous, particularly the nearer we approached the city. We passed the little village of Calebasses and Terre Rouge, which, with the exception of a station house, police quarters, and half-a-dozen small cottages, are mere collections of Indian huts. Then we came to the new Cemetery of Bois Marchand, with its glaring red earth and rows on rows of graves of the fever victims. Along this route we see a range of hills, which is a branch of the Peter Both Mountain. The varied peaks are most picturesque, and in the distance stands the far-famed giant himself. Seen from this point of view, the summit of it presents the appearance of a lady in long sweeping robes, and a regal tiara on her head, a fair imaginary likeness of Queen Victoria with her sceptre in her hand. All is beautiful as we raise our eyes to these heights; but lower them to our surroundings, and the contrast is strikingly disagreeable. The whole foreground is filled with dirty Malabar camps, that lie in a waste of long coarse grass and wild aloes, with a few straggling Tamarind or Bois noir trees.

To the left, as you approach the city, is the Valley des Prêtres, at the far end of which stands the pretty little Catholic Church of St.-Croix, densely shaded with trees. The Latanier River, sacred to the Indians, runs through this valley; and there are many small gardens where vegetables are grown for the market.

The main Pamplemousses road crosses what were formerly the limits of Port Louis. A line of defence extended from the Fanfaron Battery across this road, and terminated in a small redoubt on the crest of one of the ridges that branch out from the Pouce. Another line ran down the rocky base of the Mountain de Découverte to the Moka Road, and the plain between this and Fort William (then Fort Blanc) was defended by three redoubts; but all were more or less dilapidated, even at the surrender of the Island in 1810. Now little remains, save a few earthworks here and there, and occasionally a few of the old guns are planted in the ground as boundary marks round the police stations.

The change of atmosphere, so perceptible as you near the city, is felt on rising the hill at its northern entrance. The bustle and din of the docks to our right, the mule-carts urged along by the loud discordant voices of the Malabars, the cries of itinerant vendors of vegetables—'Bouteilles vides,' 'Gonys,' 'Du lait,' &c. &c., all screaming out, told us plainly enough of our whereabouts.

Our long trip was over, and we were not sorry to regain the comforts of home. All were delighted with our ramble, and we had succeeded in our object of viewing the principal parts of the Island, and had added largely to our stores of marine plants, shells, specimens of Natural History, &c., to say nothing of the stock of health laid in by breathing so long the cool bracing air.

As I have said before, Mauritius is a country of exceeding interest to the geologist and naturalist, and one in which a sojourn may be made very profitably for the advancement of science. The whole of it, with the exception of a few mountain-tops, is accessible. Much of it is wearisome and monotonous in the extreme to pass over; and, beautiful as a cane-field is, the eye tires when an endless succession of them is presented.

None, however, can view the innumerable and fantastic peaks, some bare and precipitous, striking boldly against the sky, others broken into pinnacles, bulky fragments that seem tottering, ready to fall and overwhelm all beneath; the gorges and ravines, the rough work of the long extinct volcano, and ever-wearing Time; the over-hanging rocks, with their feathery foliage to the water's edge; the deep river, or limpid stream, both alike hurrying on to be lost in the ocean; none, or very few, I think, can gaze on these without emotions of deepest delight. There are soft landscapes, delicious sea-views, that will leave pleasant memories for life; and, though I may be far from the 'Gem of the Ocean,' when this volume is published, I can never forget the enjoyment I have received amongst its glorious old hills, nor will the remembrance of the friends who shared my many excursions ever fade.

I will close this long chapter by quoting the words of one of

Nature's true poets, whose verses, though addressed to scenes far distant, will admirably express my feelings on the subject, by only substituting *cane* for *corn* lands in the fourth line :—

Homeward once again. Ah ! vanished mountains,
Like old friends, your faces, many a day,
O'er the bowery woods shall rise before me
And the level *cane* lands far away.

Yet I bear with me a new possession ;
For the memory of all beauteous things,
Over dusty tracks of straitened duties,
Many a waft of balmy fragrance brings.

Was it thriftless waste of golden moments
That I watched the seaward, burning west,
That I sought the sweet rare mountain flowers,
That I climbed the rugged mountain-crest ?

Let me rather dream that I have gathered,
On the lustrous shore and gleamy hill,
Strength to bravely do the daily duty,
Strength to calmly bear the chancing ill.

SKETCH OF ISLAND.

CHAPTER XXIV.

THE HISTORY OF MAURITIUS.

From its Discovery by the Portuguese, in 1505, through the various Changes of Government it has undergone during its Possession by the Dutch, then by the French, and lastly, by the English, to February 1871.

THE Island of Mauritius is situated between the tropics, within three degrees of Capricorn, 100 miles NE. of Bourbon and E. of Madagascar. Its greatest length is 39 miles, and breadth nearly 34. The area is about 700 square miles, the exact measurement being given as 432,680 acres. The length of the coast-line is about 135 miles.

It was not until the sixteenth century that the existence of this island was known to the civilised world. Don Pedro de Mascaregnas, in 1505, during the first year of the administration of Almeida, Governor-General of the Portuguese possessions of India, when exploring these seas, discovered this and the sister isle; to the latter he gave his own name, and called the former Cerné; why is unknown, except that it might be a fanciful allusion to the Dodo, or to some other bird of the same species that he found on its shores. The Portuguese, however, did not avail themselves of their new acquisitions. They contented themselves with fixing their geographical positions, and landing some deer, goats, monkeys and pigs, the descendants of which are still found wild, in retired parts of the Island. Though they retained the Isle of Cerné till 1598, they seem only to have considered it as a simple station for taking in refreshments, believing that this route would always be kept a secret, and that they had nothing to fear from any encroachment of other European powers on their monopoly of commerce with India.

On May 1, 1598, a squadron of eight ships, under the command of Admiral Wybrand von Warwick, left the Texel to repair to the Dutch possessions in Batavia. These vessels were dispersed off the Cape of Good Hope by a violent storm, and several of them, including the Admiral's ship, sighted the Isle of Cerné on September 17.

The Dutch, not knowing its name, sent two boats to reconnoitre the shores, and discovered a harbour on the SE. Being ignorant if the Island was inhabited or not, the Admiral used the greatest caution, on account of the sickly state of his crews. He landed a large party of his men, and took up such a position as to prevent surprise. On the following day, boats were sent out to examine the other parts of the Island, and find out if there were any inhabitants. His men met with a great variety of birds, which surprised them by their familiarity, and the facility with which they were taken. They discovered water in abundance, and an astonishing vegetation. On the shore was found 300 cwt. of bees' wax, a hanging stage, the spar of a capstan, and a large yard, evidently the relics of some unfortunate vessel that had been buried in the waves. They found no other traces of human beings. After having returned thanks to God, for having brought them to so fair a harbour, the Vice-Admiral named the Island 'Mauritius,' after Count Maurice of Nassau, then Stadtholder of Holland, and the port 'Warwick Harbour,' after himself.

He left no settlers here, but ordered a board to be fixed to a tree, bearing the arms of Holland, and planted a piece of ground with vegetable seeds, as an experiment on the soil. A year after he returned to Mauritius, and was enabled to supply his ships with abundance of fish, fowl, and fruits.

From this period it does not appear that the Island was revisited till May 12, 1601 when Hermansen availed himself of its recent discovery to supply his ship with provisions and water.

The period at which the Dutch formed their first settlement is doubtful; but in 1613 it became the resort of the pirates who infested the Indian Seas. This circumstance, and the threatening aspect of European affairs, caused the Dutch to turn their attention to the Island so long neglected; but it was not till 1644 that a permanent establishment took place.

It is said that at this time the SE. port was chosen for the first colonisation of the Island. The Governor selected was Van der Mester; who, after a areful examination of the resources of the place, saw that the energies of the new colony would be greatly hindered for want of labourers. He therefore sent a vessel to Madagascar to buy slaves, in order to supply this deficiency. Pronis, the French Governor, acceded to this proposal, and kidnapped a number of Malagashes, who had settled themselves under his protection. This breach of faith, which was the ruin of both colonies, was considerably aggravated in the eyes of the natives, when they discovered that amongst the captives were sixteen women of the race of the Lohariths (a superior caste).

Scarcely had they landed at Mauritius, when a great part of them escaped to the woods; and the rest, goaded by their severe treatment, soon followed this example.

It was thus that the body of men called Maroons (i.e. outlaws) was formed, which, forced by the pains of hunger and the desire of vengeance, was ever on the alert to attack and insult its oppressors.

The Dutch, harassed on one side by these depredators, and on the other checked by the parsimony of the East India Company, were forced to abandon the Island.

The Maroons, fearing their return, still kept to their mountain fastnesses, whence sallying forth on the crews of vessels which came to the Island for refreshments, they frequently surprised and cut them off.

To remedy these disasters, it was resolved in the General Council of Batavia that the Dutch should re-establish themselves in Mauritius. Three settlements were immediately formed: one on the NW., another upon the SE., and a third upon the Rivière Noire. M. la Mocuis was named Governor. State criminals from Batavia and other of the Dutch possessions were now banished to Mauritius. M. Rodolphe Deodate, a native of Geneva, and a man of feeble character, succeeded M. la Mocuis.

The Dutch raised a fort in the SE. called Frédéric-Henri, which was entirely burnt by the blacks; but in 1694, it was rebuilt of stone. This fortress was armed with twenty pieces of cannon, with a garrison of fifty soldiers, and enclosed the Governor's house, the magazines, and the principal buildings of the Company. The planters, numbering about forty families, spread over the district of Flacq, where the Company established gardens, and drew thence such supplies of fruit and vegetables as were required for the garrison. A few inhabitants settled at the NW. port, called 'Camp,' and three or four families went to the district of the Rivière Noire. Their principal occupation was the culture of tobacco.

Towards the commencement of the eighteenth century, the Dutch East India Company, finding that their possession of the Island was only a source of continued troubles, resolved to abandon it a second time. Their troops were sent to the Cape of Good Hope, and tne occupation of Mauritius by the Dutch ceased entirely.

Mauritius under French Rule.

The final abandonment of the Island by the Dutch did not long escape the observation of the French at Bourbon. M. de Beauvilliers, then Governor of that island, sent M. Dufresne, captain of the ship 'Chasseur,' to take formal possession of Mauritius, in the name of the King of France, on the 20th of September, 1715, and its name was changed to that of Isle of France. Notwithstanding this, and the founding of an establishment at the NW. port (Port Louis), Dufresne departed without leaving anyone to maintain the new acquisition; and it was only at the end of 1721 that a permanent settlement was effected. On the 25th of September of that year, Le Chevalier Jean-Baptiste Garnier de Fougerai, commander of the 'Triton' of St. Malo, retook possession in the name of the French East India Company, to whom it had been ceded by the King. M. de Nyon, a knight of the order of St. Louis, was selected by M. de Beauvilliers, in October, to fill the place of Governor, but he did not arrive till January 1722.

He commenced his administration by the establishment of a provincial council, composed of six of the principal inhabitants; dependent, however, on the principal council of Bourbon.

M. de Nyon, following the example of the Dutch, fixed the seat of government at the SE. port. The only events that marked his administration were an attempted sedition by a part of the troops, which was soon appeased, and the increased penalties attached to 'Maroonage,' on account of the number of recently imported slaves, who had escaped to the Maroons left by the Dutch. On the 26th of August, 1726, M. Dumas was chosen Governor-General of the two colonies; but, as his residence was in Bourbon, the resources of the Isle of France were not developed. The French East India Company were several times on the point of giving up a colony that, as affairs were conducted, was only an expense, but some event always occurred to hinder their design. M. Dumas was succeeded, in October 1728, by M. de Maupin, who, like his predecessor, was Governor of both islands.

The most violent hurricane till then experienced by the colonists was felt during his administration, and the terror occasioned by this disaster was increased by an unexpected irruption of Maroons, who drove out the inhabitants of the district of Flacq.

About this time, the East India Company, wishing to render the Island of some use, sent out M. de Cossigny, an engineer, to make a more minute survey of it. From his report the Company saw at once that the position of the Island was advantageous for commerce with the East. In order to put an end to the anarchy and confusion then reigning, and to provide means of defence for both islands, in November 1734, Mahé de Labourdonnais, who had already visited the Island, was named Governor, with full powers to carry out the projects of the Company. The stringent measures they ordered him to enforce placed serious difficulties in the way of his success. On his arrival in 1735, his first care was to ascertain the resources of the Island. Finding that the SE. port presented no advantages, either as a seat of Government or for outward commerce, he resolved to abandon it, and turned his whole attention to the NW. port, or Port Louis. One of his first acts was to procure letters patent from the King, to confer superiority in the Council of the Isle of France over that of Bourbon. This was attended with the most successful results, as it put an end to the discord prevalent in the two councils till this period; and during the eleven years of his government there was but one lawsuit, as he accommodated all disputes by his own amiable interposition.

With great trouble he succeeded in destroying the formidable band of Maroons, which still spread terror over the Island. Of commerce there was scarcely a trace on his arrival. He began by planting the sugar-cane, and so successfully, that in 1750, the sugar works which he constructed produced a clear annual revenue to the Company of 60,000 livres.

He established manufactures of cotton and indigo, for which he found a market at Surat, Mocha, Ormuz, and in Europe.

The inhabitants, sunk in apathy and indolence, had utterly neglected the advantages agriculture offered, but the indomitable energy of the Governor at length awoke a spirit of enterprise and activity in the people. He induced them to cultivate the grains necessary to the subsistence of the two islands, that they might be no longer subject to the almost periodical dearths. He introduced the manioc from St. Iago and the Brazils, but had great difficulty in overcoming the prejudices of the planters against it. There was neither engineer nor architect in the Island. Fortunately M. de Labourdonnais united both in himself; and, in the face of obstacles few would have had the courage to surmount, he carried out his projects for the prosperity of Mauritius. Trees were felled, and stone quarried; carts constructed, and roads made, for up to that time transport by land was almost impracticable. The only hospital was a large hut containing about thirty beds. He ordered the construction of one in which from four to five hundred beds could be placed.

A detail of all the works erected would be far too long for this summary; suffice it to observe, they consisted of magazines, arsenals, batteries, fortifications, barracks, mills, quays, offices, shops, canals, and aqueducts. Previous to his arrival, water had to be sought at a league from town; so he caused an aqueduct to be constructed nearly six miles in length (the remains of which still exist), which was of inexpressible advantage both to the inhabitants and ships which touched there for refreshment.

So ignorant were the people of even the rudiments of shipbuilding, that, to mend their fishing boats, they were obliged to have recourse to the ships' carpenters. M. de Labourdonnais, grieved to see an island so neglected, which from its central position might be a second Batavia, or at least an entrepôt for the commerce of the Indian Ocean, and a refuge for the Company's vessels, directed his genius to the improvement of its maritime advantages. His efforts were rewarded so well, that in a few years there were wet and dry docks, and a ship of war was built at Port Louis, and sent to France, where it was received with great approval. Ships could be refitted with as much facility as at any port in the East. But all these gigantic enterprises, and his untiring energy for the benefit of the colony, only served to excite jealousy and calumny, and his detractors spared no pains to blacken and defame his character. He received little appreciation of his services even from the East India Company; and when obliged to return to France, on the death of his wife, in 1740, he found so strong a prejudice against him from the reports of his secret enemies, that he demanded a public investigation of his conduct. This trial was so favourable for him, that both the ministers and directors of the Company expressed their approbation of his conduct, and refused to accept his resignation. As war was then imminent between the European Powers, he was sent out, on April 5, 1741, with a squadron for the East.

He arrived at the Isle of France in August, and ordered a fortress to be erected for the defence of Port Louis, and directed the inhabitants to be trained to the use of arms. He departed for Bourbon to arrange for the protection of that island also. He visited all the dependencies, and gave his name Mahé to the chief of the Seychelles group, on his way to Pondicherry. His management of affairs there was such as to merit the highest approbation, and on his return to his government, in 1742, letters patent of nobility were sent to him from the King. But the Governor's efforts for the increase of commerce were checked by the Company's orders to disarm his squadron. In 1744, finding himself obliged to remain in his government, he himself set to work for the internal progress of the colony.

It is needless to enter into detail of the ruinous policy of the French in their Eastern possessions, after war was declared with England. It is sufficient to say that all the efforts of M. de Labourdonnais for their protection were rendered abortive by the vacillating conduct of the Company. Still more to disable him, an extraordinary drought had occasioned an alarming scarcity, and the harvests of the current year were ravaged by locusts, so that he was destitute of provisions for his ships of war. The 'St.-Geran,' a large ship laden with stores for the island, was wrecked on the Isle d'Ambre, in 1745. This disaster inspired Bernardin de St.-Pierre with his delightful romance of 'Paul and Virginia'; but it struck such terror into the inhabitants of both islands, that it was with extreme difficulty the Governor could procure crews for his ships.

In March 1746, he set sail for India, leaving M. de St.-Martin as Deputy-Governor, and Baron Grant was intrusted with the military defences. The limits of this short history will not allow of our following this great man in his military career. On his return to the Isle of France, he found that M. David had been sent out to make fresh enquiries into his conduct, and to supplant him as Governor; but his acts during the whole of his administration were found so irreproachable, that M. David did not hesitate to deliver to him the order of the King, to command the squadron then leaving for Europe. Thus terminated the connection of M. de Labourdonnais with the Isle of France, which had lasted eleven years—years fruitful in events of the utmost importance to the colony. Indeed, he may be said to be the founder of Mauritius. 'His memory,' says a local historian, 'still remains in every heart; his portrait is in every house, his memoirs in every library, and his statue in the Place d'Armes.'

The government of M. David was of little importance, except that the manufactures of cotton and indigo were nearly abandoned as failures. In 1748, an attempt was made by the English to take thae Island; but Admiral Boscawen, deceived as to the strength of its defences, and the show of resistance, thought success impossible with the force then available, and relinquished the design.

M. David was succeeded in 1750 by his brother-in-law, M. Bouvet. About this time were sent out, for scientific purposes, M. Daprès Mannevillette and the Abbé de la Caille. The former became distinguished for his acquirements in hydrography, and published a series of charts that have been little invalidated by recent discoveries.

In 1754 the small-pox broke out, and a severe hurricane devastated the Island.

M. Magon succeeded M. Bouvet in 1755, and began his government by a general permission to cut wood; which was done to such a ruinous extent, that in 1761 the East India Company sent particular directions to the Governor to stop the evil, and actually forbid the stripping the shores of wood near the port.

M. Desforges Boucher, the last of the Company's governors, followed M. Magon in 1759. His principal attention was devoted to the cultivation of Reduit, which had been founded by M. David, and where a botanical garden was begun.

After all the exertions of M. de Labourdonnais, the Isle of France was quite unable to supply sufficient provisions even for the inhabitants. The commercial retrospect gives proof of the violent restrictions on the part of the Company to every effort for the advancement of individual enterprise. All agricultural benefits were monopolised. Men were sent out from the mother-country who were unused to labour, and who understood nothing of husbandry. Lands were distributed at a venture; and out of 149,067 acres ceded, only 6,335 were in cultivation.

Notwithstanding the arbitrary measures adopted by the Company in all the Eastern possessions, the war had so reduced the finances that they were obliged to renounce them all, including the Isles of France and Bourbon, to meet the demands of their creditors; and thus in 1767, the Island reverted to the crown of France.

According to the Abbé Raynal, the population at this period amounted only to 3,163 whites, 587 free people, and 15,022 slaves. The produce did not exceed 105,712*l.*, and about twenty bales of cotton: valued in francs as follows, wheat, 320,600; rice, 474,000; maize, 1,570,000; beans, 142,700; oats, 135,500.

No sooner had the King taken over the Isle of France, than a total change was effected in its government. In July 1767, MM. Dumas and Poivre were sent out, one as Governor, the other as Intendant and Commissary-General of the Marine.

During the rule of the East India Company, the laws and customs of Paris were followed; and when under kingly government, the laws put in force were, first, the customs of Paris; second, those laws and ordinances made for the mother-country, which were ordered to be registered and published in the colony; third, the laws and bye-laws made expressly for the Island, and which are comprised in the Code Laleu. M. Dumas was recalled at the expiration of a year, and was temporarily replaced by M. Steinhaven. The Superior Council was reformed, and was composed of those colonists remarkable for wealth and intelligence, and soon after became both a legislative and judicial body. The governors were enjoined in every case to give the preference to native colonists for all public functions.

The harbour of Port Louis, having been obstructed to such a degree as to cause serious inconveniences to the shipping, was cleansed and deepened by M. Fromelin. M. Poivre, the Intendant, had been connected with the Isle of France, by a series of essential services, long before his appointment to the newly created office. He was an eminent naturalist and philosopher. One of his first projects was the transplantation of the spices to the Isles of France and Bourbon, the culture of which was concentrated at the Moluccas.

After great difficulties too long to narrate here, he succeeded in introducing the nutmeg and clove, and enriched the Island with a large collection of valuable and ornamental trees and shrubs procured from the East.

This was about the time when the power of the Company was in decadence; but when the King resumed the control of these Eastern possessions, the ministry pressed the return of M. Poivre, as the only man who could repair the disasters that had ensued since the time of M. de Labourdonnais; and, much against his will, he was sent out as Intendant, with the cordon of St. Michael and letters of nobility.

He was not long in putting things on their former footing; and such was his activity, that in spite of the two successive hurricanes that ravaged the islands in one year (when the 'Vert Gallant' was sunk, and the 'Ambulant' wrecked in the pass at Morne Brabant), under his encouragement, the produce of both was so increased as to bring in abundant crops of maize, rice, and other grains; and from the resources his foresight had provided, he served both troops and fleet that had been sent out by the ministers to carry on the war.

He introduced from Madagascar, the Cape, and India, every domestic animal and production suited to the consumption of the inhabitants, and imported a number of cattle and sheep to stock the Island.

In 1772 arrived the Chevalier de Ternay and Maillard Dumeste, the former as Governor, the latter as Intendant, to replace MM. Desroches and Poivre.

A weekly journal was established, which the increasing population and extension of commerce rendered necessary.

The Island was reduced to eight districts, in lieu of eleven, as had been fixed by the Ordinance of August 6, 1768. Additional administration and police regulations were also enacted.

At this time M. Poivre purchased an enclosure, at some distance from Port Louis, called Mon Plasir, where he formed a magnificent garden, containing every plant he could procure from both hemispheres. He instructed M. Ceré in all the details of Asiatic cultivation of the spices he had so successfully planted, and soon after ceded the place to the King, for the original price he had given for it; and this became the now celebrated King's Garden at Pamplemousses.

M. Ceré so well carried out the plans of M. Poivre after his departure, that he secured the first harvest of cloves and nutmegs in 1777. The joy then felt is unappreciable now, as the clove-trees propagated in the several districts have all been destroyed to make way for the sugar-cane.

In 1773 a violent hurricane occurred, which laid in ruins 300 houses in Port Louis; thirty-two ships were stranded on the banks of the harbour, and the church fell in, crushing several people in its ruins.

In 1744, the powder-mills exploded with great loss of life to the military, and the ship 'Mars' was burned in the harbour.

M. Ferney, who was much more feared than loved, was relieved by the Chevalier de Giran la Brillane, December, 1777. Frustrated in all his efforts for the good of the colony, after two years of inquietude, he died, and was buried with few marks of respect. The Vicomte Souillac, Governor of Bourbon, arrived on the death of M. la Brillane. The war at this time, so far from proving a check to the prosperity of the Island, brought a crowd of vessels, which, by introducing abundance, changed into luxury the simple manners of the inhabitants. Seconded so well by M. Foucault, Intendant in 1777, afterwards by M. Chevrau, 1781, and lastly by M. Mortens de Narbonne, in 1785, the Vicomte supplied the wants of the squadrons of M. Orve and Admiral Suffrieu, and the armies of MM. Duchenian and Dubussey so effectually that the attention of the mother-country was again called to the importance of the colony.

The old East India Company was dissolved and a new one formed, with the enjoyment of a monopoly of trade between France, India, and China. As a special mark of favour to the Isles of Bourbon and France, permission was given to the inhabitants to trade with the East (mostly benefiting the latter, since it alone possessed harbours where ships could anchor in safety). Thus the ships of the Company and the two colonies were able to navigate the Indian Ocean, to the exclusion of all the other French ships. These latter were allowed to convey European merchandise to the Isle of France, to be disposed of in the East (China excepted). This measure rendered the colony a vast entrepôt between Europe and Asia, and hence arose a sudden and factitious prosperity. Industry was turned to commerce alone, and agriculture was again neglected. The Vicomte Souillac sailed for India in 1706, leaving the government in the hands of M. de Fleury. The Island had been for thirteen years without a hurricane, but this year it was again visited by that scourge.

The latter part of the administration of the Vicomte, and the two years of that of M. d'Entrecastreaux, who arrived in 1787, were passed in tranquillity, with the exception of a hurricane, in which the frigate 'Venus' perished, with fifteen children of the best families, who had embarked for France, sent by their parents to finish their education. In 1789, the Comte de Conway relieved M. d'Entrecastreaux, and M. Dupuy succeeded M. de Narbonne as Intendant-General.

The power enjoyed by the Governors and Intendants having been of late exercised in an arbitrary manner, the inhabitants, anxious to free themselves from it, looked forward with impatience to the news of the French Revolution, which broke out in 1789. A vessel from Bordeaux, in 1790, brought the intelligence of the great power the National Assembly of France had usurped to itself. On the landing of the captain, officers, and crew who had assumed the tri-coloured cockade, and on their relating the occurrences in France, the flames of revolutionary violence burst forth in all parts of the colony, and the tricolour was everywhere adopted.

Assemblies were formed to draw up memorials of demands and claims, and a most tumultuous meeting took place in the church. The Comte de Conway, with all the prejudices of the old noblesse, made no concessions to calm the popular spirit, but sent a party of soldiers to arrest the men who had posted up the placards and planted the tricoloured flag, and went to the Intendant's house to consult about measures for resistance; but the people rescued the prisoners on their way to gaol, and, following the Governor, compelled him to wear the national cockade.

Fruitless were all the efforts of the Superior Council to maintain peace and order; excesses of all kinds were committed, ending in the murder of M. de Macnamara, Commandant of the French Marine in the Indian Ocean, in the principal street of Port Louis. The crime was unpunished, as it was not thought advisable to carry out the orders for bringing the perpetrators to justice; but the horror excited by this bloody outrage, the first that had stained the annals of the Island with crime, restrained in a great measure the violence which inundated France and her other colonies with the blood of victims to barbarity and injustice.

The Comte de Conway, unable to reconcile his principles with the feelings of the times, resigned the reins of government into the hands of M. de Fleury, July 12, 1790. M. de Malartic was named Governor-General by Louis XVI., a short time before his deposition, and arrived in June 1792.

He found the two colonies each governed by its particular Assembly, whose decrees had the force of laws after receiving the sanction of the Governor. The National Assembly of France had expressly recognised the new order of things, and an attempt was made to effect the gradual removal of abuses by three decrees: one of which forbade the mutilation of Maroons or fugitive slaves after capture; the second abolished the trade in slaves; and the third established political equality between the whites and free citizens of colour, a class of recent origin.

The paternal administration of the new Governor tended greatly to quiet the agitation of the colony; but the news of the dominancy of the Jacobins and the anarchy in France again roused the passions of the people.

In this state of things, the most prudent and influential united their efforts with the Governor and the majority of the Colonial Assembly; but they were not able to hinder the formation of a Jacobin club, called the Chaumière, and the erection of a guillotine in the public square. The new club soon rivalled the constituted authority, and compelled M. de Malartic to grant them a sloop to send 100 men to Bourbon to arrest M. Duplessis Vigoureux, the Governor; M. Fayal, the Civil Commissary; and M. de St.-Félix, with some others, under the pretext that they were in correspondence with the English.

On the arrival of the prisoners, they were fettered and thrown into a dungeon, where they remained six months. Orders were given that they should be judged by a court-martial alone, named by all the citizens of the colony, united in assemblies each in its own district. The delay occasioned by this proceeding at length succeeded in putting a stop to the effervescence of the Jacobins, and the guillotine, undefiled by human blood, became a simple Jacobin formality, in happy contrast to that terrible instrument of slaughter in France. Before the trial could come on, a decree arrived from the General Convention, abolishing slavery in all the colonies and dependencies of France. In a community of 59,000 persons, where 49,000 were slaves, such a summary decree, without a word of compensation, may be well supposed to have created universal alarm.

The Jacobin club was annihilated, the guillotine removed, the prisoners released, and about thirty of the principal Jacobins arrested, and at once deported to France.

The planters knew not what step to take, believing that if the decree were not annulled, similar scenes to the recent horrors in St. Domingo were inevitable. Some proposed to declare the colony independent, others sought to stay the promulgation of the decree.

M. de Malartic, profiting by the authority he had obtained, in reserving to himself the execution of the laws, induced the Assembly to pass a resolution by which no laws or revolutionary decrees emanating from France, unless previously examined and sanctioned, should be published or executed in the Isle of France. While deliberating, four frigates, under Vice-Admiral Percy, arrived with two agents from the French Directory, named Braco and Brunel.

The colonists protested against their landing, but in vain. Dressed in Dictatorial costume, they landed in state, and proceeded to take on themselves the government of the Assembly.

Before three days had passed, the menacing tone of the agents was such as to give serious alarm. They threatened to guillotine the Governor, and proceeded to such severe measures, that at length it became evident that it was their intention to execute the decree for the abolition of slavery and the slave trade.

The inhabitants, awakened to a sense of their imminent danger, determined at once to enforce the deportation of the agents, and but for the exertions of the Governor and others, who arrested them and sent them on board under a strong escort, they would never have escaped alive.

A conspiracy amongst the soldiers, to assist in emancipating the slaves, gave further trouble; but the energetic conduct of Governor (now General) Malartic soon put a stop to it, by forcing all the disaffected, to the number of 800, to embark in a vessel then leaving for France.

The colony now looked forward with confidence to a state of comparative tranquillity; but disputes soon arose with respect to the laws about to be enacted for the reimbursement of the debts contracted in paper currency (bullion not being obtainable), the depreciation of which had increased in such a proportion as to bear a real value less by a thousandth part than the sum it nominally represented. In the *mêlée* of discordant interests, the Colonial Assembly endeavoured to adopt a mode of payment founded on just principles, when the creditors entered into a conspiracy with the Sans-culottes, and a number of lawless adventurers, to dissolve the Assembly.

In November, 1799, the conspiracy broke out, and, for a time, Port Louis bore the appearance of a civil war.

The insurgents at length, in spite of the bravery and spirit of the President of the Assembly, Citizen Journel, forced the Governor to sign the arrest of twelve members, and eventually to dissolve the Assembly; and it was only after grievous outrages had been committed that order was restored.

The Assembly was then reformed, and the members limited to twenty-one, instead of fifty-one as formerly.

From 1794 the French squadron had been incessantly engaged with English ships of war in the Indian seas, nearly always with success to the former. This may be attributed to the shelter afforded by Port Louis to shipping, and the resources for the equipment and victualling ships of war, which enabled Percy Linois, Bergeret, Hamelin, Duperre, and other enterprising French officers to inflict incalculable injury on the British.

In 1798 the taxes began to suffice for the interior expenses of the Isle of France, as the Assembly established a Custom-house to receive a tax on importation, from five to ten per cent. on all merchandise brought to the colony by neutral ships : the tax was reduced to two-thirds for French vessels.

On the 20th of July, 1800, the day of his anniversary, at the moment he was going to church, the Governor was seized with apoplexy, from which he died two days afterwards, having held the reins of government through eight stormy years. He was universally regretted, for he had won, by his sagacity and firmness, the esteem and affection of the inhabitants, under the most trying circumstances. Even the English squadron, then on a cruise before the Island, while the colony paid the last tribute of respect to its chief, proposed a suspension of arms; and the vessels, hoisting the national standard, thus honoured the death of their brave adversary, with whom for six years they had waged a murderous warfare. His funeral was celebrated with the greatest pomp, and his remains deposited in the Champ de Mars. The Assembly decreed that a suitable monument should be raised, with the inscription 'Au Sauveur de la Colonie.' It was not, however, until the administration of Sir William Gomm that it was completed ; Lady Gomm, by means of a fancy fair, having raised sufficient funds for its erection.

General Magellan de Molière was proclaimed Governor on the death of M. de Malartic.

After the establishment of Consuls in France, M. de Cossigny, the ex-deputy, was sent out to take charge of the powder mills, and it was supposed that he had a secret mission to effect the emancipation of the slaves ; but when the Governor refused assent to the demands for his departure, the Assembly resigned to a man, and in 1801 M. de Cossigny left voluntarily. In the same year took place the resistance to the decree of the Home Government to purge France by sending away its most violent characters to places in the Indian seas. A law was voted by the new House of Assembly, punishing with death any convict who should set foot on the Isle of France.

The year 1802 saw an end to the fears as to the abolition of slavery, as a law was passed by Buonaparte re-establishing the trade in slaves. News of peace arrived, and with it also the expression of the First Consul's disposition to the sister isles, which was so flattering, that the act which proclaimed him Consul for life was received with the greatest transports of joy. In September 1803, hopes of peace were dissipated by the arrival of General Decaen, who took possession of the government, dissolved the colonial assembly, abolished the whole existing system by a proclamation of twelve lines, and promulgated the new constitution formed for the colony by the Consuls, in virtue of which all the executive legislation and judicial powers were committed to three high functionaries, styled the Captain-General, Colonial Prefect, and Commissary of Justice.

General Decaen changed the name of the Port North-West to that of Port Napoléon, and that on the South-East to Port Impérial. It was with difficulty he could get this change acceded to by either soldiers or citizens, as the Emperor had expressly forbidden any town been called after him. However, the General persisted in using the new names, and actually got a decree from the Court in France sanctioning them.

In 1809, when the injuries sustained from the French had exceeded all bounds; when the East India Company complained, on the one hand, of the loss of their ships, and the merchants, on the other, could no longer be slighted; when the British Navy, everywhere else triumphant, could not succeed either by blockade or by bringing their ships into action, the Indian Governor resolved on the conquest of the colony. Since the departure of the Marquis of Wellesley from India, who had long before insisted on this step in all his Despatches, it had been procrastinated, which may be owing in a measure to General Decaen's using every endeavour to conceal the real state of the defences. A detachment of the 56th Regiment, with a large body of Sepoys, was sent, under the command of Lieutenant-Colonel Keating, early in 1806, to take possession of Rodrigues; and in September, a successful descent was made on St. Paul's, at Bourbon. Government stores were destroyed to the value of a million sterling, and a large booty carried away.

The first attempt to land in the Isle of France was made at Black River and Jacotet. After a long and brave defence, in spite of every obstacle, a landing was effected, the batteries dashed upon, and in less than ten minutes taken possession of; the troops put to flight, and their officers and guns in the hands of the assailants. It was then found imperative to take the battery on the Souillac side of the Rivière des Galets, which was almost impassable from the strong current caused by heavy rains, and the precipitous and strongly guarded banks. It was, however, crossed without loss, and the party, giving three hearty cheers, charged with the bayonet, and carried the hills and batteries in the most brilliant manner. After destroying the gun carriages, spiking the guns, and removing the field pieces on board the frigate, the English carried off a schooner, and re-embarked, with the loss of only one man killed and seven wounded. In the succeeding months attacks were made on Belombre, and the post of the Cap de Savane, but with little success.

Bourbon also was abandoned, as the force there was not considered strong enough to retain possession of the island. In June 1810, a force of 4,000 men was sent from Madras to Rodrigues, to be employed later against the Isle of France. Meantime they all attacked Grande Chaloupe and Ste.-Marie; and on the 9th of July, the Island surrendered, and M. R. T. Farquhar was left, with a great portion of the troops, as temporary Governor. In the next month, Captain Pym, of the 'Sirius' frigate, succeeded in gaining the Isle de Passe, a coral islet in which was a circular battery and barracks, distant about a league from the mainland, defending the entrance to Grand Port. A series of successes to the British arms followed; but their progress was suddenly checked by the loss of the two East Indiamen, the 'Wyndham' and 'Ceylon,' on their passage to India from the Cape, which were taken by the French squadron off Mayotta.

The tide of victory which had so lately set in, almost unbroken, in favour of Britain was completely turned; disaster followed disaster, as if the expiring genius of Gallo-India power should emit one flashing ray previous to its utter extinction. On the 20th of August began a murderous conflict off the Isle de Passe, one of the most disastrous to the English they had ever experienced.

It only ended with the capture of the frigates 'Sirius,' 'Néréïde,' and 'Iphigenia,' and the loss of the 'Magicienne,' which was set on fire to prevent its falling into the enemy's hands.

The Isle de Passe was retaken, and prisoners to the number of 100 naval and military officers, and 2,600 soldiers and seamen, were taken into Grand Port.

The French pledged themselves to forward their prisoners in a month to the Cape, or to send them home on parole; instead of which, the officers were treated with the greatest hardship, and even some ladies, taken on board the Indiamen, were imprisoned. Flushed with success, General Decaen, after the battle of Grand Port, considered the French naval force sufficient to destroy the remainder of the British squadron, stationed at Bourbon, and to render unavailing the immense preparations at Rodrigues for the subjection of the Island.

Several other desperate sea-fights occurred, with great loss of men, but little permanent advantage on either side. While these various successes and reverses were going on by sea, the colonists could not be blind to the fact, that the British were meditating a most powerful attack on the Island. To aid the apathy and cover with indifference the exhausted patience of the more quietly-disposed inhabitants, the exactions of the rulers, and the impoverished state to which the colony was reduced, forcibly contributed. Public credit had fallen so low that the Colonial Intendant could not raise money under his official guarantee, unless his clerks endorsed his bills.

Although the preparations at Rodrigues were well known, they were treated with indifference; and the signals which announced, on the morning of the 26th of November, 1810, the approach of twenty-four vessels met with few hostile preparations on the part of the inhabitants. But the number of sail augmenting, the former warlike spirit of the people was roused, and orders were sent to all the districts to hold themselves in readiness. On the 28th seventy-six sail were in sight.

The great obstacle opposed to the attack on the Island was the difficulty of landing, in consequence of the coral reefs which surround every part of the coast. By the indefatigable exertions of Commodore Rowley, assisted by several Madras engineers, this hindrance was removed.

Every part of the leeward side of the Island had been minutely examined and sounded, and it was found that a fleet might anchor in the narrow passage formed by the small island called the Gunners' Quoin and the mainland, and that there were openings for boats through the reefs.

The point of debarkation considered most favourable was Grande Baie, or Mapou, about seventeen miles from Port Louis. The troops, to the number of 10,000, landed before nightfall without opposition. The fleet was directed to maintain the blockade of Port Louis, protect the convoy at the anchorage, and to keep up a communication with the army on shore. By daybreak the troops were on their march, with the intention of delaying no more till they arrived at Port Louis; but at noon General Abercrombie was forced to halt his men at Powder Mills, about seven miles from the Port, for they were exhausted from want of water. Here a small picquet was cut off in the woods by a party sent out by General Decaen to reconnoitre. Lieutenant-Colonel McLeod seized upon the batteries of Tombeau and Tortue, and thus kept open communication with the fleet. The French endeavoured to destroy the bridge at Rivière Sèche, but were prevented in time, so that the soldiers were enabled to pass, though they had great trouble in dragging the guns through the rocky bed of the river.

The enemy's line supported itself on the east of Peter Both Mountain, extending nearly parallel to the wood, at a distance of nearly 200 paces from it. The French force there consisted of 3,500 men, with several field-pieces, under General Vandermassen. The chief force of General Decaen remained within the lines. Several sharp skirmishes took place before the head of the column, under Lieutenant-Colonel Campbell, of the 33rd, had emerged from the wood, and formed with as much regularity as the broken nature of the ground would permit. Exposed to a storm of grape, the grenadiers were next formed, and, being supported by all the flank companies of the reserve, they rushed to the charge with great spirit.

The French waited till they were within fifty paces, when they broke and precipitately retired, leaving the field-pieces in possession of the English.

This advantage, however, was purchased with the life of Lieutenant-Colonel Campbell, and Major O'Keefe, of the 12th, both excellent officers. A corps now ascended the mount, and pulled down the French standard, hoisting the English one, with hearty cheers. In the course of the forenoon, a position, in front of the enemy's lines, but beyond cannon-range, was occupied by the British.

The heat of the weather and fatigue of the men prevented further action till the morrow.

The French were disturbed by a false alarm of an attack, during which the irresolution of the National Guard, taken in conjunction with the appearance of a reinforcement of troops, which disembarked in safety at Petite Rivière, induced General Decaen to propose terms of capitulation. He sent a flag of truce to the outposts, which did not prevent the progress of arrangements for a general assault. Many of the articles appearing inadmissible to both naval and military commanders, General Abercrombie gave orders for a general attack on the following morning. Upon this, General Decaen offered to revise his propositions; and, finally, he was obliged to accede to the terms of the British—nothing less than the complete surrender of the Island, which was ratified on the 3rd of December.

On the same day, at six o'clock, the grenadiers marched into the lines, and occupied the principal batteries of Port Louis; while the fleet took possession of the forts and roads; and the French squadron was subsequently given up to Admiral Bertie, by order of General Decaen. The inhabitants awaited with the deepest inquietude the arrival of the British troops in the town, anticipating scenes of pillage and disorder; and it is not easy to express their surprise, when they beheld 20,000 men, flushed with victory, enter without molesting a single individual.

A few instances occurred of foraging parties unscrupulously taking possession of cattle, but orders were at once given for compensation to be made to the sufferers.

The next day the shops were all open, displaying their finest wares; hotels and canteens were crowded; the most perfect harmony prevailed amongst the sailors, soldiers, and inhabitants—no one would have supposed it was a city only the day previously in a state of siege.

A few days after, Port Louis resembled a vast bazaar, where Indian and European met for trade, the only difficulty being ignorance of each other's language. Three Company's vessels were loaded at once for London with coffee, sugar, pepper, and other merchandise that had been lying for years in store. Ships in the harbour, unable before to land their goods, were now able to do so, and to dispose of them at a fair price. The amount of money in circulation the first month after the capture was incalculable. The Treasury was turned into a bank, where everyone could get accommodation to send to any part of the world. Credits were opened with Europe, India, and China; and it may well be imagined that the impulse given to commerce, after the circumscribed state it had been in for some time, induced the people to look with complacency on their conquerors. Their flag was changed, but so little else for a long time, that the change of masters was scarcely felt.

On the 5th of December, Mr. R. Townsend Farquhar, having taken over the government, issued his first proclamation, informing the inhabitants that the civil and judiciary administration would be carried on as before.

In this proclamation the old names, Isle Maurice, Port Louis, and Grand Port, were substituted for Isle de France, Port Napoléon, and Port Impérial, and they have ever since retained them.

The office of Intendant was abolished, and the Governor united in his own person the executive and legislative powers. The principal part of the officials were allowed at their option to remain in office; a permission of which most availed themselves. The utmost liberty was given to all enterprises. Those who received pensions under the French Government were invited to produce their titles, and, after examination, were continued on the list.

On the 20th of December another proclamation was issued, calling upon all the inhabitants to take the oath of allegiance to the King, which at first caused great alarm; but the mild measures and conciliatory tone adopted by the Governor soon laid aside the mistrust and prejudice between the English and French; and it was not long before matrimonial alliances were formed between the colonists and the new comers. After four months of administration, Mr. Farquhar was ordered to hand over the government of the Isle of France to Major-General Henry Warde, and to assume that of Bourbon.

On the 8th of April, 1811, General Warde, in notifying his appointment, stated his being named by the King Governor of Mauritius; and from that period the name of the Isle of France has ceased to exist in all official records. Few changes took place; but the Governor insisted on everyone taking the oath of allegiance, and threatened all who did not comply before the 18th of April with forced departure from the colony.

He re-established the Colonial College, which had been taken temporarily for a hospital during the attack on the Island.

Balls, soirées, amusements of all kinds followed, and at these *réunions* English and French alike enjoyed the festive season; and the anniversary of the King's birthday, the 4th of June, was numerously attended by both nations.

On July 11th, Mr. Farquhar received new commands to resume the reins of government; and a few days after his return he announced free trade with the Cape, which had been prohibited in May preceding.

Several aliens having refused to take the oath of allegiance, new orders were issued to do so or leave the colony. Strict measures were taken to preserve the *vaccine virus*, as vaccination had recently saved the Island from the disastrous effects of the small-pox which had broken out.

In 1812, the first races were run in Mauritius, under the direction of Col. Draper, who was a member of the Jockey Club.

The month of January, 1813, is remarkable for the publication of the Act abolishing the slave trade, and the suppression of the premium given to the proprietors of slaves killed when Maroons, and an increase granted for every Maroon caught alive.

Hydrophobia made its appearance this year, and its first victim was the son of an influential proprietor, M. Gonderville.

In April, Mr. Farquhar named in Port Louis Commissaries with police attributes; but few persons were willing to accept the office. In July a Colonial Bank was established, but soon after suppressed.

In 1813, Lord Moira, Governor-General of India, during a sojourn in the Island, laid the first stone of the present Catholic Church, clad in his masonic robes, and attended by all the masons of all the lodges.[1]

In 1814, when Louis XVIII. remounted the throne of France, Mauritius was definitely ceded to Great Britain, and Bourbon, under the same treaty, was restored to France.

[1] This is a curious fact, when we remember a late Catholic Bishop refusing to admit persons who were masons to receive the Sacrament in that very church, and even excommunicated two gentlemen who would not consent to quit their lodges.

A proclamation was issued about this time to close Port Louis harbour to the ships of all foreign nations.

On the sudden arrival of Napoleon in Paris, plots were laid to gain possession of the Island for the Emperor.

An insurrection, headed by M. Perrat, was discovered at Grand Port, and matters threatened to assume a serious aspect; but the prompt measures of the Governor succeeded in quieting the conspirators, and the disorders ceased on the defeat of Bonaparte.

The year 1816 is memorable for the diplomatic and commercial relations entered into between the Mauritian Government and Radama, King of the Hovas, who, from a petty chief in the north of Madagascar, had gradually extended his authority over the greater part of the island. Two sons of Radama were sent for their education to England. The King himself engaged to suppress the slave trade on payment of a subsidy; he offered advantages to mechanics and others who would reside in his dominions. Civilisation was advancing with rapid strides when death cut short his career.

In September a fire broke out which destroyed a great part of Port Louis, causing distress to such an extent that the Governor at once issued a Provisional Act, suspending all civil and judiciary proceedings.

Food and clothing were supplied, and money advanced from the Treasury to aid the burnt-out proprietors. That education might not be delayed, the Government maintained at school the children of those who had severely suffered by the fire. A vast and commodious market was built, and stalls in it assigned to those who had no place to display their goods.

Two brigades of firemen, with engines and all accessories, were at this time established.

In December the Governor laid the first stone of the Quays that now surround the harbour.

Complaints having been made at home, Mr. Farquhar obtained leave of absence; and taking with him all the principal archives of the colony to afford information, and accompanied by Baron d'Unienville, amidst the profound regret of all classes, he embarked for England November 19, 1817, leaving the reins of government in the hands of the senior military officer, Major-General Hall.

His first official act of note was to annul the disposition of Governor Farquhar in favour of the Society of Arts; in consequence of which its fate was sealed, and for years it was unheard of.

The year 1818 is memorable for a terrific hurricane, followed by an epidemic sore-throat, that carried off victims from all classes of society.[1]

At the beginning of this year, Commander Purvis, of the 'Magicienne,' seized the Hamburgh, American, and French vessels then in port, under the pretext of infringement of the navigation laws.

The case was, however, dismissed by the Commissary Justice, Mr. Smith, greatly to the displeasure of the Governor, who soon after turned out Mr. Smith from his post, and took that office on himself.

He then suspended Col. Draper, Collector of Customs, on account of the part he had taken in trying to prove the innocence of the proprietors of the above-mentioned vessels, of contravening the laws by landing goods from foreign vessels.

The year was marked by continual troubles from the tyranny of the Governor; but a new spirit infused itself into all classes when orders came from home for the General to leave; and on the 10th of December, Lieut.-Col. John Dalrymple was received with every manifestation of joy as temporary Governor.[2]

[1] An address was presented by the principal inhabitants to the Major-General, suggesting measures for repairing the great damages done by the hurricane, and remedying some of its worst effects, and offering to second the Government in any scheme that should be proposed for alleviating the distress. But he was too busy to heed their supplications, being engaged in sending out his emissaries after new slaves reported to him as having been landed, and spies to arrest those he suspected of evading the laws, then being put in force, as to slaves and slave-holders.

When he replied, instead of sympathising with the people in their calamity, he wrote, 'Instead of writing to him with a pathetic story about the misfortunes of the country, it would be far better to put an end to the infamous commerce in slaves.' 'What do you complain of?' he writes of hurricanes, why you are better off than the Antilles, for they get one every year. You fear famine? open subscriptions, and get provisions for the unfortunate; or rather open the shops of the rice monopolisers, and rice won't be wanting!' and for the future, he advised them to keep their advice to themselves, and not trouble him with it.

[2] General Hall not only undid, as far as lay in his power, the beneficent acts of Sir R. Farquhar, but in all his despatches home he vilified the colonists and tried to influence the Government against them, but fortunately without success.

In the year 1819, the Island was visited by three violent hurricanes. In February, Major-General Ralph Darling was proclaimed Governor.

In November, the cholera suddenly broke out in Port Louis, and spread with terrible rapidity to the country districts. It continued its ravages till April in the following year, and carried off nearly 12,000 persons.

On the 6th of July, 1820, Governor Farquhar, arriving with the title of Baronet, resumed the administration, and expressed his intention of carrying on all his former measures for the welfare of the colony—a task not easy of accomplishment, from the constant dissensions between the late Governors, the Council, and the people, and the financial difficulties he found resulting from the recent scourges that had so severely afflicted the colony.

In January 1821, the Common Council was dissolved; Port Louis was re-opened to foreign trading vessels under certain restrictions; the Dyot Canal was finished, and the present Bathurst Canal was begun; and in June the new Theatre was opened.

After having rendered many important services to the colony, Sir R. T. Farquhar retired, and was succeeded, in May 1823, by Sir Galbraith Lowry Cole.

A local historian speaks of his departure as a misfortune severely felt. During his government the resources of the colony were greatly developed, and commerce revived; and the manner in which he endeavoured to heal the wound inflicted by the separation of the colony from France is worthy of all commendation.

In 1823, a resolution was passed in Parliament for the introduction of a progressive system of amelioration in the state and condition of the slaves in the British Colonies, and this with the avowed intention of abolishing later altogether the slave trade—that social anomaly in the dependencies of a professedly free country.

From the time the first idea of abolishing this traffic was mooted, there appears to have been a rebellious feeling ever surging up amongst the colonists.

As a preliminary step, a fixed and inflexible rule was established, that the immediate representative of His Majesty, as well as chief magistrates and other officers, administrative and judicial, should not directly nor indirectly be possessed of slaves, or land cultivated by slave labour, or of mortgages on such estates. The directions to this effect bear date 1824.

Then was shown how sturdy a resistance was to be expected in those countries where slavery had been encouraged for centuries; as all views tending to emancipation were looked on as chimerical and ruinous.

An Act of the highest import to the colony was passed, in June 1825, by the Imperial Parliament, permitting the importation of the products of the colony into the British markets; and this admission caused everyone to turn his attention to the culture of sugar, to the neglect of all others.[1] Letters patent were sent out to ordain a Council, to consult with the Governor and assist him in the administration of the government; and from this period the laws were no longer in the shape of proclamations, but ordinances of the Governor in Council.

In 1826, the Bathurst Canal was completed, thus giving the town a plentiful supply of water.

In 1827, a Chamber of Commerce was established, the president of which was to be a Government officer. In February 1828, the streets were re-named, and houses numbered; and petitions sent to Government, begging to have the town lighted, in consequence of the night robberies becoming so frequent.

In June, Sir Lowry Cole was succeeded by Sir Charles Colville, K.C.B.

In November, the Chamber of Commerce was reformed, and was to consist of twelve members; three of the dignitaries to be elected by a general meeting of the commercial body.

In 1829, an Order in Council was promulgated, abolishing all

[1] This, which was in reality a valuable privilege if used with prudence, became from its abuse a source of endless trouble to the colony.

Nearly the whole colony embarked in the most hazardous speculations; landed estates acquired double and triple value; the Creole imagination of the inhabitants became heated to such a degree, that there was no price to which landed property could limit itself: the wildest extravagance and luxury were the consequence. England and India poured forth their millions, which were expended on this rock.

At length these moments of prosperity reached their term: a contraction was perceptible, and the illusion vanished—failures, bankruptcies, foreclosures, unusual distress, the entire destruction of credit, and all the long list of evils that ever follow in the train of mercantile speculations conducted on false principles.

the distinctions existing between the whites and free citizens of colour, and enjoining that the births and deaths of both should henceforth be registered in the same books.

An attempt was made to introduce Chinese and Indian labourers, but with so little success that they were sent back to their own countries.

Numerous dissensions arose, after the death of King Radama, between the governments of Madagascar, Bourbon, and Mauritius, but they were soon amicably arranged.

In the year 1830, the colonists resolved, after long deliberation, to despatch an agent to lay their claims before the Home Government for more liberal concessions; and Mr. Adrien d'Epinay was chosen, and left for England on the 10th of October. He returned the following year, and reported that he had been favourably received by Lord Goderich, the Secretary of State.

The creation of a legislative council, half the members to be chosen from the principal merchants and proprietors, and liberty of the press, which till then had been under the censorship of the Secretary of State, were among the first results of his mission.

About this time a gradual estrangement was taking place between the English and French; and so far from time enfeebling this alienation, it assumed day by day a new energy, and all the efforts of Sir Charles and Lady Colville to bring about a better feeling amongst all parties were unavailing.

In 1832, new laws were enacted for regulating the duties of masters and servants.

At this time an attempt was made to bring about the emancipation of the slaves, which roused the fears of the people to such a point that the whole Island was in commotion. To suppress an expected movement amongst the slaves a Volunteer Corps was formed.

In June, Mr. Jeremie was sent out as Procureur and Advocate-General, to arrange for the emancipation, but the people refused to allow him even to take his seat in the council.[1] The

[1] An eye-witness thus describes the state of the town, the morning after Mr. Jeremie's arrival:—'Every third person was armed in the streets; Port Louis rather resembled a citadel than a commercial town. The Bazaar was cleared of produce, the shops closed, the cart and boat establishments refused to work.' The committee of the malcontents had drawn up a resolution that no business should

most violent scenes ensued; and the disturbances only ceased when the Governor consented to send Mr. Jeremie out of the Island.

On the 31st of January, 1833, Sir William Nicolay became Governor in the place of Sir C. Colville, who had requested permission to retire to England.

On the 4th of February Sir William Nicolay published an order in council, directing the dissolution of the Volunteer Corps. Colonel Draper, and Mr. Virieux, President of the Supreme Court, were suspended for the part they had taken in the proceedings against Mr. Jeremie. In April, that General returned, with the 9th Regiment, and entered the same day on his functions of Procureur and Advocate-General.

In May, a proclamation was issued for all persons to give up their arms. On June the 19th, notice was given that all situations, including those of the learned professions, would henceforth be reserved for British subjects, or persons becoming so by treaty; and a few days after, by another notice, a knowledge of English was made a *sine quâ non* for employment in the service.

The rest of the year was passed in plots against the Government, and in consequent arrests.

The year 1834 opened with the publication of an Act memorable to all ages—the abolition of slavery in all the King's dominions.

But the laws respective thereto were to remain in force till February 1st, 1835; and from that date, all persons aged six years, duly registered, would become apprentice labourers, and continue so till February 1st, 1839, for those non-attached.

The year 1835 began by the arrival of Indian labourers from Calcutta for the plantations.

The first stone of Fort Adelaide, on the Little Mountain, was laid by the Governor.

In February the commission of indemnity began the valuation of slaves, and in December, the mode of division was made

be done, no taxes paid, that the courts should be closed, and no attention paid to police orders. This was circulated everywhere, and acted on to the letter. After Mr. Jeremie was sworn in as a Privy Councillor, the press unanimously refused to print it.

known. Mauritius received 2,112,632*l.* for 68,613 slaves, about an average of 69*l.* 14*s.* 3*d.* each.

In 1836, the Port of Mahébourg was opened for trading vessels, and a weekly post was established between it and Port Louis.

On the 29th of August, Mr. Jeremie was dismissed from his post, and very soon after left the colony.

On the 1st of January, 1837, the Savings' Bank was established; and on the 9th was laid the first stone of the Grand River Suspension Bridge. In 1838, Indian immigration was again suspended; and the Commercial Bank opened. In 1839, when the apprentices were freed, a general disorganisation took place, the ex-slaves refusing to work, and the streets of the town were crowded with them.

On the 20th of February, 1840, Sir W. Nicolay took his departure, and Col. Power succeeded for the short space of five months.

During this time a committee was formed and blended with its predecessor, under the name of the 'Free Labour Association,' for facilitating the introduction of labourers: it was presided over by Capt. Dick, Colonial Secretary. On the 16th of July, Sir Lionel Smith became Governor; and the principal events of importance during his government were—M. H. Adams received letters of naturalisation, the first who had enjoyed that privilege in Mauritius; and the Home Government refused to allow immigration from the coast of Africa.

In July 1841, it was announced that the English text of all laws published in the colony would be the only legal version.

On the 2nd of January, 1842, Sir Lionel Smith died suddenly at Reduit, and in three days was followed by Lady Smith. Until the arrival of the new Governor, the senior commanding officer, Lieut.-Col. Stavely, was appointed as Acting Governor.

Little of interest took place at this time, if we except the severe financial embarrassment in May and June. On the 21st of November, 1842, Sir William Gomm arrived; and it required stringent measures on the part of Government to allay the ferment caused by the difficulties on all sides from the immense amount of small paper notes the banks had been putting in circulation. The premium on gold at this time had risen to 20 per cent., and on silver to 12 per cent.

Sir William took considerable interest in the cause of immigration, and obtained leave to introduce 6,000 labourers annually, also a large number of Indian women, which had never been permitted previously.

In 1844, he urged upon the inhabitants to plant provisions for their men, to meet the frequent emergencies when the price of imported goods was so high.

In May an auto-da-fé was made of the notes of the Committee of Finance, but so carelessly that large bundles were rescued from the flames to pass again into circulation. In 1845, a despatch was published authorising the Government to send to England yearly the pupil who had most distinguished himself.

A contagious epidemic broke out amongst the cattle, and raged for months, till it was feared that the whole bovine race would disappear. Upwards of 12,000 cattle and 6,000 pigs, besides goats, were swept away.

At this time the commercial body signed a convention to accept the rupee at the uniform rate of two shillings, the former value being only one and tenpence.

Affairs in Madagascar were in a very unsettled state. The widow of Radama, Ranavalona Manjaka, followed just the opposite course of policy to that of the late king. So far from encouraging settlers, she expelled the missionaries, and prohibited Christianity. Extortions to the greatest extent were practised on foreigners, and a peremptory order was at last issued for all strangers to depart.

Time was refused them even to arrange their affairs, and matters were carried so far that the Government was obliged to interfere. Captain Rolly, of the 'Conway,' was sent down to protect the British subjects, and he was joined by a French man-of-war, under command of Commodore Romain Desfosses. Persuasion and entreaty being alike in vain to obtain time for the settlers, orders were given to bombard Tamatave; but it was so well defended, that the attacking force was quite unequal to its conquest, and had to retire, leaving behind even its dead.

Ranavalona then ordered all trade to cease, which caused great distress in Mauritius, as Madagascar was the principal source whence cattle for the market and agricultural purposes were brought—distress doubly felt on account of the late murrain.

Trade also suffered, as cotton goods, cutlery, and iron ware all found a good market there.

Ample details of the whole affair were sent to England, and Sir W. Gomm even recommended that a sufficient armament should be sent out to subdue the island.

Possibly it might have been attended to but for the views and claims of the French, and political events in Europe soon absorbed the project.

In 1844, the new system of manipulating sugar by the vacuum-pan was introduced and effectually established on the Labourdonnais and Phœnix Estates. By the adoption of this valuable discovery the quality of the sugar was so much raised that Mauritius could then compete with any country in the world. About the same time another improvement called the 'Wetzell,' after its inventor, was introduced by M. Huguin.

In 1846 a peculiar blight attacked the sugar-canes, destroying thousands of acres of the white cane.

This calamity was in one respect useful, as it caused a more careful cultivation of the plant, and greater attention in choosing the canes, as it was proved that not a red cane was touched.

In this year a census was taken of the people, with the following result:—

	Males.	Females.
General Population . .	30,148	25,331
Ex-Apprentices „ . .	28,142	21,223
Indian . „ . .	48,935	7,310
	107,225	53,864

The first stone of St. Thomas' Church, at Plaines Wilhems, was laid by Lady Gomm in 1845, and opened for divine service on October 1846; and Sir William laid the first stone of St. John's, at Moka, the same year; and both contributed largely to these edifices.

The patent slip of Messrs. Scott and Murray was begun this year.

The great crisis which shook the whole commercial world at this time terribly affected Mauritius.

All the principal mercantile houses stopped payment. A

petition was sent to the Queen setting forth their grievances; the principal result of which has been ever since felt in the reduction of the salaries of almost all the subordinate officers of Government, the abolition of minor situations, and a general reduction of taxes. The immigration stamp-tax on Indian engagements was abolished; and many important items were either abandoned or greatly reduced to such an extent, that the revenue suddenly fell to so low a figure that the Secretary of State gave orders for the re-establishing of the stamp-tax at once.

Sir William took deep interest in the cause of education. A number of Government schools were established and supported at its expense. An ordinance was also passed, setting aside a sum to be paid annually into the Treasury for Church building purposes.

The representative committee at last perceived a favourable prospect, from the energies aroused by their correspondence with England, in favour of immigration, steam communication, and elective bodies.

The present currency of Government notes was prepared during the last months of Sir William's administration.

The overland mail of February 1849 announced that Sir William was appointed Commander-in-chief of the Indian Army; and his Excellency embarked for Calcutta, leaving the government in the hands of Lieutenant-Colonel Blanchard, who was only a month in office, and was followed by Lieutenant-Colonel H. Lewis Sweeting, who in turn gave place to the new Governor, Sir George Anderson, who arrived on the 8th of June.

He at once set to work energetically, and issued a proclamation to all the inhabitants to assist him in the administration of government. A draft of ordinance was laid before the Council by the Governor, for allowing three years' engagements of labourers, and was passed at once.

On the 1st of September our present currency of notes was issued; an arrangement having been concluded with the Commercial Bank, by which the pecuniary affairs of government were to be carried on from that date.

At the end of this year an ordinance was passed to constitute a municipal corporation; and the preliminaries were carried on so rapidly, that on the 4th of March, 1850, the Governor notified that he had selected, as the first Mayor of Port Louis, Louis Lechelle, Esquire, and Felix Kœnig, Esquire, as his Deputy.

This year was ushered in by great changes in the Courts of Justice. The Supreme Court was to consist of one chief Judge and two or more puisne Judges, which court was invested with the powers of the Queen's Bench, and made a court of equity. District Courts were also established, trial by jury introduced, and many other judicial ordinances were passed to be put in force in 1852. This year the 'turbine,' the greatest improvement in sugar making since the steam-engine, was brought into use in the colony.

A petition was presented to the Governor, in June, for the erection of lighthouses on the coast, to avoid the repeated disasters and shipwrecks from the shoals and currents.

Sir George was occupying himself with many matters of public utility when he received news of his appointment to the Government of Ceylon, and he left Mauritius, to the infinite regret of all parties.

Major-General Sutherland was appointed Acting Governor October 19, but his brief administration offers nothing of interest.

In January, 1851, Mr. James Macauley Higginson arrived in the colony from Ceylon, where he met Sir G. Anderson, and doubtless their conferences aided him greatly in carrying out the important measures planned by Sir George before his departure.

A project was set on foot at this time to introduce the culture of the silkworm, and it was proved that silk of a very superior quality could be produced here; but the apathy of the working classes rendered all such attempts futile. The first question to which the Governor directed his attention was to procure free labourers from the coast of Madagascar, to make good the deficiency of the labour market. The next measures were those of steam communication, and the extension of the limits previously fixed for the annual introduction of labourers from India.

By a new enactment, a provision of 500*l.* was allowed to the Mayor, whose services were previously gratuitous.

By this time the financial difficulties, so serious during the latter part of Sir W. Gomm's government, began to improve so much from reaction and increasing prosperity, that there was now a considerable surplus in the hands of Government. The Governor advised using part of this for opening up new roads into the interior; but to accomplish this he proposed plans that did not meet with general approbation, and they thus proved in a great degree abortive.

At this time Mr. Wilson, manager of the Cape gas works, visited the colony, and obtained a concession of land for establishing a gasometer for lighting the town with gas, in place of the dull oil lamps that alone glimmered in the extensive and only city of Mauritius.

Propositions were made for a regular monthly communication with England by steamer, and the Council voted 12,000*l.* a year as a subvention, for a period not exceeding five years; Messrs. Blythe Bros. having proposed to establish the line.

The year 1852 began with the new judicial changes, by which local courts were established, and the present organization of the Supreme Courts, nearly as planned by Sir G. Anderson, were put into operation.

The trade with Madagascar was temporarily renewed, and petitions were presented to the Governor to take measures to try and adjust the difference that had existed since the rupture at Tamatave.

Arrangements having been made with the G.S.S. Company, the first fine steamer, the 'Queen of the South,' arrived after a passage of forty-three days.

In August the first annual report of the Meteorological Society was published.

The year 1853 began by an appeal of Mr. Tropier to the inhabitants for funds to erect a monument to M. de Labourdonnais. The Governor headed the list, and a subscription was quickly raised, but it was not till some years later that it was erected. The prospects of the colony brightened more and more, and the mail steamers succeeded each other regularly.

The question of lighthouses progressed to a solution, and there was every appearance of a renewal of the Madagascar trade, the Government offering to advance the required indemnity.

The Governor occupied himself with innumerable matters for the progress of the colony; but his health and sight began to fail, and as a sea voyage was recommended, he went by the mail steamer to Seychelles, leaving General Sutherland to replace him in his absence. On the 11th of September, on the return of His Excellency, commissioners were sent to Madagascar, and all differences were amicably adjusted, the ports re-opened, and trade in cattle, rice, mats, cloths, &c. was renewed.

In April 1854, the Governor's health still declining, he left for England, and General Sutherland was again left in charge.

At this time broke out serious dissensions between the Roman Catholic clergy and the Freemasons, the former refusing to administer the sacrament to any of the order. During the administration of General Sutherland, the island was visited by sorrow and desolation. The cholera broke out in the prisons of Port Louis, and once outside the walls it spread with such alarming rapidity, that the inhabitants of the city fled on all sides.

During the progress of this terrible plague, almost every family had to bewail the loss of some member of it, for it spared neither rank, nor age, nor sex.

Amongst the most universally regretted were Dr. Rogers and the Rev. Mr. Banks, who fell victims to their untiring devotion, wherever their services could avail. 7,650 persons were carried off.

General Hay succeeded in January 1855, and held the reins for the remaining six months of the leave of absence of the Governor.

Sir Herbert de Lisle, a highly talented man, Governor of the sister island, spent a short time in Mauritius in May, and on his return carried with him the pleasantest souvenirs of his visit.

In July a second patent slip was erected by Mr. Prout, and it was at once in full activity.

On the first day of Mr. Higginson's return, it was notified by letters patent under the great seal, dated November 1854, that Mauritius and its dependencies were erected into an episcopal see and diocese, and that the Right Reverend Vincent William Ryan, D.D., who arrived on the 18th of June, was appointed the first Bishop thereof.

During the absence of the Governor in England, he had actively employed himself in the interests of the colony, both in respect to immigration and steam communication, and with favourable results.

Small-pox visited the island severely this year, which was introduced in consequence of imperfect or too brief quarantine.

In November a large meeting took place to petition the Queen to allow the French language to be used in the courts, and all judicial and administrative Acts; and in December a counter petition was got up, asking for the optional use of both the French and English languages. At this time the new lighthouse on Flat Island was at last completed, which added greatly to the safety of foreign vessels entering the harbour.

The year 1856 opened with the most brilliant prospects, as sugars increased in prices past expectation; but during this year the borer made its appearance in the canes, and has since done much mischief in the plantations.

By despatches in February, the Secretary of State approved of two pupils being sent home by the colony from the Royal College, and being educated there at Government expense; also authority was received for the local Government to enter into a contract with Messrs. Menon and Co. for a steam postal communication between Mauritius and Aden.

There being no proper quarantine station, in March the colony was again invaded by cholera, some vessels arriving with the disease on board.

The immigrants were landed at Gabriel Island, and underwent the severest hardships and sufferings from want of shelter and provisions; and as there was constant communication between Gabriel and Flat Islands, the cholera was soon brought to Port Louis. The first death in hospital occurred on the 6th of March, and the dire plague did not cease till the 7th of June, when its victims numbered 3,532. Soon after the Government voted 55,000*l.* for quarantine accommodation at Flat Island and Cannonier's Point.

In 1856 Dr. Ulcocq, being in England, brought to the serious consideration of the Secretary of State the advisability of a railroad in the colony. On the 27th of December the steamer 'Governor Higginson' left Port Louis on her first voyage to Aden; and on the 27th of January, 1857, it arrived with the mails, and thus proved that the route by Aden was the most prompt and advantageous for the colony.

This year may be considered one of the most prosperous ever experienced in Mauritius.

In the month of May the Council voted 1,000*l.* to be supplied to the establishment of a Sailors' Home, subject to a like sum being raised by voluntary contributions.

On the 26th of June the most favourable news was received from Europe, announcing a large rise in the staple product of the colony, just as they were about to harvest the largest crop ever grown, and the removal of the interdiction to immigration from India. In this month was laid the first stone of the Protestant church at Pamplemousses by Lady Higginson. The happy news from England was, however, speedily followed by tidings of the revolt in India, which spread momentary dismay, and caused the principal provision of the labourer, rice, to rise from 14*s.* to 21*s.* in forty-eight hours, everyone rushing to procure a supply, as if the island was menaced by a famine.

The new Mauritius Dry Dock was publicly opened on July 13th, in presence of the Governor and the most influential members of colonial society.

About this time it was recommended by the chief medical officer that coolies should only be brought from Madras and Bombay, as they would be more likely to be healthy than those brought from Calcutta. On the 10th of September his Excellency, now Sir James Higginson, K.C.B., left the colony, accompanied by his family.

Sir James was replaced for the few days intervening between that date and the 21st by Major-General Hay, when Sir William Stevenson arrived, and received the government from his hands.

This gentleman, born of one of the best planter's families in Jamaica, began his political career in that country by resigning his office as puisne judge rather than involve the Government in disputes on his behalf, a sacrifice of position to principle so well appreciated by the Crown, that later he was appointed Superintendent of Honduras. His singular capacity for business, and his unrivalled administrative abilities, were thought so highly of in Downing Street that they procured him the Government of Mauritius.

On presiding for the first time in the Legislative Council, he traced out the programme of his projects; and they embraced public institutions, material and intellectual wants, finance, agriculture and commerce, education, sanitary measures, immigration and postal communication; and the promises then held forth were well carried out in the execution.

The two subjects to which His Excellency first turned his attention were immigration and the postal service.

He succeeded in gaining what had been refused to his predecessors—liberty to engage labourers in India for five years' service on the estates, a most important measure for the planters; and he encouraged an abundant supply of labour to develope the resources of the colony.

The next step was to change the irregular overland postal service into a well-organised arrangement, guaranteed by contract with the P. and O. Company.

At the earnest solicitation of the inhabitants, he applied for a skilful engineer to indicate the best lines for railways, and to estimate their cost and revenue.

He thoroughly re-organised the police force, which was till then a disjointed, incomplete, and undisciplined service. A police court was established, and stipendiary magistrates for the districts, a great boon for both planters and Indians.

The fullest enquiries were made into the system of education at the Royal College; and he upheld the new rector, who with determined, though too hasty, hand had tried to rectify the abuses caused by the negligence of his predecessors.

He founded the Orphan Asylum at Powder Mills, and with Lady Stevenson gave it great encouragement.

A vast improvement was made in Government schools, and almost the last time he appeared in public he promised a prize of 50*l.* from his private purse for the most successful examination at the training school for teachers.

His repeated advice was to put Port Louis in a condition to repel the irruption of epidemics, and he went largely into the question of sanitary reforms. Well would it be now for Mauritius had his counsels been carried out; it might perhaps have saved thousands from the hecatombs of victims slain by the present fever scourge.

Great reforms took place in the Civil Service, and he devised plans for the better division of district hospitals, from which complaints were brought to his notice.

He personally visited them to see that the evils were rectified; and touched with the zealous labours of the sisters of charity elsewhere, he aided in gaining their services for the sick in the hospitals. He took a warm interest in scientific progress. The Meteorological and Arts and Science Societies, botanical gardens, &c., are deeply indebted to his lucid and practical ideas on all subjects connected with them.

Under his auspices the Young Men's Association was formed, and he delivered an address to them which displayed remarkable talent, and was full of the sterling eloquence so peculiarly his own.

Commerce and agriculture received every attention from him, particularly the latter, in which he always evinced great pleasure when attending to its details.

He upheld the Municipal Corporation, though attempts were made to turn popular feeling against him by the most unfounded accusations of carelessness of the public welfare; but, conscious in his own integrity, his calm attitude, and the moderation, tolerance, and loyalty he displayed, disarmed all adversaries, and conciliated all parties.

He strictly enforced the quarantine laws, the subject at that time of endless controversy.

On the death of the Queen of Madagascar he sent a mission to King Radama II., congratulating him upon his accession to the throne, and upon the liberal policy he had decided to pursue towards foreigners. The gentlemen of the mission were received with every honour by the king, and it was hoped a new era for Christianity and civilisation had begun in Madagascar.

This able and esteemed Governor was attacked on January 4th, 1863, with dysentery, which soon assumed a serious character, and on the 9th he breathed his last. The health of His Excellency was failing for some time before his death. The previous hot season, with an epidemic raging in the island, and much anxiety, correspondence, and care thence arising, had already greatly tried his strength, and his sensitive, nervous system and kindly heart.

It is believed that, but for this excessive and wearying application to duty, without adequate relaxation and repose, the dysentery which caused his death would not, humanly speaking, have proved fatal, but for the prolonged and insidious operations of the above-mentioned debilitating agencies. His remains were brought from Reduit to Port Louis, and thence a large concourse of the inhabitants, in spite of an incessant rain, accompanied it to St. John's Church, Moka.

Addresses of the deepest sympathy were forwarded to Lady Stevenson, who, only a few weeks previously, had received the heartiest congratulations on the birth of a son.

When the news arrived in Downing Street, the Duke of Newcastle wrote to General Johnson, then acting Governor:—

'I have received with the deepest sorrow and regret your despatch, marked "separate," of the 24th of January, reporting the death of the late Governor of Mauritius.

'Looking to the services which Sir W. Stevenson had rendered, and those which he was capable of rendering, had his life been prolonged, there is no possible event by which the Colonial service could have sustained a greater loss.

'He had evinced in the administration of his government a pure public spirit, unbiassed for a moment by any personal feelings or considerations, great administrative ability, untiring energy, and a devotion to labour, unfortunately carried to an excess, and leading at last to the sacrifice of his life. He was one of the most able, zealous, and honourable men with whom official life has brought me into contact.

'I have, &c.,

'(Signed) NEWCASTLE.'

The affairs of Government were left in such good working order by the late Governor, that Major-General Johnson, the senior officer in command, had little difficulty in carrying out his plans for general improvement and progress.

In April 1863 the project for a Credit Foncier was set on foot, and M. de Manteuil was sent to Europe, by subscription of the planters, to obtain the assistance required in the way of capital.

News was in May brought from Madagascar, threatening to destroy the new alliance between the English and that country. On the 12th instant King Radama was strangled by the Hovas, and at the same time all his ministers shared the same fate.

Immediately afterwards, Queen Raboda, his wife, was placed on the throne, with the title of Queen Rasoerina. Later intelligence allayed the fears this tragic act aroused, as the queen was said to have expressed her wish to continue the friendly relations between herself and foreign nations, and to carry out the treaties lately entered into.

About this time a low sort of fever broke out, commonly known as the Bombay fever, and carried off a great number of Indians on the estates.

In this month died also Dr. Philip Bernard Ayres, after a short illness. He arrived in Mauritius, January 1856, as Superintendent of Quarantine and the improvement of its laws: the excellent accommodation for Indians, and the Lazarets at Flat Island and Cannonier's Point, are mainly due to his earnest representations.

At the time of his death he was intent on writing a Flora of Mauritius, and each moment he could snatch from professional business was devoted to botany; but death prevented the completion of this work.

Little of interest took place till November 26th, when Sir Henry Barkly arrived with the *prestige* of the experience gained by having governed two important British Colonies in the West Indies, and that of Victoria in Australia, which gave great hopes of his competence to hold the reins of a Government composed of such diverse and discordant elements as those that existed in the Mauritian population.

On the morning of his arrival, the new Governor took the oath, and the same day the usual proclamation was issued, calling upon the inhabitants and servants of the Crown to co-operate with him and aid him in carrying out all projects for the welfare and progress of the colony.

On the 2nd of December His Excellency held a levée, which was numerously attended, and the Chambers of Commerce and Agriculture presented him with addresses that were well received, and frankly and favourably replied to.

Sir Henry lost no time in inspecting the line of railway, then nearly completed, and expressed his approbation of the works. He visited some of the principal estates of the Island, and studied for himself the pros and cons of that *vexata quæstio*, differential duties, and others of vital importance to the planters.

It need scarcely be said with what hearty welcome the Governor and his lady were everywhere received in his progress through the island.

In January 1864 an Embassy was sent from the Court of Antananarivo, Madagascar, consisting of two officers of the 14th and 15th Honowes Rainiferuigia and Rainandrainandriana, and a Protestant clergyman as interpreter, to the Courts of England and France.

At this time the offer of Messrs. Hanna, Donald, and Wilson was accepted by the Municipal Corporation, to light the town of Port Louis with gas.

On the 21st of May the northern line of railway was opened, and a large party left town for Grand River, SE., where an inaugural breakfast was given at Beauchamp Estate by the Government.

Two Credit Foncier Companies were now in full operation, which it was hoped would be of great assistance to the planters. Three companies were formed, two in London and one in the colony. They offered money for thirty years, to be repaid in capital and interest at 10 per cent. premium. The introduction of this alleviation to industry, and encouragement to the landed proprietor, was publicly celebrated, as not only those who borrowed were benefited, but all estates and land acquired a more solid and certain value. The commercial crisis in England checked the operations of these companies; but the money already advanced greatly aided agriculture and commerce to tide over a difficult moment, when the produce market was declining and crops reduced. On the 18th of August the Messageries Impériales steamer 'Ermine' opened the new line from Réunion and Mauritius to Suez, thus giving a second postal communication per month.

A new Protestant church for the Bengali population was consecrated by the Lord Bishop of Mauritius, the erection of which was mainly due to the benevolence of one of the most influential members of the Chambers of Commerce and Agriculture.

In January 1865 steam was first applied here to the printing press by Mr. Channel, the enterprising editor and publisher of the 'Commercial Gazette,' the only English newspaper in Mauritius.

A terrible calamity occurred in the following February. After several days of heavy rains, on the evening of the 12th, a torrent rushed down the mountains above Port Louis, and meeting the streams of the town, formed a vast expanse of raging waters violently seeking an outlet into the sea. The whole of the lower part of the town was inundated; private houses, shops, sugar stores, all were buried under a thick residuum of mud, entailing heavy losses of property, and in many instances of life. A complete stagnation of business ensued; the railways were stopped for a time, as the whole of the rivers in the island overflowed, and did considerable damage in the country, but not to the extent of that in town.

The total losses were estimated at three-quarters of a million of dollars.

Great complaints were made to the Municipality and Government about the sanitary condition of Port Louis, as its state was such that should cholera or any epidemic break out it would to a certainty ravage the place.

Dr. Edwards, who had been sent out as chief sanitary inspector, was urgent as to the measures that ought to be adopted to lessen the death-rate, then at far too high a figure. According to his estimate fever was fast becoming endemic, and therefore more formidable than cholera.

A petition was forwarded to Her Majesty in the name of the Council, praying that goods and passengers might be conveyed to and from Seychelles in foreign vessels, as up to this time the trade was entirely restricted to British coasting vessels.

News arrived from Madagascar confirming the signing of the treaty with England at the capital, where great rejoicing took place.

This treaty provided for a consular office at Tamatave, with power over all British subjects; consuls and agents to reside in the dominions of the contracting powers.

Exports and imports (except spirits) to pay ten per cent. The exportation of cows and timber prohibited, and the importation of munitions of war to be the exclusive right of the Queen of Madagascar.

British ships to have free entry into all ports, and to be assisted in case of shipwreck, and protected against plunder. The English were to have full power of purchasing land, renting and leasing houses, and trading everywhere in the island, except the three holy cities. The utmost toleration in religion was accorded, the tolerance to extend to Malagash converts.

The whole treaty was highly satisfactory, and gave equal advantage to both countries.

In answer to the Governor's proposition, the Secretary of State authorised a special appropriation of 1,000*l.* to be expended, under the sanction of the Governor in Council, in payment of stipends to missionary clergymen or catechists capable of teaching Christianity through the medium of any of the languages current amongst the Indian immigrants.

On the receipt of the news of the assassination of President Lincoln, of the United States of America, a letter was sent to Mr. Mellen, the United States Consul, from the Governor and Council, expressing their detestation of the deed, and their sympathy with the American people and Mrs. Lincoln in their bereavement; and it was answered by the Consul in the most flattering terms.

In October the Midland Line of railway was opened, which passes over several handsome bridges; one in particular, the Grand River Bridge, is a splendid specimen of its kind, and displays what science can do in conquering difficulties, and would be a triumph of art in any capital of Europe, combining lightness and elegance with solidity.

An important concession was made to the Royal College by the University College of London, through the exertions of His Excellency, to the effect that the students should be permitted to obtain their B.A. degree without the necessity of leaving the colony, conditionally on their passing a rigid examination there. For a long time affairs at the college had given the greatest discontent from the unpopularity of the rector; and at last an enquiry was entered into on his conduct, with but little effect, and nothing but his removal from office seemed likely to place matters on a different footing.

Education generally was, however, making rapid strides. At the annual distribution of prizes it was mentioned that in 1857 there were only twenty-four Government schools, but that in eight years they had increased to forty-four, entirely supported by Government, and fifty-three assisted by grants in aid.

On the 9th of November, the anniversary of the birthday of H.R.H. the Prince of Wales, the first lighting of the town with gas was celebrated by an illumination at Government House and the Place d'Armes, and since then the principal streets of Port Louis have had the miserable cocoa-nut oil lamps replaced by gas.

The year 1865 was a trying one to the colony. The borer in the canes, disease, and unfavourable weather brought short crops. The inundation causing such extensive damage and stagnation in business; rice and provisions for animals becoming excessively dear, in consequence of the famine in India, and thus heightening the planter's expenses, at a time when sugars were falling in prices, all threw a gloom over the closing year.

So many large failures ensued amongst the planters and merchants, that at one time there were twenty-four fine estates in the market at once, at the moment when money was very scarce.

The indefatigable and talented secretary to the Meteorological Society, Mr. Meldrum, left for England, to carry out the purpose of making Mauritius the reliable centre of meteorological and magnetic observations in the Indian Ocean. He intended visiting the great observatories of Europe, in order to render the new one designed to be built in Port Louis as complete and convenient as possible. The great luminaries Humboldt, Herschel, Fitzroy, and others had always marked out Mauritius as the most desirable station for a fixed land observatory. Another object in view was to examine the new delicate standard instruments for some time waiting him in England, destined for the new observatory.

The inauguration of the statue of Mr. Adrien d'Epinay took place in the presence of the Governor and Lady Barkly, and a large concourse of spectators, including the *élite* of the Mauritian community.

When the statue was unveiled, the Mayor, deputy-Mayor, and others eloquently described the career of the patriot, and then His Excellency addressed the assembly, and expressed the heartiest sympathy with the grateful conduct of the people of the colony to their once fellow-citizen.

A visit was paid to Flat Island by the Governor and a large party of officials to examine a convenient place for laying an electric cable from this island to Port Louis, a distance of seven miles, a measure calculated to be of great advantage to the shipping interest, and particularly to the quarantine station.

A difficult operation in mechanical science was successfully performed, which demonstrated the resources and ingenuity of Mauritius. The 'Egmont,' Captain Inglis, bound for Victoria, Vancouver's Island, arrived with the telegraph cable on board, which was to complete the 'girdle round the earth' by uniting the continents of Asia and America at Behring's Straits.

The vessel met with heavy gales off the Cape in the memorable storms of the 22nd to the 25th of June, and was so strained as to leak alarmingly, and put into Port Louis for repairs. The whole of the 275 miles of cable had to be discharged, and in a comparatively short time the ship was efficiently repaired, and the cable re-shipped without the slightest injury.

The last months of 1866 were marked by drought, which did so much mischief to the plantations as to preclude all hopes of a fair crop in 1867. The great reduction of crops in 1866, and the certainty of a still further one in 1867, seriously affected the colony, and rendered necessary important modifications in the estimates of the revenue for 1867, as the customs, internal revenue, and railways all declined in their receipts.

In the meantime many social benefits had accrued to the colony.

Prisons and prison discipline had been improved, sanitary laws remodelled, and medical care rendered available to the labouring classes. A reformatory school was projected, the Orphan Asylum and other benevolent institutions well maintained, and both Catholic and Protestant clergy were zealous to spread religious instruction over the Island.

The Union Steam Company's ships replaced the P. & O. Company satisfactorily; the central railway station was completed, and electric telegraphs commenced on each line of railway. Jurisprudence received considerable improvement in some important items ; amongst others a law was passed to facilitate taking evidence in cases of abduction of children ; and another to abolish judicial mortgages. Commerce too had its share of the consideration of the Council; an ordinance was passed regulating imported goods ; another remedied abuses in collecting debts at Rodrigues ; and a third extended the disciplinary powers of the Chamber of Brokers.

The distillery laws were amended, and a draft ordinance introduced to establish reformatory schools.

Immigration in 1866 was on a comparatively limited scale, but quite equal to the requirements of the planters. A medical pharmaceutic society was formed, its regulations permitting of deliberations on every branch of medical and scientific study.

The president appointed was Dr. C. Regnaud, and the society was formed of all the medical faculty in the island.

The Church of England Young Men's Association was reopened by a lecture delivered by Sir Henry Barkly, on English literature, which united a comprehensive and erudite view of the subject with attraction enough to keep a large audience attentive the whole evening.

The intense heat and the continued drought at the beginning of the year encouraged the spread of the fever, which had been insidiously making its way through Port Louis and the surrounding districts for some time ; and the death-rate steadily progressed, till it reached the enormous figure of 200 *per diem* in Port Louis alone. The prevalence of this epidemic put a stop to trade with the exception of articles of absolute necessity. The position of affairs was greatly aggravated by a total want of quinine. A small quantity was brought from Bourbon, and realised $135 per oz.! The humane foresight of the Governor greatly alleviated this trouble, as he addressed despatches to the Governors of Madras and Ceylon, requesting them to send supplies of quinine, which were quickly responded to.

Hospitals, dispensaries, depôts for provisions, every effort the Municipality could make, did not keep pace with the rage of the epidemic, which devastated all classes of society. The effects of it were almost too terrible to relate ; 10,000 perished in the month of April alone. The banks and public offices, courts of justice, railways, nearly all were at a standstill for want of hands.

Everything that could be done by the Governor, officials, clergy, and men of property was done; but in the presence of such overwhelming misery, with thousands of widows and orphans left destitute, all their efforts fell short of the necessities of the case.

In June the statue of Sir W. Stevenson was inaugurated at Government House.

A salute was fired from the citadel as it was unveiled, and an address was delivered by Sir H. Barkly, well setting forth the claims of the good and great man to the country's gratitude. His Excellency was followed by Sir Gabriel Tropier, the Hon. E. Pitot, Mayor of Port Louis, and others; and all joined their testimony of respect and esteem to the public and private virtues of the late Governor.

This statue, as well as that of Mr. A. d'Epinay, was the work of a young creole sculptor, Mr. P. d'Epinay, whose remarkable talents had procured him the notice of H.R.H. the Prince of Wales, by whom he was deputed to model three busts of the Princess Alexandra.

Subscriptions were raised at home, and reached Mauritius in August, to the amount of 2,567*l.* 15*s.* 6*d.*, but even this only partially arrested the tide of want and misery.

The mortality was declining, but so severe a blow had been given to commerce by the fever, and to agriculture by the drought, that the calamity fell heavily on the Island at a time when its productions were declining and its burdens augmenting.

On the 3rd and 4th of January, 1868, a strong gale passed over the Island, which did some mischief among the shipping, and stranded the United States steamer 'Warrior' and the English ship 'Bury St. Edmonds.' At the same time an islet was formed at the mouth of the harbour, which received the name of Barkly Island. Little injury was, however, done to the plantations, and great hopes were entertained that the ensuing crops would be heavy, and alleviate in some measure the distress of the place.

The events of 1867 form a dark chapter in the history of Mauritius. The pestilence swept off 30,000 of the inhabitants;

the taxes for sanitary measures were greatly increased; commerce suffered severely, and the harbour was almost emptied of its shipping, for masters of vessels were afraid of entering, as their crews were sure to be attacked with fever on landing.

Societies for social advancement were paralysed, and the churches were very thinly attended.

All who could fled from the city to the higher parts of the Island, Savanne, &c., thus leaving a large number of houses untenanted, and reducing the value of property greatly. The finances of the colony were seriously affected. Notwithstanding considerable reductions in the expenditure to meet the falling off in the revenue, it was necessary to have recourse to additional taxation. Wine, beer, tobacco, and opium were the articles chosen, which would bear an extra impost without weighing unduly on the industrial classes.

The railway receipts were so greatly diminished, that the establishment was overwhelmed with debts and difficulties; but it was hoped that if the improved crops were realised, and the epidemic ceased, it would also have a share in the return of prosperity.

Amongst the most important legislative measures were some especially affecting the jurisprudence of the colony. An ordinance was passed for amending the law of forcible ejectments, &c., which it was hoped would prove of eminent service in suppressing abuses long existing with regard to immovable property; one for enabling natural children to inherit property, and another respecting the Master's Court and land surveyors, were also passed.

The office of Queen's Advocate for the Land Court was established, and a draft to codify and amend the laws of judicial sales was before the Council.

An ordinance was passed, codifying and amending the laws affecting the status of Indian immigrants, sanctioning restrictive provisions, which the increase of crime by bands of vagrants rendered necessary.

By this Act they were obliged to give an account of their means of subsistence, or be sent to the depôt, and, if they then refused to work, they would be treated as vagrants.

Educational progress had been greatly checked the whole year. Many of the schools had been closed altogether. The Royal College was thoroughly disorganised by the incapacity of its Rector, as well as by its ranks being thinned by fever, so that it had been for a long time in a state of retrogression.

Nothing but a thoroughly efficient Rector, and judicious filling-up of the vacant Professorships, could give it a hope of success for the future. Several of its ablest Professors had succumbed to fever.

Immigration from the Presidencies had entirely ceased during 1867 ; but the planters were less distressed for hands than might have been supposed possible. From the excellent system of medical assistance on the estates, the deaths among the plantation labourers were, in proportion, fewer than among any other class.

The Dry Docks and Customs necessarily felt severely the scarcity of vessels in the harbour during the whole year ; in fact, it would be difficult to say what sources of revenue, public or private, did not suffer more or less.

A sum of 400*l.* was voted by Council for sending Dr. Meller, Director of the Botanical Gardens, to Hong Kong, Japan, the Philippine Islands, New Caledonia, New Hebrides, Society Islands, and Queensland, to search for new and healthy canes to renew the old, diseased, and profitless ones in Mauritius.

During January, the epidemic steadily increased. Even in the districts of Savane, Grand Port, and others that had hitherto almost escaped, it spread with such rapidity that the mortality of the Island for that month amounted to 2,981 victims.

The Crédit Foncier de l'Isle Maurice, Société Coloniale, proved a total failure; but the other two Crédit Foncier Companies succeeded well, and stood high in the opinion of merchants in London and Paris.

They, doubtless, by their timely aid, saved many a planter from ruin, and enabled him to tide over this trying period.

In February, the western cemeteries within the town limits were permanently closed ; and about 400 acres of land were purchased at Bois Marchand for new ones, far beyond the precincts of the town, yet easily accessible by rail.

At length, driven to it by pressure of circumstances, and it appearing that nothing else would do, serious discussions began to take place relative to the drainage of the city, as the only means to restore Port Louis to anything like a sanatory state; and estimates were required as to a survey of the whole place.

An order in Council was passed, allowing the Procureur-Général, or his substitute, to plead for private individuals, which gave great offence generally.

From the 12th to the 14th of March, the Island was visited by one of the most terrific hurricanes of this century, which did incalculable mischief both in town and country. Few of the vessels in harbour escaped without more or less injury—some were complete wrecks.

This put the climax to the misery of the colonists. The short crops, decline in public revenue, and fever had brought the Island apparently to its lowest point; and, with the additional burden of dwelling-houses and stores, sugar houses, railway and other bridges, and public works injured or destroyed, the universal distress may be better imagined than described.

It needed undaunted courage and perseverance on all sides to bear up under so many misfortunes.

Further taxation was out of the question, for the losses were estimated at a million of dollars.

Fever still raged everywhere, especially in the city, and this was aided by the masses of vegetable and other *débris* in all directions, caused by the cyclone; the cartage not being sufficient to clear it rapidly away.

The Mail service to Galle, by the Union Company's steamers, was stopped, nine months before the contract expired, by paying an indemnity of 7,500*l.*

Great excitement was caused in England at the Horse Guards, by the 86th Regiment being landed against orders, and from exaggerated statements in some leading journals as to the 'Decimation of the troops.' It turned out that only *two* men had then died from the fever; but when this news was reported, nothing was heard of any sympathy in the same quarter for the thousands of civilian victims who were dying monthly.

Appeals were made to the Home Government against the colony having to pay 45,000*l.* to England for military defence, when it had been declared that only a small contingent was necessary in Mauritius. His Excellency applied for a reduction of 32,000*l.* yearly, but up to this time (May) no answer had been received.

It was proposed to augment the Police force to such an extent that troops would not be required, and that the colony should pay from 20,000*l.* to 25,000*l.* for an efficient Reserve Police force.

News was brought from Madagascar of the death of the queen, and conspiracies on all sides and consequent arrests. All, however, ended quietly; and a new queen was proclaimed, under the title of Ranavala Manjaka II. Mr. Cruaux, the English Consular officer, was officially informed that the treaty with England would be respected. According to Malagash law, on the death of a queen, every man, woman, and child is obliged to cut off the hair of the head quite close, go bareheaded and barefooted, and, no matter what the weather, wear the *Lamba* under the arms, instead of covering the shoulders. To show the progress of civilisation in the capital, the late queen, on account of serious illness, paid a visit to the sea-side, the first time such an event had ever taken place in the royal annals of Madagascar.

So heavy were the damages by the cyclone to public works, that it was found necessary to borrow 100,000*l.* for governmental purposes.

In June, a Minute was read in Council by His Excellency, expressing the great sympathy of Her Majesty the Queen with the sufferings of her subjects in Mauritius.

On the 22nd of this month, the colony had to deplore the loss of one of its ablest men, the Hon. Sholto James Douglas, Acting Procureur-Général.

He met with an accident at a friend's house, and fractured his leg badly, so that, in a fortnight's time, lock-jaw set in, and he died in forty-eight hours afterwards. He was universally regretted.

The Legislative Council, Supreme Court, Chamber of Agriculture and Municipal Council, all bore testimony to the high character of this gentleman; and his benevolence and widespread charity, especially during the epidemic, had earned for him the expressive title of the 'Friend of the poor.'

A despatch was received from His Grace the Duke of Buckingham to the effect that no diminution could be made in the annual expenditure of 45,000*l.* for the troops kept in Mauritius.

The character of the Mauritians must have greatly changed

since 1826. Lieutenant-General Sir A. Campbell, when speaking to the Minister on the repeated turbulence of the people, thus described them:—

'They are so docile and gentle, they could be managed by four men and a corporal!'

But now a regiment is required to keep the peace of the Island, at a cost of 45,000*l.*

A new asylum for the poor was opened at Beau Bassin, in one of the healthiest parts of Plaines Wilhelms, with hospitals, sanatoriums, and cottages, which bids fair to be of the greatest benefit, particularly as it was intended to make it self-supporting.

On July 14 medals were distributed by the Governor to six of the police force. These men, under Major O'Brien, Inspector General of Police, have been well drilled, and become a very efficient well-disciplined corps, and during the epidemic have done good service in town and country.

After almost insuperable difficulties from the limited means at command, the Grand River railway bridge, which was so severely injured in the hurricane, was repaired sufficiently for all purposes of traffic, pending the arrival of new iron girders from England. This was done by means of what is called the 'Howe Truss,' from its inventor, an American. The work was completed by Mr. Payne, in the most skilful and successful manner.

The difficulties of such an undertaking may be appreciated when it is considered that there were four trusses to be hoisted, each 125 feet long by 19, and each weighing about thirty tons. These had to be elevated 120 feet; and to perform this, heavy hoisting derricks of 25 feet high had to be erected on the top of the columns.

In September the old question of Indian villages was revived, as an additional sanatory measure, to prevent the crowding of Indians in the miserable huts they had always occupied; but as usual, so much debating *pro* and *con* took place, that nothing was decided on, and it seems very doubtful if this justly needed step will ever be taken.

Discussions with regard to the drainage of the city constantly went on, but with incessant opposition.

In a Minute in Council, the Governor, after setting forth ably the advantages of the measure, concluded with these emphatic words :—'It is very hard that it required an epidemic of such unexampled severity, as to force and duration, to establish this truth. There were statistics in abundance to prove that the colony was fast settling down into a chronic insanatory condition: they were utterly disregarded! There were continual exhortings from wise and prudent men to put "our house in order" while there was yet time; but no one stirred! Government, municipality, and people remained unmoved. Surely we have all been to blame for not making vigorous efforts, in the face of such fearful statistics, to arrest the waste of human life. Surely it should not have needed the subsequent lessons of pestilence to induce us to follow the example of other communities by improving the drainage and sewerage of this city.'

Some idea of the depreciation of property in Port Louis may be judged of when the mayor publicly expressed the opinion that the actual rateable property in Port Louis was something short of a million sterling to that assigned to it in the then existing assessment roll.

A terrible disappointment took place when the time for the sugar harvest arrived. The crops, from which so much was expected, in consequence of the heavy rains and winds during and after the cyclone, fell so far short that only 75,000 tons were actually realised, instead of the hoped-for amount of 150,000.

Towards the end of the year fever abated, but it was greatly feared that with the intense heat of summer it would again raise its malignant head.

In December very warm discussions took place as to the reduction of the salaries of all the Government officials, with no result.

The year 1869 began with hopes that a favourable change might take place in the fortunes of the colony, so long crushed by troubles of all kinds. Serious financial difficulties were, however, still to be encountered. The expenditure of Government was expected to be barely met by the revenue, yet the inofficial members of the Council refused consent even to a conditional reduction of 10 per cent. on the establishments. Recourse was necessarily obliged to be had to further taxation, and a draft ordinance was passed to increase the revenue by new stamp duties.

In March various important ordinances became law. Amongst others was one compelling all ships carrying more than ten passengers to be provided with a life boat, two buoys, and all necessaries for use, before putting to sea. In case of neglect, a fine was to be inflicted, not exceeding 100*l.* if the fault of the owners, or 50*l.* if with the master. The game-laws were amended, and every person carrying arms was compelled to have a license under penalty. Stringent laws were put in force to check cruelty to animals, for the Indians, who have so little regard for human life, are, as a rule, exceedingly cruel to dumb animals.

Sanitary taxes continued very high, as a large establishment was obliged to be kept up to relieve the immense amount of distress, and with that it was with difficulty the still increasing poor could be assisted.

Reports were brought about this time of valuable gold fields supposed to have been discovered near Natal, and attempts were made to get up a party to proceed thither, but failed.

A petition was presented to the Chamber of Agriculture, praying for a reduction of the judicial rate of interest from nine and twelve per cent. to seven, as a boon to the planters and merchants, to lessen the speculative tone engendered by exorbitant rates of interest; for various reasons, however, it was not complied with.

In April, letters were received from Earl Granville on the sanitary condition of Port Louis, stating that the eminent engineer, Mr. Bazalgette, had been appointed to make a survey of the city, and report as to the practicability of underground drainage.

The same mail brought news of the death of Mr. James Morris, in London, who had been appointed Commissioner for the colony at the Paris and Dublin Exhibitions, and who had served as General Government Agent for sixteen years: his loss was much regretted.

In June a revival of the question of Sericiculture, or silk-growing, took place. Numerous letters were written to the Royal Society of Arts and Sciences, and it was again shown beyond a doubt that silk might be profitably raised to a considerable amount in the colony: but with as little result as formerly. The manufacture of various fibres was also again brought forward, particularly of the various kinds of aloes with which the country abounds. The experiment is being made at Petite Rivière, where a small manufacture is established for the conversion of aloe fibre into cordage. To be made profitable, the aloes will require cultivation on a large scale, and good steam machinery will be necessary; but labour is so dear that it is doubtful if it can ever prove a success in Mauritius. There would be no cause for doubt if they could compel all the unemployed and almost starving Indians to work for reasonable wages; but that appears to be one of the great difficulties under which the colony labours. As to the capability of the soil for producing aloes in as great quantities as could be required, there need be no question of that; and many a plain, now waste land, unfit for cane or other culture, could be planted with these hardy fibre-producing plants.

Despatches were received from Downing Street, fixing the amount of troops decided on by the British Government to be kept in Mauritius. The following table will show of what the force is to be composed:—

Artillery Battery . . .	106	of all ranks.
Engineers' Corps . . .	98	,,
Infantry Regiment . . .	898	,,
Hospital Corps . . .	4	,,

To be paid at the rate of 40*l.* per man for infantry, and 70*l.* for artillery and engineers, the same as the Australian rate.

No Bishop having been appointed since the departure of Bishop Ryan in 1868, the Rev. S. G. Hatchard was at length installed as Lord Bishop of Mauritius and the Dependencies, and in July arrived with Mrs. Hatchard and family.

Though apparently a change for the better took place in the sanitary condition of the Island, the death-rate was still heavy. During the year 1869, 11,495 deaths were registered, at least half of them from fever.

Considerable progress was made in the manufacture of sugar by the use of Dr. Icery's process, though a great decline in the amount of sugar raised was inevitable from the great mortality of late years, and the comparatively few Indian immigrants introduced. In the course of this year many important draft ordinances were passed, besides those above mentioned. Imprisonment for debt was abolished; the illegal practice of medicine and surgery prevented; the sale of poisons and other matters relative to pharmacy regulated; the extension of the powers of the District Courts allowed; measures taken for the prevention and punishment of arson; extension of relief for distressed seamen; a central rum warehouse established, &c.

The number of bankruptcies and consequent sales and depreciation of valuable property were much less frequent in 1869 than in the two previous years. The Crédit Foncier of Mauritius, Limited, was gradually growing into importance; its large capital was securely employed and its affairs prosperous, while its utility to agriculture and British capitalists was daily more appreciated. Taken altogether, the year 1870 opened with fairer prospects in many ways than had been seen since the beginning of the terrible epidemic. In February 1870 the colony was shocked by the announcement of the death of the recently installed Lord Bishop. After barely two days of illness from fever, death had ensued before any, save those near him, knew of his illness; just when he was acquiring a knowledge of the spiritual requirements of his diocese, and becoming intimate with the various congregations in the Island.

Continuous dry weather at this time excited great fears in the public mind as to the coming crops, and the subject of irrigation was brought before the Chamber of Agriculture. A plan was projected for directing the waters of the Mare aux Vacoas, in the centre of the Island, to the plains below. The original plan appears to have involved a very large outlay, with scarcely adequate results, but it is likely it may eventually be adopted in a modified form. The subjects of preserving the forests and re-wooding the country were again hotly discussed in Council, and draft ordinances were brought forward, but none were unanimously received.

Proposals were made for connecting Mauritius with the various ports on the Indian Ocean and the Cape of Good Hope by submarine telegraph, a scheme of the greatest benefit to the colony at large. It was, however, negatived for the time; but hopes were held out that by the time the company was formed in Europe the Island would be in a condition to meet its share of the expense.

In April, a despatch was received from Lord Granville relative to the report of Mr. Bazalgette on the underground drainage.

Most violent opposition to the project was manifested by a large portion of the community ; in fact, they went so far as to petition the Queen against it. One plea urged was that the turning up of all the ground in the city, so long saturated from the drains, would be fatal to the public health ;[1] and also on account of the heavy expense it would incur. Year after year this goes on, and little is done to get rid of the pestilential gutters and drains in use, not to speak of other nuisances ; meanwhile death is reaping a heavy harvest while the people are quarrelling as to how the city shall be cleansed, and no one seems able to propose any feasible plan that will solve the difficulty.

It having been at last decided that the visit of H.R.H. the Duke of Edinburgh, so long delayed on account of the epidemic, should positively take place in 1870, great preparations were made to receive the first Prince of royal English blood that had ever approached these shores. News was brought that in May the royal visitor might be expected. A Committee, styled the Duke of Edinburgh's, was appointed ; horses were sent for from the Cape, wines and provisions from Europe ; Government House was furbished up ; the streets newly macadamised ; paint and whitewash everywhere ; triumphal arches constructed ; and amusements of all sorts planned. The members of the Royal Society of Arts and Sciences agreed to get up an exhibition of the various products of the Island, and all was excitement and anticipation.

By the April mail the Flag arrived, selected for Mauritius by the Naval Authorities of Great Britain. It consists of a blue ensign, in the fly of which is a shield quartered severally with a ship, three cane plants, a key, and a star rising from the ocean. The motto is 'Stella clavisque maris Indicis.' It was intended to first unfurl this flag on welcoming His Royal Highness to Mauritius when landing from the 'Galatea.'

The Duke was at this time being fêted at Ceylon ; and the May mail brought the news that the august visitor would arrive about the 18th.

The whole place was in a flutter ; the shops were gay with

[1] Query—Would not the leaving that saturated subsoil be still more fatal than having it turned out and done with for ever ? Is it not daily doing mischief when the mephitic vapours it engenders are forced into the atmosphere through the open drains?

finery for the coming fêtes; and most unusual bustle pervaded everywhere.

Sad disappointment was experienced when the 18th arrived, but no Prince. Day after day passed, and Her Majesty's loyal Mauritian subjects began to fear that all the addresses and speeches prepared for royal ears were vain, and that some cause had again turned the 'Galatea' from their port. The spirits of the people were still further depressed by the death, on the 23rd, of one of the members of the Legislative Council, the Hon. H. Kœnig, a distinguished veteran of the Mauritius bar.

Every day the programme for the Duke's entertainment was changed; and it was not till about 11 A.M. on the 24th that the Union Jack on Signal Mount announced the approach of the 'Galatea.' At 4.30 P.M. she anchored, and after a salute from the forts, his Excellency the Governor, attended by his aid-de camp, Major O'Brien, extra aid-de-camp for the occasion, and Mr. Arthur Barkly, his private secretary, repaired on board to welcome the Prince. The same evening a quiet landing was effected; and he dined with the Governor, returning in the same manner, to sleep on board.

The following programme will show the arrangements made by the committee for the Prince's welcome. It was arranged on the supposition of his arriving on the 20th; but being delayed four days later, the whole had to be somewhat modified to compress it into a shorter space of time.

1870.

May 20.—Friday. Arrived.

„ 21.—Saturday. Lands officially at noon—Levee at 2 P.M.—In the evening Lady Barkly's reception.

„ 22.—Sunday.

„ 23.—Monday. Laying of foundation-stone of the Meteorological Observatory at twelve o'clock—Botanical Gardens at Pamplemousses at 1 P.M. Evening—Municipal banquet.

„ 24.—Tuesday. Queen's Levee—Regatta—State dinner.

„ 25.—Wednesday. Morning concert—Queen's ball in the evening.

„ 26.—Thursday. *Chasse* at Fressanges.

„ 27.—Friday. *Chasse* at and return from Fressanges—Masonic Ball

May 28.—Saturday. Races—Theatre in the evening.
„ 29.—Sunday.
„ 30.—Monday. Mahébourg—Entertainments by the 86th R.C.D. Regiment.
„ 31.—Tuesday. Exhibition—Cricket ball.
June 1.—Wednesday. Departure for Bois Sec.
„ 2.—Thursday. *Chasse* at Bois Sec.
„ 3.—Friday. Lawn party at Reduit.
„ 4.—Saturday. Departure.

Numerous addresses were also presented to the Prince.

This, of course, is not the place to comment on *how* the arrangements were carried out; suffice it to say, His Royal Highness expressed himself greatly pleased with his visit to Mauritius.

The last few days were all hurry and bustle, for His Excellency and family were on the point of leaving for England, his term of office having expired.

On the 3rd of June, by the Mail steamer, Sir H. Barkly, his lady and daughter, left Mauritius, taking with them regrets from all classes, not only for his zeal and incessant application to business, and his earnest endeavours to promote the welfare of the colony, but for the kindliness and warmth of feeling shown in the trials the Island had passed through during his administration. It is only necessary to mention the inundation of 1865, the fevers of 1867, 1868, and 1869, and the hurricanes of 1868, to recall the many acts of sympathy by which the Governor testified his feelings for the people under his temporary rule.

When the Mail steamer had left the harbour, she was followed by the 'Galatea,' slowly steaming away from the shores of Mauritius, putting an end to the short-lived gaiety, and leaving Port Louis to sink back to its normal dulness.

The following day, His Honour, Brigadier-General E. S. Smythe, senior officer commanding the troops in Mauritius, was sworn in as officer administering the government, until such time as the new Governor, Mr. Arthur Gordon, should arrive.

February 21, 1871, the Hon. Arthur Hamilton Gordon, C.M.G., landed in Mauritius, and assumed the Governorship of the colony.

CHAPTER XXV.

BRIEF SUMMARY OF THE GEOGRAPHY OF MAURITIUS, ITS DEPENDENCIES, CIVIL AND MILITARY STATISTICS, VARIOUS INDUSTRIES, COMMERCE, &c.

The Geography of Mauritius—Its Physical Aspect and Climate—Its Dependencies—Account of Seychelles—Internal Communication—Post Office and Foreign Telegraph Scheme—Hackney Coaches, &c.—Defences, Military, Police and Naval—Money, Weights, and Measures—Banks—Crédit Foncier, &c.—The various Industries of Mauritius—Foreign Commerce—Decadence of Commercial Affairs generally.

THE Island of Mauritius lies just within the Tropics, of irregular shape; at its greatest length, viz. from Cape Malheureux to Pointe Dernis, it measures 39 miles, and at its widest part, about 34 across, though from the coast of Petite Rivière to Point Quatre Cocos, in Flacq, its breadth is only 28 miles.

Its distance from the nearest land (Réunion) is about 115 miles; from Madagascar, 500; Rodrigues, 300; Seychelles, 915; Cape Comorin, 2,000; the Cape of Good Hope, 2,300; the nearest point in Australia (Cape Cuvier), 3,000; nearly 11,000 from England, *viâ* the Cape, or 7,000 by the overland route.

It possesses an area of about 700 square miles, giving in exact measurement 432,689 acres.

The physical aspect of the Island is in general picturesque, from the bold and grand outlines of the lofty hills, with their peculiarly formed and varied summits. The north is, for the most part, a vast plain, covered with cane lands, and the centre an elevated plateau, rising to above 1,500 feet beyond sea-level. From this elevation, the principal mountain-ranges diverge, and the land descends gradually from Curepipe to Grand Port, The eastern side presents a rich and well-cultivated district.

The coast is deeply indented with bays; but there are only

three safe approaches for vessels—the Harbour of Port Louis, the Bay of Grand Port, and the Baie de la Rivière Noire.

Islands are very numerous, but all small. The principal are Isle aux Tonneliers, near Port Louis, connected with it by a causeway, on which stands Fort George, commanding the entrance to the harbour; the Coin de Mire, Isle Platte, Le Colombier, Gabriel, Isle Ronde, and Isle aux Serpents, to the north of Mauritius; Butte à l'Herbe and Isle d'Ambre, on the coast of the Rivière du Rempart; Isle aux Cerfs and des Roches, near Flacq; Isles Marianne, aux Fouguets, aux Vacoas, de la Passe, aux Singes, and des Aigrettes, near Grand Port; and on the coast of the Rivière Noire, the Isles aux Fourneaux, du Morne, and des Bénitiers.

Mountains.

There are three principal ranges of mountains. The first, called the Port Louis Group, encircles the city, extending towards Pamplemousses. One line of the group includes Mountains Ory, the Pouce, Peter Both, and the Callebasses Mountains. One spur terminates abruptly in the cliffs of the Signal Mountain, above the western surburb of Port Louis; another, to the east, is Petite Montagne, surmounted by the Citadel, and rising from the great plain of the Champ de Mars; behind it lies the Montagne des Prêtres, and de l'Embrasure; and, still farther, the Montagne Longue, de Ripaille, and the Nouvelle Découverte. The principal elevations of this group, according to French authorities, are: Peter Both, 2,874 feet; Pouce, 2,707 feet; Montagne Longue, 611 feet; Signal Mountain, 1,136 feet. Most of these mountains are covered only with rank coarse grass and stunted shrubs; a few are wooded to their summits.

The second group commences with the Mountains of the Corps de Garde and those of the Plaines of St. Pierre; and in this chain are included the Trois Mamelles and the Rempart Mountains. Between these mountains lies the basin of the Rivière du Rempart, and almost parallel with them run the Brise de Fer, Tamarin, and Des Vacoas Mountains. Those of the Terre Rouge shoot off into Savane, and the mountains of the Rivière Noire terminate with the Morne Brabant and Piton de la Fougue; the Mountains of Savane forming the southern extremity.

The Piton of the Rivière Noire is the highest mountain in Mauritius, being 2,902 feet above the sea, thus exceeding the Peter Both by 28 feet; the Rempart Mountains, 2,710 feet, Corps de Garde, 2,525 feet; Savane, 2,429 feet; the highest of the Trois Mamelles, 2,340; and Morne Brabant, 1,937 feet.

The third, or south-western group, extends from Grand River, SE. to the centre of the Island. Various spurs run southwards, the principal of which are the Cent Gaulettes, Créoles, Camisard, Grand Port, Bambou, Diable, and Feuilles.

The highest of these are the Bambou, 2,204 feet; Grand Port, 1,703 feet; and Créoles, 1,286. Those near the coast are mostly rugged and barren, while the mountains towards the interior of the Island are well wooded, and of great interest to the naturalist.

There are often elevations not included in these groups, all more or less isolated; the principal of which are, Le Piton du Milieu de l'Isle, in Moka; Fayence and Montagne Blanche, in Flacq; Le Grand and Petit Malabar, La Meule à Foin, La Motte à Thérèse, Le Piton, La Butte des Papayers, and Mounts Oret, Mascal, and Candos. A chain of signal stations is established round the Island, the principal one being on the Port Louis Mountain. From it ships can be seen at a great distance; and on clear days, in certain states of the atmosphere, Bourbon is said to be visible. On it is a time-ball which falls daily at one o'clock, very exact when it does work, but not unfrequently out of order. A telegraph wire connects the station with the Post Office. A zigzag path has been cut up the east face of the mountain, so that it is easily ascended. It well repays climbing, if only for the fine view of the city and harbour it affords, and the pure bracing air, so invigorating when once the base of the mountain is scaled.

Between these varied groups of mountains are many beautiful valleys. In the first group is the Anse Courtois, between Mount Ory and Port Louis; that in which the city lies, the upper part called the Vallée of the Pouce; the Vallée Pitot, and Vallée des Prêtres, beyond the Citadel towards Mount Longue; and the Vallées de Peter Both and La Nicolière. The valleys of the second group of mountains are little worthy of notice; but in the third group are the Vallée des Cent Gaulettes, comprising a large part of the district of Grand Port, well watered and possessing a rich soil, and greater humidity from the large quantity of rain that falls here compared with the rest of the Island. The Plaine des Hollandais, part of which is called Beau Vallon, was the site of the first Dutch settlement. Les Bambous is also another fine valley of about 1,500 acres, &c.

The centre plateau, comprising the districts of Moka and Plaines Wilhelms, on account of its coolness, especially the latter, is rapidly increasing its population. It is principally in these districts that the country houses of merchants and others are situated, who come into Port Louis by rail every morning, returning home in the evening. The climate at Curepipe and Vacoas is cool early and late in the day (though hot at noon) even in summer, and is positively cold in winter, which can scarcely be said of Port Louis at any time.

Rivers.

As may be supposed from so much mountain and table-land the Island is abundantly watered. There are no less than sixty rivers and streams flowing to the sea, but all are small; very many cease to flow in dry weather, and the largest are only full after heavy rains, when their rise is so rapid as often to occasion much mischief—but they descend to their ordinary level with equal rapidity.

Taking the first group of mountains as the first watershed, we have the Ruisseau St. Louis running through the city, the Créoles, Pouce, La Butte à Tonier, des Pucelles, and the Fanfaron; all (except the latter, where the docks are) filthy streams, stagnant the greater part of the year, most fertile sources of malaria. Then the rivers Lataniers, sacred to Indian rites, Terre Rouge, Sèche, Tombeau, and Pamplemousses drain the north-western slope; while the Rivières du Rempart, Françoise, and Poste du Flacq drain the other slope.

The central table-land forms a second watershed, whence flow the Grande Rivière NW. on the west, and Grande Rivière SE. on the east.

From the third group the Nyon, Champagne, des Créoles and de la Chaux rise.

The Black River and Savane Mountains are a fourth watershed. Their south-eastern slope is drained by the Tabac, du

Poste, des Anguilles, de la Savane, des Galets, des Citronniers, du Cap, and other streams; through their gorges on the west flow the rivers Noire, du Tamarin, du Rempart, des Galets, Dragon, Belle Isle, and Petite Rivière.

Mares, &c.

There are several natural collections of water, which take the name either of Bassins or Mares. The principal of these is the Grand Bassin among the mountains of Savane. The Bassin Blanc in the same district is dry during a part of the year. La Mare aux Vacoas is shallow, but has an extent of nearly two square miles in rainy weather, feeding many small streams. It is purposed to utilise its waters by constructing dams, &c., which will be a boon to the residents near it in dry weather.

In Flacq are the Mares la Boue, St. Amand, aux Fougères, and Lubines, the latter near the sea, and influenced by the tides.

In Grand Port are large mares, but, except in the wet season, they are only insignificant pools. The Mare de la Violette and Les Mares have the same outlet for their waters. La Mare la Sablonnière covers several acres in the rainy season, when it has a depth of fifteen to twenty feet in places.

In the district of Moka, in the Quartiers militaires, are the Mares Delvoye and Rameau.

Divisions, Towns, &c.

Mauritius is divided into nine districts, viz.:—Port Louis, Pamplemousses, Rivière du Rempart, Flacq, Grand Port, Savane, Rivière Noire, Plaines Wilhelms, and Moka.

Port Louis.

Its greatest length is five and a half miles from east to west, and its breadth four miles from north to south. It extends from Grand River to the left bank of Terre Rouge River. Its coast, including indentations, is about seven miles. The principal places are Port Louis, aux Pailles, La Grande Rivière, Roche Bois, and La Vallée des Prêtres.

Port Louis, the capital of Mauritius, lies in the NW. of the Island.

Since 1850, it has been placed under a Municipal Corporation, consisting of a mayor, deputy-mayor, and sixteen councillors.

Aux Pailles consists principally of country cottages belonging to persons employed in the city; and there are numerous market gardens cultivated by Indians, the red earth of which, when well watered, being singularly fertile.

At Grande Rivière are the lunatic asylum and a vagrant depôt; and a suspension bridge spans the river.

At Roche Bois are also country houses, many on a very diminutive scale; but all the gardens are uncared for, and the whole place has a desolate look: there are many kilns here for burning coral. It is frequently resorted to for sea-bathing; this shore being better adapted for that purpose than any other part of Port Louis.

At the last census the city had a population of 74,128, or 7,413 persons to the square mile. No wonder in such a hot-bed that an epidemic carried off so many thousands! It has now only a very greatly diminished number of inhabitants.[1]

Pamplemousses.

It is thirteen miles from N. to S., and as many from E. to W., and takes its name from the Shaddock, called here Pamplemousses. The coast is about fifteen miles in length, entirely defended by coral reefs.

It is divided into eight cantons: viz. Montagne Longue, Le Piton, Peter Both, La Rivière des Callebasses, La Villebague, Bois Rouge, Mapou, and Le Tombeau.

The principal places are, Pamplemousses, La Terre Rouge, L'Arsenal, La Villebague, Le Trou aux Biches, La Grande Baie, Riche Terre, Powder Mills, La Pointe aux Piments.

At Pamplemousses are the famous Botanical Gardens.

Powder Mills has an orphan asylum. At Riche Terre is a large nunnery.

The population was 53,598, or 615 persons to the square mile.

Rivière du Rempart.

This district is fourteen miles from N. to S. and six from E. to W., and owes its name to the principal river in it.

The coast is deeply indented, but has no harbour for large

[1] The population given is taken from the Census before the epidemic.

vessels: including the bays, it extends about thirty-five miles. It has seven cantons: Bois Rouge, Le Mapou, Poudre d'Or, Le Piton, La Plaine, St. Cloud, Rivière du Rempart, and La Plaine des Roches; all having villages of the same name.

Population 19,331, or 333 persons to the square mile.

Flacq.

This district, the first in size, and third in population, has an area of 113 square miles. It acquired its name from the Dutch, but 'Flat' can only apply to those parts near the sea. The indentations are few, and the coast-line about twenty miles in length.

It has eight cantons: Flacq, La Mare aux Lubines, Les Quatre Cocos, Trou d'Eau douce, La Rivière Sèche, La Mare aux Fougères, Les Trois Îlots, and Camp de Masque.

Formerly, the Poste du Flacq was the principal village, but one has sprung up near the railway station which is now the more important, and where the district court is held.

Population 41,468, or 367 persons to the square mile.

Grand Port.

The fine bay gives its name to this district, which has an area of 112 square miles.

The coast, including openings, measures twenty-nine miles.

It has seven cantons: Les Mares d'Albert, Plein Bois, La Mare du Tabac, Les Cents Gaulettes, La Rivière la Chaux, La Rivière des Créoles and la Côte.

Population 35,564, or 317 persons to the square mile.

Savane.

This district has an area of ninety-two miles, and takes its name from a large savannah or plain in its eastern district.

It has a coast-line of about eighteen miles, which is principally devoid of reefs, and the surf breaks direct on the shore.

There are only two cantons: La Grande and La Petite Savane; their two principal places are Souillac and Jacotet.

The population is 21,026, giving 228 persons to the square mile.

Rivière Noire.

One of the largest rivers gives the name to the district, which has an area of about ninety-four square miles.

There are several bays on its coast, which, including them, is about thirty-five miles in length.

It is divided into six cantons: La Petite Rivière Noire, La Plaine St. Pierre, Le Tamarin, La Rivière Noire, Le Côteau Rapu, and Les Gorges du Cap.

The principal places are Rivière Noire, Tamarin, Bambou, Petite Rivière Noire, and Morne Brabant.

At the village of Bambou are the courts of the district, and stipendiary magistrates, police station, &c.

Population 17,171, or 182 persons to the square mile.

Plaines Wilhelms.

This fine district has an area of about seventy square miles, and derived its name from two brothers, Dutchmen, who settled here in 1690.

It has only about fourteen miles of coast.

It is divided into Upper and Lower Plaines Wilhelms, and these are again subdivided into four cantons: La Terre Rouge, Les Quatre Bornes, Le Bassin, and Les Vacoas; and the principal places are Plaines Wilhelms, Le Trou aux Cerfs, Curepipe, Les Vacoas, Petite Rivière.

Population 28,014, or 400 persons to the square mile.

This district has a larger number of Europeans residing in it than any other in the Island.

Moka.

It was here the coffee tree was planted when introduced from Mocha, in Arabia, and thus its name.

It has an area of sixty-eight square miles, but no coast, as it lies between the districts of Port Louis, Flacq, Plaines Wilhelms, and Grand Port.

It has six cantons: Les Pailles, Moka, La Terre Rouge, and the Quartiers Militaires; and its three principal places are Moka, Malagassy Village, and Réduit. The latter is the country residence of the Governor. The former has both Catholic and Protestant churches; and Malagassy Village is said to have been formed by a number of natives of Madagascar, who escaped from the persecutions to which the professors of Christianity were exposed in that country.

Population 17,704, or 260 persons to the square mile.

Climate.

Mauritius, though within the Tropics, enjoys on the whole a very fair climate, and were the sanitary regulations of both city and country well carried out, it might be a very healthy one. The sky is remarkably clear, and except in hurricane weather there are few days in the year in which walking is impossible during some part of the day.

From December to April the heat is intense in Port Louis, frequently as bad by night as by day. About this time the evenings and mornings begin to cool a little, and by the middle of May, the heat is bearable; and till November the climate is fine, with occasional exceptions. There is a vast difference in the country, on the Plaines Wilhelms' side especially. There the temperature varies many degrees from that of Port Louis: the nights are cool even in summer, and in winter, on the heights of Curepipe and Vacoas, a fire is welcome; a luxury rarely to be procured, as there are only two or three grates, I believe, in the Island. It should be stated that such articles (so suggestive of pleasant evenings at home) would be but superfluities in other than the above-mentioned districts. I give the following note, the result of a series of observations made at Powder Mills, a few miles from Port Louis. The mean annual height of the thermometer for the year at sunrise was 70°, in the afternoon 86°, and at sunset 72°; the maximum was 90°, and the minimum 61° 5′. This, I should think, would be a fair average for Port Louis, Pamplemousses, and Flacq; so it may be well seen how little the residents in these districts require any artificial heat in their dwellings.

The hurricane season in Mauritius extends from about the beginning of December to the middle of April, and the cyclones, so dreaded by mariners, and often so destructive to life and property, range from about 8° to 30° S. latitude. There are certain signs by which their approach is indicated, thus giving warning to masters of vessels and others to prepare for the coming storm—a falling barometer, sombre atmosphere, the clouds of a yellowish grey shade, sultry oppressive weather, an irregular wind, and generally rain in fitful gusts.

In general, on the eve of the storm, the mountains are misty, white clouds are detached from a black ground, and chase each other violently. At sunset the sky looks coppery; squalls from the SE. are followed by sudden calms. The barometer sensibly lowers, and if the squalls become stronger and more frequent, a cyclone is pretty sure to follow. The roaring of the wind is so loud during one of these storms that the growling of the thunder is almost unheard. It is rarely that cyclones pass over Mauritius for two consecutive years, though it is an exceptional case when it does not get the fag end of one or more. The years which pass without sharp storms may be marked with a black letter, for they are as a rule most unhealthy, and have but too often been visited by some dire disease.

Slight shocks of earthquake have been occasionally felt here, but I am not aware that they were ever accompanied with damage.

The longest days are at the December solstice, and the shortest at the June solstice. The length of the longest day from sunrise to sunset is thirteen hours twelve minutes; the shortest, ten hours forty-eight minutes. The difference of time between the observatories of Greenwich and Port Louis is three hours forty-nine minutes fifty-eight seconds, the latter of course in advance of the former.

Hail, though it very rarely falls, yet does sometimes fall in Mauritius, principally in the district of Grand Port.

There has been no active volcano here within the memory of man, though the continuous streams of lava found all over the Island, that once flowed to the sea in every direction from the craters formerly active, show that the eruptions must have been on the grandest scale. In the sister isle of Bourbon is a volcano constantly in eruption.

The prevailing wind in Mauritius is the SE. trade wind; from the middle of May to the middle of October it blows chiefly from SE. and ESE., passing occasionally to N. and NW During the rest of the year it is chiefly from ESE. to ENE.; as a general rule, it veers from SE. to E., NNW., and W., veering seldom in the contrary direction. When the wind sets in from the W., or the 'vent du large,' everyone is complaining, *migraines* and nervous complaints are prevalent.

The rains are very irregular: in some years genial showers fall during most months, rendering the whole Island fertile, and spreading verdure to the mountain summits, and a pleasing murmur of content spreads through the land, in anticipation of good crops, on which the whole prosperity of the place depends; in other years, such heavy incessant torrents fall (especially in those visited by hurricanes), that the canes imbibe too much moisture, and their precious juice is deteriorated. Bad as this is, it is comparatively trifling to the mischief done in the frequent long droughts, when months pass, and scarcely more rain falls than suffices to keep trees and canes alive. Every shade of grass dries up, and the heavy look of care in the face of every planter you meet but too well accords with the dreary aspect of nature.

Then, again, the rainfall differs greatly in various parts of the Island: near the forest lands, steady regular rains fall, and the crops are fine; whereas to the north everything is parched up for want of rain, and there is no means of irrigation.

The following table will show the difference of the rainfall for a series of years, as figured in the Transactions of the Meteorological Society; taking Cluny in Grand Port as the maximum, Labourdonnais in Rivière du Rempart as the medium, and Port Louis as the minimum.

	CLUNY	LABOURDONNAIS	PORT LOUIS
	Inches	Inches	Inches
Total fall in 1869	129·37	63·73	54·57½
1868	183·74	70·46	64·18
1867	141·23	56·99	35·970
1866	129·42	50·29	20·741
1865	192·45	87·63	44·737
1864	122·48	57·25	24·147
1863	147·09	70·72	33·420
1862	122·54	52·23	28·397

The 'monthly means of the barometer, dry and wet bulb thermometers, dew point, elastic force of vapour, relative humidity, amount of cloud, and force of wind,' during the year 1869, as published in the Blue Book, will give a fair general idea of the average of the above meteorological features, in years when there are no hurricanes and a small rainfall. This table has been derived from the four observations taken daily at 3.30 A.M. 9.30 A.M. 3.30 P. M. and 9.30 P.M. The highest and lowest reading of the dry and wet bulb thermometers are obtained from self-registering thermometers:—

The mean height of the barometer for the year was	30·084	
Highest reading (corrected) of barometer . .	30·372 at 9½ A.M. Aug. 8	
Lowest " " . .	29·717 at 3½ P.M. Feb 7	
Mean daily barometric oscillation	0· 60	
Mean temperature of year	79· 2°	
Highest reading of maximum dry bulb ther. in shade	93· 2° Feb. 19	Range 25.6°
Lowest " minimum " "	67· 6° Aug. 23	
Highest reading of maximum wet bulb "	82· 0° Jan. 26	Range 24·1°
Lowest " minimum " "	57· 9° Aug. 7	
Highest dew point (from the six-hourly observations)	77· 7° Jan. 25	Range 28·7°
Lowest " " "	49· 0° Aug. 6	
Highest tension of vapour	·949 Jan. 2	Range ·602
Lowest "	·347 Aug. 5	
Highest relative humidity (1·0 = compl. sat.) .	·865 Feb. 2	Range ·445
Lowest " "	·410 Dec. 14	
Rainfall during the year	54·535 inches.	
Greatest fall in twenty-four hours	8·00 inches.	
Number of days on which rain fell . . .	120	

Dependencies of Mauritius.

The following islands are reckoned in the Dependencies of Mauritius, and receive supplies of all sorts from it.

There are many other small islands, but mostly barren rocks. Some are merely coral atolls, notably so the Cosmoledo group. The two small islands, St. Paul and Amsterdam, so far south as 37° and 38° S. lat., 78° E. long., also form part of the dependencies of Mauritius, though seldom visited, except by the whalers of the Southern Seas.

From the six islands great quantities of cocoa-nut oil are sent yearly to Mauritius, and salted fish from the St. Brandon Isles and Rodrigues. Our American whalemen cruise constantly in the waters near these islands, and numbers of vessels are annually laden with the spoils of the monster sperm whales found in this vicinity. The whole of the islands have dangerous reefs near them, compelling the most careful navigation when approaching them. Many a fine vessel has come to grief on these treacherous rocks, and has had to be abandoned, an utter wreck.

Curious and valuable marine and land shells abound, and might easily be procured if the fishermen could be induced to take a little trouble in collecting them. St. Brandon is noted for the beautiful scarlet coral, the *Tubifora musica.*

Names	Latitude S.	Longitude E.	Occupations
	Between	Between	
	° ′ ° ′	° ′ ° ′	
The Cargados Carayos, or St. Brandon Isles, sixteen in number.	16 15 and 16 57	50 0 and 60 0	Fishing.
Agalega	10 30	56 30	Cocoa-nut plantations.
Cortivy	7 30	56 30	Ditto.
The Perhos Banhos, twenty-five in number.	5 10 and 5 25	71 45 and 72 0	Ditto.
Solomon's or Onze Isles .	5 17 and 5 22	71 13 and 73 18	Ditto and wood-cutting.
Nelson Island or Ségour .	5 41	72 22	
Trois Frères . . .	6 6 and 6 10	71 34 and 71 38	Ditto.
Eagle Isles, two in number.	6 10 and 6 15	71 21 and 71 24	
Isle au Danger . .	6 23	71 17	
The Six Islands . .	6 39	71 20 and 71 27	Ditto.
Diego Garcia . . .	70 0	72 0 and 73 0	Ditto.
Rodrigues . . .	19 41	63 23	Various.
The Seychelles, thirty-five or thirty-six in number.	3 43 and 5 45	55 13 and 56 10	Cotton and Sugar, Tobacco, Maize, Oranges, Coffee and the Coco de Mer.
The Cosmoledo group, four or five in n u mbe	9 50 and 10 0	48 35 and 48 44	
Providence . . .	9 12	51 10	Fishing.
Astove	10 9	47 48	Ditto.
Isle St. Pierre . .	9 18	50 53	Ditto.
Assumption . . .	9 44	46 34	Ditto.
Aldabra	9 22	45 50	Ditto.
The Amirautés, seventeen in number.	40 51 and 6 15	53 56 and 53 43	Cocoa-nut plantations.

The most important of all the groups is that of the Seychelles. I have always had a great wish to visit it, but have hitherto been unable to accomplish it. The few notices of the islands I have met with are so scanty, that I gladly avail myself of the permission to use some notes lent me by my good friend the Hon. Swinbourne Ward, made at the time he was Civil Commissioner at Mahé. These notes are very copious, especially on the natural history of the Seychelles (on which it is not my intention to touch, except very lightly.) And it is to them I am indebted for the information now given. The group constituting the Seychelles Archipelago was discovered by the Portuguese, but not thought worth their occupation. It was taken possession of by the French in 1742, and it was named

Les Isles des Labourdonnais; but later the name was changed to that of Seychelles, after Viscount Hérault de Seychelles. In 1792 they were captured by the British man-of-war 'Orpheus,' under Captain Newcombe. The French commandant capitulated, and was allowed to retire with the honours of war. However, as Captain Newcombe could not remain to take possession, he requested the French officer to continue his governorship under the British flag. This curious arrangement actually took place, and lasted for some years. The French still kept a sort of hold there, and it was not till the peace in 1814 that the Seychelles was definitely ceded to Britain.

Shortly after this period these islands attained a high degree of prosperity. Large quantities of cotton were grown of the finest quality, and many fortunes were made. A great change however took place in 1827, when America began to fill the European markets with her cotton; prices lowered, and the trade gradually dwindled away.

Mahé, the principal of the group, named after Labourdonnais, is about seventeen miles long. Only the littoral, and a portion of the south of the Island, are available for purposes of agriculture; the rest being a series of lofty mountains, of granite formation, the 'Morne Blanc' rising to the height of 2,000 feet. In the interstices of the enormous granite boulders and on the plateaux grow fine timber trees.

The town of Port Victoria overlooks a fine harbour, extending four miles each way, enclosed on all sides but the north by a chain of small islets, forming a natural breakwater. The harbour will contain at least 300 vessels, but on account of the vast coral beds, and numerous reefs, it is a difficult port to make. It is impossible to enter it without a pilot at night, from the intricate and badly marked-out channel.

The temperature of the Seychelles, though they lie so near the Line, is much cooler than might be expected. The average mean day temperature is from 80° to 87° Far.; the night, from 70° to 74°. May is the hottest month. The constant breeze prevents the heat being oppressive, and it is always healthy, and blow which way it will, there are no marshes for it to pass over, and become laden with miasmatic vapours. Either 'Siroc' or 'Land Wind' is unknown. Healthy as the climate is, with epidemics unheard of, the inhabitants are yet subject to some of the direst diseases that afflict the human frame. They are far from cleanly in their habits and persons, and their principal meat is pork, and such pork, mostly fed on the garbage of the streets. The constant use of this most unwholesome food in a tropical climate poisons the blood, and is the root of many of the hideous diseases the people suffer from—hydrocele, sarcocele, elephantiasis, leprosy, &c. It is easy to trace its work—indigestion, dyspepsia, scrofula, leprosy, death!

The inhabitants are mostly mixed races. Some few of pure French descent remain; but the great admixture of African blood has brought African indolence, want of truth, addiction to sensual pleasures, and an amount of *want* of energy so great, that such a *rara avis* as a hard-working man scarcely exists in the island.

Life is so easy; and their only luxuries being rum and tobacco, which are so easily produced, no one takes more trouble than he or she can possibly help. The waters all round the shore abound with fine fish, captured without any difficulty; manioc, their principal food, only requires a piece of the cut stalk to be placed in the ground, where it grows of itself; the juice of the sugar-cane gives them rum, and can be bought at 1*s.* 6*d.* a bottle; and the finest tobacco is grown with little or no cultivation.

The only item of any financial importance of the present day is cocoa-nut oil, for which a good market is always found at Mauritius. In 1862 the value of oil exported was over 10,000*l.*; and if proper machinery were used, instead of the old wooden mills, a sort of pestle-and-mortar affair, and worked by an ox, such as has been used from time immemorial in India and Ceylon, the yield would be double that quantity.

Vacoa bags for sugar are made by the lower class of women.

Tobacco might be exported very largely, and of the best quality, but no care is taken in its manufacture, which is of the rudest.

The coasts abound with green turtle, and the hawk's-bill turtle, from which the tortoise-shell of commerce is procured. The latter are, however, daily diminishing, and the former will soon abandon these shores to seek for a more undisturbed retreat to lay their eggs in. The flesh of the green turtle is used largely as food, and is, in fact, their beef. Only a very small portion of the shell can be used, and that merely for the commonest veneering purposes, yet enormous numbers are killed for that alone. In 1862, 600 lbs. of 'cawan,' as it is called, were exported, and it is calculated 1,800 turtles were sacrificed for it, leaving, on an average, 490,000 lbs. weight of flesh to rot on the beach.

The Bêche de Mer, or Trepang, is very abundant near some of the islands, and might be made a profitable article of export to Singapore, also the fins and flukes of sharks. Many kinds of voracious monsters are common here:—*Trygon Uarnak* (M. and H.), the ferocious Hammerhead, *Zygæna malleus* (Shaw), the 'Demoiselle,' or Tiger Shark, *Stegostoma fasciatum* (Mull. and Hen.). The 'L'Endormi,' or Basking Shark, *Rhynchobatus ancylostomus* (Blk.), grows large, but has no teeth, only a hard long ridge; is harmless and stupid. The 'Chagrin,' *Rhinodon typicus* (Smith), is frequently found fifty feet long. Two species of sawfish are known to the fishermen—the *Pristis antiquorum* and *Pristiphorus cirratus*. The 'Ray bouclé, *Urogymnus asperrimus*, and 'Ray Vache,' *Aëtotatis narinari* (Mull. and Hen.), are caught near the shores, and easily speared with the grains of a three-pronged harpoon: a single barbed spear is not enough to hold them. The Bone Shark, described by whalemen as often seventy feet long, will yield as much as 500 gallons of oil from its liver. The 'Devil Fish' is another monster of these seas, and gives rare sport in its capture; and among the giants of the deep must not be forgotten the 'Predatory Whale,' *Ginglymostoma brevicaudatum* (Gunth).

Smaller fish of hundreds of species are so abundant near many of the islands, that it is a common saying among the the fishermen, that 'There's more fish than water.'

Internal Communication, &c., in Mauritius.

There are main roads leading from Port Louis to the principal places in the Island. Nearly all are macadamised and kept in order by Government, while those diverging to various estates are attended to by the owners. Where pains are taken by the proprietors to improve the appearance of their plantations as well as their profits, the roads through the cane-fields are bordered with the Vetivert, *Anatherum muricatum* (Beauv.), a pretty fragrant grass, a native of India, from which a fine essence is extracted. Formerly the roads were made by the soldiers; then by Sepoys, convicts from India; and now by bands of Indians, mostly prisoners, employed under the supervision of inspectors.

For some years two lines of railway have been in use, and have wonderfully changed the character of the inland traffic. They have become invaluable to the colony since the great influx of people into the country, away from the vitiated air of Port Louis. They are beginning now to bring in all the produce of the estates by rail; and, as the wishes and convenience of the majority of the proprietors are being studied by the Government, it is hoped they will be able to liquidate very soon some of the heavy debt incurred in the construction.

The North line, opened for traffic in May, 1864, passes the following stations:—Terre Rouge, Callebasses, Pamplemousses, Mapou, Poudre d'Or, Rivière du Rempart, Flacq, Argy, and Rivière Sèche, terminating at Grand River SE., a distance of thirty miles from the city. This route has little interest, beyond the Pamplemousses gardens and village, and the ranges of hills lying to the right of the road. Nearly the whole is laid out in cane fields; and the country is monotonous in the extreme, especially in long protracted dry weather, when the canes look miserable, and all nature generally lies under a heavy coating of dust.

The maximum gradient on this line is 1 in 80 feet; and, at its highest, only rises to the height of 329 feet above the sea, a little beyond Pamplemousses. There are fourteen bridges of stone and iron, with spans varying from twenty-five to eighty feet.

The Midland line is far more interesting. It passes the stations of Pailles, Coromandel, Petite Rivière, Beau Bassin, Rose Hill, Quatre Bornes, Phœnix, Vacoas, Curepipe, Cluny, Rose Belle, Mare d'Albert, and Union Vale, terminating at Mahébourg, a distance of 35¼ miles.

The gradients of this line are very steep, frequently 1 in 27 feet. Just beyond Curepipe the elevation is 1,822 feet above sea-level. There are 21 bridges. The principal are:—the St. Louis River bridge, with a single span of 90 feet, 25 feet from the bed of the river, and the viaduct over Grand River of 5 spans, 126 feet each, supported on fine pillars, and rising to a height of 140 feet above the ravine, through which Grand River flows. From the time of leaving Port Louis the scenery is grand on this line, that is, for those with an appreciative eye for mountain ranges. Their forms change with every turn of the road, and as you gradually rise to Curepipe the configuration of the Island is admirably seen. Those magnificent broken walls of the old-time craters, gigantic barriers of long extinguished fires, stand, and most likely will stand while time lasts, as open books, wherein are clearly recorded the wondrous facts of other eras. Of all classes, those who seem most to appreciate the iron roads are the Indians, who use them on every possible occasion, and on fête days they swarm like bees round every station. The rates of traffic have been, and indeed still are, very high; but the directors have seen fit to make some concessions to the public of late, and they are already finding their benefit in it. The planters of Savane are trying to get a branch line to their district, which produces sugar largely, and it is possible they may succeed when the railway debt is worked down to somewhat lesser dimensions.

The inland mails were formerly despatched in mail carts daily to the principal places in the Island; but now a post office is established at nearly all the stations, a great convenience for those in the country. They have not, however, discovered the advantages of a penny post, for that sum is required for a newspaper, and twopence for a letter.

A telegraph has been established along the railway lines, but does not as yet appear to give much satisfaction.

Post-Office and Foreign Telegraph Scheme.

The General Post-Office, as well as all other civil establishments, is in Port Louis. There are letter-boxes disposed in various parts of the city, and two daily deliveries of letters take place. The mails for Europe and elsewhere leave once a month by the steamers of the Messageries Impériales Company, at a great cost to the colony. Formerly the service was performed by the steamers of the P. & O. Company, for which was paid 36,000*l.* annually. Foreign postage is very high, particularly *viâ* Marseilles; and freights for packages most extortionate, 1*l.* per square foot being exacted.

Once a month also arrive the mails, and only those who have lived in the Colonies can realise the excitement of this one day. Telescopes are incessantly levelled at the signal mountains in city and country; and when the double balls are seen at the top of the signal mast, the Place d'Armes, quays and docks are gradually thronged. As soon as the steamer anchors, boats innumerable put off up the harbour, and only wait the signal that she has received pratique (that is, shown a good bill of health), when her decks are at once crowded to get the first items of news, and welcome the passengers. A rise or fall in sugar, war or peace news, flies like magic to the shore and spreads through the city. Then the tedious waiting for letters. Supposing the mail arrives early morning, it will be at least two or three o'clock before any letters are delivered, save Government despatches.

After being accustomed to the constant delivery of mails in America, I found it very trying to have to wait a whole month for news; and such constant changes are made in the departure of mails, that often when our solitary one arrives, the chances are half our letters do not come, our friends not being at once aware of the change of date. When the colony was more prosperous there was a second mail per month, *viâ* Aden, and one by the United States Ship Company, *viâ* the Cape. But these are of the things that were, and I doubt will be long ere they are again.

There has been much talk of a marine telegraph to connect Mauritius with India and Australia, and proposals have been talked over with both the Cape and India, but no result hitherto; the finances of the colony not allowing of the necessary expenditure. Mauritius must, I suppose, in the ordinary course of things, be one day included in the 'Girdle round the world,' but he would be a rash man who predicted *when* such an event would take place. It took about sixteen or eighteen years for gas to be *talked over* before it became an accomplished fact. I believe the Mauritians beat the Yankees out and out in *talk*. They have been *talking* of sanitary measures for Port Louis for twenty years, and yet its gutters still give forth the foulest stenches.

Hackney Coaches, &c.

Port Louis has a supply of vehicles for hire always ready on the Place d'Armes, and at several livery stables. The owners are obliged to have a tariff of charges posted up in their carriages (as they are called) and carrioles. The ordinary fare of the former for a single person is one shilling, and half price for a second to any place within the city limits, and two shillings for the longer distances, as prescribed by law. They may, however, be hired for a dollar the hour for three or four passengers. Almost all have been private carriages, too shabby for their owners, sold cheaply and furbished up a little for the stand. Formerly, these carriages were the only means of transport to the country, when the proprietor could make his own bargain, as he can now for that matter, anywhere beyond the prescribed limits. Of course there is but little call for hired carriages into the country since the establishment of railways, but incessant and regular traffic to and from the central station in Port Louis, especially on a rainy day, must nearly be an equivalent for the loss.

The carrioles are two-wheeled vehicles, most miserable shaky affairs, with no steps, and only a seat behind the driver, but in great request with Indians; the Chinamen, however, principally affect the carriages.

Defences: Military, Naval, and Police.

The position of Mauritius and its possession of so fine a harbour, docks, &c., have always rendered it of great importance to its government, giving it the command of the Indian Seas. With it France kept her footing in the waters, and was enabled to do infinite mischief to the Indian commerce of all other nations—a power lost to her for ever since the conquest of their Isle de France. England ruled this ocean for years after she became mistress of the Island, and it was literally a 'Half-way house' to all outward or homeward bound vessels to and from the East. It was strongly fortified, and could, if well defended, have defied its enemies. Forts George and William protect the harbour, Fort Adelaide commands the city; Mahébourg has a battery; there are military posts at Black River, Flacq, Grand Rivers NW. and SE., and many others now given up to the police. All this sounds well, but with the appliances and material of modern warfare, Mauritius would be 'knocked into a cocked hat' in no time.

Two regiments of the line, and detachments from the Royal Artillery and Engineers, were regularly stationed here, making a total force of 2,000 men. Now it is not considered necessary to keep more than a single battalion, with a few artillery and engineers. This is a great relief to the heavily taxed colony, which had to pay 45,000*l.* annually as its quota towards the military establishment.

Many causes have concurred to place Mauritius in a far different position from that it formerly enjoyed. The prevalence of steamers over sailing vessels, preventing the necessity for constantly calling here for water and provisions; the opening of the Suez Canal, giving a nearer route to the East than the long voyage round the Cape; the terrible reverses of the colony, compelling them to relinquish direct communication with India and the Cape, except by the single monthly mail; all have had a telling effect on the Island. Besides these outward influences, there are many internal ones which have a powerful tendency to assist in her depreciation.

The whole system of the customs, port dues, and in fact all connected with the shipping, is calculated to prevent foreign ships entering. No appeals are of any effect to get fair and liberal arrangements, and the decline in the shipping tells its own tale. Formerly, nearly all our large fleet of whalemen put in here, and left an enormous sum annually for supplies. They have, however, been charged such exorbitant rates for everything, from money downwards, and such heavy fees for custom and port duties, that they are nearly all leaving for Bourbon and the Cape. These places welcome them gladly, and give them fair and reasonable accommodation. The docks erected at such expense, where every repair a vessel needs can be done, yet lie idle two-thirds of the time, vessels fearing to come here on account of the extravagant charges for the smallest repairs. The Cape Town Docks will cut out the Mauritius ones, on account of their liberal terms, and the greater expedition of the work.

The police force has increased greatly of late years, and is taking the place of the military. They are in a fair state of discipline, considering the heterogeneous, and difficult to deal with, classes it is composed of—runaway sailors, discharged whalemen, seedy clerks, loafers of all nations, and men of all colours and races.

They are under an inspector-general (of late years always a military officer), a superintendent, and adjutant; and they have a large staff of inspectors, sergeants, and corporals, besides the numerous body of constables. The cost to the colony yearly for police, prisons, &c., is nearly 70,000*l.*

The naval defence of these seas consists of seven of H. B. M.'s men-of-war, with their head-quarters at the Cape, and others called the Western African Division. It is rarely that any one of these vessels visits Mauritius, but they can easily be brought if required.

Money, Weights and Measures, &c.

The coinage in use in ordinary transactions is chiefly decimal. All persons in business use dollars and centièmes; the dollar, a fictitious coin of 100 centièmes, passing for 4*s.* ordinarily, but in reality only worth 95 cents. Then all English coins pass: the rupee 2*s.* or 50 cents, half a crown 2*s.* 6*d.* or 62½ cents, shilling or 25 cents, sixpence or 12½ cents, with threepenny and fourpenny pieces, pennies 2 cents, or a gros cash, half-pennies, centièmes or cash; silver 3 cent pieces or 6 sous, farthings or sous, and a 3-farthing or 3 sous. The French francs, 20 cents, and half francs 10 cents, were in constant use till lately, but are not now legal tender. Besides these, the livre, also 10 cents, though only a nominal coin, was in great vogue, and the Creoles still use it. Such an amount of coins in circulation, and their various names, make a curious jumble, and it gives a stranger no end of worry, time and trouble, before he can become familiar with them. The Indians are not nearly such ready reckoners as the Creoles. They know little of the decimal parts of the various coins. They would not understand 93 centièmes, but tell them a thing costs a dollar less 7 cents, and they are all right. They have certain standpoints, but they are mostly taken from livres; thus, 3 livres 10 sous or 35 cents, 7 livres 10 sous or 75 cents, 6 livres 5 sous or 62½ cents, and so on, and any between sums you must count as so many *cash*, less or more than one of these standpoints. They know all English coins well enough, and their English names too, and never fail to take advantage of your lack of knowledge in *cashes.* The 3 sous or marquee is invaluable in the petty dealings with the Chinamen, and it is curious to see how many things are sold by a 3-sous worth. It is a queer thin flat coin, with the fleur-de-lis of France on one side, and a palm tree on the reverse, with a motto showing its destination was the Isle of France and

Bourbon. I have some dated 1775 still in good preservation. It appears to have been a universal coin in the old slave times, and is a favourite way of calculating amongst the older Creoles; thus, 25 marquees are 37½ cents or 1*s.* 6*d.*, 16 for a shilling, 8 for sixpence, and so on; and all the cake-sellers (who are Legion) always vend their wares by 3 sous or 6 sous.

In Government offices, English pounds shillings and pence are the legal tender; other coins are used, and the following table will show their value.[1]

GOLD.

	£	s.	d.
Doubloon of Spain, Mexico, or the States of South America	3	4	0
Gold mohur of the East India Company, coined since September 1, 1835 . .	1	9	2
Twenty-franc piece of France	0	15	10

SILVER.

	£	s.	d.
Rupee of East India Company Territory, coined since September 1, 1835 . .	0	1	10
Dollar of Spain, Mexico and States of South America	0	4	2
Five, two, and one franc pieces of France; five francs of English Colonial money coined at the Royal Mint, of the same weight and fineness of Spanish dollar	0	3	10½
Dollar	0	4	4
Half dollar	0	2	2
Quarter dollar	0	1	1
Eighth dollar	0	0	6½
Sixteenth dollar	0	0	3¼
Dollar Decaen	0	4	0
Token	0	0	8

The following are the weights and measures in general use in the colony:—

In the transactions with the Military Commissariat Department, imperial weights are used; in other transactions they are the same as those in France before the introduction of the metrical system in 1799, viz.:—

[1] See Blue Book for 1869.

100 lbs. French, *Poids de marc*, equal to 108 lbs. English, and the same proportions in the subdivisions, which are the ounce, gros, and grains.

16 ounces	make	one	pound
8 gros	,,	,,	ounce
72 grains	,,	,,	gros.

The Quintal is 100 lbs. French.

The Ton 20 quintals.

Sugar is reckoned per pound or per quintal.

Coffee per bag or 100 lbs. nett French.

Cotton per bale or 250 lbs.

Rice is sold per bag of 150 lbs.

Measures.—In military transactions only imperial measures are used, but those for other purposes are French.

The French foot is to the English in the proportion of 100 to 92·89, or in common practice as 16 to 15.

12 lines	make	one	inch
12 inches	,,	,,	foot
6 feet	,,	,,	toise
5 feet	,,	,,	fathom.

The Aune is forty-four inches, and is to the English yard as nine to seven; every kind of cloth is measured and sold in this Island by the aune or ell.

The Velte is equal to one gallon, seven pints 4-5 English, but is always taken as two gallons. One gallon = 0·608915 veltes, 5 gallons = 3 veltes.

In commercial transactions it is by the velte that every liquid is measured.

3 gills / 4 ,,	make	one	pint
2 pints	,,	,,	quart
3 quarts	,,	,,	gallon
2 gallons	,,	,,	velte.

Nine English quart-bottles are generally considered equal to a velte and 40 drams to a gallon.

A cask measures 30 veltes.

The ton of sugar 2,000 lbs. French

,, coffee 1,400 ,, ,,

,, ebony wood 2,000 lbs. French.

The ton of cotton 750 lbs. French.
" cloves 1,000 " "
" grain 2,000 lbs. or 13 bags of 150 lbs.
" liquids 120 veltes.
" square cut timber 32 cubic feet.
" boards 386 feet.
" shingles 3,000 in number.
The arpent or acre is 100 square perches.
The perch is 20 feet French.
The tonnage of cases is 42 cubic feet measurement.

These are all the legal weights and measures as published in the Government Blue Books.

'Thus the limit of *mass* is the French pound.[1] The unit of *length* is the *toise* of 6 feet. The *toise* of *Pérou*, made in Paris, 1735, by Langlois, under the direction of Godin, is a bar of iron which has its standard length at the temperature of 13° Réaumur. It is known as the toise of Pérou because it was used by the French Academicians, Bougner and La Condamine, in their measurement of an arc of the meridian in Peru.

'The unit of area for land is the arpent of 40,000 French or 45,434 English feet; i.e. add 4⅓ per cent. to convert arpents into English acres.

'Water from canals is estimated by the *prise*, or quantity that issues from a circular orifice of specified diameter and immersion, equal to 5 gallons English per minute.

'The force of *gravity* has been determined for Mauritius experimentally by Freycinnet and Duperez, using the second for the unit of time, and the English foot for the unit of space, and the mean value obtained in absolute units was 32·115; the calculated value.

'Claraut's formula is 32·108 for sea-level, and 32·102 for 2,000 feet altitude. It may be noted the value for Greenwich is 32,191, whence, in a comparison of the mercurial barometer with Greenwich or Masses by spring balances, a small correction becomes necessary.

'The *range* of the tide has never been very accurately determined for this Island; but approximately it may be taken at

[1] See Mauritius Almanack for 1870—article by M. Connal, Esq. C.E.

2 feet for spring tide, and the complement of the Port at one hour.'

It would appear that the British Government, after the conquest of the Island, to conciliate the French inhabitants, left them the greater part of their laws as well as their language; and in over sixty years little change has been made, which renders it very difficult for Englishmen and foreigners to become conversant with the intricacies of the laws and commercial regulations. Instead of a thorough knowledge of English being the absolute necessity for the English colony of Mauritius, it is imperative on anyone hoping to succeed to have the French language at his finger ends, or at least the French spoken here, which is far from being Parisian.[1]

Banks, Crédit Foncier, &c.

There are three banks established, the Commercial Bank, the oldest here, a branch of the Chartered Mercantile Bank of India, London and China, and the Oriental Bank Corporation. The latter owns a fine property in the Chaussée, where a large staff of clerks find constant employment. The building is commodious and handsomely furnished. The clerks are, most of them, sent from England, and the continuation of their appointments rests on their good behaviour: they receive large salaries, and are most of them young gentlemen of good education. They keep up their English proclivities by their hospitable entertainments; and once a year they give a select dancing party, at which the Governor and his lady attend.

A large business is carried on by this bank, and a good deal of accommodation is allowed to planters; but as a rule their rates of interest are higher than those of the other two banks.

The Crédit Foncier of Mauritius, Limited, and a branch of

[1] I beg leave to quote the words of a friend (an Englishman) which appear to me particularly appropriate to this subject.

'One great mistake we have always made in our colonies and conquests. Few or no attempts have been tried to introduce our language, habits, and laws, and unless acquainted with all these, it is impossible a stranger can perfectly comprehend our character. They appreciate the justice of laws, and fairness of our rule over that of many other nations, and yet we have taken little pains to enforce them. It would be a hard matter now to substitute English laws, as the French system is far more lucrative for the swarms of lawyers who crowd every court of justice in the Island.'

the Ceylon Company, Limited, are both in a flourishing condition. These have for their object to make advances to the planters for the efficient working of their estates.

There are no less than nineteen Insurance offices; four local, the rest agencies for European and Australian Companies.

Chambers of Commerce and Agriculture.

Everything in the Island connected with its commercial and agricultural affairs is regulated by the Chambers of Commerce and Agriculture. The members of both are chosen from the leading men of the colony, and are frequently called upon as arbitrators in difficult cases in which the above interests are concerned. Their endeavours are also directed towards the advancement of any industry available for the colony.

The Various Industries of Mauritius.

Of course, pre-eminent stands the culture of sugar, which is carried to great perfection; and the distilling of rum from the dregs of the sugar is next in importance. There are no less than 255 sugar estates, all in work, and 41 distilleries, the latter yielding nearly 500,000 gallons annually, and the former averaging between two and three million pounds a year.

With the increase of sugar estates in cultivation has grown a corresponding increase in mechanical trades. Blacksmiths, coopers, wheelwrights, saddlers, workers in machinery, are numerous. Carpenters and stonemasons are in constant request; all kinds of buildings requiring incessant attention to repairs, from the destructive action of the climate upon woodwork, and the inferior quality of the lime used for mortar rendering even stonework perishable, to say nothing of the ever-encroaching *caries*, wherever damp enters. Yet, in spite of this, house-owners appear to possess all the *laissez-aller* of the Island; for it is not uncommon to see a fine building in a most dilapidated condition before its proprietor thinks it worth his while to repair it, and then most probably it has to be half pulled to pieces to get out all the caries-eaten wood.

During the hurricane season large numbers of workmen obtain employment in the docks; and at such seasons, and when the sugar crop is ready for shipping, all trades flourish that are connected with the marine.

Jewellers' shops abound, from the grand establishment in the Chaussée, where you may gratify your taste in French gold and jewels, and lighten your pocket of fabulous sums, to the little rooms, a few feet square, where an Indian works all day mending trinkets for his countrywomen, or boring holes in gold and silver coins, for necklaces for these same jewel-loving dames. Very often when the possessor is hard up, these holes are filled with some base metal, and the coins passed at the boutiques. So great indeed was the trade in them, that it was taken in hand by the police, and it is now illegal to pass any coin that has been bored. They are, however, so cunningly wrought that you have to look out sharply when you take change from Creole, Chinaman, or Indian, and, even then, the chances are that *you're done.*

Provision shops seem to be the most numerous of any in the Island: whole streets are lined with them. Some stored with delicacies from France and England; but hundreds of them so dingy and dirty, that one wonders how anyone could be tempted to eat anything out of them, eyes and nose being equally disgusted.

In numbers of the stores you may purchase a vast diversity of articles; for instance, in your ironmonger's you may order a ream of writing paper with your saucepans, and seeds for your garden with the spade to dig it.

Foreign Commerce.

The Foreign Commerce of Mauritius extends to every quarter of the globe. Ships showing the flags of all nations may be seen during the year in the harbour of Port Louis.

Sugar and rum being the only staple articles of export, everything for the general wants of the inhabitants must be imported. It is curious to read the lists of imported articles supposed to be requisites for general need. The most incongruous possible, or would be so, but for the strangely mixed population. The imports appear to be very large for so small a place; but it serves now as an entrepôt for Madagascar, and the Dependencies are supplied from it. In one year the value of these imports amounted to 12,190,000 dollars.

The principal countries from which they are derived are: Great Britain, India, Australia, France, the Cape, Madagascar,

Peru, Pondicherry, Singapore, Réunion, United States, Ceylon, the Dependencies, &c.

The following items will show the extent of trade carried on when the colony is flourishing during a single year:—

10,980 oxen; 220 horses; 1,194 mules; 73,000 gunny bags and 47,500 vacoa bags, for sugar; 864,000 bricks and tiles; 118 carriages; 19,000 tons of coal; 75,000 cwts. of dholl; 171,000 cwts. of grain; 1,109,603 cwts. of rice; 38,800 qrs. wheat; 29,459 cwts. of flour; cotton goods to the value of 500,000*l.*; 215,893 pieces of glassware; 20,926 looking-glasses; haberdashery and millinery valued at 56,280*l.*; hardware and cutlery, 91,624*l.*; 420 tons of ice; 1,744 cwts. of leather; and 178,599 boots and shoes; machinery to the value of 25,500*l.*; 5,691 cwts. potatoes; 14,000 yards of silk; 56,000 gallons of brandy; 26,713 lbs. of tea; 986,898 lbs. of manufactured tobacco: 25,143 hhds. and 25,271 dozens of wine, &c. &c. These are only a very small portion of the imports, but they will give a fair idea of their range.

Since the fever, a change has taken place in the imports of articles of luxury, which are greatly reduced; though recovering from the effects of the epidemic, the failure of the crops for several years, in comparison with the expectations, has caused a general decadence in all commercial affairs. Fewer ships are needed to convey the sugar, and less goods can be imported; business of all kinds suffers, everything connected with the marine is stagnant, and universal complaints are heard, and not without cause. It is difficult to surmise at the present time what *can* give new life to the colony, except very heavy crops, and they will soon be subject to such competition from other countries, that new industries *must* be found, if Mauritius is ever to make head against her commercial embarrassments.

CHAPTER XXVI.

THE GOVERNMENT OF MAURITIUS AND ITS VARIOUS ESTABLISHMENTS, WITH THE DIFFERENT RELIGIONS IN THE COLONY.

The Chief Officers of the Government—The various Departments—Savings' Bank—Episcopal Church of Port Louis—Other Protestant Churches in the Colony—Roman Catholic Sacred Edifices—Convents—Mohammedan Mosque—Its Worship—Fast and Feast—Catholic Fête-Dieu—Procession—Raising the Host, &c.

LIKE all the British Colonies, Mauritius is under the control of the Secretary of State for the Colonies, who appoints a Governor, subject to Her Majesty's approval, and is assisted by a Legislative Council.

The official members are :—

His Excellency the Governor, the officer commanding the troops, the Colonial Secretary, the Procureur and Advocate-General, the Colonial Treasurer, the Auditor-General, the Collector of Internal Revenues, and the Collector of Customs. The four first named constitute the Executive Council.

The ten non-official members are selected by the Governor, nominated for life, but subject to the Queen's approval.

The laws passed by the Council are called 'Ordinances,' and discussions, amendments, and additions accompany every Act.

From a mixture of the English and French laws being in use, the government is a very complex affair. Most of the laws of the Code Napoléon are still in force, though now greatly modified.

I will enumerate the various departments, which will show what intricate machinery has to be daily set going and kept in working order to carry on the government of this speck in the ocean :—

The Council Office, Colonial Secretary's Office, the Treasury,

Savings' Bank and Audit Office, Survey or General Department, Botanical Gardens, Observatory, Museum, Civil Status, Customs, Port Department, Internal Revenue, Registration and Mortgage Departments, Post Office, Supreme Court, Procureur and Advocate-General's Office, Vice-Admiralty Court.

District magistracy, senior and junior magistrates of Port Louis, stipendiary magistrates for Pamplemousses, Rivière du Rempart, Grand Port, and Plaines Wilhelms. Police force and gaols.

District and stipendiary magistracy for Flacq, Savane, Black River and Moka.

Churches of England and Scotland.

Roman Catholic clergy.

Royal College Government schools, Orphan Asylum.

Medical department, Quarantine establishment.

General Board of Health.

Commissariat and Stamp office.

Land Court and Archives.

Railway construction and working department.

Poor Law Commission, and Immigrant department, Crown agents, and the affairs of Seychelles and Rodrigues.

No wonder the sum of 800,000*l.* or 900,000*l.* per annum is demanded. The Governor alone of this little Island receives nearly 7,000*l.*, while the President of the United States only has 25,000 dollars, and all other Government officers are paid in proportion.

In a work like this it would be out of place to enter into a detail of the functions of all the above establishments, which would demand volumes to perform satisfactorily, and write of all their uses, and a considerable amount of abuses in many of them. I will merely mention the Savings' Bank, which is beginning to play an important part with the Indian population. It was long before they could be brought to trust their earnings out of their own hands. They are excessively suspicious, and the slightest circumstance is sufficient to induce them to withdraw their money. A very little would destroy their confidence, and cause a run on the bank. However, by convincing them that they can draw out their money at any time, they are, by degrees, changing from a most improvident to a thrifty race. It is but fair to say they distrust each other equally, if not more so, than they do the whites. It is curious to see how readily they avail themselves of the stamped papers, lately made obligatory for all receipts, in their transactions with each other.

In most of the departments the heads are chosen from English, either here or sent from England. Great numbers of Creoles are employed, but almost all in subordinate offices.

The different Forms of Religious Worship, with the principal Sacred Edifices in the Island.

The Episcopal Church is represented by a Bishop, under the title of 'Lord Bishop of Mauritius and its Dependencies' (his diocese extending to the Seychelles Islands), civil and military chaplains; several English clergymen; two native ones for the Tamul and Bengalee churches, and one for the mariners.

The principal building for the use of the Established Church is St. James's Cathedral before mentioned. It was erected, in 1741, for a powder magazine, with walls from eight feet to ten feet thick, a dome-shaped roof, bomb proof, and slits for its only openings. When the British took Mauritius, this ungainly building being no longer required for its original purpose, it was proposed to use it for a Protestant Church. (Would to God that every powder magazine in the whole world could be converted thus!) Square windows were let into the walls, and in 1828 the dome was changed for a new roof, and the present steeple and porticoes were added.

In 1846 the congregation had so increased that two wings were built on, giving it the form of a cross, and an organ gallery was raised. The pews are all of teak wood, and the Communion window is of stained glass, presented by one of the church members. Marble *in-memoriam* slabs cover the walls; and a handsome Gothic monument adorns the chancel, raised to the memory of the Rev. Mr. Banks, who lost his life through his untiring zeal in behalf of the sufferers by the cholera of 1854.

The grounds round the Cathedral are enclosed by a high iron railing, and the avenues to the different entrances are shaded by fine Banyan, and the lovely Bauhinia, and Flamboyant trees.

There are three full services here every Sunday, two in English and one in French, besides one in the early morning for the military when the troops are in Port Louis.

On Wednesday evenings service is also held, but the attendance is very poor since so many English have left the city. There is a school-room attached, but no school has been held there since the time of Bishop Ryan: it is now, however, used for the congregation of St. Mary's, while that church is being rebuilt.

At Pailles, Pamplemousses, Moka, Grand Port, Vacoa, and Plaines Wilhelms are churches, besides temporary ones in various parts of the Island. The Church Missionary and London Societies have been working since 1814, principally among the Indian population.

There are Tamul schools for religious instruction in various places. At Crêve-Cœur there is the principal mission school, where the children are also taught all kinds of useful work. The Rev. Mr. Hobbs and his wife are most energetic in their endeavours to spread the light of Christianity in the dense darkness of superstition and idolatry still surrounding thousands of the population in Mauritius; and though their progress is slow, it will surely do much eventually in changing the moral condition of the Indian races.

In Poudrière Street is a chapel for the Independents, for many years under the charge of the Rev. Mr. Le Brun, and now in his son's hands. Great good has been done among the Creole population (of whom there is a large congregation on Sundays and week evenings) from their system of house to house visiting.

The Wesleyans have lately appeared in the field. A minister was sent here about two years ago, and it is said that he made a great many converts among the soldiers: be that as it may, I believe he has already left the colony, and has not been replaced. They have no chapel.

The only church for the Presbyterian form of worship is well attended.

There is a small number of members of the New Church; but they have no public building for divine service, so for the present they meet at the house of Mr. de Chazal.

The Roman Catholic religion is certainly the prevailing one, and is coeval with the settlement of the French in the Island. It is presided over by a Bishop, who is called 'the Bishop of Port

Louis,' and a large staff of priests. The Catholics, however, like the Protestants, are at this moment without a head. They have seventeen churches and about thirty-two chapels in the different districts.

Their principal building, the Cathedral of Port Louis, is in Government Street, standing in a square shaded by old trees, and its western façade has a distant resemblance to that of Notre Dame in Paris. In front is a fountain, with a large cross near it about ten or twelve feet high. This, on certain days, is hung over with garlands of flowers, and bouquets are placed at its foot in such quantities that I have seen it almost buried beneath them. The Cathedral has the best clock in the city, and its deep tones may be heard nearly to its limits. On the roof are two very unsacerdotal ornaments, two small cannons, that used to be fired on the day of the Fête-Dieu, at the moment the Host is raised on the Champ de Mars. The inside is very plain, the whitewashed walls are covered with a series of paintings representing the various scenes of our Saviour's sufferings previous to His crucifixion. There is a fine altar-piece, and the usual display of golden candlesticks, statues of the Virgin and Saints, and the ordinary paraphernalia of the altar, interspersed with large vases filled with artificial flowers, all votive offerings.

In the month of May, or 'Mois de Marie,' the altar and walls are profusely decorated, at a great expense, with flowers made by the ladies of the congregation, under the superintendence of the Dames de St. Paul.

There are Catholic chapels in all the villages; but the only other in the city is that of the 'Immaculée Conception,' in St. George's Street, a temporary building, in wood, far more elegantly decorated than the Cathedral. This is used pending the erection of a fine edifice in stone, which will be the chef-d'œuvre of the city when completed. I fear this generation will not enjoy its beauty, as it is over twelve years since its foundation-stone was laid, and, except a part of the clock tower, the walls are only about ten or twelve feet high.

There are two Convents, one in Rempart, and the other in Bourbon Street. The former is occupied by the Sœurs de Charité, who devote the greatest part of their time to the care of the sick. They have an hospital adjoining the convent, where many a poor wretch, sick unto death with cholera or fever, has blessed their pious cares and gently tending.

At the Convent of Loretto is a school where numbers of young ladies are educated, or sent for the seclusion necessary for the preparation attendant on their first communion. Behind the Cathedral of Port Louis is the Roman Catholic Bishop's residence; Palace it is called, but realises little of one's ideas of a palatial house, entirely surrounded by an upper and lower verandah, doubtless rendering it very cool in the heat of summer.

In Royal Street stands the Mohammedan Mosque, conspicuous from its white dome and minarets. When completed it will be a fine structure; the small part within that is finished is very handsome, with its tessellated pavement and carved pillars. In the court is a fountain of deliciously cool water, to which descend a flight of steps, where the faithful wash their feet, and leave their slippers before entering the sacred precincts. The whole of the front is a mere shell at present, and a wooden partition screens it from the street, outside of which are little shops of a few feet square lighted up at night, where may be bought cakes, cigars and Turkish slippers, and a barber plies his trade.

This mosque has been already twenty years in building, and it is expected to take ten more before it is completed. The expenses are defrayed by the Arabs and Lascars of the Mohammedan persuasion, and a large fund is yearly raised by an impost of a halfpenny on every bag of rice sold to them. All the stone, lime, and wood are sent from Bombay, and the workmen are nearly all from Calcutta. During the time they are at work, they remain together in the mosque, sleeping and eating under the pillared arches of the outer court.

Every evening the priest calls to the faithful from the minareted roof to come to prayers, and after gun-fire, or 8 o'clock P.M., they begin to pour in.

In the centre of the court is a Badamia tree; and as you stand under it on a clear night, myriads of stars glittering over head, it is not difficult to fancy yourself transported to some Oriental land, where Allah alone is worshipped. The recess where prayers are read is resplendent with the brilliant light from the large chandeliers; the tall white-robed Arabs, after their ablutions, lay aside their belts and upper coats that the free motion of the body may not be impeded during their numerous genuflexions;

and you gaze wonderingly as they keep up an incessant bowing with their foreheads to the ground and rising up to their full height, muttering monotonous responses to the prayers. It appears like a dream as you watch them, and but for the quiet earnestness of their manner, showing their thorough belief in what they are about, it would provoke a smile.

During the daytime they will allow a heretic to enter and examine the place, but in the evening admission is only given to certain limits. They will, however, answer any questions with a politeness which puts to shame the *brusquerie* of English pew-openers.

The 15th of January is the new year of the Mohammedans, and for forty days previously a fast is held, called 'Eid,' during which time food is only allowed to be taken in the evening after sunset. It terminates on this day; and after morning prayers a feast is given in the mosque to all the poor, halt, and blind of their persuasion, who have seats placed for them, and after a hearty breakfast each has a piece of money given him. Every attendant at prayers on the 15th and the preceding day is expected to take some present, either rice, fruit, or money, which is all scrupulously devoted to the feast of the poor.

There is a small mosque at Plaine Vert, for the Lascars, who appear to follow a spurious kind of Mohammedanism.

While on the subject of the various forms of religious worship exercised in Port Louis, it may not be out of place to give a short description of how the principal fête of the Roman Catholics is carried out in Mauritius—the Fête-Dieu.

The Fête-Dieu.

The very words will recall the imposing ceremonies in the imperial city—its interminable processions displaying all the pomp of papacy.

But, alas, what a falling off is here! However small an affair it is to those accustomed to the religious fête days of Italy and Spain, it is a grand day for Port Louis.

From earliest morn the bells of the Cathedral and Church of the Immaculée Conception ring out loudly to call all devout Catholics to the services of the day. It is a general holiday; all public offices are closed, and few women servants are supposed to be in attendance on that occasion.

For weeks previously a special toilette is in course of preparation; many a poor family could speak of scant dinners that all may shine resplendently in new costumes at the Fête-Dieu.

Towards noon crowds pour up the different thoroughfares to the Cathedral, which is decked outside with greenery, and the large cross facing it hung with garlands, and the steps to it covered with bouquets.

Rows of palm and cocoa-nut leaves are carried up Government Street, and continued to the top of the Champ de Mars, where an altar is erected under a sort of arbour.

The police keep the way clear from carriages, and after considerable trouble the procession begins.

Files of women of every shade, from tawny to black, crowned with wreaths of roses, or white veils, or both (contrasting curiously with their dark skins), proceed leisurely up the street; delicate fair girls, dressed in the prettiest costumes, veiled, booted, all in pure white, but in a shower of ribbons and flowers that flutter down from the silken embroidered banners they bear.

Very small fairies, aptly termed 'Les Anges,' trip along, carrying baskets of flowers, and they also wear dainty white satin shoes. I was told that only a few years ago a number of little children, chosen from the best families, were always present, dressed in a white gauzy texture with wings, and their pretty little feet bare. Heat and fatigue and often a heavy shower wetting them through caused such severe illnesses that generally one or more fell victims to the cruel practice, so it has happily been abandoned.

The children of the different Catholic girls' schools are there in great force with their teachers, all in white; but each *pension* has its own peculiar colour for ribbons, trimming, &c. Very demure the older girls look, and the little ones try to imitate them; but it is a failure, their little sparkling eyes betraying their enjoyment of the scene, and that only the severe looks of Madame or Mademoiselle restrain the pretty little romps in order, or the sharp but subdued 'Attention, Mesdemoiselles!' heard along the line.

The boys' schools muster also, dressed in their best.

All the nuns and priests of Port Louis, the Catholic soldiers of the different regiments, the (*soi-disant*) converted Malabars, and crowds of spectators fill up the procession.

In the centre, under a heavy gold embroidered canopy, supported by four gentlemen, walks Monseigneur, bearing the sacred burden with uplifted hands.

The present Bishop[1] is a fine handsome man, and he needs to be a strong one to support the weight of velvet, satin fringes, and tassels he wears, and the heat and fatigue of the procession.

Little boys, in flowing garments, hover round him swinging censers that send forth clouds of incense at intervals. The band of the regiment is in attendance, and plays the most solemn music; and as they cease, the strains are caught up by the priests, and an especial service is chanted nearly the whole way, occasionally joined in by everyone.

Slowly they reach the altar at the head of the Champ de Mars; file after file passes, humbly saluting the raised Cross, and they descend the avenue of palm-leaves in the centre.

By the time Monseigneur arrives at the altar the vast plain is filled with spectators, mostly on foot. As soon as the Bishop prostrates himself before the Cross, a suppressed murmur sweeps through the crowd announcing the fact; a sudden halt takes place, and down on their knees go the whole assembled multitude.

Silence the most profound reigns, as Monseigneur kisses and holds up the Host. Turning to face the crowd, he appeared to be pronouncing a blessing, but, of course, too indistinct to be heard far off. Every male head is uncovered, unless a few not of this faith should be there, and they are instantly conspicuous by the erect posture and hatted head.

After kneeling some time, they rise with a triumphant song of praise that resounds to the farthest limits of the Champ de Mars.

All return down the central avenue to the Cathedral, and often the ceremony is not over till quite dark.

It not unfrequently happens that a smart shower overtakes them when high up on the plain, and then they return home with draggled dresses and drooping banners, in a woful plight.

Formerly the moment the Host was raised, guns were fired from the roof of the Cathedral, but this custom is now dispensed with.

[1] Since writing the above, this gentleman left for the Œcumenical Council, and was taken ill and died in Rome.

CHAPTER XXVII.

THE ROYAL COLLEGE, PRIVATE AND GOVERNMENT SCHOOLS, AND THE MUSEUM.

Schools when the Island was under French Rule—M. Boyer—Assistance given to him—Rules and Course of Instruction in the Colonial College—Its Use as a Hospital—Its Rehabilitation, and new Title—Pupils sent to the Royal College from Abroad—Hurricane in 1824—Repairing Damages—A Pupil sent yearly to England—Disciplinary Reform by Mr. Redle—Causes of Failure—A more practical Education required—A new Rector and new Hopes—Schools suffering from the Fever in 1867—English taught, but small Results—Effect and Show too much sought for in Education—Music—Boys' Schools—Government Schools—Unwillingness of Coolies to be taught—Sums collected notwithstanding Fever—Curious Notes on the Effect of Fever on various Studies—Oriental and Creole Characters—Course of Studies—Number of Schools, Teachers, &c.—Visit to the 'Asile'—State of the Place when first occupied—Its present Aspect—Varied Races—Products of Grounds—Rules and Regulations—Dinner—Drill—Bed-time—First Natural History Society—Its Aims—Its Prospects under Governors Farquhar and Hall—The Society of 1829—Baron Cuvier—Foreign Correspondents and Members—Allowance for a Curator—MM. Desjardins and d'Épinay—The Society's Name in 1847—Exhibitions—The one in 1860—Early Morning Scenes at an Exhibition—Ordinary Articles exhibited—The Visitors—Collections in the Museum—Paintings—M. Louis Bouton.

Several public establishments for the instruction of youth had been tried by the colonists before the one now existing under the title of the Royal College, but although more or less sustained by Government, they never appeared to answer their original purpose, and were all successively abandoned by their promoters.

The best known of these were, the school founded by M. Challan; that of M. Michelet, which bore the title of College, in 1791; and one established by MM. Jobert and Bellon, in 1792, near the Champ de Mars. To these succeeded the collegiate institution of M. Boyer, which may be called the cradle of the present College, which numbered many pupils, and was the most esteemed of all. At this period coloured children were not educated with those of the white population, but there were private schools for them in different parts of the town.

The question of education seems to have been one of great difficulty in those days. It was a choice between sending their children to Europe, to encounter the dangers of the passage and the uncertainty of their being properly cared for when they arrived; or keeping them here under the parental eye, and confiding their instruction to incompetent professors.

Great anxiety was felt as to M. Boyer's success, and when it was found that failure was inevitable unless the Government came to his rescue, the case was laid before the Assembly in 1797. Measures were taken to assist M. Boyer in sustaining his college, to whom a fixed sum was paid monthly from the Treasury.

The establishment then received the title of 'Colonial College;' a committee was chosen from the members of the colonial assembly, which, under the names of 'Instituteurs honoraires,' was charged with the surveillance of this college, and all the schools in the Island.

Fixed rules were laid down for the instruction to be adopted, and a place called 'Vauxhall,' at the Champ de Lort, was chosen where another school, called 'L'École centrale,' was established, to be the fountain head of all other schools, and to it was annexed a drawing department, and one for hydrography.

The Principal and professors were all paid by Government. Annual distributions of prizes were also established, and everything connected with education was entrusted to the commission, and its president received the title of 'Director-general of Public Instruction.'

The central school changed its name under General Decaen to the 'Lycée des Isles des France et Réunion,' some amendments were made in the studies, &c., and military training was added, to the great delight of the pupils.

The taking of the Island by the British gave a temporary shock to this institution. The Lyceum had been evacuated by the pupils by Government order on the expected descent on the town. It was transformed into a hospital for the sick and wounded of the British army. The inhabitants feared this would be the annihilation of their College, but as soon as the most urgent needs of the new government were cared for, Mr. Farquhar took measures to reinstate it; and, after an interval of six months, the 'Colonial College' was re-opened, June 15, 1814. During the time of the French, twenty-four boarders were admitted free by Government, and the English added to them twelve half-boarders.[1]

There were at that time 250 pupils. Boarders paid twenty dollars a month, and half-boarders twelve; day scholars only paying five dollars. They all wore a uniform jacket, with blue sleeves, red collars, and gilt buttons. In 1813 a Professor was appointed to teach the Malagash language, in order to facilitate the intercourse with the island of Madagascar.

Education was ever one of the principal objects of solicitude to Governor Farquhar. He placed the institution under the protection of H. R. H. the Prince Regent (afterwards George IV.), who was graciously pleased to order that for the future it should be called the Royal College, and the choice of professors and committee was reserved for the home Government.

Two vacations of a fortnight only were allowed during the year, which were always preceded by public examinations, and succeeded by a distribution of prizes, given with much ceremony, in presence of the Governor, the civil and military authorities, and a large concourse of spectators. Monthly examinations also took place of the different classes, when silver crosses and divers coloured ribbons were awarded.

To excite the zeal of the students still further, additional prizes were granted, the recipients to be chosen by Government, to enable the pupils whose progress merited such honour to be sent to the European universities. The professors taught the English, French, Latin, and Greek languages; writing, geography, history; mathematics, including navigation, drawing, architecture, botany, physics, and the elements of chemistry.

Such was the estimation in which the College was held, that pupils were constantly sent to it from India, Bourbon, &c.

In 1819 a hurricane injured the building severely, but the still more violent one of February 23, 1823, drove the whole upper part off the basement. One of the professors was seriously injured; and but for the courage of the Rector and professors most of the pupils would have been sacrificed. Sir G. Lowry Cole caused the edifice to be rebuilt on a solid foundation, but it

[1] These were added on the condition that a third of the whole should be of English origin.

was long before its completion. However, a temporary residence was found, and the studies were continued in it with little interruption.

The two former stories of wood were raised on a good stone foundation, and flanked by two wings, each 66 feet long by 30, also of stone.

After the re-opening of the College, the red collar of the uniform was exchanged for a yellow one, and the price of the day scholars was raised to six dollars.

In 1838 great complaints were made as to the changes in the manner of education, and the disorders prevalent.

In 1845 a despatch was published, authorizing the Government to send to England yearly the pupil who most distinguished himself.

It would appear that there must have been lax discipline for many years, till the evil had become so hydra-headed as to need a thorough reorganisation of the whole system.

Disciplinary reform, well conceived and absolutely necessary, was attempted by the late Rector, Mr. Redle, on his arrival.

Some few abuses were corrected, but the new order of things proved a total failure. That gentleman was totally unfitted for his task. In the first place, the fact of his being an Austrian displeased both English and French; his overbearing temper and utter want of conciliation and tact, the 'fortiter in re' ever employed and the 'sauviter in modo' equally ignored, in a post rendered exceedingly difficult to hold in the then state of affairs, prevented the hoped-for advantages accruing from the really commendable reforms he tried to establish. There was constant war between the rector and professors, and the pupils gradually fell off. Mr. Redle through all his career showed himself to be one of those square men, who always try to fit themselves into a round hole; the result may be imagined.

There has always been a magic to the Mauritian people in the words 'Royal College,' which was long the academic grove whence the brightest intelligences received their culture. The rectorship of Mr. Redle nearly ruined it, and notwithstanding its old *prestige*, it will take time before its popularity can be restored. At the present time the private schools are far outstripping the College pupils.

The needful studies for fitting boys for filling positions in the world as engineers, architects, merchants, planters, &c., are completely ignored, whilst too much importance is given to acquiring a little Latin and Greek. Of course the College has sent forth many bright scholars who have done honour to both school and professors, but in the present day they are the exceptions, not the rule.

A fair field is opened to youths both white and coloured, all meet now on equal terms to try the superiority of their intellects. Many of the coloured lads have attained honourable posts by their perseverance; many of those sent to England by Government have belonged to this class, and they have returned to Mauritius as doctors, lawyers, &c.

It is to be hoped that such a thorough reform will take place under the Rector newly installed, that the Royal College will rise again to its former place in the estimation of its true friends. From the prospectus proposed by Mr. Bruce he evidently appears to see very accurately what the requirements of the case are, and if properly aided, will, I do not doubt, prove to be the right man in the right place.

Private and Government Schools.

When everything else was at a standstill during the fever, in 1867, schools naturally suffered to a great extent; and when re-opened, it was long ere parents could be induced to send their children regularly, whilst liable to be struck down at any moment, and perhaps before they could be taken home, the attack was so serious, as either to end fatally, or leave the poor little patient ill for weeks.

Some of the old established schools were nearly ruined; and it was only towards the middle of 1868, that confidence was sufficiently restored for the usual course of study to be resumed.

English is taught in all the schools, but judging from the small amount of it spoken, with no great results; English being the exceptional, not the ruling language.

The rising generation is, however, making greater progress, and I have conversed with young men who have not left the Island who speak well, and write far better English. Some letters I have received from clerks applying for places, or on business, display an amount of grandiloquence quite astounding; though nothing can beat the letters of the Indian Creoles who can write English at all. I have a specimen by me I copy for the benefit of future applicants for help under interesting circumstances.[1]

I find many more English ladies speak French than the reverse. French ladies as a rule are very shy of sporting their knowledge of our language; but I am sure, if they knew how prettily and softly their English with a French accent falls on our ears from their lips, they would be less chary of their speech.

The boys seem to have a better education than the girls, though theirs is far below the European or American standard.

In the schools for the latter, they go in too much for long recitations (for which they have marvellous memories), music, embroidery, and other things that make a show, to leave room for a very solid foundation, except where private tuition has been employed, and there the result is markedly different.

Music is a Creole passion, and it is greatly cultivated, and with success. There are plenty of excellent pianists as teachers, and the most difficult music of the German masters is found in very many families. The system employed, however, tends to make dashing performers, and one often longs for something softer and quieter than a brilliant *morceau* from an opera. Ballad music, except in a few English houses, is unknown; and sacred music, except with the few who sing in the churches, is unheard. Every piano seems scrupulously closed on Sunday; unless in some Catholic family you may chance to hear a stirring waltz or polka, when their day's devotions are over.

The boys' schools are many of them ably conducted, and they have turned out many accomplished scholars. I find amongst the boys generally a woful deficiency in geographical science. It appears to hold the lowest place in Creole estimation, whilst in reality it should be made the connecting link with so many other sciences.

The Government schools have increased greatly within the last twenty years, in spite of the periodical troubles they have passed through since 1850.

I glean the following information from a Report on schools, by Mr. J. Comber Browne, superintendent of government schools, who kindly placed it at my disposal.

[1] See Appendix, p. 511.

Since 1850, repeated visitations of cholera, and the long protracted malarial fever, each in turn nearly brought the schools to a dead stop. In every instance, however, they have survived the shock, and shown a degree of vitality and elasticity truly remarkable.

It is to be regretted, however, that the machinery is still inadequate to meet the growing wants of the colony. Thousands of children are yet unreached, and uninfluenced by any direct civilising agent whatever.

At one time the greatest indisposition was shown by the coolies to submit to any kind of education. This has been overcome, and teachers have been found to undertake the irksome task : funds alone are wanting to carry on the work.

The Government schools are professedly secular as to their curriculum of studies, but in most all the ministers of different creeds have ample facilities for instructing the children in their religious duties.

Since the fever, there have been great difficulties in collecting the fees under pressure of circumstances. 1,050 orphans are on the books ; 870 have lost one parent, and 180 both : of course, on the latter it was impossible to impose a fee. 50 pupils died, and 500 were withdrawn, mostly from sickness. Nevertheless, the sum of 490*l.* was collected during the year 1868.

It appears from official returns that these schools have been productive of great good ; only nine pupils have been tried, and convicted of any crime by the magistrates.

It is stated that a decline of 30 per cent. in point of proficiency in the general range of instruction has taken place.

It is rather curious to note Mr. Browne's remarks on this subject, and they might serve as fertile ideas to be worked out by some philosophic brain.

He says: 'The mechanical subjects, such as mapping and penmanship have not fallen off much ; nor has mental arithmetic fallen greatly into arrear ; but languages and their auxiliaries have suffered considerably.'

The teachers have uphill work to contend with in the peculiar vices of the native population. Falsehood, petty thefts, and absence of self-help are rampant in every school ; and I fear it will be long before these truly Oriental characteristics will be eradicated, if ever. The superintendent has had long experience of both Indian and Creole characters, and he thus emphatically writes: 'Comparing the apprentice with the poor Indian labourer, the contrast is by no means favourable to the former. While at work, and in the receipt of good pay, he is improvident and a spendthrift; out of work, a helpless pauper. Should sickness overtake him, he flies to his priest for aid, and to his relations for shelter; these failing, he soon starves and dies; and no one can deny that this has been the fate of hundreds during the epidemic.'

I can endorse this statement from my own observation.

That they have no idea of self-help is true to the letter. I have seen poor wretched starving Indians gladly earning a few pence to get a meal, and making the most of it; and again strong able Creoles who will beg from anyone they think likely to give. When offered a day's work, they will either refuse it, if it requires much personal exertion, or demand a high price, which if given, they loiter half their time away to spin out the work; and if refused, they go off in a huff, and resume their begging.

In spite of all the obstacles to success, the Government schools during the year 1868 sent out boys to fill the following positions: Twenty-two were apprenticed to carpenters; twenty-three as clerks in mercantile, telegraph, and other offices; thirteen are employed by engineers; seven engaged in sugar factories; six have become assistants in schools; twenty-five have been distributed among the trades of smith, mason, coach builder, painter, &c., and two have obtained Royal College scholarships. All this speaks well for the practical nature of the studies in these schools.

The course of instruction comprises English reading and translating into French; French reading and translating into English, Geography, the world in general, and England and Mauritius in particular; outline mapping and physical geography; English and French grammar; arithmetic; the respective values of Imperial and Colonial money, making out accounts applicable to the requirements of the colony, calculating interest, &c. &c.

The school staff consists of fifty-three masters, twenty-one mistresses, and eighteen assistants. The official work is carried on by the superintendent (who is also Secretary to the Committee of Education, and Inspector of Elementary Schools and Reformatories), an accountant, and copyist.

The number of Government schools is	52
Schools assisted by grants	42
Reformatories	2
	96

There are also departments under Creole and Indian teachers, which raise the number to 117.

Sixteen elementary schools were obliged to close on account of fever; yet at the end of the year there were 5,821 children on the books.

Besides the above, there is the Indian Orphan Asylum at Powder Mills. Death made sad havoc among these children during the epidemic, and there appears to have been a good deal of mismanagement since.

It is now, however, affiliated with the Reformatory at the 'Asile' in its vicinity, which is under the immediate direction of the Police department.

The annual amount voted by the legislature for the payment of salaries, rents, grants to elementary schools, books, stationery, and other contingencies, is 16,596*l.*

Having been induced to pay a visit to one of the Government reformatories, I give a short account of it. I as a stranger was so interested in all I saw, that I think it would be well for many others, who seem to know nothing of it save its existence, to do all in their power to encourage an institution that must, if continued successfully, be of incalculable benefit to the future of the colony.

It is carrying out the New World recognised fact that, for a country to prosper, its vagabond children must be cared for whilst mind and body are so plastic as to be capable of moulding to good uses, an almost impossibility with adults. If this is proved to be a necessity elsewhere, how much more so must it be in a place where there is such a mixture of races as in Mauritius!

The Reformatory, known generally as the 'Asile,' is about six miles distant from Port Louis. In 1868, the happy idea was conceived by His Excellency the Governor of converting an old abandoned, broken-down sugar estate, taken over for debt by the Government Savings' Bank, into what is eventually intended to be the model farm of the Island. To Major O'Brien, the Inspector General of Police, the carrying out of the scheme is due. When this gentleman first visited the place he found it in a most deplorable state—'roads almost impassable, covered with weeds and grass six feet high, buildings without exception uninhabitable, nearly all unroofed by the hurricane of 1868, swamps, and rank vegetation everywhere.'

He saw before him a truly herculean task, but he set about it undaunted, for his heart was in this good work. None knew better than he, from his daily experience amongst all classes, of the dire need of such an institution, of the great importance of rescuing the hundreds of homeless boys, eking out a miserable existence by theft and worse crimes. Numbers of these boys were brought to the vagrants' depôt, but being placed indiscriminately with older offenders, more harm than good was done by their detention.

On June 26, 1868, Major O'Brien sent fifteen boys with a band of vagrants, under superintendence, to begin the contemplated work. A temporary shelter was made by covering part of the house with tarpaulins, and by degrees most of the ruinous tenements were made habitable. When these were completed, attention was turned to the grounds, and there a systematic clearance was carried on.

Roads were cleaned and mended; the old basins, covered with fetid mud, were filled up, and fresh ones made, while floodgates were built to allow the ingress and egress of water to them; the bridge over the Citron River repaired, drains were dug to clear the unhealthy, swampy land, and walls reared.

It was a little more than a year after its inauguration that I visited the Asile, and I was astonished to see so much accomplished, and the order, cleanliness, and neatness that prevailed made it an example to many another place in Mauritius that might advantageously copy it in these respects. A fine metalled road had been made from the highway, leading to the main house, and as I drove up the whole place had a pleasant aspect. All the buildings were whitewashed, the grounds laid out in vegetable and flower gardens, and close to the house was a pretty little fernery.

The principal rooms used for school and office purposes were surrounded with a grove of mango trees. Here I was shown the handiwork of the boys: tin plates, watering-cans, baskets, and mats, and all very creditably done. It was with pleasure I witnessed the progress many of the boys had made, who did not know a letter when they entered the 'Asile.' English is the rule, the different vernaculars only being used when explanations require them. Some of the lads I examined could read English, and wrote it on their slates very fairly. Simple arithmetic they acquire with great facility, as most Indians do.

There are children of Indian, Creole, Coringhy, African, and Bourbon parentage; and the Superintendent told me they were most of them very tractable, and few attempt escape except new comers, who find the discipline irksome to their vagabond habits.

Every kind of household and other occupations connected with the institution are taught first. Cooking, cleaning, washing and mending clothes, ornamental and vegetable gardening, field work, carpentering, brick and basket making, masonry, tin and blacksmith's work, attending to horses and cattle, and driving the mule carts used on the place; everything which can be useful to them, and help to make the institution self-supporting. There were 227 boys in the Asile there, and already 78 acres of land were in cultivation.

Most of the roads were skirted with Filaos, Palmistes and other trees. All kinds of vegetables are grown, which are sent into the bazaar daily, where they have a stand set apart for them; and experiments are being made (with an eye to future use) in growing coffee, tea, China grass, vanilla, poppies, and tobacco.

Very firm and excellent rules have been issued for the government of the establishment, and the regulation of the various duties of the boys; and a register is kept in which is noted every particular respecting their conduct from the time of their entry into the Asile.

They are divided into squads of from ten to fifteen; and the boys who, by being first in their classes, and at work, and meriting it by general good conduct, are appointed overseers, or sirdars, are answerable for the cleanliness and order of their respective squads.

This responsibility seems to have a very beneficial effect, and inspires emulation in the boys to attain the post; and a slight distinction of dress is also made, which is another attraction to them. Each boy is put to some trade, at which he works for a certain time ; should he then wish to change he can do so, but his decision must be final. Good workmen are chosen to teach the several trades. A capital rule is made about these workmen and the teachers—their increase of pay, &c., are made to depend upon the progress of the taught ; a rule that would be of infinite service if applied to schools and trades generally, here and elsewhere.

During the last six months before the expiration of their time, a part of each boy's earnings is laid aside to form a fund for providing him with clothes, tools, and other necessaries when he makes a start in life. Seventeen is the prescribed age for leaving, but if a good offer for an apprentice is made, with the consent of the superintendent, they can leave much earlier. Should circumstances deprive them of a home before their apprenticeship is closed, they may return temporarily to the Asile.

The simplest forms of prayer and religious instruction are given, irrespective of creeds, the bases of which are the Lord's Prayer and the Ten Commandments ; no catechism whatever is allowed to be taught, but access is given to all ministers of religion when requested by parents.

Their days, summer and winter, are pretty equally divided with work, school, drill and recreation.

It was late when I paid my visit, and the boys were about to be marshalled to their evening meal, which in summer time is given them under the mango trees. They marched along like soldiers, and filed off to their respective places, facing inward at the word of command. All remained motionless till the order was given to sit down to their meal, which was done without confusion, and in perfect silence. When all had finished, they were marched off, and drawn up in front of the dormitories.

Here the superintendent talked to them, and asked if any of them had any complaint to make ; but all expressed themselves satisfied, except one little fellow, who wanted to change his trade of stonemason for that of carpenter. The boys looked up at the Major as children would do to a kind friend. It was quite evident, though the rules are strictly carried out, and disobedience sharply punished, that this kind-hearted man has not forgotten that they are children he has to deal with, and that gentleness and kindness will win their way even with the roughest and apparently most hopeless subject.

Here they were drilled, and a smart little fellow put them through their manœuvres in capital style. He entered heartily into the spirit of the thing, and I have no doubt was as proud of his post as a general at the head of his army. At last they were marched in line to where their hammocks hung, and at the word of command they opened them out, and slung them up as promptly as if trained on board a man-of-war. These hammocks have been used to replace the awkward prison bedsteads, as cleaner and healthier, and allowing of the room to be used in the daytime for other purposes.

PISTACHE NUT.

I was shown a temporary hospital, where a few boys lay sick of fever. The poor little fellows raised their heads as I entered to look at me, and get a kind word from the Major. Very few had touched the meal that lay on a stool beside them. Everything was clean and neat, and the boys looked as comfortable as possible when suffering from such a miserable disease. I was informed that they are about to build a permanent hospital. I saw the prison for the incorrigibles, one of whom was punished for theft in presence of the whole gang, as a warning to the rest.

I left much pleased with my visit, and wished every success to so useful and benevolent an undertaking.

The Natural History Society, Museum, &c.

In 1805 an association was formed, under the title of the 'Société d'Émulation,' to occupy itself with everything connected with science, agriculture, commerce, and navigation.

This society was formed by a few intelligent men, and a number of members soon joined it, till its correspondence extended to India, Seychelles, Bourbon, the Cape, and France.

Its principal objects were to aid navigation in the Indian seas, improve agriculture in Mauritius, and acquire a knowledge of the natives of Madagascar and Africa. Some important services had been rendered in all these branches, when the society began to languish. However, after the British conquest of the Island, Governor Farquhar raised its drooping wings, placed it under the protection of Government, and personally expressed his interest in its transactions. He was elected a member, and soon infused into it new life and spirit.

In 1817, before his departure for England, the rules were remodelled, and its name changed to the 'Society for the Encouragement of the Arts and Sciences.' When General Hall was Governor *ad interim*, it was naturally supposed he would have respected the wishes of the actual chief, only temporarily absent. But no; he appears to have put a veto on everything that could conduce to the progress of the colony. He inaugurated his official acts by a proclamation annulling the dispositions made in favour of the Society, and very soon little was known of it save its name.

It was not until 1829, under the administration of Sir Charles Colville, that it revived, principally through the agency of the Curator of vacant estates. It received a new title, the 'Natural History Society,' and was composed chiefly of young men, under the direction of Mr. Charles Telfair, Dr. Lial, and Mr. W. Bojer, Professor of Botany at the Royal College.

The day of the re-opening was the auspicious one of the 22nd of August, the sixtieth anniversary of the birth of Baron George Cuvier. This distinguished man took great interest in the revivified society; and in 1831 sent it a present of a fine marble bust of himself and a copy of his valuable works, which are still its most cherished treasures.

Meetings were held once a month for scientific purposes, based on the rules of the 'Société d'Histoire naturelle,' in Paris. This association comprises a president and vice-president, secretary and vice-secretary, treasurer, resident and corresponding members. Amongst the latter are names well known to fame in the scientific world. I cite a few at random:—Sir Alexander and Sir William Buckland, Sir A. Johnson, Rev. J. Adamson, Sir W. Hooker, Geoffroy St.-Hilaire, A. P. de Candolle, Le Comte Dejean, Sir J. Herschel, Von Martins, Adrien Jussieu, Professor J. Lindley, C. D. Schreiber, Dr. Stewart, Professor Agassiz, Madame Ida Pfeiffer, &c. &c. A correspondence is also kept up with all the leading societies in India, Australia, the Cape, Europe, and America; whilst the best names Mauritius can boast have been enrolled amongst its members.

In 1835 a present of shells was sent it from Bourbon; and I find that the Custom House in those days played as unpleasant a part to the scientific world then as it does to ordinary individuals in the present day. Weeks elapsed before the cases could be procured, and then there were grave doubts as to their being intact.

In 1842 the acting chief officer, Colonel Stavely, sanctioned an allowance for a curator with a grant of 240*l.* a year. Another grant was also given from the public chest of 200*l.* per annum to meet expenses. This amount was to be employed for cost of printing the 'Reports of the Transactions of the Society,' which are issued once a year and sent to all foreign correspondents; for medals and prizes granted each year to the best pupils in agricultural chemistry at the Royal College; also to the planters, small cultivators, artisans, manufacturers, and others at the annual exhibitions.

Just previously to the above grants, the death of one of the most zealous of its members took place, that of M. Desjardins, who had filled the post of hon. secretary from 1829. His widow presented his valuable museum to the society on a guarantee being given her that it should be well cared for. The condition was willingly accepted, and this donation formed the nucleus of the present museum. M. Adrien d'Épinay, dying about the same time, bequeathed his library to his late colleagues, and in consequence of these bequests the office of Curator mentioned above was instituted.

M. Bojer was appointed to fill this post, and apartments in one of the wings of the College were set apart, to which the museum and library were removed, and which have been their abode ever since.

In 1847 the word 'Royal' was allowed to be added to the title, and thenceforth it has been known as the 'Royal Society of Arts and Sciences in Mauritius.'

About this time or a little earlier, an exhibition of sugars, vegetables, flowers, &c., took place, and the exhibitors were rewarded with medals and prizes in money. It was so favourably received that one or more has taken place every year since, with the exception of 1867. In 1850, twenty medals were given for sugars and other produce; and there was a competition for the best essay on the cultivation of the sugar-cane. The prize was divided between M. Gallet and M. Autard, and honourable mention was made of several others.

I find that in 1852 a prize of *50l.* was awarded to Mr. Hounslow, of the engineer department, for ameliorating the dwellings of the poor, and presented to him by the then president, the Hon. R. W. Rawson. I have, however, yet to learn what good results have accrued to the town from this liberality.

It appears that the society has been unremitting in its endeavours for the encouragement of different articles of produce, both for export and home consumption, but from one circumstance or other all seem to have failed but the everlasting sugar-cane.

In 1860 an intercolonial exhibition was held at Government House. Sir William Stevenson threw open house and grounds to the public for three days. Seychelles, Rodrigues, and Bourbon sent their choicest productions; and from all accounts it appears to have been the best thing of the kind ever held in the colony.

In 1867, when the Great Exhibition took place in Paris, an effort was made to represent Mauritius there. Sugars were sent of very fine qualities, and colonial rum, tanned hides, tobacco and cigars, fibres, vanilla, arrowroot, specimens of indigenous woods fit for building and other purposes, and a variety of produce. Drawings of Mauritius scenery and views of Bourbon were forwarded, with some of the elegant basket-work made from the leaves of the coco-de-mer, and shell-flowers, cleverly constructed from the various tinted tellinas, Venuses, and the opercula of different shells, the effect of which is charming when made with taste.

As a whole I believe Mauritius looked very insignificant at the 'World's Fair in Paris.' She comes out better at home.

I have been present at two of these shows, and a curious sight they present. They are held in the upper half of the bazaar, which is closed to the public during the previous day, to undergo a thorough cleansing and adornment with greenery.

Early in the morning of *the day* carts are crowding up, laden with flower plants or vegetables from the various districts, to be arranged in their allotted spaces. Moka is always strongest in flowers, from its peculiar damp climate, and from its possessing the only nursery garden in the colony.

For some hours a babel rages inside and out of the building. I pitied the poor secretary, who has to settle all differences, write out tickets, find the best places for everybody, never to make a mistake; and whether he does or not he is safe to be abused right and left, everyone shouting at him at once and few helping.

One minute it is a heap of fresh butter which somebody dabs down on a basket of strawberries or violets, or a lady's cushion; then a couple of pigs, or a pair of carriage wheels: very lucky if the porkers don't get the tickets of their neighbours, the Cochin fowls. Then a basket of monster patates, or a bouquet fit for a lady's dress, or large enough to fill a good-sized round table, and so on. Every one, of course, is in a hurry, and must have his or her ticket at once. However, by a good deal of tact and patience and unflagging zeal, matters are pretty amicably arranged by eleven o'clock, when the judges enter to award the prizes, which are marked in large letters on each article. It would be unfair to draw comparisons with exhibitions elsewhere, but for so small a place they are very creditable.

Place aux dames! The ladies' work, millinery, artificial flowers, and other feminine fabrics, might pass muster anywhere. The fairy Creole fingers do not restrict their handiwork to fineries; large pats of sweet fresh butter, most appetising preserves, and pickles attest their skill.

A partition is covered with paintings and photographs; the latter, besides portraits, showing some good views of Mauritian scenery. Vegetables are fine and well assorted; tobacco and colonial-made cigars very good; liqueurs, Vanilla fruits, and many other things (as the advertisements say) far too numerous to mention.

The flowers and bouquets of all shapes and sizes show well, and there is generally a fine display of ferns, principally those of Lady Barkly.

Towards two o'clock His Excellency with his lady and suite arrive; the band strikes up, and in pour the *élite*, the demi-monde, any one fortunate enough to hold a ticket, but all orderly, and the lowest well and cleanly dressed. One half of the visitors at least goes to see the other half. I confess, as I sat quietly gazing on the varied scene, I was perfectly astounded at the extensiveness of the dress of the femininity.

Every exaggeration, from the hideous chignon to the two-inch heels that throw the figure off the perpendicular and into the Grecian Bend. Every combination of colour was there; I need not define in which class. All, however, seemed gay and festive, and glad to chat, flirt, and air their finery.

At four o'clock the prizes are given by the Governor; the band plays 'God save the Queen,' the representative of royalty disappears, and, by half-past five, the scene has again changed to the confusion of tongues of the morning, as the various objects are carried away by their owners, till night closes in.

The Natural History collections of the Society in their museum are fine and rare, but not extensive. Besides the Fauna of Mauritius, that of Madagascar, Southern Africa, and the neighbouring islands is well represented. The fish of the surrounding seas are in great numbers. The monsters of the deep show their hideous maws at every step The very staircase is lined with gigantic heads of sharks, their triple tiers of teeth grinning horribly. It makes one's hair stand on end, when viewing these dry bones, to think that it is in the region where these insatiate animals abound that the Indian diver seeks the treasures of the ocean.

It is quite a relief to turn to the cases of many-hued shells, for which Mauritius is famous. To this department all the Dependencies and the Far East have contributed. India and Africa send a large collection of reptiles, well preserved. Ccrals, of course, are not wanting; and there is a small collection of minerals, principally from Australia and South America, but not of great value.

Round the room are hung a few large pictures: one, a copy of Murillo's 'Holy Family,' was painted at Paris by M. Michel, and presented to the Society. Attached to the museum is the library, which now numbers over 2,000 volumes, many very costly, and some invaluable as books of reference. The whole is under the care of M. Louis Bouton.

This gentleman has made a very large and rare collection of the indigenous plants of Mauritius. He sent a duplicate of them to the Paris Exhibition of 1867, and the originals have been removed to the Pamplemousses Gardens, and were placed under the care of the late Dr. Meller, whose loss the colony has so recently deplored.

CHAPTER XXVIII.

IMMIGRATION.

A new Era for English Colonies—When and How the Abolition Act was brought in Force—Number of Slaves—Introduction of Coolies—Bad Management-Valuation of Slaves — Ex-Apprentices — Immigration renewed — Cholera — Agricultural Progress—Changed Condition of Malabars after residing here—Tickets and Photographs—Camps—Fever—Death-Rate—Report of Mr. Beyts—Cost of Establishment and other Statistics—Arrears of Wages—Immigration Tables—Facts respecting various Castes of Indians.

THE year 1834 was the beginning of a new era for all the Colonies of Great Britain. From that date all traffic in human flesh virtually ceased for ever, where England held sway. Though the Act for the Abolition of Slavery was passed in this year, the laws respecting thereto were to remain in force till February 1st, 1835. From this period all slaves of six years old and upwards, duly registered, became apprentice labourers, and continued so till February 1st, 1841, as regarded field labourers, and until February 1839 for those non-attached. There were at this time in the colony 39,464 men and boys, and 25,856 women and girls, making a total of 65,320 slaves.

From symptoms of disaffection amongst the soon-to-be liberated slaves, it was evident to the planters that no time was to be lost in procuring men to till the soil; and the introduction of labourers from India was attempted.

The Government offered no obstacle to the project; and, as no restrictions were laid as to the number to be brought in each vessel, by the year 1838, no less than 24,566 coolies had arrived from Calcutta.[1]

[1] These labourers engaged to work at field labour for a term of five years, at the rate of five rupees a month, with rations.

A certain sum was to be retained of these wages, to pay for a return passage to India if desired at the expiration of their engagement.

The bad management in the shipment of these Indians led to serious complaints being laid before the Home Government, as well as the Government of India. In consequence of these and other remonstrances, immigration was suspended in 1838.

In February 1835, the Commission of Indemnity began the valuation of slaves, which was completed by the end of the year, resulting in the sum of 2,112,632*l*., which was paid by England to the planters of Mauritius, being at the rate of 69*l*. 14*s*. 3*d*. per slave.

When the ex-apprentices were freed in 1839, scenes of riot and disturbance took place all over the Island.

The ex-slaves refused to work, alleging, for one reason, that they had been ill-treated by their former masters having sent to India for labourers; but the truth was, they considered that their freedom would be incomplete without an entire abandonment of their former labours.

Like all large bodies of men when all restraint is suddenly withdrawn, they launched into violent excesses. Every street in Port Louis swarmed with them, much to the annoyance of the more quietly disposed population. It was only positive hunger and want that compelled them at last to seek employment, but in so desultory a way that it was found no certainty could be placed on their work.

In 1840, during the time Colonel Power was Acting Governor, a committee was formed, under the presidence of Captain Dick, Colonial Secretary, to organise some plan for the continuance of immigration. The 'Free Labour Association' was the title of this new society, and its object was to facilitate in every way the introduction of labour into the colony. It was forbidden by the Government to bring immigrants from the coast of Africa, so that from India alone could they look for working men.

In 1842, Sir William Gomm obtained leave to introduce 6,000 labourers annually. In 1849, a draft ordinance was passed, allowing only of engagements for a term of three years.

The new system of immigration did not apparently answer all its requirements, for I find, in 1851, Mr. Higginson, the then Governor, endeavouring to obtain free labourers from the coast of Madagascar, to make good the deficiency in the labour market.

In 1854, the cholera was brought to Mauritius by an immigrant ship from Calcutta, where the terrible pest is indigenous to the soil, having its head-quarters in the Delta of the Ganges.

So dire were the effects of this disease on the colony, that in 1857 it was proposed by the chief medical officer that coolies should only be brought from the presidencies of Madras and Bombay; the natives from these districts being healthier than those from Calcutta.

In Sir William Stevenson's time, liberty was granted to the planters to engage their labourers for a period of five years, which proved of great advantage to all concerned.

The progress of agricultural industry has been rapid and regular, and the increase of the productions of the soil has been in the same proportion as the introduction of Indian labourers.

The tables at the end of this chapter will show the exports of the main staple in the times of slave and free labour of the colony.

The coolies number two-thirds of the population, and, as far as I am able to judge, are as well cared for and protected by the Government as any other class in Mauritius. I have visited many estates and found the labourers apparently contented and happy, and certainly better off than they ever were before.

Look at the thin frail form of the Malabar when he arrives from India, and see him after some years' residence in the Island. His form assumes a roundness and his muscles a development, from exercise, wholesome and sufficient food, and being well cared for, which speak volumes in praise of the civilising influence he is unconsciously undergoing, and if its effects are not very evident in this generation they will be most unmistakably in the next.

Every coolie carries a small tin case attached to his waist, containing his certificates of arrival, age, personal description, with a photograph, engagement, &c. He never ventures into the street without this, as he is liable to be stopped at any moment by the police; and if his papers are not all correct, he is at once arrested till he can give a satisfactory account of himself. If a domestic servant gets leave to go into the country, he must have a pass from his master, specifying the number of days he has permission to be absent, and the place of his destination. The photograph system has been adopted to compel every Indian to show his own ticket. Formerly there was any amount of rascality carried on. If a man lost his own ticket, he would beg, borrow, or steal his friend's, or get one forged for a trifle, all of which tricks are useless now. The dated passports not only prevent vagabondage, but put a stop in a great measure to runaway servants, who on the slightest provocation would formerly abscond.

Every sugar estate has what is called a 'Camp' attached to it, where the labourers reside. The houses are principally thatched, but many of them are built of stone on the larger plantations, and there is always a good supply of water for drinking and washing purposes.

Near the 'Camp,' on a site chosen by a medical officer appointed for that purpose, a hospital is erected, and proper attendants duly qualified by certificates for waiting on the sick are appointed.

The sanitary condition of both camps and hospitals is examined into, and reported on yearly to Government.

During the epidemic the greatest care was bestowed on the labourers, and the deaths were less in proportion to the great numbers employed than in any other class.[1]

The death-rates amongst the Indians during the fever were as follow per 1,000:—

Adults	37·4
In total population of estates	44·5

At the same time, in the districts, it was forty-five per 1,000, and in Port Louis eighty! which means decimation in fifteen months, and annihilation in twelve years.

Many of the Indians are frugal, and manage to save enough to remit home to India, either for investment in land there, or for the support of aged relatives; to invest in small stores here or to return to India. In 1869, there were 69,032*l.* standing to the credit of Indians in the Savings' Bank, and this sum is yearly steadily increasing as they begin to have confidence in the security of the bank. No less than 17,158*l.* were remitted last year on behalf of immigrants to Bombay, Madras, and Calcutta. This does not include large sums sent home through merchants, or taken in specie by the immigrants themselves.

[1] Besides the hospitals on the estates, five public hospitals and thirty-two dispensaries have been established in various parts of the Island.

A convincing proof of their appreciation of the benefits to be derived in the colony, is given in the numbers constantly coming back to the Island and setting up in some way of business, or returning as servants to their former masters.

For the following account of the present state of the Indian immigrants, and the statistics respecting them, I draw my information from the able reports of the Hon. Mr. Beyts, who is at the head of the Immigration Office, and whoso long experience makes him the best authority on the subject. This gentleman has for years rendered most valuable services to the colony in his department, and has also been up to India on an important mission for the Government to further the cause of immigration.

From the great care bestowed of late years on the immigrant ships to Mauritius, the ratio of deaths is small compared with that in vessels conveying Indian immigrants to other colonies.

The costs of the establishment connected with immigration for 1869 were 7,882*l.* 8*s.* 10*d.*

The Indian population amounted at this time to 206,771.

With the coolies usually arrive a number of free passengers, many of them old hands, who return, paying their passage and bringing friends with them, especially Dhobies, induced by their representations to visit Mauritius in quest of fortune. Six immigrant ships arrived in the course of the year, four from Madras, and two from Calcutta, bringing a total of 1,682 souls.

The departures, as compared with other years, show a great decrease (though they exceeded the arrivals), viz. 2,320 left. The following table will show the difference in these years.

Departures in 1866	2,815
„ 1867	3,398
„ 1868	2,544
„ 1869	2,320

The precise number of Indian Creoles now in the colony cannot be accurately ascertained, but an idea may be derived of the pace at which they are increasing by the fact that the births in the Indian population during the last ten years give an average of more than 6,000 per annum.

There are 223 sugar estates in the Island, the total Indian

population of which has been represented by the stipendiary magistrates to be as follows:—

	M.	F.	Total.
Adults	71,906	25,710	97,616
Children under ten . .	12,773	12,060	24,833
	84,679	37,770	122,449

The vagrants were formerly a serious grievance, but laws for the suppression of vagrancy have now been for some time in force, and appear to be working satisfactorily. The complaints

CREOLE SITTING.

of masters against servants, and *vice versâ*, have increased of late years. Those of the former were principally for unlawful absence and desertion; those of the latter for arrears of wages.

The great irregularity of the payment of wages has been due to the severe financial crisis the colony has been passing through. Such heavy arrears were due on some estates that it necessitated the intervention of the Procureur-General and the Protector of immigrants (Mr. Beyts). A more satisfactory state of things is, however, now prevalent, and by the latest reports scarcely any estate is now more than three months in arrear.

Another change for the better I see is going on. Formerly, few if any women could be got to work on estates, but during the last year 993 were engaged in agricultural work.

On thirty plantations schools are established that give instruction to 1,092 pupils, nine-tenths of whom are boys. As the Indians when they choose to learn are a quick-witted race, this must tell well on the next generation.

It appears that the principal part of the arrivals during 1869 were from Madras and Calcutta. Owing to the establishment

INDIAN WOMAN.

of large cotton and other factories, the demand for labour has been so great that emigration thence has for the time ceased.

It seems that Indians get home-sickness as well as the rest of the world. Large numbers present themselves daily to be invalided and sent back to India. So determined are they when once they have this idea, that if they are refused they will work it out even if it cost their life. The Inspector says: 'An Indian, if bent on return to India, though possibly, nay probably, only for a visit, will starve, vagabondise till he is arrested as a vagrant, and then tamper with his eyes, irritating them with lime and other substances, till he frequently loses his sight; or will irritate any little scratch till it becomes an ulcer of so malignant a form as to end in amputation, or death. Should he survive he returns to the depôt a most pitiable object, and with great need of invaliding.

INDIAN MAN.

INDIAN WOMAN.

The accompanying account of some of the principal of the numerous castes into which Indians are divided was sent me by an intelligent Indian merchant, and may interest those far away from India and its strange people.

The following tables will give an idea of the classes of men employed by contract, and the average amount of wages paid at different ages for field-labourers, artisans, domestic servants, and others, with their general rations.

Information on Indians, communicated by an Indian.

The four grand divisions of the people of India into castes are, the Brahmins, the Cshatryas, the Vaisyas, and the Sudras. Let us first consider what caste is? It is an institution by which extraordinary distinctions are sanctioned, and at the same time reconciled so as to preserve from disorganisation a community in which certain interests and occupations are kept in immutable subordination. It effected a separation among certain orders of society, as if they had been of different species. Its power was at one time immense, but it is daily on the decrease. Caste as existing at present is not caste as it existed in the olden days. It has been stripped of the countless restrictions, numberless severities, and religious bigotry, which foully stained it in days of old. Caste, as it exists at present, is no more than a division of people into the higher and lower classes. Castes are distinguished simply by the different forms of worship, the different prayers uttered mornings and evenings. If Sanscrit were made the vehicle by which the prayers of the Brahmin are to be conveyed to heaven, Tamil and Telugu are for the rest. But what element of discord and disunion can be found in these external differences, these differences in ceremonies and formalities? Have these differences conferred on the Brahmin any weapon of torture or oppression, under which his fellow countrymen groan, and must fall in with him? Nothing of the kind, and I do not see why, notwithstanding the external differences mentioned, men of all castes cannot agree in political, educational, or any other measures that effect them all alike; and why children of different castes cannot commingle their concerns and interests, blending in a common cause. Such considerations alone have led the educated Hindoos in India to form themselves into associations, such as the Bramho Somaj of India, the Veda Somaj of Madras, and the Prathana Somaj of Bombay, with their branches in the interior.

STATEMENT SHOWING THE CLASSES OF MEN WITH WHOM CONTRACTS OF SERVICE WERE ENTERED INTO IN EACH DISTRICT OF THE COLONY DURING THE YEAR 1868.

		Number of men engaged to new masters										Number of men engaged to same masters									
		Port Louis	Pamplemousses	Flacq	Riv. du Rempart	Black River	Moka	Plaines Wilhems	Grand Port	Savane	Total	Port Louis	Pamplemousses	Flacq	Riv. du Rempart	Black River	Moka	Plaines Wilhems	Grand Port	Savane	Tota
Indian Immigrants .	New	790	54	86	19	21	141	51	59	55	1276	26	35	60	,,	5	20	4	36	45	231
	Old	5125	4600	4934	1558	1421	2243	3941	4228	2724	30774	753	3690	7941	2983	1619	2894	2748	5331	4053	32012
Other Registered Immigrants .		530	31	46	70	3	10	,,	51	55	796	,,	31	40	7	3	,,	,,	43	28	152
Creoles		409	115	179	7	55	24	210	226	66	1291	51	89	218	18	56	4	53	210	58	757
Europeans		11	,,	,,	,,	,,	,,	,,	,,	,,	11	,,	,,	,,	,,	,,	,,	,,		,,	,,
		6865	4800	5245	1654	1500	2418	4202	4564	2900	34148	830	3845	8259	3008	1683	2918	2805	5620	4184	33152

STATEMENT SHOWING THE PRESENT AVERAGE RATE OF WAGES AND ALLOWANCES OF AGRICULTURAL LABOURERS, TRADESMEN, ARTISANS AND DOMESTIC SERVANTS.

First : Ordinary Agricultural Labourers.

New Immigrants

Age	Wages per Month					Rations	lbs.	ozs.
	First Year	Second Year	Third Year	Fourth Year	Fifth Year			
From ten to eleven years inclusive.	5	6	7	8	9	rice per diem	1	8
,, twelve to fourteen ,,	6	7	8	9	10	or maize pounded	2	0
,, fifteen to seventeen ,,	7	8	9	10	11	or manioc (cooked)	2	8
,, eighteen years and upwards	8	9	10	11	12	or ,, raw	5	,,
						Dholl per mensem.	2	,,
						salt fish ,,	2	,,
						ghee, or oil ,,	1	,,
						salt	1	,,

Old Immigrants

Age	Wages per Month			Rations	lbs.	ozs.
	Minimum	Maximum	Average			
	sh d	sh d	sh d			
From ten to eleven years inclusive	4	10	7	rice per diem	1	8
,, twelve to fourteen ,,	6	12	9	or maize pounded	2	,,
,, fifteen to seventeen ,,	8	14	11	or manioc (cooked)	2	8
,, eighteen years and upwards	12	18	15	or ,, raw	5	,,
				Dholl per mensem	2	,,
				salt fish ,,	2	,,
				ghee, or oil ,,	1	,,
				salt	1	,,

Remarks.—Very few receive maize or manioc instead of rice.

Secondly: Tradesmen, Artisans, Domestic Servants.

	Wages per Month								
	Old Immigrants								
	Minimum			Maximum			Average		
	£	s.	d.	£	s.	d.	£	s.	d.
Carpenters	2	0	0	4	0	0	3	0	0
Joiners	2	0	0	4	0	0	3	0	0
Cartwrights	0	14	0	2	6	0	1	10	0
Blacksmiths	0	11	0	2	0	0	1	5	6
Coopers	1	10	0	3	0	0	2	5	0
Tinsmiths	1	10	0	3	0	0	2	5	0
Farriers	0	15	0	1	12	0	1	3	6
Harness makers	0	11	0	1	16	0	1	3	6
Painters or Glaziers	1	0	0	3	0	0	2	0	0
Masons	0	14	0	3	0	0	1	17	0
Stone cutters	1	0	0	1	6	0	1	3	0
Sawyers	1	3	0	1	14	0	1	8	6
Timber squarers	1	0	0	2	0	0	1	10	0
Tobacconists	0	10	0	1	0	0	0	15	0
Gardeners	0	4	0	1	8	0	0	16	0
Cooks	0	15	0	2	0	0	1	7	6
Table servants	0	2	0	1	0	0	1	1	0
Coachmen	0	15	0	2	0	0	1	7	6
Grooms	0	9	0	1	7	0	0	18	0
Tailors	1	2	0	1	14	0	1	8	0
Washermen	0	12	0	2	0	0	1	6	0
Sugar makers	0	17	0	4	0	0	2	8	6
Mill drivers	1	0	0	4	18	0	2	19	0
Sailors	0	14	0	1	8	0	0	16	0
Jewellers	0	9	0	2	0	0	1	4	6

	Minimum		Maximum		Average	
	lbs.	ozs.	lbs.	ozs.	lbs.	ozs.
Rice per mensem	30	,,	104	,,	67	,,
Dholl ,,	2	,,	8	,,	5	,,
Salt fish ,,	2	,,	8	,,	5	,,
Ghee, or oil ,,	1	,,	2	,,	1	8
Salt ,,	1	,,	2	,,	1	8

For the last two years, no requisitions have been received for Artisans or Domestic Servants.

The object of these Somajens is, 'the establishment of universal brotherhood irrespective of all prejudices, national and sectarian, and the obtainment of religious freedom by bringing back Hindoos from idolatry to a true faith.' The rules of the Veda Somaj are as follows :—

'I shall worship through love of Him and the performance of the work He loveth—the Supreme Being, the Creator, the Preserver, the Destroyer, the Giver of Salvation, the Omniscient, the Omnipotent, the Blissful, the Good, the Formless, the One only without a second, and none of the created objects, subject to the following conditions: I shall labour to compose and gradually bring into practice a ritual agreeable to the spirit of pure Theism, and free from the superstitions and absurdities which at present characterise Hindoo ceremonies. In the meantime I shall observe the ceremonies now in force, but only in cases where ceremonies are indispensable, as in marriages and funerals, or where their omission will do more violence to the feelings of the Hindoo community, than is consistent with the proper interests of the Veda Somaj as in Sastras. And I shall go through such ceremonies, where they are not conformable to pure Theism, as mere matters of routine, destitute of all religious significance, as the lifeless remains of a superstition which has passed away.'

To attempt to furnish a detailed and correct account of the different races of the Indian population is no easy task. Deep research and careful inquiry are necessary to render any satisfactory information on the points requiring elucidation. But, so far as Southern India or the presidency of Madras is concerned, I may assert that representatives of all castes and races are to be found in the colony, namely, from the divine Brahmin to the degraded Pariah. It must be remarked here, that, with rare exceptions, the ignorant and the worst characters alone come out to this place. These men, either from their intercourse with foreigners or from the freedom they enjoy here in the use of brandy, and other alcoholic spirits (the use of which is strictly prohibited among the higher classes of people in India, and the eating and drinking particular kinds of food are the chief among deadly sins which subject the perpetrator to the loss of caste), have thrown aside their original habits of cleanliness, and have adopted theoretically European habits in respect to dressing and eating, but no improvement is perceptible in their intellectual and moral character.

A few Hindoos have embraced Christianity, more from curiosity and associations than from any actual appreciation of its high principles of morality and religious obligations. Others who have saved a fortune either by semi-starvation, or by strict economical use of their gains, and who still persist in the preservation and practice of their old superstitious habits and customs, notwithstanding their long residence in the colony, take a pride in bringing up their children after Creole fashion, by giving a smattering of education in French and English: and when such children attain to their age, they are inclined, against the will and consent of their parents, to marry a Creole young man or Creole young woman, as the case may be; while their parents wish them to marry their own kinsmen and kinswomen, either in the colony or expected from India. These boys and girls desire Creole connections simply because they associate with that class of people from their infant days, and whose language they have adopted, neglecting altogether a knowledge of their own mother tongue, which is neither imparted in government schools nor by their own parents, most of whom are themselves ignorant and perhaps not even able to sign their names. Hence convivial mingling and inter-marriages (which are prohibited in India, and the introduction of which is thought by the educated Indian public of the day as a stepping-stone for the removal of that 'monster evil' caste) are in daily practice here without any appreciation of its advantages, inasmuch as the parties in general are of no intelligence, position, and influence in Indian society. Inter-marriages have tended to produce bad results; in fact, the morality of the Indian community, including men and women, is not worthy of imitation. A respectable Hindoo lady would no doubt be ashamed to reside in the colony, and a residence for some time would taint her morals and reputation, such is the vicious company she will have to keep. In a word, the Indians in Mauritius, though they have partially overcome caste prejudices, as above mentioned, yet have little concern for their intellectual, moral, and social improvement; nor do they care about the public rights and privileges, which as citizens they can enjoy under British Government. They have lost almost all the noble qualities, such as bravery, patriotism, love of liberty, true ambition, and self-respect. Their chief aim is to make money, either by honest or foul means, without any sense of *self-respect.*

There are a few heathen schools here and there, and the education given in them is of a secular character, consisting of Tamil and English. The standard is very low, and in fact the teachers themselves are not able to impart more than an elementary education, and that too in an imperfect manner. They are therefore next to nothing. Hence it is necessary that the Government should direct their attention towards improving the Indian character by opening fresh schools to impart Vernacular and English education of a more useful kind than they are imparting at present. With these remarks, I shall briefly describe the caste, religion, and habits of the population of Southern India, who are also to be found in the colony.

Of *Brahmins* and *Cshatryas* little need be said, as it is a notorious fact, that the duty of the former is to perform Sacerdotal functions, and that they subsist on alms. Sacred books relate the miraculous powers exerted by them in drying up the sea, vomiting fire on their enemies, &c., and as such they once enjoyed, and in some places do still enjoy, a rank almost equal to divinity. The Cshatryas, or the military class during the era of Hindoo independence, were not only great warriors, but even kings were chosen from this body. They are now in a state of depression. Very few of these two castemen are to be found in the colony.

Vaisyas, or traders dealing in different commodities, are divided into several sub-divisions according to the nature of their business. By tradition we hear that the Brahmins, Cshatryas and Vaisyas are strict vegetarians, but the Vaisyas now eat animal food. These are generally known by the name of Chetty or Chettiar; such as Caniety Chetty, Bari Chetty, and Telugu Chetty. Oil-mongers who profess to belong to the Vaisya caste are to be found here in immense numbers, most of them carrying on trade.

Sudras.—The original occupation of this caste is agricultural labour, yet certain people, forming sub-divisions, exercise various trades and handicrafts. Great exclusiveness prevails among these classes. They will not even eat their meals in the presence of each other. Their employments are transmitted by hereditary descent from father to son.

The *Vellalers*, whose language is Tamil, are of different grades. Their occupations are chiefly the cultivation of the earth, and trade. They worship Seva. Most of them are vegetarians. The vegetarians or Sival never keep their mustaches. The Vellalers are known by the appellation of Moodelliar or Pillay. Some of them are rich landed proprietors, and are of a charitable disposition.

Naicks and *Reddies*.—Their language is Telugu. Occupation, cultivators. They worship Vishnu. There seems but little difference between Naicks and Reddies. They are tall, muscular, and well made, and are the finest class of men; they make excellent soldiers. They use all animal food, saving the cow. The males, like the Vellalers, wear a pigtail or 'Kudumay,' and on the death of parents shave this as well as mustaches, in token of mourning. A singular custom exists among the Reddies as regards marriage. A young woman of fifteen or twenty years of age may be married to a boy of five or six years. She, however, lives with some other adult male, perhaps a maternal uncle or cousin, but is not allowed to form a connection with the father's relatives; occasionally it may be the boy husband's father himself, that is, the woman's father-in-law! Should there be children from these liasons, they are fathered on the boy husband.

When the boy grows up, the wife is either old or past child-bearing, when he in his turn takes up with some 'boy's' wife in a manner precisely similar to his own, and procreates children for the boy husband.

The *Yerkalas* or *Koravers*.—A wild tribe of India: they eat flesh meats of all kinds, in which they are by no means nice. The jungle herbs, roots, and fruits also furnish them with food. The majority of them pretend to fortune-telling, to which men and women are addicted. They also take to basket, mat, and wooden comb-making; for the former two they use the mid ribs and leaves of the date palm, and occasionally work as coolies. Sometimes wealthy men of the tribe settle down in places, and engage in cultivation. There appear to be many sub-divisions among them, which consist in the variety of their occupations; most of them confine themselves to particular ones, such as firewood sellers, salt sellers, basket makers, and coolies, &c. There is nothing remarkable in their physical structure; they are usually dark-coloured. Their bodies are usually filthy, and as a rule they wear nothing except a small piece of cloth. As a race they are low in the scale of civilisation; and while they pretend to a show of industry during the day, there is no doubt, from the large proportion they form as inmates of jails, that their habits at nights are decidedly of a predatory nature. They form bands of dacoits and thieves, and prefer living by theft to honest industry.

They are said to be the most troublesome of any of the wanderers. A similar tribe under the name of Oopoo Floraver is found in South Arcot.

Their language seems to be a medley of Tamil and Telugu. They have rude ideas of religion, and will worship any Hindoo deity; their old men are the priests of their community. Most of them have some household god, which they carry about with them in their constant travels. Polygamy prevails amongst them, and the number of wives is according to the means of the husband: the marriage string is tied round the neck of the wife.

Marriages are only contracted between adults. The ceremony is usually conducted on a Sunday, preceded by a poojah on the Saturday. Rice mixed with tumeric is bound on the heads of the married couple, and when the marriage string is tied the ceremony is complete. Marriages within certain degrees of relationship are not allowed, and widow re-marriages are not permitted; they may occasionally live in concubinage. A custom prevails among them by which the first two daughters of a family may be claimed by the maternal uncle as wives for his sons.

The value of a wife is fixed at twenty pagodas. The maternal uncle's right to the two first daughters is valued at eight out of twenty pagodas, and is carried out thus. If he urges his claim, and marries his own sons to his nieces, he pays for each only twelve pagodas, and similarly, if he, from not having sons, or any other cause, forego his claim, he receives eight pagodas of the twenty paid to the girl's parents by any one else who may marry them. There is a kind of clanship among these people. Each gang comprises many distinct families, each having their own family names; and, like the Hindoos, they form undivided families.

Wodders.—These are tank diggers, and are common throughout the country. They engage in the carrying trade, but more frequently move about from place to place in search of work. Besides Telugu, they have a peculiar dialect among themselves. They have nothing peculiar about their rites and ceremonies. Widow re-marriage is permitted. Occupation, labourers. There are some fine, well-made men among the tribe.

Lubbays are to be found in large numbers, chiefly between Pulicat on the north, and Negapatam on the south; their head-quarters being near Nagore, near Negapatam, the burial-place

INDIAN WOMAN AND CHILD.

of their patron saint, Nagore Meera Saib, to whose shrine numerous pilgrimages are made by the tribe. They are believed to be the descendants of Mohammedans and Hindoos, and are supposed to have come into existence during the Mohammedan conquest, when numbers of Hindoos were forcibly converted to the Mohammedan faith. They are followers of Mahomet, and practise circumcision. Physically they are a good-looking race, tallish, of light complexion, and well-developed limbs. They are generally attired in Loongees (cloths loosely fastened round the waist, and extending below the knees); they also wear bright-coloured jackets, occasionally turbans; the most frequent head-gear being a skull cap fitting closely to a shaved head.

Like Mussulmans they live freely on animals and vegetables, making use of all kinds of flesh meats, saving pork, for which they have a religious abhorrence. Their language is Tamil, though some talk a little Hindoostanee. They are exceedingly industrious and enterprising in their habits and pursuits, there being hardly a trade or calling in which they do not try to succeed. They make persevering fishermen and good boatmen. They are lapidaries, weavers, dyers, mat makers, jewellers, gardeners, bazaarmen, grocers, boat-makers and owners, and merchants. As regards the leather and horn trade, they excel as merchants; in short, there are few classes of natives in Southern India who in energy, industry, and perseverance can compete with the Lubbays.

Maravers.—These are believed to be descendants of lineal representatives of the Pandean dynasty.

The Maravers are a robust, hardy race. They are believed to be, by birth and profession, thieves and robbers, and have been from time immemorial employed as village watchmen, for which service they are paid in kind by the villagers for the protection of their property. They are true to their trust in their own village, but at night form large gangs, with a view of pillaging villages in remote places. If thwarted in their designs on these occasions, they become reckless, and frequently commit murder. To avoid being taken, they divest themselves of clothing, and oil their skins freely. They are prone to Hindooism; they make use of all flesh meats, except beef. They seldom cover their heads: the few that do so simply tie a long coloured handkerchief about the head. In their marriages difference of age, or the absence of the bridegroom, is of no consequence. The ceremony is contracted by the friends and relatives of either party, without the consent of the individual himself, and a block of wood is employed as proxy for the absent groom; and who, should he be absent from the village, knows nothing of the rite until his return, when he finds a wife to receive him. The rules of the tribe enforce the acceptance of the wife selected for him without his knowledge and consent. But these marriages are as readily dissolved as they are contracted; all that is necessary being for the dissentient party to cut the marriage string or thalee, and all is over. The man is bound to support his children. Their religion is a species of demonology and the worship of evil spirits, to whom bloody sacrifices are offered occasionally. There are devil dances, and these are introduced especially during the prevalence of cholera and small-pox, when the whole village is thrown into a state of excitement.

Shanars.—These are believed to be emigrants from Ceylon, from whence they migrated, and found their way into Madura and Tinnevelly, bringing with them the Palmyra palm seeds; and, having obtained the sandy wastes of these district coasts, they began cultivation. Their language is Tamil; and a very large proportion, more than one half, are either Protestant or Roman Catholic Christians, whilst their heathen fellows practise demonology, with its attendant bloody offerings and devil dances; when one or more become possessed with the devil, and get quite excited with their gestures, and are consulted by the people as to their fortunes. At present their chief occupation consists in attending to and collecting the juice of the palms. They are very timid and superstitious people.

Sembadaver.—These people live along the sea-coast, and follow the occupation of fishing. They own a number of boats, and proceed several miles out to sea before daylight; they return again about noon; they use nets, hooks, and lines. They are nominally Roman Catholics in creed. They certainly observe the Sabbath. As a race, they are addicted to drink, and are dissolute in their habits.

Suckilier or *Chucklers.*—These are considered low in the social scale, and form a sub-division of the Pariahs. They eat all kinds of animal food, and are particularly partial to horse-flesh, and will carry away and devour all diseased carcases of horses. In some places they, like the Pariahs, claim as their peculiar perquisite all cows, buffaloes, horses, and tattoos that have died of disease in their vicinity, over which they quarrel, the quarrel sometimes ending in murder. As a class, they are a dissolute, disorderly body, given to intoxication, and carry out the functions of hangmen in all stations where individuals are legally executed.

Kuller.—These people profess themselves to be of superior caste, than Maravers, though their habits, manners, religion, and occupation are identical with those of Maravers. Of these there are a few in the southern districts of the Madras presidency possessed of extensive landed property.

Yanadies, *Lumbadies*, and *Dombras* or *Jugglers*, are of the same class as Yerkalies or Koravers, viz. wild tribes, but they only differ from each other as regards occupation.

Shader, *Shanier*, and *Kykalaveer*.—These people, though divided into different classes, still all of them are weavers by occupation, and inclined to Hindooism. Their language is Tamil and Telugu.

Pattoonoalkarer.—These are silk manufacturers. There is nothing peculiar in their habits and manners. They are Hindoos, and they have a dialect of their own.

Cunnadier.—There are divisions and sub-divisions among this class of people, following several trades and callings. Some of them are priests, performing certain rites and ceremonies on funeral occasions among lower castes of Sudras; whereas such ceremonies among higher class Sudras are performed by the Brahmins. And a few live solely by selling curd, which they carry on their heads in large earthen pots to towns and places of public gathering for sale. Their language is Kannadum, a language in which all the revenue accounts were kept in the Madras Presidency, and which formed a branch of study in the Presidency College; but it has lately been discontinued, since the system of keeping the official accounts in that language was abolished.

Padyachy, *Gownden*, and *Pully*.—These are a sub-division of the Sudra caste. Their occupation is tillage. They are held to be somewhat low in the social scale. Those residing in towns take the title of Moodelliars and Naicks so as to conceal their real caste, as also to avoid the degradation they would otherwise be subjected to.

Janapper.—Another sub-division of the Sudra caste. They are generally ignorant, and deal in crockery, gunny bags, and tarpaulin. Some of them are hawkers, and others work as coolies. These are also held low in the social scale. They live on all animal food, saving the cow, but they are partial to bandicout flesh.

Nathaman.—These are a class of Roman Catholic Christians converted from Hindooism, who still retain certain habits and customs peculiar to the Hindoos. Their language is Tamil and Telugu.

Puller and *Pariah.*—These are by birth a degraded class, but of no caste. They are employed in the meanest offices, such as scavengers, and the rudest description of country labour. They usually dwell without the walls of the cities and villages, which present a disgusting sight. The touch, or even the close approach, of them is considered as a pollution by caste men. In Malabar a Nayror noble is legally authorised to kill a Pariah approaching his august presence.

CHAPTER XXIX.

SUGAR AND THE SUGAR-CANE.

Its History—Mode of Culture—Parasites that attack it—Its Manufacture—Amount exported and monetary Value—Dr. Icery's Process.

As Mauritius produces about one-ninth of the sugar grown in the whole world, it deserves a special mention ; and perhaps a slight sketch of its early history may not be without interest.

The best authorities of ancient and modern times lead to the conclusion that China was the first to cultivate the cane and manufacture sugar, and that its use was known there two thousand years before its adoption by Europeans.

Slowly the culture of the cane made its way to India, Arabia, and Egypt. The Phœnicians are supposed to have taken it to Greece, and the early Greek writers mention it as 'Indian salt.'

Its progress amongst civilised nations was very slow, on account of the jealousy of Indian cultivators, who feared the secret of its culture and manufacture spreading to the West ; also from the merchant vessels, in the early ages of navigation, being of such small dimensions, that sugar was too bulky an article for freight—the trader naturally seeking for the least weighty, and most profitable, articles of commerce.

It would be too long to trace its gradual introduction into different countries ; suffice it to say, that in the thirteenth century it was planted in Sicily, and the king, William II., gave the monks of St. Bennet a mill for grinding the canes ; but the sugar made was greatly inferior to that of the East.

In 1420, Dom Henry, Regent of Portugal, introduced it into the Madeiras and Canaries, with great success. After the discovery of America, it spread with such surprising rapidity, that in 1518 the proceeds of the port duties on sugar imported from Hispaniola were so enormous, that the magnificent palaces of Madrid and Toledo were erected from them. In 1520, St. Thomas had sixty sugar manufactories, and made 4,650,000 lbs. annually.[1]

In 1644, the English began to increase the manufactories in their possessions, and refining sugar was well known and practised at that period. It was, however, rarely used in England then, except for medicines, or as an article of extreme luxury, first, on account of its dearness, and, secondly, from a prejudice against it, as possessing unwholesome properties if taken in any but the smallest quantities.[2]

In the early part of the eighteenth century, the sugar-cane was introduced by Mahé de Labourdonnais into the Isle of France. It was with difficulty he could succeed in inducing the inhabitants to attend to its culture. Cloves, indigo, coffee, cotton, and different cereals so occupied the planters, that it was long before sugar took its place as an article of supreme importance for exportation. When once it had gained the palm, everything else gradually succumbed to it, and for years it has reigned paramount in Mauritius, not one of the above-named articles being now grown for commerce. The soil of this Island has proved remarkably propitious to the culture of the canes. Vast sums have been expended in procuring the best machines that Europe could produce, and the most skilful English and French engineers. Labour at great cost has been brought from India; no expense has been spared; and this little colony, in the year 1863, produced 122,432 tons of sugar of very superior quality, perhaps equal to any in the world, and commanded the best prices.

But, since that period, a general decadence has taken place, from a combination of unfortunate circumstances, such as droughts, fever, cyclones, and others, over which the planter had no control; and again, from those that result from overtaxing the energies of the land, faulty manuring, and other causes, within his own power to remedy, and to which planters generally are growing very wide awake.

[1] I am partially indebted for the above information to some stray leaves given to me of a large book on the sugar-cane. I know not the author, but should he be amongst my readers, and able to claim some of the remarks as his own, I beg him to accept my best thanks for them.

[2] This Island is no longer a sugar-producing one.

The yield since the above-mentioned period has been gradually less, till in 1868 it fell to 70,000 tons.

The cyclone of March 1868 put the climax to the distress long felt on every plantation; the violence of the wind prostrated and otherwise damaged the canes to a great extent. They were in a weakly state, and the roots not strong enough to give to the wind; and I found, on a careful examination of some of the injured plants, that the spongioles of the radicles were greatly hurt.

They were, however, apparently resuscitated by the continuous rains that fell soon after, and they appeared restored to more than ordinary vigour and luxuriant vegetation. The planters all looked forward to heavy crops, to make up their deficiencies, and the damage done to their mills and other buildings by the cyclone. When the time of the coupe (as the crop season is called here) arrived, dire was the disappointment. Abundance of juice was given, but it contained less than ordinary of saccharine matter.[1] I can well imagine the anxiety with which all looked to the results of the coupe. Many a once-wealthy planter, as he watched the work go on day by day, must have felt his last hope die out of saving the property on which he had bestowed so many years of labour and expense. Already heavily burthened with debt, accumulating at compound interest, nothing was left but bankruptcy. During the last three years, many of the finest and oldest estates have passed away from their original proprietors, and been brought to the hammer, and, I fear, many more will be before this crisis be past.

The simple plant that is the cause of so much anxiety to thousands of growers, buyers, and sellers; that has slain its hecatombs of victims, before the abolition of the slave trade; that, from its valuable qualities, has become an item of the highest importance in the commerce of all nations; for which the brains of men of the highest intellectual order have been racked to prepare the costliest machines for extracting its luscious juice—this

[1] One writer on the sugar-cane says, 'The soil most favourable to the sugar-cane is a rich and moist, but not a wet one. An excess of soluble mineral constituents in the soil is said to prevent the maturation of the cane, and it certainly has the effect of introducing into its juice soluble salts which injure the sugar and diminish the yield.' From January 1868 to May the rainfall was in such excess, that it doubtless caused a failure in the yield from the reasons given in the above note.

simple plant belongs to the large natural order of the Gramineæ or grasses. It is the *Saccharum officinarum*, also called *Arundo saccharifera*, an endogen, or inwardly developing plant.[1]

There appear to be three chief stocks from which most of the varieties now cultivated in Mauritius are derived—viz. the Creole, originally indigenous to India, the Batavian, and Otaheitan.

The principal sorts most in favour at the present day are: the white and red belloguet, the white diard, white-striped and red bamboo, white renang and guinghan. The latter canes, being harder, require, of course, stronger machinery to crush them, and, coming to maturity all at once, require to be cut down with great expedition; and this, again, exacts a superior plant to work it through rapidly.

The canes attain ordinarily from ten to fourteen feet in height, and three to six inches in circumference, according to the kind or favourable soil.

The cane, as in all reeds, has a knotty stalk, and at each knob a joint, or leaf.

The number of joints on the stalk varies from thirty to forty. The roots are very slender, seldom more than a foot long, with a few fibres at their extremities.

The cane requires from ten to twenty months after planting to arrive at maturity.

It is cultivated either by planting the top of the cut cane, or by allowing the parent stole to put forth new ones, and to form new ratoons.

In both cases the new canes are derived from buds, which are situated on the alternate sides of the cane at the joints. The buds at the lower and upper extremities of the cane retain the power of vegetation the longest, the former being protected by the earth, and the latter by the tuft of leaves at the top, from drought. Every joint of the cane and stole contains all the organs necessary for an entire plant.

The wood exists in the body of the cane in long tubular cells,

[1] I have collected the above information from the best authorities on the sugar-cane; amongst others, I would mention the pamphlets by Messrs. Antelme, Bouton, Autard de Bragard, and Dr. F. Guthrie. I am also under obligations to the courtesy of many gentlemen owning and belonging to different estates, and otherwise connected with the staple product of the Island.

which extend from joint to joint. Their form is hexagonal, and their function to hold the cane juice. Towards the circumference, these cells become flatter, and their capacity less. They form at last a hard, compact, woody envelope. The quantity of wax and silica gives to the rind its peculiar hardness and power to repel water.

Mauritius offers everywhere to the eye spacious cane fields, with here and there the long chimneys rising high above the surrounding buildings, that generally lie embowered in a grove of trees, often the only ones visible for miles.

The forests, which formerly covered the Island to the water's edge, even close to Port Louis, have gradually disappeared, a few only remaining in the interior. Strict laws have long been in existence for the preservation of the forests, but they do not seem to have been enforced much. As wood and charcoal are the only things used as fuel, the destruction is still going on.

Could Labourdonnais see his much-loved isle in the present day, he would scarcely recognise any part of it. Where once stood the monarchs of the forest are now fields of waving canes, or arid plains, every stream long dried up. Through districts only intersected then by cattle tracks are now wide roads, and over them rush the railway trains bearing their freights of the precious substance to be shipped to all parts of the world. All is changed, and by the very people he fought so bravely to keep from getting a footing in the Isle of France—by them have all his hopes and plans been brought to fruition. Unlike many other sugar-growing countries, in Mauritius the planter is also the manufacturer of sugar, which multiplies tenfold the difficulty of the administration of an estate.[1]

The first operations when a field is marked out for cultivation are to extirpate all weeds, root up old stocks, and lift away the rocks and stones which more or less encumber all ground, and place them in even rows.

Between these at set distances, about eighteen or twenty inches apart, holes are dug twelve inches and a half deep, eighteen long, and eight wide.

Generally before planting, about ten or twelve pounds of well-

[1] For the same man to grow the cane, crush it, boil the juice, and make the sugar, points to a system as relatively imperfect as that when the farmer is also the miller and baker.

decomposed stable manure are placed in each hole, and pressed down by the feet of the labourer, when it is covered with a light layer of earth.

The cuttings are made from the five or six tender joints or knobs nearest the heart of the cane; two, three, or four of which are put into each hole, according to the locality or season.

The best months for planting are December, January, February, and March.

In the quarters most exposed to droughts, after planting, the holes are filled up with dried leaves or grass, to protect the young shoots from the ardour of the sun.

The cuttings are placed lengthwise in the holes, taking care that the eyes of each are turned in opposite directions, so as not to impede each other's growth.

At the expiration of the time necessary for the shooting of the canes, the dead, fermented, and those with sickly buds are replaced by fresh ones.

The cuttings of the virgin or first canes are preferred, as being more healthy than those of the second.

To free the canes, before planting, from the insects that infest them, they are plunged from ten to twelve hours in a mixture of phœnique or carbolic acid and water—an infallible remedy.

Sometimes manuring is done after planting, but then the litter is placed between the rows of canes, or in a circular trench dug round the stocks of the young plants.

But all this is only a slight portion of the work required in sugar culture.

Then comes the clearing the young canes of the weeds and runners which invade them, and pioching up the earth so as to render it permeable to air and water.

The weeds grow with such marvellous rapidity, that the planters are obliged to watch the tender canes with the greatest care. The number of clearings depends on the soil, climate, and nature of the weeds on various estates. The different earths are divided into the rocky and free (to use a colonial expression). Nearly the whole of the land of Mauritius on the littoral is rocky, in fact to such an extent in some parts, that, with the stones cleared off them, walls from two to four feet high are raised between the rows of canes; yet they are of the greatest fertility, very porous, and easily imbibing water, and yielding good crops with proper manurings and rest.

The free earths are not, as their name would intimate, destitute of rocks, but are only less encumbered than the rocky. These lands lie more in the interior, except in some parts of Savane and Grand Port, where they extend to the sea-shore. Loose volcanic, rocky debris and stones are found from the coast to the tops of the mountains.

Constant turning up is required in the free soils, for the introduction of air, and to decompose the vegetable matter in the earth. In some places a plough might be advantageously used in planting, but it has not yet been adopted I believe.

The stables and cattle folds are the two great sources of manure for the plantations; and the heads and leaves of the canes employed as food or litter afford them ample materials.

Except in the more humid localities where wood is plentiful all the sugar houses employ bagasse[1] and cane leaves as fuel Every plantation has then a great quantity of ashes, which wher returned to the earth form its most valuable renovator. One of the principal planters writes, 'Long experience has shown that the ashes ought to be previously mixed with vegetable matter in fermentation; and when the skimmings of sugar are added, and the fibrils of the bagasse, they act promptly and energetically on the canes.'

This appears to me most sensible advice; but unfortunately too many take away everything from the soil, returning little to it of the actual ingredients required to give the juice the proper quantity of saccharine matter.

Of late years the most prominent place as a renovator has been held by guano. Its stimulating properties increase the production twofold for a time, and it has made the fortune of many planters.

In the end it is like killing the goose for her eggs, for it is certain loss eventually, when injudiciously used, as too many have already found in their failing crops.

The above-mentioned writer says, and most correctly, 'Invaluable as guano undoubtedly is, its analysis proves it does not

[1] Bagasse is the word applied in Mauritius to designate the fibrous and spongy parts left from the canes that have passed through the mill.

contain all the mineral substances that enter into the composition of the cane; therefore, it is certain that those planters who do not restore to the soil the ashes and other debris of the cane, will find the fertility of their lands gradually diminish.' This is so true that already in many localities exhaustion has set in.

Nearly 130,000*l.* annually are spent in guano, and, according to one authority, two-thirds of that quantity are wasted, from the guano possessing an amount of extraneous matter, such as nitrogen, &c., which is not required at all, and is therefore so much waste. So many cheaper manures may be had, possessing *all* the ingredients required by the cane.

When there is such a waste daily going on in the city of Port Louis, of matter enough to enrich every plantation in the Island, it is a pity some intelligent practical man does not set about what would be the greatest benefaction to the colony as well as boundless profit to himself.

Never was any place in such a deplorable state as to its sewage. Though efforts have been lately made to put things on a more decent footing than formerly, yet all in connection with this question is wofully behind the age.

I believe that a proper system of sewage would not only soon defray all expenses of the present plan of draining the city, but it would soon save the 130,000*l.*, now paid for guano, to the colony.

I see by a late paper that the Metropolitan and Essex Reclamation Company are showing on a large scale the value of sewage as a fertilising agent in England; and one especial passage I notice, 'The sewage when used is colourless, and free from taint and odour.'

To use the sewage of Mauritius thus would, I feel sure, restore it to its once healthy condition, for it would do away with the greatest source of disease in the Island. But the system must be carried on over every estate to be really beneficial, and the planter would soon reap his profit in the increase of health and strength in his camp.

In some parts of the Island the rainfall is sufficient for the canes, but in those utterly denuded of forests they suffer frequently from drought. Irrigation is resorted to, but in many places it is an expensive and tedious process; and the failure of the streams in very dry weather renders it often totally impracticable. The leaves grow yellow and withered, and unless the canes get rain before they are dried to a certain point a failure of the juice is certain.

Some of the planters have well studied the advantages of a change of crops. After the canes have yielded for two seasons, the ground is either allowed to lie fallow or is planted with manioc, which serves as food for the cattle; several kinds of peas, called ambrevades—the black pea being eaten greedily by oxen, sheep, goats and pigs, and the yellow flowered one being used both by men and animals; arrowroot, which the Island produces in abundance, the whitest and best in the world, and maize.

Three years is the time usually given to the land between the cane crops.

Every one who has thus carried out the system of a rotation of crops has reaped the benefit of it.

It is a fact known by every farmer all the world over, and yet how many planters go on, year by year, planting the same fields, and over-manuring; and the result is much of the misery of the present day.

I do not doubt that the diseases in the cane have been brought about in a great measure by the above practices.

There are two enemies the planter has had to fight against, most deadly ones—the pou blanc as it is called here, and the borer.

The latter, or *Proceras sacchariphagus*, made its appearance in 1850. Some canes were imported from Ceylon in 1848 that were pronounced to be all attacked by a boring caterpillar, a plague well known to exist in some parts of that island. It was thought so dangerous to plant them that they were all condemned. They lay however for some days under the shed near the port office, whence it is supposed some of the cuttings were clandestinely removed and planted at Flacq.

The man who committed such an insane act had better have applied a torch to his plantation.

Two years after, the canes at Grand Baie were attacked by an insect recognised as the same as those on the Ceylon canes.

It also appeared at Labourdonnais the same year, though then imagined to have been brought in some canes imported from Java; but it has since been stated that the borer is unknown there.

The depredations of this insect were frightful, as it soon ravaged whole plantations in every part of the Island.

When the eggs of the borer are hatched, the caterpillar remains on the leaves until it is strong enough to attack the cane.

It possesses two powerful mandibles, and its mouth is armed with a lance-like instrument, which serves it to pierce the flinty cuticle of the cane. When it has once made good its entry it mines it with frightful rapidity, and as soon as it attacks the heart the plant withers and dies. It is one of the most voracious of insects.

When hatched it is only 1¼ line large, but at the end of thirty-one or thirty-two days it is of the thickness of a quill. It then begins to spin its envelope, which it lines with debris of the cane and leaves. The chrysalis state lasts about fifteen days, and it then emerges a fly of a reddish colour on a silver grey ground, covered with powdery scales that fly off with every movement of the insect.

During the next five days it lays its eggs, to the number of 130, and then dies.

This destructive insect has an inveterate enemy in the ant tribe that wages continual war on it, and they, being so small, are able to pursue wherever the borer hides. Many birds also devour it greedily; but, in spite of all its enemies, it has continued its ravages even to the present day. It has partially disappeared in some districts, but will I fear never be eradicated.

The pou blanc is of the genus Coccus, and a most destructive insect. It will stand the highest and lowest temperatures, and I have seen it in the three parts of the world I have visited. There are many species of it, and all of them generally attack sickly plants and trees. It is possible that the diseased state of the canes in 1848, a short time previously to the appearance of this insect, induced its ravages; for wherever an unhealthy plant is, there is sure to be some parasite, often one quite unknown in the vicinity previously. The coccus on the Mauritian canes deposits about 150 eggs under its carapace or shell. This takes place after the female has done feeding for the season.

Some days are occupied in depositing these eggs, which are

enveloped in a web that she spins round them, raising the carapace, and exhibiting a white cottony substance beneath.

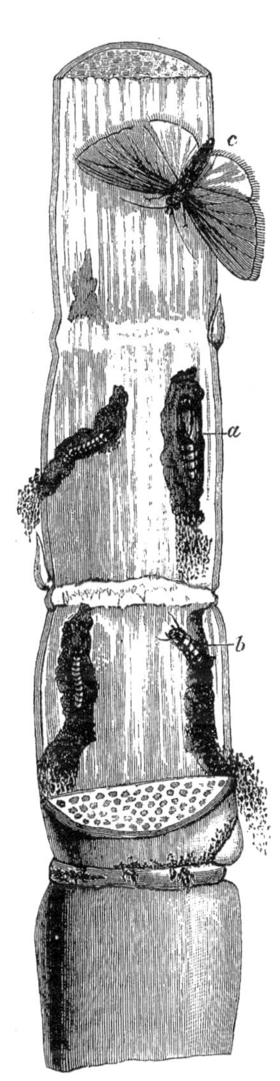

LARVA AND PUPA.

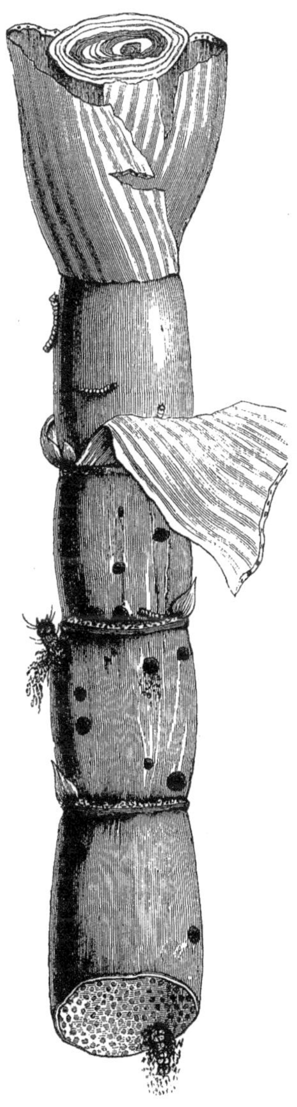
DISEASED SUGAR-CANE.

If the weather is favourable, in a few days the young appear, and are very active, running about on the green shoots and leaves, until they find a spot that suits them to fix themselves for life.

They are armed with a sharp probe as long as the body, which they insert in the young sap-wood, and suck away the life-juices of the plant, sometimes quite destroying it.

On cutting branches that have become fibrous where these insects have been at work, the whole medullary system seems so deranged that circulation appears almost impossible.

This insect spreads and multiplies rapidly. It has one inveterate enemy, the ant, which annoys it by tickling it with its forefeet while eating, and causing it to disgorge the juices it has fed on, which it devours greedily, till the pou shrinks up and dies, starved out. I gave a full description of this insect, in a treatise I published on the vine disease in 1853.

This coccus has been very destructive in different cities of America.

Newhaven in the United States is known as the 'City of Elms,' from its streets and squares being planted with these magnificent trees. They were all attacked a few years ago by the coccus, or cotton louse as it is called there, and numbers of them were destroyed. A reward was offered for the prevention of this pest.

Amongst other propositions was one to scrape the trees, and shower them with a solution of blubber oil and water, which proved effectual in eradicating the insect from the city.

No sooner, however, had they got rid of one plague, than another appeared. On examination, it was found that the trees were diseased at their roots, owing partially to the gas pipes passing close to them; also from their inhaling the impure air from the gases emanating from the general use of hard coal in the city. In most of the towns of the United States the trees sicken from the same causes.

The coccus will not attack plants and trees that are not previously in a diseased or sickly state. I will mention an instance of this.

In front of my own residence in New York I had planted, at great expense, many fine trees on the lawn. Among them were some magnolias, one of which was injured in transplanting. This tree put forth its leaves in the spring, but looked so sickly that I concluded it would die in the fall. By midsummer, the tree was covered with the cotton louse, which killed it, but none were found on the healthy plants.

It is my conviction that the canes had been so over-stimulated by guano, that they were in a fit state for the attacks of the pou blanc. Wherever this exists, if the plant is examined, the roots will be found diseased, and the medullary system filled with a gummy substance, which prevents the circulation.

During the entrecoupe, the sugar houses are thoroughly cleaned and painted, the machinery repaired, and everything put in order; a notable instance of which may be seen on the Labour-

CANE PLANT.

donnais estate, which I can best describe by saying that it is a model of cleanliness and order within and without, and does infinite credit to the manager and his staff of superintendents and workmen.

As soon as the coupe begins, all is activity; no time for idlers then, and the anxiety of the proprietor is ceaseless till he sees the returns his canes are likely to yield.

In September the canes generally arrive at maturity, but according to locality, time of planting &c.: they are often not ripe for cutting till October or November.

When a field is pronounced fit to cut, a third of the labourers with a small hatchet chop off the canes close to the earth, another third clear them from the leaves, and the rest pack them upright in carts, and take them to the mill.

After many tons of canes have been cut and carted to the sugar house, steam is put on the engine; and if the mill is powerful, say of 35-horse power, and rollers fifty by thirty, it will require about twenty coolies to supply it with canes. In the process of feeding the mill the coolies proceed in rotation on each side of the feed-plate, fetching up a dozen or two canes on their shoulders, pitching them in without much regard to order, and, with one turn of the huge roller the greater part come out on the other side crushed to dry chips, which are carted away, and spread out in the sun to dry.

This refuse is the bagasse, and when thoroughly dried is stacked in ricks or covered sheds for future use as fuel for the engine.

In this first process lies one great cause of loss to the planters. Some attribute it to the use of plated rollers; however that may be, it is certain from some cause, in the crushing of the canes the planter's loss is serious, said to be equal from three to eight lbs. in the 100 lbs. of sugar. To give an instance; a rich proprietor has obtained by a powerful mill 4,550 lbs. of juice from 7,500 lbs. of canes, the mean rendering being 60 to 68 per cent.

This loss is equivalent to 2,860 lbs. of sugar to an arpent.[1]

This planter cultivates from 700 to 800 arpents, so that he loses the frightful quantity of from 2,002,000 lbs. to 2,288,000 lbs. yearly.

The liquor, now called Vesou, that flows from the mill (looking like water disgustingly muddy) is at once conducted by wooden or cast-iron gutters to the steam defecators of 300 gallons each, where it is heated to boiling point.

The vesou flowing thence into the first pans of the battery, ebullition commences in those next the furnace; as it boils up at a temperature not exceeding 140°, it is constantly skimmed and ladled from pan to pan, until relieved of its impurities.

The vesou is then run into clarifiers of the same size, where lime is added, about 3 lbs to each 300 gallons.

[1] An arpent is 100 square perches, and a perch is 20 feet French.

It is stirred up and then allowed to rest for fifteen or twenty minutes, when it is drawn off and evaporated to 25° Réaumur in cast-iron pans.

The liquor, now designated Clairée, is sent into large cisterns, where it remains for twenty-four hours. And thus it goes on: as long as the mill is working the battery works too, defecating and concentrating. The vacuum pan now comes into operation. Steam is put on the pan, an engine with pumps for exhaustion is set going, and, when a vacuum of 25° is attained, about 500 gallons of Clairée are admitted into the pan; and when once grains are formed in that quantity, more and more is allowed to flow in as granulation takes place.

The temperature of the pan is always kept at 170°, and in about four hours, or less with a good pan, nearly four tons of sugar will be taken out. The sugar runs from the pan along wooden troughs into large shallow wooden cisterns, where it remains from six to ten hours for cooling, till it is ready for the centrifugal machines called turbines, which purge and drain the sugar.

These machines revolve at the rapid rate of about 1,200 rotations per minute, and separate the syrup from the sugar, which flows through a pipe in the side of the turbine into large vats under the sugar house. It is then called molasses, and is sold to the distillers for the manufacture of rum.

When the turbine is in motion a small quantity of water is thrown in, and the sugar can be made extremely white. On some of the estates it is made into large crystals. On leaving the turbines the sugar is packed into gunny and Vacoa bags, and is then ready for the market.

Many of the planters still use the wetzells, a machine far inferior to the vacuum pan, but on all the large estates the latter is used.

During the whole of the coupe, the air on the plantations is filled with the powerful odour of the boiling sugar. Everywhere you hear but the one topic, sugar, sugar, and still sugar, or crops.

On the arrival of the monthly mail, all are eager for the latest sugar quotations, and the first question is always, Are sugars up or down?

I fear Mauritius has produced more than she ever will again, and that real capital will have to be introduced in order to carry on the plantations profitably. Most of the planters are bankrupt, and even the few who still keep their heads above water do so by paying enormous percentage for capital.

Annexed to this is a table of the exportation of sugar from 1812 to 1870, together with its value in pounds sterling, &c.

EXPORTATION OF SUGAR FROM 1812 TO 1869.

YEARS	Sugar lbs. French	Sugar English Weight			
		Tons	cwts.	qrs.	lbs.
1812 . . .	969,264	467	6	1	25
1813 . .	549,465	264	18	1	18
1814 . . .	1,034,294	498	13	2	5
1815 . . .	2,504,957	1,207	14	3	21
1816 . . .	8,296,352	4,000	0	2	4
1817 . . .	6,583,457	3,174	3	1	9
1818 . . .	7,908,380	3,812	19	1	14
1819 . . .	5,678,888	2,738	0	2	23
1820 . . .	15,524,755	7,485	2	3	27
1821 . . .	20,410,053	9,840	11	0	25
1822 . . .	23,403,644	11,283	17	3	27
1823 . . .	27,400,887	13,211	2	3	9
1824 . . .	24,334,553	11,732	14	2	13
1825 . . .	21,739,766	10,481	13	1	23
1826 . . .	42,489,416	20,485	19	1	13
1827 . . .	40,619,254	19,584	5	2	18
1828 . . .	48,350,101	23,311	13	0	13
1829 . . .	58,431,538	28,172	6	3	25
1830 . . .	67,926,692	32,750	7	1	15
1831 . . .	70,203,676	33,848	4	0	2
1832 . . .	73,594,778	35,483	3	3	20
1833 . . .	67,482,800	32,536	7	—	—
1834 . . .	71,143,851	34,301	9	3	27
1835 . . .	64,876,825	31,279	17	3	23
1836 . . .	63,333,513	30,535	16	0	2
1837 . . .	68,275,065	32,918	6	2	22
1838 . . .	72,002,226	34,715	7	0	20
1839 . . .	68,572,979	33,061	19	1	21
1840 . . .	82,048,509	39,559	2	0	5
1841 . . .	78,969,678	38,074	13	1	8
1842 . . .	71,225,151	34,340	13	3	23
1843 . . .	55,026,564	26,530	13	1	5
1844 . . .	72,656,720	35,030	18	1	13
1845 . . .	87,561,994	42,217	7	3	5
1846 . . .	127,531,510	61,488	8	0	14
1847 . . .	118,291,246	57,033	5	2	9
1848 . . .	114,653,469	55,279	7	0	2
1849 . . .	133,418,250	64,326	13	0	14
1850 . . .	114,393,223	55,153	17	2	—
1851 . . .	138,123,365	66,595	3	3	14
1852 . . .	148,550,169	71,622	8	0	6
1853 . . .	190,342,546	91,772	5	3	25

EXPORTATION OF SUGAR—*continued.*

YEARS	Sugar lbs. French	Sugar English Weight			
		Tons	cwts.	qrs.	lbs.
1854 . . .	176,116,461	84,913	5	3	13
1855 . . .	204,081,115	127,324	16	1	24
1856 . . .	244,667,523	117,964	13	3	24
1857 . . .	240,910,000	116,153	0	2	24
1858 . . .	246,229,138	118,717	12	1	17
1859 . . .	256,981,607	123,901	16	3	19
1860 . . .	271,807,107	131,049	17	0	11
1861 . . .	220,631,916	106,376	2	0	5
1862 . . .	268,162,551	129,292	13	0	19
1863 . . .	274,548,961	132,371	16	1	17
1864 . . .	233,440,106	112,551	9	2	10
1865 . . .	270,026,937	130,191	11	0	19
1866 . . .	247,383,011	119,273	19	0	3
1867 . . .	200,895,816	96,860	9	2	17
1868 . . .	198,601,676	95,754	7	2	10
1869 . . .	213,766,517	103,065	19	3	26

This return represents the annual exportation of sugar from January 1 to December 31 of each year.

Dr. Icery has invented what he calls the mono-sulphite of lime for purifying sugar. He gives practical instructions for its manufacture and use. He gives a diagram of machinery that can be easily added to the sugar-house, and the article can be made at an extremely low price. To use Dr. Icery's own words, 'This process consists of an altogether special method of preparing sulphite of lime, and of applying it in the decoloration and purification of cane juice and syrups. The apparatus, by its solidity, its particular arrangement, and the perfect regularity of its action, satisfies as nearly as is possible the exigencies and usages of colonial manufacture. The syrups remaining from the turbinage of sugars, when treated with mono-sulphite of lime, give most advantageous results. Under the influence of that agent syrups become purified, decolorised, and crystallised with remarkable facility.

'Manufactured by this process, syrup sugars have a perfect grain and fine colour ; not entirely due to the direct influence of the substance employed, but from the purification to which the vesou has already been submitted, and the absence in the syrup

EXPORTATION OF SUGAR FROM MAURITIUS TO DIFFERENT PLACES FROM THE CROP 1843–44 TO THE CROP 1869–70.

[*Kindly furnished by the Editor of the 'Commercial Gazette.'*]

CROPS	United Kingdom	France	Australian Colonies	Cape	India	Other Places	TOTAL
	lbs.	lbs.	lbs.	lbs.	lbs.	lbs.	lbs.
1843–44 . .	56,941,099	—	213,529	2,370,475	—	20,772	59,545,875
1844–45 . .	73,152,498	—	3,694,450	1,282,030	—	36,128	78,165,106
1845–46 . .	94,837,167	—	4,090,759	3,216,513	—	23,729	102,168,168
1846–47 . .	124,912,296	—	3,856,880	4,304,937	—	336,090	133,410,203
1847–48 . .	103,674,275	—	10,317,053	8,571,344	—	264,616	122,827,288
1848–49 . .	93,953,789	—	7,418,812	4,883,146	—	14,842	106,270,598
1849–50 . .	107,355,498	—	6,432,266	6,233,774	—	501,957	120,523,495
1850–51 . .	106,539,801	—	5,497,469	4,254,903	—	794,233	117,086,406
1851–52 . .	114,859,749	—	9,271,133	13,098,867	—	145,430	137,375,179
1852–53 . .	137,617,792	—	16,230,021	7,395,471	—	84,504	161,327,788
1853–54 . .	173,212,219	349,797	22,992,073	5,836,576	—	881,340	203,272,005
1854–55 . .	153,645,610	26,037,768	26,500,630	11,285,845	—	3,039,182	220,509,035
1855–56 . .	178,176,094	16,867,241	28,885,626	5,816,358	—	338,849	230,084,168
1856–57 . .	125,532,100	48,523,297	37,689,275	7,280,144	—	3,448,702	222,473,518
1857–58 . .	116,896,933	34,337,965	49,273,860	11,767,840	—	5,804,352	218,080,950
1858–59 . .	133,213,960	41,944,694	47,581,513	10,622,440	—	4,536,312	237,898,919
1859–60 . .	108,238,079	59,905,435	43,751,932	10,100,726	—	4,950,140	226,946,312
1860–61 . .	185,572,459	27,399,837	43,053,751	9,258,895	—	6,714,209	271,999,151
1861–62 . .	82,718,558	50,047,715	67,207,552	12,835,521	—	7,607,891	220,417,237
1862–63 . .	170,709,066	42,199,734	69,916,628	13,817,204	17,551,200	2,128,444	316,322,276
1863–64 . .	118,255,069	36,702,080	59,397,235	9,354,230	19,199,598	524,313	243,432,525
1864–65 . .	116,825,885	48,837,456	61,408,877	9,326 914	22,853,945	1,079,974	260,333,051
1865–66 . .	131,463,429	3,620,722	69,623,783	4,486,299	30,708,980	1,513,057	241,416,270
1866–67 . .	51,423,733	11,223,163	100,360,454	6,469,993	44,938,743	2,059,076	216,475,162
1867–68 . .	102,550,997	3,309,362	70,617,653	3,655,330	51,760,761	1,087,583	232,981,686
1868–69 . .	43,808,898	9,957,359	73,420,247	1,507,740	26,658,466	1,210,574	156,563,284
1869–70 . .	76,212,485	22,310,088	99,748,587	4,751,588	59,209,368	2,273,428	264,505,545

This return represents the exportation of sugar of each annual crop, i.e. from July to July.

of those foreign soluble matters which are the principal obstacles to the crystallisation of sugars of the second boiling.'

Dr. Icery's process seems to be gaining ground, and is already employed on many estates, as it has been proved that a larger quantity and better quality of sugar is obtained from the syrup, in addition to which the process is more economical.

THE AUTHOR'S DOG 'QUILP.'

APPENDIX.

THE following letter was sent to me by an Indian Creole, and is about the best begging letter I ever received. It speaks for itself without any comment of mine, so I give it verbatim, also preserving the punctuation.

TO THE HONORABLE PRESENCE OF MISTER THE COUNCEL OF THE AMERICAN COUNTRY.

The Humble Petition of Surwurrah.

Assured of your Benevolences and Sympathy, your needy ; most respectfully, as well as humbly, begs to offer this small acknowledgement of your great favour, and kindness in aiding him with several good things, while he was sick on his bed with the fever.

Your Humble Petitioner is in a miserable condition at present ; having no families or kindreds, in this Colony of Mauritius his Father and Mother being died of the Fever, so ; as to care for him, and keep up his things, without wasting in vain, the Benefits of his travailes ; he thinks it necessary to marry a wife, and he has found a good match for him, with whom he has engaged to be married on the 25th Instant.

The, Baptised name of your Poor Petitioner is Christian, having, no means, or influence to perform his marriage he humbly as well as, very Confidently solicit your Honor, of your Clemency have an eye of Sympathy, and lend him some money, which will be considered a great help to finish his marriage. He pays your Honor now some monies of a former account, and for the money you will lend hereafter, he can pay in 5 months. The God almighty will reward you and, incress your Stores.

SURWURRAH.

BURTON'S LAKE REGIONS OF CENTRAL AFRICA. The Lake Regions of Central Africa. A Picture of Exploration. By RICHARD F. BURTON, Captain H. M.'s Indian Army, Fellow and Gold Medalist of the Royal Geographical Society. With Maps and Engravings on Wood. 8vo, Cloth, $3 50.

BURTON'S CITY OF THE SAINTS. The City of the Saints; and Across the Rocky Mountains to California. By Captain RICHARD F. BURTON, Fellow and Gold Medalist of the Royal Geographical Societies of France and England, H. M.'s Consul in West Africa. With Maps and numerous Illustrations. 8vo, Cloth, $3 50.

BELLOWS'S TRAVELS. The Old World in its New Face: Impressions of Europe in 1867, 1868. By HENRY W. BELLOWS. 2 vols., 12mo, Cloth, $3 50.

CURTIS'S THE HOWADJI IN SYRIA. By GEORGE WILLIAM CURTIS. 12mo, Cloth, $1 50.

CURTIS'S NILE NOTES OF A HOWADJI. By GEORGE WILLIAM CURTIS. 12mo, Cloth, $1 50.

CUMMING'S HUNTER'S LIFE IN AFRICA. Five Years of a Hunter's Life in the far Interior of South Africa. With Notices of the Native Tribes, and Anecdotes of the Chase of the Lion, Elephant, Hippopotamus, Giraffe, Rhinoceros, &c. With Illustrations. By R. GORDON CUMMING. 2 vols., 12mo, Cloth, $3 00.

DAVIS'S CARTHAGE. Carthage and her Remains: being an Account of the Excavations and Researches on the Site of the Phœnician Metropolis in Africa and other Adjacent Places. Conducted under the Auspices of Her Majesty's Government. By Dr. N. DAVIS, F.R.G.S. Profusely Illustrated with Maps, Woodcuts, Chromo-Lithographs, &c. 8vo, Cloth, $4 00.

DILKE'S GREATER BRITAIN. Greater Britain: a Record of Travel in English-speaking Countries during 1866 and 1867. By CHARLES WENTWORTH DILKE. With Maps and Illustrations. 12mo, Cloth, $1 00.

DOOLITTLE'S CHINA. Social Life of the Chinese; with some Account of their Religious, Governmental, Educational, and Business Customs and Opinions. With special but not exclusive Reference to Fuhchau. By Rev. JUSTUS DOOLITTLE, Fourteen Years Member of the Fuhchau Mission of the American Board. Illustrated with more than 150 characteristic Engravings on Wood. 2 vols., 12mo, Cloth, $5 00.

DU CHAILLU'S AFRICA. Explorations and Adventures in Equatorial Africa; with Accounts of the Manners and Customs of the People, and of the Chase of the Gorilla, the Crocodile, Leopard, Elephant, Hippopotamus, and other Animals. By PAUL B. DU CHAILLU, Corresponding Member of the American Ethnological Society, of the Geographical and Statistical Society of New York, and of the Boston Society of Natural History. With numerous Illustrations. 8vo, Cloth, $5 00.

DU CHAILLU'S ASHANGO LAND. A Journey to Ashango Land, and Further Penetration into Equatorial Africa. By PAUL B. DU CHAILLU. New Edition. Handsomely Illustrated. 8vo, Cloth, $5 00.

EWBANK'S BRAZIL. Life in Brazil; or, a Journal of a Visit to the Land of the Cocoa and the Palm. With an Appendix, containing Illustrations of Ancient and South American Arts, in recently discovered Implements and Products of Domestic Industry, and Works in Stone, Pottery, Gold, Silver, Bronze, &c. By THOMAS EWBANK. With over 100 Illustrations. 8vo, Cloth, $3 00.

ELLIS'S MADAGASCAR. Three Visits to Madagascar, during the Years 1853, 1854, 1856. Including a Journey to the Capital, with Notices of the Natural History of the Country, and of the Present Civilization of the People. By the Rev. WILLIAM ELLIS, F.H.S. Illustrated by a Map and Woodcuts from Photographs, &c. 8vo, Cloth, $3 50.

HALL'S ARCTIC RESEARCHES. Arctic Researches and Life among the Esquimaux: being the Narrative of an Expedition in Search of Sir John Franklin, in the Years 1860, 1861, and 1862. By CHARLES FRANCIS HALL. With Maps and 100 Illustrations. 8vo, Cloth, Beveled, $5 00.

HERODOTUS, LIFE AND TRAVELS OF. The Life and Travels of Herodotus in the Fifth Century before Christ: an Imaginary Biography founded on Fact, illustrative of the History, Manners, Religion, Literature, Arts, and Social Condition of the Greeks, Egyptians, Persians, Babylonians, Hebrews, Scythians, and other Ancient Nations, in the Days of Pericles and Nehemiah. By J. TALBOYS WHEELER, F.R.G.S. Map. 2 vols., 12mo, Cloth, $3 50.

HOLTON'S NEW GRANADA. Twenty Months in the Andes. By I. F. HOLTON. Illustrations and Maps. 8vo, Cloth, $3 00.

KINGSLEY'S WEST INDIES. At Last: A Christmas in the West Indies. By CHARLES KINGSLEY, Author of "Alton Locke," "Yeast," &c., &c. Illustrated. 12mo, Cloth, $1 50.

LIVINGSTONE'S SOUTH AFRICA. Missionary Travels and Researches in South Africa; including a Sketch of Sixteen Years' Residence in the Interior of Africa, and a Journey from the Cape of Good Hope to Loando on the West Coast; thence across the Continent, down the River Zambesi, to the Eastern Ocean. By DAVID LIVINGSTONE, LL.D., D.C.L. With Portrait, Maps by Arrowsmith, and numerous Illustrations. 8vo, Cloth, $4 50.

LIVINGSTONE'S EXPEDITION TO THE ZAMBESI. Narrative of an Expedition to the Zambesi and its Tributaries; and of the Discovery of the Lakes Shirwa and Nyassa. 1858–1864. By DAVID and CHARLES LIVINGSTONE. With Map and Illustrations. 8vo, Cloth, $5 00.

LAYARD'S NINEVEH. A Popular Account of the Discoveries at Nineveh. By AUSTEN HENRY LAYARD. Abridged by him from his larger Work. With numerous Wood Engravings. 12mo, Cloth, $1 75.

LAYARD'S FRESH DISCOVERIES AT NINEVEH. Fresh Discoveries at Nineveh and Babylon; with Travels in Armenia, Kurdistan, and the Desert. Being the Result of a Second Expedition undertaken for the Trustees of the British Museum. By AUSTEN HENRY LAYARD, M.P. With all the Maps and Engravings in the English Edition. 8vo, Cloth, $4 00.

MARCY'S ARMY LIFE ON THE BORDER. Thirty Years of Army Life on the Border. Comprising Descriptions of the Indian Nomads of the Plains; Explorations of New Territory; a Trip across the Rocky Mountains in the Winter; Descriptions of the Habits of Different Animals found in the West, and the Methods of Hunting them; with Incidents in the Lives of different Frontier Men, &c., &c. By Brevet Brig.-General R. B. MARCY, U. S. A. 8vo, Cloth, Beveled Edges, $3 00.

MOWRY'S ARIZONA AND SONORA. Arizona and Sonora. The Geography, History, and Resources of the Silver Region of North America. By SYLVESTER MOWRY, of Arizona, Graduate of the U. S. Military Academy at West Point, late Lieutenant Third Artillery, U. S. A., Corresponding Member of the American Institute, late U. S. Boundary Commissioner, &c., &c. 12mo, Cloth, $1 50.

MACGREGOR'S ROB ROY ON THE JORDAN. The Rob Roy on the Jordan, Nile, Red Sea, and Gennesareth, &c. A Canoe Cruise in Palestine and Egypt, and the Waters of Damascus. By J. MACGREGOR, M.A. With Maps and Illustrations. Crown 8vo, Cloth, $2 50.

NEVIUS'S CHINA. China and the Chinese: a General Description of the Country and its Inhabitants; its Civilization and Form of Government; its Religious and Social Institutions; its Intercourse with other Nations; and its Present Condition and Prospects. By the Rev. JOHN L. NEVIUS, Ten Years a Missionary in China. With a Map and Illustrations. 12mo, Cloth, $1 75.

NEWMAN'S FROM DAN TO BEERSHEBA. From Dan to Beersheba; or, the Land of Promise as it now appears. Including a Description of the Boundaries, Topography, Agriculture, Antiquities, Cities, and Present Inhabitants of that Wonderful Land. With Illustrations of the Remarkable Accuracy of the Sacred Writers in their Allusions to their Native Country. By Rev. J. P. NEWMAN, D.D. Maps and Engravings. 12mo, Cloth, $1 75.

OLIPHANT'S CHINA AND JAPAN. Narrative of the Earl of Elgin's Mission to China and Japan, in the Years 1857, '58, '59. By LAURENCE OLIPHANT, Private Secretary to Lord Elgin. Illustrations. 8vo, Cloth, $3 50.

ORTON'S ANDES AND THE AMAZON. The Andes and the Amazon; or, Across the Continent of South America. By JAMES ORTON, M.A., Professor of Natural History in Vassar College, Poughkeepsie, N. Y., and Corresponding Member of the Academy of Natural Sciences, Philadelphia. With a New Map of Equatorial America and numerous Illustrations. Crown 8vo, Cloth, $2 00.

PAGE'S LA PLATA. La Plata, the Argentine Confederation, and Paraguay. Being a Narrative of the Exploration of the Tributaries of the River La Plata and Adjacent Countries during the Years 1853, '54, '55, and '56, under the Orders of the United States Government. New Edition, containing Farther Explorations in La Plata during 1859 and 1860. By THOMAS J. PAGE, U. S. N., Commander of the Expeditions. With Map and numerous Engravings. 8vo, Cloth, $5 00.

PRIME'S (S. I.) TRAVELS IN EUROPE AND THE EAST. Travels in Europe and the East. A Year in England, Scotland, Ireland, Wales, France, Belgium, Holland, Germany, Austria, Italy, Greece, Turkey, Syria, Palestine, and Egypt. By Rev. SAMUEL IRENÆUS PRIME, D.D. Engravings. 2 vols., large 12mo, Cloth, $3 00.

READE'S SAVAGE AFRICA. Western Africa: being the Narrative of a Tour in Equatorial, Southwestern, and Northwestern Africa; with Notes on the Habits of the Gorilla; on the Existence of Unicorns and Tailed Men; on the Slave Trade; on the Origin, Character, and Capabilities of the Negro, and on the Future Civilization of Western Africa. By W. WINWOOD READE, Fellow of the Geographical and Anthropological Society of London, and Corresponding Member of the Geographical Society of Paris. With Illustrations and a Map. 8vo, Cloth, $4 00.

REINDEER, DOGS, AND SNOW-SHOES. A Journal of Siberian Travel and Explorations made in the Years 1865–'67. By RICHARD J. BUSH, late of the Russo-American Telegraph Expedition. Illustrated. Crown 8vo, Cloth, $3 00.

PRIME'S (W. C.) BOAT-LIFE IN EGYPT. Boat-Life in Egypt and Nubia. By WILLIAM C. PRIME. Illustrations. 12mo, Cloth, $2 00.

PRIME'S (W. C.) TENT-LIFE IN THE HOLY LAND. By WILLIAM C. PRIME. Illustrations. 12mo, Cloth, $2 00.

SQUIER'S CENTRAL AMERICA. The States of Central America: their Geography, Topography, Climate, Population, Resources, Productions, Commerce, Political Organization, Aborigines, &c., &c. Comprising Chapters on Honduras, San Salvador, Nicaragua, Costa Rica, Guatemala, Belize, the Bay Islands, the Mosquito Shore, and the Honduras Inter-Oceanic Railway. By E. G. SQUIER, formerly Chargé d'Affairs of the United States to the Republics of Central America. With numerous Original Maps and Illustrations. 8vo, Cloth, $4 00.

SQUIER'S NICARAGUA. Nicaragua: its People, Scenery, Monuments, Resources, Condition, and Proposed Canal. With One Hundred Maps and Illustrations. By E. G. SQUIER. 8vo, Cloth, $4 00.

SQUIER'S WAIKNA. Waikna; or, Adventures on the Mosquito Shore. By E. G. SQUIER. With a Map and upward of Sixty Illustrations. 12mo, Cloth, $1 50.

SPEKE'S AFRICA. Journal of the Discovery of the Source of the Nile. By Captain JOHN HANNING SPEKE, Captain H. M.'s Indian Army, Fellow and Gold Medalist of the Royal Geographical Society, Hon. Corresponding Member and Gold Medalist of the French Geographical Society, &c. With Maps and Portraits and numerous Illustrations, chiefly from Drawings by Captain Grant. 8vo, Cloth, $4 00.

STEPHENS'S TRAVELS IN CENTRAL AMERICA. Travels in Central America, Chiapas, and Yucatan. By J. L. STEPHENS. With a Map and 88 Engravings. 2 vols., 8vo, Cloth, $6 00.

STEPHENS'S TRAVELS IN YUCATAN. Incidents of Travel in Yucatan. By J. L. STEPHENS. 120 Engravings, from Drawings by F. Catherwood. 2 vols., 8vo, Cloth, $6 00.

STEPHENS'S TRAVELS IN EGYPT. Travels in Egypt, Arabia Petræa, and the Holy Land. By J. L. STEPHENS. Engravings. 2 vols., 12mo, Cloth, $3 00.

STEPHENS'S TRAVELS IN GREECE. Travels in Greece, Turkey, Russia, and Poland. By J. L. STEPHENS. Engravings. 2 vols., 12mo, Cloth, $3 00.

THOMSON'S LAND AND BOOK. The Land and the Book; or, Biblical Illustrations drawn from the Manners and Customs, the Scenes and the Scenery of the Holy Land. By W. M. THOMSON, D.D., Twenty-five Years a Missionary of the A.B.C.F.M. in Syria and Palestine. With Two elaborate Maps of Palestine, an accurate Plan of Jerusalem, and *Several Hundred Engravings*, representing the Scenery, Topography, and Productions of the Holy Land, and the Costumes, Manners, and Habits of the People. Two large 12mo Volumes, Cloth, $5 00.

VÁMBÉRY'S CENTRAL ASIA. Travels in Central Asia: being the Account of a Journey from Teheran across the Turkoman Desert, on the Eastern Shore of the Caspian, to Khiva, Bokhara, and Samarcand, performed in the Year 1863. By ARMINIUS VÁMBÉRY, Member of the Hungarian Academy of Pesth, by whom he was sent on this Scientific Mission. With Map and Woodcuts. 8vo, Cloth, $4 50.

VIRGINIA ILLUSTRATED: containing a Visit to the Virginian Canaan, and the Adventures of Porte Crayon and his Cousins. Illustrated from Drawings by PORTE CRAYON. 8vo, Cloth, $3 50.

WALLACE'S MALAY ARCHIPELAGO. The Malay Archipelago: the Land of the Orang-Utan and the Bird of Paradise. A Narrative of Travel, 1854–'62. With Studies of Man and Nature. By ALFRED RUSSEL WALLACE. With Maps and numerous Illustrations. Crown 8vo, Cloth, $2 50.

WELLS'S EXPLORATIONS IN HONDURAS. Explorations and Adventures in Honduras; comprising Sketches of Travel in the Gold Regions of Olancho, and a Review of the History and General Resources of Central America. By WILLIAM V. WELLS. With Original Maps and numerous Illustrations. 8vo, Cloth, $3 50.

WHYMPER'S ALASKA. Travel and Adventure in the Territory of Alaska, formerly Russian America—now ceded to the United States—and in various other Parts of the North Pacific. By FREDERICK WHYMPER. With Map and Illustrations. Crown 8vo, Cloth, $2 50.

WILKINSON'S ANCIENT EGYPTIANS. A Popular Account of the Ancient Egyptians. Revised and abridged from his larger Work. By Sir J. GARDNER WILKINSON, D.C.L., F.R.S., &c. Illustrated with 500 Woodcuts. 2 vols., 12mo, Cloth, $3 50.